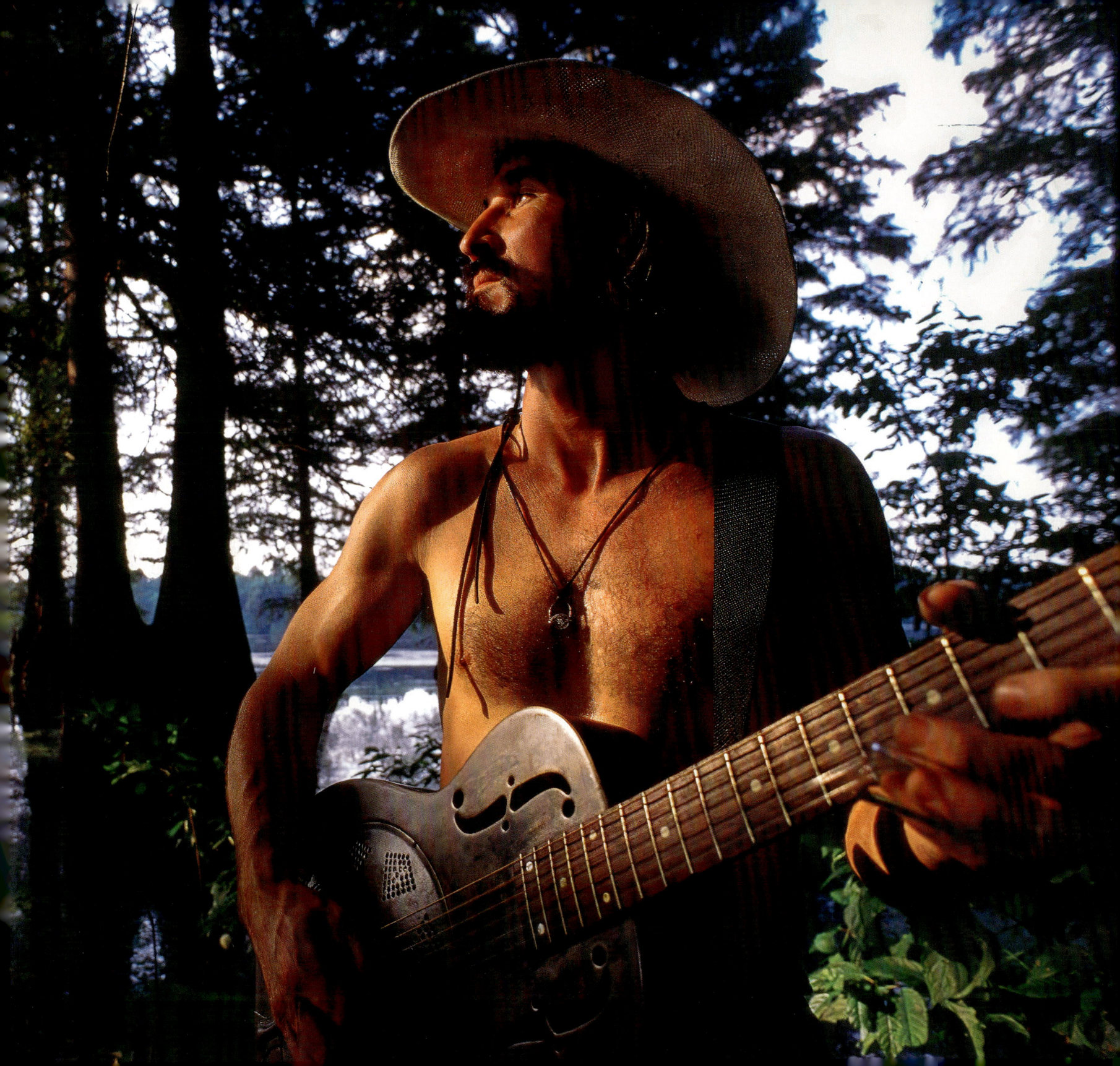

Skyhorse Publishing books may be purchased in bulk at special discounts for sales promotion, corporate gifts, fund-raising, or educational purposes. Special editions can also be created to specifications. For details, contact the Special Sales Department, Skyhorse Publishing, 307 West 36th Street, 11th Floor, New York, NY 10018 or info@skyhorsepublishing.com.

Skyhorse® and Skyhorse Publishing® are registered trademarks of Skyhorse Publishing, Inc.®, a Delaware corporation.

Visit our website at www.skyhorsepublishing.com

Please follow our publisher Tony Lyons on Instagram @tonylyonsisuncertain.

10 9 8 7 6 5 4 3 2 1

Library of Congress Cataloging-in-Publication Data is available on file.

Hardcover ISBN: 978-1-5107-8041-5
Ebook ISBN: 978-1-5107-8042-2

Cover design by Kai Texel
Cover photographs by Peter Guttman

Printed in China

Joyously dedicated to the wildly original cast of family characters whose engaging personalities have in no small measure helped nurture my curiosity and spark my passions—my dad Arthur's brilliant genius, my mom Judith's ebullient spirit, my wife Lori's enthralling effervescence, my son Chase's intrepid creativity, and my brother Gary's iconoclastic artistry.

INTRODUCTION

Character counts. At least the prevailing winds of modern American society seem to tell us that, but it's actually a bit more complicated. A vibrant nation so thickly speckled by an infinite array of genetic heritage, religious convictions, diverse lifestyles, philosophical undergirdings, and regional attitudes would at first blush appear completely unable to form any national consensus or identifying characteristic. Yet, there appears to be a nearly universal conviction amongst its citizens that there is indeed an unusually distinguishing, anthem-worthy American Character which seems almost tangible and completely worthy of admiration. Unlike virtually any other country on earth, most of this country's principles in their purest form point to an intellectual concept based not on religion or heritage, but rather upon delicate equipoise between individual freedom and a common good. That seesawing balance does not always enjoy a level equilibrium and is actually the pivot point on which most of the country's political struggles often teeters. In a nation that has increasingly been picking sides against one another, the dilemma seems to be that character may well be defined quite differently depending on exactly where you stand. Where one stands might well be determined by where you sit on that seesaw.

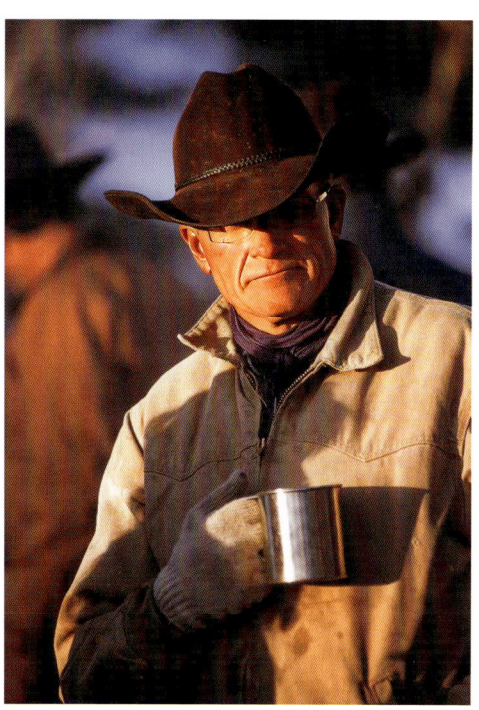

I have always had an insatiable curiosity about the very planet I've been spinning around on. Admittedly a childhood nerd of sorts, my earliest pre-teen obsession with developing an internal drive powering artificial hearts had been profiled in medical magazines and seemed to have had me destined for pre-med career tracks, however that passion plowed headlong into my infatuation with earth's geographical wonders and the colorful cultural traditions of its people. It's no wonder that my premature midlife crisis occurred while only nineteen years old. As a result, I nabbed an unconventional geography degree, sadly rare in this country. Its first occupational manifestation for me was as a tour guide, engaging my captive audience with microphone in hand on an air-conditioned motorcoach filled with forty or so excited vacationers hoping to explore the North American continent during journeys of up to 31 days. My determination to inspire, educate, and entertain was certainly stress-tested during an era that had not yet seen the existence of Walkmans, iPods, or onboard television diversions as my Casser Tours motorcoach barreled headlong toward its next destination across wheat-field-flat landscapes filling Nebraska's horizon on a seemingly interminable ramrod-straight highway. While honing my photographic skills on those journeys, I also continued an admittedly insane lifelong documentation that delineated my travels. An exacting, highly eccentric, and perhaps unprecedented linear display charted my entire peripatetic existence on a national AAA map that would eventually morph into slightly dog-eared two-dimensional spaghetti strands of dense ballpoint pen tracings.

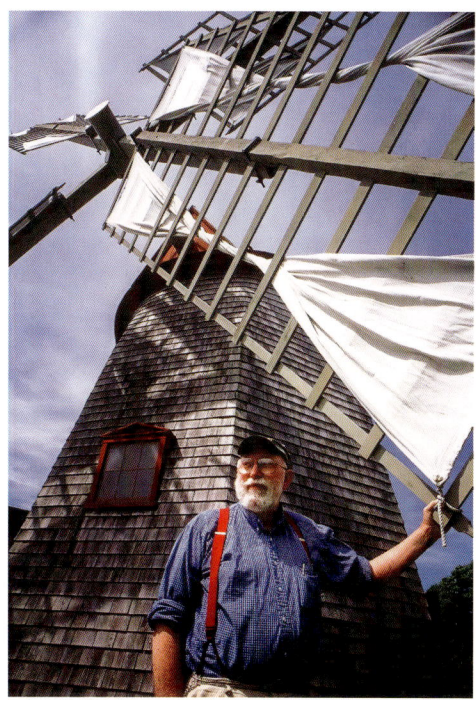

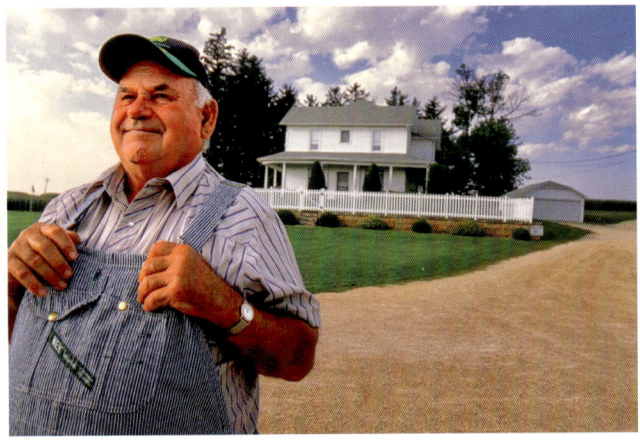

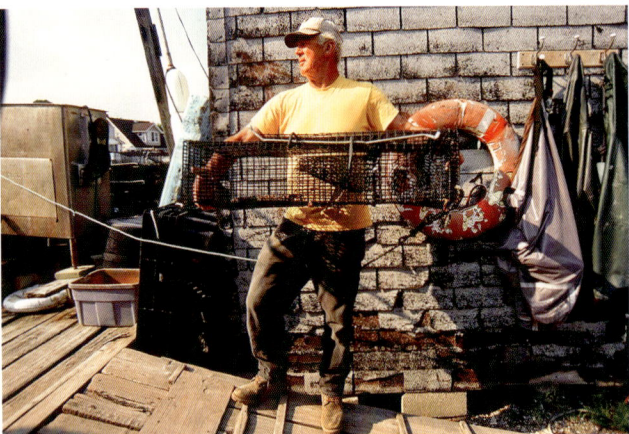

Beyond the borders of my United States map, later explorations as a travel journalist led me to shoot during assignments on all seven continents and over 250 countries, seeking out disappearing Indigenous groups like those fiercely cannibalistic Asmat warriors who raid mosquito-infested coastlines that edge New Guinea or recently discovered facially painted Melpa Wigmen further ensconced within that island's corrugated mountain folds. I spent time deep in Peru's steamy Amazon with riverbank-dwelling, palm fiber-wearing Yagua; seldom-visited, shaman-consulting Wai Wai playing flute amongst nearly inaccessible Guyanese rainforests; hardy Nenet reindeer herders snugly clad inside animal-skin parkas while they drove their hoofed herd along frigid Siberian coastline far above the Arctic Circle; and Vanuatu's spry Naghol land divers who apparently invented bungee jumping on South Pacific's tiny Pentecost Island when leaping with only ankle-tied vines from rickety bamboo towers to ensure successful yam harvests. That wide spectrum of existences emblazons our planet with a cultural vitality that is essential to defining our deeply textured human civilization.

Returning home, I could better appreciate that the United States of America, which aside from containing, hands down, earth's largest medley of landscapes to be found anywhere on its surface, also comprises a sweeping population containing perhaps this world's most diversified citizenry. Multi-pronged mingling between historical and societal influences has shaped the differing characters that drove this country's development, while helping rack up an amazingly rich assortment of hardy, self-reliant individuals stubbornly defying modern society—grizzled eel trappers, bundled ice harvesters, Cajun swamp denizens, cautious rattlesnake wranglers, or even hopeful bigfoot trackers. The fact that fearless beekeepers, toiling chile pickers, and Yupik walrus hunters are thriving in a land of seemingly endless opportunities while coexisting, perhaps unknowingly, with nuclear physicists, lonely lighthouse keepers, octogenarian ballerinas, exacting topiary gardeners, daredevil tornado chasers, pensive Buddhist monks, or limber contortionists thrilled me almost beyond any reason. Each character, busily engaging in their anthropologically fascinating roles, helps contribute an essential thread to the breathtaking American fabric. An even greater catalog filled with iconoclastic bohemians, eccentric mavericks, or scheming renegades found their way to my wide-angle lens during unfolding investigative decades of additional Bic-inscribed lines, leading me into remote corners of this country's physical, cultural, and spiritual edges.

Though honored recently as an inducted Fellow of the Explorers Club, where I was welcomed into ranks shared by Ernest Shackleton, Jacques Cousteau, and Buzz Aldrin, it still feels oddly fitting somehow to perceive the nation of my birth as a truly exotic subject for investigation. After all, it's here that my earliest boyhood wanderlust was quickly recognized and appreciated by loving family members. I actually remember my bemused mother and father exercising tremendous patience as their five-year-old son meticulously collected license plate numbers off the rear end of out-of-state automobiles with comically naive assumptions that I'd later contact its owners to learn all about life in their states. While my spirited mom may have mostly filled our domestic household with laughter, it was a brilliantly creative dad who skillfully carved exquisite wooden figurines that echoed the tribal Makonde and their East African traditions. Further cementing an eager fascination with other far-flung cultures were almost five dozen childhood visits to the New York World's Fair, conveniently located only a few miles from my house, and almost exactly in between both sets of grandparents.

Having survived the Great Depression, it must have been some great relief to my doting grandparents that I always provided a reliably cheap playdate. Long before video games or the internet, just one dime would buy my grandpa and me a truly unforgettable ride atop an elevated, foreign tongue-filled Number 7 Flushing subway line from his neighborhood apartment in Queens into Manhattan's Times Square before reversing course without ever exiting that subway. It was quite enough for me to be in that front car, with my nose pressed up against the forward glass window while, through foggy breath, surveying those rails during a thrilling roller-coaster expedition over bustling ethnic neighborhoods crowned by sagging rooftops. My other grandpa would drive me in his tailfin-tipped Oldsmobile 88 to Idlewild Airport, its name before President Kennedy's assassination. There, I would visit foreign currency exchange shops and occasionally be treated to the lower denominations of exotic alien currencies, then watch from observation decks as planes took off for mysterious unknown destinations.

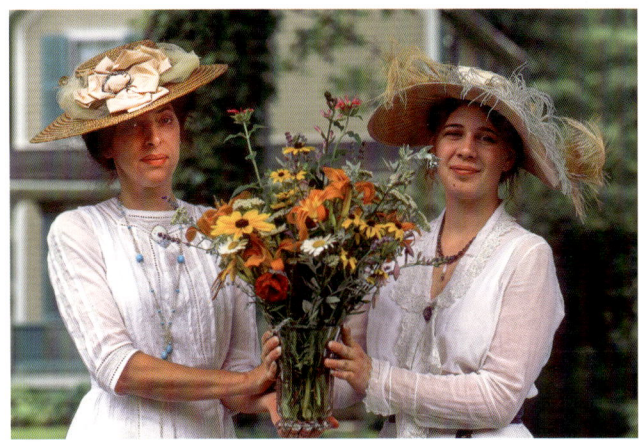

Decades later during my own numerous domestic airplane flights, I have found window seats richly meditative thrones upon which to consider not only life or abstract philosophical concepts, but the profoundly telling character of our American landscape itself. That panorama in many ways forges the lives and destinies of those people it cradles. Employing minimal discipline, I will ignore several dozen spoon-fed channels and often inane movies streaming mere inches from my eyeballs, and with some soothing assistance from white noise-generating engines allow views unfolding below to generate an intriguing series of ponderable notions. Obsessed with the astonishing history of this country's changing landscapes and dynamic people, that towering perch helps empower my perspective into America's metamorphic drama.

Taking off from my nearby airport the jet plane banks, suddenly revealing coastline tracing southern New England as it curls away toward Cape Cod shores. There seventeenth-century pilgrims once disembarked after fleeing religious persecution before making temporary peace with that region's Indigenous people. Their initially harmonious interactions later evolved into town hall meetings, perhaps the nation's purest form of democracy. I soon spot the spindly stem of one mighty river, whose inviting mouth

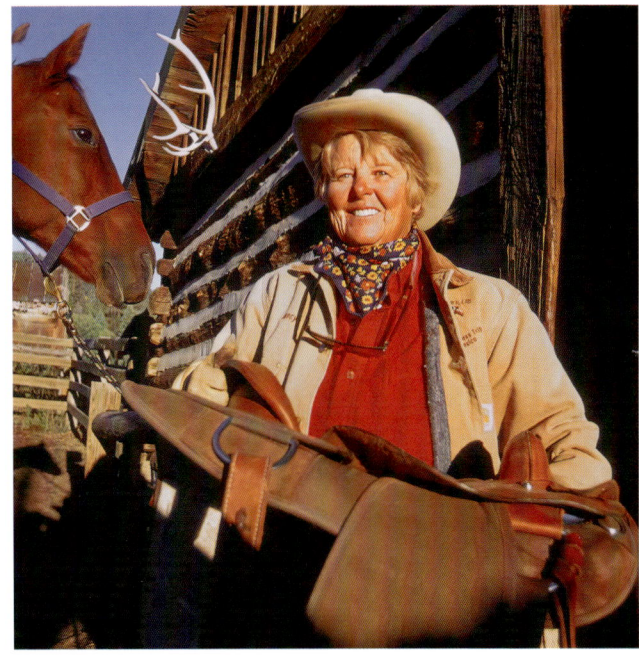

helped develop a bustling harbor that lured greater immigration and sparked industrial enterprises along its shores. The Hudson's fjord-like course appears to dwindle into fading horizons and toward its innovative Erie Canal branch-off, which was so instrumental in America's westward expansion and first spurred shipping industries within this nation's interior.

After the 10,000-foot-high announcement approving usage of portable devices, this westbound journey flies above increasingly smaller cities, then towns, country villages, and rural hamlets. Finally, a glimpse of rising mountains appears. This country's first geologic chain link fence is a two-thousand-mile range now hosting earth's longest hiking trail. That mountainous chain hemmed in nineteenth-century fertile valleys where greater agricultural demands metastasized the already tragic slavery system, further fueled both by property-owning British aristocracy and continued arrivals of slave ships from Africa. The Appalachian range also largely held back spreading European development until uncontainable demands for additional farming land and rumors of gold-based wealth busted the proverbial dam. This profit-hungry thirst for opportunities farther west unleashed pioneering explorations and entrepreneurial imperatives that helped forge wagon trails which began their infiltration across the continent.

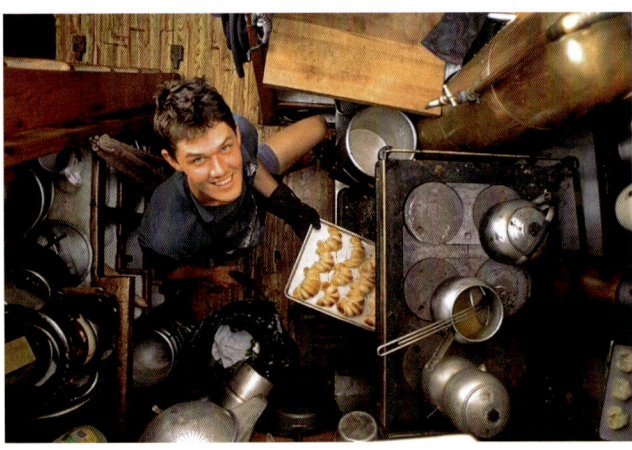

Just above I see the seatbelt sign has been turned off. After leaving rolling plateaus behind we soon approach the Midwest where native peoples were continually displaced, as a sometimes-violent frontier line kept receding westward. In this new land of opportunities, the stubborn, self-righteous vision promoting manifest destiny provided a moral and religious permission slip to overlook greediness or even genocide. During this time, the continent's abundant resources coupled with greater social mobility and need for self-sufficiency helped engender a uniquely American spirit spawning nineteenth-century rugged individualism, which to this day kindles many of their descendant's suspicions over governmental supervision. Below, the mighty Mississippi River once plied by steam-powered riverboats is now sliced with tug-ushered barges hauling several thousand tons of petroleum and grain products within quarter-mile-long containers. The river that once provided a gateway for adventure-seeking traders, trappers, and troubadours now serves as a vital artery for this nation's industrial survival while signaling that distinctive midway point between both coasts.

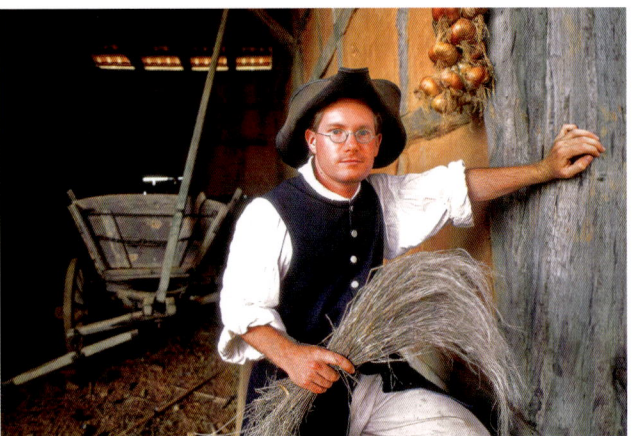

Having already reached cruising altitude and leveling off, the dramatic scope of this great American heartland completely reveals itself while looking down onto earth's surface. Eastern America's circuitous tracings of hillside roads now seem to have been organized into the Midwest's ruler-straight checkerboards marked by highways and fields. Alternating squares of agricultural activity appear to indicate corn, wheat, and alfalfa. The immigrants from Northern Europe settled here and cultivated their more rigid cultures and lifestyles. Circular patterns of radial irrigation soon superimpose farmland rectangles and stamp their design on terrain increasingly thirsty for water resources. These crops help supply feed for ranching, a modern-day manifestation of lengthy cattle drives that once crisscrossed the ranges herding bovine traffic towards hungry markets farther east. That cowboy culture originated in Mexico and spread Spanish influences into America's southwestern corners, which in some locales only joined this nation during the twentieth century.

Flying over Rocky Mountain ranges, topography becomes more dramatic just beyond those wingtips as snow clad alps yield to tortured red rock country. An insistent Colorado River drilled into high altitude plateaus in this area and helped display the baked geological layer cake at the Grand Canyon. Nearby, Native reservations ably clawed back the remains of their ancestral territory, held sacred by tribal communities still maintaining traditional powwows, dances, sweat lodges, and original languages. Drier, cloudless skies here in the Southwest yield little precipitation which created intense friction over water supplies, irrigation access, and dam building. These struggles became critical to needy cities throughout California, a longtime promised land sought by fortune seekers, and today hosting thriving tech companies reaching for twenty-first-century innovations. After wing flap deployment and touching down at a west coast airport, I'd allow myself to be snapped out of airborne contemplations while leaving my window seat and removing baggage from the overhead bins. I'll remember that where I stand is determined by where I sit.

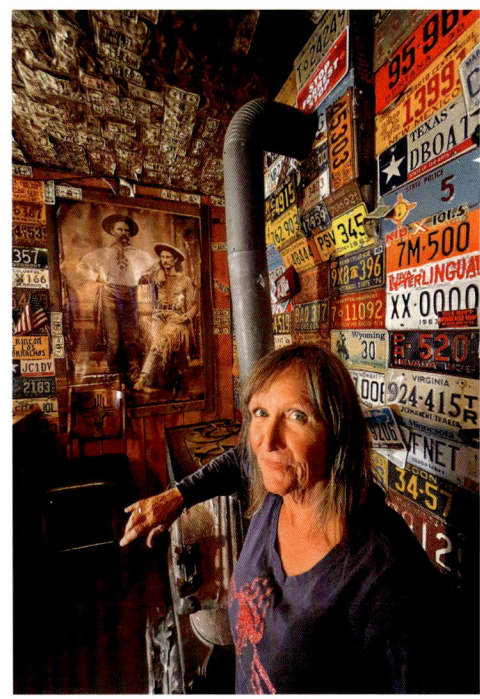

American Character: A Surprising Portrait of an Unseen Nation is a visual treasury representing an almost four decades-long labor of love. With eyes wide open, an accepting heart, and a determined embrace of new experiences and hidden corners, my exhausting erstwhile journeys yielded myriad serendipitous encounters. Some meetups actually resulted in sleepover-level friendships, while other interactions may have only lasted mere seconds. On the whole, they graciously provided me fascinating glimpses into worlds that I might have been less than familiar with, enabling deeper introspection into my own lifelong pathways and creating a vivid picture of our collective American experience. In my accompanying stories, I've attempted to first construct the historical or geographical stage set for these mostly environmental portraits, before finally placing those subjects on that podium for their spotlight.

For most of us, in an increasingly impersonal, digitized world there are underlying yearnings to renew human contact and intimacy. In this nation's ineffably vast constellation of people striving to make their time on earth have some meaning, it might prove both comforting and perhaps even energizing to more closely explore those seldom-visited side streets that approach our common humanity. Perhaps for at least one brief moment we should even pack political baggage or biases away in the trunk, readjust our rearview mirror, and head toward that unifying boulevard where fellow citizens are endeavoring to steer their own distinctive versions of American character.

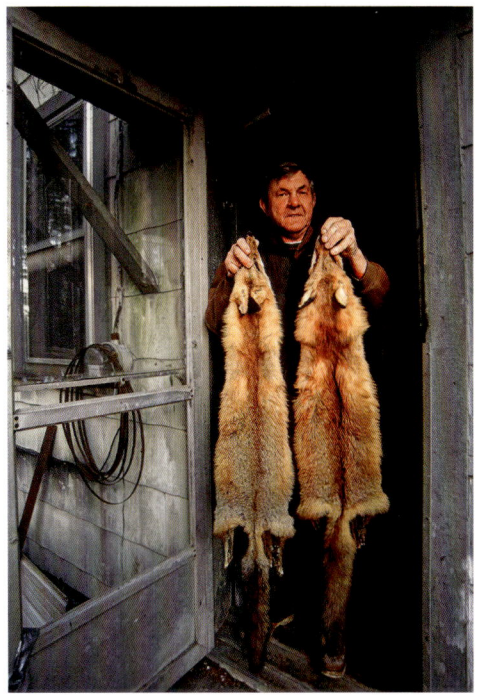

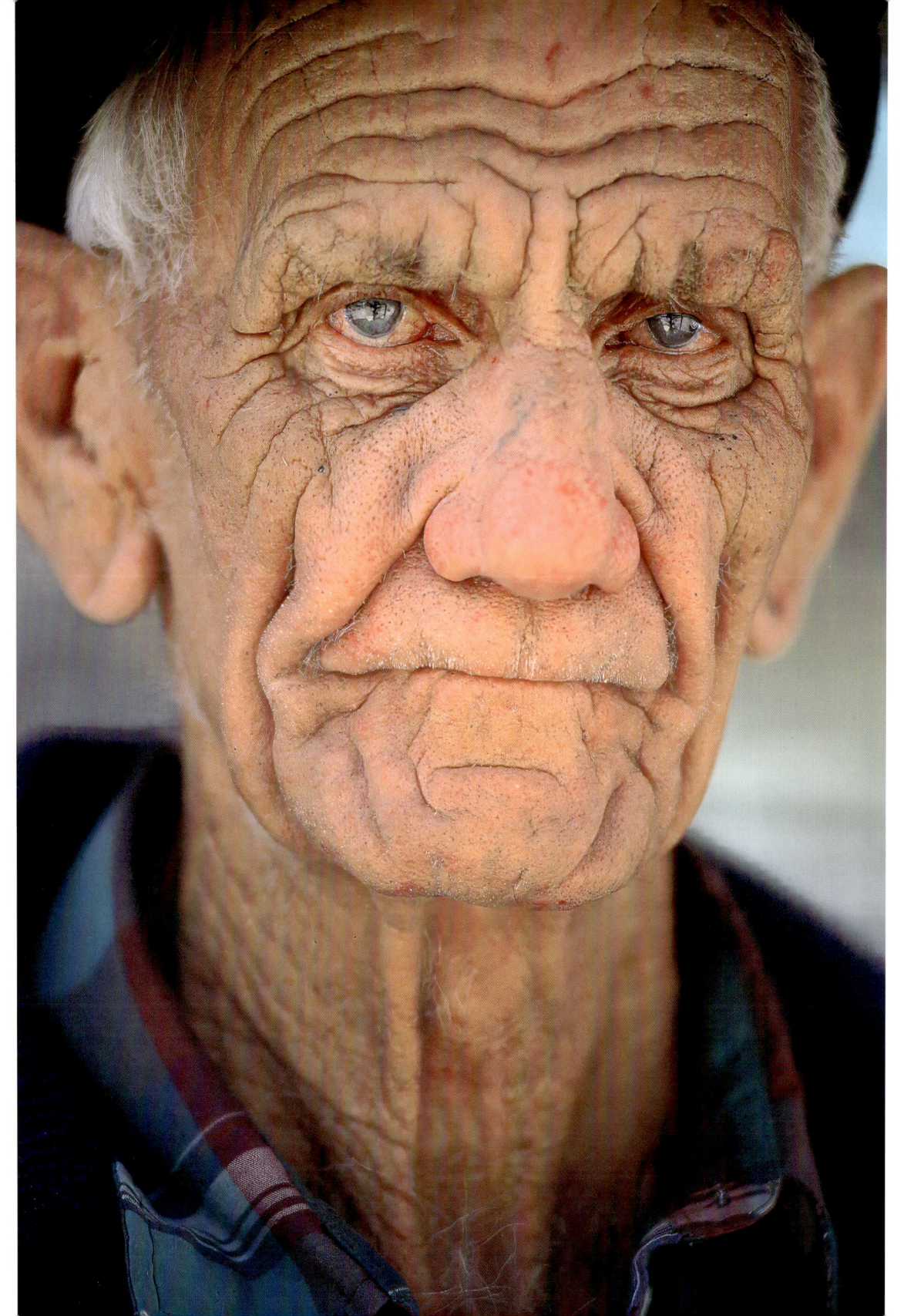

ZINC PROSPECTOR

Blue Eye, Arkansas

Though primarily saddling Arkansas and Missouri, the Ozarks arguably touch up to six states. Virtually alone amongst rugged landscapes between Appalachian summits and the Rockies, this Ozark region is often mistakenly referred to as mountains but is actually eroded upland plateaus. Its indented topography was mostly unsuitable for farming, which obviated the widespread demand for slave labor. Early settlers arrived mostly from the British Isles, traveling in oxen-drawn wagons over wilderness roads and settling in valley hollers, butchering hogs for meat and making soap out of their rendered fat. The area's porous limestone karst topography harbored crystalline lead and zinc forms, creating mining industries which produced more of these minerals than anywhere in America. Zinc, now the fourth most-used metal on earth, first became a useful alloy as anti-corrosion coatings for steel or brass, instrumental in pharmaceuticals, cosmetics, and paints. Depleted resources eventually left behind mining ghost towns and the skeletons of stone smelters. Regions of intense poverty arose, often leaving working men largely unemployed and killing time by whittling their wooden sticks on benches surrounding tiny town squares. In the border settlement of Blue Eye, named for the alluring gaze of its first postmaster's daughter, passing time would mean playing marbles, as the Irish pioneers who settled here brought their homeland passion for this game. They became acclaimed for deft skills with baked clay marbles, plunking their taw at boulders within a hand-drawn court. They never played for keeps, as these handmade orbs were passed down to each succeeding generation, perhaps as their most valuable asset.

Rural hardships from a weary life toiling in the Ozarks are deeply etched into creases on this retired zinc miner's expression, reflecting the craggy landscapes of local holler-filled mineral-rich hills, once teeming with underground workers scurrying beneath hardened caps lit by kerosene and lard. That wrinkled facial topography on this Blue Eye resident indeed seems to provide something of a dermal roadmap charting the worrying plight of those left behind in an increasingly technological world.

BEEKEEPER

Middletown, New York

There's an obvious reason that often-dreaded parental discussions about birds and the bees gets employed as a preamble for understanding life's development. A crucial keystone element to our globe's biodiversity, honeybees are critical pollinators responsible for at least one third of earth's food supply, while also maintaining the lungs of planet earth. The growth of trees, fruits, vegetables, and plants needed to feed animals relies very heavily on pollination that *Apis mellifera* provide. Floral rewards found in nectar or pollen, bees' main protein source, are picked up by electrostatic forces on that insect's stiff hairs, then inadvertently spread after flitting from male stamen filaments onto sticky female pistils inside the next visited flower. Flying a seemingly physics-defying flight pattern at average speeds reaching 15 mph, their wings will flap at an astonishing 230 beats per second while they buzz away in the key of C-flat. Giant-eyed male drones mate mid-air with virgin queen bees from different hives to maintain genetic diversity. They will die shortly thereafter, as the powerful ejaculation ruptures their endophallus. Back at the hive, worker bees stockpile gathered honey within hexagonal honeycombed lockers, adding to their supply of nectar and pollen mixtures. Bees just returning into their hives from foraging will waggle and shake during vibration dances that signal distances or directions toward floral food sources, spurring motivation for other bees getting down to business. Benefitting from their horticultural labors, honey offers easily stored, antibacterial sweeteners, beeswax that's employed for candles, seals, or lip balm, while resinous propolis yields flu remedies and violin wood finishes. Nine millennia ago, honey's viscous liquids offered up mead as the world's very earliest fermented beverage, first evidenced in northern China's Henan Province, and actually predating an advent of agriculture.

Beekeepers have for millennia assisted with the maintenance of an apiary's healthy hives, replacing combs or adding queen bees as needed, while employing pacifying smokers and protective garb to help minimize stings. Taking care not to sneeze while letting serenity reign, an unruffled beekeeper bravely hosts hordes of ten thousand buzzing honeybees clustered around the one queen caged in his improvised necklace. At Orange County's agricultural fair, this act of apiarian courage actually follows a centuries-old bee beard sideshow tradition.

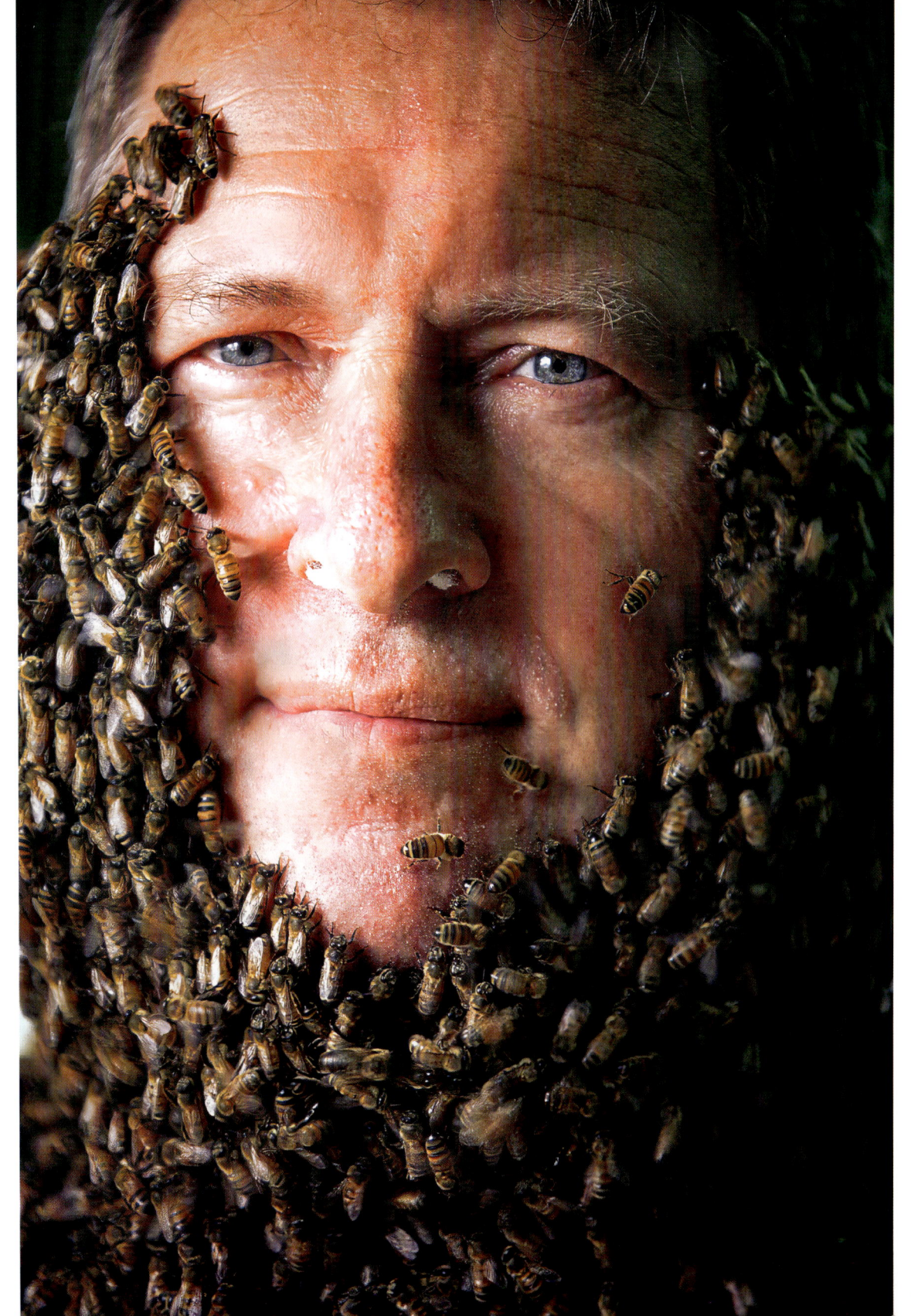

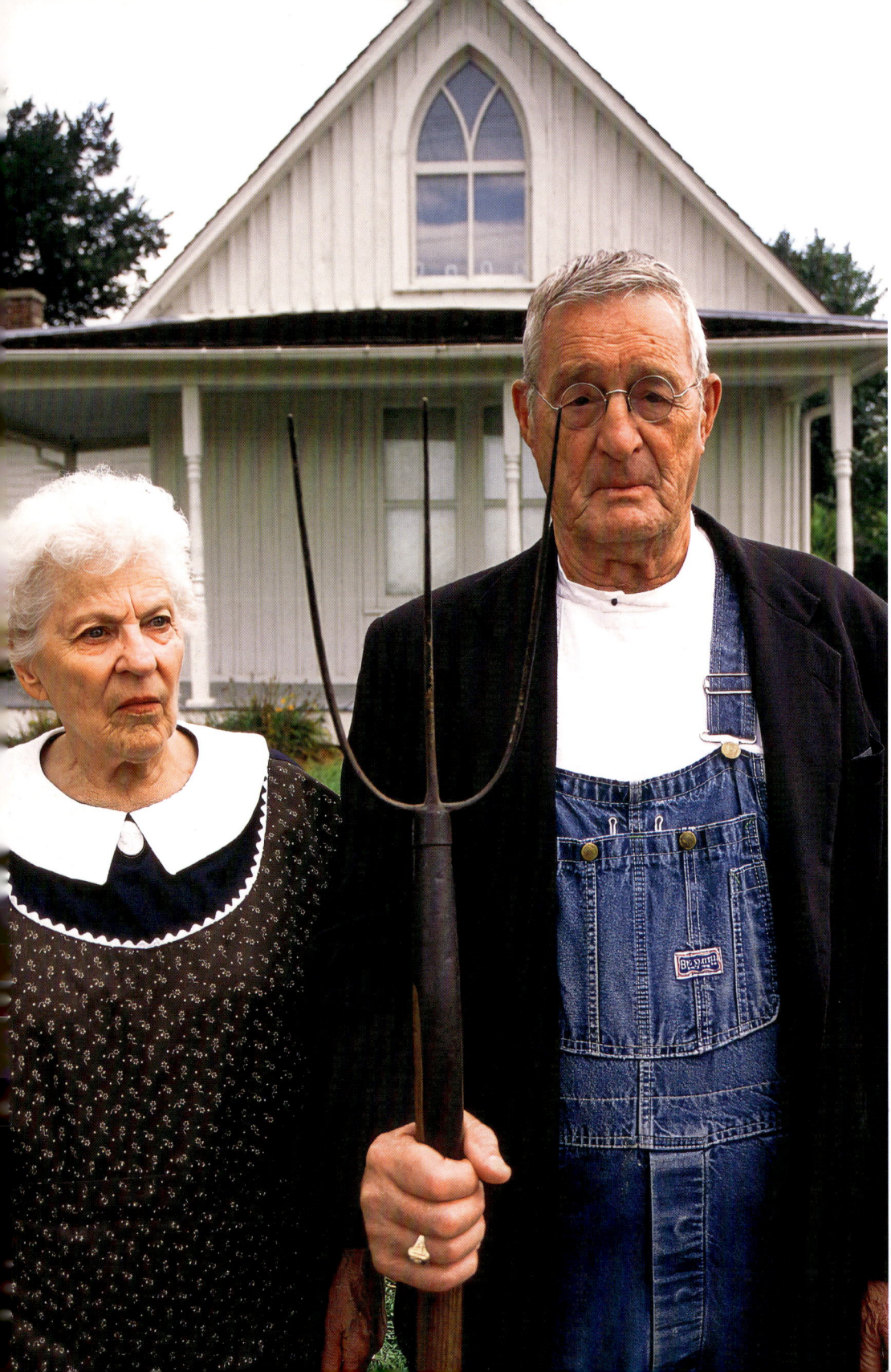

FARMHOUSE COUPLE

Eldon, Iowa

Iowans' cold, chip-on-the-shoulder attitudes, as portrayed by local resident Meredith Willson in that acclaimed 1962 Tony-winning theatrical *The Music Man*, captured not only a portrait of stoic Midwestern sensibilities but also the first Grammy ever won for Best Musical. However, its depiction of small town, church-driven virtues perhaps originally drew its inspiration from *American Gothic*, an iconic, much parodied 1930 tableau that featured rural demeanor and was painted by regional artist Grant Wood in Eldon, a Rock Island Line railway stop. That scene was created with oil paints on his beaver board panel, and, contrary to popular belief, was meant to represent a father and his grown daughter who seems to evoke an aging tintype from an old family album. The artist's sister modeled as that cameo-clad daughter, while his dentist portrayed a bespectacled dad. Behind them, an 1882 Carpenter Gothic home features ogive-shaped windows, a chapel-like facade adding to its charm, and was probably ordered from Sears Roebuck catalogs before catching the eye of this scene's painter during his drive through town.

Mirroring the classic painting at its original site, unblinkingly stoic, faith-filled expressions stand sentry before this humble Iowan farmhouse, guarding tightly fitted compositions that join overalls, a patterned, rickrack-trimmed apron, and his three-tined hay fork. With a somewhat sardonic nod to the fastidious sensibilities inhabiting Hawkeye State residents, locals volunteer their personas for an echoing of the region's earlier agrarian lifestyles.

AGING HIPPIE

Woodstock, New York

Domestic frustration and rage over escalating warfare in Vietnam dominated this nation's news during much of the sixties. In 1965, famed beat poet Allen Ginsberg proposed transforming angry war protests into spectacles of passive resistance. Embracing that symbolism, disaffected hippies who voluntarily estranged from society began garbing themselves with vibrant, embroidered colors and flowers tucked in their hair. This movement toward flower power began infiltrating gatherings and musical movements, a trend further supercharged by The Beatles or other experimental rock bands. The anti-authoritarian counterculture heralded a psychedelic era of head shops, black light posters, groovy lava lamps and exploratory drug usage, an LSD-inflected artistic wave that permeated discs spun across newly adopted stereo rhythms on FM radio. As that movement began reaching its fever pitch, the seminal event of this decade seemed to almost magically mushroom in upstate New York's Catskills across grassy slopes on an undulating 650-cow dairy farm owned by a conservative Republican who supported war efforts in Vietnam. On August 15, 1969, almost a half million people clogged this region's roads and converged on what was billed as "An Aquarian Exposition: 3 Days of Peace & Music," otherwise known as the Woodstock Festival. It was named for its originally intended mountain town site which, as the dove flies, is 45 miles northeast of Max Yasgur's meadow, where despite torrential thunderstorms and muddy fields, musical legends like Jefferson Airplane, The Who, Grateful Dead, Jimi Hendrix, Janis Joplin, plus Santana among dozens of other star-studded names performed through the days and nights to a peaceful, stoned, skinny-dipping sea of blissed out humanity.

Just off a village green in front of Woodstock's eighteenth-century Dutch Reformed Church, a wizard-capped apparition of the 1960s, Allyn Richardson holds court. Better known for decades as Grandpa Woodstock, Richardson attended that Woodstock Festival at the age of 25, ignoring warnings about consuming brown acid. In later years he viewed his full-time job as spreading peace and love from his embellished tricycle, a mobile pulpit and campground equipped with an old car battery-powered sewing machine to mend flower-patterned attire. Amongst baubles, gewgaws, and floral fandangles is Snoopy's yellow avian companion Woodstock, just beneath ruby red fingernails that help flash the peace sign, a gesture first made widely known by Winston Churchill before its permanent adaptation by flower children or hippies.

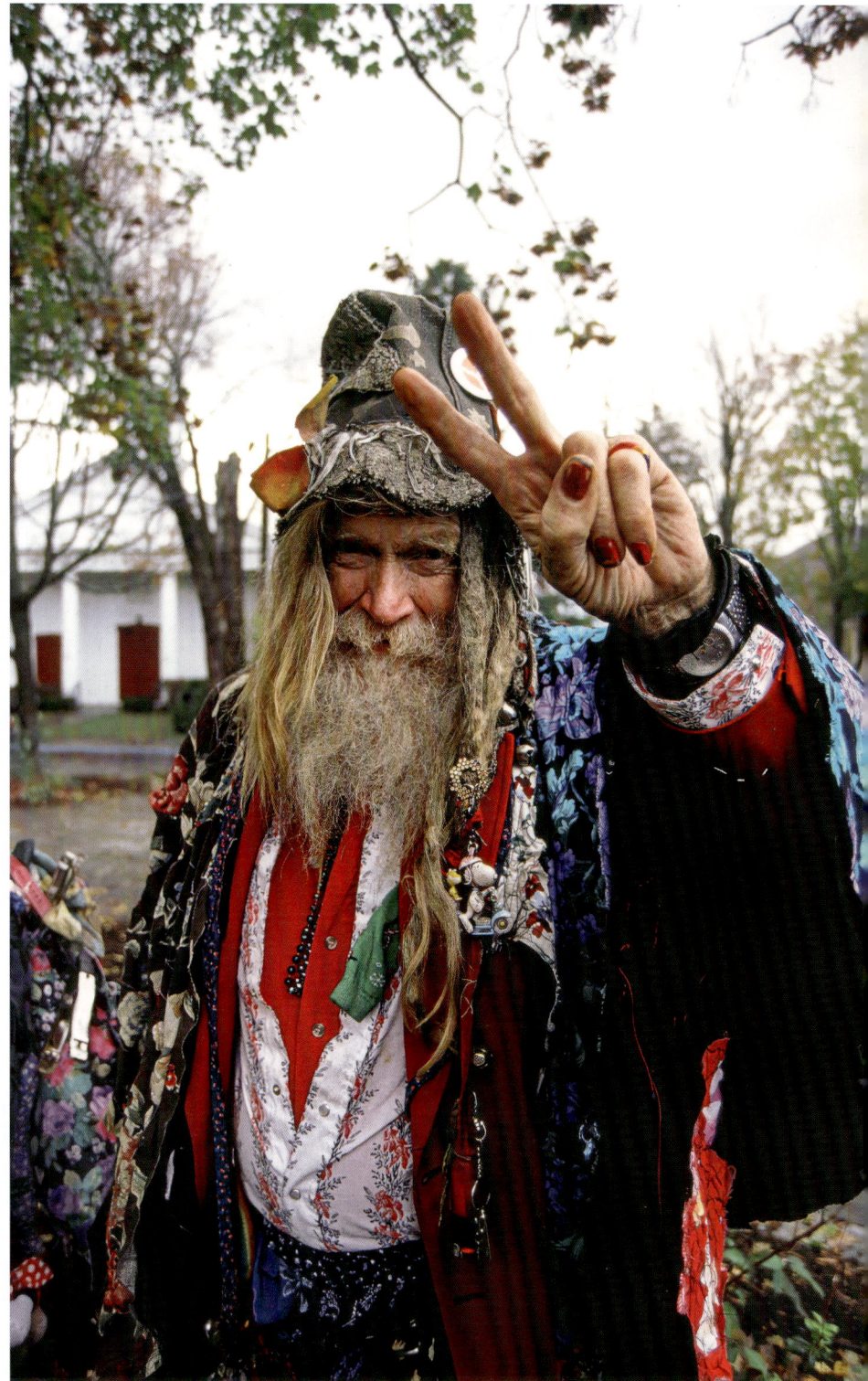

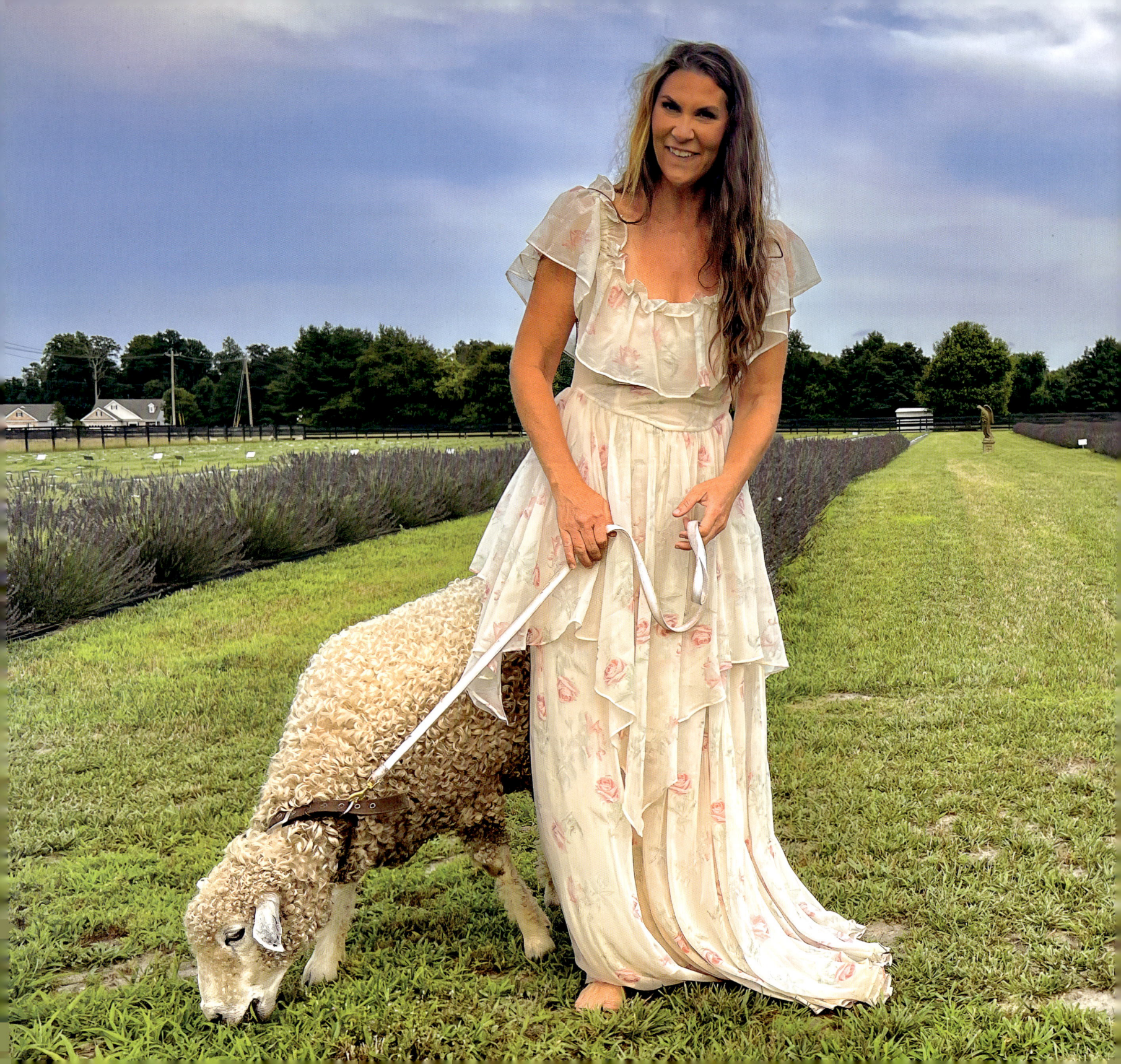

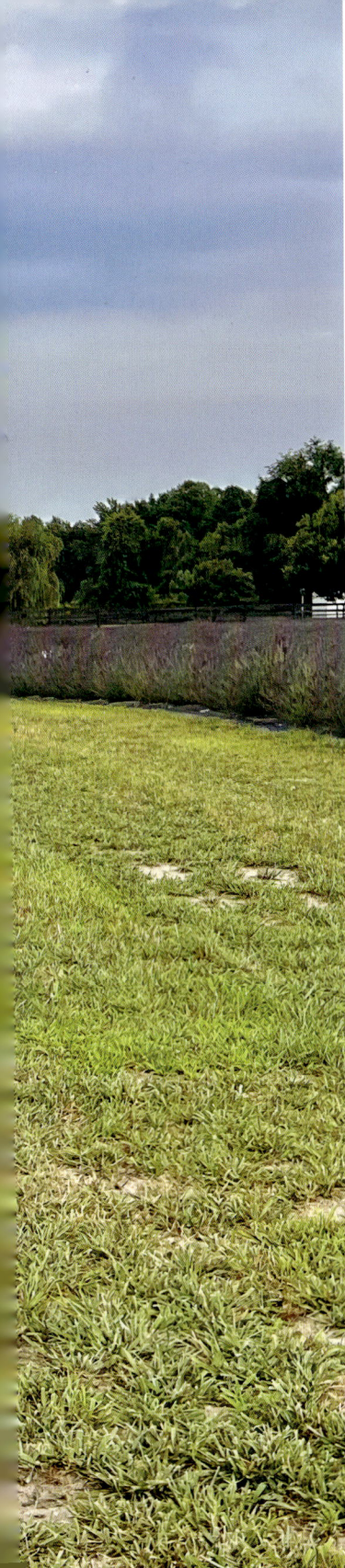

LAVENDER FARMER

Millsboro, Delaware

With the lowest elevation of any state, moderate climates cradling Delaware's flat, clay-rich coastal plains create fertile grounds for farming activities. However, stubbornly insistent suburban sprawl has lately threatened the historic proliferation of small family farms. At Brittingham Farms, four generations of agricultural efforts have played out across a relatively small tract of 350 acres where diversification has proven the key to survival. A transition to growing lavender has sparked deepening interest in the fragrant herb. Throughout history, the ancient crop was used variously for mummification, insect repellent, nerve calming tea, washing hair, plus famously applied by Cleopatra to seduce Julius Caesar and Mark Antony. At the farm, essential oils and moisturizing hydrosol are lovingly handcrafted at an artisanal copper distillery in their handsome barn, and aromatic rows of honeybee-speckled crop may be strolled while enjoying homemade lavender ice cream.

Amidst this fairytale setting, an ebullient Laura Brittingham accompanies one of her many Leicester Longwool sheep, a heritage breed valued in colonial times for their long, curly wool used in cloaks and bed blankets. In fact, George Washington wrote often in his farm journals at Mount Vernon about the utility of these docile creatures and their coarse fibers. These days at this flourishing homestead, a member of the flock might even play an occasional cameo as entree during one of their meadowside farm-to-table dinners.

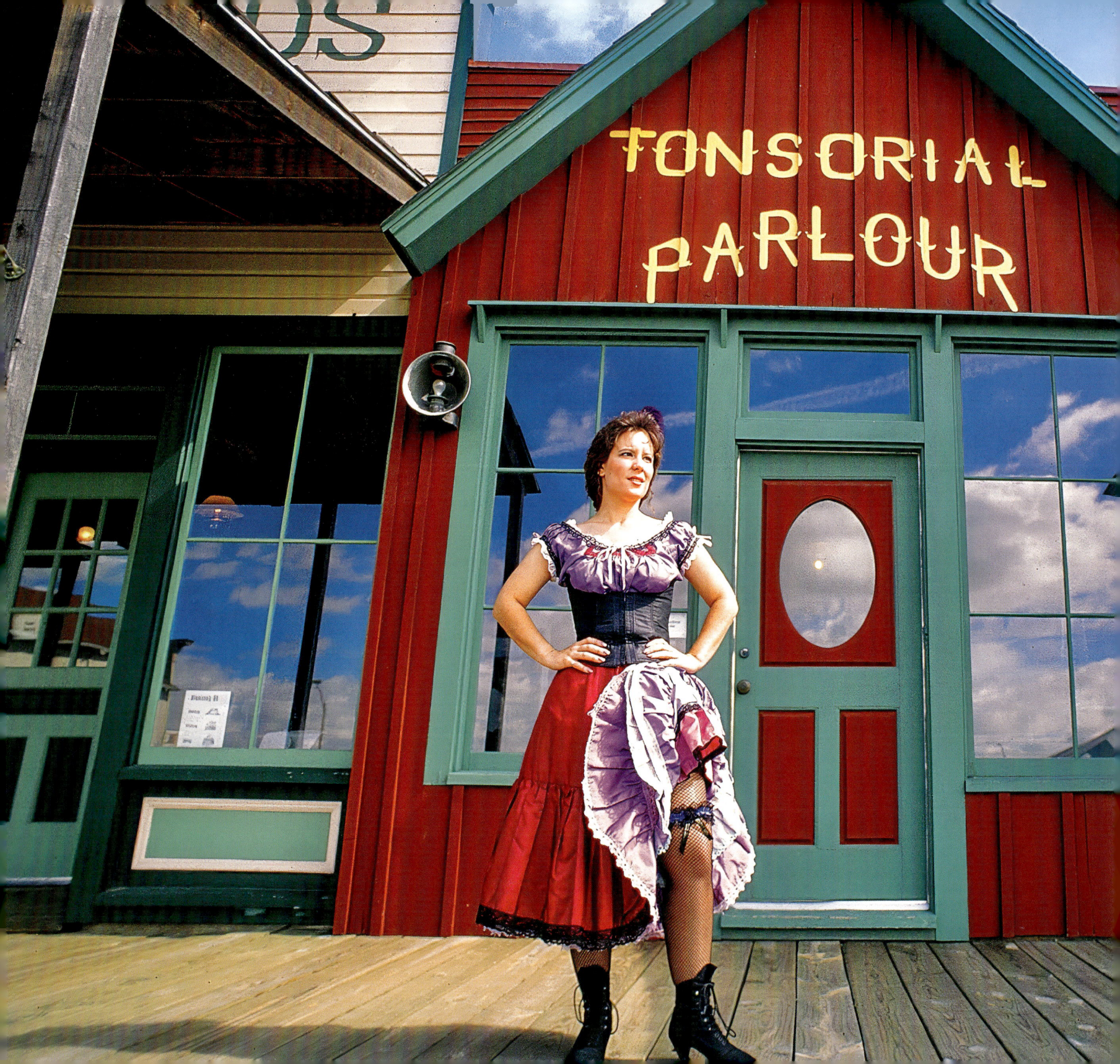

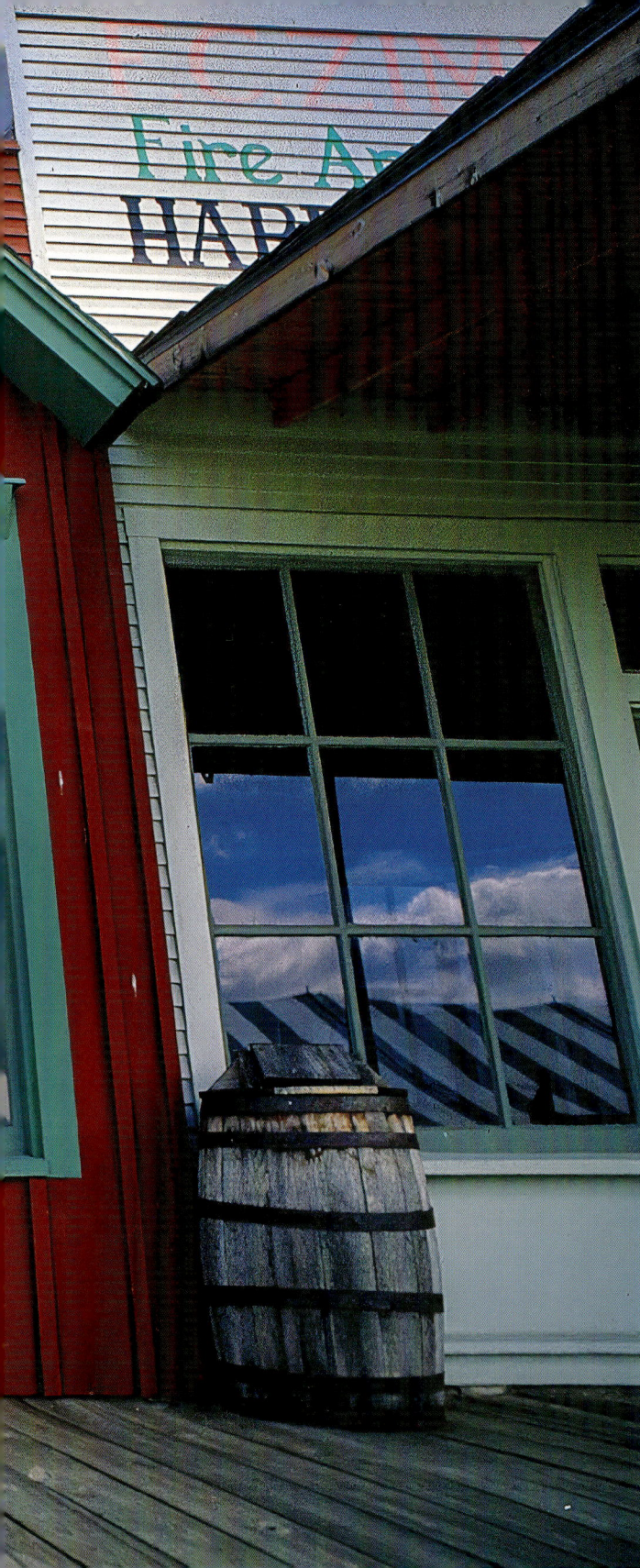

PROSTITUTE IMPRESSIONIST

Dodge City, Kansas

An urgent imperative of a hasty departure has been neatly encompassed in that expression "get the hell out of Dodge." This dark admonition joined America's lexicon after frequent repetition on *Gunsmoke*, the longest-running dramatic series in network television history. The show mythologized the often lawless, southern Kansas cowboy community of Dodge City, long serving as a barometer for American moral character. Its outlaw image developed during the town's 1872 founding as an outpost for trading buffalo hide, and shortly thereafter becoming a railway trailhead for movements of dust-kicking cattle arriving from Texas. Legendary lawmen Wyatt Earp and Bat Masterson arrived in town to fill an unenviable position of sheriff at a place where more gunfighters roamed than any other frontier outpost around the nation. Pistol duels still recur regularly here on Front Street during summer months along wooden sidewalks where cowboys, railway workers, and harlots would once commingle amongst the inebriated, spilling from packed saloons—one for every fifty residents. Virtue was subordinated to growth as a profusion of gambling rooms, drinking emporiums, or bawdy houses existed cheek by jowl with dry goods and hardware stores.

A palimpsest of the wickedest place in the west may be found along a false front streetscape at present-day Boot Hill Museum, named for an adjacent cemetery where villainous gunslingers were said to have been buried with their boots on. Nearby, overlooking busy railroad tracks, the Red Light House no longer exists but in its day saw a healthy patronage seeking that world's oldest profession and was said to have spawned the phrase "red light district." Facing stiff competition, ladies of ill repute might reveal a bit of leg to drum up some brothel-bound business. Where even horse thieves and desperadoes needed some moments of relaxation, an evocative figure strikes a defiant, corseted stance in front of John Tyler's Tonsorial Parlour, where barbers had not only cut hair but performed bloodletting, tooth extractions, leeching, and enemas.

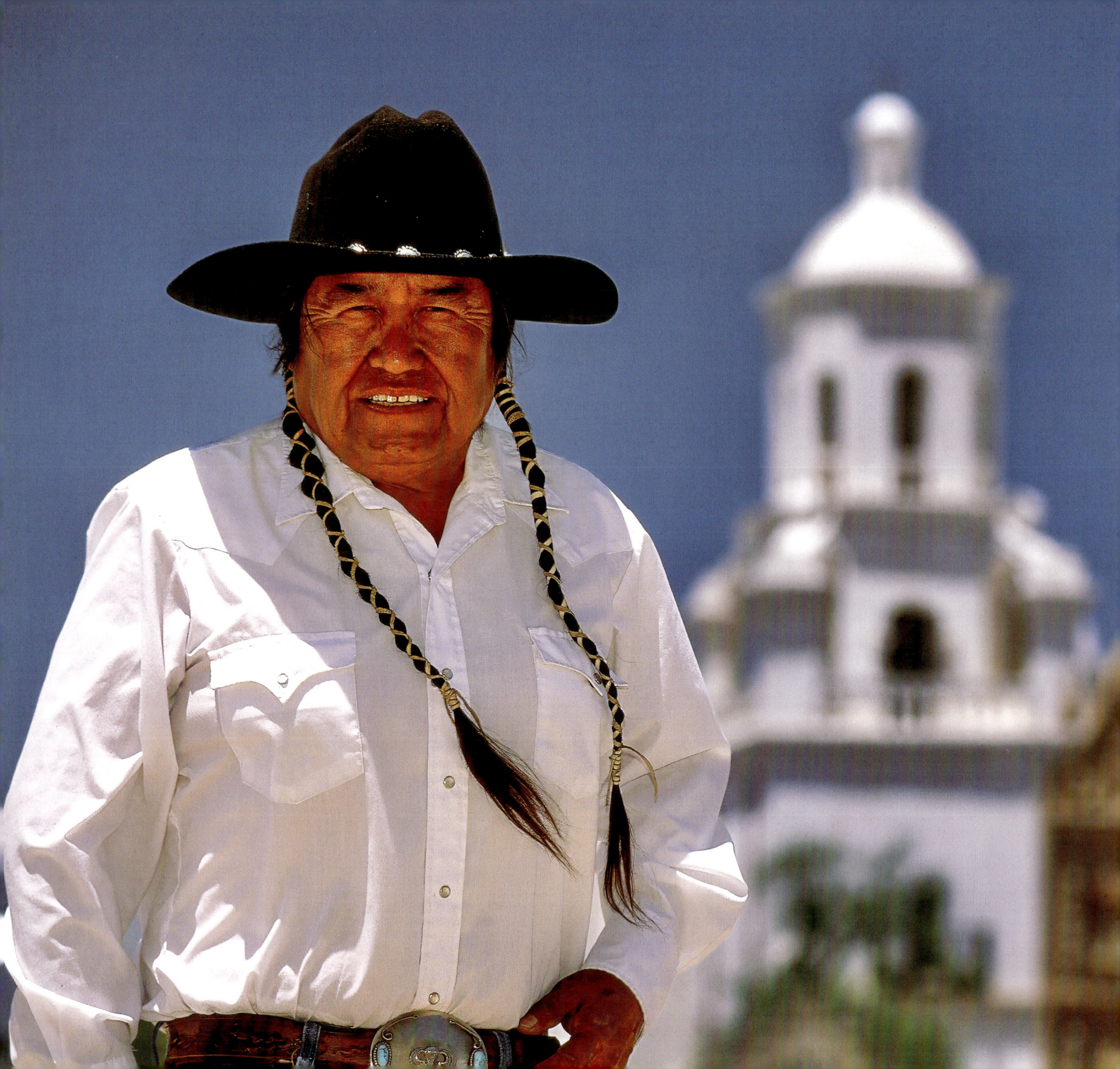

TOHONO O'ODHAM TRIBAL ELDER

Tucson, Arizona

Living amongst parched, cactus-littered plains, the native Tohono O'odham cleverly made their Sonoran Desert homes alongside alluvial plains. That enabled a natural funneling of mountain runoff during rare late summer monsoon rainstorms and channeled nourishing waters into adjacent agricultural fields which then enjoyed long growing seasons. Older girls would fetch the water while boys snatched small game. As men farmed the fields, women laboriously wove yucca grass baskets and created pottery. In winter older men would hunt bighorn sheep or pronghorn antelope, sharing their catch with all their fellow villagers. Diets there were supplemented by honey mesquite, tepary beans, hog potatoes, and organ pipe cactus fruit. Tohono O'odham cooks whipped up porridge from the edible seeds of saguaro cactus, its fruits transformed into jams and ceremonial wines. The challenges of desert survival in this inhospitable landscape were exacerbated during agricultural shoplifting by raiding Apache parties, then compounded with dwindling water supplies that accompanied European colonization as they soon introduced detrimental habits including ranching and well drilling. As Spaniards engaged in their Catholic vision promoting church development, they employed the Tohono for construction of Mission San Xavier del Bac, completed by 1797. This building rose under watchful supervision from Franciscan priests, creating America's finest example of Spanish Colonial design and the oldest European structure in Arizona. Knocked by earthquakes while also struck by lightning, its miraculously surviving interior is filled with frescoes, ornate gilded carvings, and trompe l'oeil. The astonishing structure became a much-revered pilgrimage site, attended by nearly a quarter million worshippers arriving either on foot or horseback during cavalcade processions. On the grounds, its pomegranate and fig tree-studded Mission Gardens, enlivened with acequias irrigation, Tarahumara chicken coops, and ocotillo ramadas represent 4,000 years of gardening along with the longest continually cultivated area in this country.

Requiring fourteen years to construct, the twin towers of Mission San Xavier del Bac seems to match tones with the double-pocketed white shirt held in place by a turquoise-studded buckle that helps girdle this proud, sun-wrinkled Tohono O'odham native whose long pigtails might well symbolize the longevity of his people. First constructed within Mexico's borders, it was only after an 1854 Gadsden Purchase that this mission could claim residency in the United States of America. While famed singer Linda Ronstadt baptized all her children here, Reverend Martin Luther King Jr. attended during the only time he ever visited a Native American reservation.

PUEBLO PATRIARCH

Taos Pueblo, New Mexico

Cradled beneath shadows from the serrated Sangre de Cristo Range, one of North America's oldest continuously inhabited communities still practices their ancient traditions. Amongst the surrounding piñon pine wilderness, a cubist, thousand-year-old apartment building of mud-baked adobe soars up to five stories in viga-supported sections of its sprawling rectilinear compartments. Originally, these individual units were improbably entered from holes in the roof, first reached by climbing ladders before a Santa-like descent into their homes with another ladder. During threats of Spanish attack, first noticed outside from terraced platforms, the exterior ladders were pulled up, denying invaders any possible access. The native language of the inhabitants at this northernmost of New Mexico's pueblos is Tiwa, probably spoken by less than two thousand people on earth. Scores of residents still live inside its four-foot-thick earthen walls, lacking electricity, plumbing, and any running water as decreed by the Tribal Council. Outside, red chiles are strung near ramadas of drying corn, as fluffy bread is yanked from cedar-fueled, beehive-shaped horno baking ovens. Water is hauled from crystal currents flowing through Red Willow Creek, which traverses a main plaza, and whose sacred source emanates from mountainous Blue Lake, whispered in secretive legends as the spiritual birthplace of all Pueblo people.

A wizened tribal elder prepares for the next day's Turtle Dance, when gourd rattles and pine boughs are gyrated by waves of shirtless men. Across their snow-dappled compound, solemn processions shuffle along as leg-strapped bells chime rhythmically in the cold of New Year's Day.

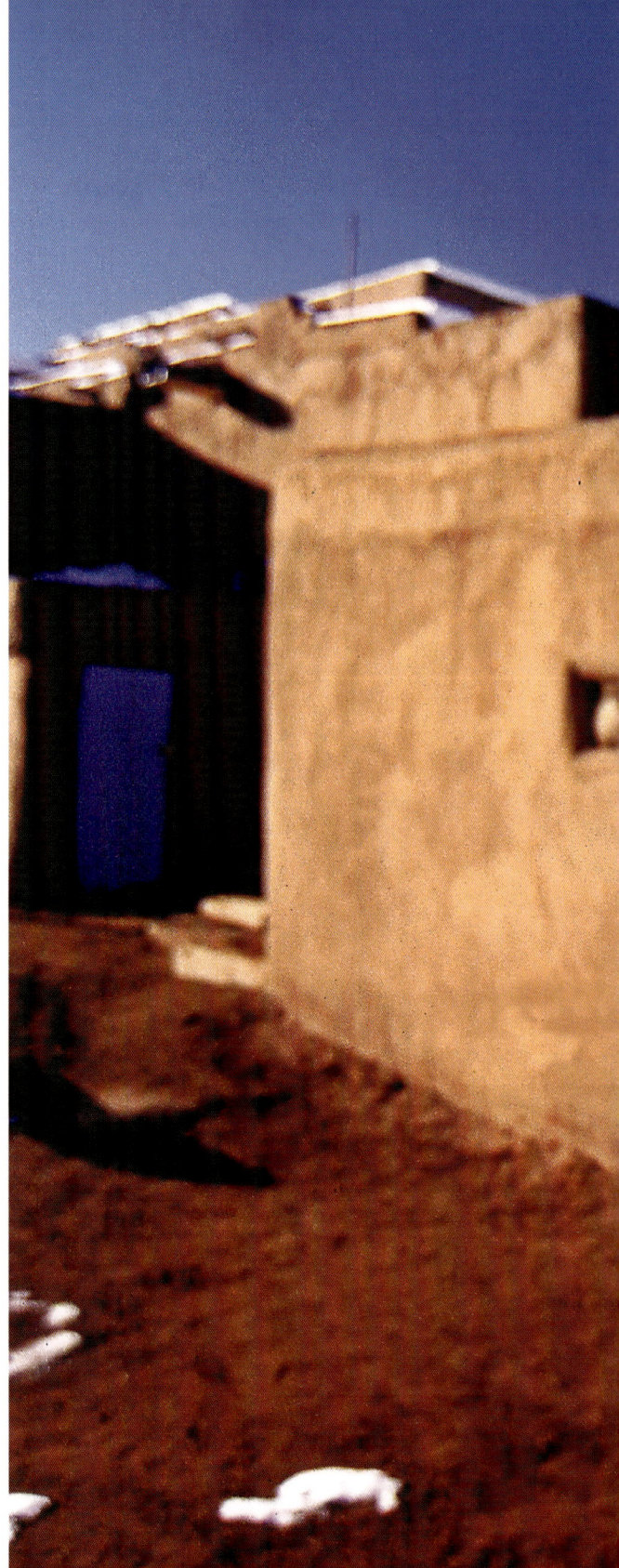

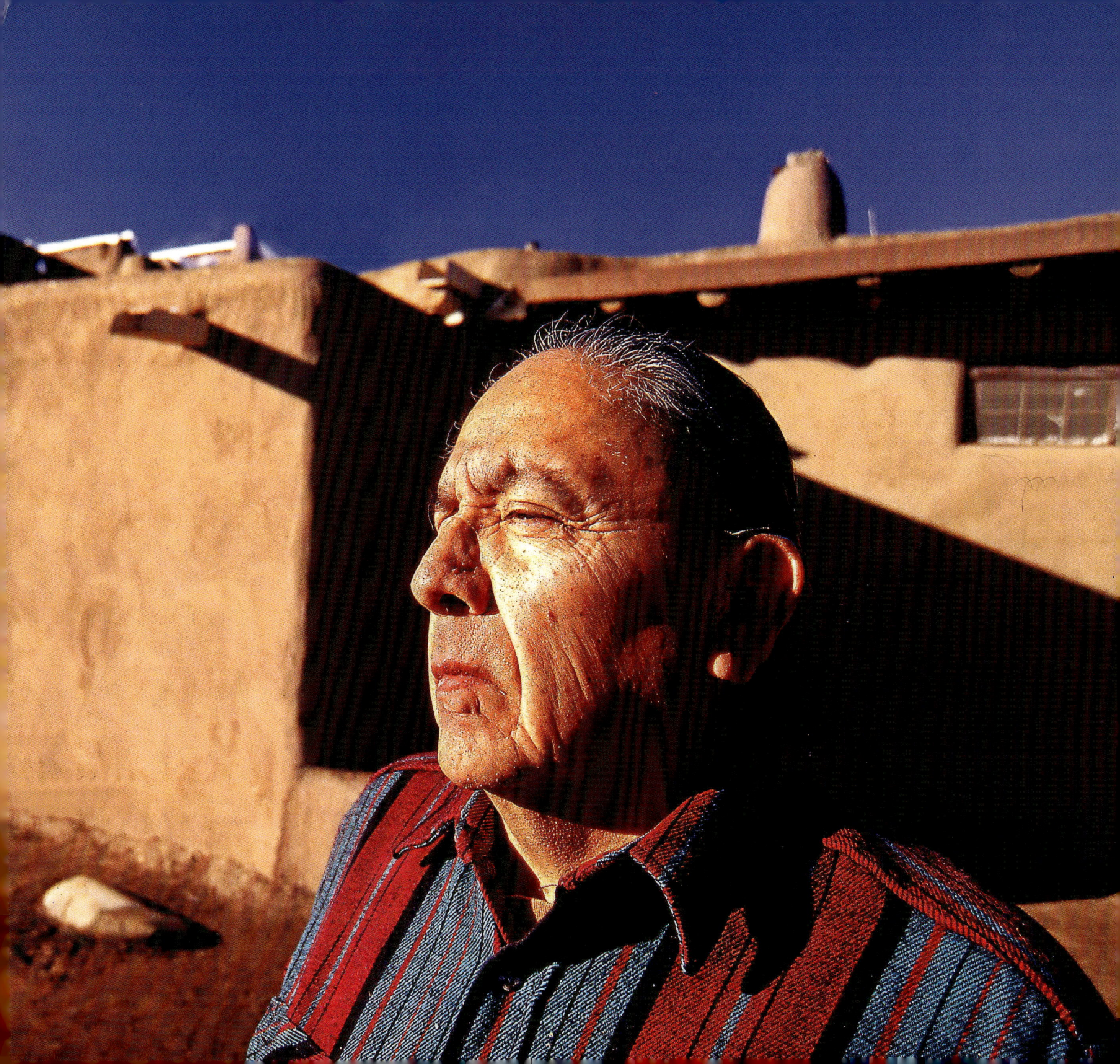

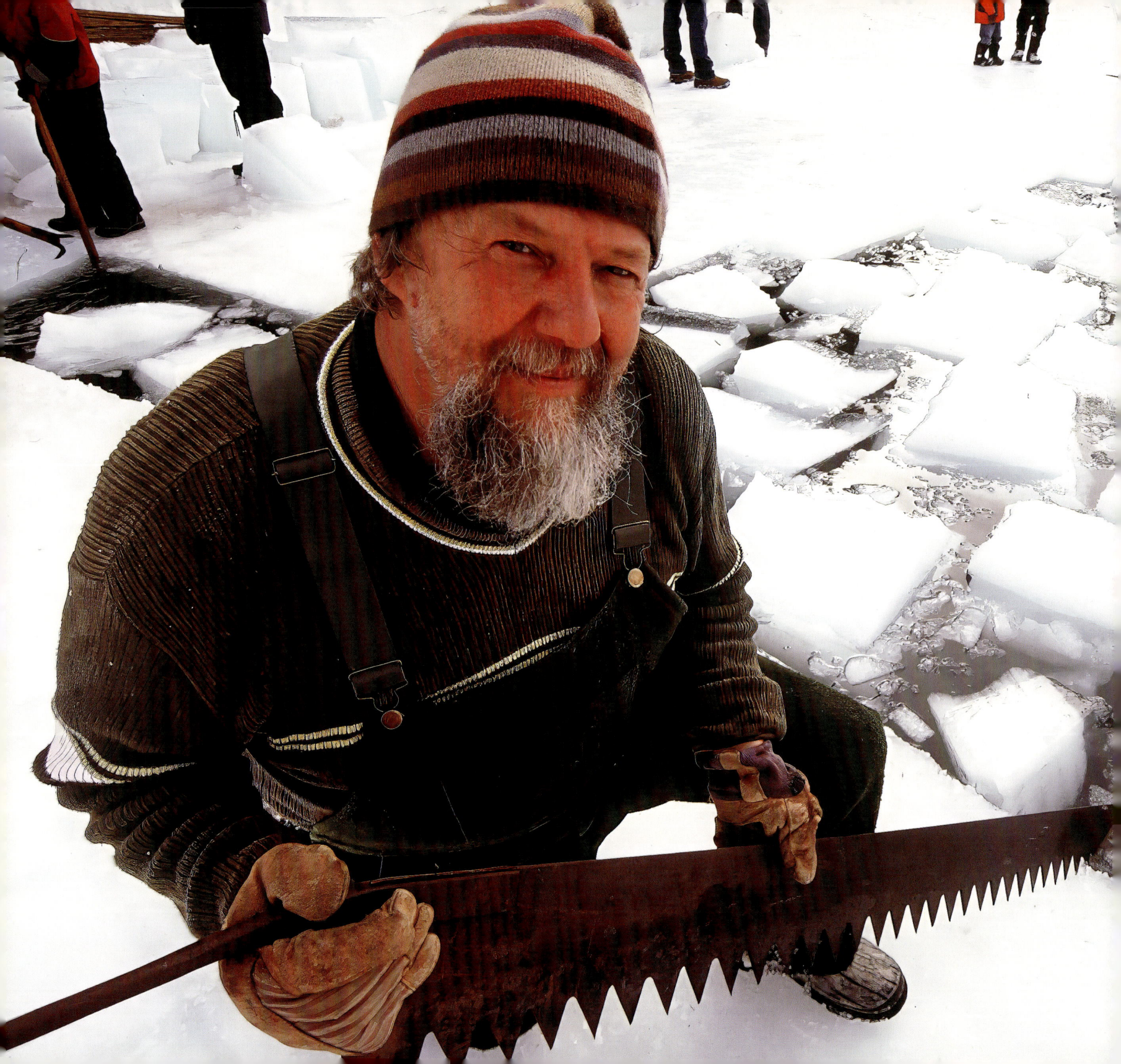

ICE HARVESTER

Tully, New York

An atmospheric conveyor belt of frigid Canadian air traveling over warmer, lengthy Lake Ontario produces the country's largest daily snowfalls. Firmly in the lake effect's target zone is Tully, New York, once a burgeoning railroad town that sits aside numerous shallow bodies of water. These lakes, freezing earlier than their deeper counterparts, have historically been important centers of ice production during the nineteenth century's pre-refrigeration era.

The frozen lakeside expanse at Green Lake, once over 12 inches thick, are still cleared by horse-hitched plows. Joining his neighbors, a stalwart, thermally prepared villager uses five-foot-long saws and pike poles to dissect its surface, creating channels for floating the freezing blocks to shore. Then the 300-pound chunks are tong-loaded onto equine-powered pickups for its sleigh journey to a nearby two-story ice house, where they are carefully insulated with sawdust. The coldest crop once waited there to be shipped by rail to New York City for their iceman's daily home delivery. These days, the slippery cubes will re-emerge in early summer to serve as a crucial ingredient for their local strawberry ice cream festival. In the meantime, as nearby ice fishermen trawl for panfish and pickerel, these wintry community gatherings serve as chilly reminder of bygone days before refrigerators caused an icy industry to totally melt away.

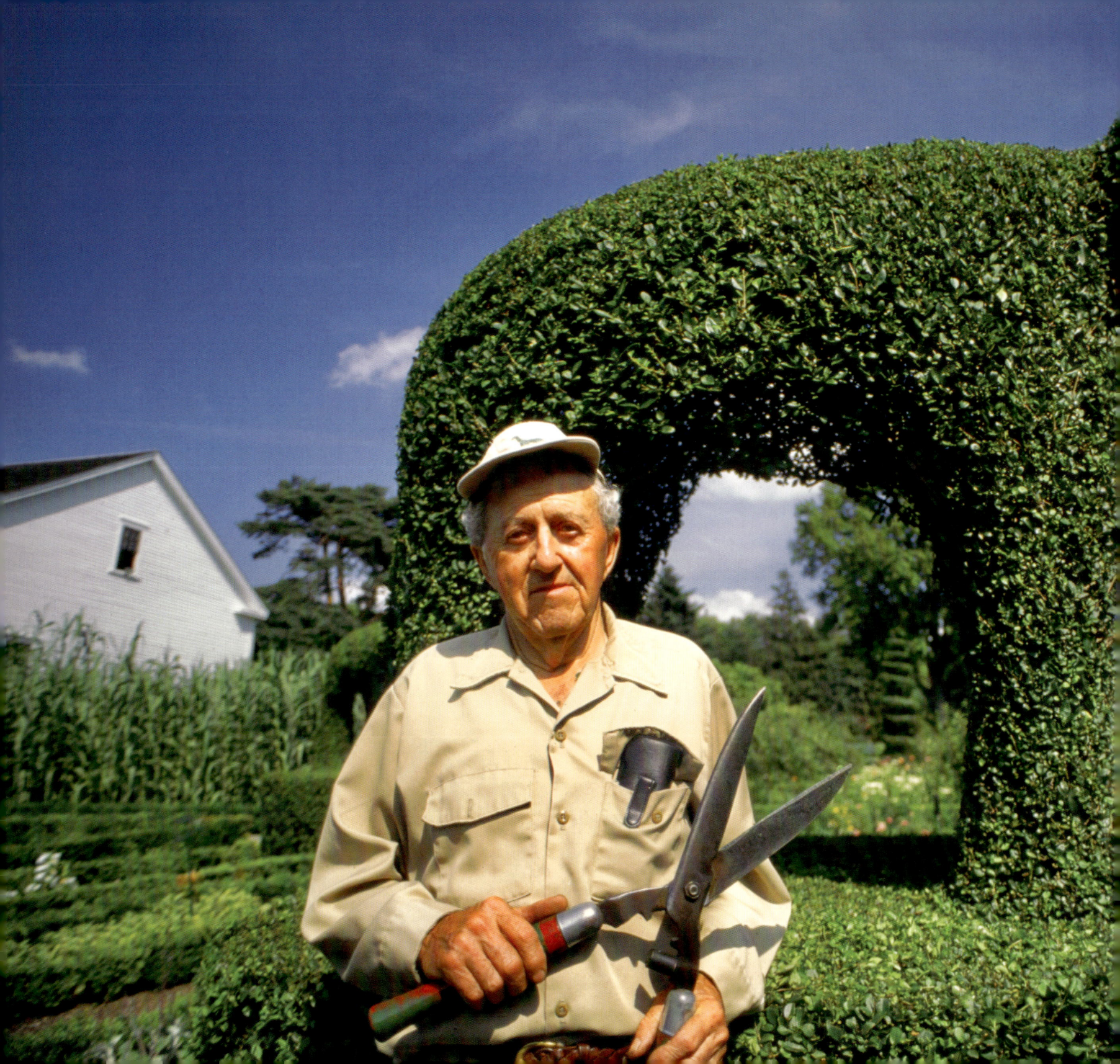

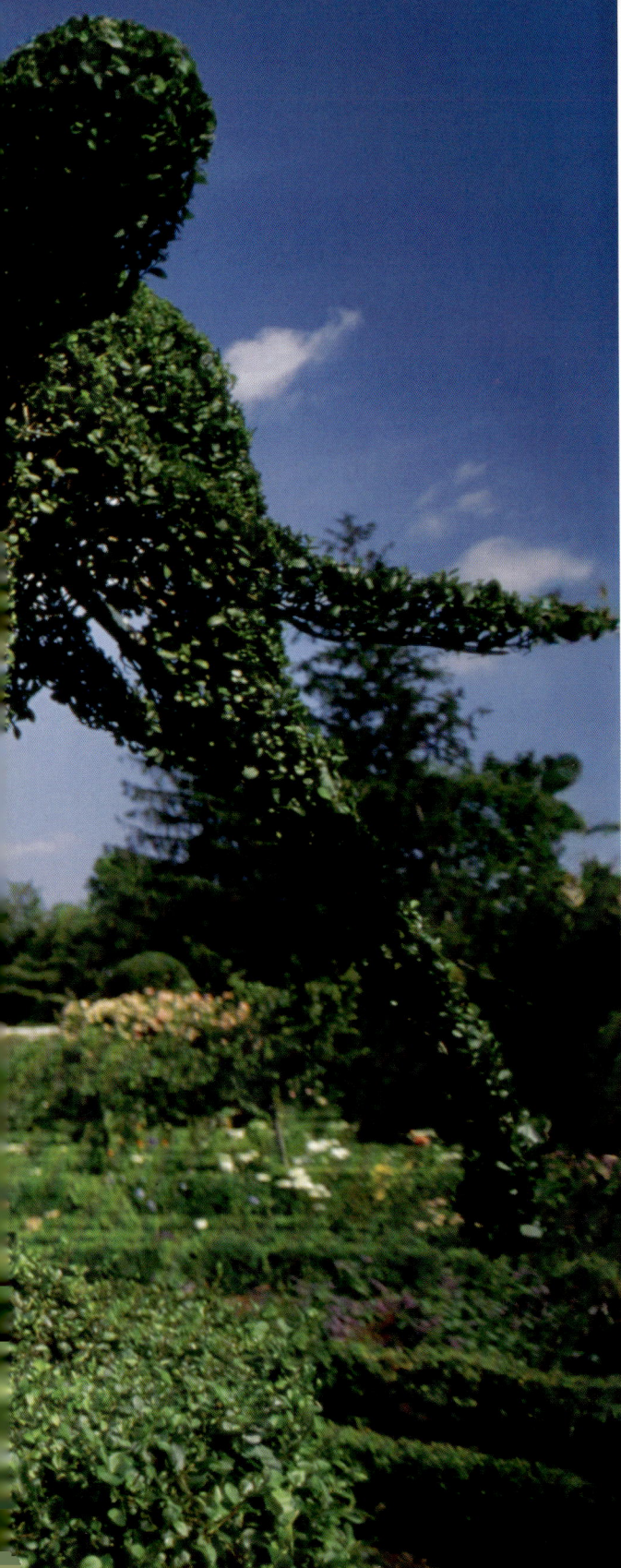

TOPIARY GARDENER
Portsmouth, Rhode Island

A magical variety of fanciful gardening, topiary's early roots date back to Pliny the Elder, a naturalist, philosopher, and army commander during the early Roman Empire who described that practice of barbered groves in his *Naturalis Historia*, an ancient encyclopedia originally published in 77 CE and considered perhaps this world's very first such compilation. The work inspired Gaius Matius, a close friend of Julius Caesar, who in turn popularized topiary all throughout his global domain, as clipped cypress expressed elaborate figures of obelisks, cyphers, and even animals, motifs that eventually infiltrated many wealthy villas. As the empire collapsed, medieval monks preserved this tradition of growing herbs and manicuring hedges in their monastery's cloistered courtyards. During the Renaissance, French landscapers expanded Italy's geometric gardens emphasizing proportion and symmetry, which culminated in splendid displays at Versailles, while Dutch greenskeepers introduced a whimsical complexity to their own sculpted displays. These meticulously crafted forms required a nurseryman's patience and finesse to snip phantasmagorical botanical critters into living testaments of horticultural creativity. Verdant beasts seemed to rampage across a delicately arranged parterre, while boxwood ships might find themselves smoothly sailing toward espaliered fruit trees.

America's first and northernmost topiary gardens were created at Green Animals, a small 1859 country estate overlooking Narragansett Bay. Since 1912, this Victorian summer retreat has hosted a zoological menagerie of privet, yew, and boxwood creatures that have been hemmed in by arbors, geometric pathways, and over 35 formal flower beds on seven fragrant acres offering a captivating blend seeding nature with artistry. In 1948 the gardens hosted the coming-out party of Jackie Bouvier, who went on to become First Lady and widow of John Kennedy, and then her decidedly less fashionable predecessor Mamie Eisenhower. George Mendonça, a determined gardener, is poised with gargantuan pruning scissors to make skillfully quick trimming work out of elephantine shrubbery lording over his enclosure penning blooming roses and spiraling hedges. This estate's superintendent, Mendonça was a featured subject in *Fast, Cheap & Out of Control*, an arresting documentary by Academy Award-winning director Errol Morris. That acclaimed film further raked up the longevity of this horticultural savant who departed earth at age 101, just one day behind his wife.

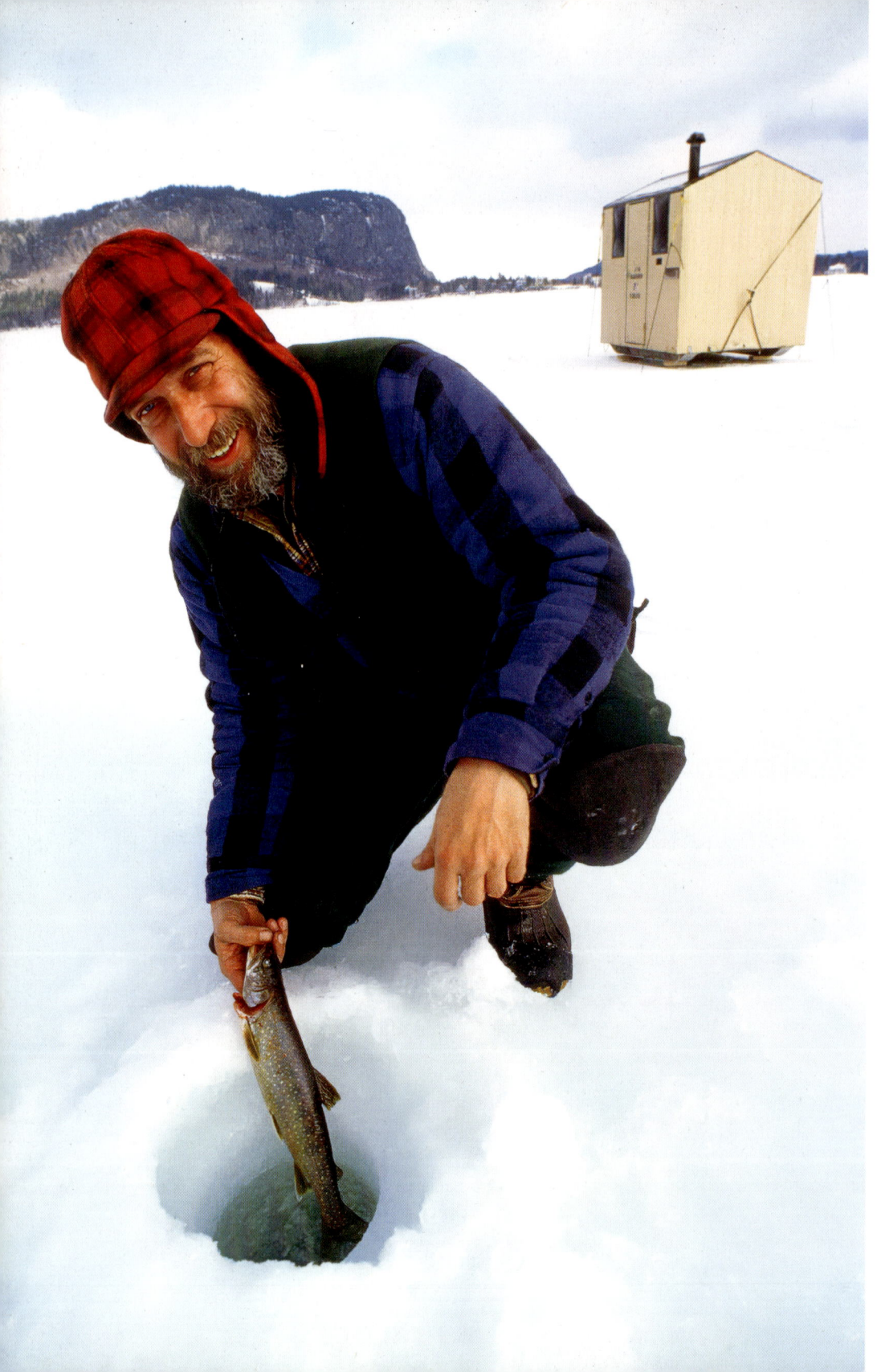

ICE FISHERMAN
Mount Kineo, Maine

From the air Moosehead Lake truly does resemble its namesake's head, that of North America's tallest mammal. Glaciated shorelines around Maine's largest lake form convincing moose antler silhouettes, found here crowning some of their densest populations in the lower 48 states, as they outnumber humans by more than three to one. Dominating Moosehead Lake is Mount Kineo, one of New England's most prominent geological landmarks whose dramatic slopes were shaped by mile-thick ice sheets about 15,000 years ago. Left behind is the world's largest chunk of rhyolite, a prime component for flint. That mineral was first utilized by the native Maliseet tribe for sharpening tools and later as a crucial ingredient in sparking lighters which now might ignite wood stoves warming ice fishermen. Despite concerns about frostbite, ice fishing's lure grabs those who crave a rugged wilderness experience with no chance of annoying bug bites. With fewer insects or crawfish available in the winter, hungry fish are much more willing to take risks and try snacking on a line. Weathering these frozen conditions also confirms mankind's primal instinct for hunting and gathering, as well as the questionable impression that human beings sit atop the food chain. After drilling holes with an auger through ice that might well be two feet thick, green water shoots up like uncorked champagne. Beneath the ice, landlocked salmon, togue, cusk, and trout all congregate beneath a catch-alerting tip-up's flag, which when sprung would certainly justify for that hardy troller any frigid snowmobile trip needed to reach this spot.

After some time, a lake trout reluctantly emerges from the state's second deepest lake. Obviously, patience and some jigging with bucktail bait pays off, spawning delight beneath the flannel ear-flapped hat capping a stout, well-insulated ice fisherman. He'll dine heartily beneath the smoking chimney at his tiny skid house warming hut, where chowder of freshly caught cusk proves a worthy starting appetizer.

RATTLESNAKE WRANGLER

Sweetwater, Texas

Dust and tumbleweed sweep across desolate West Texas prairie, a favorite habitat of the western diamondback. Overpopulation among these serpentine pit vipers, more aggressive than any other rattlesnake species, is a major concern to local ranchers fearing for the safety of unsuspecting children and livestock. Out amongst the cactus and sagebrush, only the brave or foolish dare attempt gathering one of earth's most deadly predators. Despite its less than optimum vision, the six-foot slithering reptile can track its prey with heat-sensing facial pits and a flicking tongue that enables olfactory detection, while vertical pupils help somewhat with depth perception. Hidden limestone rock-protected dens may signal a horde of coiled snakes, unveiled by using small handheld mirrors to reflect the searing sun into subterranean passages. When disturbed, its hissing maraca-pitched tail-shaker can rattle up to ninety times per second, the world's fastest firing muscle. Their rattles grow by one segment every skin shedding and are composed of keratin, the same substance in human fingernails.

After wielding his pinner with adept hooking finesse, a steady-nerved, Kevlar-legged wrangler immobilizes that prey beneath a shading, snake-skin-banded cowboy hat. For the five-dollar-a-pound bounty, this sure-footed hunter will then deftly fling rattlers into wooden boxes, eventually supplying milking-delivered antidotes from their hinged fang's concentrated, tissue-destroying, hemorrhage-inducing venom.

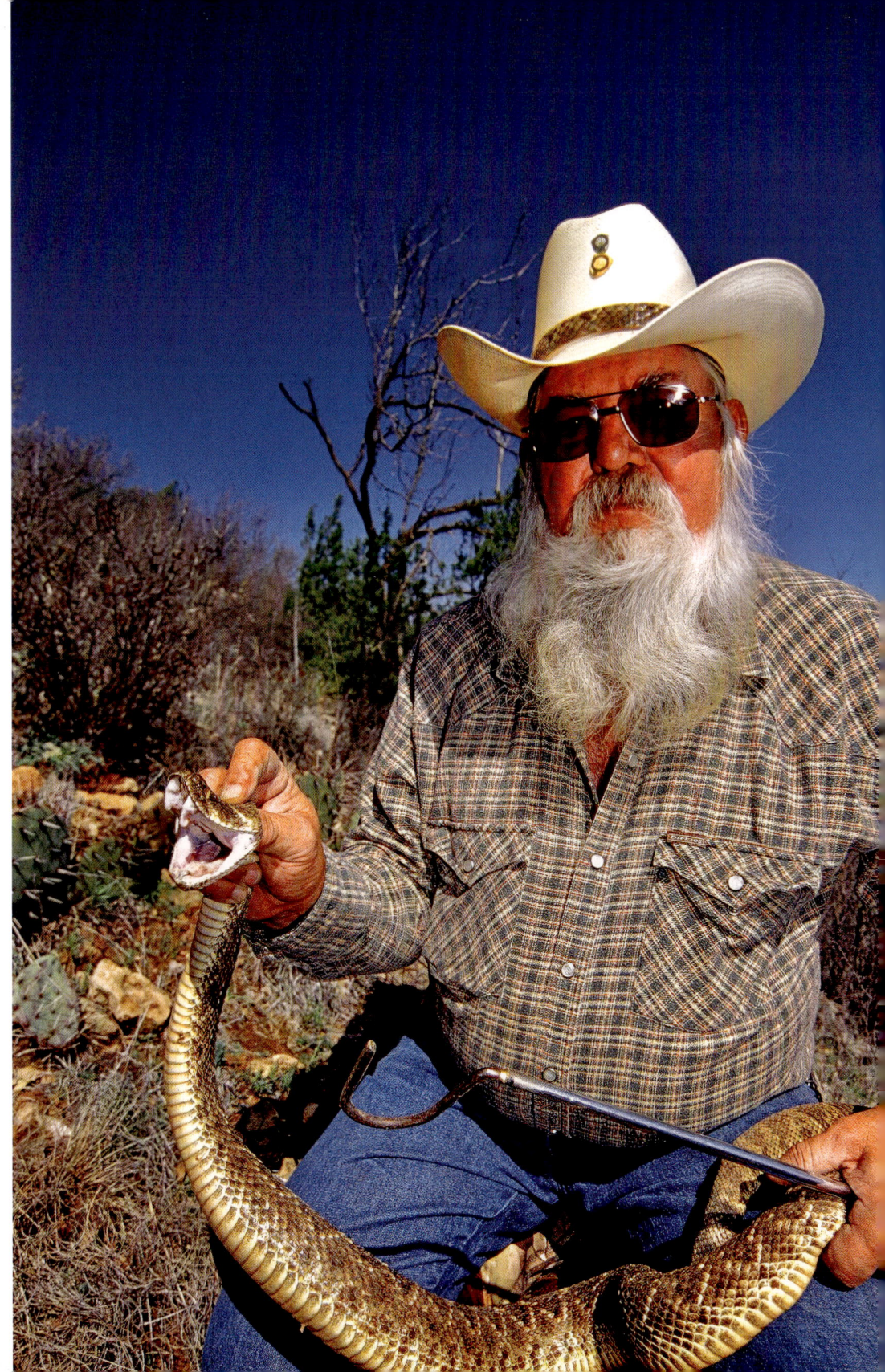

EEL TRAPPER

Hancock, New York

In the western Catskills' rural Sullivan County, shortened daylight hours during autumn inhibit chlorophyll production within deciduous forest leaves that soon adopt their new seasonal palette. Their branches frame swollen currents on the Delaware River, carving its way through mountainous topography. When a new moon and steady rain coincide sometime in late September, slithering American eels ride these gurgling downstream cascades by the thousands during one of nature's most mysterious and seldom-seen migrations. Oriented by earth's magnetic field, this slippery catadromous species are instinctively determined to head toward their point of origin at spawning grounds near Bermuda, in the seaweed-choked Sargasso Sea.

Intending mass interceptions, grizzled iconoclast and eel trapper Ray Turner annually goes about backbreaking construction of an elaborate stone weir that funnels the gourmet delicacy into its hand-built wooden multi-stage contraption, where they are gathered daily into his smokehouse-bound canoe. Aromatically fumed eels are a widely sought delicacy snatched by savvy customers who venture down bumpy dirt roads past his fenced pet emu and toward an off-the-grid riverside cabin.

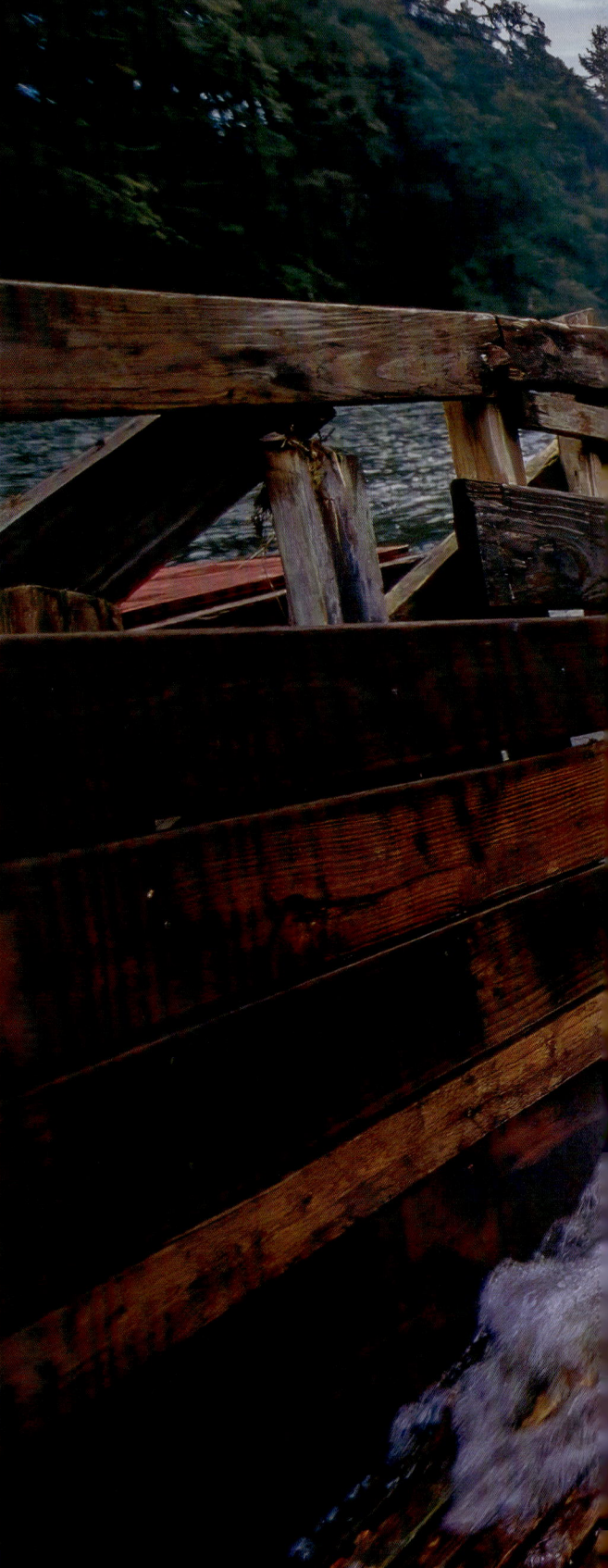

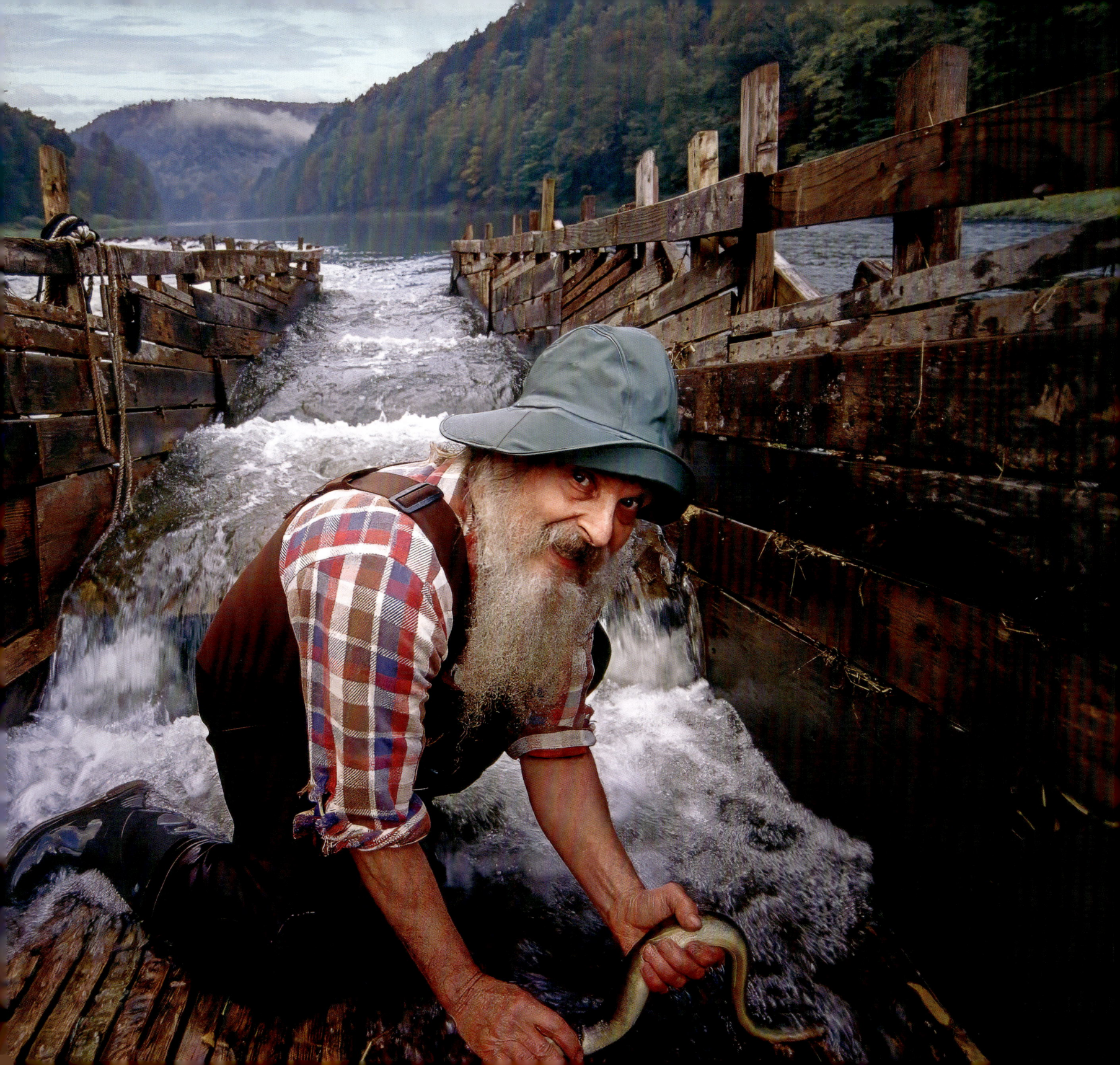

COTTON FIELD WORKER

Mattson, Mississippi

Testing America's brand-new patent system, Eli Whitney received recognition for his invention, assigned early number 72X in the nation's march into the industrial revolution. His cotton engine, whose last word became *gin* for short, was the subject of much litigation during numerous contesting court claims that followed. Consequently, this iconic inventor failed to reap much profit from his major innovation but instead managed to inadvertently spark a reinvigoration of southern slavery, and ultimately create geopolitical conditions for the Civil War. His simple gin pressed raw cotton against mesh screens, catching seeds, while wire hooks on the other side pulled its fluffy white substance through and a moving brush removed loose lint while collecting cleaned fiber. As a result, the prohibitive, extremely labor-intensive methods previously employed could be supplanted by new efficient productions that lowered costs and increased profitable demands from European markets for cotton products. Plantations thrived as cotton fields flourished in the Deep South, particularly across fertile, river-enriched Mississippi Delta soils. Their enslaved population grew exponentially as this planet's first agricultural powerhouse produced three-quarters of cotton's global supply.

Scattered remnants of late nineteenth-century sharecropping and tenant farming culture still sprout amongst cotton pickers scouring bountiful fields that can yield up to three bales per acre. As whitened rows of bolls bloom, sun-drenched, back-breaking labor helps to stuff bulging burlap sacks in the fertile, sediment-fortified delta. During the midday Mississippi heat, a stoic picker is almost finished filling just one of his many tattered bags after gathering with caution to reduce hand injuries. Twisting cotton out of the bolls from its base exposes busy fingers to sharp and pointy edges on this plant. In the meantime, its seeds have planted a flag in the culinary world as it provides cottonseed oil, once a main component of Crisco shortening and still found in supermarkets as an ingredient for potato chips and mayonnaise.

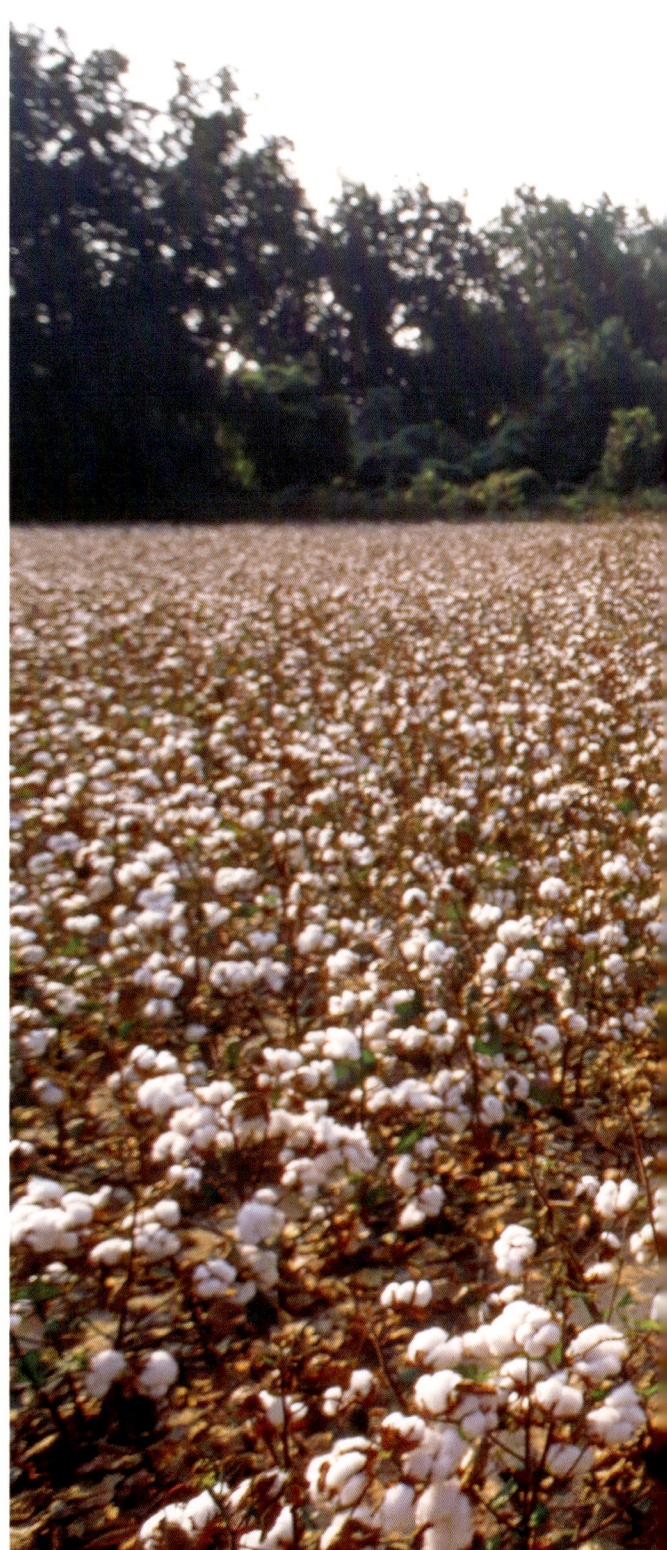

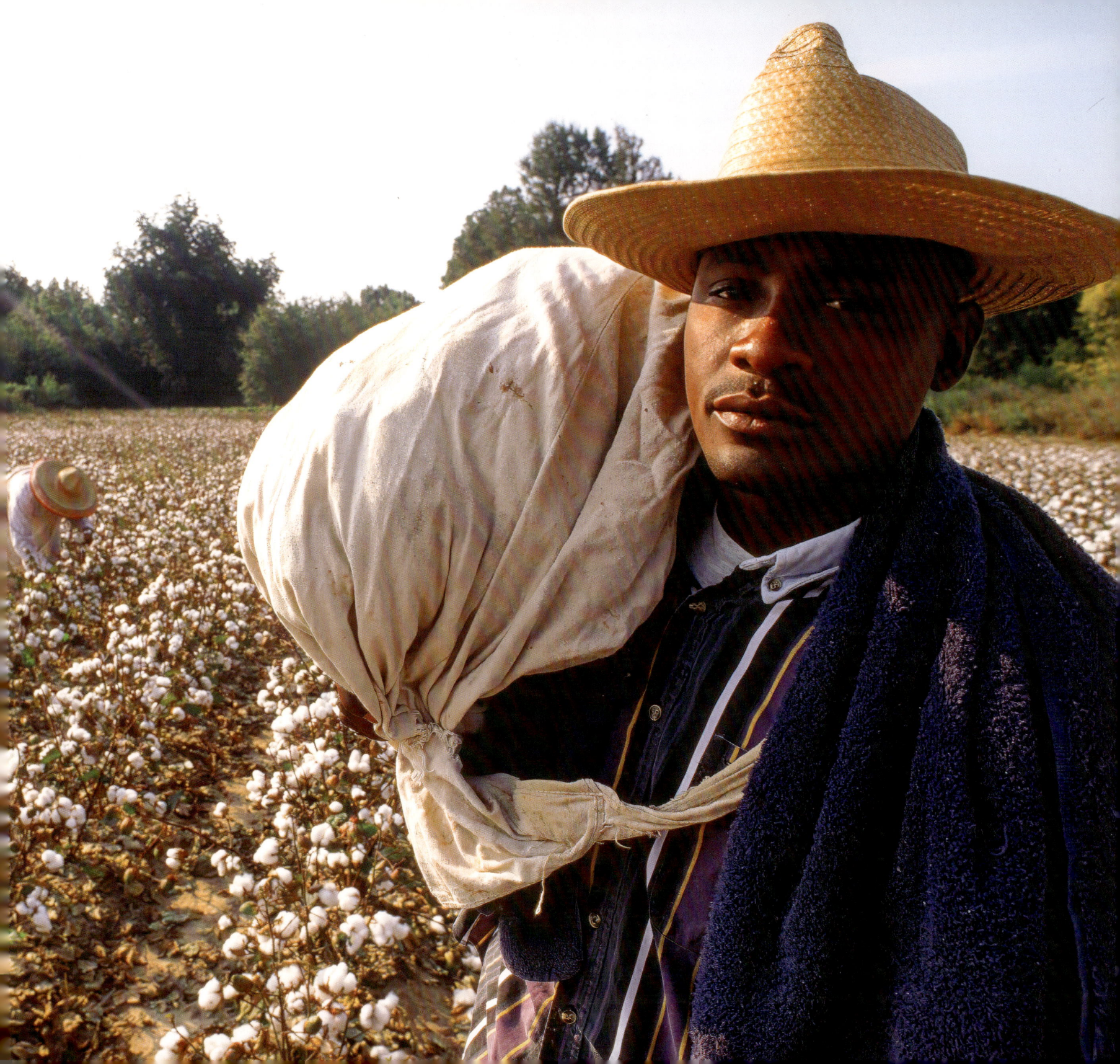

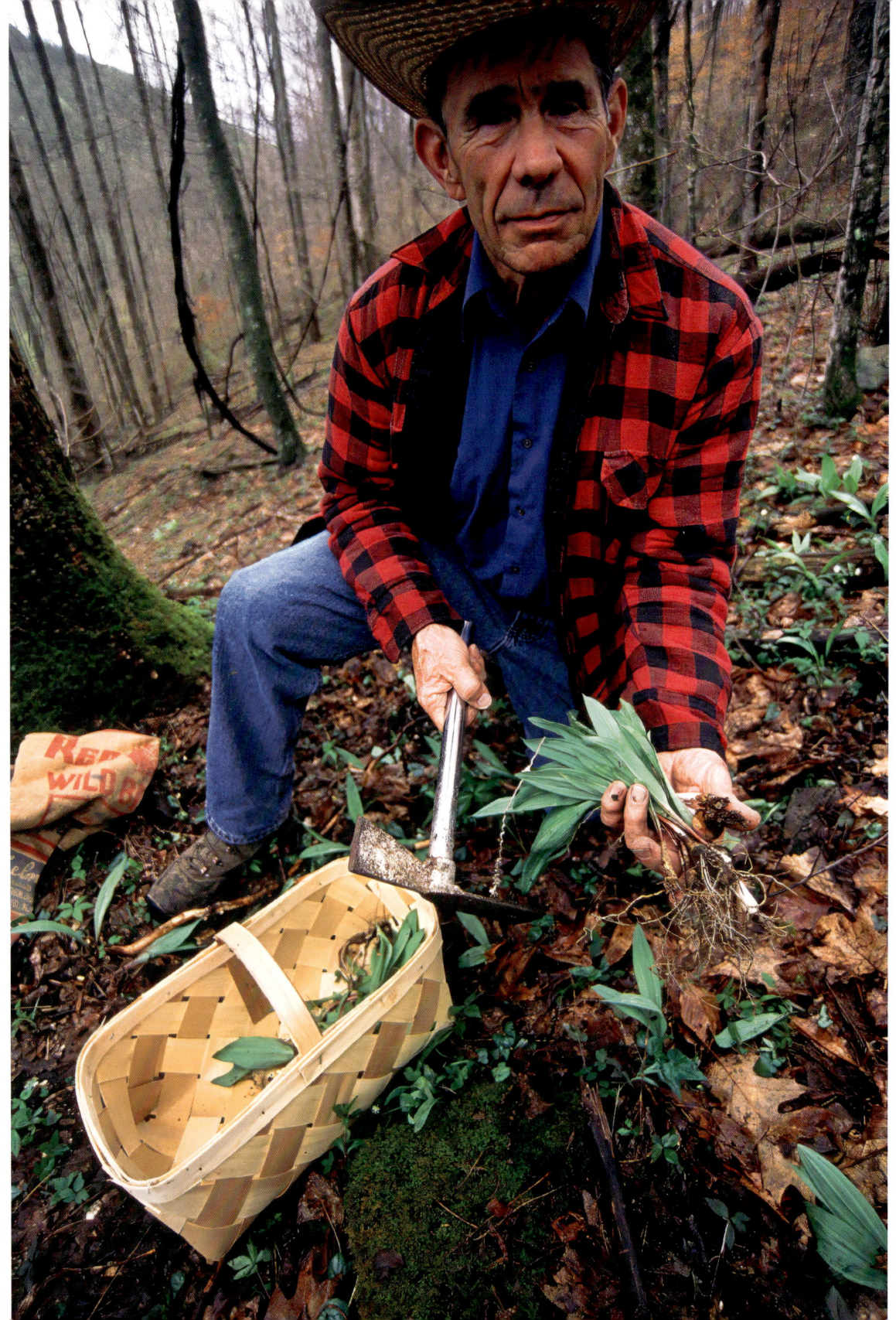

RAMP FORAGER

Richwood, West Virginia

Aptly nicknamed Mountain State, rugged West Virginia is indeed this country's highest east of the Mississippi River. This nation's third most forested state is the only one completely situated within Appalachian Mountain ridges, where some wondrous culinary secrets hide partially buried within rolling hillside folds. Soon after the snow melts, pungent odors may be detected by vigilant foragers with keen olfactory senses, as they zero in on a patch of unfurling ramps, one certain harbinger that spring has sprung. These seasonally edible greens, shade-loving wild leeks, a member of the lily family, can best be spotted along steep, north-facing slopes. While treasured by local Cherokee people as their spring tonic, a cold remedy and sinus cleanser, subsequent mountain settlers found the garlicky, red-stalked plant to be an important nutritional supplement after their difficult winter of only dried corn and beans. Today the undomesticated edible, available fresh merely for just several weeks, has become a much-coveted item in high-end restaurants where celebrity chefs like Emeril Lagasse and Jean-Georges Vongerichten feature the ramps on their seasonal menus.

After trudging across leaf-littered petrichor in the heart of these Monongahela hills, an intrepid, plaid-jacketed forager discovers his trove as he predicted beneath bare oak trees. Armed with pickax and trowel, he prepares to fill his basket and return to salivating appetites gathering at Richwood, proclaimed "ramp capital of the world." Up to two thousand pounds of odoriferous vegetables are cooked at this Feast of the Ramson and served as crowned ramp queens flash their smiles amid flavor-bursting meals. Throughout the region ramp feeds may include pickled, fried, or boiled ramps, in addition to its incorporation in burgers, eggs, casseroles, risotto, jam, and even wine. Back in Richwood, drinks of choice remain sassafras tea to wash things down, though an often-three-day stench from stinky bulbs is hardly remedied by this town's mayor, who greets each arriving diner at the door with one free breath mint.

CHILE PEPPER PICKER

Hatch, New Mexico

From the vantage point of autumn migration's soaring sandhill cranes, a skinny olive swirl tracing river-nourished fields snake conspicuously through rust-colored thrusts that form cradling mountains in southern New Mexico. Their rocky slopes hem in fertile terroir bursting with Hatch chile peppers, said by gourmands to be the world's finest. The gurgling Rio Grande offers a soothing soundtrack for labor intensive harvesting as an agricultural hive of activity centers on dexterous hands, bent spines, and hoisted baskets brimming with pods. Embracing lightning efficiency, pickers scamper across rows of the floodplain's lush vegetation to deposit their tasty load into awaiting tractor-hauled cartons. Hatch chile is prized for a perfect balance of smoky and sweet heat, its pungency offering rich and sometimes buttery flavor. Brought into town for flame roasting, hand-cranked cages sizzle with fragrances that actually prompted the state legislature to designate a first-ever official aroma. The growing notoriety of this regional culinary jewel has prompted an annual red ristra-strung Labor Day festival that swells the town's population fifteen-fold. They'll converge on Sparky's, housed in an antique-stuffed 1926 mercantile building, and feast on this event's gustatory star, hand peeled and chopped, dressing enchiladas, stews, cheeseburgers, or even the restaurant's signature green chile milkshakes.

Soon after sunrise, a pepper picker only briefly pauses beneath the generous shade of his expansive straw hat. His quick pace seems assured, as wooden coins determine payment and are carefully doled out near that tractor upon the deposit of a full container. As the rapidly brightening sun continues a blistering ascension, its strength might seem surpassed only by searing heat emanating from these chile peppers onto taste buds as accurately measured on their Scoville scale.

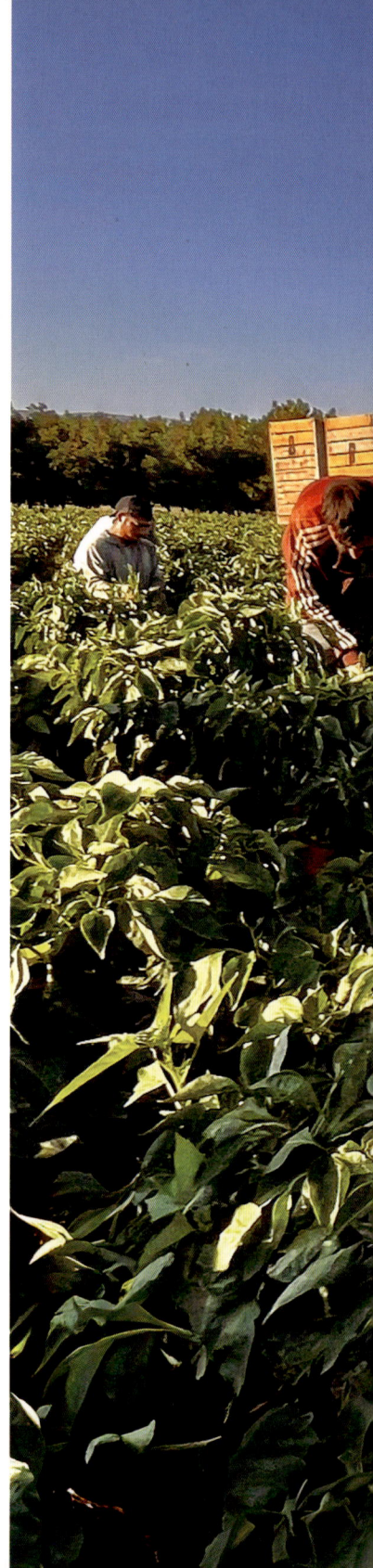

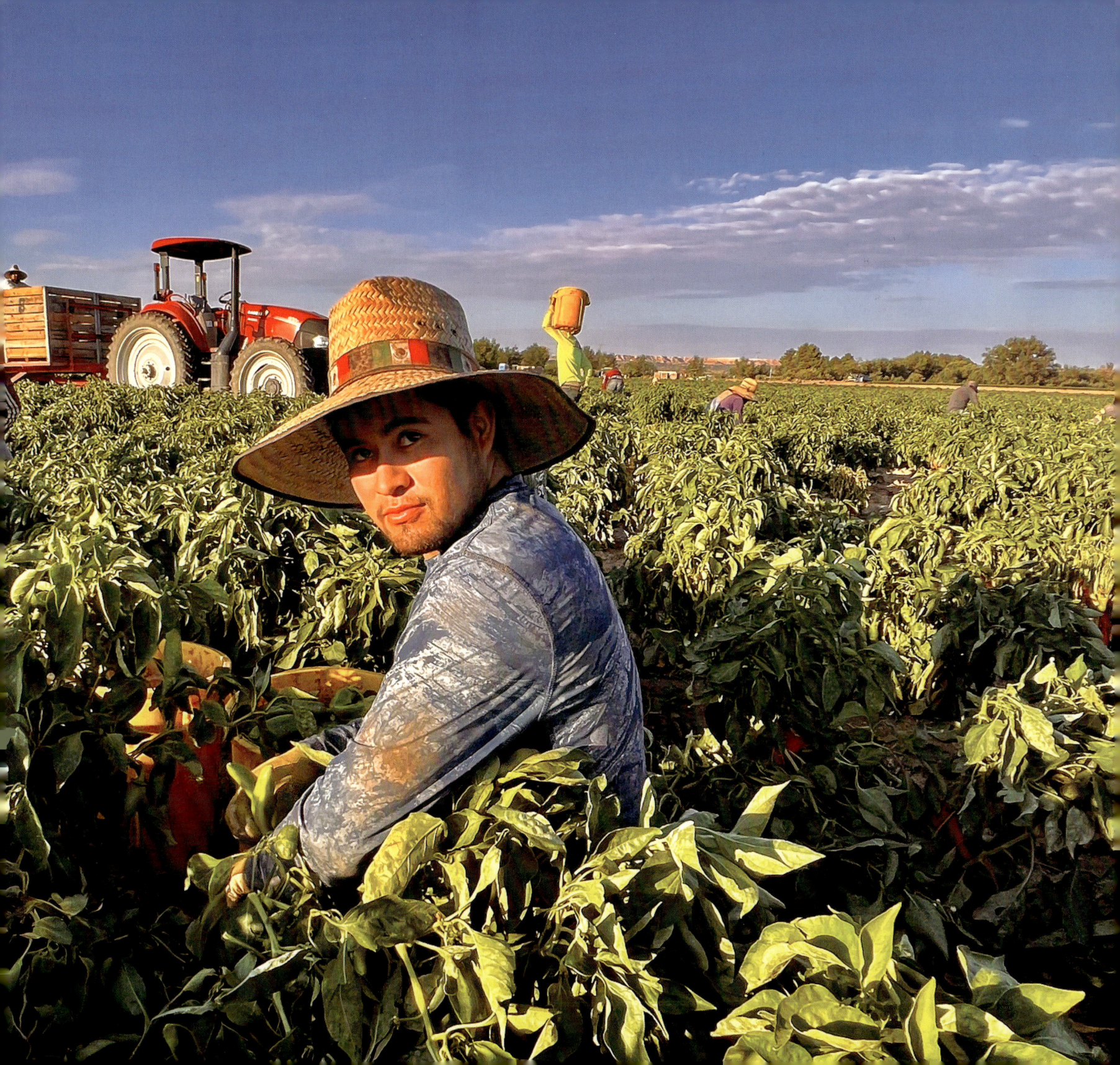

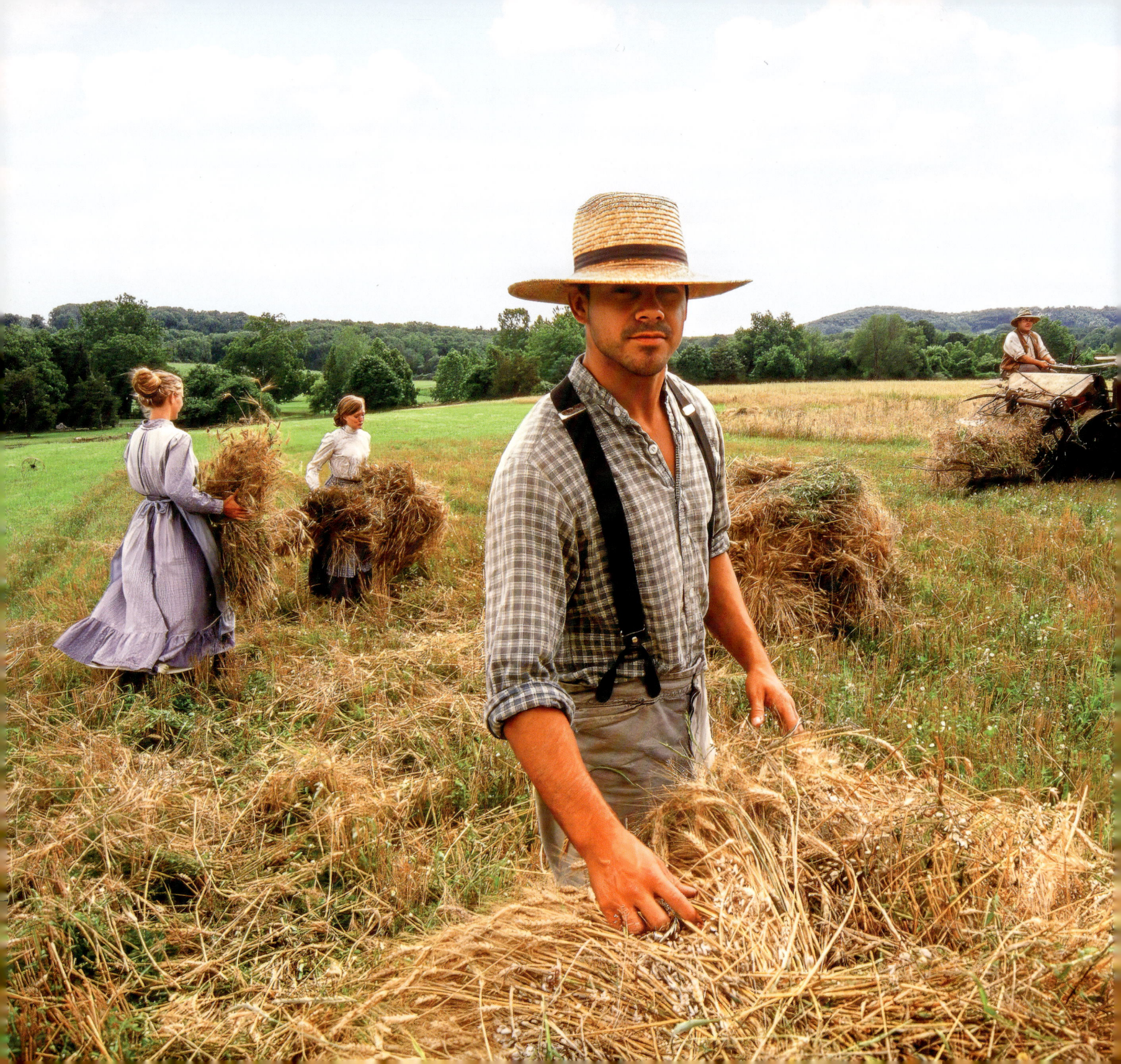

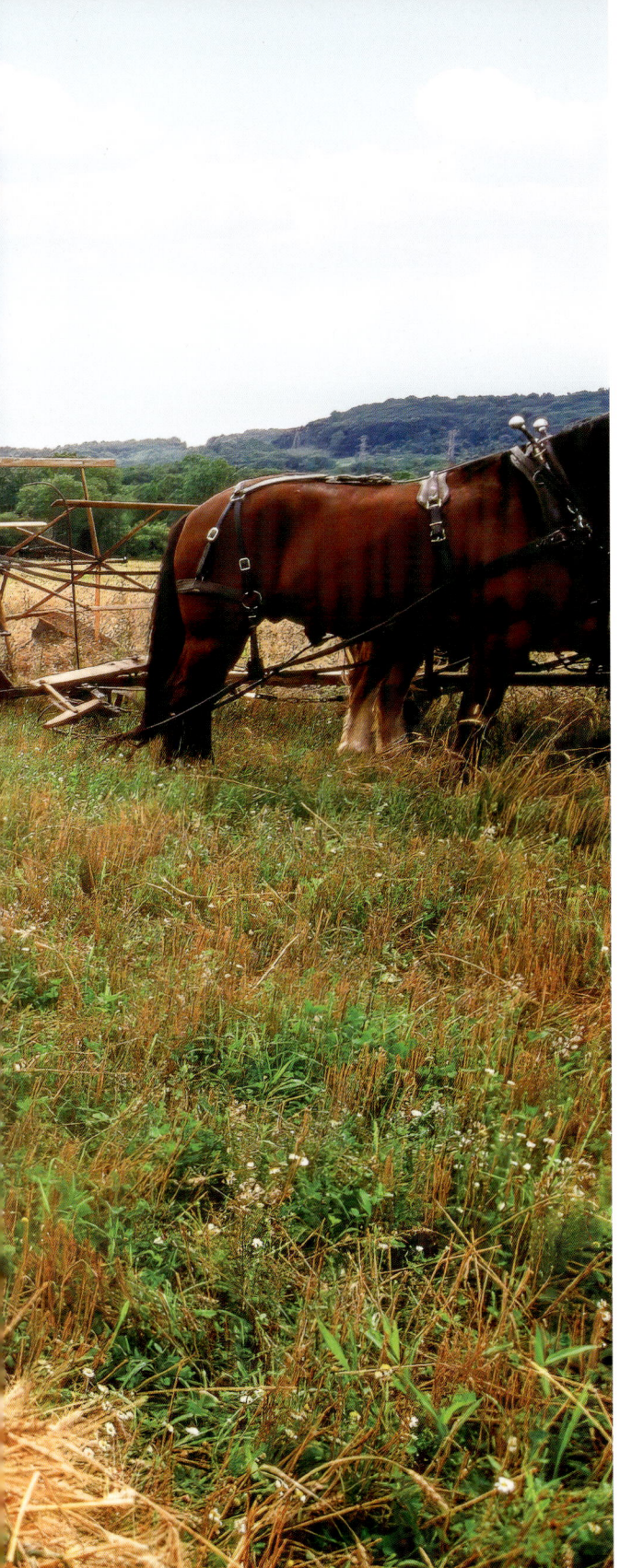

WHEAT REAPER

Titusville, New Jersey

The Roman goddess of agriculture is Ceres, who helped to christen that word cereal, a grass whose cultivation has been foundational to human civilization. Its most important grain is wheat, grown on more land area than any other food crop in the world. In the 1830s, however, wheat-growing farmland acreage was restricted due to scarce farm labor which at the time had to hand cut cereal grain with a scythe. Facing their short harvest season, a typical backbreaking day of manually gathering the crop might cover only two acres as fatigued workers would feverishly attempt to reap what they sowed. After failed attempts by his inventor father, Cyrus McCormick eventually succeeded through arduous experiments in creating the mechanical reaper, sparking a revolution that forged modern agriculture by enabling larger regions to be cultivated utilizing much fewer workers. The draft horse-pulled mechanical reaper incorporated sharp, vibrating cutting blades along with a spinning reel that grabbed the wheat within its reach and an open platform designed to catch any falling grain. A binder would fasten these sheaves of grain, depositing them on the ground for later collection. Today in New Jersey, Howell Living History Farm is nestled within Mercer County's remaining pastoral nook and preserves these rural traditions from the earliest moments of our last century.

This clattering, Clydesdale-drawn McCormick Reaper-Binder from the late 1880s grinds to an abrupt halt after plowing through amber waves of ripened grain, cutting and bundling golden harvests of winter wheat into sheaves, directly inspiring a noted nineteenth-century Protestant church hymn. Its catchy chorus has often been repeated, whether in a John Wayne western or an episode of *The Simpsons*. Wearing prairie dresses, female workers carry sheaves that will be gathered into a stook, arranged to keep grain heads off the ground. Amidst 130 acres of fertile fields, a suspender-supported farmhand momentarily breaks from chores, and will no doubt doubly enjoy the homemade wheat bread baking back at the 1809 Joseph Phillips Farmhouse.

FLAX SCUTCHERS

Stahlstown, Pennsylvania

The first clothing known to man was created in Asia from twisted flax fibers found in Georgia's Dzudzuana Cave and radiocarbon-dated back to 36,000 years ago. Extensively cultivated in ancient Egypt, flowering flax adorned temple walls and its linen fibers were employed to embalm mummies. Considered a cloth of purity, this ancient textile garbed priests and was later used to swaddle Jesus Christ one final time at burial. That reputed linen and its facial imprint has been exhibited very arguably as the Shroud of Turin, now preserved in an argon-filled airtight case. Flax was one of the first plants grown by colonists settling the American frontier, which lessened reliance on Europe and helped create some conditions for independence. Before Eli Whitney's cotton gin, linen was the most commonly used fabric in this growing nation. In Pennsylvania's Ligonier Valley, it was descendants of these flax-growing settlers who stubbornly kept alive the traditions of this important crop. They created the Western Hemisphere's oldest flax-scutching festival dating back to 1907 and since held annually amongst its blooming fields. Scutching turns flax fiber into linen cloth as the plant is held against an old wooden board and scraped with a paddle. When first harvested, flax is pulled from the ground and not cut, then spread across meadows to dry out during a retting process before being pummeled with a hinged breaker to crack its woody pith and loosen fine fiber. Those golden strands are known as tow and helped originate the word "towheaded" to describe a temporarily blond child. After scutching, the fibers are brushed with hackling combs before being spun into thread on spinning wheels and then onto bobbins, which are placed into a linen loom where they will be shuttled back and forth to create cloth. That alternating movement of these bobbins was eventual inspiration for the term "shuttle bus."

The piercing blue eyes on this flax scutcher appear to interrupt the sepia-toned sea of brown shades staining the wooden frames siding an agricultural workshop. David Pletcher and his son Bryce are just two-thirds of three generations still working hard to keep alive the agrarian traditions in this region. David grasps the pulled crop along with a flax ripple used to remove its valuable seed heads for linseed oil, instrumental in linoleum, paints, and nutritional supplements. Bryce holds a scutching knife, wavy tow fibers, and the hackles used for its combing. His handmade shirt is largely from woven flax, less flexible and much more durable than cotton, even if in some quarters a tad less fashionable.

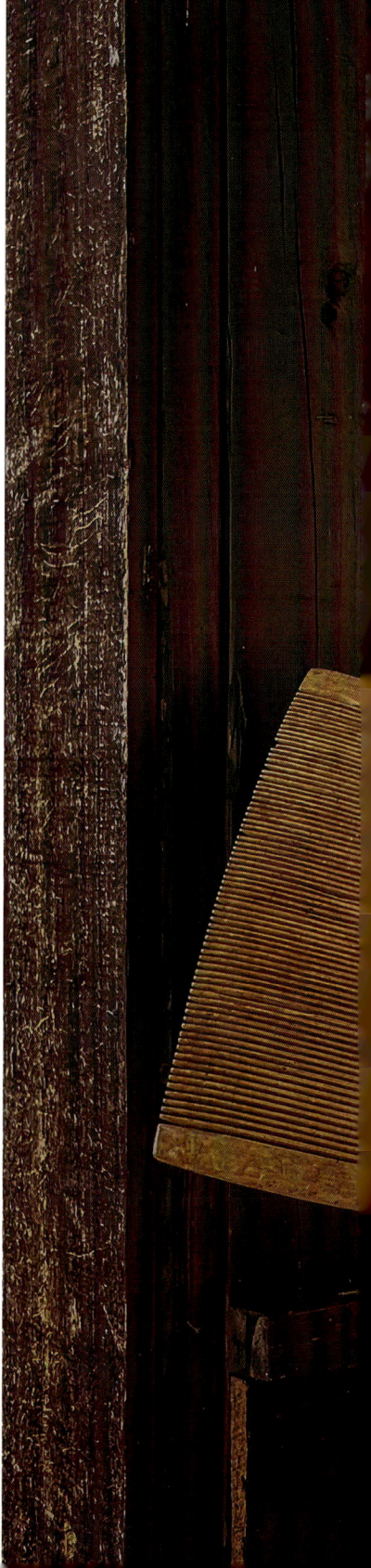

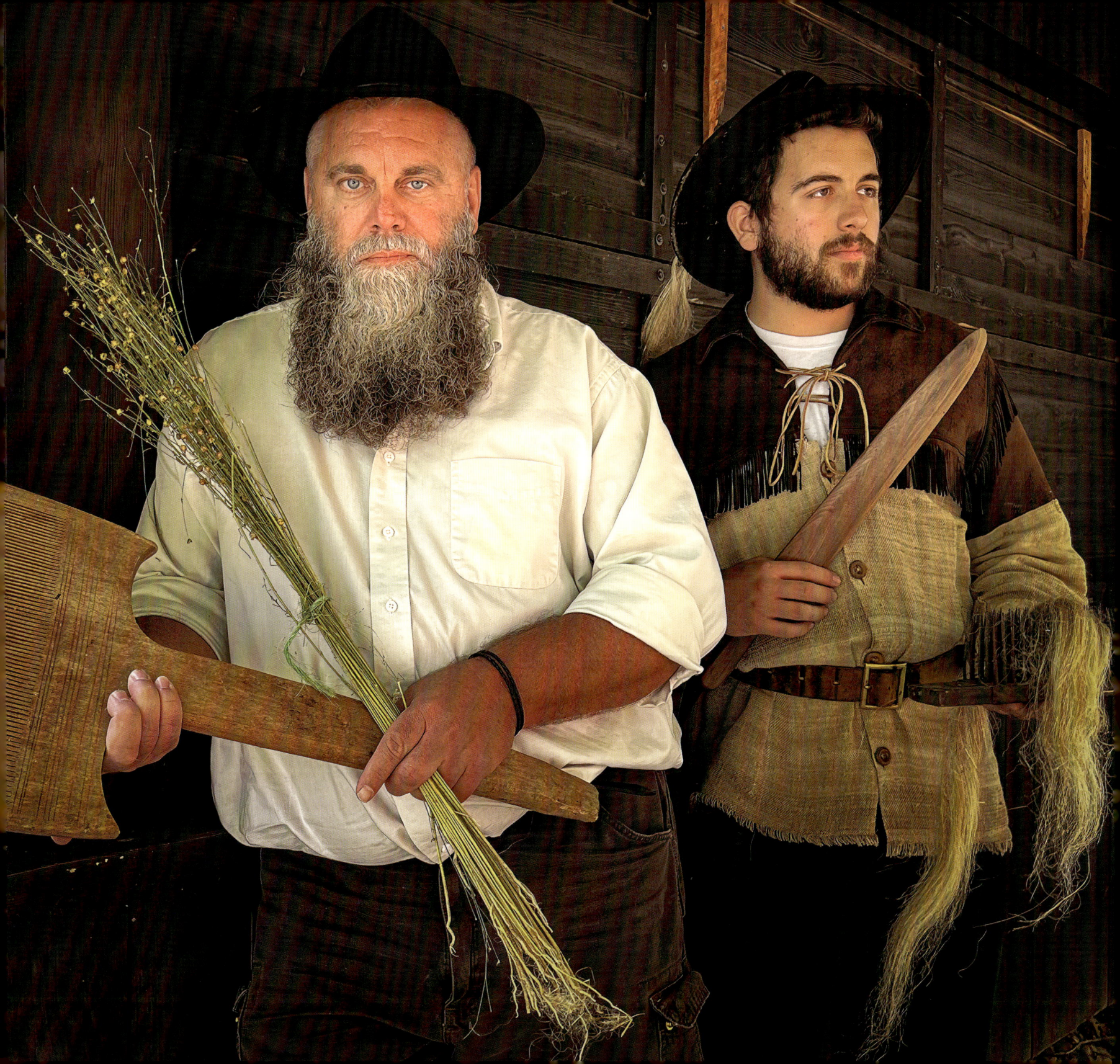

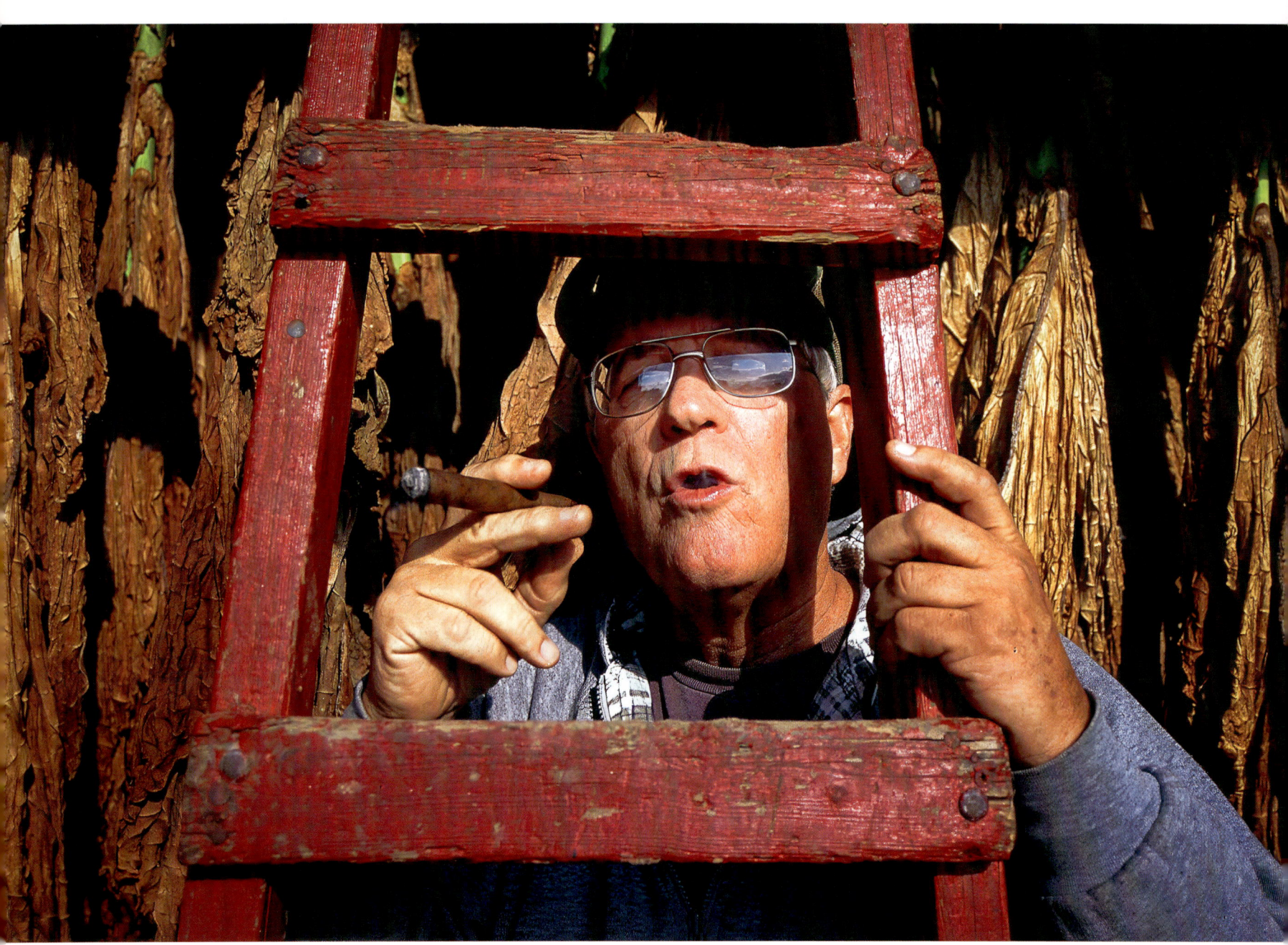

TOBACCO GROWER

Southwick, Massachusetts

As a reaction against urbanization in nineteenth-century America, this nation's first landscape paintings were spawned from an overlook atop the Connecticut River as it threaded its way through Massachusetts's verdant Pioneer Valley. Its shores were once densely speckled with open-slatted, rust-colored barns whose multi-story beams helped hoist an upended profusion of large leaves hanging in bunches. Earliest settlers here learned from the native Mohawk many secrets of tobacco cultivation first used predominantly for smoking pipes. As tastes evolved towards cigarettes and cigars, refinement of this finicky cash crop still required hot, humid conditions tempered by moistures that the nearby river best provided. Amongst swirling vestiges of oxbow bends that twist along New England's longest river, rich silt and loam soil deposits contain a fine, sandy base that quickly leeches mold-inducing rainwater away from the growing plant. This region had long been famed for shade tobacco, known for distinctive, mild flavors and prized by cigarmakers for its silky-smooth wrapper, ensuring a supposedly elegant finishing touch to the leafy, rolled binder envelope. This aptly named cultivar is nurtured beneath those tempering effects of sunlight-dimming cheesecloth that mimics the atmospheric growing conditions found in competing rainforest jungles throughout Sumatra.

Closely following in those dirt-caked footsteps through an agricultural lineage that toiled across these fertile floodplains since the 1830s, hardworking farmer David Arnold appears to delight in the fruit of his labor. Savoring aromas inhaled from the shade tobacco wrapper, he pauses by a rustic ladder that provides access to soaring rafters at one of his curing sheds. The family operation is still surviving, more engaged now in growing asparagus and strawberries, but still trying to protect their heritage by producing a unique strain of tobacco that converts to lower level of carcinogens. Despite the late twentieth-century proliferation of cigar bars and speakeasies, a fuller awareness regarding smoking's cancer-related consequences have proven irresistible for real estate-hungry developers, looking to manifest commuter-friendly suburban developments throughout this picturesque agrarian valley, which just might before too long vanish in a puff of smoke.

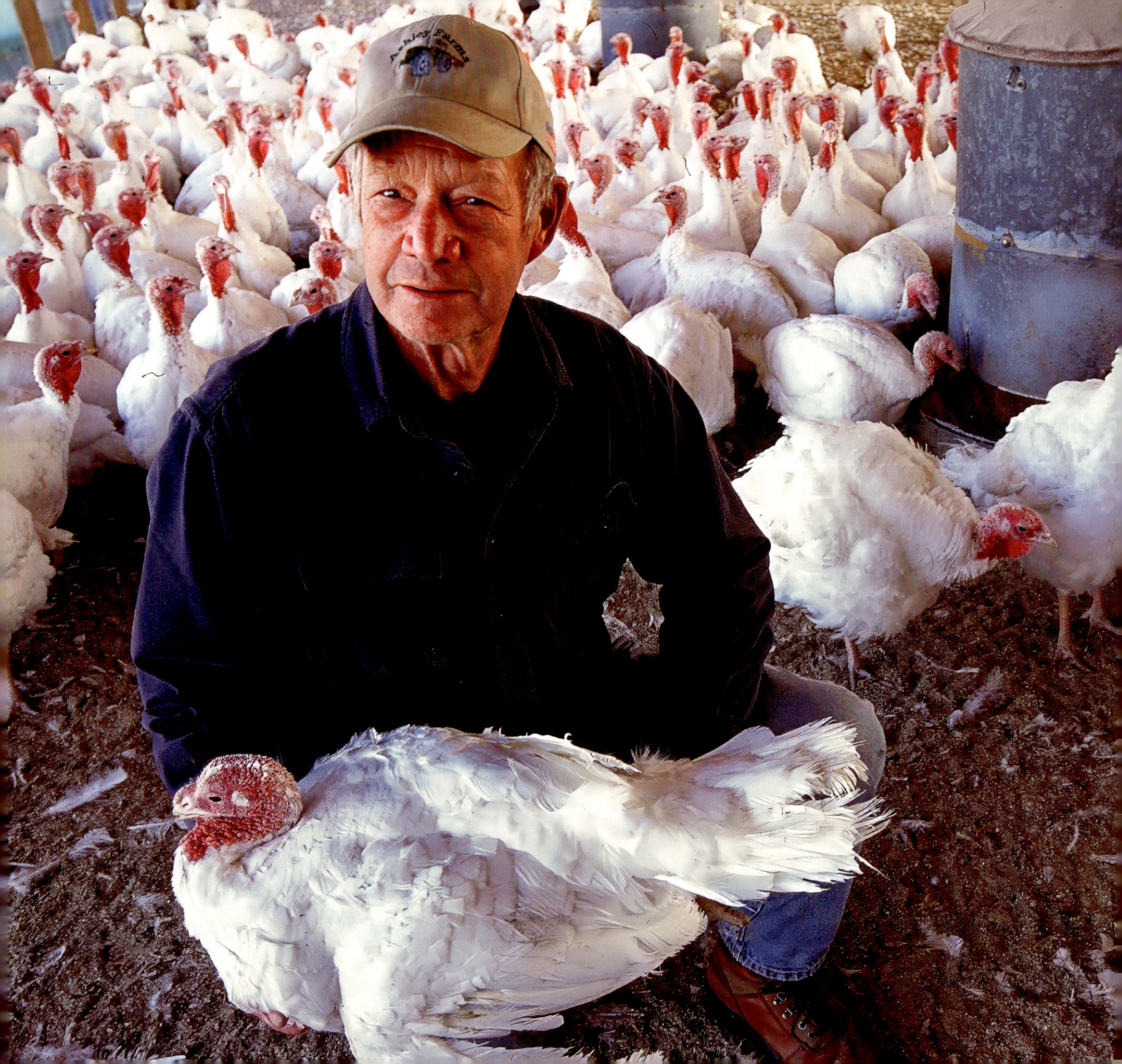

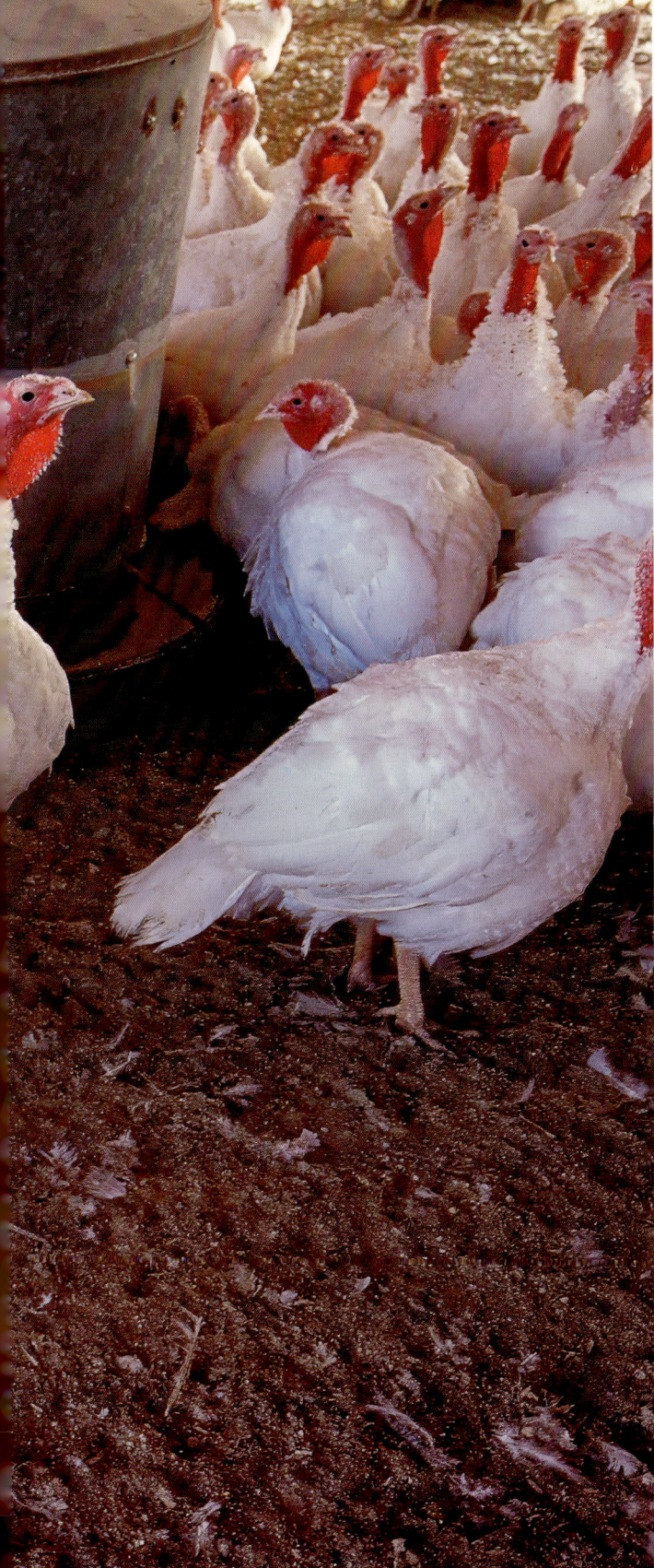

POULTRYMAN

Flanders, New Jersey

Actually, ducks or geese were the most probable contribution brought by colonists to their feast with Wampanoag people during their communal meal in late autumn of 1621. Rather than turkey, that reputedly first meal of Thanksgiving in the New World was supplemented by their deer-hunting Native neighbors' venison. Notwithstanding that myth of Benjamin Franklin's advocacy for this avian creature to be named a national bird, it still took more than two centuries before wild turkeys, indigenous in America and one common farmyard resident, would be accepted as gastronomic anchor at the traditional holiday meal. Numerous famished diners could be satiated with its tryptophan-laced presence when, during the measurably largest eating event in this country, up to four thousand calories might be consumed along with a vast constellation of savory fixings.

At a fourth-generation family farm, Larry Ashley, an unruffled poultryman grabs heaving feathers inside his raucous turkey coop thronged by strutting hens and gobbling toms scarfing down their custom soybean or cornmeal recipe. Across rural Ashley Farms these high strung, red-wattled fowl ululate in unison, and live out their final weeks before a starring nationwide role atop Thanksgiving Day tables.

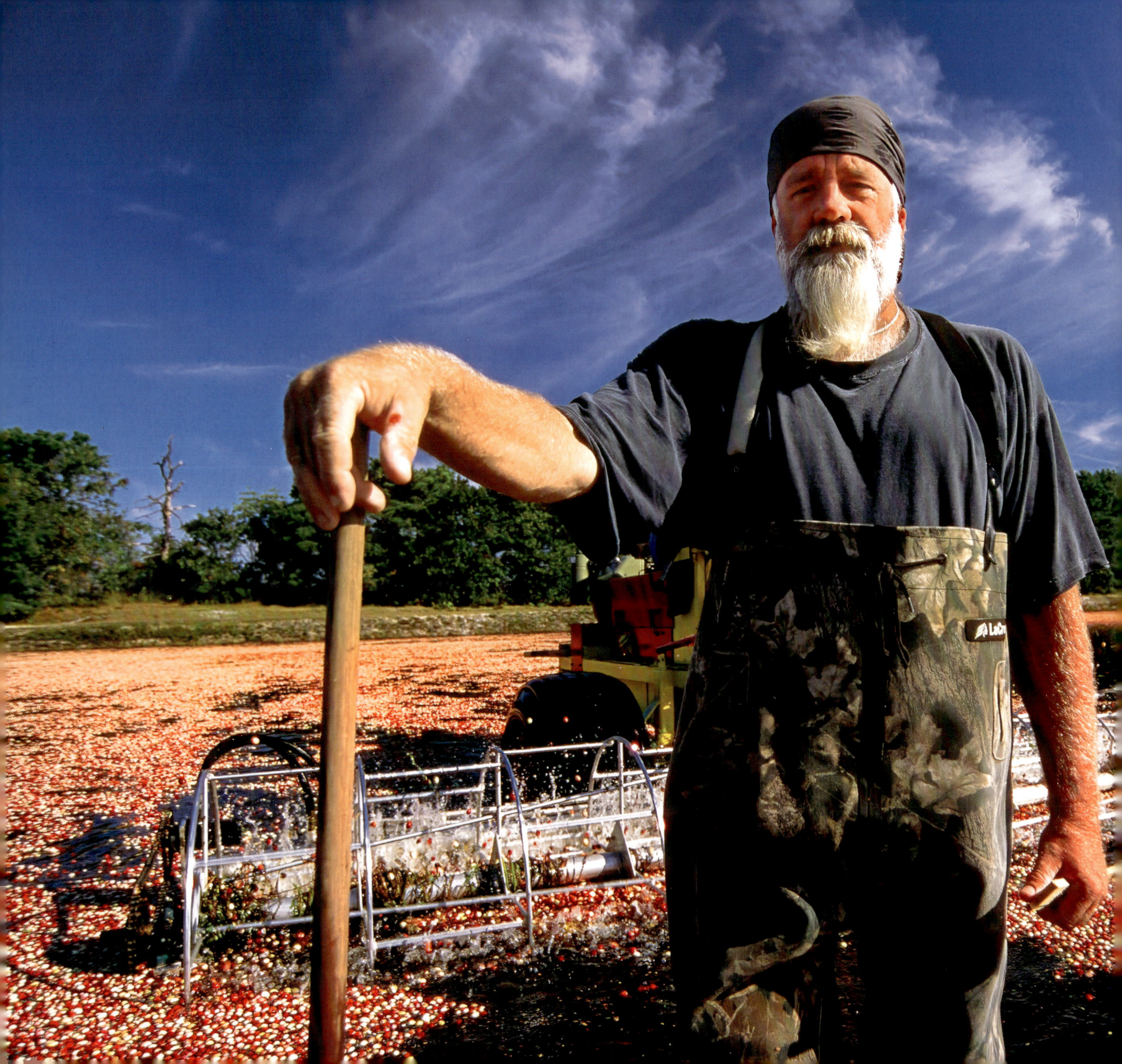

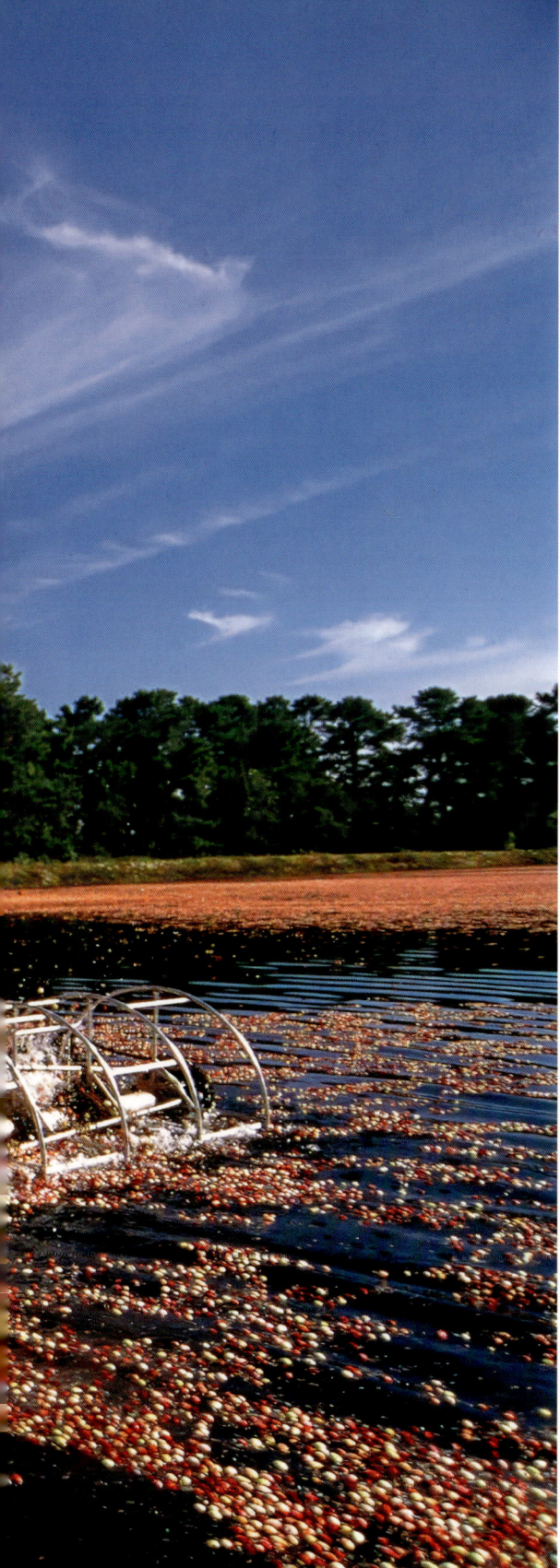

CRANBERRY BOG GATHERER

Chatsworth, New Jersey

Stubbornly resisting settlement in this country's densest state, New Jersey's immense Pine Barrens is the largest remaining forested stretch along America's eastern seaboard between Maine's North Woods and Florida's Everglades. Its vast million acres sit atop a subterranean reservoir of bacterially sterile, chemically immaculate waters that are among the world's very purest. Here within the Garden State's pygmy pitch pines where a Jersey Devil reputedly lurks, its sandy, acidic soil nurtures carnivorous plants and orchids, yet are virtually unsuitable for growing any crops. Nevertheless, beside stream banks and bogs, savory cranberries grow in wild profusion, clustered along creeping evergreen shrubs. Before European arrival here, Native Lenni Lenape mixed the salubrious fruit with deer meat to make easily preserved pemmican, an Aboriginal energy bar. They also used the cranberry for medicinal poultices to draw poison away from arrowhead wounds and utilized their juices for dying cloth and blankets. Later christened by Pilgrims as crane berries for its vine's pink flower, which resembled that bird's head, the ruby red produce is one of only three truly indigenous foods to be found in supermarkets.

Since the 1930s, Ocean Spray cooperative growers have choreographed autumnal harvesting spectacles where marshy depressions slathered with ripened cranberry vines are carefully flooded through pump house valve openings. Those submerged berries become dislodged when beaten which allows their buoyant four-chambered interior to the surface where they're corralled with floating booms then scooped by workers onto conveyer belts and into awaiting trucks. Immersed in an orb-filled, buoyant crimson carpet, and probing the depths of drowned bogs while employing his rod, a burly harvester prepares to lead early morning processions with eggbeater-like water reels mowing bobbing cranberries from their underwater shrubs and toward eventual breakfast tables.

BUDDHIST MONK

Beecher Lake, New York

Originating in the fifth century BCE, Buddhism is an ancient philosophical tradition that's followed by over 550 million adherents, making it this planet's fourth-largest religion. This immensely influential spiritual movement was founded by Siddhartha Gautama, commonly known as the Buddha, who was born a mere five miles north of present-day borders with India in Lumbini, Nepal. Renouncing his wealthy family at the age of 29, he wandered as an ascetic for six years venturing into India along tributaries to the Ganges, finally attaining enlightenment beneath heart-shaped leaves on a sacred bodhi fig tree. Now considered the holiest spot in Buddhism, it marks where he determined to take a Middle Way between asceticism and luxury, reputedly freeing himself completely from lust, rage, and delusion, while eventually enabling an entrance to Nirvana. Buddhist monasteries were established by disciples as missionaries were deployed and his philosophies traveled along the Silk Road, fanning out all through Asia. The faith's Mahayana movement seeped across the Far East into Japan, where deep beliefs in ancestral figures and devotion to honoring family helped spawn an Obon religious ceremony, now practiced for over five centuries and performed during a summer's full moon.

Surrounded by 1,400 acres of forest and meadow on banks of the Catskills' highest lake, Zen monastery Dai Bosatsu Zendo holds a heart-purifying reunion with deceased loved ones. After prayerful fireside ceremonies accompanied by temple gongs, the abbott leads a silent, candlelit procession down to the moonlit waters, where a yukata-robed Buddhist monk tenderly launches illuminated spirit lanterns. The memorial Obon flotilla will drift off across a shimmering tarn deep into the night, releasing gratitude and guiding spirits back to their world as mesmerizing chants pay homage to compassionate wisdom.

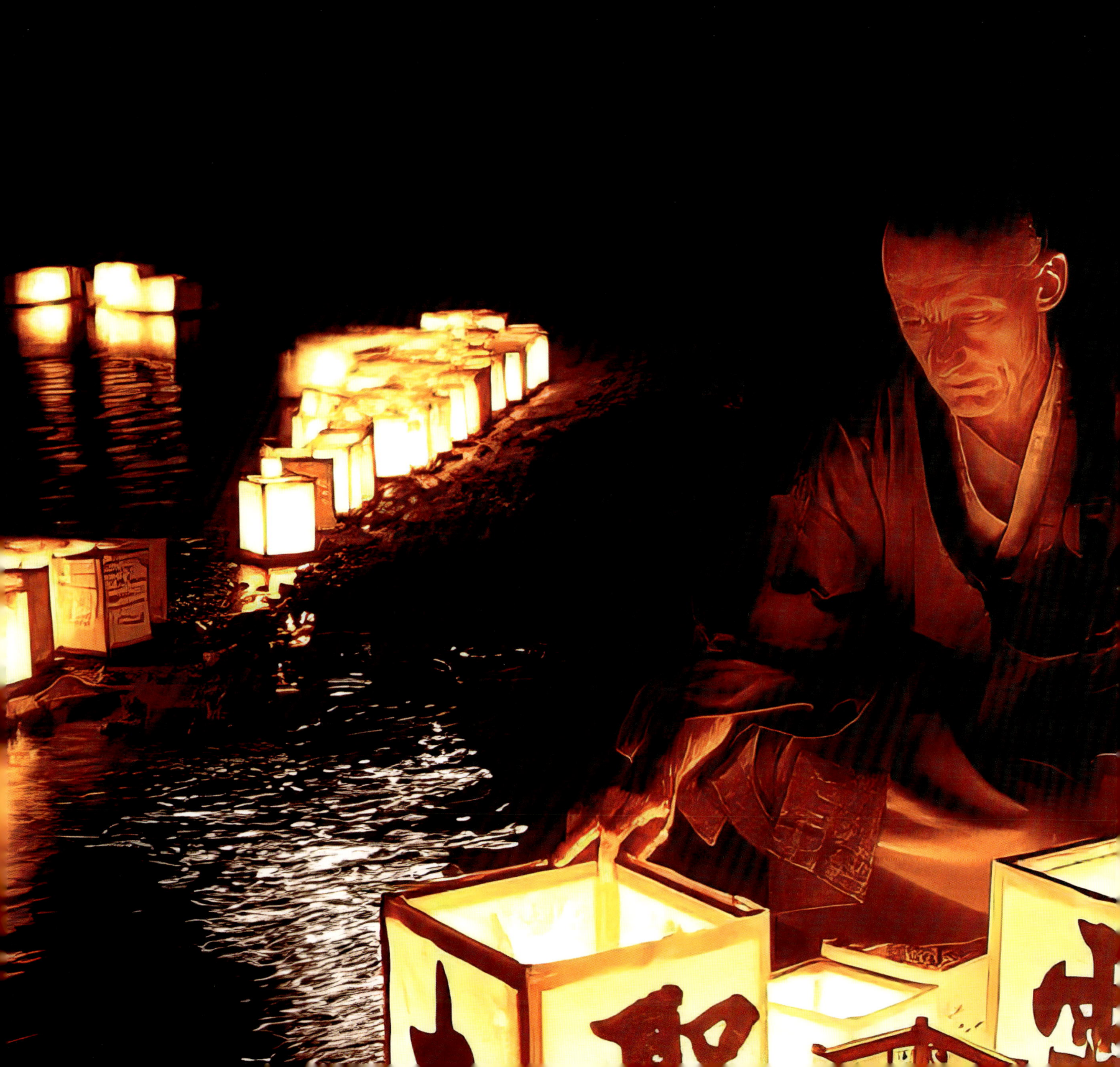

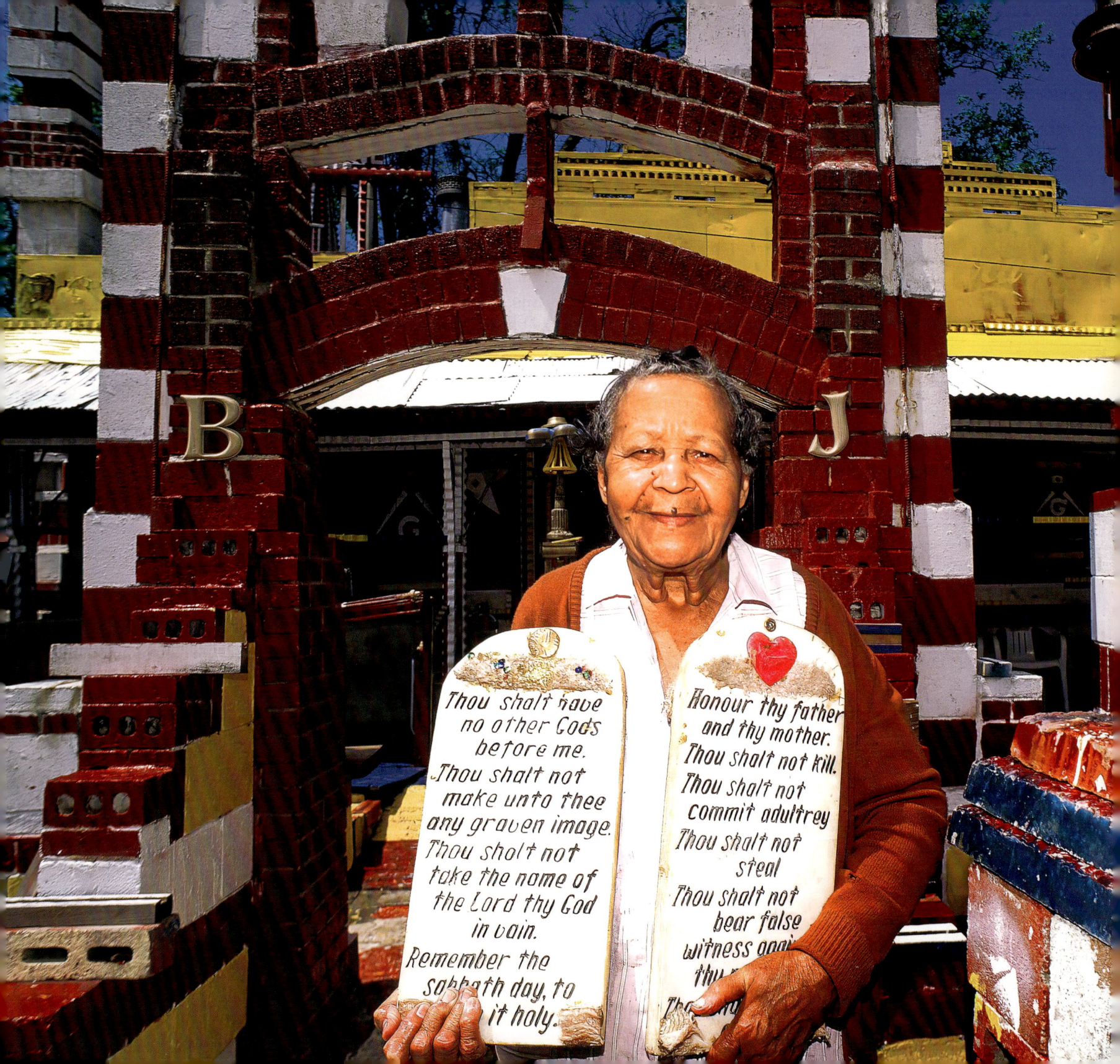

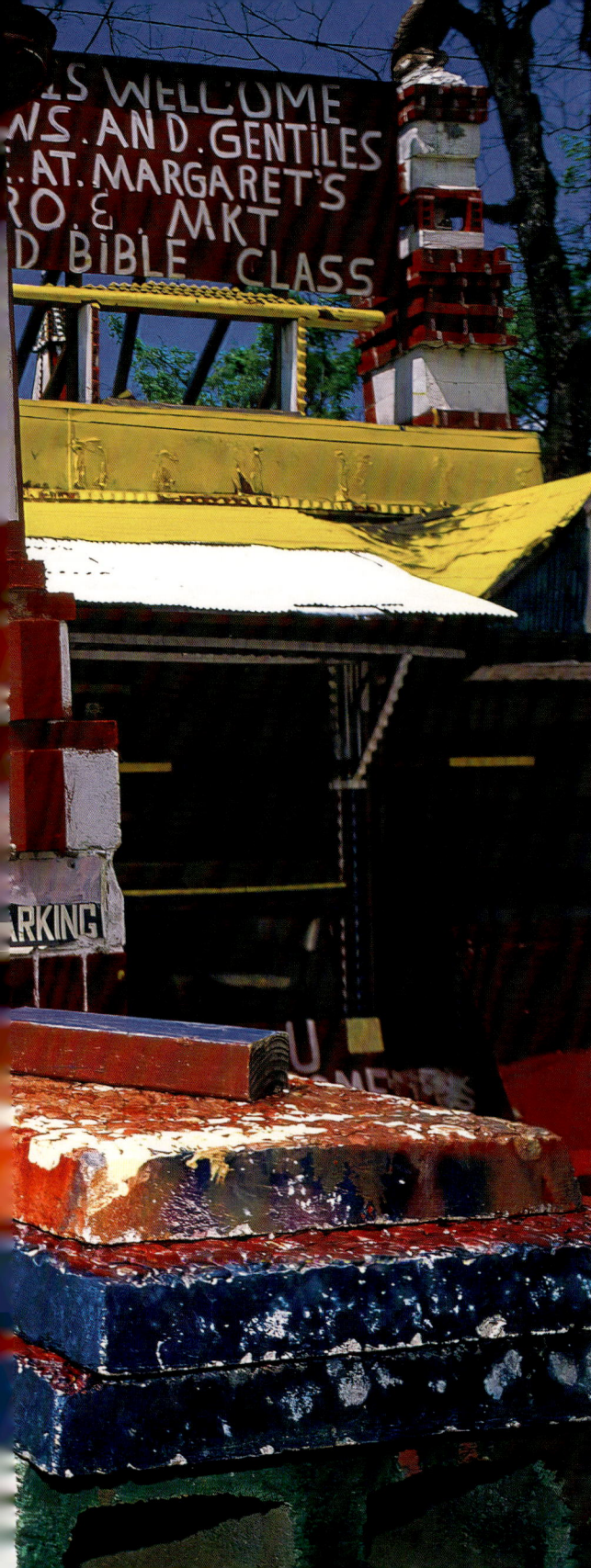

BIBLE PARK STEWARD

Vicksburg, Mississippi

Just beside lanes pulsing with pickup trucks along famed US Highway 61, a rural grocery store dispensed the likes of toilet paper, kerosene, and hogsheads cheese to the accompaniment of music emanating from its corner jukebox. When the proprietor of the shop was killed in a robbery, his wife Margaret Rogers became one of Mississippi's first Black woman business owners. She later met Reverend H.D. Dennis inside the store and it was love at first sight. Vowing to build an on-site castle proclaiming his adoration in exchange for marriage, the two transformed their surroundings, as Margaret disposed of her jukebox and stopped selling beer, while the preacher went about the business of creating a dizzying spiritual theme park. Before long, rising candyland confections of polychromatic towers and gates were smothered by a chockablock of biblical references and Hallelujah-inspired sentiments. An old city school bus was transformed into a mobile chapel for the itinerant preacher, encrusted in bulb-festooned ornamentation and gilded Ark of the Covenant. Upon eventual return to his permanent parking spot by the old grocery, its steering column and wheel were ripped out to be replaced by an ornate pulpit.

Surrounded by her vivid theological emporium, ardent Margaret Rogers Dennis offers guidance to any wayward visitor with armfuls of biblical prohibitions. Signage helpfully explains that both Jews and gentiles are welcome at Margaret's Grocery & Market and Bible Class, where both folk-art wisdom and the Ten Commandments imperatives commingle in Deep South eccentricity.

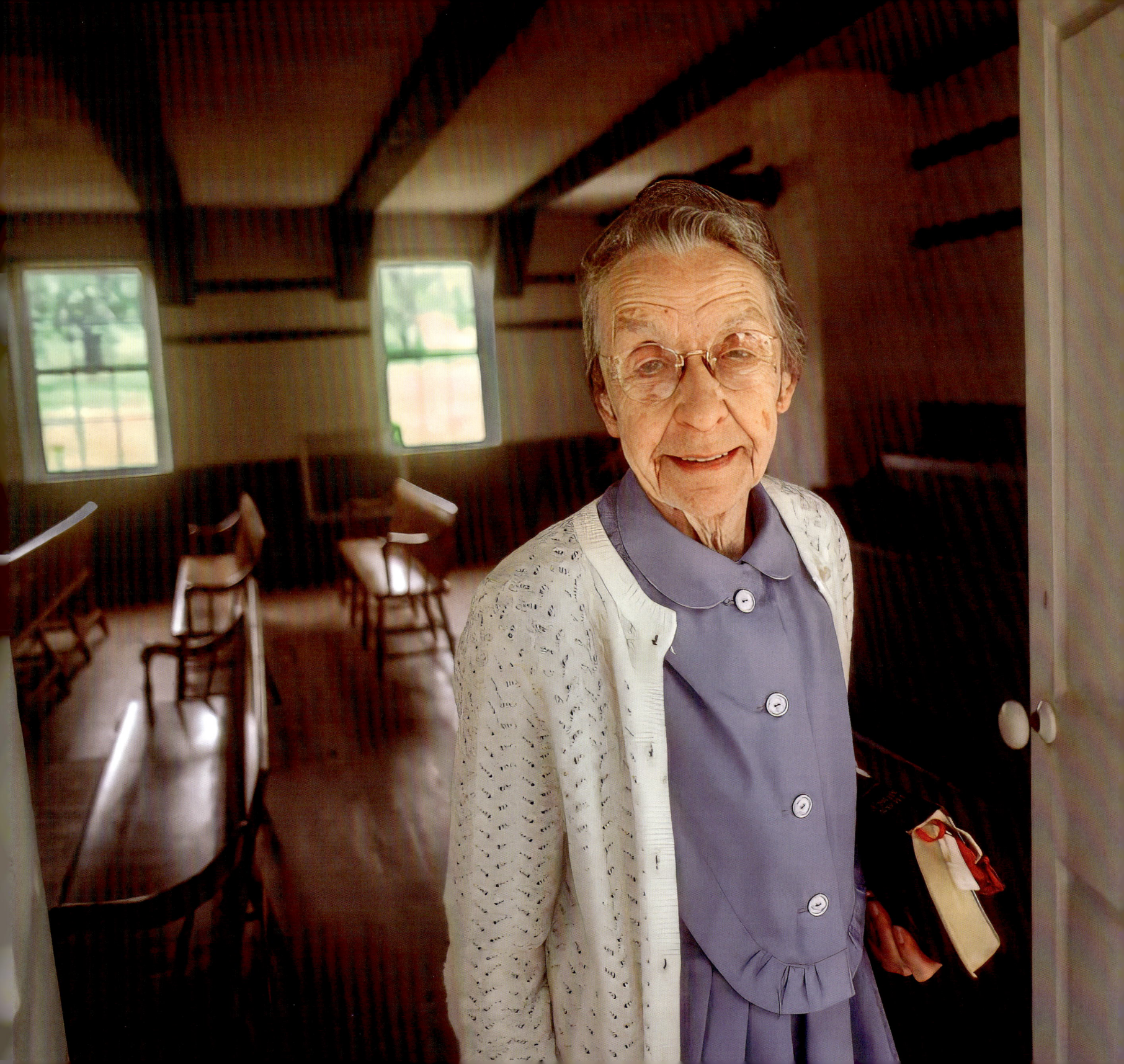

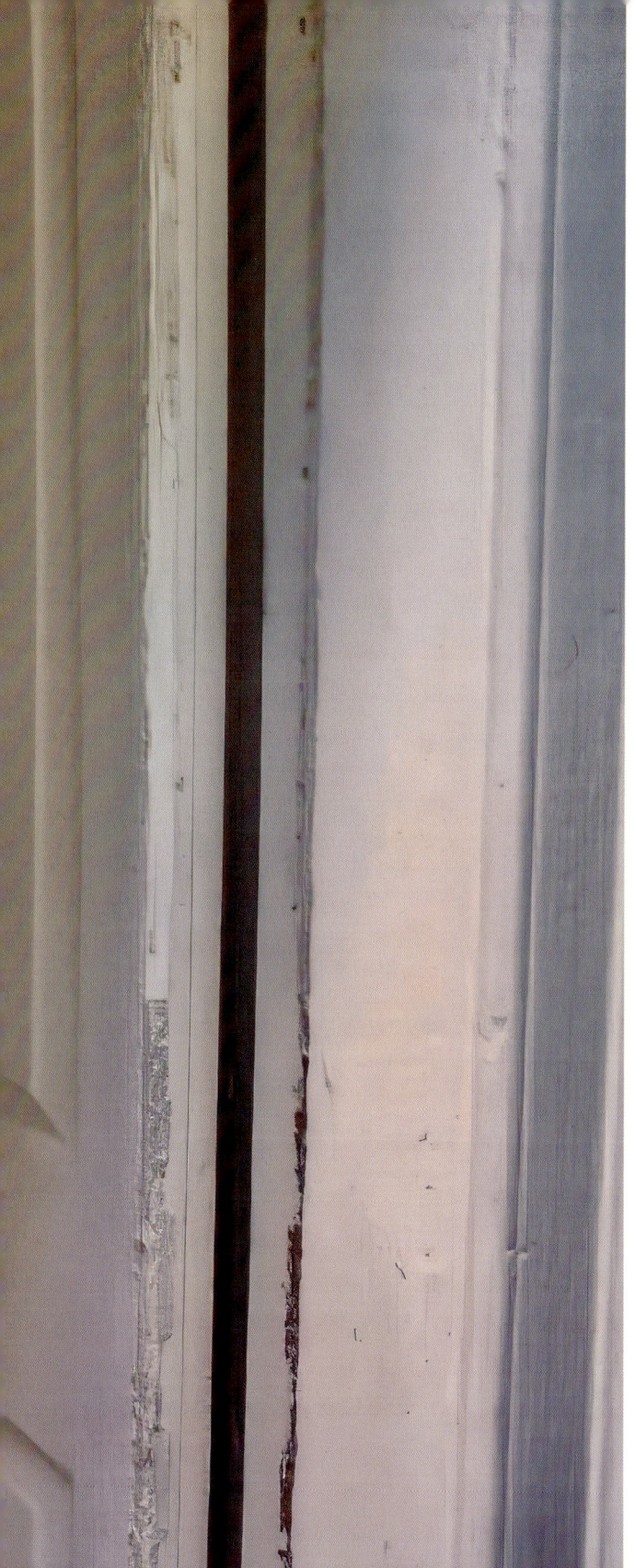

SHAKER ELDRESS

Sabbathday Lake, Maine

A religion now sitting on the very precipice of complete extinction, this unique Shaker faith once stamped its distinct influence upon American society. At its height around the Civil War's onset, there were over eighteen thriving communities of worship scattered across the country's northeastern quadrant. Perhaps alone amongst our world's religions, its revelation-spurred founder and Christ-level embodiment of belief was a woman, Mother Ann Lee, who departed England to reestablish her flock in the New World. Disciplined levels of craftsmanship along with clever ingeniousness were hallmarks and key to their religious devotion. The Shakers attained great notoriety for their invention of clothespins, flat brooms, and washing machines. The community's horticultural expertise with medicinal herbs and seed cultivation inspired culinary movements. Named for their vigorously ecstatic gyrations during prayer, Shakers created uplifting hymns of sublime beauty, first attaining true acclaim after famed composer Aaron Copland sampled one classic within his 1944 ballet's finale. Yet perhaps what most distinguished this once burgeoning theology was its celibacy-affirming limits on any procreation. With group adoptions no longer allowable, and recruitments dwindling amongst an increasingly industrialized society, there currently remains just one community in southern Maine with two aging adherents clinging to the last strands of a great legacy.

Clutching her worn, bookmarked bible, Mildred Barker, a pious Shaker eldress, is clothed as always in handmade garments and heads into Sunday worship at this scarcely furnished 1794 meeting house, trademarked by the Shakers' lovingly crafted, spare wooden furniture. Once placed in charge of the village's candy making, Barker's valiant efforts toward keeping alive their treasured but simple musical anthems, led to her eventually helming spiritual activities within this handsome agrarian community at Sabbathday Lake.

INNKEEPER

Tangier Island, Virginia

Time is ticking. At this bed and breakfast, that clock in the kitchen background might be keeping time until morning meals arrive on its table, yet also serves as a constant reminder of nature's impatience. A distinctive culture and vanishing lifestyle is now highly endangered by climate change as scientists and climatologists agree it is only a matter of three decades before Tangier Island, now clinging to existence after its constant battery from rising seas and gnawing waves, becomes completely unlivable. In the midst of vast, wave-tossed Chesapeake Bay, this fragile, postage stamp-sized speck hosts marshland and scattered ridges topping out at a mere four feet above sea level are stitched by creaky footbridges. Since 1850, the unrelenting bay has swallowed up two-thirds of its mass, endangering eighty still-existing habitable acres with just one remaining shrinking village. In its center, an occasional smattering of white clapboard cottages is ornamented by pastel hydrangeas bursting through picket fences that line the narrow island pathways. At their hub, an imposing Methodist Church is passed by pedaling female septuagenarians toting a week's worth of groceries in the baskets of their tricycles. Hardy watermen gather down by shoreline docks bantering in a highly unique Elizabethan English, reputedly imported their seventeenth-century arrival from Cornwall and Devon and kept unhindered in this pristinely isolated corner of the world. Garlanding this car-free island is a profusion of offshore, weather-beaten crab shanties, where vigilant eyes monitor that moment peelers will disrobe from their hard casings and unveil themselves as the famed soft-shell crabs for which Tangier proudly proclaims itself its global capital. An irony sometimes overlooked by local watermen is those same waters providing the fruits of their labor and hard-earned income also threaten to doom a deeply cherished existence.

In the meantime, hand-cleaned lump crab filling savory golden-brown crabcakes or buttery soft shell crabs, along with clam fritters, Virginia ham, corn pudding, and pickled beets became the much noted, all-you-can-eat hallmark of Hilda Crockett's Chesapeake House which first flung open its doors to a hungry crowd of guests in 1939. The most voracious hoard of visitors, however, are bloodthirsty mosquitos who inhabit their next-door marshes, and on windless days make themselves at home in town, where a welcoming innkeeper stands protected by these ever-present insect screens found across this island. Thick mosquito populations here will surely outlast the human one, now down to about 400 people, at least until this island totally disappears in relatively quick fashion during the warming passage of time.

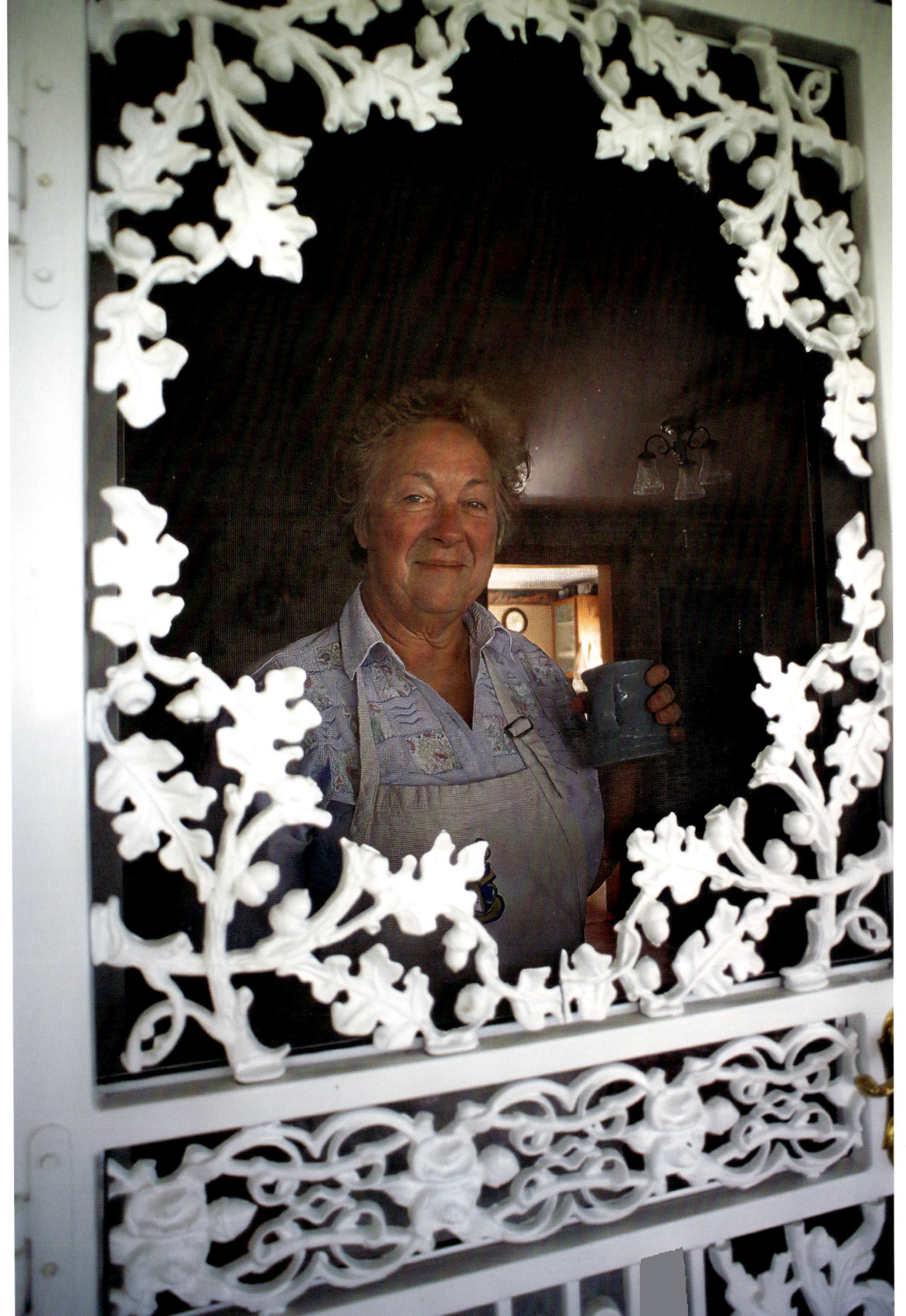

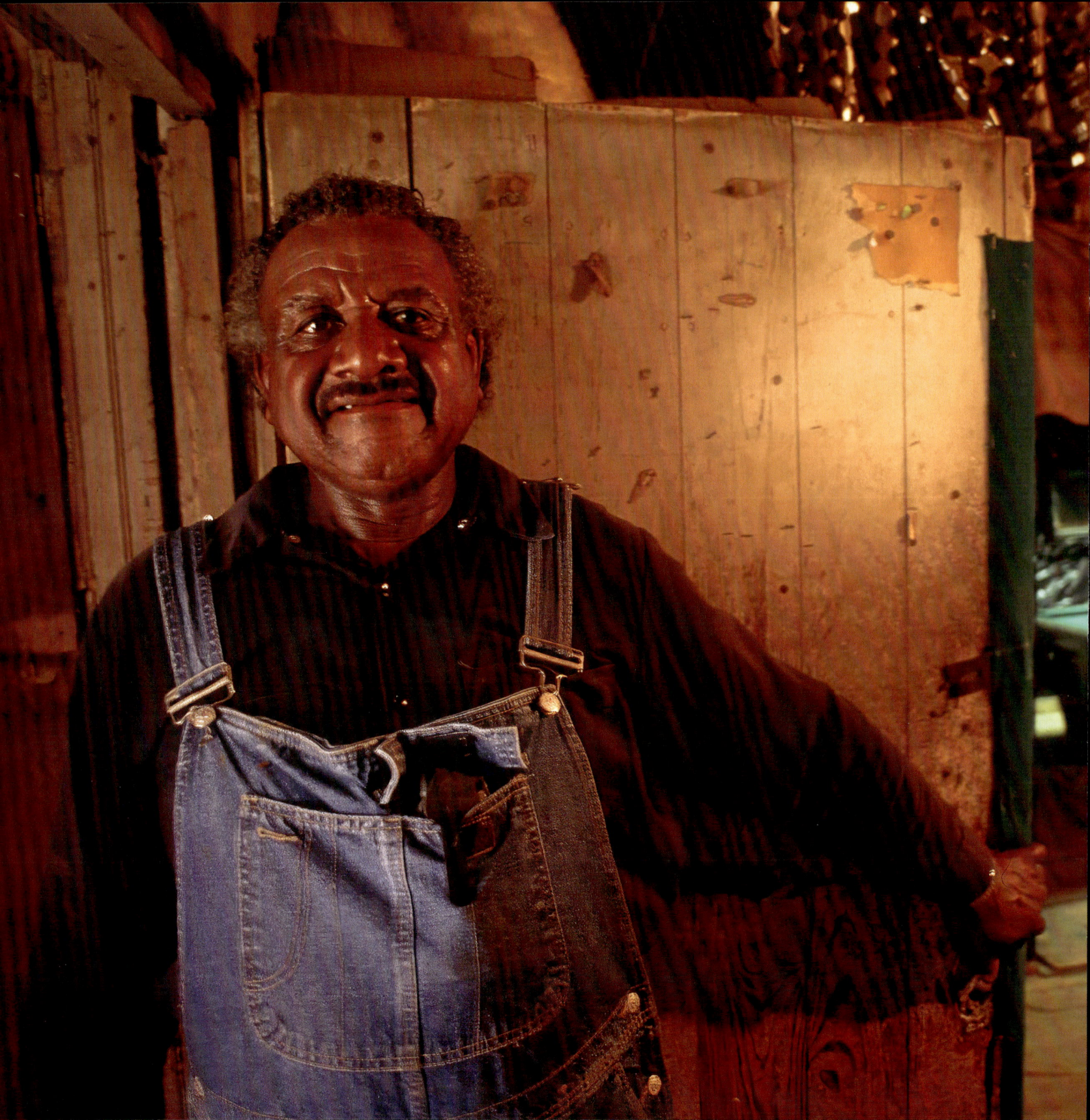

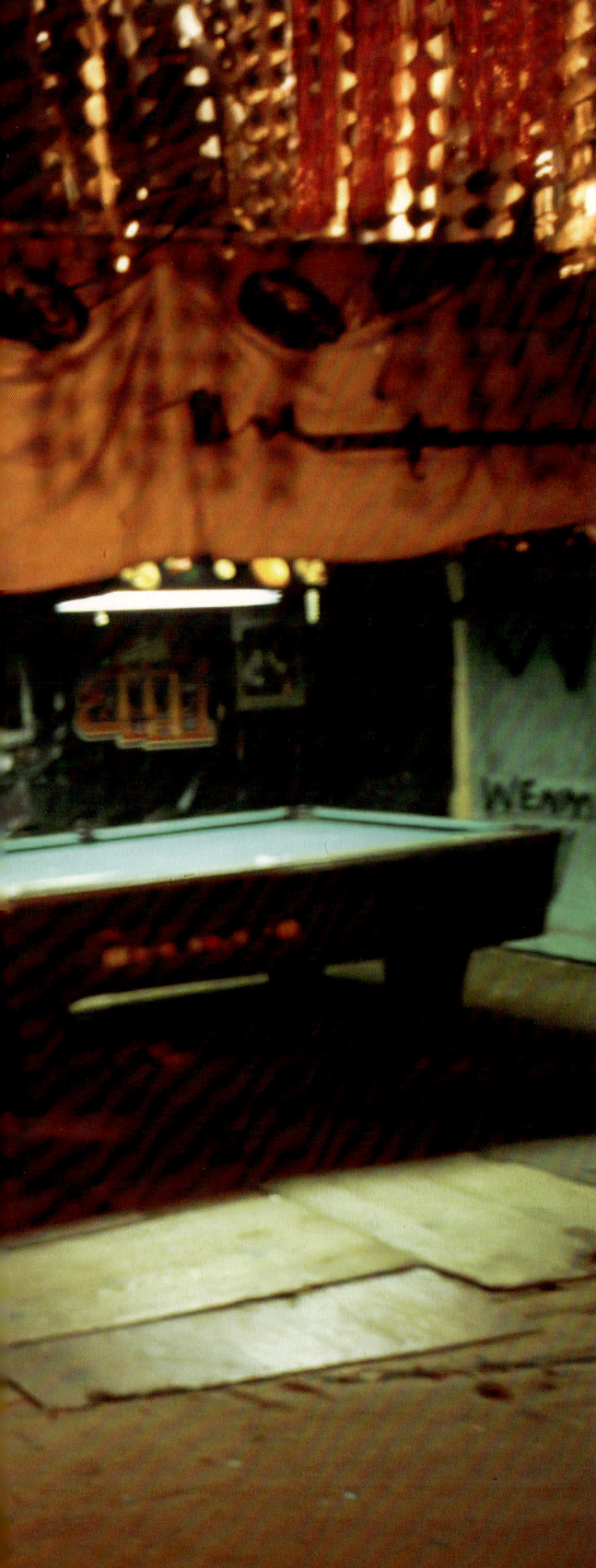

JUKE JOINT HOST

Merigold, Mississippi

Deep in the Mississippi Delta, alongside a skinny curl of Jones Bayou, gravel roads were obscured on Thursday evenings by determined, dust-kicking pickup trucks hurling toward one solitary, ramshackle sharecropper shack. While its rustic 1920s exterior is plastered with stern admonitions about expected house rules, the interior reveals a lovingly furnished assemblage of stuffed animals, tinsel, pool table and jukebox. For over five decades Po' Monkey's Lounge provided a trustworthy beacon summoning local field hands and plantation workers that would jam the crooked floorboards of its tiny dance floor, intent on blowing off some steam from days enduring hard, sunbaked toil. Rural crossroads across the South were once dotted by these hardscrabble bastions of African American culture, whose patrons took refuge from stringent Jim Crow laws. Soon after mandated racial segregation ended, one of the country's very last remaining authentic juke joints attracted legions of barrelhouse blues aficionados from far and wide, eager to experience that raw energy expressing this delta's musical roots.

Its proud legendary proprietor Willie Seaberry gets ready to shed his overalls, transforming into a dapper backwoods concierge, overseeing the raucous throng and demanding well-mannered behavior from passionate jook devotees.

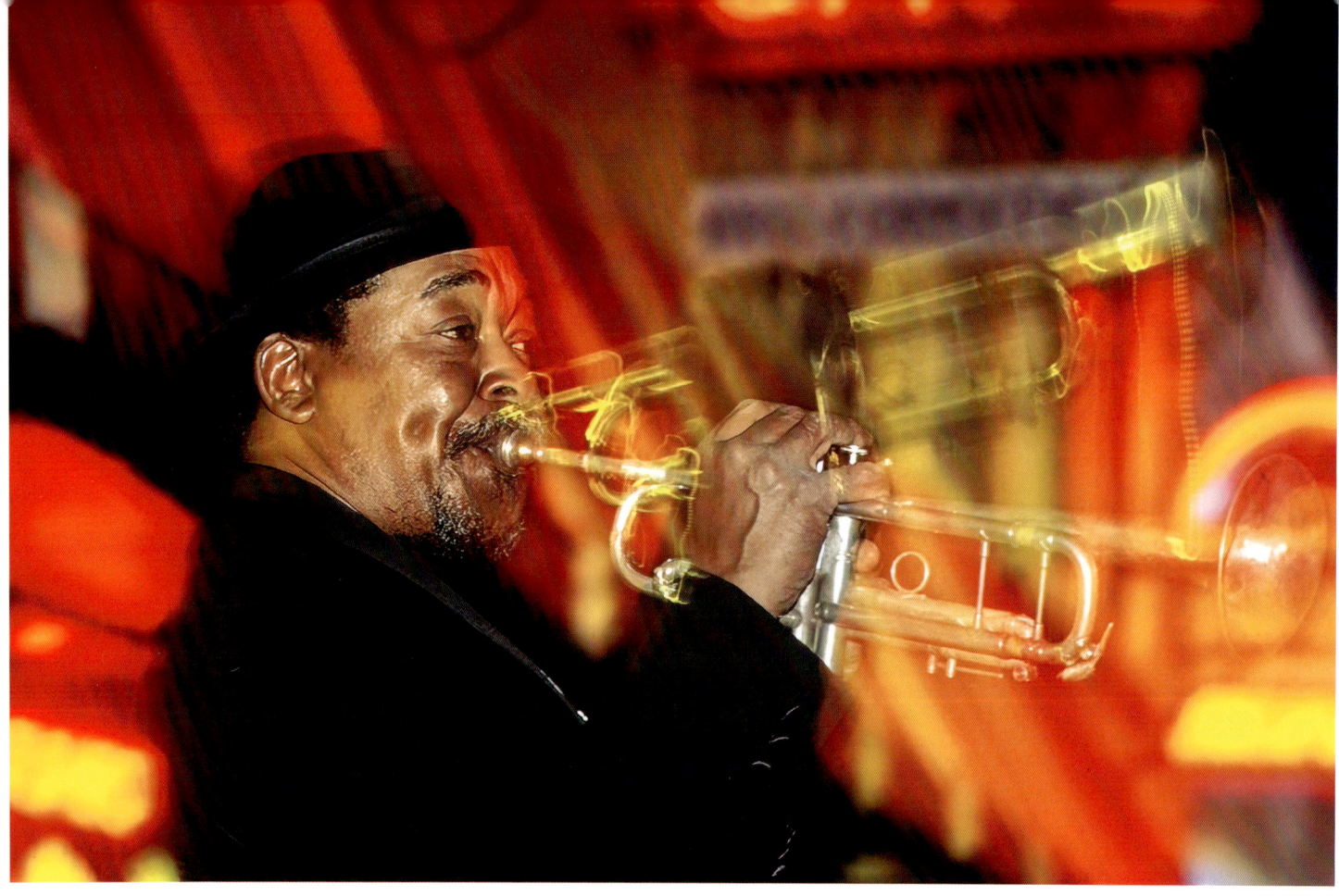

TRUMPETER

Memphis, Tennessee

Soon after a proclamation of emancipation in 1863, recently freed enslaved workers in joyous celebration of new-found liberty began expressing the musical sounds originally rooted in their ancestral West Africa. That auditory tradition incorporated ring shouts with call and response, which were inspired further with field hollers that helped to bolster spiritual melodies from their Sunday worship. As blues music slowly evolved, the repetitive effect of its trance-like rhythm created a groove in the growing genre laced with woeful narratives wailing over troubled spirits and life's hardship. The Deep South nurtured a constellation of blues musicians and when legendary song-writer bluesman and soi-disant Father of the Blues W. C. Handy moved to Memphis in 1909, he performed with his band on trumpet at various clubs along Beale Street. Black entrepreneurs opened barber shops, restaurants, and nightclubs there, as the Jazz Age soon found nonpareil performers like Louis Armstrong or Muddy Waters wandering amongst the neon-lit cobblestoned lanes to appear on one of America's most iconic streets.

Just several blocks from the Mississippi River's east bank, a soulful, derby-capped trumpeter wails away while teeth-sealed, lip-tucking embouchure struggles to find just the right heartfelt expression of his emotions. Expelled through bulging cheeks, brassy notes echo down Beale Street and past the brightly lit Kings Palace Cafe, a joint known for both B.B. King's rousing performances and Memphis barbecued ribs.

SWING DANCERS

Gruene, Texas

The Lone Star State hosts more historic dance halls than anywhere else in America. Speckling the arid landscape, these rural cathedrals of clonking, beer-fueled musical communion are most concentrated across diminutive towns throughout Hill Country. It was in this region that pioneering German and Czech immigrants seeking cheap farmland laid down roots, importing the tuneful traditions of their native homelands. Open every single night, Gruene Hall is the pulsing epicenter and linchpin for social life in its eponymous village and is this state's oldest such purveyor of nocturnal boot-scooting. Founded in 1878, the venue offered an evolving menu featuring music from its nineteenth-century brass and polka bands along with a culturally rich stew of honky tonk, blues, Tejano, and Western swing. As shifting rhythms seem to stir some migratory instinct, hesitant dancers suddenly weave their way onto an initially unfilled floor. While the gravel parking lot fills up, crooked swinging doors squeak on their hinges and side flaps are flung open to allow open air two-stepping. Beneath its highly pitched, rust-worn tin roof, growing crowds fill an original layout of 6,000 square feet, which has hardly changed during the passage of time, save a dramatic ratio shift evidenced by dwindling still-living musical icons framed alongside paint-chipped walls.

Maintaining their tight center of gravity, joyous country swing dancers effortlessly execute a cuddle dip, while cascading golden hair seems poised to sweep the creaky hardwood flooring, scuffed by more than one century of shuffling cowboys and tread by musical luminaries such as Willie Nelson or Merle Haggard.

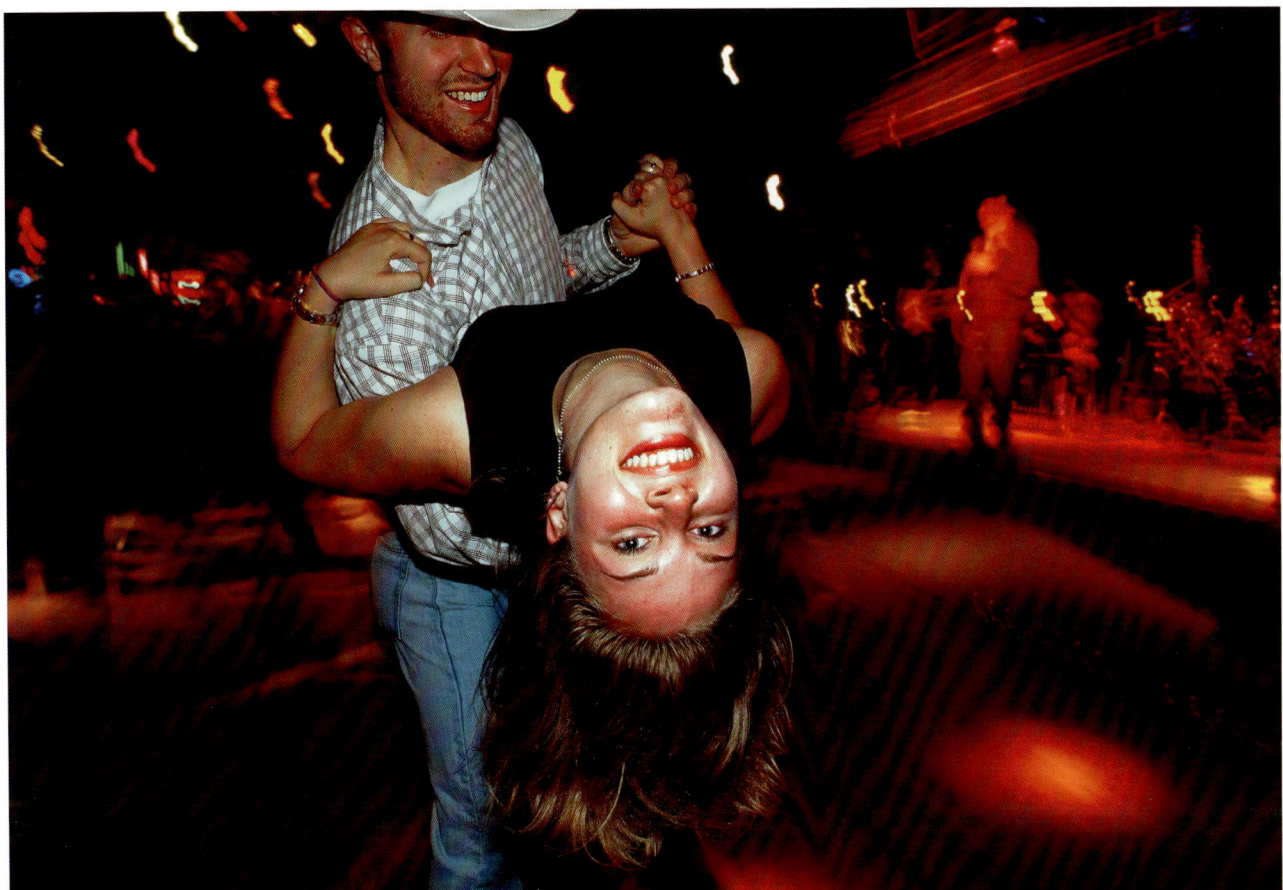

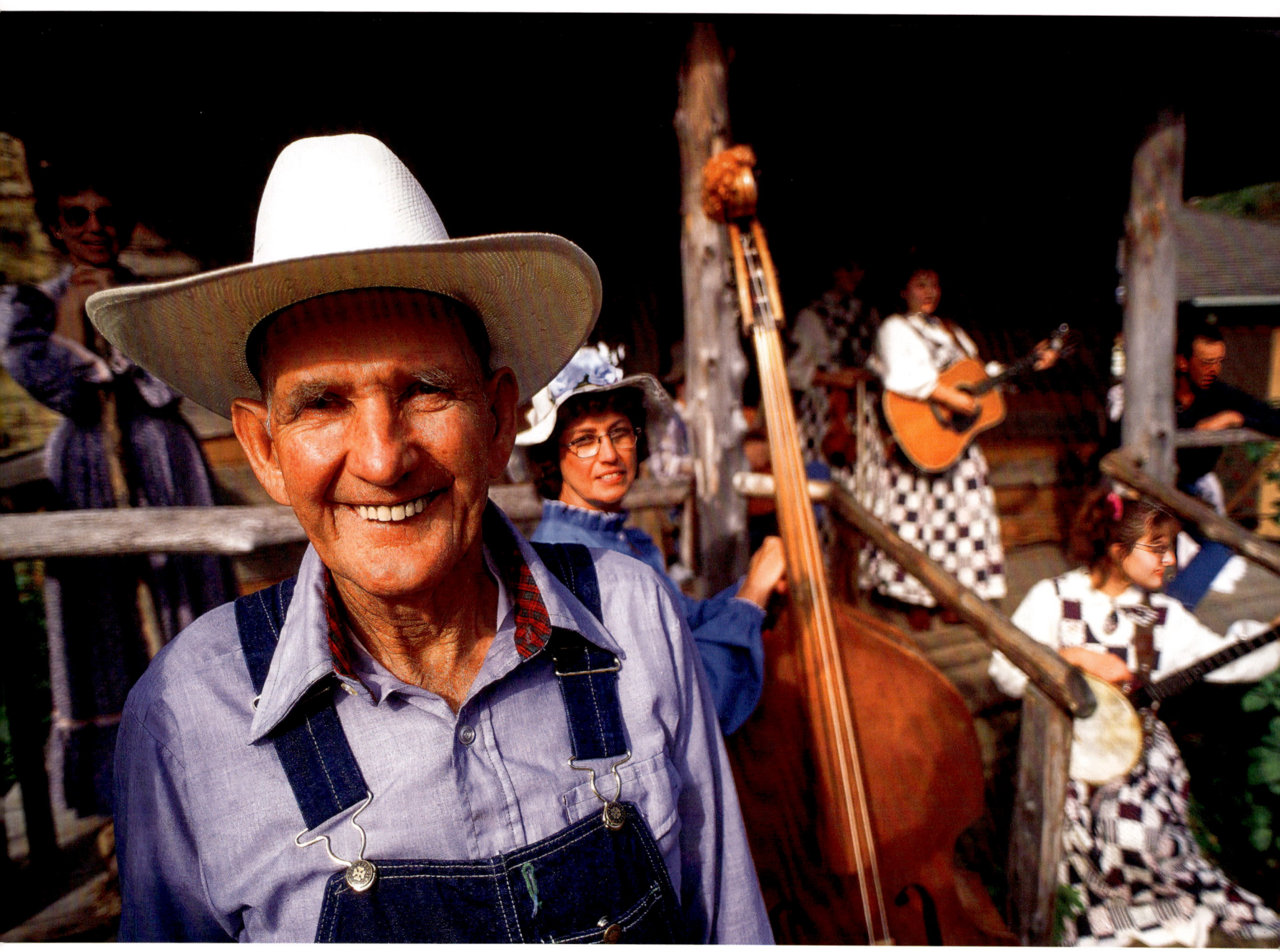

MOUNTAIN MUSIC CLOGGER

Mountain View, Arkansas

The billion-year-old Appalachian Mountains were partially created during a collision of two continents eons ago. Forming an eastern Continental Divide, its stream-separating ranges originally acted as a limiting fence for westward movement of pioneers until the French and Indian War. Seeking farming, trapping, and mining opportunities, early settlers looking farther west arrived in the Ozarks, straddling its Arkansas-Missouri border. Many of these migrants were of Scotch-Irish descent and like most settlers who had earlier traveled overseas from Europe, they brought their customs and musical traditions with them. These rugged journeys excluded large items, so the portable instruments tended to be fiddles, jaw harps, mouth bows, and spoons. Music in these mountains actually blended English and African traditions, as minstrel or medicine shows began featuring banjos, which were first developed in Arabia and brought through Muslim expansion to African coasts. The akonting, played by Jola people in Gambia, was later destined to arrive at America through slave ship transport. Crude versions of the American banjo were first created by enslaved workers using gourds. Driven by pulsing energy in reels, square dancing and frenetic banjo strumming, the fiddle's complicated rhythmic bowing would back up singers, especially after Civil War's end. Troops mingling during this war allowed young mountain men an introduction for the first time to squeeze boxes, harmonicas, and guitars. German immigrants brought their zither-like scheitholz, which evolved into the lap-cradled, three-string mountain dulcimer, usually plucked with a turkey feather. Its hypnotic strains further heightened the prominence of ballads, lyrically narrating uneven travails that daunt rural life. Isolated mountain villages across Ozark hollers, cricks, and bald knobs maintained these sonic traditions and wove them into the fabric of their lives. In aptly named Stone County, Arkansas's second-poorest such district, the limestone rock-faced Court House at Mountain View each day hosts spontaneous performances during constantly morphing ensembles of joyous, improvising mountain musicians. In perhaps one of this nation's most authentic cultural gatherings, parlor pickers and impromptu porch jams throughout town strum and fiddle away into the evening, when bonfire-filled trash cans warm gathered crowds.

Displaying that same hillbilly joie de vivre just nearby, Ozark Folk Center State Park hosts picking and grinning by century-old Shannon Cabin. Its creaky porch supports musicians wielding washboard, gutbucket bass, and banjo instruments as they join forces with the powerfully rhythmic, short bow saw-stroke techniques unfolding on a fiddle. A gleefully delighted dancer is ready to explode into sure-footed clogging displays of showmanship as infectious toe-tapping rhythms embrace their rural symphony sweetened by stringed instruments echoing across Ozark hollers.

NOTED BLUES GUITARIST

Clarksdale, Mississippi

Following emancipation of Black Americans in the Deep South, their sorry plight continued to spill its stain on our nation's quest for a more perfect union. An 1896 Supreme Court ruling, now regarded as one of the worst edicts in its history, upheld "separate but equal" segregation and ignited the spark for a series of state-issued Jim Crow laws. These newly established regulations operated along the premise of white supremacy, odiously self-perpetuating a cycle of substandard living conditions for recently freed slaves. Former plantation owners would soon benefit from the establishment of a share-cropping system, allowing them to reestablish a labor force as workers toiled under economically untenable conditions. In the agriculturally rich Mississippi Delta, railroad stops serving former plantations became hubs of newly developed settlements sorted out by their ruling class, and establishing a pattern throughout neglected, almost covert landscapes filled with minority populations. In these separated worlds, Black entertainment centered across rustic networks of weekend-only juke joints fueled by viscerally emotional musicianship where the blues sprung from their seven days a week misery. In Clarksdale, a beating heart of both the delta's thriving cotton industry and musical epicenter, the old Paramount Theater still stands with an outside stairway out back that graciously allowed Blacks to trudge up for balcony-level performances without inconveniencing its more affluent audience who enter beneath neon-lit marquees. That same town also spawned legendary musicians like Howlin' Wolf, John Lee Hooker, Sam Cooke, and Ike Turner in addition to a multitude of other greats who performed in smoke-filled clubs dotting this region.

In downtown Clarksdale, nickel strings on an aging Gretchen electric guitar are graced by the dexterous fingers of Johnnie Billington, a nattily dressed, highly noted blues guitarist. Here he belts out rhythms in front of a shuttered juke joint named The Spot, an apparent homage to nearby fabled crossroads where Robert Johnson reputedly sold his soul to the devil in exchange for musical greatness. Billington was born the child of an impoverished sharecropper, who managed a guitar gift for his son at age nine that proved instrumental. With intense practice, he was destined to perform with iconic bluesmen Muddy Waters and Elmore James, then teach underprivileged local youth to play the blues while insisting on strict moral values, partly expressed by formal dress codes for those young musicians, all performing under his tutelage in jacket and tie. With an honored invitation, he brought his musical ensemble to the White House for a performance watched by Bill Clinton, who seemed to embrace popular notions that he was this country's first Black president.

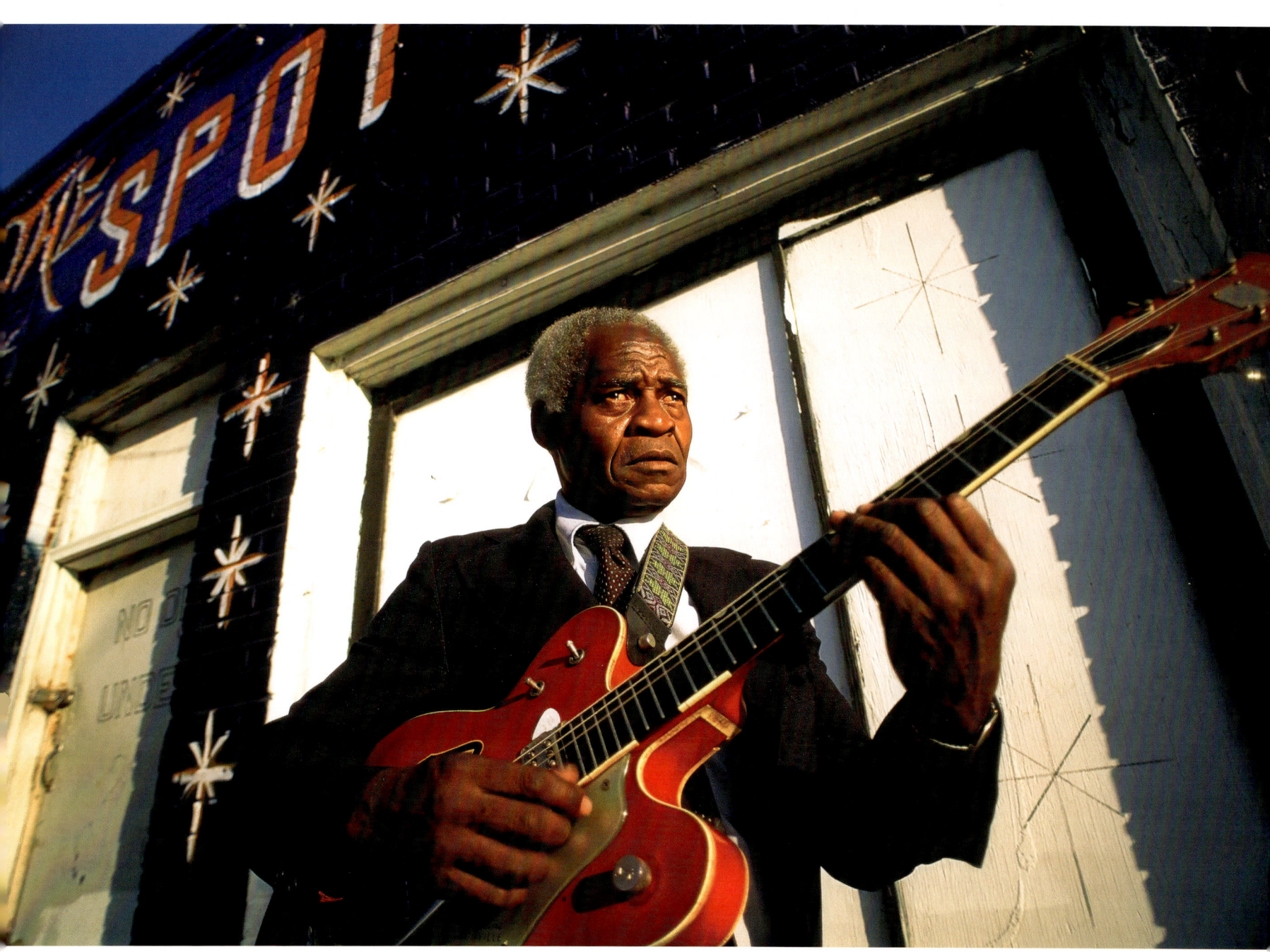

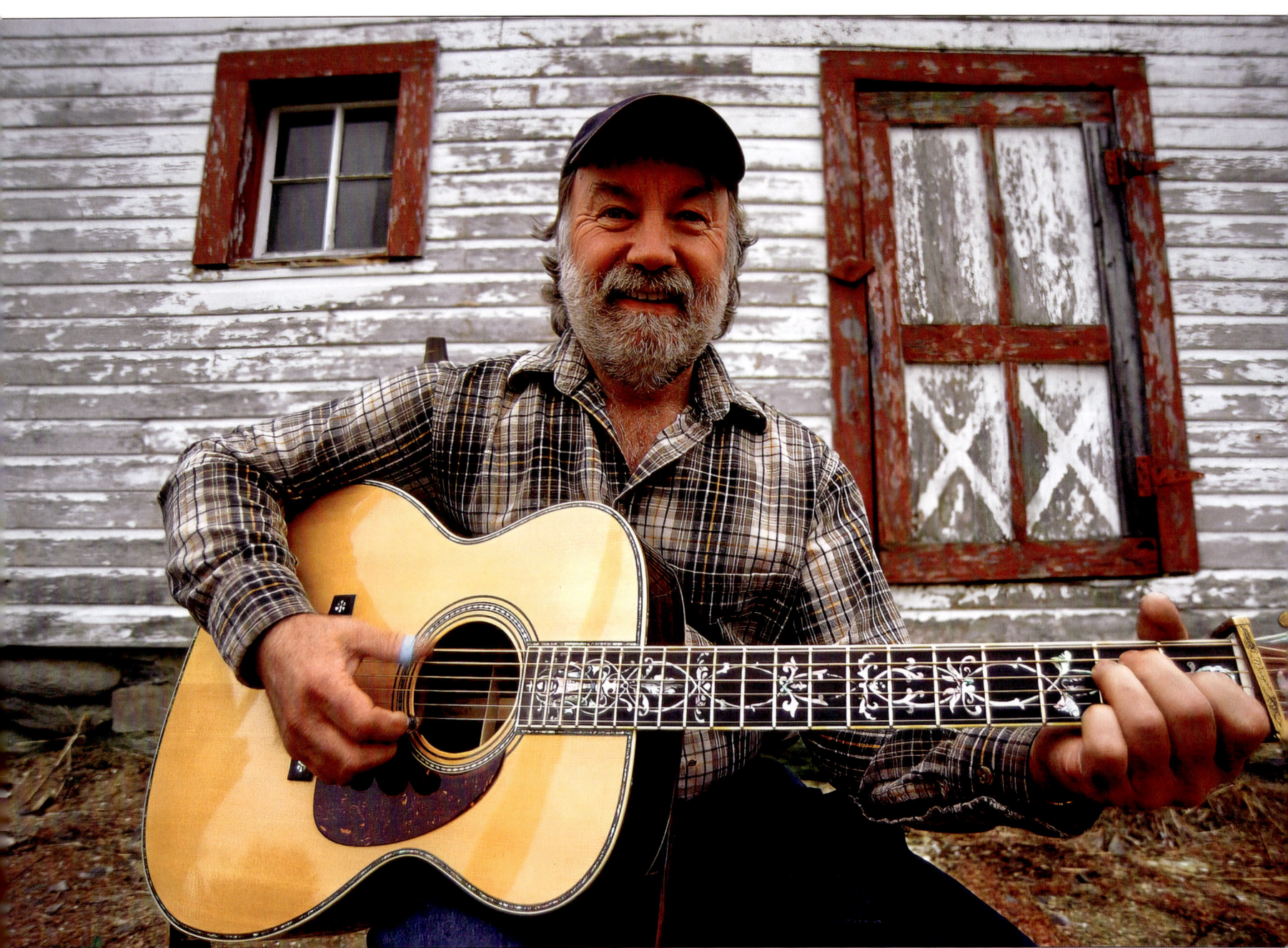

RENOWNED LUTHIER

Rugby, Virginia

Wiggling through hollers and vales across southwestern Virginia, a signposted Crooked Road connects the toe-tapping dots of mountain music with the region's cultural heritage. For over 300 miles, this rural asphalt ribbon concatenates with tobacco barn fiddle performances, barber shop banjo jams, Dairy Queen bluegrass concerts, general store hoedowns, passing dulcimer festivals and coon hunting clubs before swooping down into the minuscule Rugby settlement, housing a fairly steady residency of seven. After dusk on one edge of this hamlet, a faint fluorescent glow emanating from a long rustic woodshed reveals the fevered workshop activity of some hardworking man creating dreams for eagerly expectant patrons. A cramped array of benches, air hoses, flexible sanding blades and band saws command a floor filled with curly wood shavings, sprinkled about from laborious hours spent hand whittling, planing or scraping. An internationally acclaimed luthier sculpts honey-toned guitars, mandolins, and fiddles here, as he sands a body's sound hole, then adjusts the top bracing before nuts or saddles are hewed from his stock of aged beef bones. Using one sharp penknife, he describes how he whittles away everything that's not a guitar.

After returning from a spin through the mountains in his vintage 1957 Thunderbird, Wayne Henderson pauses outside that shop to test the fretwork action on his handmade green abalone-inlaid guitar. Known not just for the beauty of these instrumental creations but as well his brilliant bluegrass fingerstyle performances on them, Henderson keeps a waiting list for very impatient customers who will have to wait many years. He famously kept Eric Clapton on hold for one full decade. A custom order from folk and bluegrass legend Doc Watson capped their decades-long friendship, affirmed by his headlining participation in an annual music festival actually named after the famed luthier. Equally at home on a stage inside his local VFW post as one in Carnegie Hall, Henderson attracts music lovers making pilgrimages from all around the globe, usually tripling that hometown population every single day.

RIVER
ADVENTURER

Farrell, Mississippi

Drooling over one lip rimming diminutive, glacial Lake Itasca in Minnesota's red pine-scented woodland, an easily hoppable, 18-inch-deep stream will widen to over two miles as it defines borders and passes ten states during its inexorable quest to reach the Gulf of Mexico. The Mississippi River is the main trunk of this planet's fourth-largest river system. Its development into the vital lifeblood of a nation was made possible by profit-thirsty, fur-trading voyageurs in paddled birchbark canoes, later followed by Mark Twain-era's high-falutin steamboats. Heavily burdened with cargo bound for New Orleans, their cast iron boilers often needed to let off steam for prevention of common mid-channel explosions. Today, quarter-mile-long barges haul up to 2,500 tons of petroleum, chemicals, and grain products as their navigation is complicated by globally warmed droughts and lower water levels. An intricate web of locks, dams, spillways, and levees attempt to tame or divert the river during periodic flooding, segregating traditional river towns from their natural shoreline settings.

Appreciating those few remaining wild stretches of this mighty river, accomplished outfitter and paddling guide John Ruskey enlists venturesome, starry-eyed youth into exploratory adventures along the unspoiled Lower Mississippi. Having journeyed amongst frolicking otters and soaring snowy egrets, he has painstakingly established encyclopedic documentations of flourishing wildlife and riparian culture. His determined motivations were molded during astonishingly lengthy solo ventures in handmade rafts or canoes, dodging snags and dining on sandbars between daily baptisms. Ruskey's younger artistic skills and fascination with southern riverine cultures led to a stint as curator at the nearby Delta Blues Museum, where companionships with blues greats sharpened his musical talents. By a swampy oxbow lake just off the Big Muddy, he takes a short break from his intrepid river journeys. An undulating crescendo of chirping insects harmonizes with glissando resonating across his bottleneck slide guitar, plucked beside swampy cypress knees, woody projections that suggest to some the deeply rooted connections between delta blues and Ol' Man River.

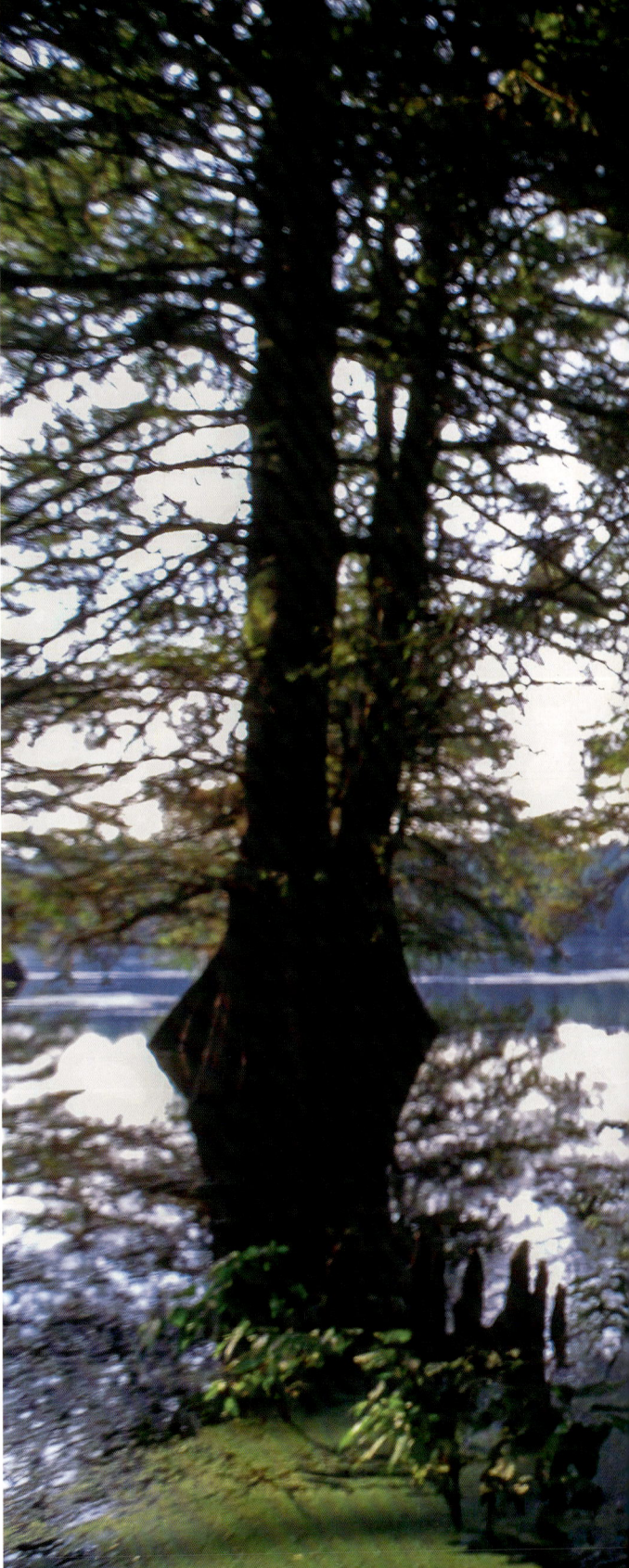

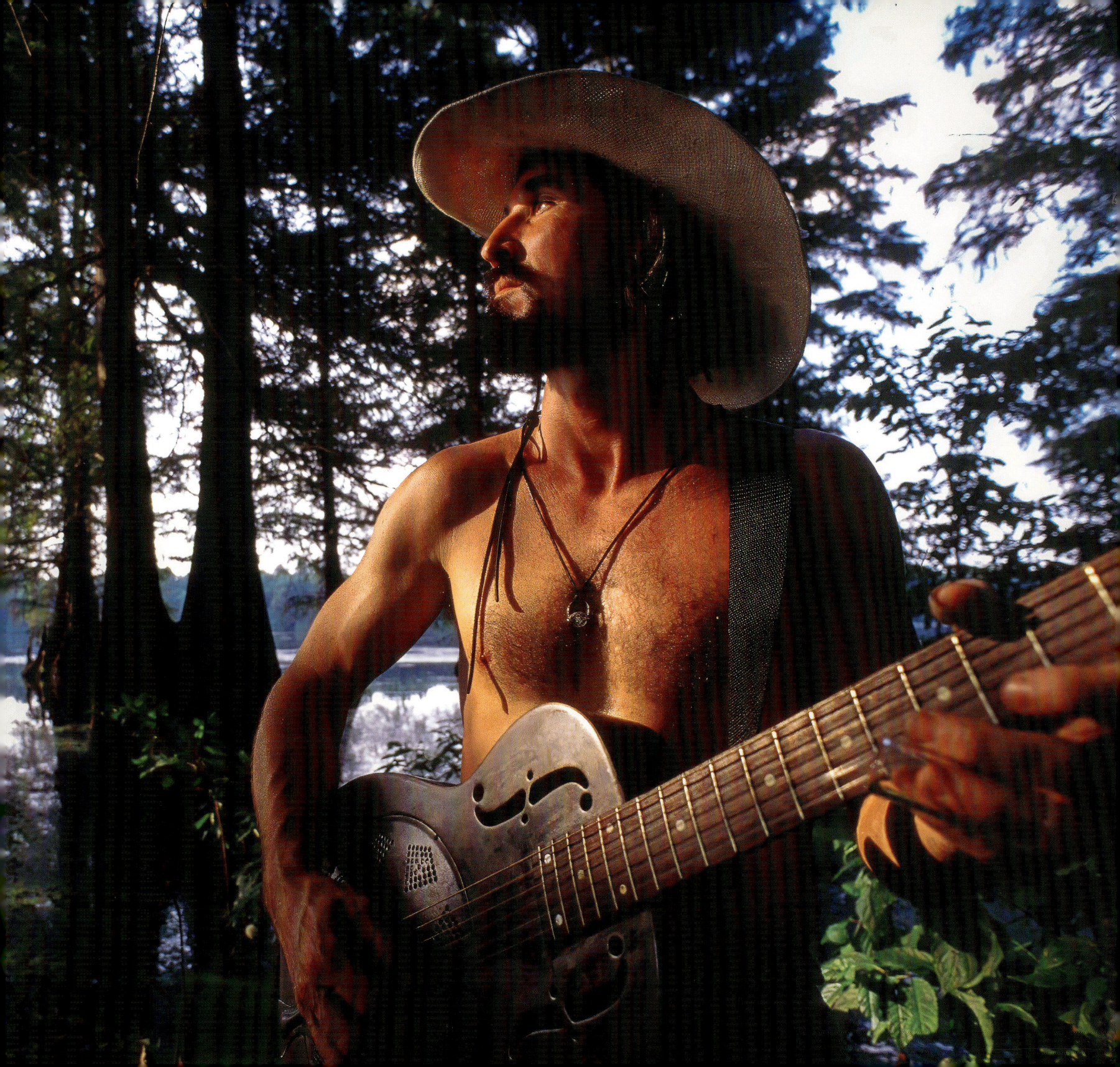

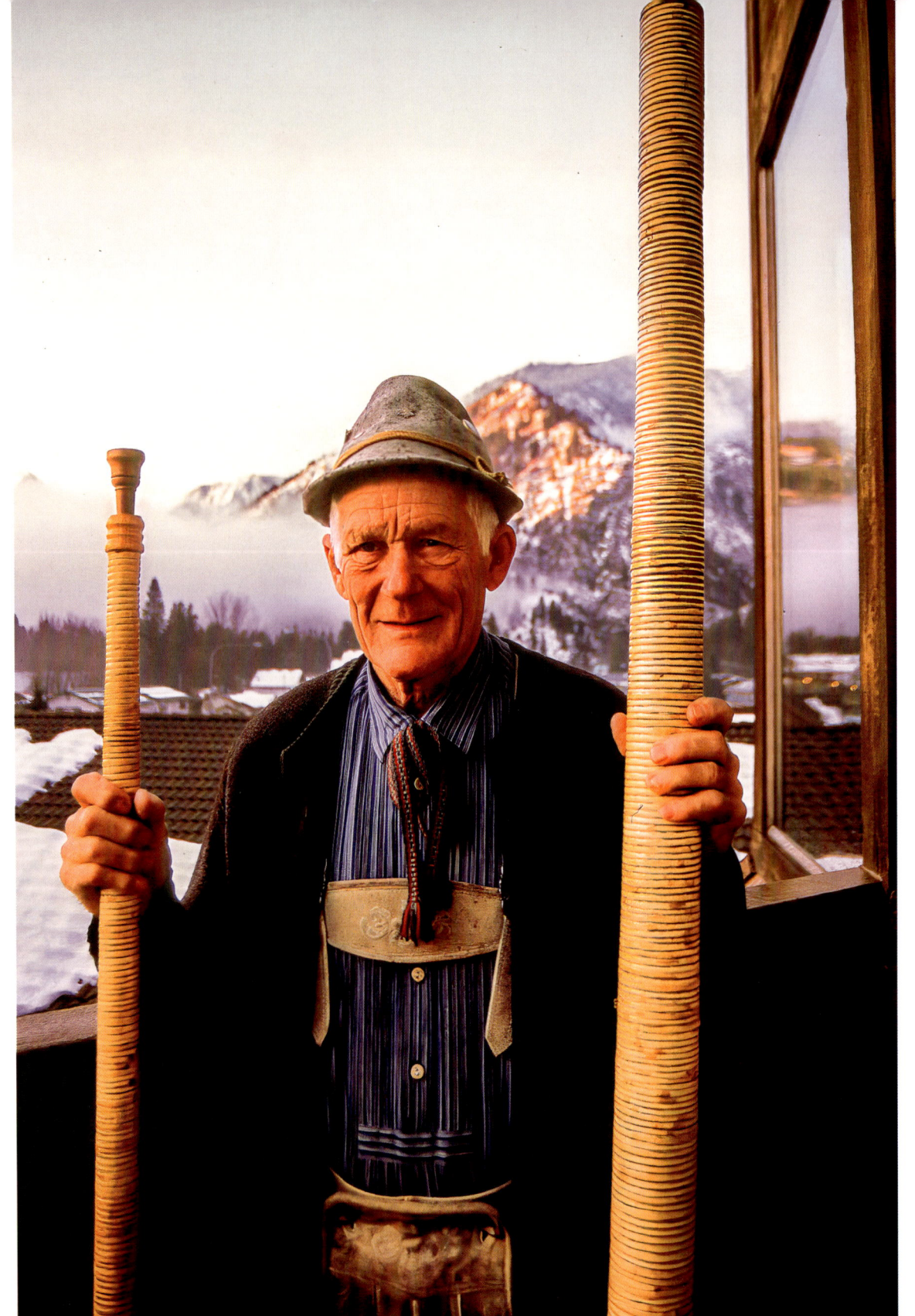

ALPHORN PLAYER

Leavenworth, Washington

The Ring of Fire is a 25,000-mile-long, horseshoe-shaped arena defined by intense geothermal activity. It is the earth's largest geographic feature, producing most of this planet's volcanic eruptions and nearly all its earthquakes. Along the Pacific Northwest's coastal edges, an immense tectonic battle occurred millions of years ago when spectacular North Cascade mountain ranges were shoved skyward and its Pacific plate slid beneath a North American counterpart. Those resulting landscapes, much resembling the Alps, were one last hindrance to explorers Lewis and Clark's expedition searching for a coastline, but subsequently helped lure gold miners or fur traders seeking their fortune in this wilderness. Eventually, burgeoning sawmill activities made the small mountainside village of Leavenworth into a trading crossroads. Later, when the economy there began to falter, an idea was hatched to enhance its town's revenue by transforming itself into a unique Bavarian-themed alpine wonderland. By its village green, an illuminated gazebo awaits wintertime's excited sledders while nearby establishments serve bratwurst and fresh baked pretzels at their beer garden's fire table, providing nourishment for a visit to the renowned next-door Nutcracker Museum. Yet the most convincing and authentic trumpeting of Bavarian lifestyles occurs daily throughout the year as a punctual morning wake up call.

Presumably inspired by climbers scaling vertiginous slopes on Dragontail Peak glimpsed just behind his shoulders, octogenarian and lodge owner Bob Johnson actually hops up along a very skinny fourth floor ledge at the Enzian Inn where for decades he serenaded waking citizenry with mellifluous tones on his 13-foot, three-inch-long aspen alphorn instrument. Dressed in deer-leather lederhosen and Tyrolean felt hat, Johnson was gifted that one alphorn by a local Swiss-born logger and then composed his own music for morning breakfast serenades, amusing dirndl-clad waitress staff and startling newcomers with visions of an elderly, precariously perched bugler on the roof.

BIGFOOT SEEKER

Grand Staircase-Escalante National Monument, Utah

Of the 7.8 million species of animals estimated by scientists to currently inhabit earth, less than a quarter have actually been identified by taxonomists, and most of those are insects. Somewhere along that spectrum of myths, legends, rumors, sightings, and documentation lies the fascinating cryptozoology field, centered on studying cryptids, rumored creatures that have become subjects in focused investigations. Amongst our planet's immense zoological stadium, new species are constantly being discovered, named, classified, and analyzed. While legends like mermaids and unicorns seem to be universally discounted, numerous rumored animals thought by most to be fictional have indeed been found or documented. Discovered only in 1798, the furry platypus from Australia, seemingly cobbled from spare parts, was originally thought by amazed biologists to be a hoax. The venomous mammals actually lay eggs, have tails resembling that of a beaver, feet just like an otter and startling duck-like bills. One subspecies of the world's largest primate, the long-rumored mountain gorilla remained a cryptid until its discovery by Europeans in 1902. Forty-foot-long sea monsters that likely inspired Norse mythology to trumpet the Kraken, giant squid were never even photographed alive until 2006. While debates rage around the Loch Ness monster actually being a humongous eel, it is Bigfoot that understandably has most captured the imagination of cryptozoologists in North America. An eight-foot-high, muscular hunk of a hairy bipedal humanoid has sporadically been sighted and poorly documented, though some distinguished, yet marginalized scientists continue to investigate its existence.

When wildlife biologist John Mionczynski noticed a monstrous hand atop his six-foot tent during one 1972 solo scientific camping expedition in Wyoming's Wind Mountains, he presented that Bigfoot encounter to nonchalant game and fish officials. Featured on National Geographic television programming for his determined searches, he spent years assessing Sasquatch habitats, setting camera traps, and trying to snare DNA. Originally famed for tracking radio-collared bighorn sheep, his deep backcountry knowledge led him to a widely acclaimed book on goat packing, an enterprise he first pioneered to assist him while carrying equipment to remote research sites. Here Mionczynski, deep within Grand Staircase-Escalante canyons, serenades his goats on a beloved accordion. His mother purchased that instrument as his therapy for an elbow crushed when he was a young boy. Since then he actually created a hidden compartment for first aid equipment and emergency food supplies inside that accordion. He performs with it at a Wyoming saloon in the remote gold mining settlement that's also his hometown. Its roadside signpost boasts a population of 57 year-round residents, which includes Mionczynski's own cabin, built from refurbished materials grabbed from the town dump for $72. In the meantime, he ruminates about his goats' odor creating a lure during future odysseys on the prowl for Bigfoot.

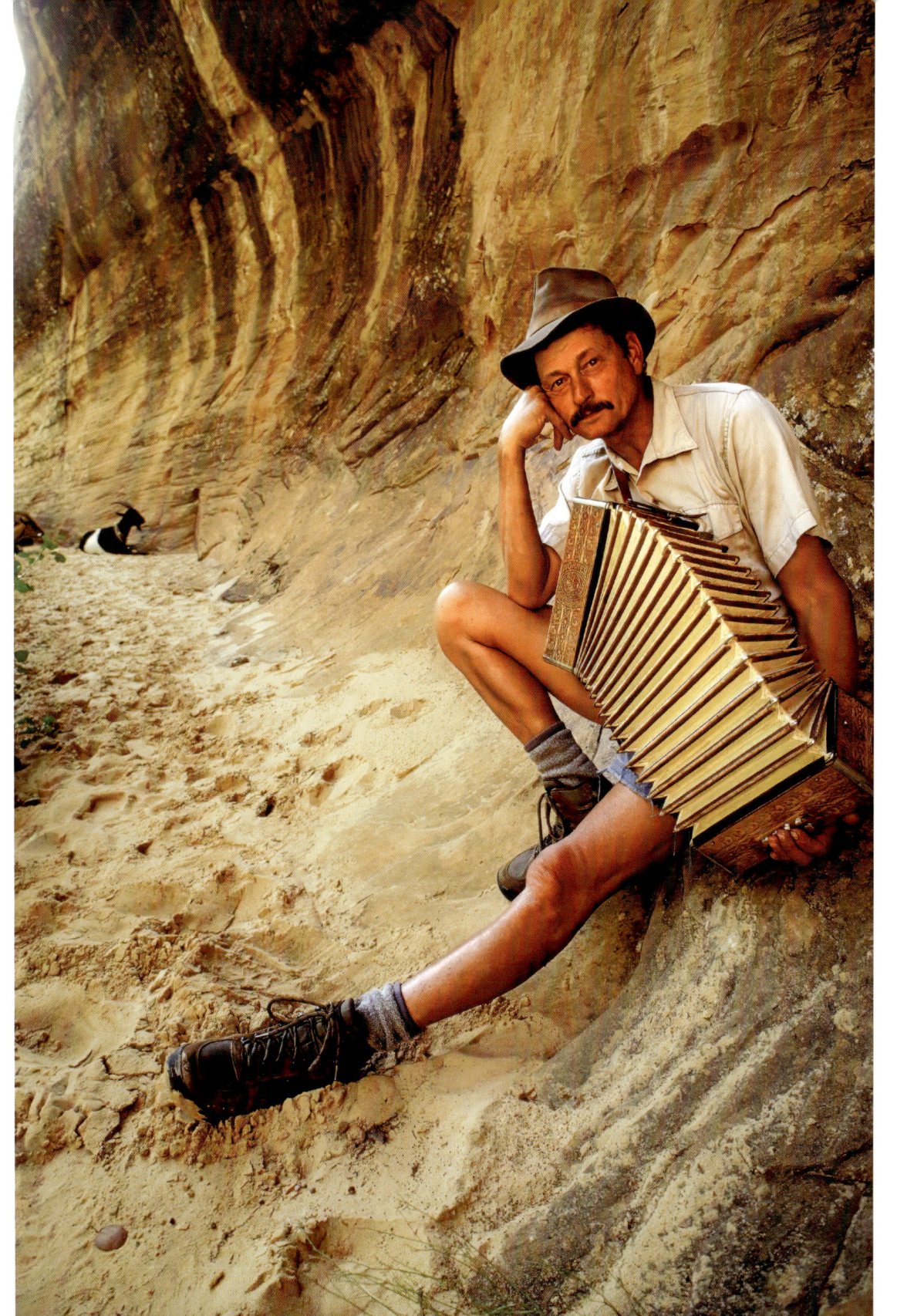

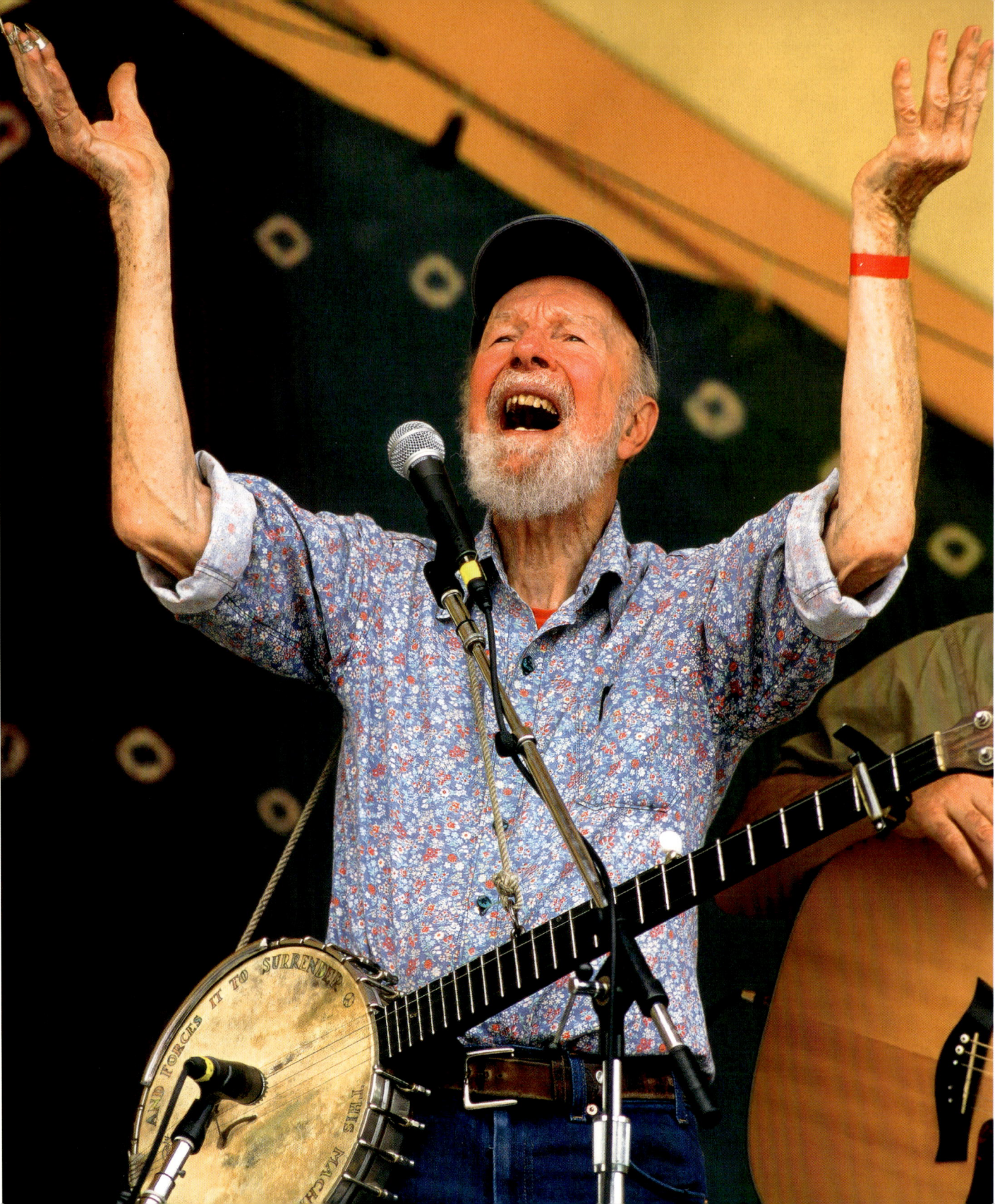

LEGENDARY FOLK SINGER

Croton-on-Hudson, New York

Musical protests have a rich history that dates back through the centuries. Their songs offered galvanizing strength, reminding dissenters of their humanity in the face of repressive, more powerful authority. Its entreaties were evidenced hundreds of years ago in Beethoven's anthem "Ode to Joy," a revolutionary call to enlightenment's freedom that rallied against war and desperation. A well-known, flute-punctuated "Yankee Doodle" was sung in defiance of British soldiers who themselves originally wrote that ditty to ridicule the American Revolution. Enslaved communities vocally mobilized behind liberating spirituals to set a pace for their field work, while in the Jim Crow-era, Billie Holiday's "Strange Fruit" provided haunting images of revolting Southern lynchings. Its jazz-inflected melodic outrage was said to have sparked an awakening of the civil rights movement. Perhaps the most iconic hymn pushing for racial equality was that gospel tune "We Shall Overcome," thought to have had its origins during a 1945 tobacco workers' strike in South Carolina, and later popularized after being rewritten by Pete Seeger. Its melody was heard during Montgomery's bus boycott, handholding marches at Selma, across Lincoln Memorial rallies in the nation's capital, and during Martin Luther King's last sermon before his assassination. Seeger, founding father for many twentieth-century protest movements, was a political activist protesting war, injustice, poverty, and racism, in addition to being an ardent folk-singing musician, armed with his long-necked five-string banjo capable of firing off numerous timeless classics. In support of the Progressive movement, the former blacklisted Communist's flagship paean "If I Had a Hammer" was originally released as a 78-rpm vinyl single, becoming an eventual top ten hit when performed by Peter, Paul and Mary. The elegiac "Where Have All the Flowers Gone?" is a plaintive cry about war's senselessness and has been covered by seemingly everyone from Marlene Dietrich to Dolly Parton. "Turn! Turn! Turn!" his plea for world peace was notably based almost verbatim on Ecclesiatic scripture, and topped music charts for The Byrds after being tweaked just a bit by Seeger. It was a rare instance that any popular song employed large portions from the Bible for its musical content.

At this nation's oldest and largest event of its kind, the Clearwater Festival features seven bio-diesel powered stages spotlighting stellar folk performers while promoting environmental awareness. Founded in 1966 by Pete Seeger and his wife Toshi, this event's eponymously named sloop sails the adjacent Hudson River to celebrate its rehabilitation from a once polluted dumping ground, one cause he persistently championed. Onstage deploying soaring lyrics and uplifted fingers clad in ready to utilize metal picks, Seeger totes his longtime faithful instrument which is lovingly inscribed around its goat-skinned banjo head with "This Machine Surrounds Hate And Forces It To Surrender." Unrelenting in pursuit of earthly justice, Seeger performed into his nineties, finally surrendering to mortality at age ninety-four, when President Obama noted quite rightly that he was America's tuning fork.

HIP-HOP DEVOTEES

Hollywood, California

In Southern California, iconic fifty-foot-high white letters erected in 1923 spelled out Hollywoodland to promote a real estate development from high atop Mount Lee until more than two decades later when the last four letters were removed. Down below, the twinkling billboard-studded, neon-adorned city of Hollywood had become synonymous with glamorous stars and filmmaking, where numerous theater houses adjoined movie palaces, which stretched across its legendary main street. There, scattered like breadcrumbs luring an endless flock of selfie-posing tourists, a terrazzo-and-brass constellation spreads its stars across one particular fifteen-block stretch lining Hollywood Boulevard, inscribing into its sidewalks stellar names in film, entertainment, or music. Just down that street from where annual Academy Award ceremonies churn out new matinee idols, and right across the way from towering music industry headquarters, Amoeba Music has located this planet's largest record store. With its quarter of a million titles the establishment beckons music lovers, most especially hip-hop devotees who bop to hypnotically insistent sounds echoing inside clubs and blaring from cruising open-topped convertibles. Though hip-hop originally emerged in the 1970s through breakdancing b-boys and battling turntablists set up on South Bronx building stoops or abandoned parking lots, California's street gang warfare with its thug life sensibilities eventually spawned Death Row Records promoting genre-busting artists like Dr. Dre, Snoop Dogg, and Tupac Shakur.

Beneath a DMX-style tank top and LL Cool J-inspired backwards baseball cap, this pair of hip-hop devotees sport apparel trumpeting iconography evoking both coasts that first nurtured evolving hip hop sounds. They're just chilling outside the neon and graffiti-splashed storefront at Amoeba Music, where this window's reflections reveal Capitol Records' profile hovering above two of that sidewalk's Walk of Fame stars, including hip-hop celebrity DJ Khaled.

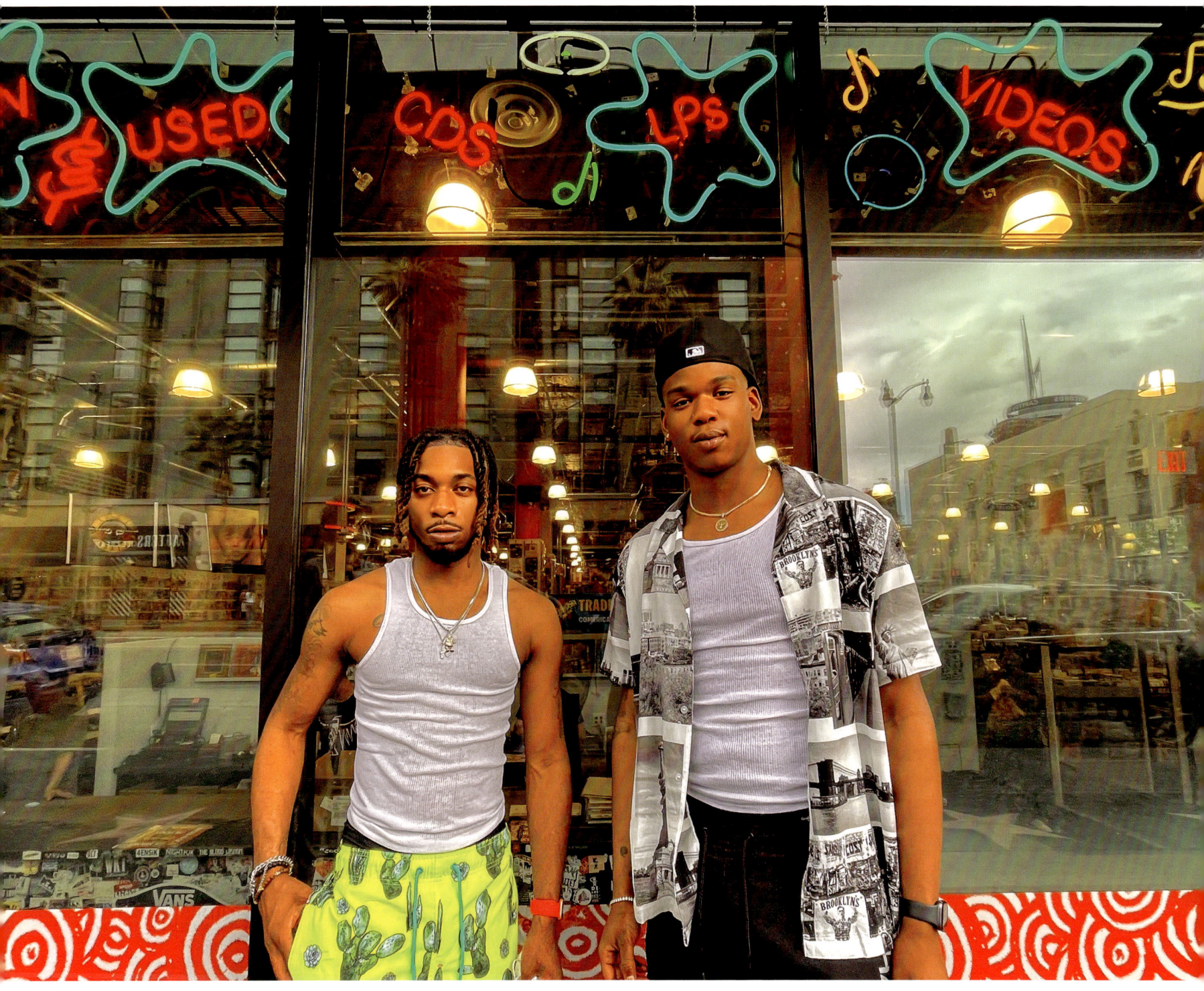

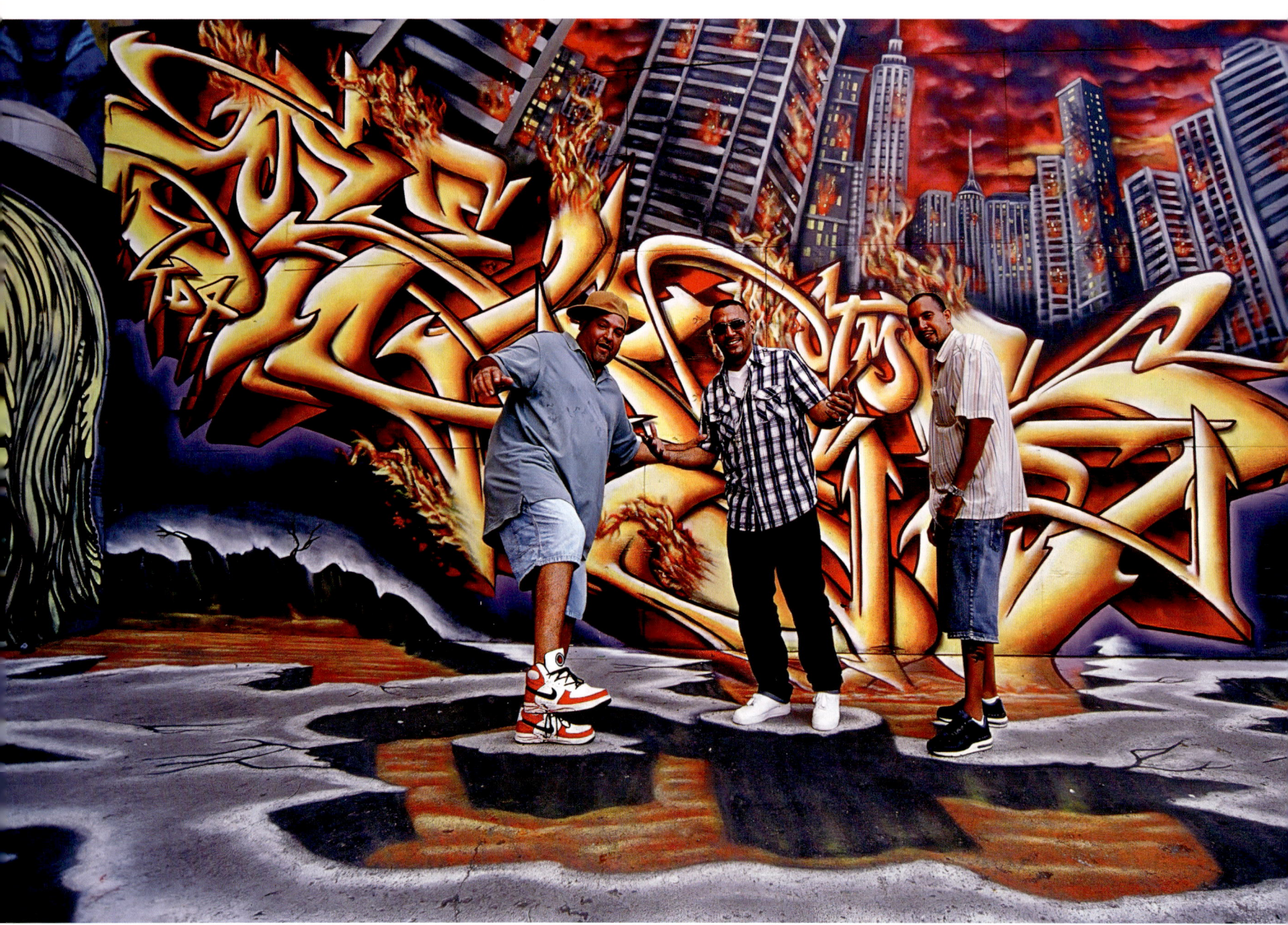

GRAFFITI ENTHUSIASTS

Long Island City, New York City, New York

Richly pigmented galloping equines and stags found in a Lascaux, France, cave are said to be 17,000 years old but are not as popularly imagined part of earth's very first ancient wall paintings. Rather, the oldest wall art ever created was some 300 centuries earlier, and only recently discovered in limestone caverns on Sulawesi, an Indonesian island. Those depictions consisted of just a few obese Pleistocene-era warty hogs, now extremely endangered animals. In Ephesus, one of antiquities' seven world wonders, drawings featured body parts that advertised brothels while within the ancient city of Pompeii, frozen in time by volcanic flows, phallic images were etched into its basilica. Conditions for contemporary graffiti were created in 1949 when paint was first placed in spray cans, which until then had only been used for deodorizers and insecticides. Yet modern day graffiti never really debuted until 1965 at a youth correctional facility in Philadelphia, where one 12-year-old troublemaker Darryl "Cornbread" McCray touted his grandmother's culinary creation through incessant scribbling. Upon his release, McCray took to city streets spreading that quick bread moniker, but fame only arrived when he broke into the Philadelphia Zoo and spray painted both sides of an elephant with his trademark tag. In New York City, Taki 183 found fame using his street number and diminutive Greek name. With it, he managed to spray paint his way into notoriety as subway cars conveniently spread that signature message across four boroughs. Before long, urban centers were steadily tattooed in hieroglyphics, and perceptual conflicts between vandalism and art generated political heat. In the 1990s, Keith Haring's distinctive graffiti-stylings were transformed into gallery-going admiration and later Banksy further elevated renegade paint attacks into auction house bidding wars. In Long Island City, a hugely inviting expanse of 200,000 square feet covering walls on an abandoned factory became a monstrously sized canvas that lured artistic expressions from spray paint-wielding artists scribbling tags, throw ups, murals, and masterpieces. Best viewed from west-facing windows on the clattering 7 subway line circling overhead, this site was the former 1896 Neptune Meter factory before becoming a hallucinatory rainbow-hued amalgam of street artist aspirations known as Five Pointz.

By loading docks inside the former water meter factory, aerosol artists, breakdancers, taggers dropping rhymes, and DJs scratching discs mix it up in a courtyard fostering hip-hop solidarity for an edgy community of creatives. Anamorphism screams to get attention as this crew of graffiti enthusiasts balance precariously amid tromp l'oeil stumps, a burning skyline, and calligraphic Wildstyle signatures that appear gasping for air. In 2013, the building's owner initiated a rudely unannounced whitewashing, bulldozing dreams of aspiring artists and replacing them with luxury condominiums touting an indoor pool.

OCTOGENARIAN BALLERINA

Death Valley Junction, California

Near the Western Hemisphere's lowest spot, earth's highest temperatures can melt pavement and often shatter records, Turkey vultures whirl overhead on patrol for carrion, while prowling coyotes dodge blowing tumbleweed. At a lonely crossroads is Death Valley Junction, with a population that usually peaks somewhere around four. It was once the hub of a thriving borax mining industry where mule teams hauled this valuable laundry detergent ingredient out from dry lake beds to be loaded onto awaiting trains by this junction's depot. All that activity supported a small Spanish Colonial Revival hotel and social hall that served area workers until the industry collapsed in the 1920s.

Decades later, at this dusty collection of abandoned adobe structures, an accomplished ballerina and dancer from New York looking to further some ambitious dreams, was driving through the region when her disabled vehicle sought refuge here. Following her fixed tire and vivid recollections of an encouraging consultation with a fortune teller, Marta Beckett decided to reconvene her creative gifts at this unlikely venue, which was purchased in one quick burst of impulsivity. She quickly got to work on her newly christened Amargosa Opera House. Metal coffee cans were repurposed into stage lights and theater curtains were sewn from discarded red corduroy. The bare interior walls beckoned as an inviting blank canvas to be slowly transformed. After six paint-splattered years of hard work, a lively crowd featuring vividly portrayed gypsies, nuns, monks, and prostitutes emerged, finally providing a dependably enthusiastic spectators for her nighttime performances in the desert. As word spread of this eccentric venue and its indefatigable performer, actual human beings began supplementing those painted versions in the audience, all apparently enthralled as they bore witness to a chimerical ballet-slippered stage performer masterfully spinning fantasies in her fading ghost town.

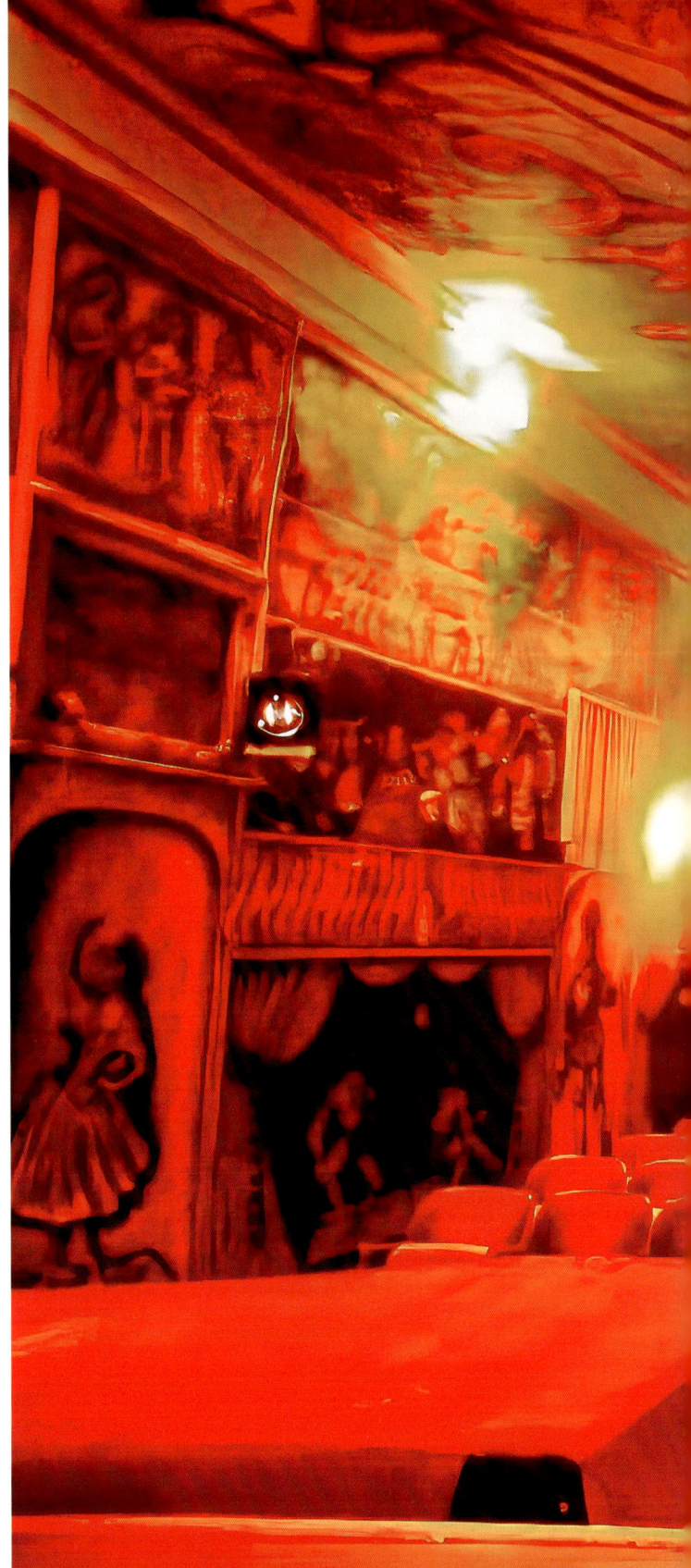

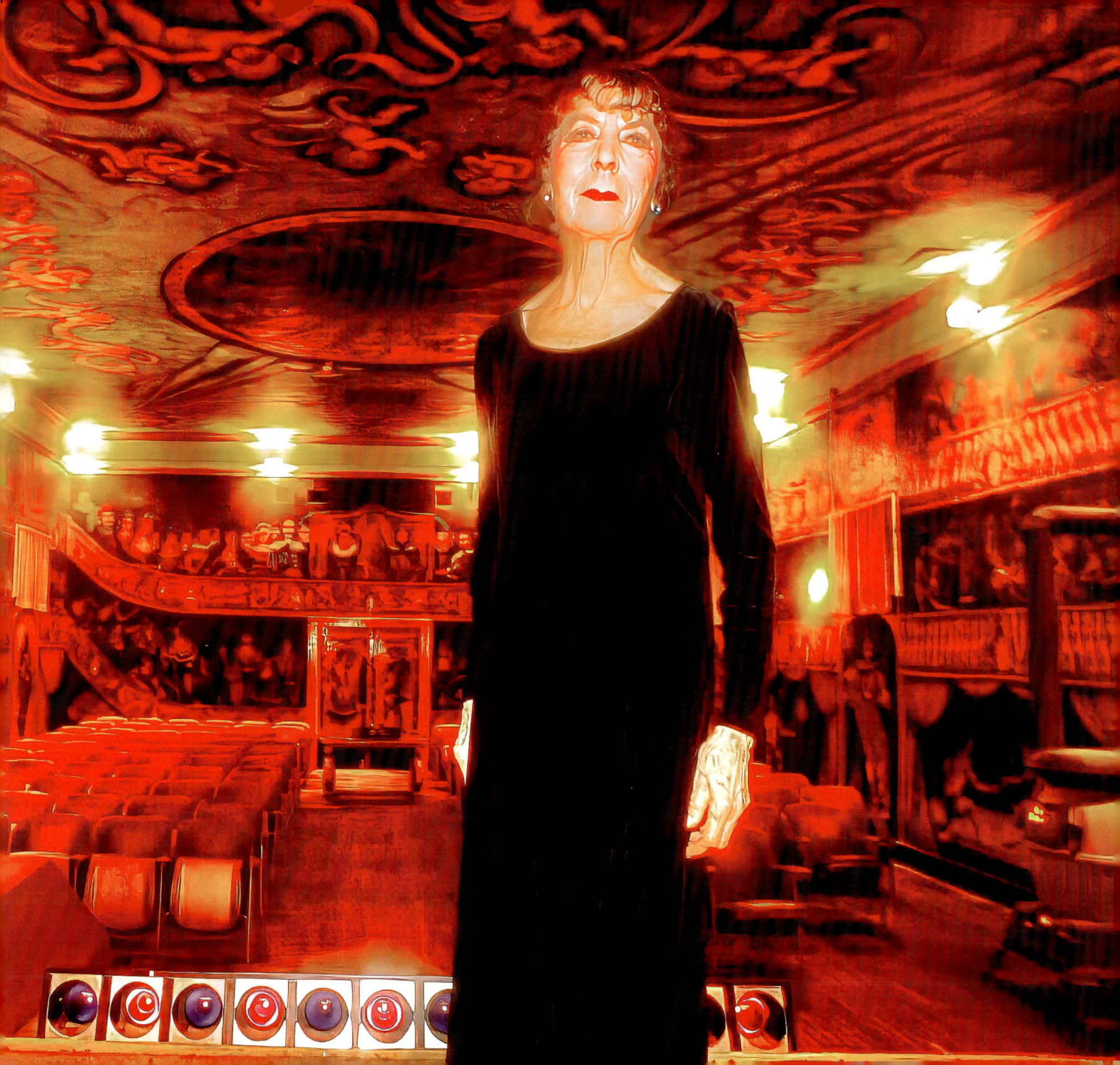

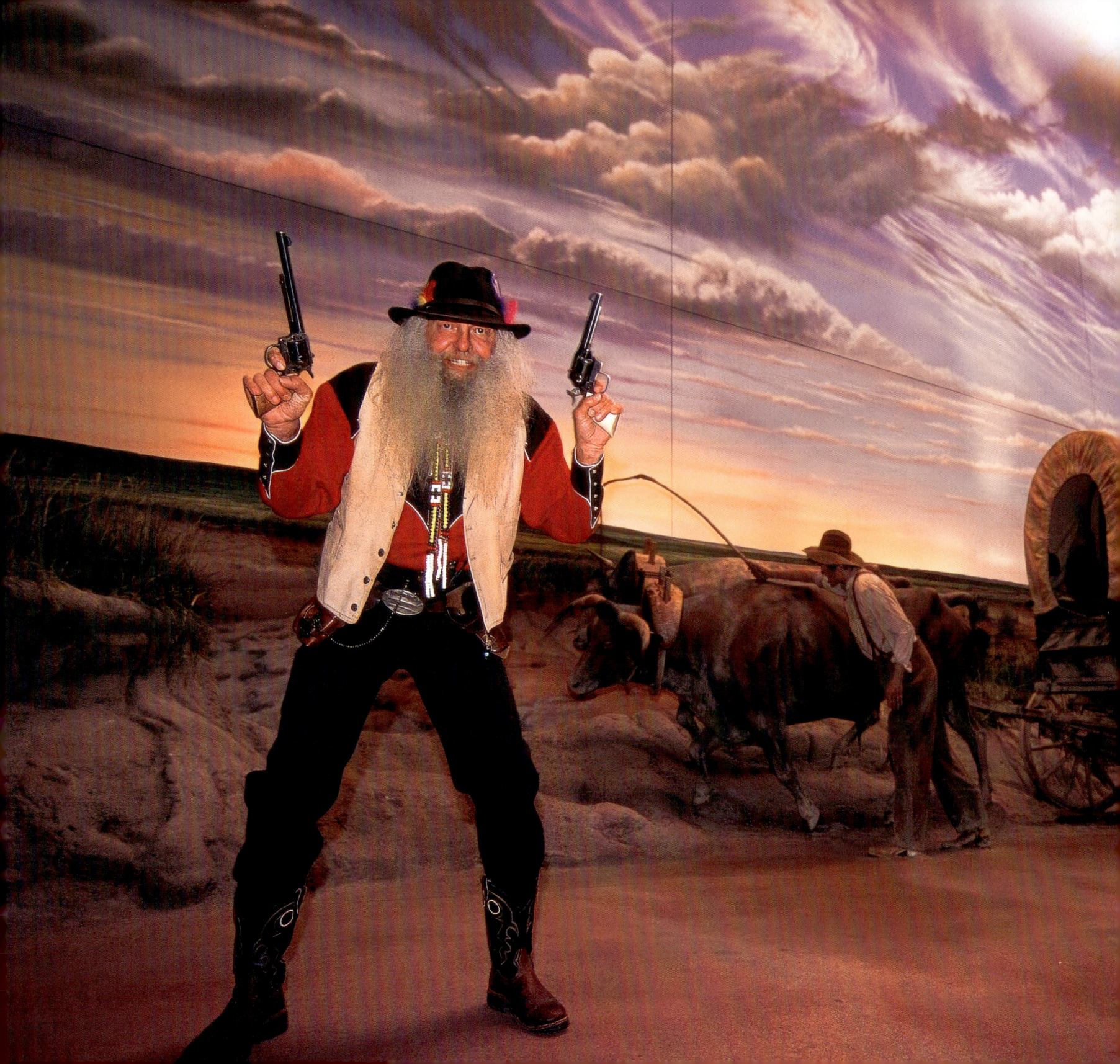

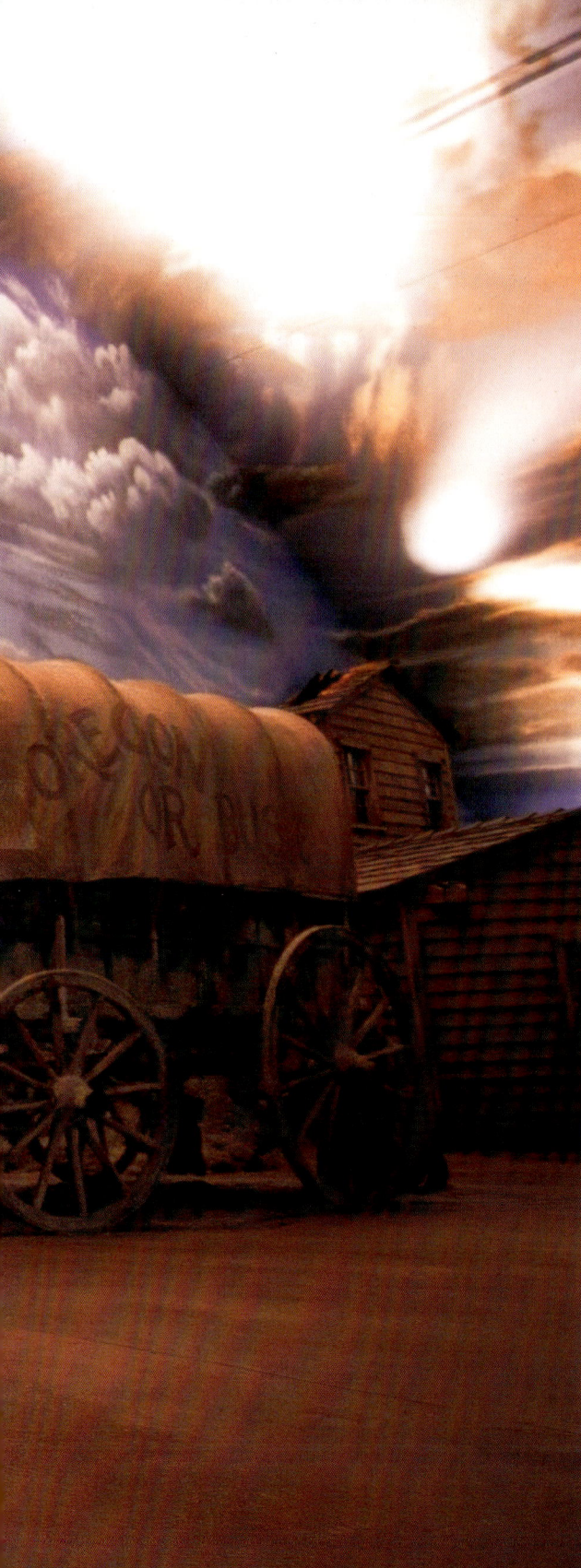

MUSEUM DOCENT

Kearney, Nebraska

During early nineteenth-century migration, emigres from harsh climates across America's heartland were lured westward by exaggerated newspaper accounts boasting about bountiful forests and temperate weather in the Pacific Northwest. In covered wagon convoys following the braided Platte River, early pioneers bounced along a rutted Oregon Trail, first blazed by fur traders and trappers. Overnighting in protective circles, they mostly sought to avoid conflict with Indigenous peoples who rightly viewed their uninvited presence as a threat to their existence. Those native concerns proved well founded as less than seven decades later, a first transcontinental automobile roadway, the Lincoln Highway, largely followed pathways of these original trails. That happened only after substantial fine-tuning by an arduous military experiment in 1919 when the First Transcontinental Motor Convoy charted a vehicular path across America. Assigned to observe and report on that endeavor was a Lieutenant Colonel Dwight Eisenhower, who later became the Supreme Commander of Allied Forces during World War ll. After Germany's defeat in the conflict, then-General Eisenhower was astonished to discover their hugely efficient, high-speed Autobahn highways, enabling rapid deployment and movement of German troops. It was after Eisenhower's election as president in 1952 that he began initiating legislation to create America's first Interstate Highway System, owned and operated by the Department of Defense with limited access entry and exit points, which could, if needed, be used for regulating troop movements. During the paranoid era of the Cold War, interstate highways were envisioned as means to escape enemy bombardments and nuclear calamities. The second-longest interstate in this nation, I-80 travels 2,920 miles from Atlantic to Pacific shores as it barrels through eleven states. The single straightest stretch of interstate roadway in this entire system occurs in Nebraska, where for some 72 miles twin ribbons of concrete travel along a ramrod straight line, never deviating beyond an occasional few yards. With its reputation as a Gateway to the West, Nebraska's Great Platte River Road Archway Monument arose over this prairie as an arresting landmark museum that actually spreads across Interstate 80 as sports cars and tractor trailers alike roar down below, some hell bent on reaching one of two different oceans a continent apart. Just above the highway, this museum traces an amazing evolution of transportation through massive dioramas featuring pioneer emigration, early motor camps, tacky motels, and greasy spoon diners.

Appearing much like some demented wax figure, a bearded, overenthusiastic gunslinger seems quite at home beneath bloodshot skies as oxen drovers deploy covered wagon traffic from Fort Kearney to points beyond. In an unusual museum of transportation, this time-traveling docent helps interpret ever-changing movements that fostered migration across a western frontier, where present-day visitors can track with radar guns the often-illegal speeds driven by actual motorists racing directly beneath the museum.

GUN RANGE INSTRUCTOR

Lajitas, Texas

In a country founded through its musket-toting revolution first lit by a shot heard around the world near Concord, Massachusetts, the American experience is often noted for its enthusiastic embrace of gun culture. Unrivaled amongst all its contiguous neighbors for an outsized devotion to firearms is the Lone Star State. Its own independent republic for over a decade, Texas was forged through the centuries by a rolling series of violent events. Long before a bolt-action rifle's scope found the skull of America's 35th president in Dallas or even decades earlier when notorious gangsters Bonnie and Clyde, born, bred, robbed, murdered, then buried in Texas, this state's history seems to have always been consecrated with gun violence. After Apache and Comanche were wrenched from their indigenous homelands, there were heroic citizens who got outgunned while fighting to their apocryphal death alongside flint-lock-armed Davy Crockett in Alamo's ill-fated courtyard, followed by bloody battles defining the Mexican-American War, a less successful Army pursuit chasing guerilla fighter Pancho Villa, and gunpoint apprehensions targeting hostile cattle rustlers, all figuring heavily into the zeitgeist of Texan annals. Utilizing his one-volume law library, much-mythologized Judge Roy Bean dispensed crazed versions of swift frontier justice from his isolated saloon courtroom while using a six-shooter revolver as a gavel. Best known for arranging an illegal championship prizefight on a sandbar in the middle of a muddy Rio Grande, he successfully outmaneuvered both Mexican and American authorities while receiving one large cut of those proceeds. Just upstream, tiny Lajitas, barely around the other side of Big Bend, was where Villa's bandits once roamed and television's *Rawhide* portrayed ranchland troubles. With its easily forded, flagstone-shelved 150-foot-wide international boundary, it became an illicit staging ground for rum running and smuggling cattle and Mexican candelilla wax, an important component for waterproofing tents. Proliferation of guns here can be traced back to the Civil War's conclusion when southern civilization lay smoldering in ruins. Deserters and desperados fled to lawless stretches across Texas with absconded weaponry, which to this day finds refuge amongst Second Amendment interpretations.

Nowadays, in a place where some preachers still pack pistols, there are more gun dealers within Texas than any other state. Rifle ranges abound even at remote outposts like Lajitas, where the nearest grocery shopping is 190 miles away. Squinting toward a blazing, late afternoon sun, an attentive rifle-toting buckskinned marksmen inspects recent ballistic handiwork from guests at this rustic shooting range amidst the arid Chihuahuan Desert's northern edge and beneath backdrops used for famed 1970s era Marlboro cigarette ads. A crumbling adobe trading post still services this remote settlement where icy Lone Star beers were actually chugged by Clay Henry Jr., a thirsty goat who was improbably elected mayor here and gave that name to the nearby saloon.

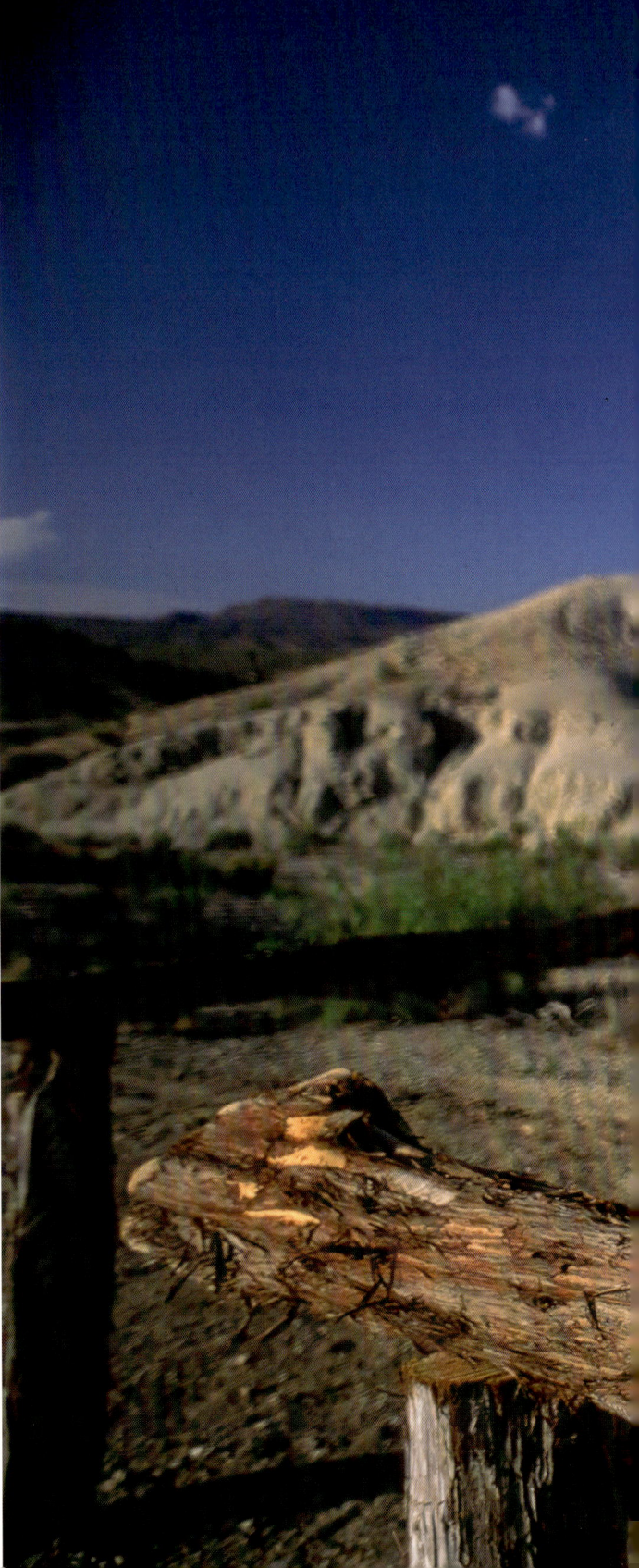

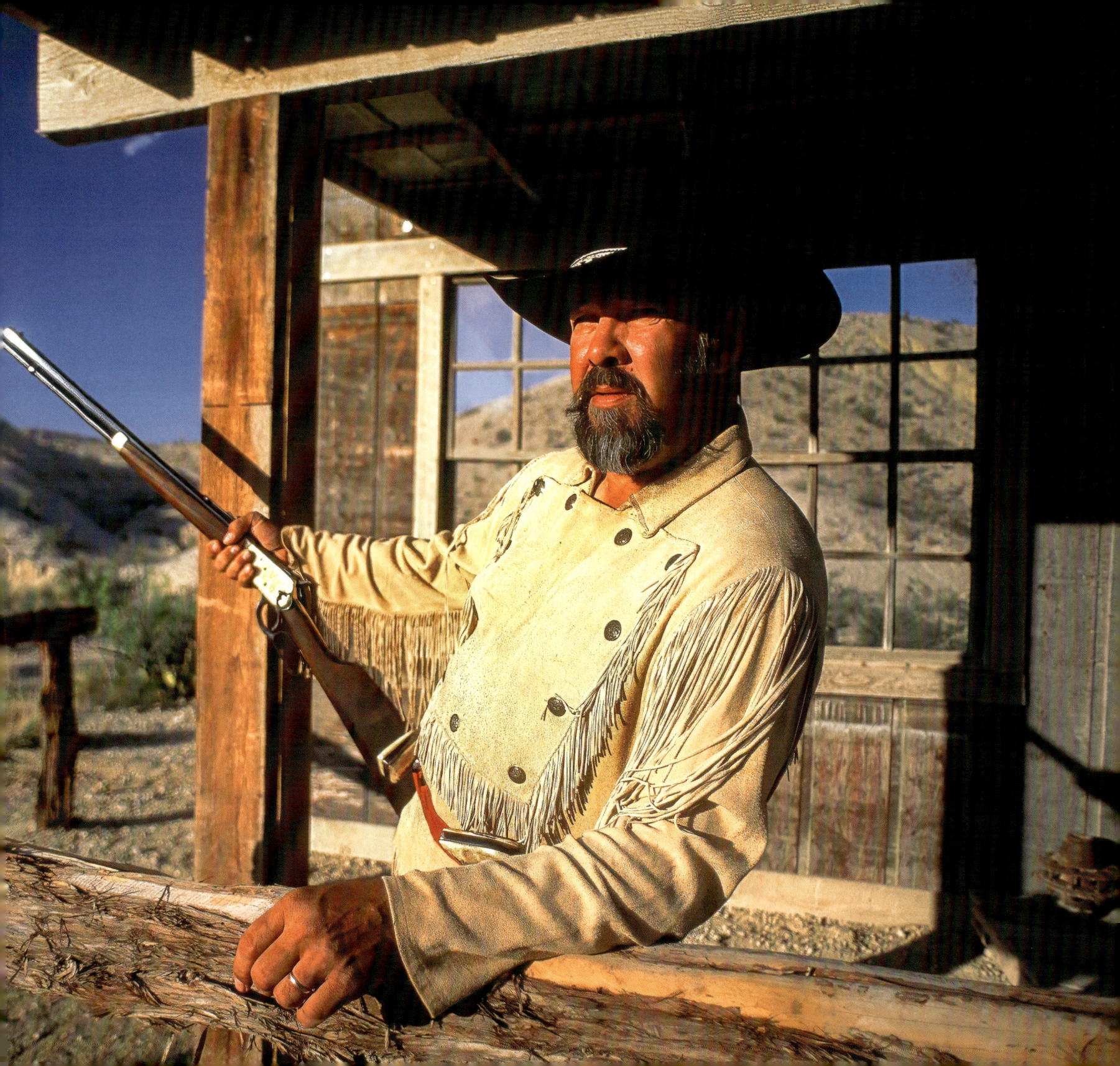

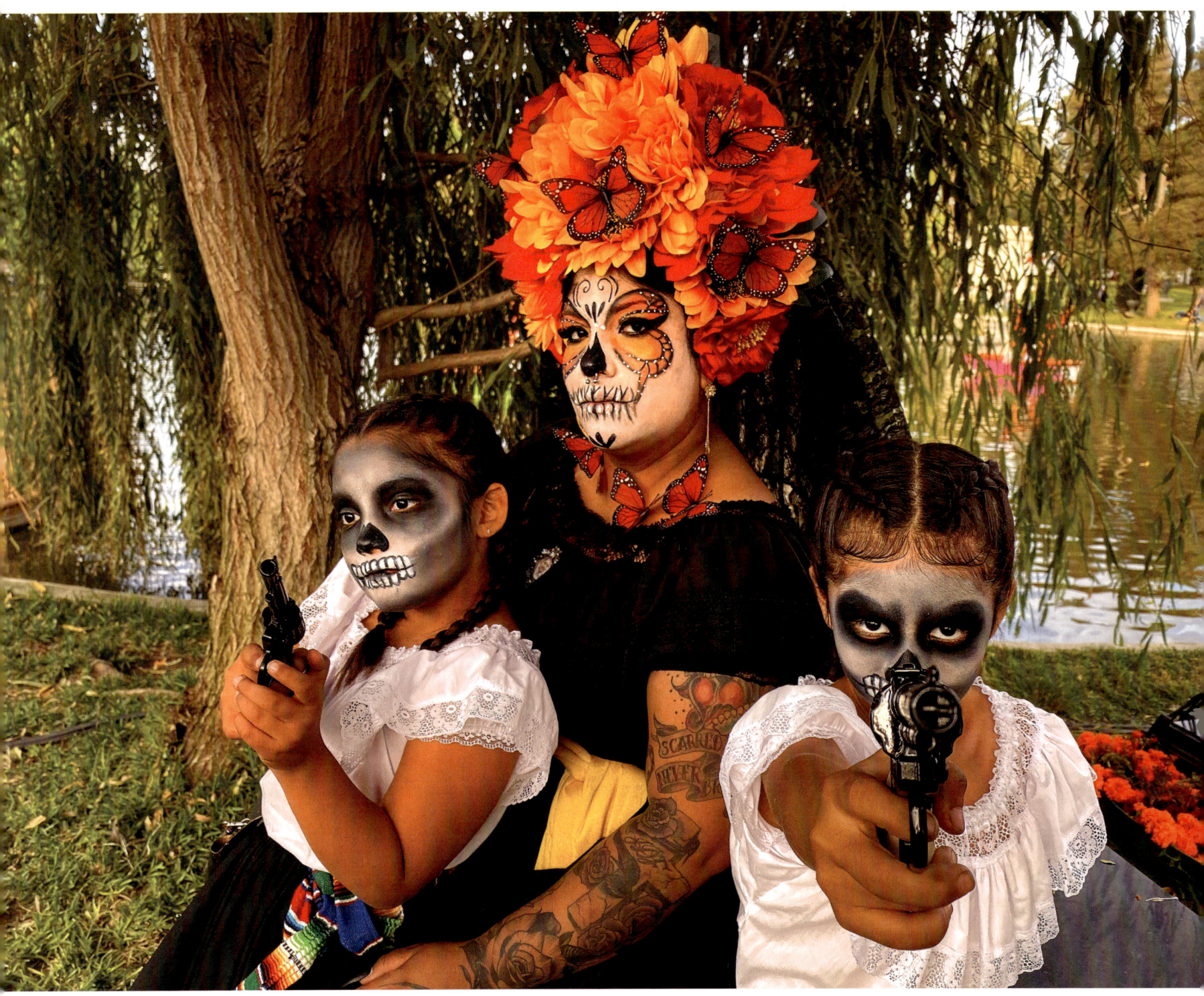

DAY OF THE DEAD MOURNERS

Hollywood, California

Fame can sometimes be fleeting, but death is usually long lasting. As one of the nation's most notable cemeteries, Hollywood Forever harkens back to 1899 and has hosted as its permanent guests cinematic luminaries Judy Garland, Cecil B. DeMille, Rudolph Valentino, and Burt Reynolds. Wandering amongst cremation niches, sepulcher urns, and ornate tombstones, taphophiles enjoy stumbling over the final resting spots of Little Rascal Alfalfa, Tinseltown titan Mickey Rooney, or gangster Bugsy Siegel. The intended remains of legendary punk guitarist Johnny Ramone is marked by his bronze guitar-playing statue, serenading lushly landscaped grounds graced by reflecting pools and tinkling fountains as nearby graceful swans glide on a pond beneath soaring palm trees. Imbuing vitality into traditionally sad landscapes, classic movies are projected onto marble mausoleum walls and sunlit yoga sessions are staged on its sprawling lawns. Within this inviting mortuarial playground, deceased ancestors might ponder return, which is at the very essence of ancient Mexican traditions that come to life every year at a vibrantly macabre celebration. Day of the Dead is a remarkable Mesoamerican reunion of families with their recently deceased loved ones. Here Aztec ritual dancers weave winding paths advancing along a hundred candlelit ofrenda altars, lovingly assembled tableaux laced with orange flowers and guarded by oversized skulls.

At the largest such event in the United States, this mourning family decked out in skeletal accouterments of ancestral connection gather rather appropriately beneath a weeping willow tree. Marigolds represent the fragility of life while its bright orange colors and musky fragrance strongly attract monarch butterflies, vibrantly depicted on both mom's headdress and reverently etched eyewear. The flying insect's spectacular annual migration in early November arriving at Mexico's Sierra Madre mountains after a mystical, distant journey is believed to be strongly indicative of ancestral souls revisiting their much-missed kinfolks. This scary point-blank brandishing of toy guns seems to suggest that a stopover at Hollywood Forever could possibly become eternal.

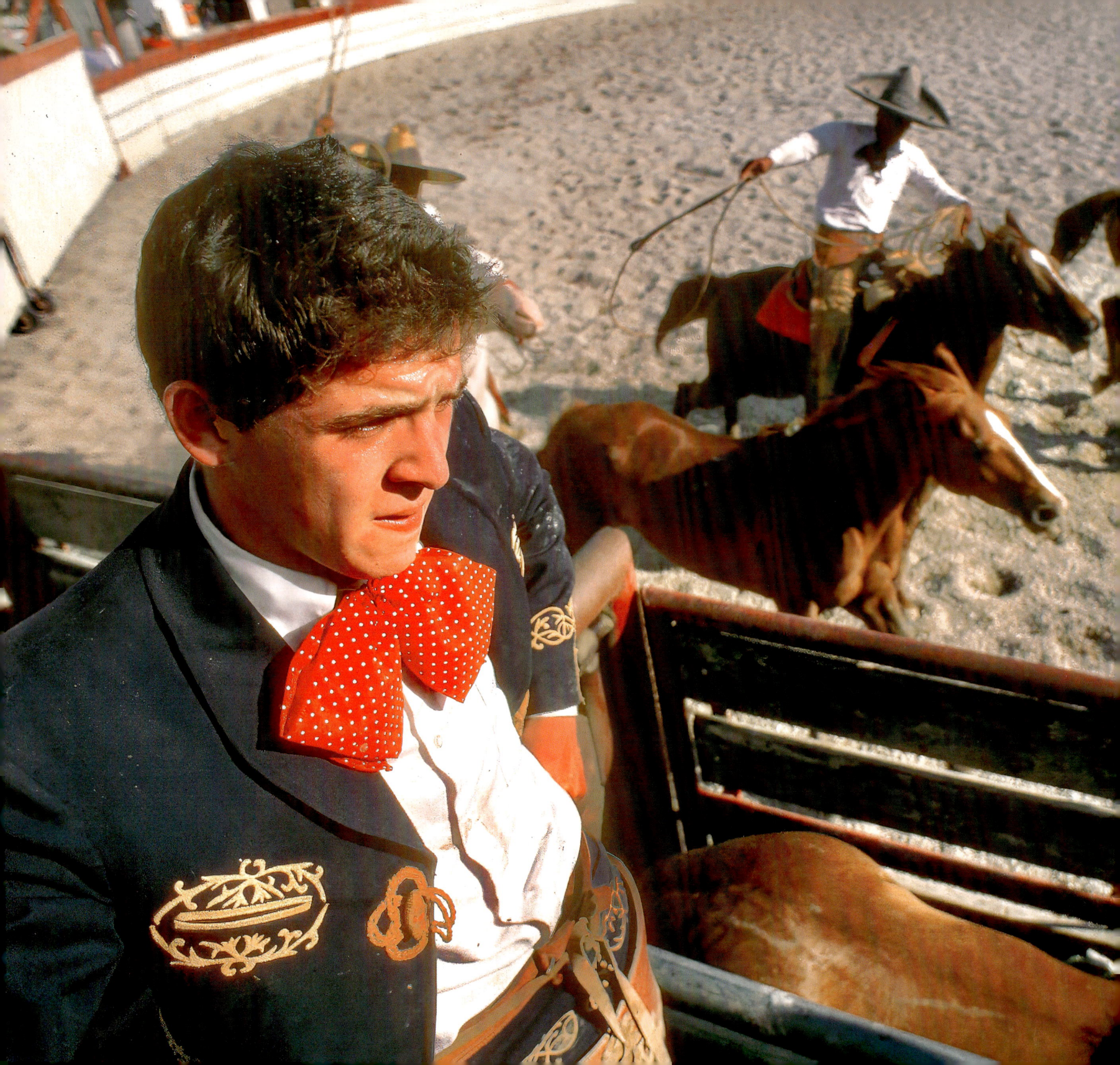

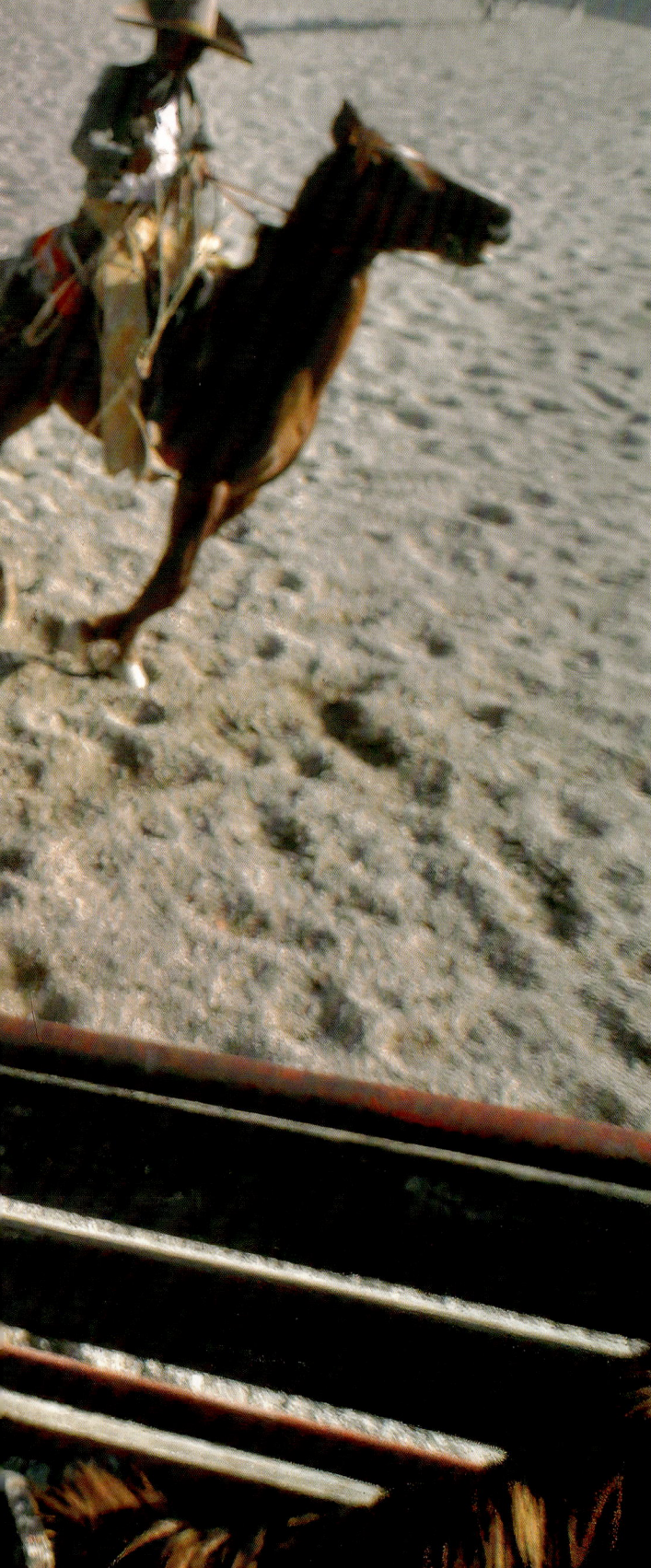

CHARRO RODEO EQUESTRIAN

San Antonio, Texas

Most often envisioned as a cowboy event springing from America's Great Plains, the rodeo's rollicking lineage can actually be first traced to charrería contests that evolved from sixteenth-century Spanish traditions of horsemanship and ranching, imported after gold-seeking conquistadors arrived in the New World from Spain. Under Spanish orders to raise horses long before Mexican independence, an equestrian-skilled society rapidly spread through establishment of the labor-intensive encomienda system permeating haciendas and their onerous ranching lifestyles. Cattle-raising vaqueros and Indigenous ranchers dwelling there sought to transform their difficult circumstances into playful bovine handling techniques, perhaps creating the world's only sport directly grown from occupational hardships. Today with family support, charrería is treated as a multi-generational lifestyle where charros practice their horsemanship skills on specially bred Azteca horses trotting within the 44-yard-diameter lienzo arena thrice daily. In Mexico's popular national pastime, intricate reining and cutting maneuvers are just one small detail in these high energy spectacles which are a direct precursor to rodeo. Tequila-fueled spectators filling this crowded stadium snack on elote (sweet corn), as they gape at the charreada's bucking broncos or light-hoofed dancing horses harnessed with gold-adorned saddles, before competitive events featuring barrel racing, bull-tailing, and lassoing trick ropers. Lariats woven from Maguey cactus threads are swung in joyous artistic expression, with airborne flowering patterns that reflect the elegance of their traditional outfits. Essentially resembling mariachi players with detailed stitching on the arms or legs, they are bow-tied and capped off by a sombrero. Their regalia actually preceded those worn by ranchera-playing roving musicians, whose outfits mimicked these heroic Mexican horse-riding icons.

As part of San Antonio's annual Fiesta, an A Day in Old Mexico celebration is presented by their Charro Association, largest and oldest of its kind this side of the Rio Grande. Elegantly jacketed, chap-garbed, and awaiting the opening of the bucking chute, this sweating charro contemplates his upcoming dangerous Paso de la Muerte event which entails leaping onto a moving, bare-backed, unbroken horse without either any reins or comforting insurance of not being trampled by three rapidly galloping rancheros.

SHEPHERD

Hailey, Idaho

For well over a dozen millennia, sheep have been amongst the earliest domesticated animals, raised for their meat, milk, and fiber. During sixteenth- and seventeenth-century encampments they were brought into the western United States by Spanish settlers, primarily through South America. Later, Basque people arriving in this region initially for mining prospects eventually became critical to sheep industry success, with many beginning their own operations in the 1850s. It was often Peruvians who filled the roles of shepherd as their experience with rugged high altitudes helped to acclimatize them during alpine labors. With the aid of highly trained sheepdogs, they would move animals by day and, as evening fell, sleep in tiny mountaintop sheep wagons, often beneath an infinite blanket of dazzling stars. During the approach of autumn's cooler weather, quaking aspen's golden veneer plasters lower elevations here at a more hospitable Wood River Valley, where gathering mobs must head to survive winter's harshness.

Almost hidden amongst dusty clouds, this last throng of sheep are ushered off an unusually steep mountain slope by a determined shepherd, topped with his Andean-style chullo, no doubt woven from the congregation's wooly strands. This seasonal rhythm of enforced migration creates sweeping spectacles filled with more than a thousand sheep whose pathway to their wintering grounds lead straight through downtown Hailey, Idaho, just below. The Trailing of the Sheep has become an annual festival where mutton is served in endlessly mouthwatering ways as eager spectators crowd shop-lined sidewalks. Shortly, its streets fill up with a sea of baaing livestock, interrupted only by a priest offering blessings to the flock, while firmly holding his ground amongst that moving ovine carpet of fleece.

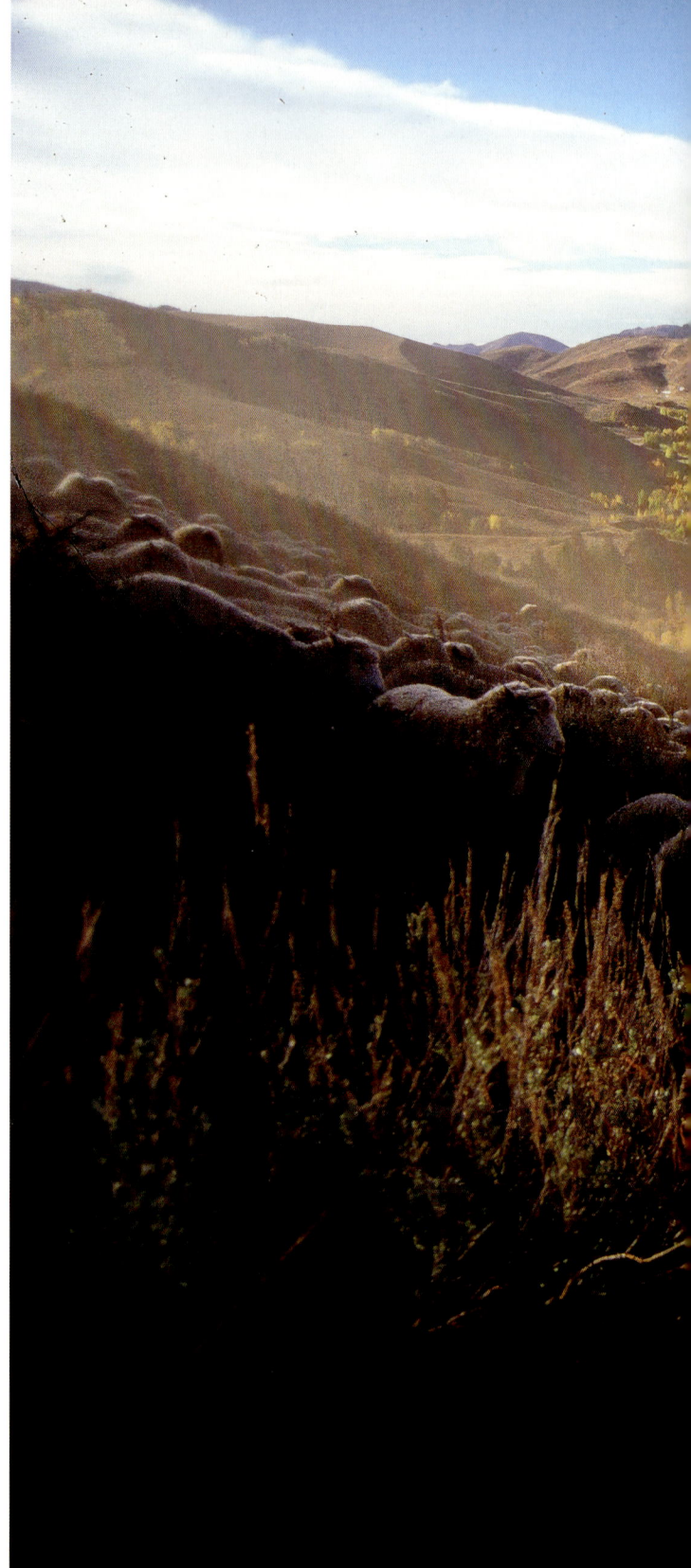

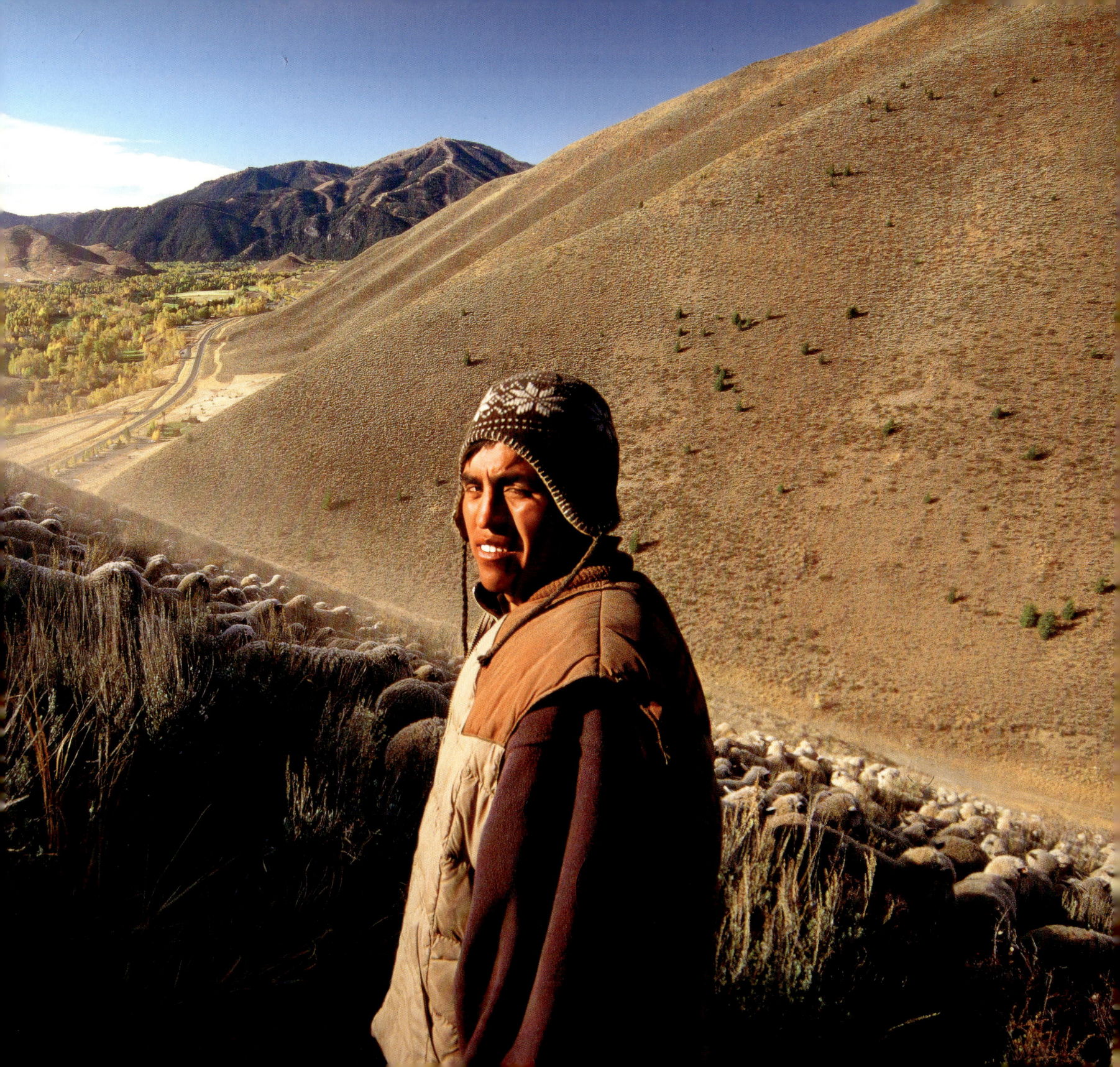

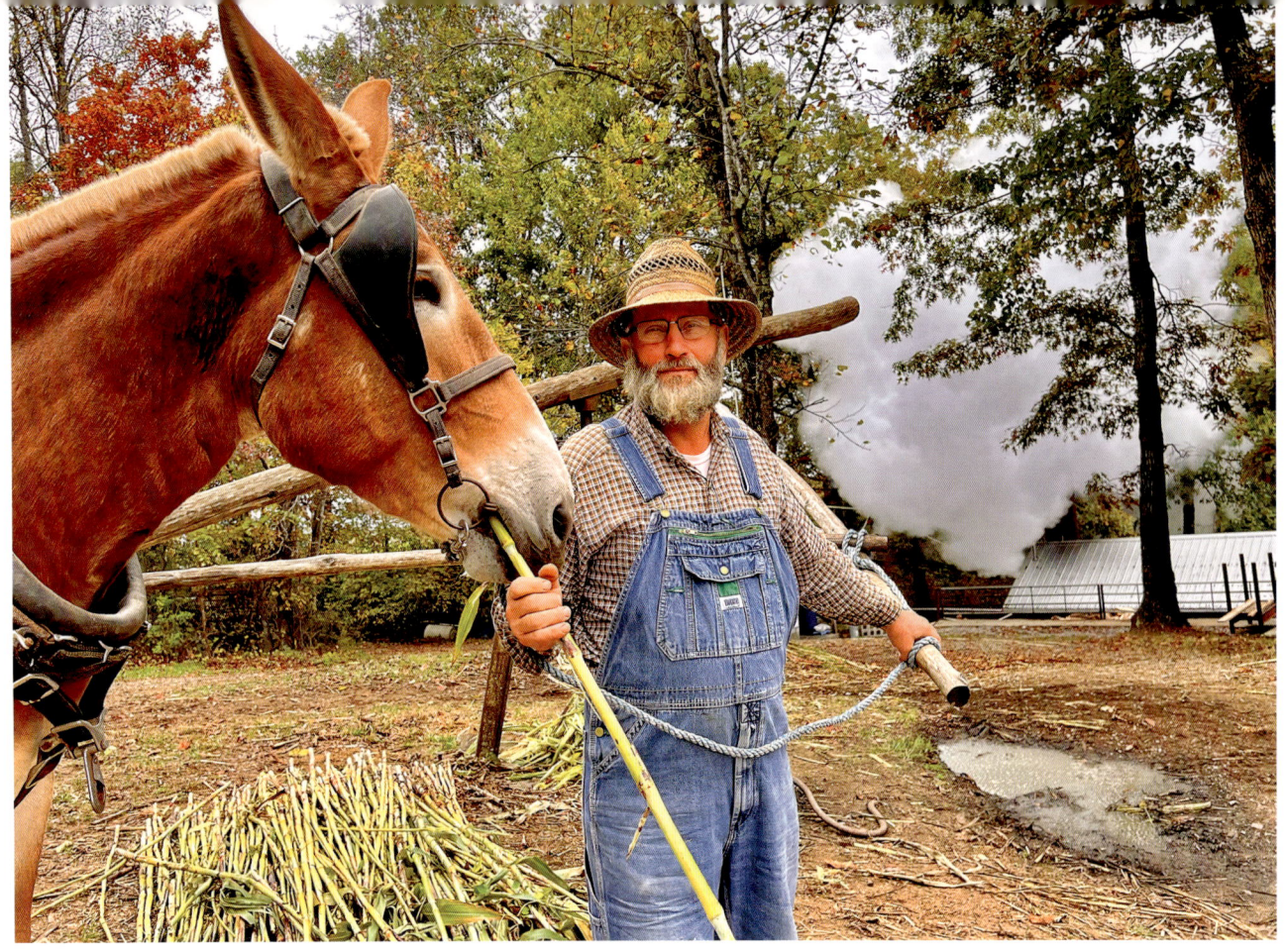

SORGHUM MILL OPERATOR

Muddy Pond, Tennessee

Come early autumn, as chilly temperatures seep into mountain folds, wafting clouds of steam fill yellowing valleys around Muddy Pond. There a tightly knit Mennonite community tenaciously clings to its past amidst the undulating hollers of Central Tennessee. Fragrant sorghum mills are in full operation, promulgating a traditional southern foodway, now quickly disappearing. As sugarcane prices exploded during the Civil War's naval blockades, its inability to flourish north of America's tropical edges made sorghum a go-to crop for this country's growing sweet tooth cravings. A member of the grass family, sorghum produces a sweet and savory molasses, rich in robustly earthy flavor. Its remarkable production at the Muddy Pond Sorghum Mill is only made possible with the tireless dedication of a four-legged beast of burden. The mule is a hybrid creature, longer living while more patient than horses, with greater intellect and less obstinacy than donkeys. During spinning of an animal-powered carousel, pre-stripped stalks are hand-fed into small clusters of 1912 mill gear at its center, wringing precious fluids into a barrel container where gravity conveniently sends juices flowing down through tubes into the boiling shed. There, amongst an aromatic fog, a serpentine tract of boiling troughs reduce the sorghum, reaching molasses perfection during those closely monitored moments.

As a final treat for all the hard circular work, overalls-clad Mark Guenther feeds Ida, who enjoys sweet juices during some cane pressing of her own doing. As evidenced by an immense pressure-relieving baritone blast from a steam locomotive engine, the syrup-processing shed below is busy boiling down over 2,000 gallons of juice from just one of 60 acres bursting with their cultivated crop. His Mennonite family share duties cutting cane, stoking the boiler's fire, managing temperatures, skimming surface chlorophyll from scalding syrup, and bottling delectable liquids. They'll say grace at their communal table after Mark drenches his roasted farm-raised pork beneath the spigot of a sorghum finishing tank.

SUGARING DROVER

Ashfield, Massachusetts

Essentially in the world's only maple syrup producing region, cold northern forests of New England produce starch-storing trees that allow for their winter survival. Within the trunks of these arboreal chemical factories, starches will turn to sugars through released amylase enzymes during March's thawing weather conditions. This warmth expands carbon dioxide within, creating pressure to squeeze the sap outward. Celebrating the season's Sugar Moon, Indigenous Iroquois in early spring performed maple dances of gratitude for sweet liquids that seemed to have blessed them. Legends suggest that Chief Woksis accidentally discovered sap oozing forth from these deciduous trees when his thrown tomahawk remained embedded in one during a chilly overnight. After its removal that next morning, warmer temperatures allowed sap to flow from this cut in the tree. Eventually flavoring their venison meats, the trick was passed on to arriving settlers who improved sap delivery with a spigot system and learned to efficiently gather its collection using buckets hung just below them. The contents were emptied and collected on foot or with horses and even oxen, who then transported their sloshing, precious liquids from the sugarbush to cupola-vented sugarhouses for boiling into syrup. Many of these traditional efforts are being quickly supplanted by modern plastic tubing, stitching trees and their sap to processing shacks steaming away down below. Importantly, mud season's ticking clock must be closely checked as sap needs gathering before the very first buds of spring start sipping up its own internal sugars.

Beneath his flannel cap, a gloved drover prods this yoked team of oxen tugging its sweetened payload toward the aging, wooden sugar shack. Soon those upper vents will be steaming forth its fragrant content and obscuring these surrounding Berkshire sugarbush woodlands ornamented with recently emptied metal buckets.

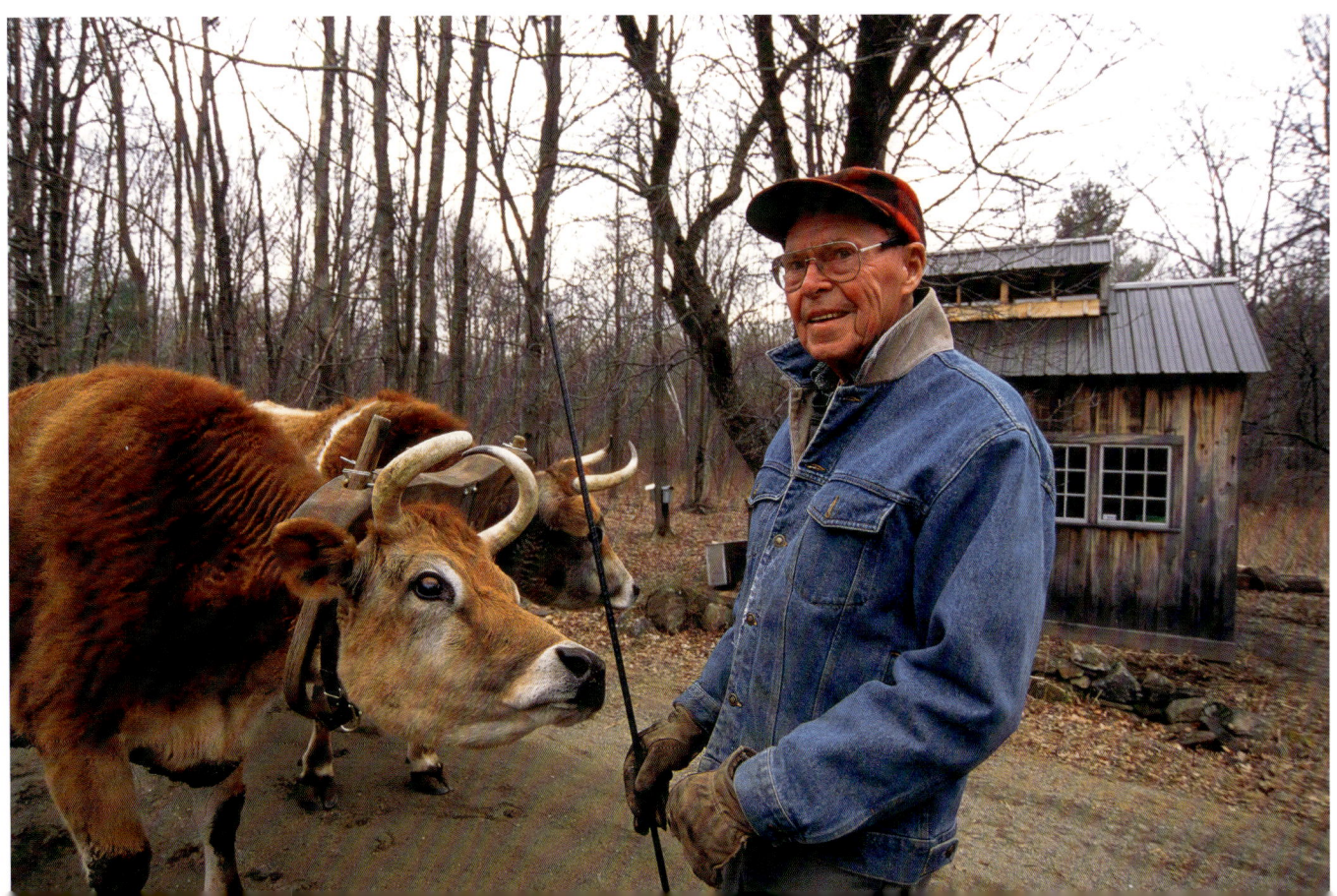

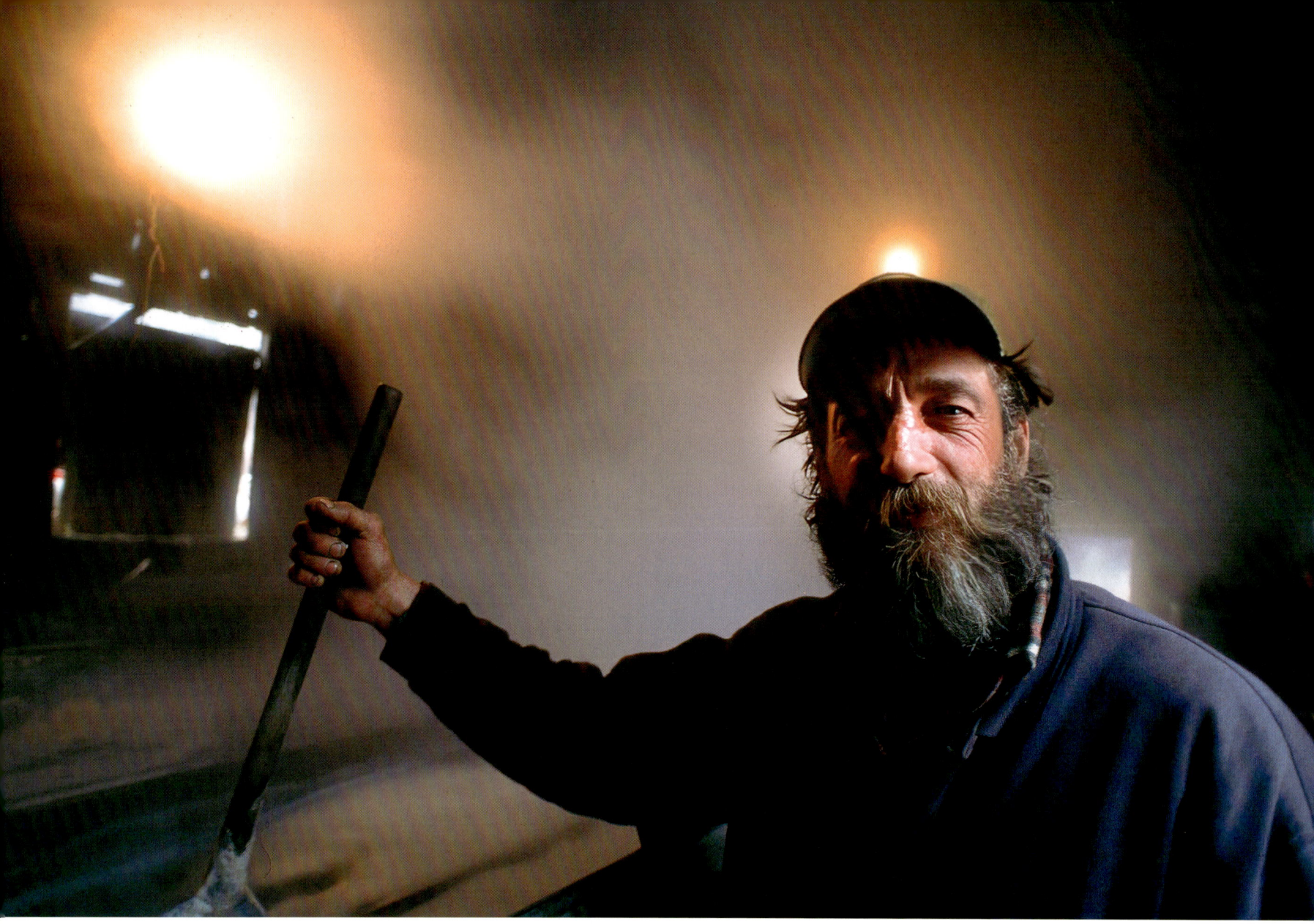

SUGARMAKER

South Reading, Vermont

Inside this South Reading, Vermont, sugar shack, precious liquid gold is boiled down to its essence, where one gallon of syrup actually requires 40 times that volume in sap. This scraggy family member of the Jenne Farm wields a dipper employed to maintain viscous consistency within the trough-like evaporator pans, which will eventually yield delectable syrup for filtering, bottling, and inevitable dousing over pancakes and waffles.

CIDERHOUSE PROPRIETOR

Weathersfield, Vermont

In the years before refrigeration, New England's bountiful apple crop faced varying time-sensitive deadlines for perishable viability. Typically, unpasteurized apple cider at room temperature would begin to ferment after about three days, while hard ciders might last a few months before turning into vinegar. Soon enough, thrifty Yankees realized they could capture the sweet essence of apple by heating these liquids until producing a boiled cider, and even further distilling it into jelly, creating year-round sweeteners for cooking or baking. Cider mills producing these apple molasses once steamed away at hill town communities all throughout Vermont, but refrigeration, changing tastes, and supermarket economies virtually eliminated the handcrafted artisanal efforts required to produce this heritage taste. Kept alive by seven generations of one family's agricultural pursuits, this rustic eighteenth-century hillside farm has at its beating heart a ciderhouse fairly bursting with an aromatic sauna of sweet apple essence. At Wood's Cider Mill an exacting blend of apple varieties, mostly helmed by McIntosh but rounded out with heirloom varieties like Golden Russets or Baldwins, are gathered from nearby orchards as 70 bushels at once are ground into a slurry. That mixture is spread across wooden trays held in place with swaths of canvas, then tightly squeezed together by the 1882 screw-cranked press. An assemblage helmed by huge iron gears squashes the pulp and its smooshed contents, oozing a luscious waterfall of honeyed elixir. The exquisite liquids are poured into huge evaporator pans, then heated by a regularly replenished wood fire burning at 1400 degrees Fahrenheit to create dense nectar and richly caramelized lager. Nine gallons of fresh cider are needed to produce just one containing an intensely tasty apple jelly.

Moisturized by a wafting curtain of fragrant steam, wool-capped Willis Wood reaches for his wooden-handled tin scoop to determine the precise consistency of his prized apple concoction. Chosen by Hollywood set designers as a location for the 1999 Academy Award-winning motion picture *The Cider House Rules*, this strikingly quaint structure features its own real drama as delicate culinary procedures unfold to create masterpieces of complex flavors.

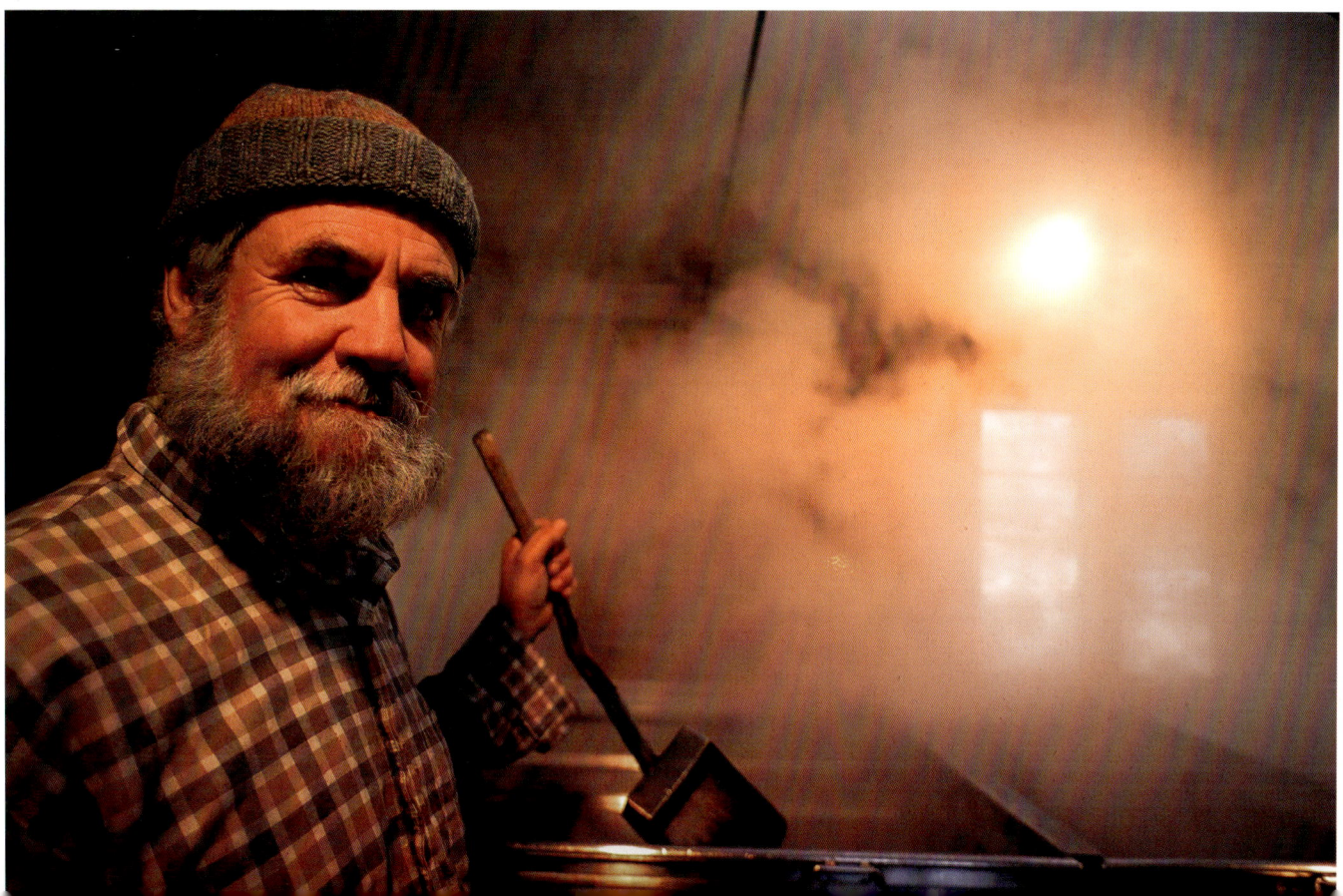

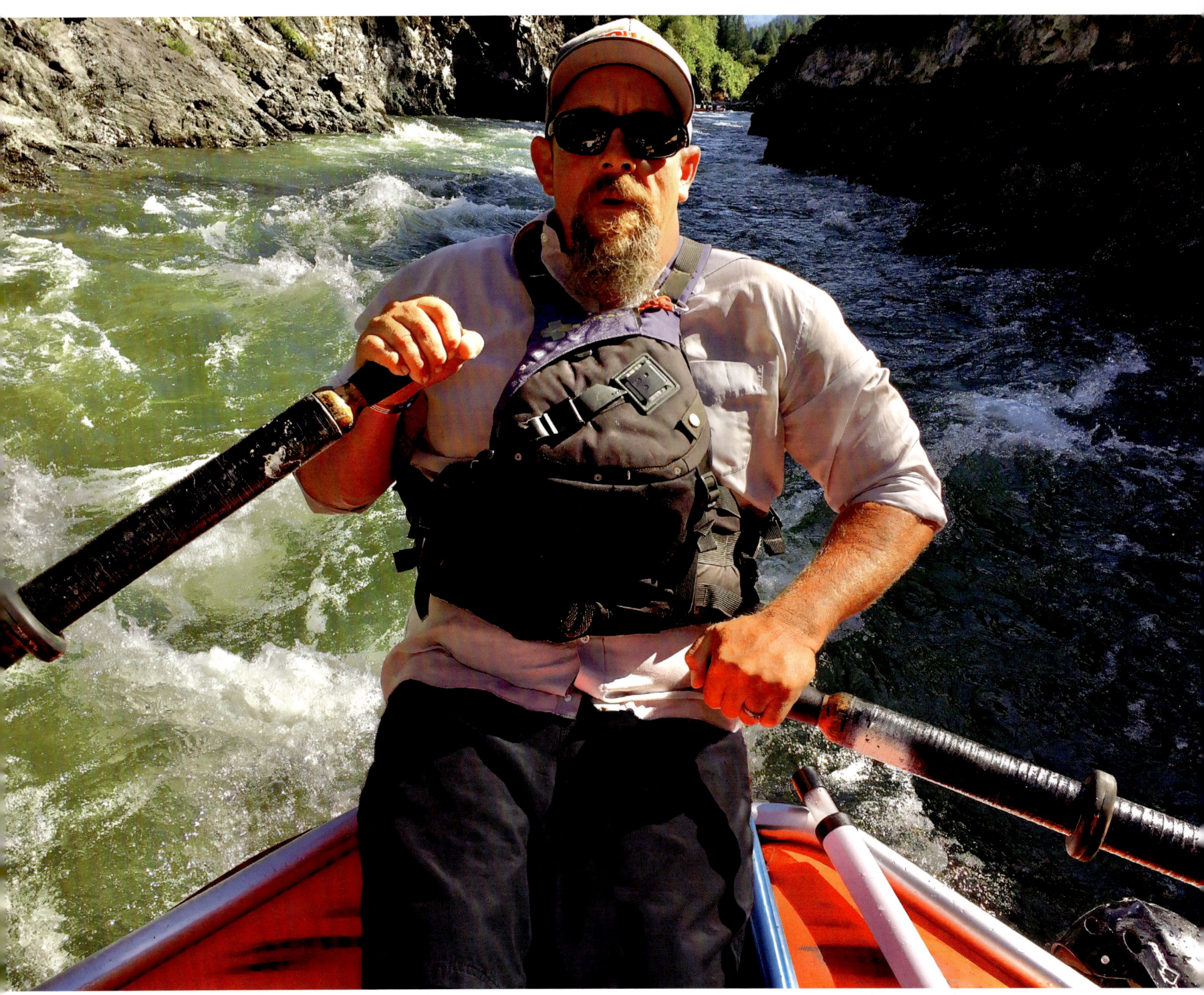

WHITEWATER RAFTING OARSMAN

Rogue River, Oregon

Crater Lake, cupping America's deepest such body of water, offers a watery genesis for the Rogue River, burbling up from its steep volcanic slopes and ultimately roaring 215 miles through Oregon before emptying out into an immense Pacific Ocean. Coursing through jagged Cascade ranges and past some of the most productive coastal forests on earth, this river system helps nourish over 3,500 different plant species marking it with great global botanical significance. Its abundant natural resources set the nineteenth-century stage for numerous hunting or gold prospecting conflicts between native Takelma and fortune-seeking miners. Those troubles inspired famed author Zane Grey to pen his 1929 novel *Rogue River Feud* from inside an old log miner's cabin along the riverbank's Winkle Bar. That small contingent of intrepid settlers who chose to inhabit this remote wilderness established orchards and diminutive farms, remaining isolated from the outside world even while receiving occasional provisions over an arduous mule trail. The United States Postal Service was persuaded to service what then had been only one dozen families and operate an almost weekly mail boat up this river toward its newly established Agness post office, named after that postmaster's daughter but permanently misspelled because of a typographical error. Propelled by sail, oars, poling, and eventually motor, it continues to operate as one of the last two mailboat routes in this country. Other evidence of the Rogue's early residents may be found at remote riverside abodes which have been converted to lodgings for adventurous rafters paddling their way to rustic cabins or comfortable lodges. Old player pianos perform inside creaky Black Bar Lodge while farther downstream, at stilted Marial Lodge, double-decker lazy Susans spin out fried chicken, corn pone, and marionberry custard. Accumulating high calorie counts is certainly a wise decision for the following day spent shredding through Class IV rapids, pinwheeling around tractor-sized boulders while getting soaked in bracing currents and adrenaline.

Plotting strategies to dodge boulder gardens and navigate hazardous rapids, burly river guide Greg Contreras bravely grips his oars in preparation for the quickly approaching descent into a whirling maelstrom. The waters here accelerate as they squeeze between narrow basalt and sandstone passages within Mule Creek Canyon, nearing raft-wrapping dangers at Blossom Bar Rapid. The Rogue River, while stunningly beautiful, has claimed numerous lives for unprepared paddlers who often need to scout ahead for the safest route of passage through what often feels like tumbling through an extra rinse cycle inside an industrial-sized washing machine.

YUPIK WALRUS HUNTER

Gambell, St. Lawrence Island, Alaska

Along North America's northwestern most edges, the sixth largest island in the United States contains not a single tree. Anchored forlornly in the Bering Sea, St. Lawrence Island remains as one last major remnant of Beringia's ancient landmass, providing an occasional glimpse of Russia scraping icy horizons a mere thirty-six miles away. The frozen landscape's barren assets are counterbalanced by a rich marine buffet of bowhead whales and walrus swept in by chilly Anadyr currents swirling past from nearby Siberia. The island's scant population speaks Siberian Yupik as a first language, and many eke out their maritime survival hunting both the world's longest living mammal (over 210 years) and its largest pinniped (two tons of whiskered pink biomass). Their meat is joyously shared amongst the Yupik village residents, providing sustenance for up to six months.

Within their windswept village, a cluster of wooden community dwellings tilt at various angles in the melting permafrost. Nearby, upended boats provide an inviting hint of shelter where, huddled beneath translucent walrus skins coating his trusty umiak, this bundled hunter inspects a traditional vessel before heading out with his harpoon into treacherous Bering Sea swells courageously searching for walrus.

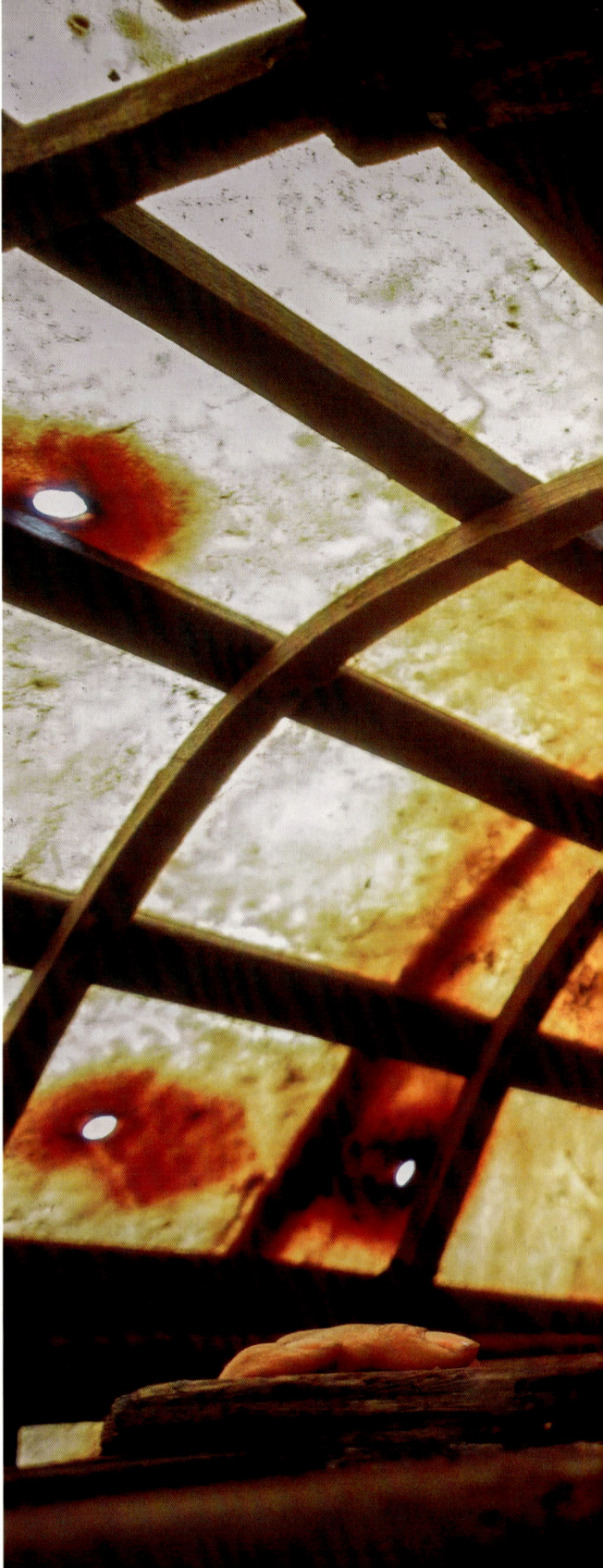

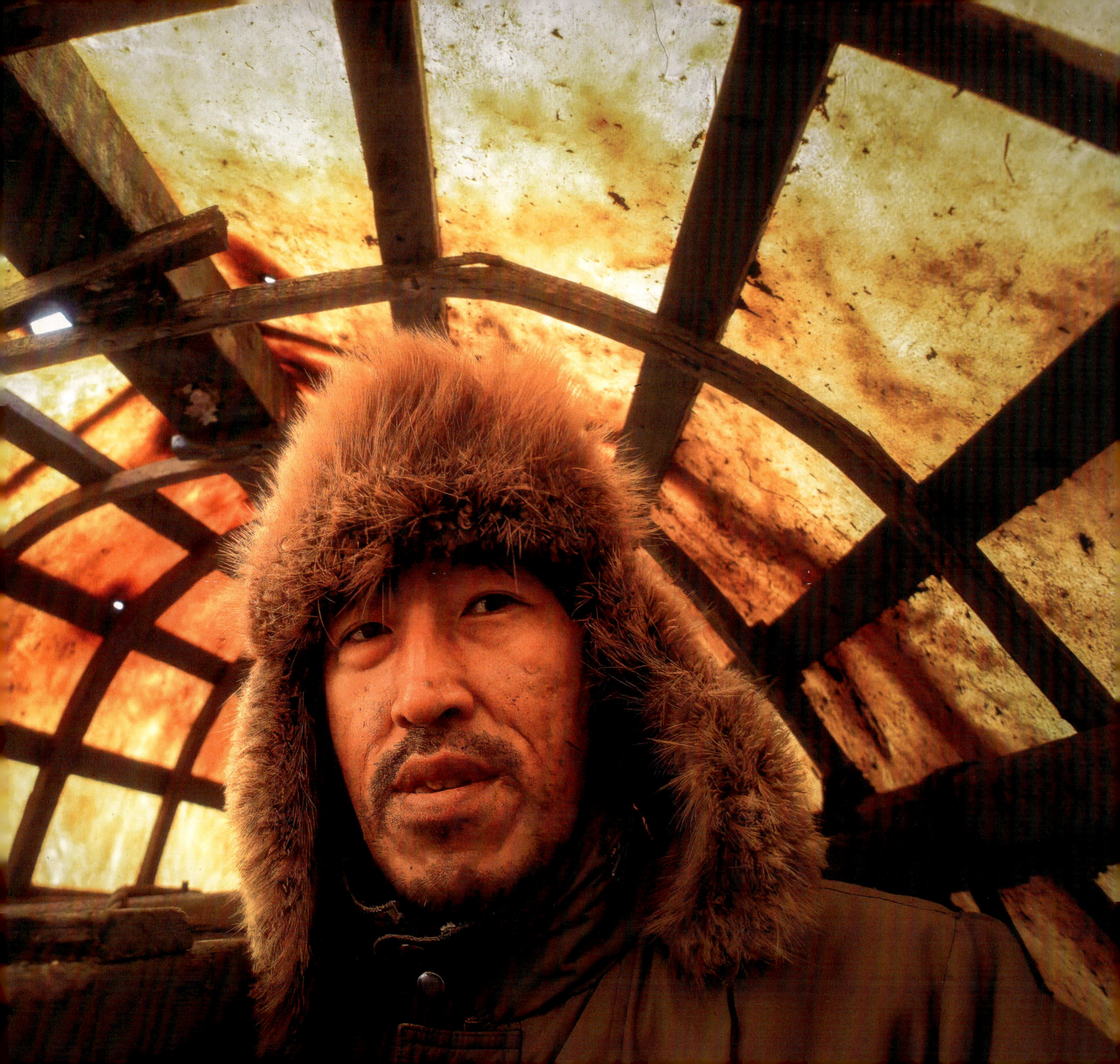

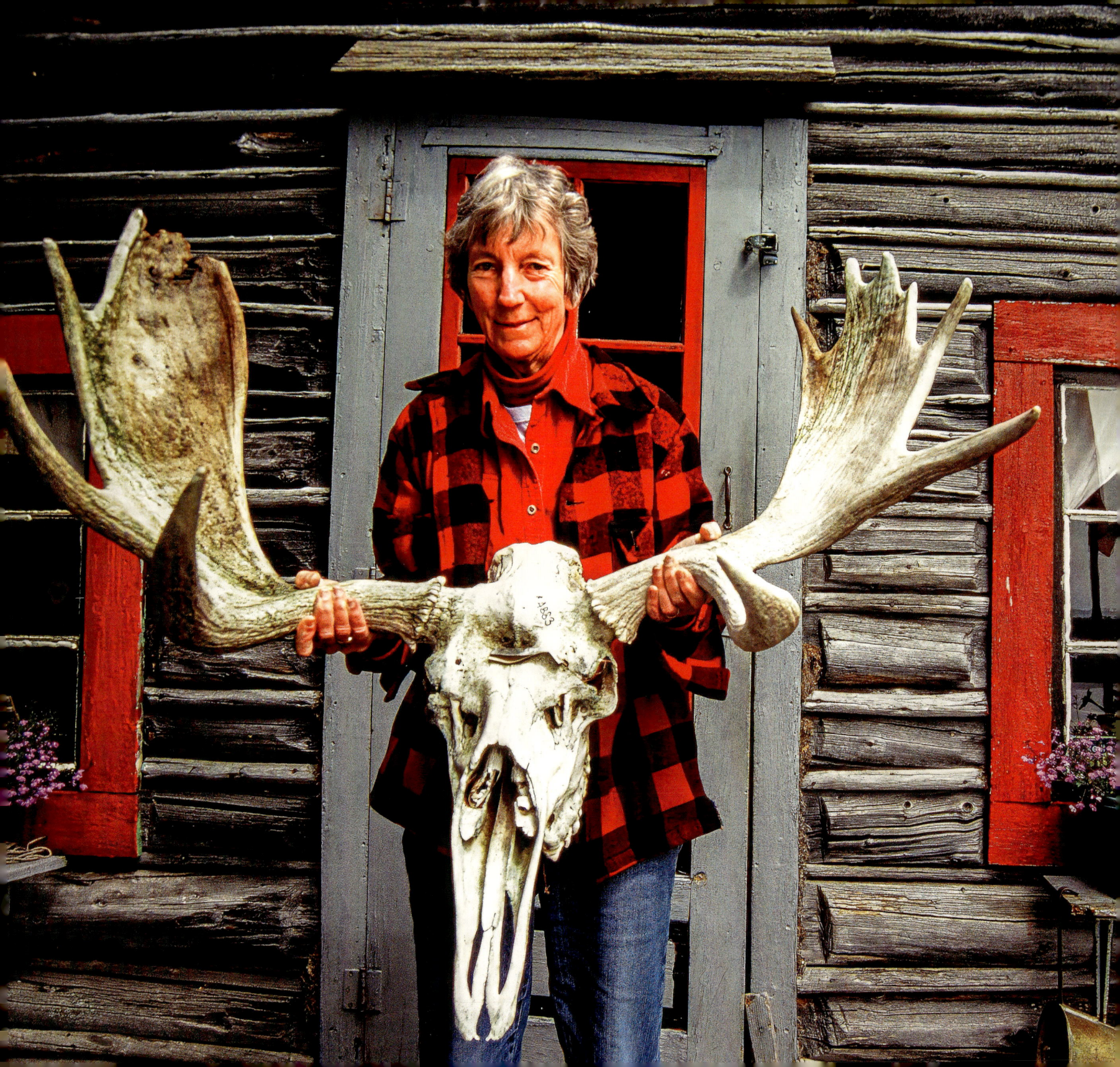

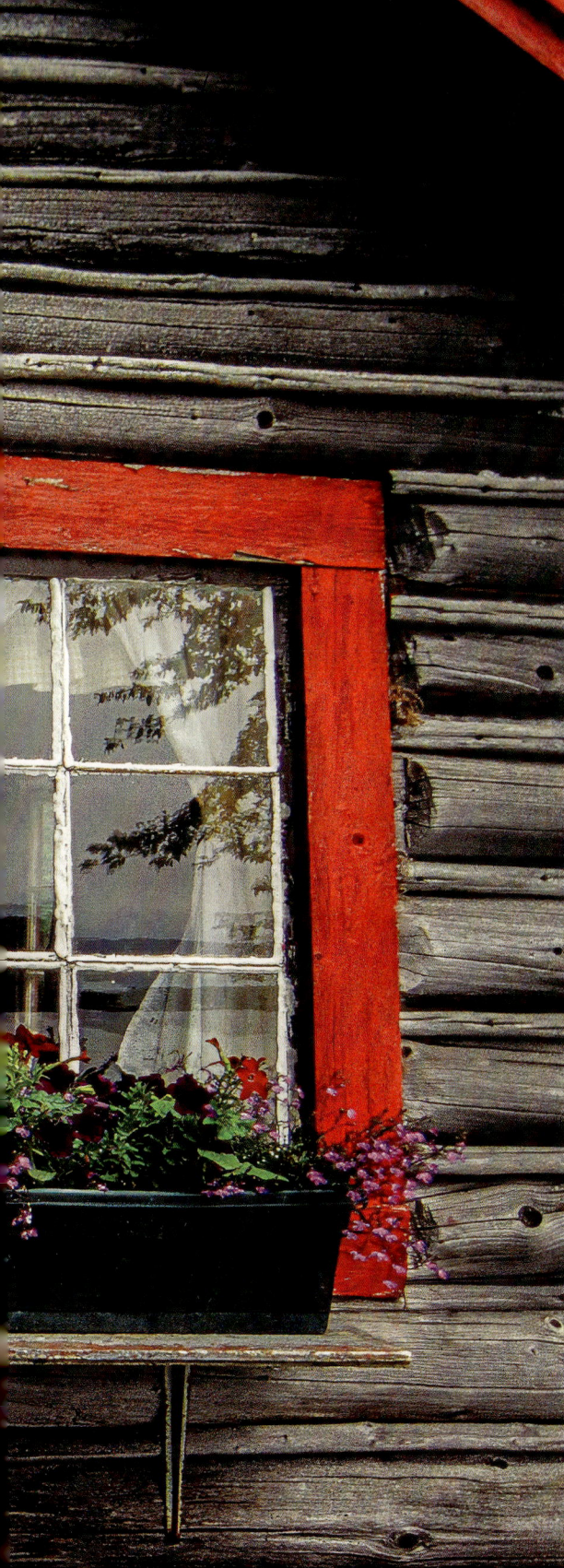

WILDERNESS BIOLOGIST

Isle Royale, Michigan

The very least visited national park in these contiguous United States is Isle Royale. Its inaccessible isolation and fierce winter conditions make it the lone such parkland to completely lock its doors to human visitors during winter season. This fourth largest lake island on earth sits out within the planet's largest freshwater lakeshore. Lake Superior often spreads a foggy blanket over the island's trembling bog carpets and thick tangles of evergreens, hiding dramatic interplay between an apex predator and its giant, one-ton prey. Pulling back the curtain on relative populations of moose and wolves that seesaw wildly over time, scientists aided by field researchers have painstakingly chronicled a fascinating ecological record. In a dynamically charged ecosystem, these wilderness detectives scrutinize teeth in moose skeletons to evaluate pollution levels and food supply, just as wolf excrement helps determine gene pools or diet habits. Out on the water, global warming controls any existence of icy pathways that wolves use to access this island, while over land, warmer temperatures threaten balsam fir that provide a primary food source for moose.

On an island with no permanent human population, Carolyn Peterson lives summer months with her husband in their rustic 1926 fishing cabin, where they have for over five decades established themselves as premiere authorities of this seldom evaluated ecology offering the world's longest continuous study involving a prey-predator system. With a sprawling skeletal boneyard of moose skulls serving as garden ornaments and an aging scat shack somewhere out back, those very few visitors who do make it out here by ferry or floatplane might stumble upon unexpectedly passionate poop collectors toiling away in the damp forest.

GOATPACKER

Evanston, Wyoming

One hundred centuries ago somewhere in Mesopotamia's Fertile Crescent, goats became the very first animal that mankind ever domesticated. Though horses, donkeys, camels, and llamas did much heavy lifting on their respective continents, in North America goats have only recently become an unlikely, somewhat comical hiking companion for backcountry enthusiasts who enjoy these porters while they climb canyon walls or navigate log-littered forests. With tightened cinch straps and fastened rump belts, a determined caravan of bleating goats might head off into alpine wetlands spreading beneath Uinta's wilderness, which encapsulates the highest east-west mountain range in this country's contiguous states. Amongst wildflower-decorated rock stones and boulder fields, these environmentally friendly, softly treading animals can nonchalantly carry sixty pounds stuffed inside each of their panniers while climbing steep quartz sandstone ledges. Fueling up during the journey, they'll browse on grassy eye-catching fast food, while keeping attention focused upon their new human playmate. Digging no holes while searching for snacks, the ungulate's "leave no trace" comportment is enhanced by odorless droppings and barely visible hoof prints. Hoisting up to a quarter of the goats' body weight, these furry station wagons prefer traveling in herds but will happily admit a recently arrived adventurer into their exclusive club. The hoofed coterie's only rule is to not touch their heat-dispersing horns that provide them with a territorial sense of well-being. After some minimal prodding they'll reluctantly hop mid-current rocks to ford tinkling mountain streams. These waters spill from nearby Ruth Lake, where this evening's substantial camping site will wholly materialize just from the emptied contents of caprine cargo. After settling in, bleating cries accompany tinkling collared bells that echo across the lake, summoning above silhouetted mountains that twinkling August ascension of Capricorn, the zodiac's smallest constellation and christened in Latin as "goat's horn."

Back home, along the southwestern edge of Wyoming, intrepid slicker-clad goatpacker Clay Zimmerman says goodbye to a bony old friend out by his immense scrubland backyard. With at least 150 square feet required to support each one of his twenty kids, the noted "goat whisperer" wanders the sagebrush expansion after springing this mischievous menagerie from a two-horse trailer and back into their pens. Offering bargain rates, he is currently the nation's only goat rental service for wilderness exploration.

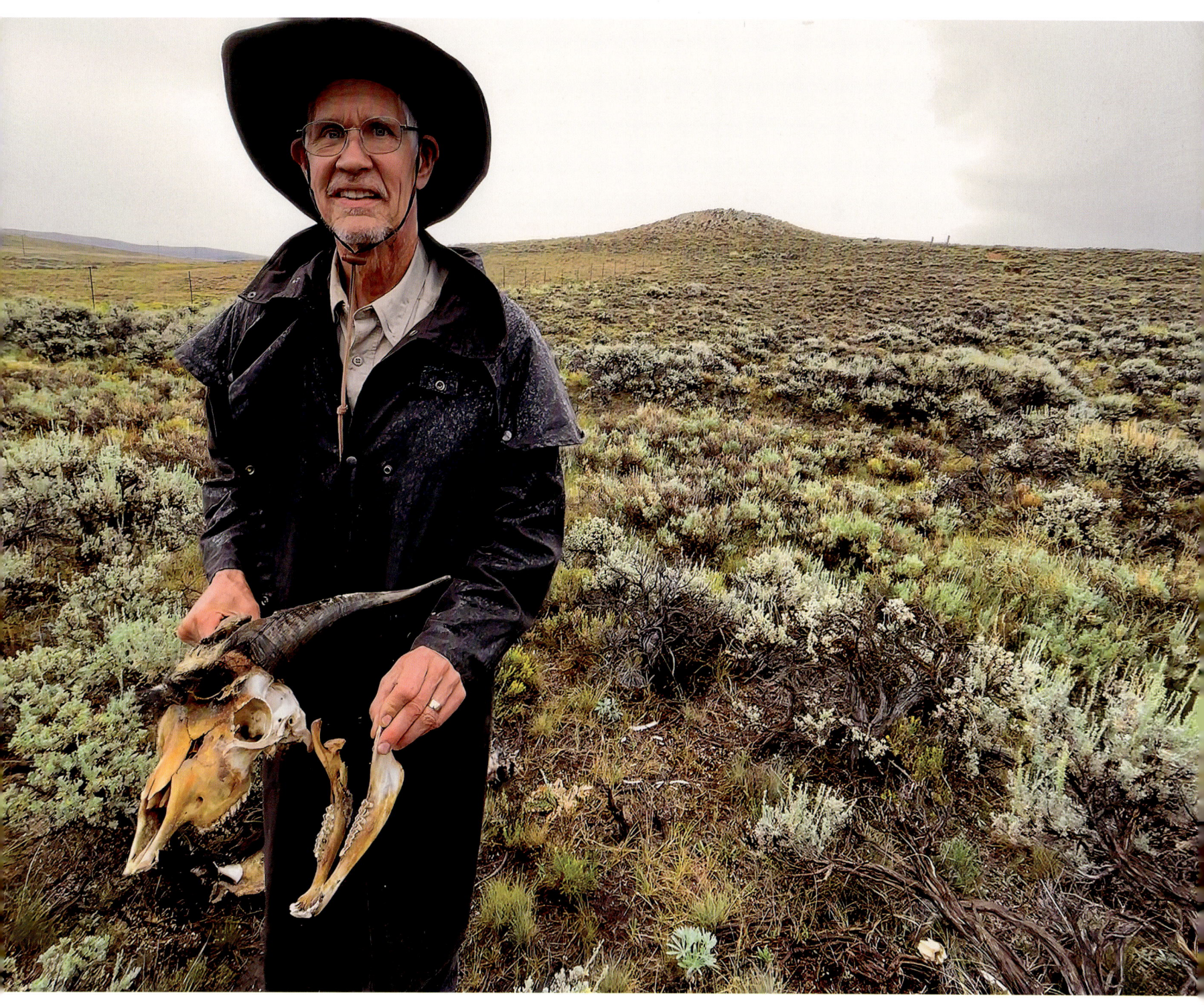

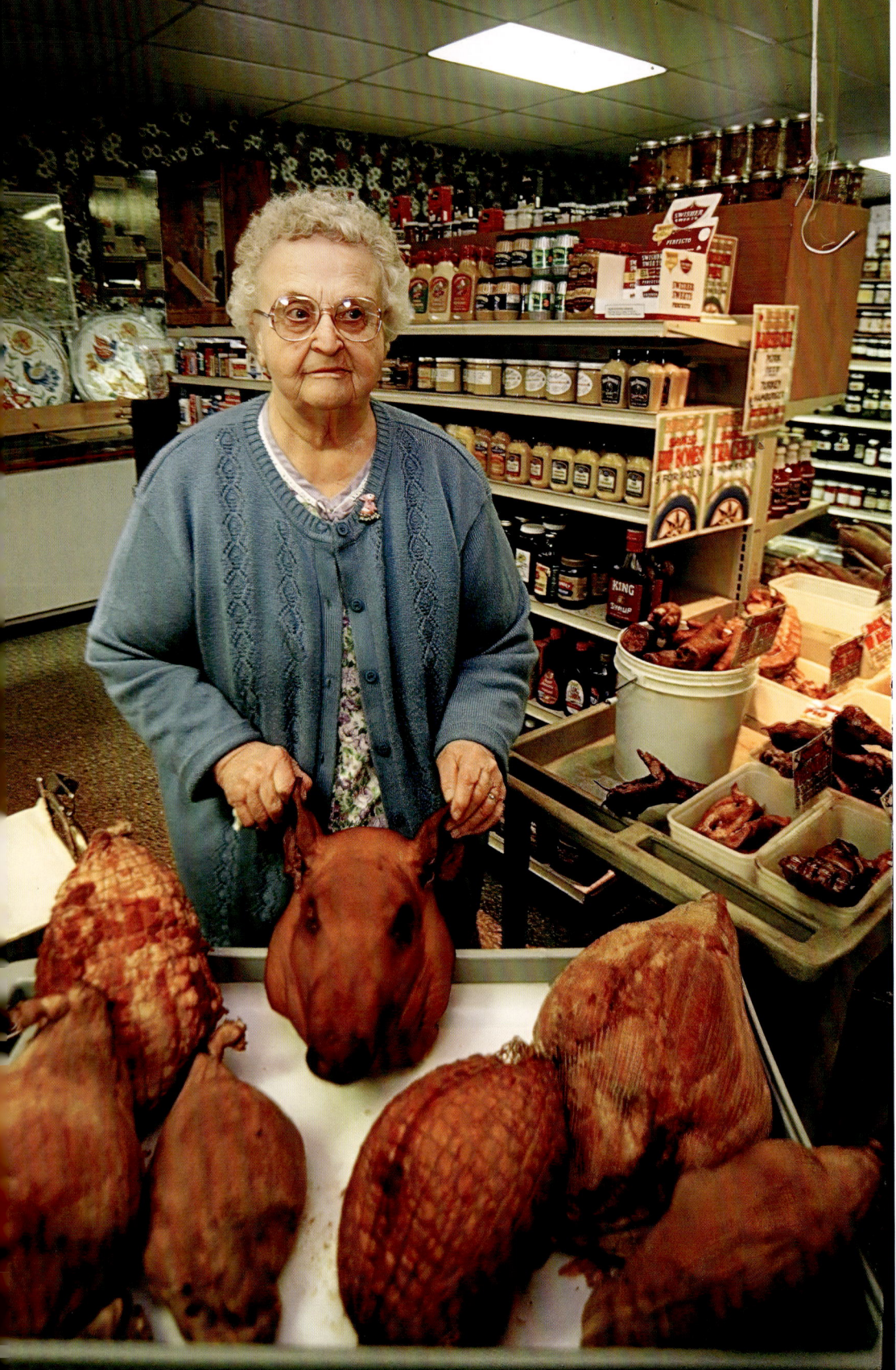

SMOKEHOUSE MATRIARCH

Krumsville, Pennsylvania

Driving buggy-filled roads winding through the fertile farmland of Berks County, one can't help but notice an agricultural art gallery dressing up oversized barnyard facades. Dazzling geometric motifs feature stars and birds, most notably the distelfink, stylized renderings depicting a goldfinch, said to rid farmer's fields of thistles. They announce the folkloric Pennsylvania Dutch influence of hex signs, incorrectly assumed to ward off evil spirits. This area actually received its appellation as a homonym-like corruption for Deutsch or German, referencing a European region noted for its centuries-old devotion to smoking their sausages, beef, pork, and even beer. Over here in the Keystone State, a most memorable aspect of this region's Teutonic influences are its unchanging, authentic foodways, best explored in Krumsville at Dietrich's Meats and Country Store. For those visitors first arriving at their oversized red barn, the destination is considered a Sistine Chapel of Penn Dutch cuisine, notable not for its painted murals but instead for intoxicating aromas wafting from an adjacent smokehouse.

Inside, a gastronomic museum offers seldom-encountered cuisine that fills shelves and counter displays with an astonishing variety of edibles awaiting the adventurous palate. Crowding out more pedestrian local options of apple butter, pepper cabbage, and chow chow are cases or buckets that display smoked frozen chicken feet, lamb tongue, head cheese, filled pig stomachs, plus everything from snout to tail but the squeal. Tenderly caressing the alert ears of her porcine comestible, nonagenarian Verna Dietrich still supervises the gourmet operations of this renowned enterprise and delights in distributing free samples. First educated in a one-room schoolhouse, she was forelady at an underwear factory, ran huckster routes selling fresh eggs, and began gaining notoriety with her late husband while debuting eye-catching produce at the local farmers market. Her radio spots or local television commercials always spun the heads of listeners and bemused audiences as she detailed the market's startling inventory.

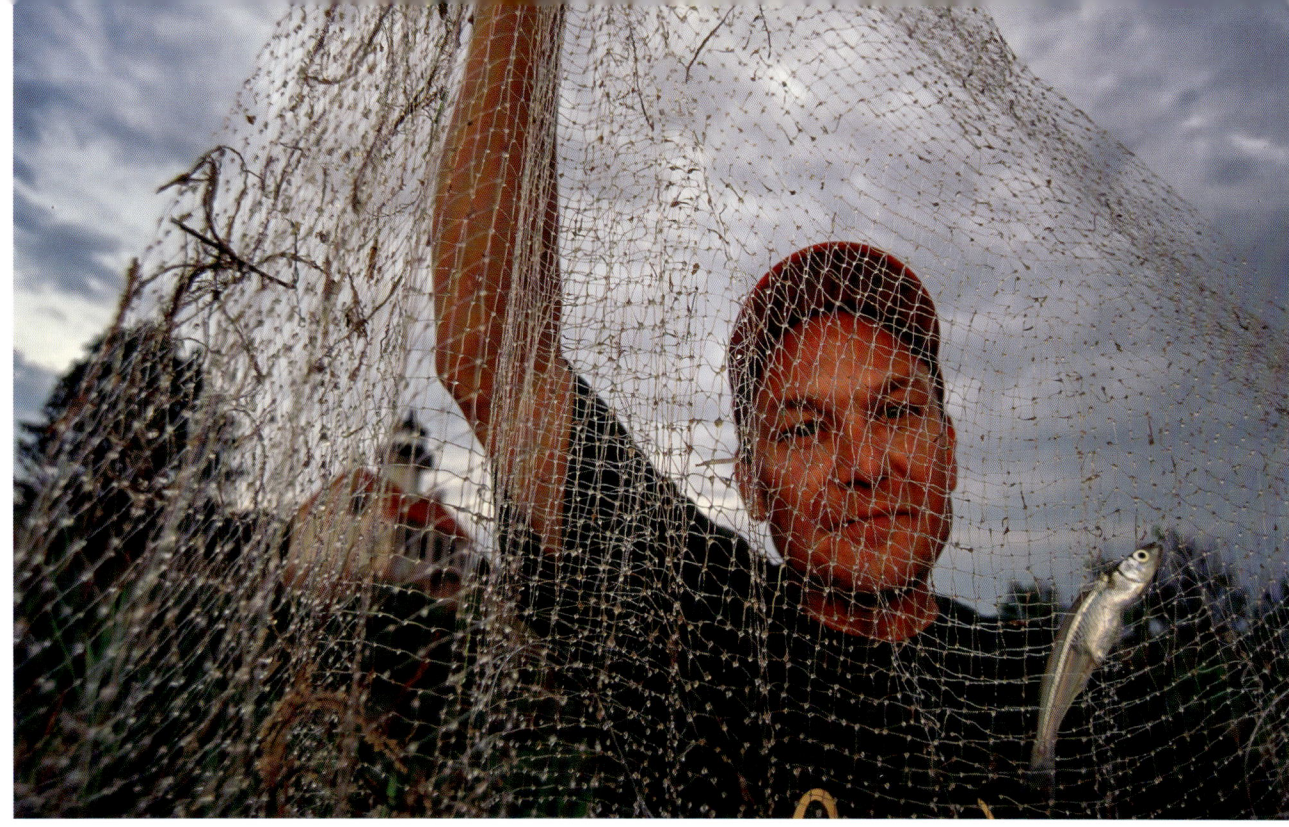

GILLNET TRAWLER

Heislerville, New Jersey

Considered the longest free-flowing, undammed river in all of America's eastern half, Delaware River's 330 miles first thread tortuously through mountainous Catskills-forested grasslands. Its widening waters spread into riffles coursing past banks lined with wading fly fisherman casting about for wild rainbow trout. These waters provide half the drinking supply for a thirsty New York City, while its crystal-clear currents define four state borders. Downstream, whitewater rafters pass upstream migrations of shad along rapids that slash through looming Kittatinny Mountains while creating the dramatic Delaware Water Gap. Farther downriver General George Washington valiantly led 6,000 troops during a pivotal Christmas night transit of ice-chocked currents to shock and defeat inebriated Hessian soldiers at their Trenton outposts. During their crossing, he was probably way too preoccupied to consider that this river's name originated from the very same British system of aristocratic nobility that his revolution was meant to overthrow. In fact the Delaware's moniker honored British nobleman Thomas West, 3rd Baron De La Warr, a descendant of King Henry VIII's second wife's sister. Lower down this watercourse, otters splash in shoreline marshes even as Philadelphia's skyline appears just adjacent to the world's largest freshwater port. As this river empties out into a widening Delaware Bay, brackish currents turn saltier and its upwelling mixture draws abundant marine life, including most notably the world's largest concentration of horseshoe crabs. Not really a crustacean, these sea creatures are related to scorpions, spiders, and ticks. Their rare blue colored, copper-based blood was highly sought after by pharmaceutical companies to test for dangerous vaccine impurities. Delaware Bay's most sharply etched example illustrating synchronous survival occurs during May's full moon as an orgy of copulating horseshoe crabs emerge from the surf. They deposit teeny eggs that are fat-filled superfood which provide an essential mid-journey fueling for red knots during their exhausting 4,000-mile winged migration from South America.

Along muddy banks, three eyeballs appear to size up the netting situation unfurling near New Jersey's 1849 East Point Lighthouse, poised for an illuminating evening aside Delaware Bay's shoreline. After removal of wayward horseshoe crabs from their entanglement in the gillnet's nylon monofilaments, the careful red-capped fisherman inspects his remaining fingerling inventory. Both white perch and the netted blueback herring are legal with a permit in New Jersey but only during several months according to strict fishing rules that regulate mesh size, fish species, and trawlers' ambitions.

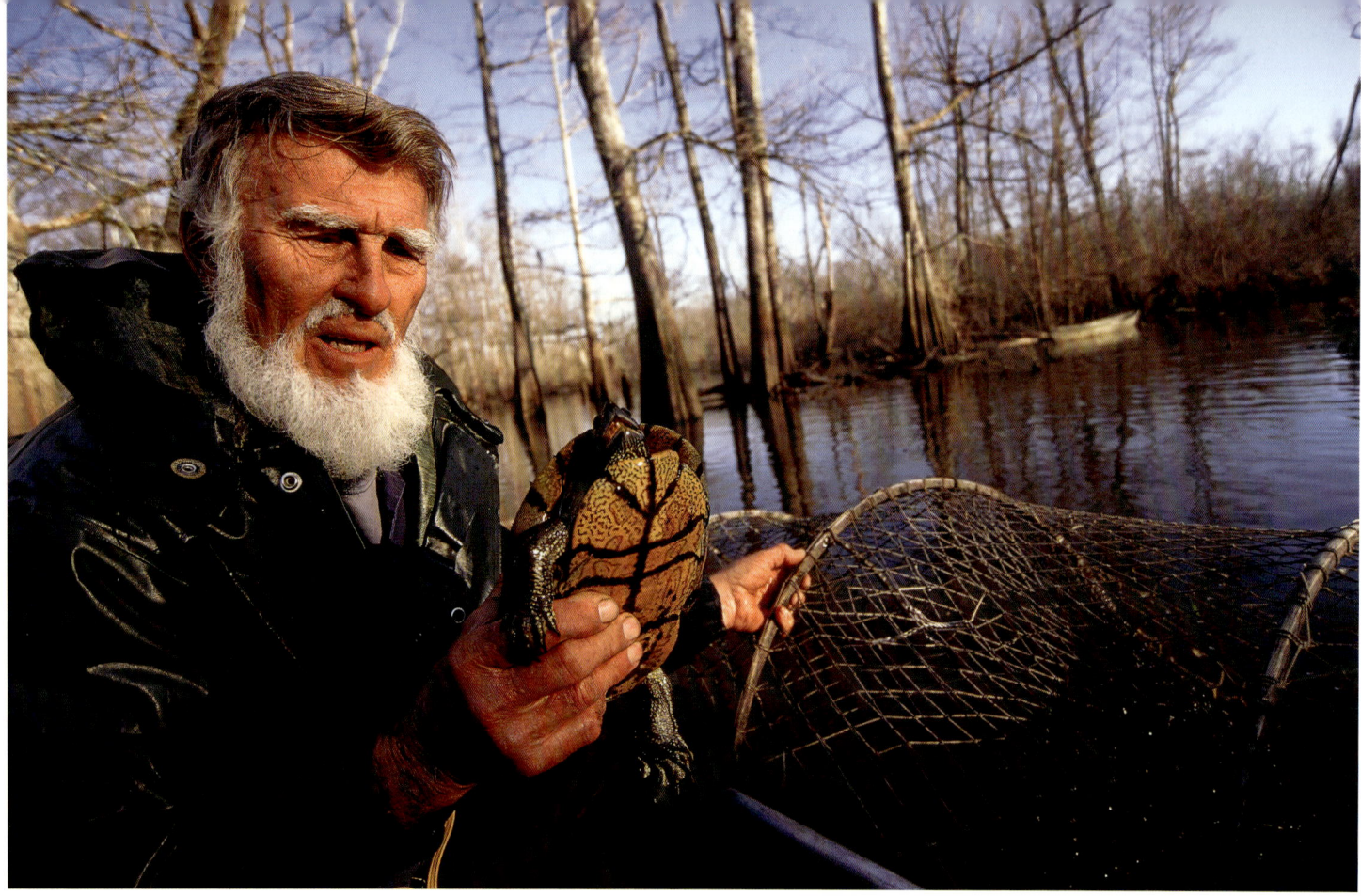

CAJUN BAYOU DWELLER

Butte La Rose, Louisiana

The Atchafalaya Basin is very sparsely populated by humans but filled with alligators, mink, nutria, and turtles dodging Spanish-moss-coated trees. The nation's largest forested swamp is known for its iconic bald cypress and soaring tupelo trees. The Cajuns still living in this remote, riparian world arrived centuries ago from thousands of miles away. Steadfastly refusing a loyalty oath to Great Britain, thousands of French-speaking Acadians in Nova Scotia were forcibly expelled from their homes around 1755. They emigrated to the warmer Francophonic life in Louisiana, then still under French control, where they cultivated an insistently vibrant lifestyle amidst this abundantly stocked ecosystem. Cajuns created their own distinct, rhythmically upbeat zydeco music for their fais do-do celebrations, characterized by fiddle, accordion, and triangle. A robustly spiced cuisine they drew from swampland creatures such as boiled crawfish, shrimp étouffée, and gumbo stews seemed to match the rich flavor of their colorfully ebullient language.

Paddling out in an oar-driven rustic pirogue from the deep thickets around floating tar paper camps, inde-fatigably intrepid swamp dwellers like this Cajun trapper eke out his rugged livelihood ensnaring wildlife while making the rounds, surveying watery grocery aisles beneath soaring egrets, where a western chicken turtle is inspected for checkout.

HASIDIC BAKERY STOREKEEPER

Williamsburg, New York City, New York

When the world's longest suspension span opened in 1903, bursting, overcrowded tenements in Manhattan's Lower East Side spilled many of its occupants as they decided to relocate just across that Williamsburg Bridge. Their new neighborhood on the bridge's other side was transformed into America's largest concentration of immigrants. Jewish populations that settled in Williamsburg further mushroomed dramatically after World War II with a new arrival of Hasidic adherents, fleeing the traumas of genocide to start their new life on a different continent. Fresh from their namesake town in present day Romania, one of their largest sects, the Satmar community, flooded many blocks across Williamsburg, mostly along Lee Avenue, bringing with them a biblically conservative worldview. Benefiting from their new country's separation of church and state, ultra-Orthodox charismatic leaders firmly established Yiddish as a lingua franca while insisting that modernity is anathema to the Torah. On Saturdays and holidays only, sons are seen with their fathers who wear imposing foxtail fur shtreimel hats, dodging tandem strollers crowding sidewalks as they lead the way to synagogue. Women are required to cover up necklines, wear long skirts with opaque stockings, and don wigs that will cover their shaved heads. Marriages are usually arranged after only eighteen years and that biblical admonition in Genesis to "be fruitful and multiply" seems seriously taken to heart as their seven-children average is among the world's highest. Yeshiva schooling teaches little if any secular curriculum, emphasizing instead the spiritual and mystical aspects of daily life, arguing that rebbe-led study of their holy Talmud texts is sufficient preparation for life's tribunals.

On Lee Avenue kosher loaves of warm, sesame-sprinkled bread are proudly displayed by the exuberantly bearded proprietor at this diminutive, heimish bake shop. A triumphant mixture between crusty and spongy textures, braided egg challah sells fast prior to Sabbath observances in this Satmar neighborhood, where the cramped quarters inside Oneg Bakery are redolent with smells emanating from hamantaschen, rugelach, and their densely riveted chocolate babka, made famous within popular culture by an absurd *Seinfeld* episode.

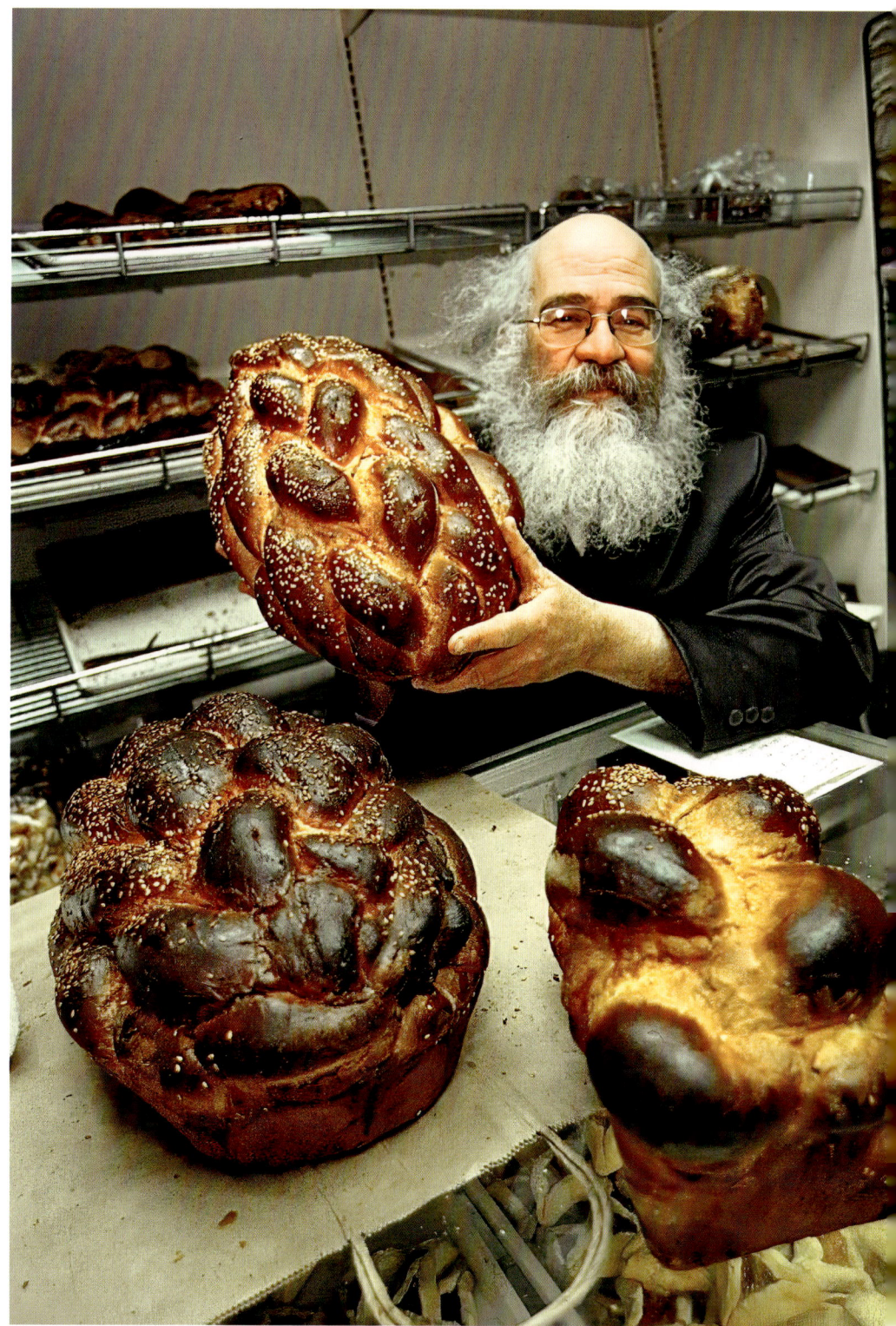

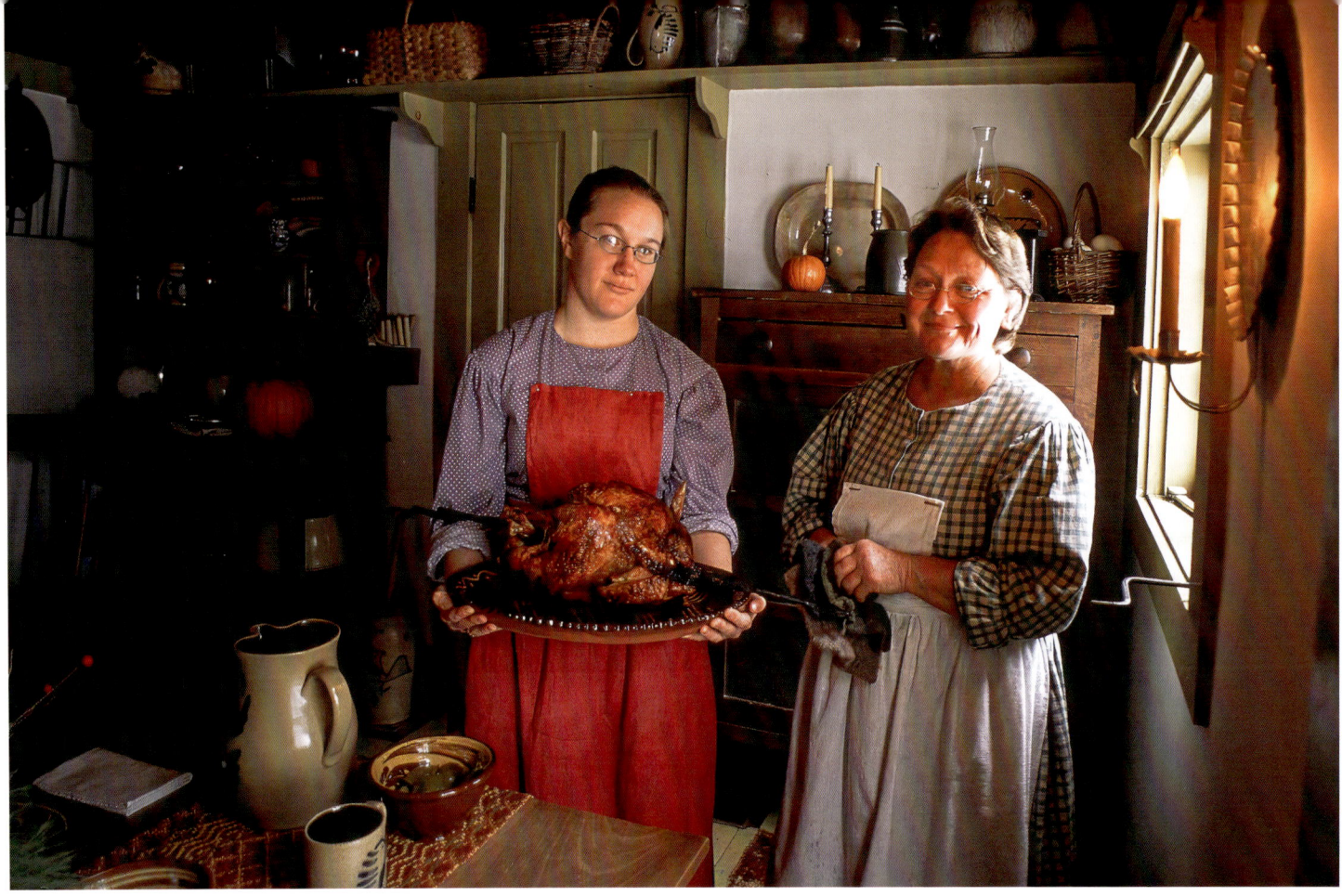

HOMESTEADERS

Wolfeboro, New Hampshire

When southern states seceded at the Civil War's outset, a table was set for a Homestead Act, which was signed into law by Abraham Lincoln in 1862. Meant to increase Union settlements through westward expansion, the government provided up to 160 acres of public land for free to settlers, on a condition of developing and improving these growing territories. That prompted railroad lines to expand, connecting communities, while further spurring growth and the national economy, which was based on a rigorous framework of self-sufficiency. This work ethic and independent rural spirit still survives today in isolated outposts and some remote pockets of society. Today's homesteaders eschew a prepackaged modern life and supermarket chains whose stocked shelves are bursting with GMO-modified products. Instead, they'll tend to their own gardens, hunt or raise poultry or livestock, and provide for their own nutritional needs. At the Farm at Frost Corners in southern New Hampshire, one such chimney-puffing homestead, built during the turn of the nineteenth century, thrives on its own horticultural wits. Recreating a lifestyle from the 1830s, turkeys roam their yards, pigs root for tubers, and eggs are swiped to provide breakfasts scrambled with heirloom tomatoes or squash cultivated in burgeoning gardens. Clothing is handsewn, and two fireplaces keep the domicile warm. For holiday dinners, turkey is trussed and speared on a spit for roasting by the fire within historic reflective ovens known as tin kitchens.

As Thanksgiving approaches, aproned Virginia Taylor along with her daughter Pip, who proudly hoists a perfectly cooked turkey, will shortly arrange placements at their dinner table, stacked with pewter dinnerware and hand-forged utensils. Colonial recipe-filled side dishes, like creamed radishes, turnip sauce, and brandied peaches accumulate before a final serving of Marlborough pie. The traditional dessert is baked alongside lemons and apples from their orchards, mixed with pounded sugar freshly snipped from its loaf. Beneath ancient timbers, her kitchen's smoky fragrance sets the stage for a time-travel banquet, experienced year-round in the cramped but cozy quarters of enterprising homesteaders.

FRIED ALLIGATOR SERVERS

Port Vincent, Louisiana

During the 1970s, Cajun naturalist Annie Miller eked out her living amongst Bayou Black, where she first grew up in the swamps trapping animals and raising her children. She and her husband would collect as many as 200 snakes in a single day, selling them to zoos or laboratories. Trapping nutria and muskrat, she tamed swamp critters as pets, while crating up trained otters for Walt Disney projects. She invented swamp tours in Louisiana, where a football field's worth of land still disappears every half-hour. Despite a shrinking state, there are now up to thirty swamp tour operators following her pioneering efforts and satiating the hunger of intrepid visitors hoping for alligator sightings. Alligators are the largest reptile in North America, and Louisiana more than any other state is populated with over a million of them. Like leathery armored battleships, they are protected by a backside's shield of horny plates and propelled from the rear by their powerful, muscular tail. Its rounded bow is guarded by eighty sharpened teeth in its jaw, which when worn down are replaced, yielding up to 3,000 fangs during a seventy-year lifespan. Even tiny hatchlings develop an egg tooth atop their snout to crack open their round-shelled prison. Surprisingly these feared creatures will chirp to alert their mother that it's time for leaving the nest. Sometimes reaching fifteen feet in length and weighing up to half a ton, this exclusively American cold-blooded animal has only injured or killed about 400 unsuspecting humans over the last several decades, so it's worth pondering whether revenge is actually top of mind for spice-happy Cajun cooks adding to their exotic repertoire of southern cuisine.

Along reptile-filled bayou, creaky wooden walkways wind beneath Spanish moss-draped bald cypress and tupelo trees to a rustic swamp cabin often thrumming with syncopated vest frottoir washboard or accordion rhythms playing deep into the night. In keeping with Cajun joie de vivre, crawfish boils and spit-roasted suckling pigs were often on tap during lively swamp-to-table dining. From atop the warping porch of Bayside Tavern, a sprawling rustic roadhouse lets the good times roll as two overall-swathed servers step out above Colyell Creek to fill empty plates. Their fried alligator crowds heaping platters that offer tender tail meat chunks, frizzled up alongside cornmeal, crushed red pepper, and a dash of Tabasco sauce, which is produced nearby at Avery Island.

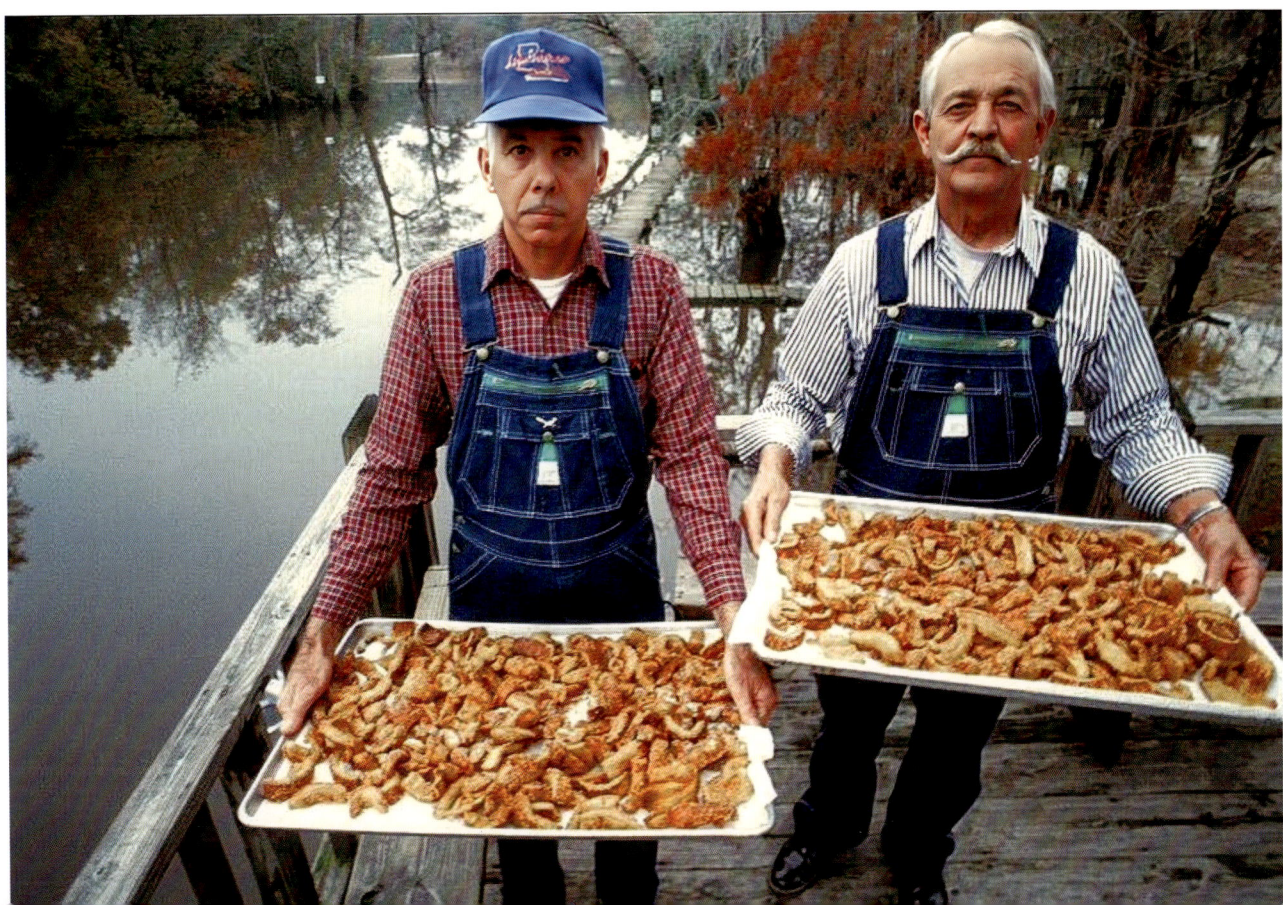

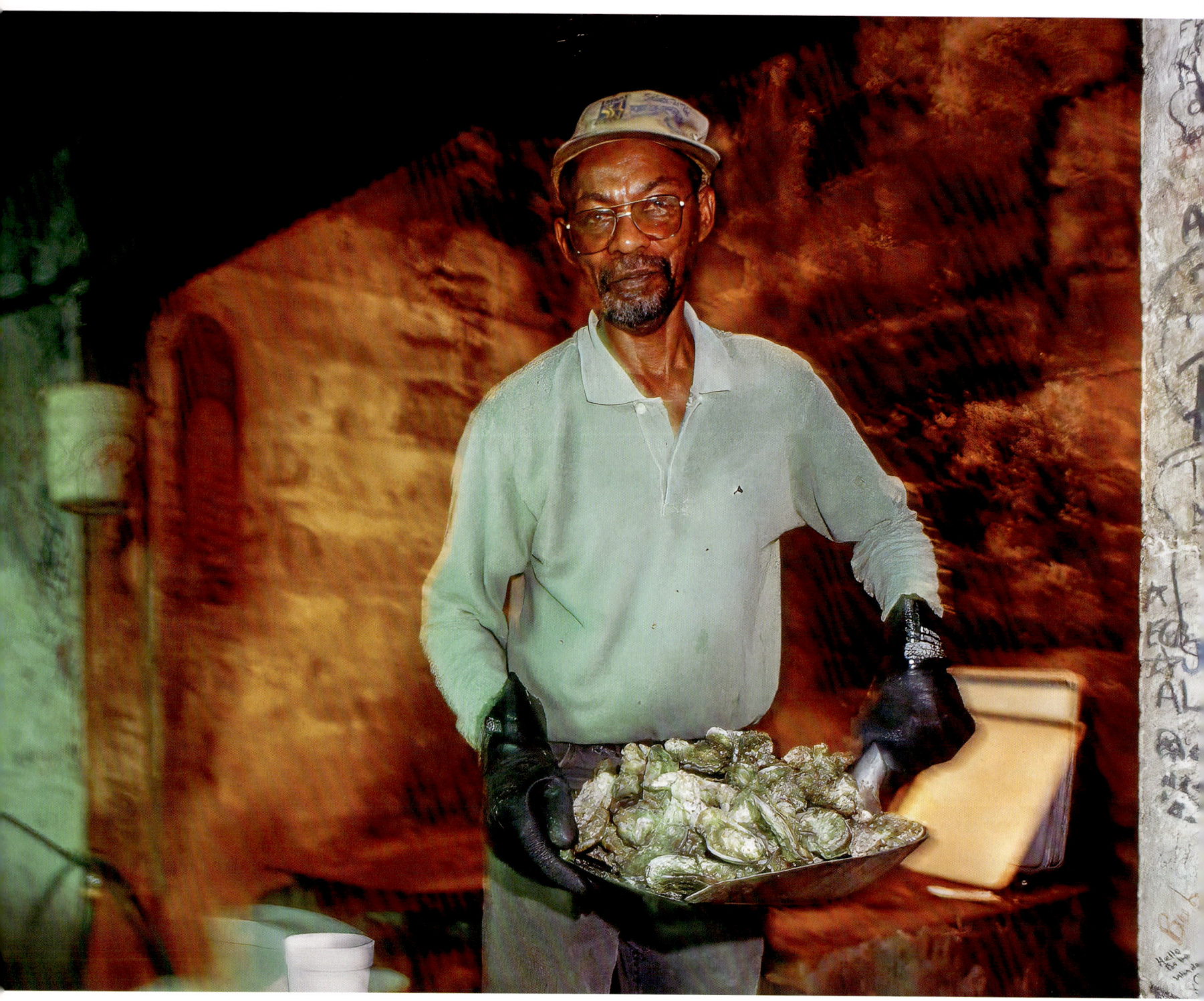

OYSTER COOK

Bowens Island, South Carolina

The first evidence of modern human behavior was presented by an amazing discovery of shellfish consumption that took place 164,000 years ago in a South African cave. As the growth of our species has often been attributed to hunting and gathering activities, oysters were destined to heavily shape America's historic development. Flourishing in shallow waters along estuary shorelines, these stationary food sources could be plucked like fruit. Before the sediments of urban growth, pristine waters offered massive oyster reefs spanning an Atlantic seaboard where native Lenape or Narragansett tribes gorged on bountiful shellfish reserves. Landscapes were subtly shaped by the resulting middens, scrap heap pilings containing enormous maritime discards assisting archaeologists with assessments of human civilization. When religious exiles first hopped onto Plymouth Rock, shorelines were littered with Eastern oysters that sometimes created navigational hazards. Dutch settlers and New York tribes traded iron implements in exchange for revealing locations of ancestral oystering grounds. Throughout the nineteenth century generous mollusk beds across New York's harbor provided this planet with its largest source of these bivalves, and the nearby islet upon which Lady Liberty now hoists its torch was referred to by immigrants as Great Oyster Island. Along Manhattan streets paved with these shucked shells, businesses and housing sprang up in buildings created from oyster paste mortar. Oyster saloons and parlors seemed to be popping up on every corner. Here raw, grilled, fried, steamed, and pickled mollusks might find themselves used in croquettes, pies, or stewed fricassees. As oyster houses flourished, Crassostrea virginica became a keystone of American diets, providing for just one penny per oyster the least expensive source of protein available. Briny bivalves were a frequent bar companion to beer, and oyster street vendors became the Victorian-era equivalent of sidewalk hotdog stands. Mark Twain revealed that oyster ice cream was a favorite flavor in his best-selling 1876 novel *The Adventures of Tom Sawyer*. Now considered considered one particularly romantic Valentine's Day specialty, oysters are rich in vitamin B12 and loaded with sex hormone-triggering amino acids, while a high zinc content may aid testosterone production. They are justifiably considered an aphrodisiac, a moody condition named for Greek goddess Aphrodite, who supposedly emerged from her opened oyster shell amongst sea foam created from severed genitals of the primordial god Ouranos.

In marshy Lowcountry, Charleston was a city literally built on oysters. In the 1830s, recycling oyster house proprietors carted off surplus shells to low lying areas. That landfill created additional real estate capable of hosting newly constructed oyster houses. Reached by dirt road, a James Beard Award–winning restaurant was an alarmingly ramshackle hideaway on its own 13-acre hammock island. For well over a decade, oyster cook Henry Gilliard kept busy stoking fires and roasting clusters in the graffiti-scratched, dungeon-like inner sanctum at Bowens Island. There, gastronomic jewels of the sea were dug from adjoining tidal marshland beds where brackish waters yielded pluff-caked clumps that were readied for fiery preparation. These gnarled mollusks were plopped beneath damp burlap to steam them open, while blazing heat infused the oyster meat in its own juices and released a briny cloud of oceanic perfume. Dramatically served by the shovelful at newspaper-lined tables, these jumbo bivalves played the title role during a succulent oyster roast. Gilliard labored only for tips, a notion reinforced for diners by that large white bucket hung beside the fire pit.

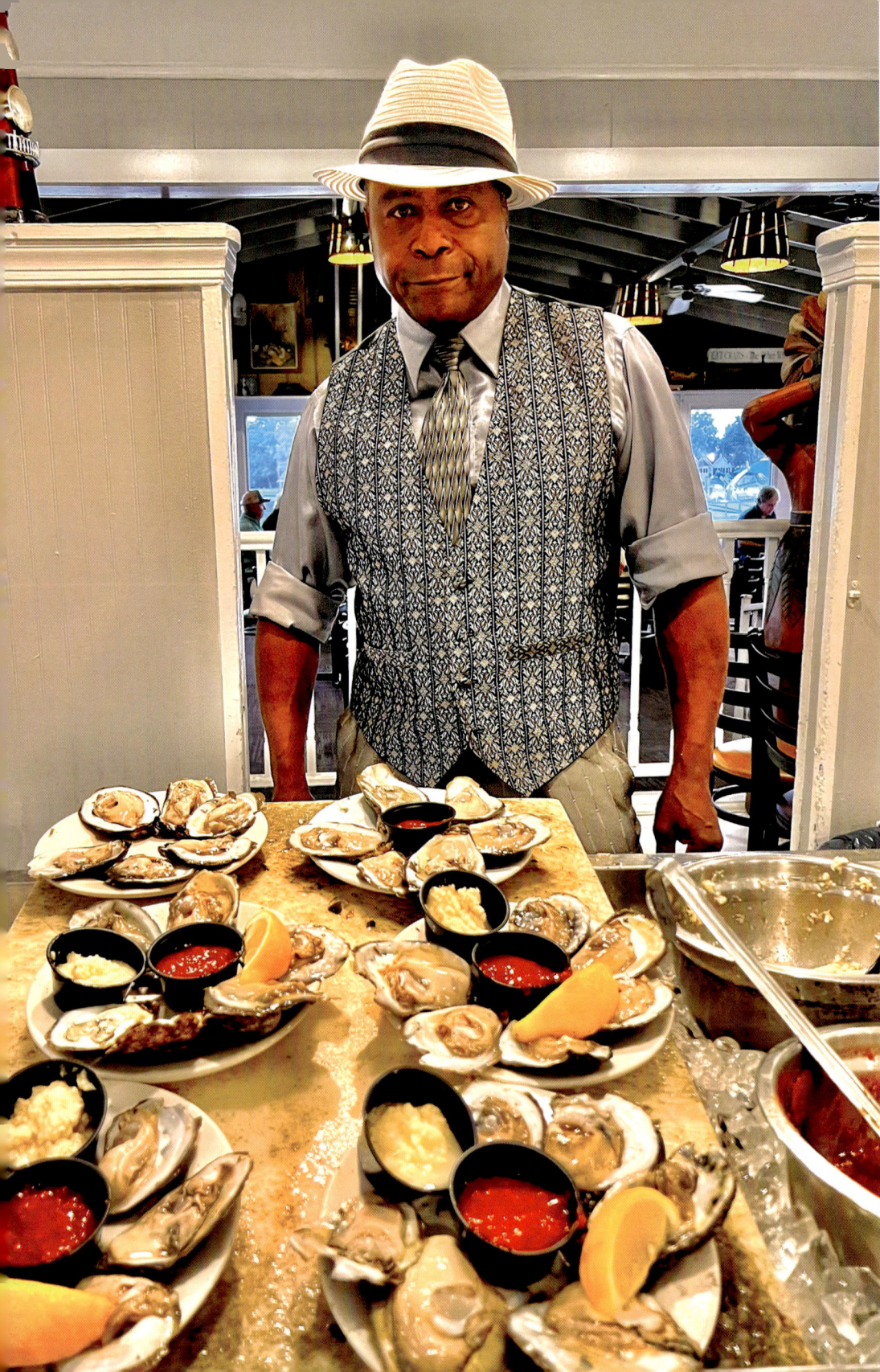

OYSTER SHUCKER

Hurlock, Maryland

Just a brief sail from the Suicide Bridge Restaurant, a freshwater Choptank River dumps its currents into marine-rich Chesapeake Bay. That body of water, America's largest estuary, is famed for its quickly vanishing, oyster-dredging skipjacks, a nineteenth-century sailing advancement over bivalve-collecting rakes and tongs. The dockside seafood emporium features an awarded champion oyster shucker, improbably clad in a tie, vest, and debonair hat. Beneath a toy lighthouse and crab basket ceiling lamps, Handy Tillman momentarily puts aside his short-bladed shucking knives used to slice the oysters' lid-releasing abductor muscles. Apparently unconcerned that an oyster is the most common animal to be eaten alive, the nattily dressed shucker seems proud to display his elegant nautical handiwork, destined for a brief lemon shower at anxiously awaiting tables.

LOBSTERMAN

Clinton, Connecticut

Often occupying the highest echelons of gourmet menus in candlelit restaurants while meant for final disposal above bibs and beneath only those most sophisticated palates, lobster was once shockingly considered a trash food, fed to pigs, goats, and paupers. They were so abundant in seventeenth-century maritime New England that the Pilgrims actually hand-picked lobsters from flooded tidepools and would use them as fertilizer or bait. Convicts were buoyed in early American penal colonies when mercifully protective regulations helped limit their forced consumption of the crustacean to only three times a week. An astonishment of nature, this cryptid-like creature seems cobbled together by spare parts. Their fertility actually increases with age, and they never stop increasing in size as their armor is shed periodically. Dining on their own discarded shell, lobsters will expand into an even larger carapace suit, and are capable of that continual refitting for nearly a century. Above stalked eyes, a lobster's wiggling antennas can smell distant prey, while they taste through their leg's chemosensory hair, chew food from inside the stomach's gastric mill, and grow back missing limbs. The pincers on their crusher claws can exert 100 pounds of pressure per square inch which come in handy as these Jurassic-era nektonic warships are adept garbage collectors, scouring benthic depths for mealtime scraps. Its greenish-brown exoskeleton cladding these arthropods keeps them obscured amongst coastal seaweed and muddy ocean bottoms. Capable of navigating backwards with ten multi-purposed legs, their big misfortune occurs when curiosity lures them into baited lobster traps, unchanged in design for almost two hundred years. When hauled up by hardworking lobstermen who buoyantly pinball between bobbing buoys, they'll be transferred from boats into saltwater confinements known as lobster pounds. It's just upon boiling that the lobster transforms into its iconic red veneer, as only astaxanthin pigments in the shell remain stable when heated, while other once dominant colorations completely disappear.

Along the marshy Connecticut coastline, gleaming eyes and reddened cheeks display awareness of culinary excellence nurtured in a shed at Lobster Landing in Clinton. Joyously gregarious Enea Bacci braves eager pincers on an immense lobster that emerges from its pound, soon to be transformed into a mouthwatering delicacy and smothered in cholesterol-fearless dowsings of drawn butter. Sitting atop pilings and surrounded by crushed clamshells, his paint-peeled, weatherbeaten, 100-year-old bait shack has survived two hurricanes with only the unrepaired dangling letter O offering mute testimony to any damage. Bacci's nautical produce is scooped daily from the sea within five miles of the dock where more than a quarter century ago he spotted an inviting "For Sale" sign when navigating with friends across Clinton Harbor. To fulfill his salt-scented dream, he made an impulsive purchase without any marital consultation, creating a seasonal gastronomic haven, nationally acclaimed for its magically luscious lobster rolls.

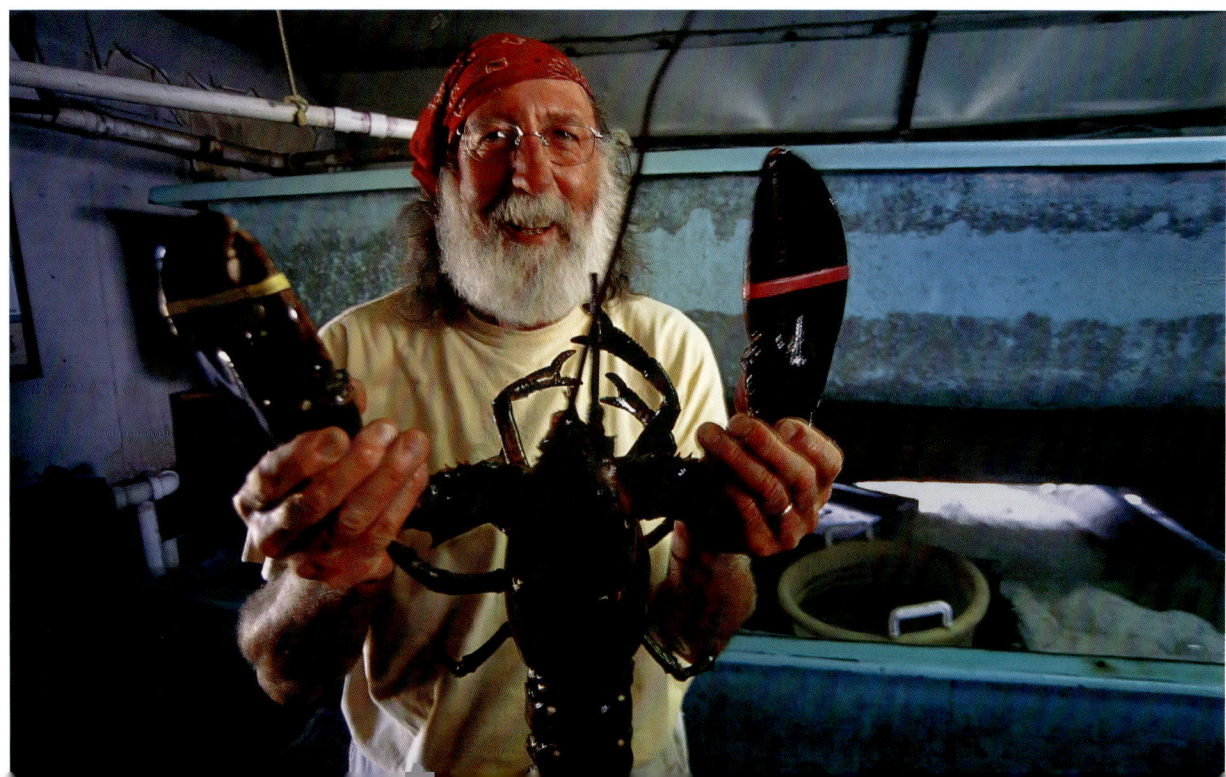

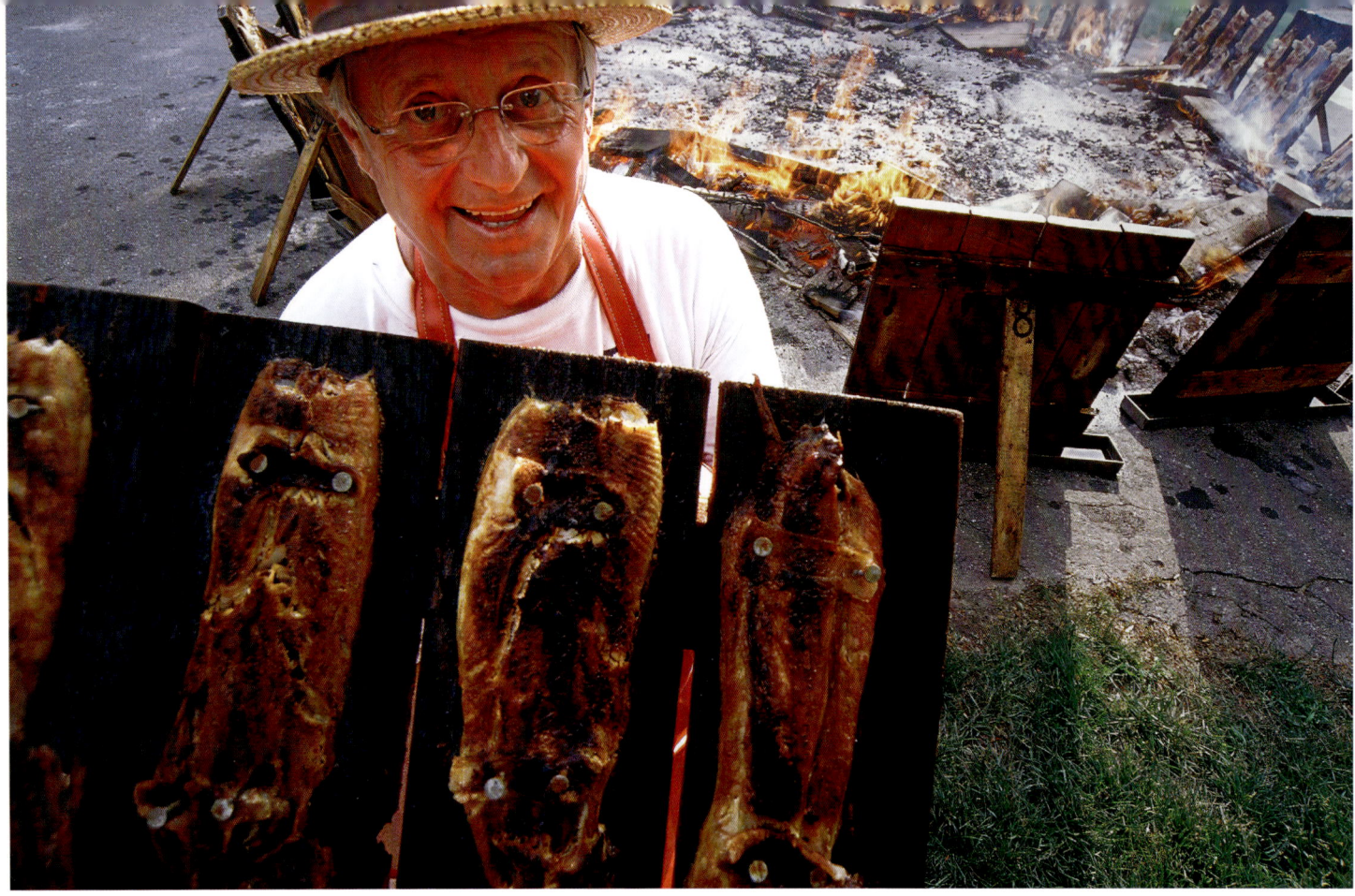

SHAD BAKE MASTER

Essex, Connecticut

For millennia, Indigenous people have relied on spring's migratory run of shad, providing sustenance throughout the year through smoking and drying. Copied by early settlers, shad rations helped George Washington's troops stave off starvation during their cruel winter encampment at Valley Forge. Shad shacks soon popped up on the banks of many northeastern rivers, most notably in Connecticut. After many years at sea, they make their way upriver though the brackish zones and then find suitable, temperature-dictated moments to spawn. As if a cog in nature's huge transmission gears, it's said that yellow blooms of forsythia bushes signal an arrival of that anadromous species, while the blossoming of lilacs some few months later calls a halt to those fishing opportunities. During that window, an almost celebratory annual ritual breaks out along Connecticut River banks as fishermen wade into a chorus line of rods. Others deploy their flotilla of flat-bottomed scows and skiffs looking for an energetic fight with the challenging catch. Fishing derbies are staged, parades feature giant, colorful shad floats, and bakes will occasionally still be held.

A straw-hatted bake master proudly exhibits perfectly cooked oak-planked fish and bacon at this annual shad festival in Essex, as old timey bands perform to hungry crowds, feasting upon smoked or pickled shad while on the prowl for some of its roe, an ultimate riverine delicacy. While precisely angling planks and slow flame-baking require some expertise, the most coveted skill sought out at these events are those of patient, knife-wielding fishmongers adroitly deboning this notoriously difficult fish. Closely holding personal fileting secrets, they'll have their hands full as shad are said to have over one thousand bones. The efforts would seem worthwhile as the alosa sapidissima species literally translates into "most delicious shad."

STEEPLECHASE TAILGATER

Winterthur, Delaware

America's only round border is a segment of circle that surveyors Mason and Dixon drew from their radius point atop the steeple on New Castle's courthouse. Separating Delaware from Pennsylvania, that delineated umbrella-shaped curve is intertwined with the pastoral Brandywine River coursing through forsythia-dotted countryside and greatly contributing to this nation's nineteenth-century industrial revolution. There by its banks, E.I. du Pont established stone-walled Eleutherian Mills, which produced explosive black gunpowder while later pioneering nylon, Teflon, and petrochemicals. This propelled his family to esteemed ranks amongst the nation's wealthiest, as its dynasty continued maintaining their fortune by carefully orchestrating arranged marriages to cousins. Not far from an elbow in the Brandywine, acclaimed horticulturalist and descendant Henry Francis du Pont brought gardening notoriety to this corner of Delaware. His 150-room country estate hosts the nation's largest procession of horse-drawn antique carriages, where dapper top-hatted gentlemen and stylish ladies trumpet their elegance through fragrant lanes filled by blooming azaleas en route to an equestrian tailgate party on lawn-like meadows at Winterthur's Point-to-Point Steeplechase.

Echoing the foxhunting heritage of this region, their furs and peacock feathers boast a sartorial menagerie that adorns an amiable tailgater. After retrieving her lavish tray filled up by appetizing canapes, tootlers replace brass horns with a glass of champagne as the grassy, horse-drawn parking lot reaches capacity for their pre-race banquet.

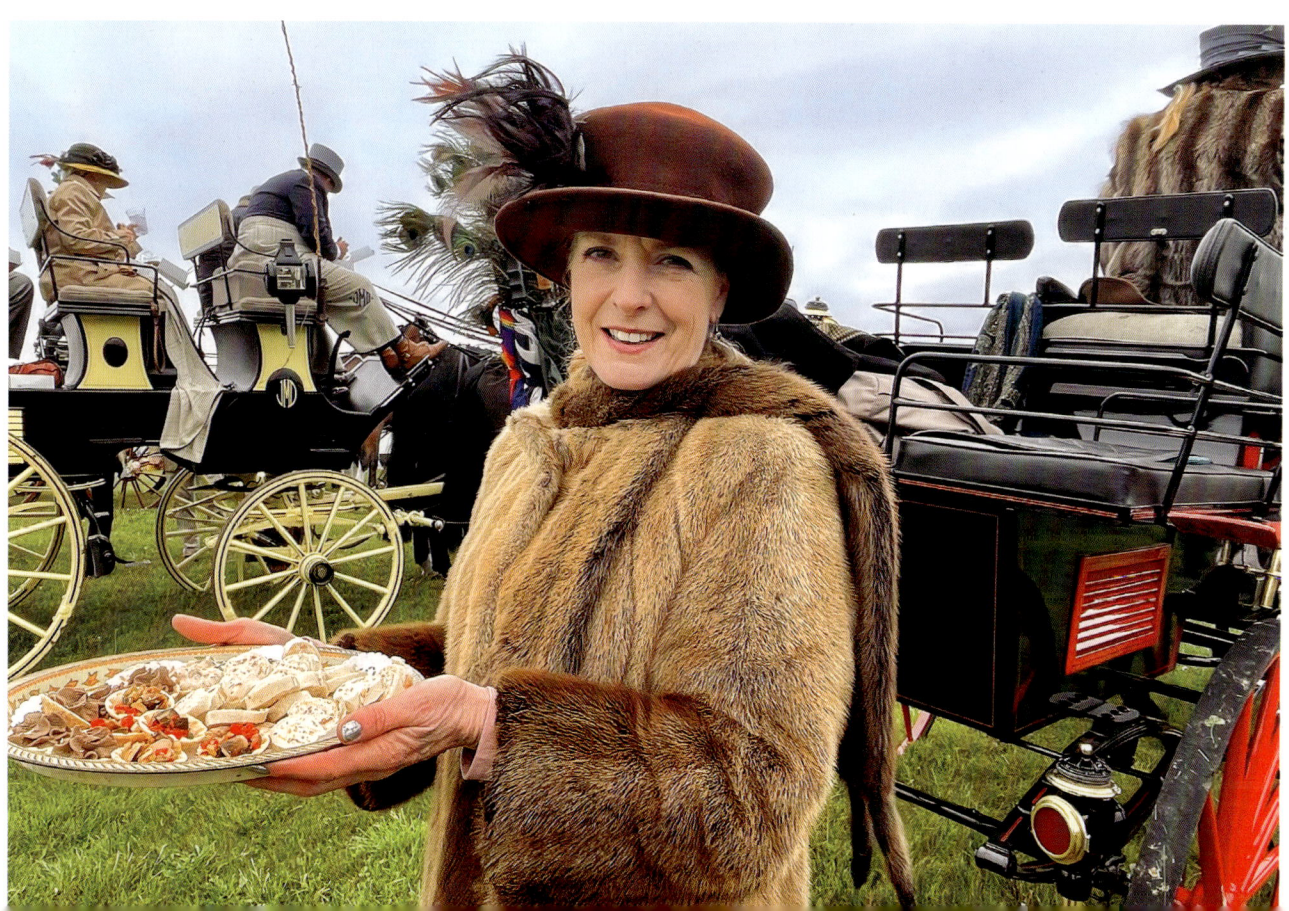

BLUEBERRY PROMOTER

Addison, Maine

Just down the road in coastal Maine, morning sunlight first glances at American soil. The granitic bedrock of Washington County was heavily raked by mammoth glacial sheets that only receded 10,000 years ago, leaving sharply indented shorelines, salt meadows, and sandy, acidic soil where blueberries first took root. Substantially smaller rakes have been used over the most recent hundred years to laboriously hand comb and extricate these gleaming, azure berries from their viny entanglement. At Wescogus Farm, a pioneering center that features sustainable cultivation and harvesting techniques, forty acres of vast, bush-coated barrens slope down toward Pleasant River's tidal valley. There the antioxidant-rich fruit are cultivated in complex, two-year cycles first learned about from native Passamaquoddy. This exhaustive horticultural nurturing requires a post-frost burning, then snow-covered incubation prior to springtime's blossoming, pollination, and slowly growing berries not to be harvested until the following autumn.

Taking a break from thrumming belts and shaking contraptions in their packing shed, Marie Emerson proudly displays one among many dozens of boxes gathered just that day. These cartons are crammed with thousands of blood pressure–lowering superfood gems, loaded with bone-building manganese and Vitamin K. This deeply passionate advocate for unmodified wild blueberries created the nearby Wild Blueberry Land, an oddly whimsical, orb-shaped theme park encompassing a blue miniature golf course, satellite dish turned blueberry pie, plus decidedly more edible jams, vinegars, and ice cream available inside. That eye-catching roadside attraction and its exhibits promote awareness of the wild blueberry, one of only three commercially available indigenous American foods.

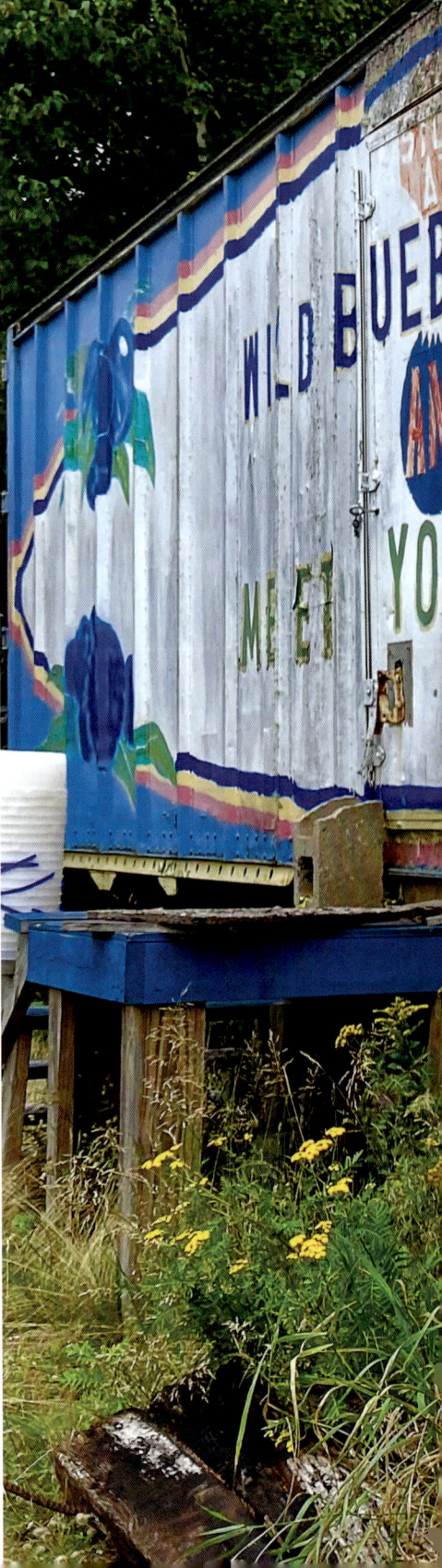

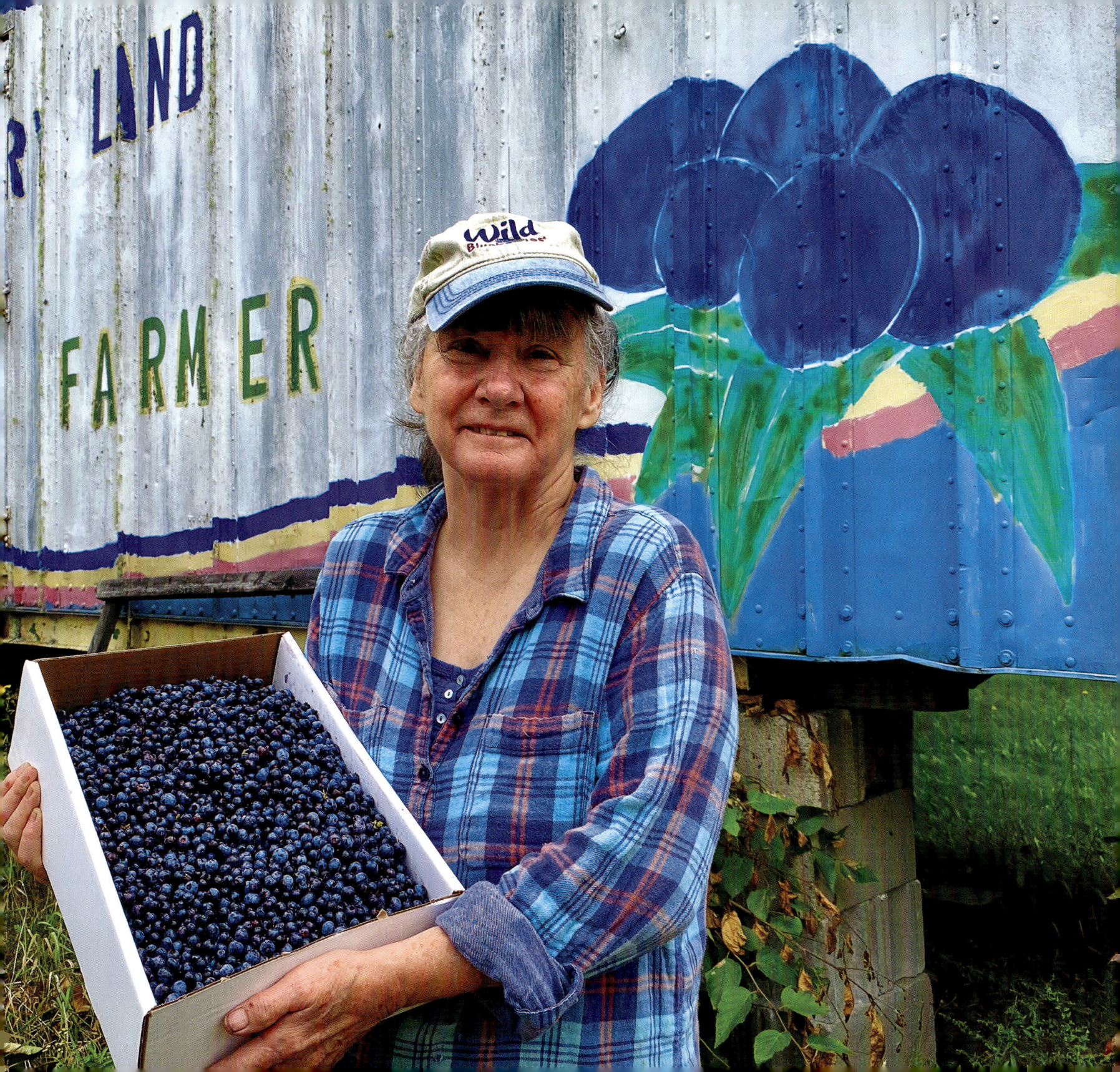

CHEESECAKE CUTTER

Lowville, New York

With more cows than humans residing in Lewis County, a glimpse across rolling hillsides just beyond the Adirondacks reveals the thick smatterings of skyscraping silos that top numerous nineteenth-century dairy barns. They'll provide nourishing feed for their Holsteins, producing up to 2,600 gallons of milk with each lactation. An essential repository for all that liquid is the 400,000-square-foot Kraft Heinz processing plant in nearby Lowville. It displays at its entrance a gargantuan replica of their starring product, a tub of Philadelphia Cream Cheese, actually invented in New York. The 150-year-old product, known for its rich, balanced flavor of locally sourced fresh milk and cream, is the nation's bestselling cream cheese, and can move from farm to fridge within six days. Though a great deal of its demand comes from urban bagel shop owners downstate, this product plays a headlining role as the prime ingredient in cheesecake, served at Lowville's annual Cream Cheese Festival.

There at the town firehouse a 6,900-pound pastry, finished off with butter, sugar, and graham cracker crust is served to about 25,000 salivating mouths while being recognized by an impressive Guinness World Record. As this giant Philadelphia-embossed dessert gets scored using industrial-sized stainless-steel rakes, cheesecake is served along with an elfin twinkle by a hair-netted employee of Kraft Heinz, relishing her festival role after spending most workdays laboring on production lines at the plant.

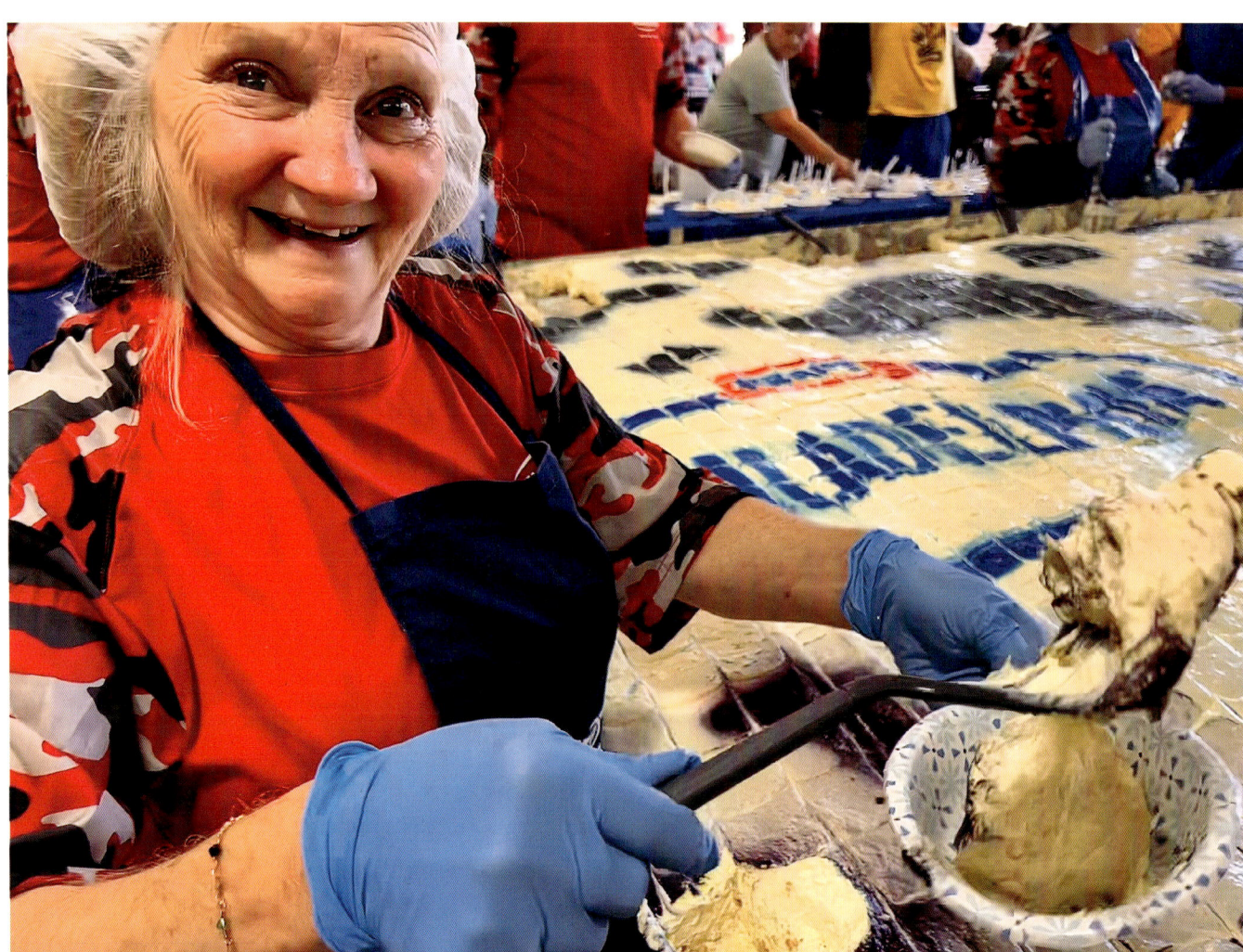

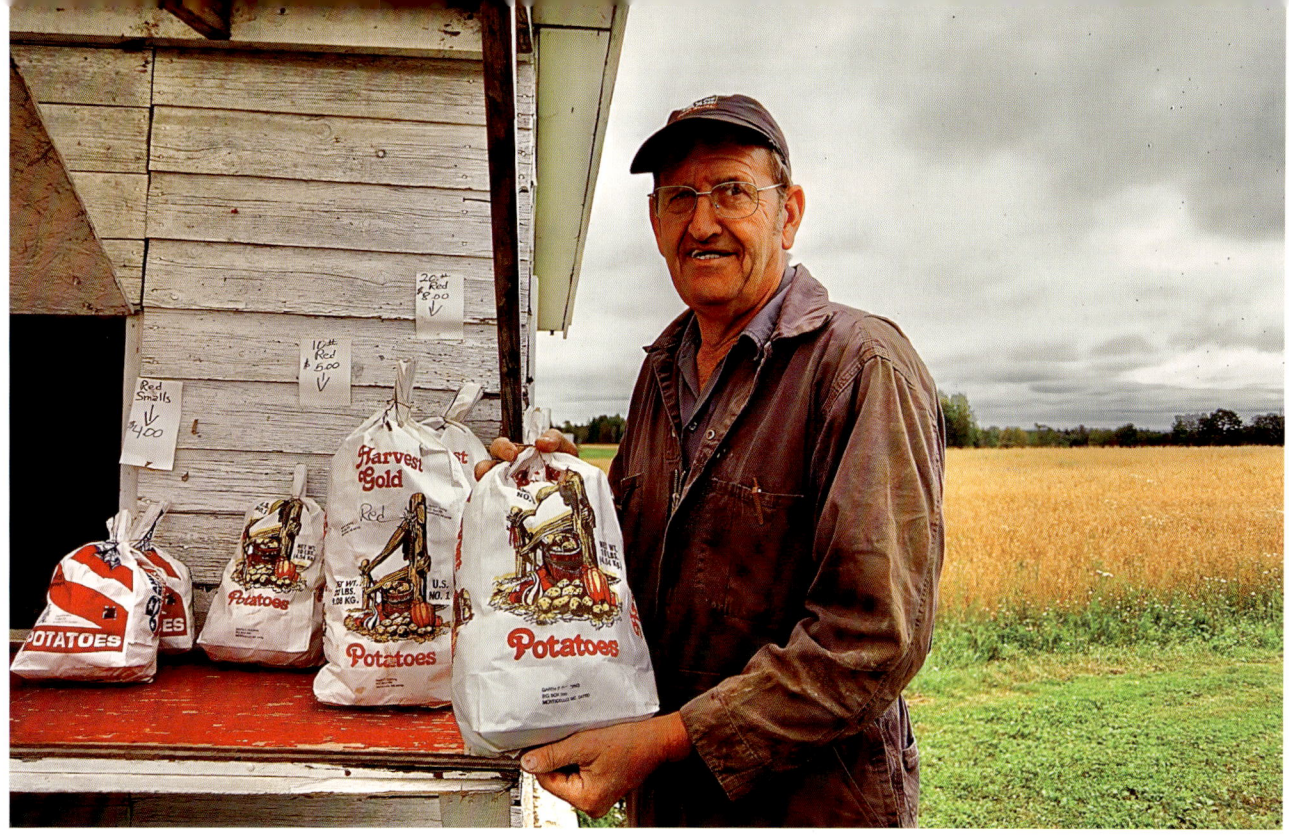

POTATO AGRICULTURALIST

Monticello, Maine

Maine's wild Allagash wilderness spreads across its immense county of Aroostook, not only second largest east of the Mississippi, but New England's northernmost one. These moose-filled forests eventually yield to vast potato fields that stretched flat as a ploye, traditional Acadian pancakes originating just across the border in French-speaking Canada. Despite Idaho's long-held claims to potato supremacy, it was here that the well-drained fields, coated by fertile loam soil, once yielded this nation's largest production of tubers. Though still nationally renowned for its taters, kudos reach a fevered pitch in July at Fort Fairfield's celebration when rows of these cultivated vegetables are lined with endless blooms exposing fragrant pink flowers. At that time, the town hosts its annual Potato Blossom Festival, which has featured potato queen pageants, picking competitions, tasting contests, and sloppily undignified wrestling in a large paddle-stirred container of mashed potatoes. When autumn approaches, the rhythmic toil of hectic potato workers fills a cultivated horizon as they immerse themselves in soil from dawn to dusk, digging, grading, and transporting spuds from their fields, over hills, and into households. Maintaining a tradition dating back to the 1940s, schoolchildren throughout Aroostook County enjoy a three-or-four week harvest break in their studies to work these fertile acreages and assist with field chores. Building resilience, discipline, and character in the region's youth, that work provides much needed benefits in this sparsely populated region, requiring extra working hands to race against time before potatoes go bad when cold sets in.

A persevering, spud-stained cultivator, Garth Golding holds aloft his hand-dug bag of taters, nearly ready for chips, fries, or melted butter. An energetic farmer, mechanic, and truck driver, Golding was also deacon at a Baptist church near his rustic roadside stand which, as is typical in the area, most often ran on the honor system.

BAR WAITRESS

Bombay Beach, California

That very same river which helped carve an eye-popping, rainbow-hued geological layer cake at the Grand Canyon was also responsible for one of earth's greatest ecological catastrophes. Flowing 1,450 miles across seven states and briefly forming an international border with Mexico, the Colorado River courses through three national parks and helped shape several more. Closer to its source, death-defying Class VI rapids cut steeply through huge elevation drops, but eventually surrounding landscapes are flattened out. Decreasing gravity slowed its movements producing a braided river delta, creeping sluggishly toward the Gulf of California. In 1900, the California Development Company began constructing irrigation canals for diversion of its waters into the dry Salton Sink, intending to create fertile agricultural farmland. Five years later, heavy rains and snowmelt upstream breached a side channel to this canal, flooding unabated over the next two years into a previously dry endorheic bathtub. The resulting Salton Sea soon became an ideal desert oasis playground with newly created yacht clubs hosting luminaries like Bing Crosby and Frank Sinatra, who cavorted along the shores of its 400 square miles. Vacationers soon came to enjoy sellout performances by Jerry Lewis or the Beach Boys, while muscle cars would cruise past glitzy resorts and palm-thatched cabanas. This resort town of Bombay Beach began fading in the 1970s when agricultural runoffs created rising salinity levels, while dwindling water supplies left once sparkling waters largely unusable. Increasingly putrefied shores showed its age with the carcasses of dead birds, rotting fish, and vanished tourists. Shorelines dried up, ghost towns emerged, and the Salton Sea is now said to be the only man-made environmental disaster visible from outer space.

Amongst an eerie, post-apocalyptic wasteland littered by rusting automobiles, half submerged couches, or disassembled refrigerators, the Ski Inn still retains a name reflective of its glorious waterskiing and powerboat racing heyday, while occasionally attracting adventurous bohemian stragglers. Plastered with dollar bills of half-inebriated desert rats, this remote eatery supports a wistful waitress awaiting the finishing touches to a takeout container filled by spicy sriracha chicken wings. A definite high point for any visitor to Bombay Beach, the Ski Inn's bar at 278 feet below sea level is the Western Hemisphere's very lowest.

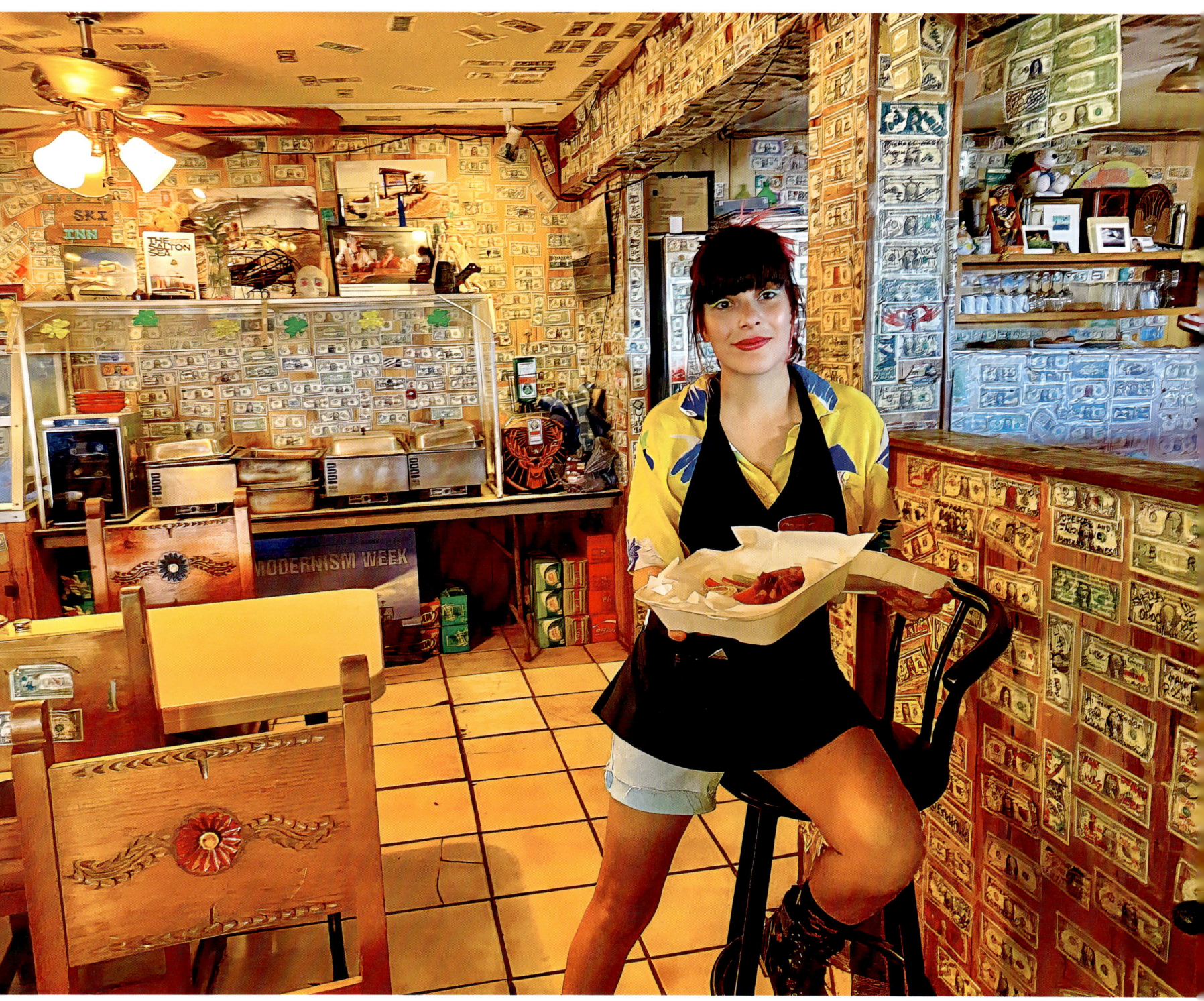

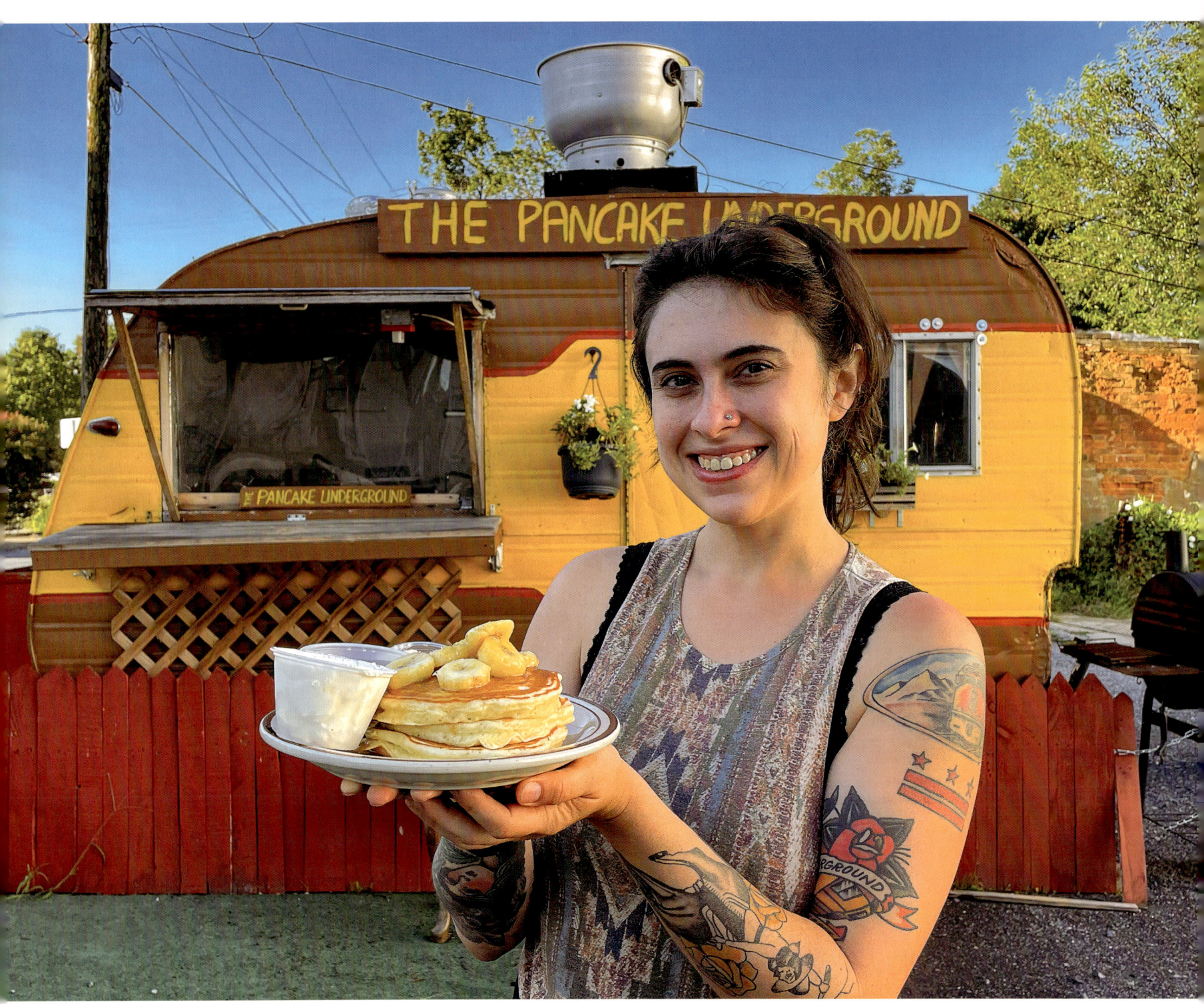

PANCAKE PARLOR PROPRIETRIX

Strasburg, Virginia

Once reverently spoken about by Thomas Jefferson himself as "one of the most stupendous scenes of nature," an unhurried Shenandoah River carved out a dynamic valley that's unusually distinct in eastern America. The forked river system predominantly flowing northward provided a busy highway for trade, fishing, military, and agricultural pursuits, as its fertile limestone river-bottom sediments spread soils that created Virginia's agriculturally rich farmlands. During the Civil War, numerous towns inside this valley changed hands between Union and Confederate forces literally scores of times during a fevered quest to control its strategic district, a topographic alleyway sculpted between mountain ridges. Known as an important "breadbasket of the Confederacy," it was a prime Union objective to destroy their critical food-supplying lifeline, which today is evidenced in numerous battlefield monuments and parks all throughout this area. Grain harvests were so instrumental here that in fact as this war began, the region hosted planet earth's largest flour mill. In quieter corners, immense water wheels helming busy grist mills powered by the river still spin away creating meal from harvests of nearby wheat fields. That flour, when paired with buttermilk, a remnant leftover after churning butter, has recently provided mouthwatering inspiration for many of the dishes served at The Pancake Underground in downtown Strasburg.

Delectably moist with perfect golden-brown crispy edges, the airy-light flapjacks are served beneath bananas or peanut butter with freshly ground grits and juicy bacon sourced by area purveyors. This distinctive breakfast eatery was commanding a new culinary wave boldly establishing itself across valley towns, as foodies have begun exploiting the cornucopia of local farm-based produce grown throughout the region. Returning for southern-style roots, Shenan Hahn and a partner hauled this battered 1957 Jewel travel-trailer camper 3,000 miles across the country to her beloved Shenandoah, from which that eponymous first name was derived. Hahn hoped this restaurant would make an oversized impact in a small hamlet, yet perhaps her greatest contribution may actually be made within the world of literature. With a master's degree in writing, her second book of poetry has recently been published, feeding hungry imaginations in addition to mealtime diners.

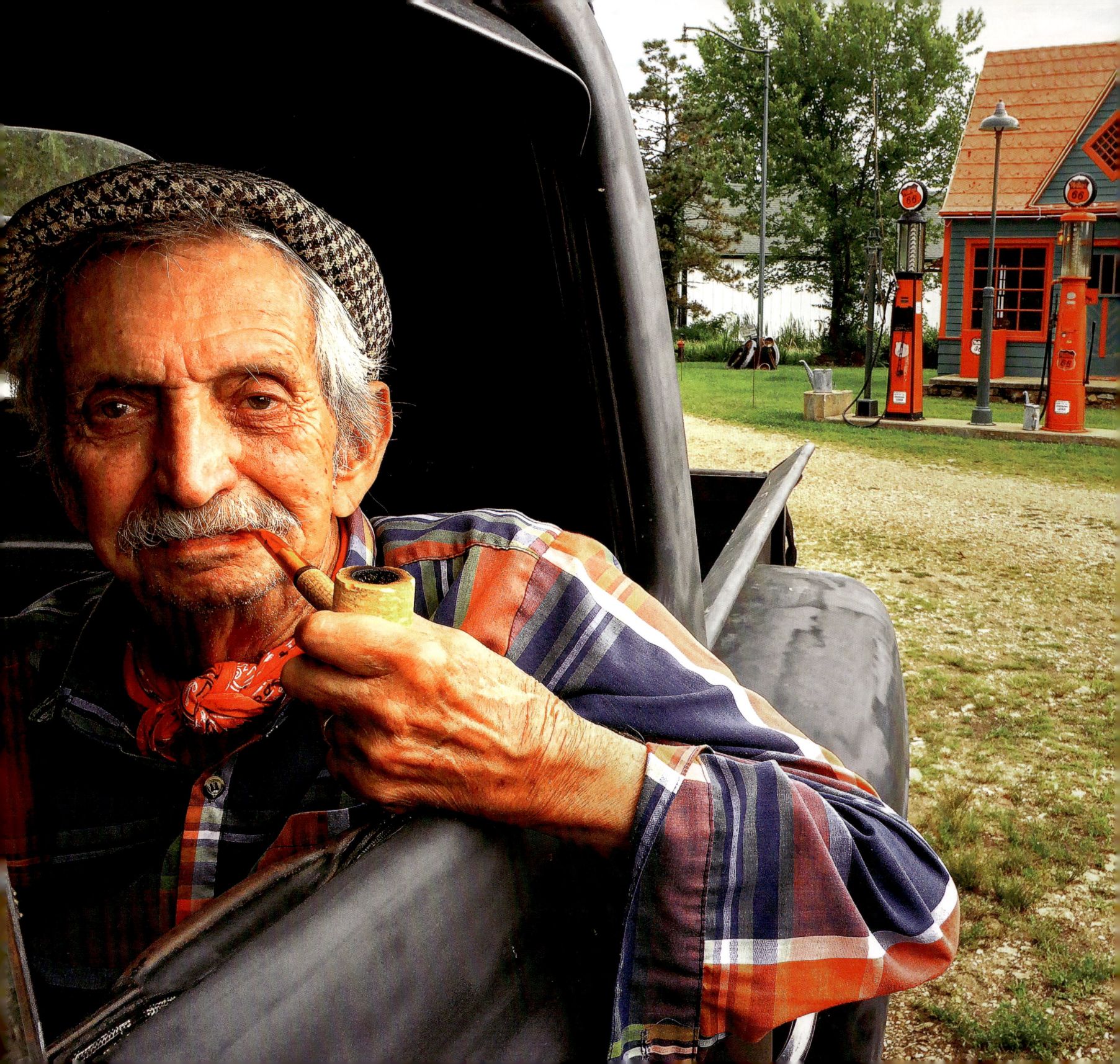

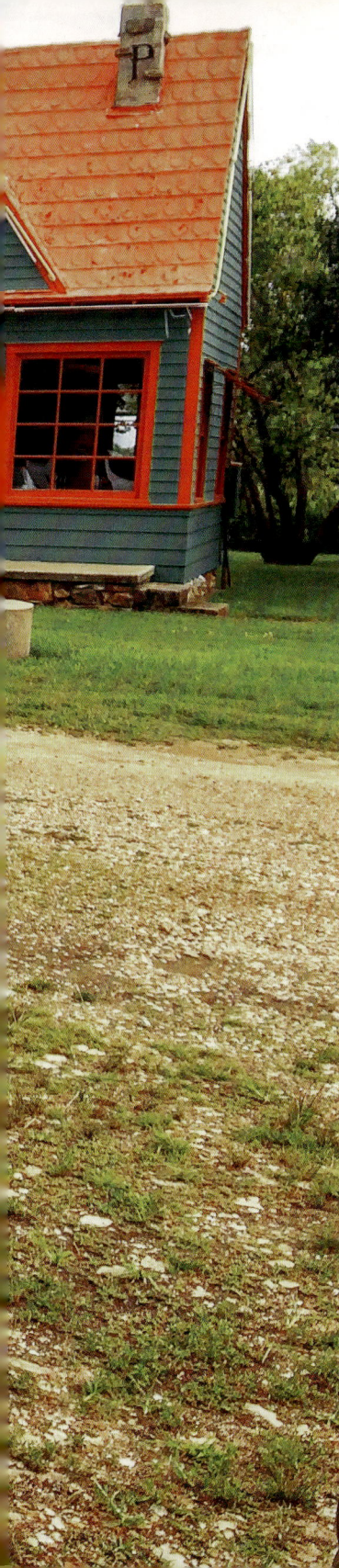

VILLAGE VISIONARY

Carthage, Missouri

Winding its circuitous way across rolling foothills in the Ozarks, the Native-trod Osage Trail, would evolve into telegraph-strung Old Wire Road and, as early twentieth-century farm-to-market thoroughfares began flourishing, these consolidated highways were braided into a newly established Route 66. That iconic national highway, transporting impoverished, dust bowl emigrants to greener pastures nearer the Pacific, unspooled 316 miles of legendary Mother Road pavement across this state of Missouri. Small towns and villages along the route grew as they catered to those fueling, dining, and bedtime needs of a surging motorist trade. Yet the late twentieth century brought a grid of homogenizing interstate highways, stamping highway exits with standardized national franchises. The superhighways bypassed local mom-and-pop establishments while precipitating a melancholic demise of numerous downtown districts, charming hamlets, and an easier, slower pace of living.

Noted corncob-smoking artist Lowell Davis made a reputation creating wistful figurines of that rural life. Desiring a return to basics, he changed gears and departed the fast lane, taking an exit ramp in nostalgic search of his boyhood village. Despairing at his finding a nearly vanished ghost town, he set about purchasing, collecting, or relocating establishments from this and other dying villages in the region, lovingly reassembling them by his farm amongst an empty cornfield. Red Oak II, is an amazingly painstaking, Route 66-era reincarnation that's a palimpsest of his childhood environment. The bucolic village is filled with lovely cottages, lanes, and gardens, helmed by a feed store, schoolhouse, and vintage 1930s Phillips filling station with hand-crank gas pumps, which once provided his family home. Possessing a world of wisdom in his eyes, this visionary creator spent the last days of his life just yards away, residing inside a former house of Belle Starr, an Annie Oakley rival and bandit outlaw consorting with Jesse James during bank robbery sprees. Amongst crowing roosters, Davis was laid to rest in the village cemetery surrounded by his surviving installation art.

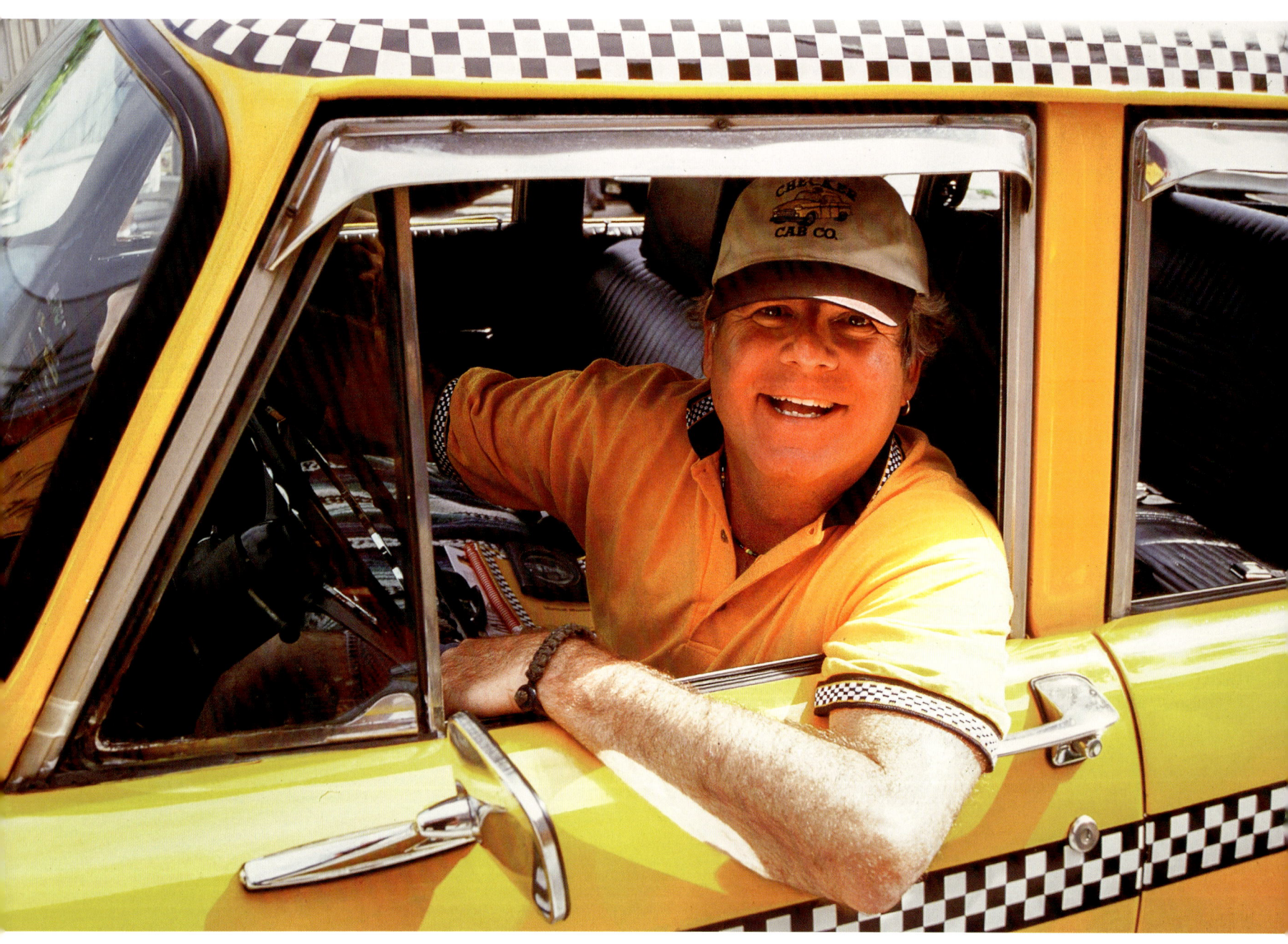

TAXICAB DRIVER

Greenpoint, New York City, New York

Just as the manure-ridden horse-drawn carriage system providing public transport in New York City required more than a touch of modernization, metered, gasoline-powered vehicles picked up their first fare in October 1907. It was the cabriolet, two-wheeled equestrian carriages known for their demonstrated speed, that lent its name to taxicab's second syllable. Originally feared for its recklessness, the very earliest recorded traffic accident in this city involved a taxi. In fact, its drivers suffered from poor reputations as being knowledgeable sources for procuring alcohol and prostitutes, while oft-times transporting pleasure-seeking residents to nearby brothels. During the Great Depression, as supply and demand for taxicabs were thrown out of whack, Mayor La Guardia instituted a medallion system, strictly limiting cab traffic scouting street hails. After the Second World War, drivers in these lemon-colored vehicles were no longer thought to have dubious character, but rather seen as philosophizing oracles, sports team prognosticators, and almanacs of useful information. Out of its Kalamazoo, Michigan, factory, the legendary two-ton, legroom-liberating Marathon vehicle came along in 1960, sporting a checkerboard motif and doorside fare rates. These bulbous yellow Checker taxicabs permeated popular culture through songs and films where Travis Bickle, the antihero of Martin Scorsese's *Taxi Driver*, preceded the sitcom *Taxi*, spotlighting along with its stellar cast, that beloved vehicular behemoth.

Over fifty Checker taxicabs converge for a reunion on Box Street in Brooklyn's industrial neighborhood of Greenpoint. With a scrapbook album boasting taxi snapshots by his side, exuberant driver Philip Arnold takes five, seemingly unconcerned about any running meter. His vintage cab was a roving workhorse and poetic symbol of New York's urban culture, rivaling bagels or pizza as the Big Apple's beloved totem.

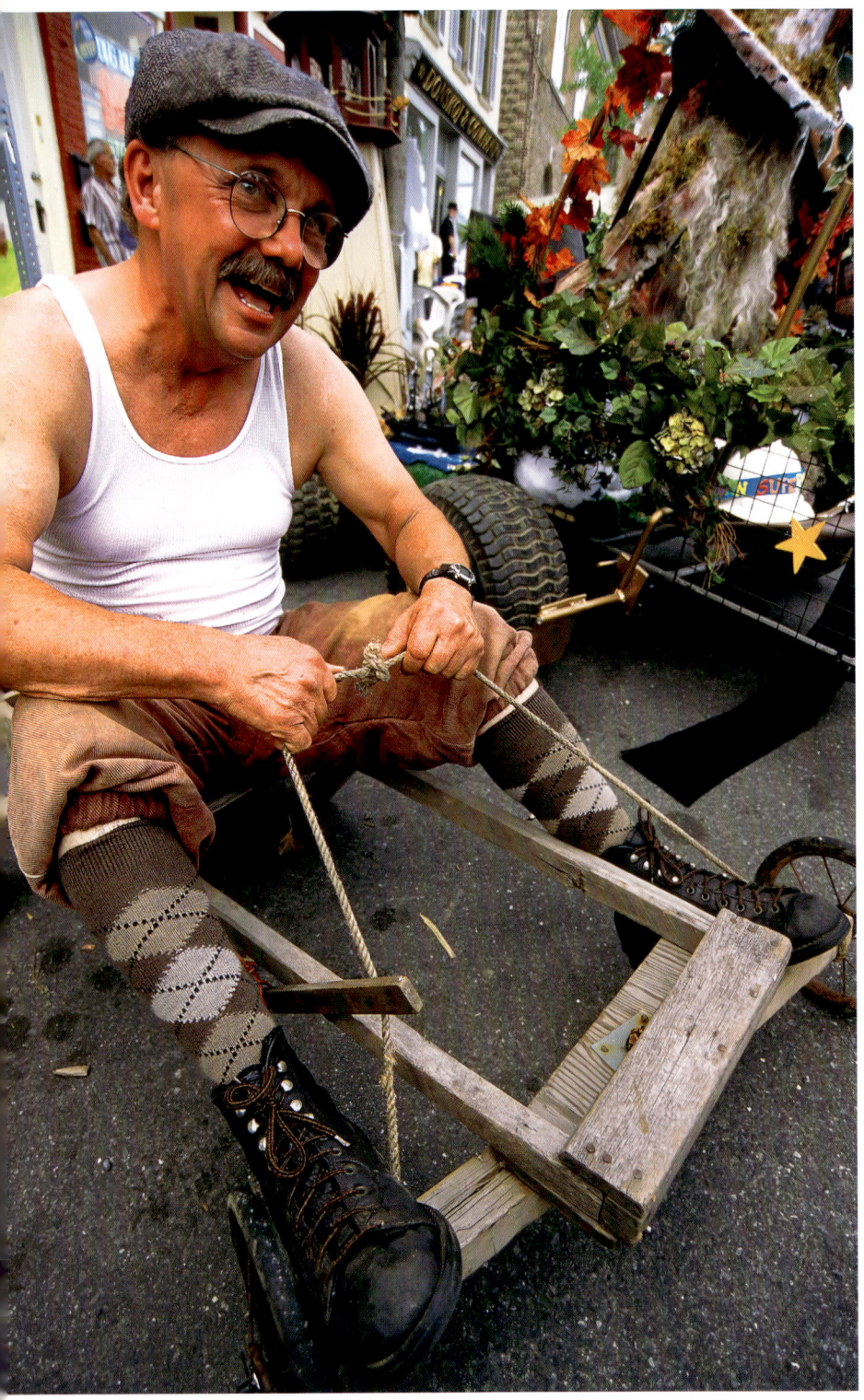

SOAPBOX DERBY CONTESTANT

Kingston, New York

Inventive tinkering must be part of the lifeblood in Dayton, Ohio, where Orville and Wilbur Wright tooled around inside their corner bicycle shop to forge history's earliest operating aircraft. Just a few decades later, that same city offered what might be the planet's first wheel-based gravity sport. The soapbox derby sprung from the childlike wonder of 25-year-old newspaper photographer Myron Scott, who had snapped images picturing six boys piloting handmade pushcarts down Big Hill Road. As was typical during the Great Depression's hardscrabble years, playtime was improvised utilizing jerry-built vehicles that were cobbled together with imagination, discarded pieces of tin, packing cases, soap boxes, or wheels pilfered from baby buggies. That photographer encouraged the children to reassemble with their friends for an event he would host and became amazed by the enlarged fleet of nineteen ragtag vehicles showing up along with their onlooker friends. Scott managed to convince his employer the *Dayton Daily News* to advertise and distribute flyers for yet another event, providing an uplifting story that would buoy their economically hapless readership. Astonishingly, 460 kids wound up taking advantage of gravity and coasted into a cheering crowd packed with 40,000 spectators. Realizing this new craze had exponential potential, he successfully sought corporate sponsorship as the Chevrolet Motor Company created an All-American Soap Box Derby, endowing both this amateur sport and youthful ingenuity for almost four decades. These days, inspired by soapbox derby traditions, aerodynamically designed gravity land speed racers have now achieved speeds of 102 miles an hour without any engines. A far less daredevil, but much more creative, manifestation echoing these early competitions can be found inside workshops of creative Hudson Valley characters preparing for the Kingston Artists Soapbox Derby. A cherished annual tradition for almost three decades, wacky assemblages of motorless, kinetic sculptures careen down Lower Broadway. They'll pass through Rondout Landing's historic shopping district filled by cheering crowds excited to view rolling bathtubs, snapping lobsters, and confetti-shooting cannons battling for their admiration.

Grabbing his reins on a homemade steering system, Marcus "Skippy" Arthur is attired in argyle socks with mid-calf lace up boots and seems to personify a middle-aged reincarnation of the Little Rascals. Ready to roll and launch his rickety transport, this madcap chauffeur must avoid roadway obstructions or vulnerable spectators lining an unusually steep thoroughfare as gravity-fueled mayhem explodes during Kingston's whimsical vehicular spectacle.

TROLLEY CONDUCTOR

East Windsor, Connecticut

Today's mammoth corporate theme parks, drawing through turnstiles millions of admission-paying visitors from around the world, actually owe their genesis to a humble streetcar trolley. During the nineteenth century, trolleys were once a chief mode of public transportation across cities and towns in North America. Before subways were constructed, these surface line railways offered pedestrians a constantly moving street hazard, and helped deliver one legendary moniker to an important major league baseball team that was originally named the Brooklyn Trolley Dodgers. To entice commuter revenue during weekend travel, trolley parks would spring up at the end of a rail line, offering refuge from city heat and growing initially into small carousel-studded lakeside or oceanfront amusement parks. At one such recreation ground along the crashing Atlantic, Coney Island welcomed Luna Park in 1903, providing saltwater fun to visiting throngs of Victorian thrill seekers. As private automobiles started populating highway landscapes, the trolley's significance began its slow decline.

In the Nutmeg State, its Hartford and Springfield line helped connect Upper and Lower Connecticut River Valley, establishing numerous suburban communities throughout this region. Helming his 24-ton 1910 trolley, an elegantly mustachioed conductor deftly applies the handle of a brass controller. Along squeaking rails, the wooden, 40-foot-long cabin is propelled forward as he works through the points of his resistor grid bringing alive both its full 600 volts charged by overhead electrical power, and a nostalgic glimpse into this bygone era of transportation.

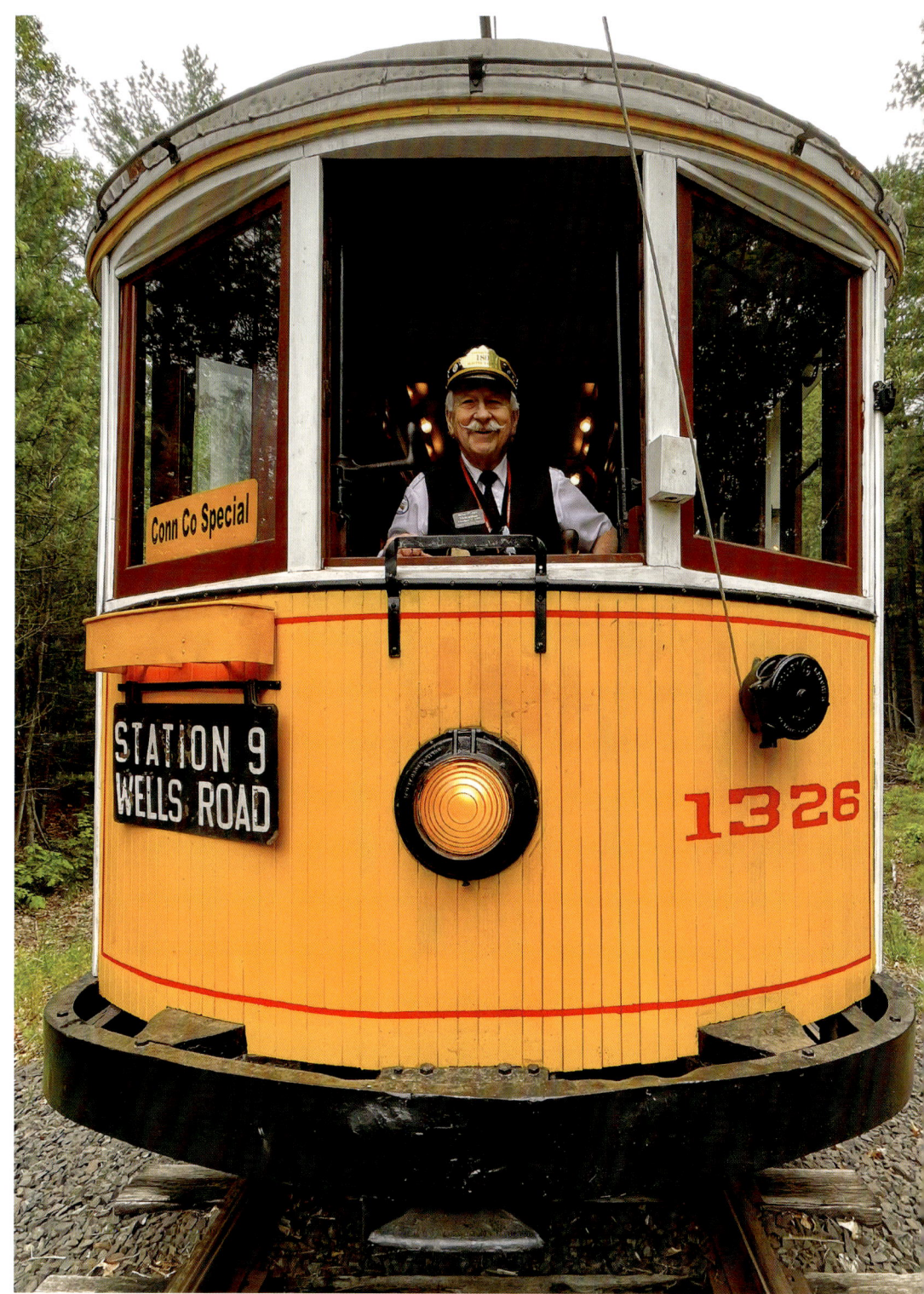

STEAM TRACTION ENGINEER

New Centerville, Pennsylvania

Steam-driven propulsion evolved during America's Industrial Revolution providing a remaining missing link in the steady progress of energy development between human muscle, horsepower, waterpower, wind power, and fuel-powered internal combustion engines. Though that golden age of steam was spread primarily across the nineteenth century, four hundred years earlier, Leonardo da Vinci's sketched papers highlighted his proposed design featuring steam-powered weapons which were operated by hot water's sudden influx into a sealed, red-hot cannon. Steam-powered railways, nautical craft, and even automobiles developed alongside the traction engine, running at 150 pounds of pressure per square inch and helping introduce agriculture to a modernizing revolution. Essentially these vehicles are fire tube boilers that can take hours to heat up because the body holds hundreds of gallons, an idea that supposedly first sparked George Frick's imagination when he watched a tea kettle whistling on his stove. Tractor engines were forerunners to today's tractors, and actually in 1878 were the very first vehicles that ever competed during a road race competition. Often too expensive for private ownership by individual farmers, they were essentially rented from threshermen and rolled into fields, where bundled stooks of grain stood ready for threshing, as their threshers, to minimize fire dangers, were hooked up through long conveyor belts with these steam-powered traction engines.

Keeping alive agricultural traditions, the annual Farmers and Threshermens Jubilee is a huge draw amongst fertile hills stretching across southwestern Pennsylvania. The unusual venue presents horse-drawn threshing, steam-engine plowing, corn shelling and even canine-powered butter churning. After a whistle-blowing grand parade of steam-powered leviathans, this 1912 Frick Eclipse traction engine stands at the ready for its evening's spark shows. Those nocturnal events were worthy fireworks substitutions during holiday celebrations when explosives proved too costly for the farmhouse family. This oil-smudged, heavily gloved steam traction engineer happily awaits sundown besides his vehicle's giant five-foot-high wheels, before opening a valve that feeds steam into the engine. Sawdust would be shoveled onto his firebox while using a prony brake until dazzling streams of glowing embers flow from its towering smokestack and into the night.

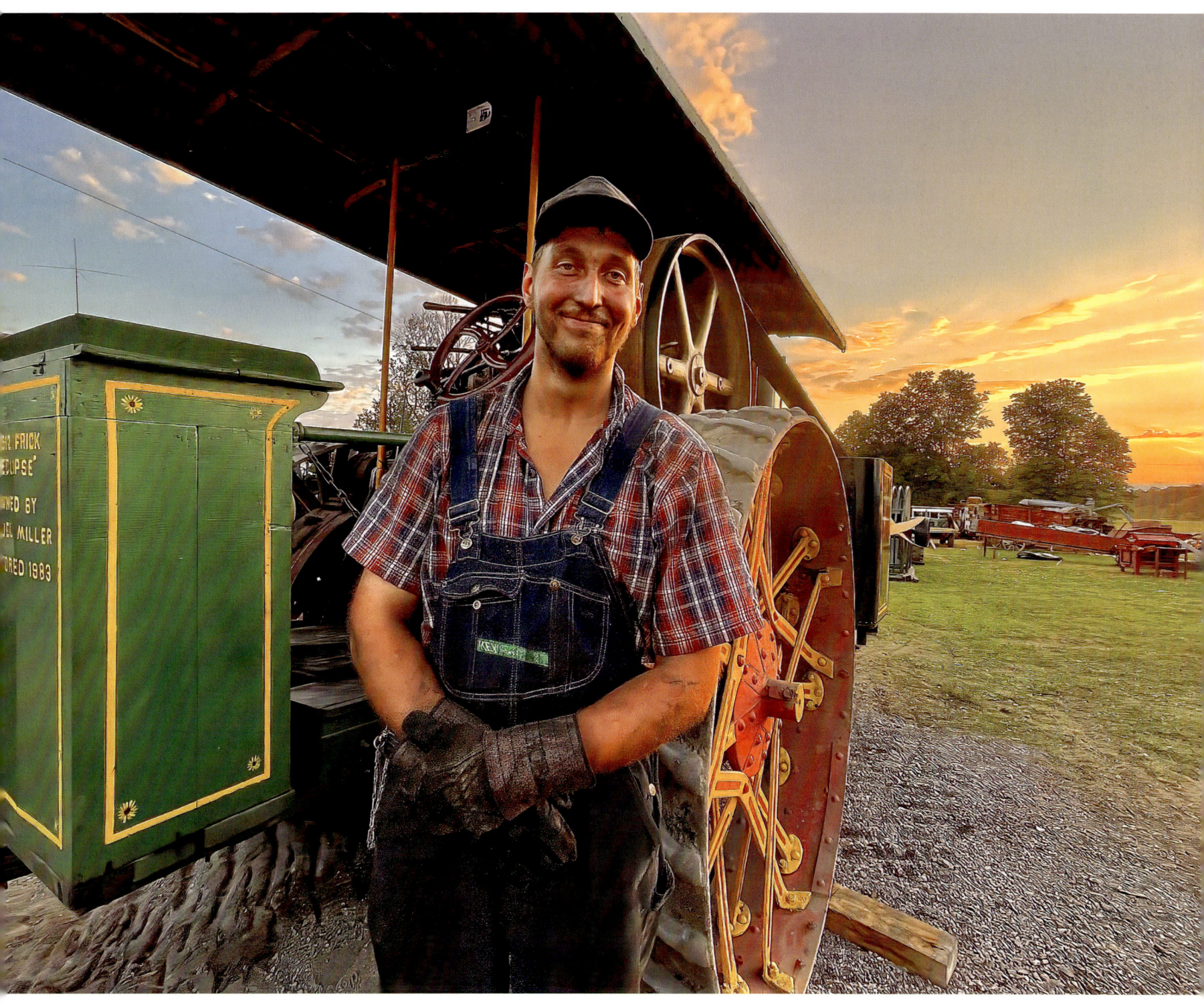

COVERED WAGON TEAMSTER

Flasher, North Dakota

Those upper reaches of North America's longest river provided a major superhighway for early nineteenth-century pioneers. An abundance of industrious beavers or frolicsome otters beside the Missouri's banks sparked a fur trade that prompted exploration by Lewis and Clark along with fortune-seeking adventurers. Waves of resolute pioneer immigrants swept across the rugged grassland in prairie schooners, their overburdened axles jostling beneath canvas-topped, flare-boxed wagons. After a day bouncing down rutted trails and kicking up clouds of dust later washed away while splashing through waist-high creeks, the wooden-wheeled convoy finally grinds to a halt and assumes its defensive circular formation. Today, intrepid travelers still soak in the historical experience, braving ballooning nimbus and violent hailstorms that often dissolve into rainbows lassoing distant cottonwood trees.

Racing sunset, boots are dried out and livestock is corralled as a hungry teamster wearily eyes his chuck wagon, where fragrant smoke will soon dance to the rhythm of an old harmonica's mournful cowboy tune.

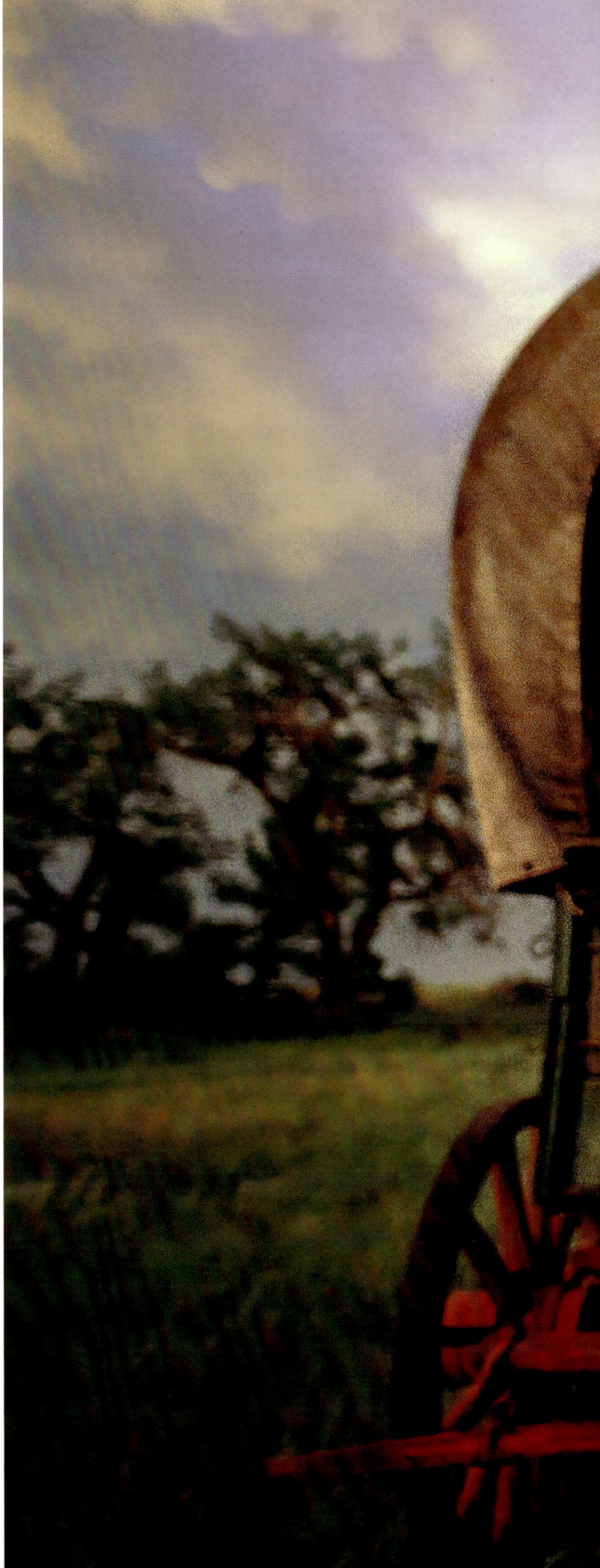

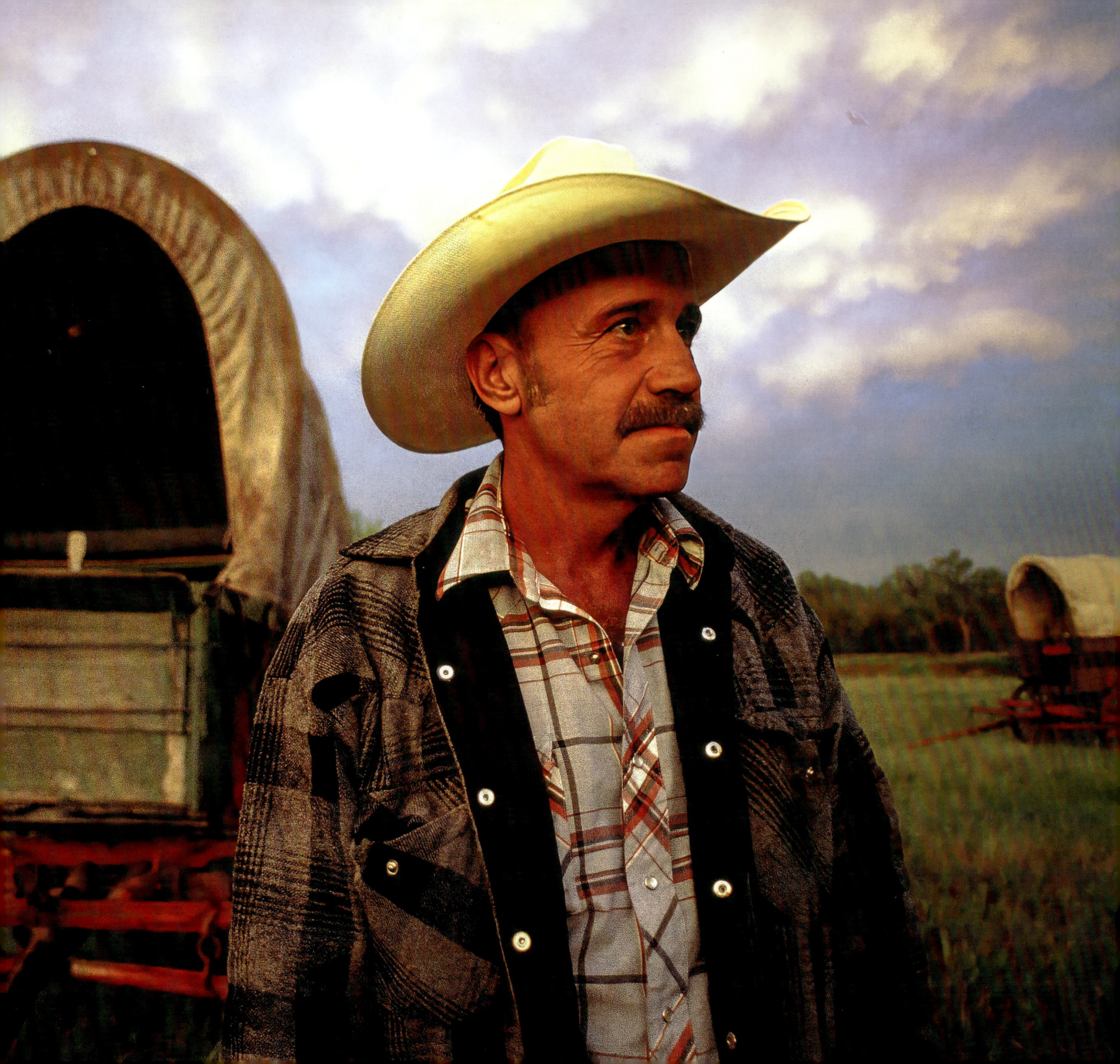

CABLE FERRY DECKHAND

Hatton, Virginia

James River is Virginia's largest and longest waterway, named after England's king during bankside construction of the New World's first English colony. Along its shores, this nation's first Thanksgiving was celebrated in 1619 and the state's present-day and previous capitals both flourished. This liquid turnpike once stitched together an uneven patchwork of plantations, where tobacco hogsheads were loaded by enslaved laborers from creaking wharves for delivery to markets downstream. Later on, that same river serviced the Underground Railroad, helping facilitate numerous escapes from slavery. Hosting church baptisms, Class V whitewater rafting, the east's largest bald eagle roosting site, and and one of earth's busiest harbors, this river is now spanned by nearly sixty bridges along with a few remaining ferries.

Two hundred years ago, there were more than a thousand non-mechanized, human-powered, poled ferries operating all across the country. Today only one remains publicly available, ping ponging its way across the James River. Strictly requiring correct water-level conditions, the steel workhorse is capable of transporting two vehicles and six passengers 700 feet across its sylvan riverine setting, just a hop from Hatton's small general store. Since the 1870s, its creaking wooden gangways access a corrugated deck which has welcomed horse-drawn carriages, pickup trucks, and motorcycles alike while gliding silently only mere inches above rapidly flowing currents. Beneath mackerel skies, a straw-hatted ferryman adjusts his wheeled winch, cable guiding an absolutely motorless flat-bottomed boat. In front of him, poling deckhands strenuously urge their wire-tethered craft toward the opposing shoreline, while keeping a very tight grip on an era that's quickly vanishing.

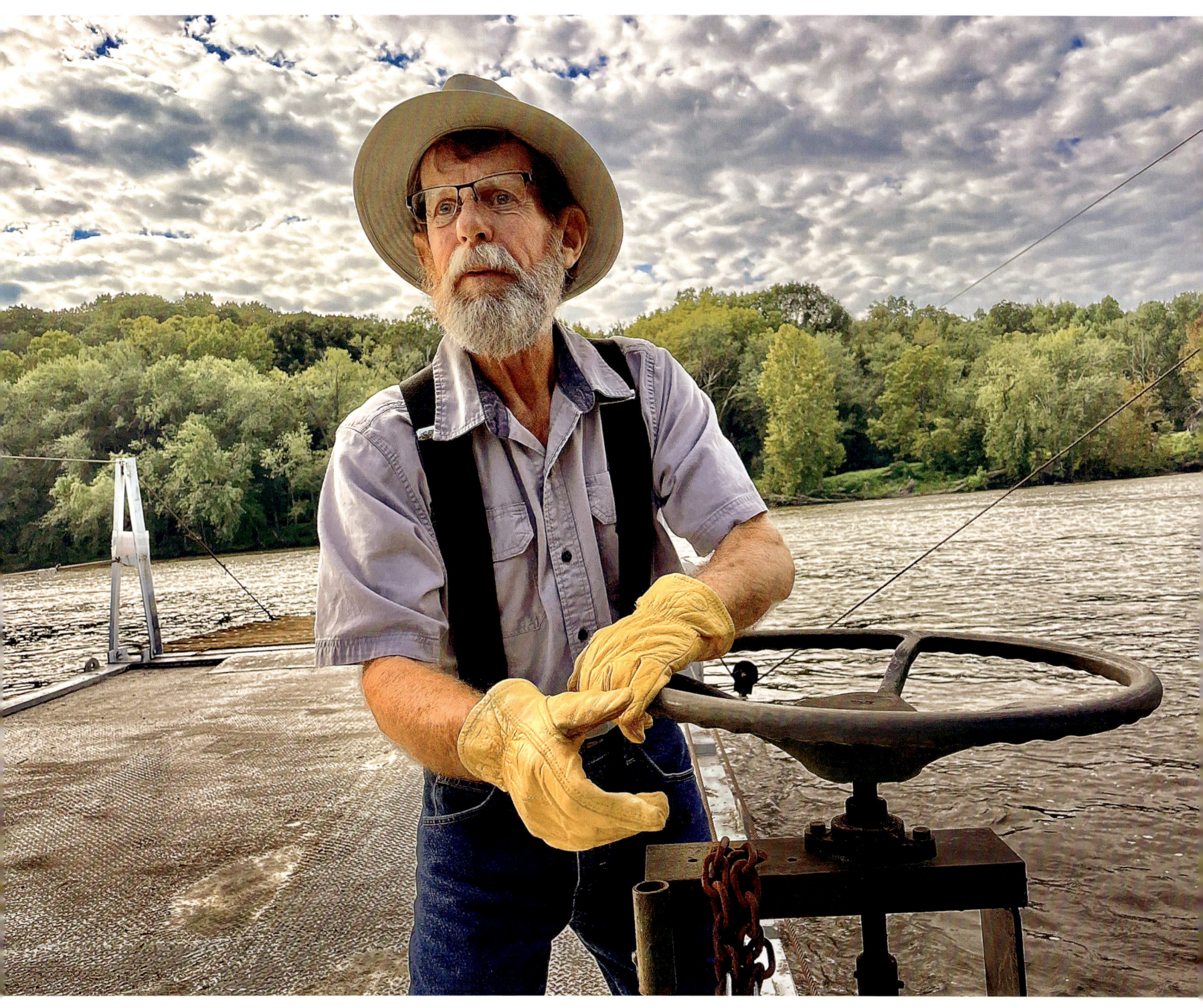

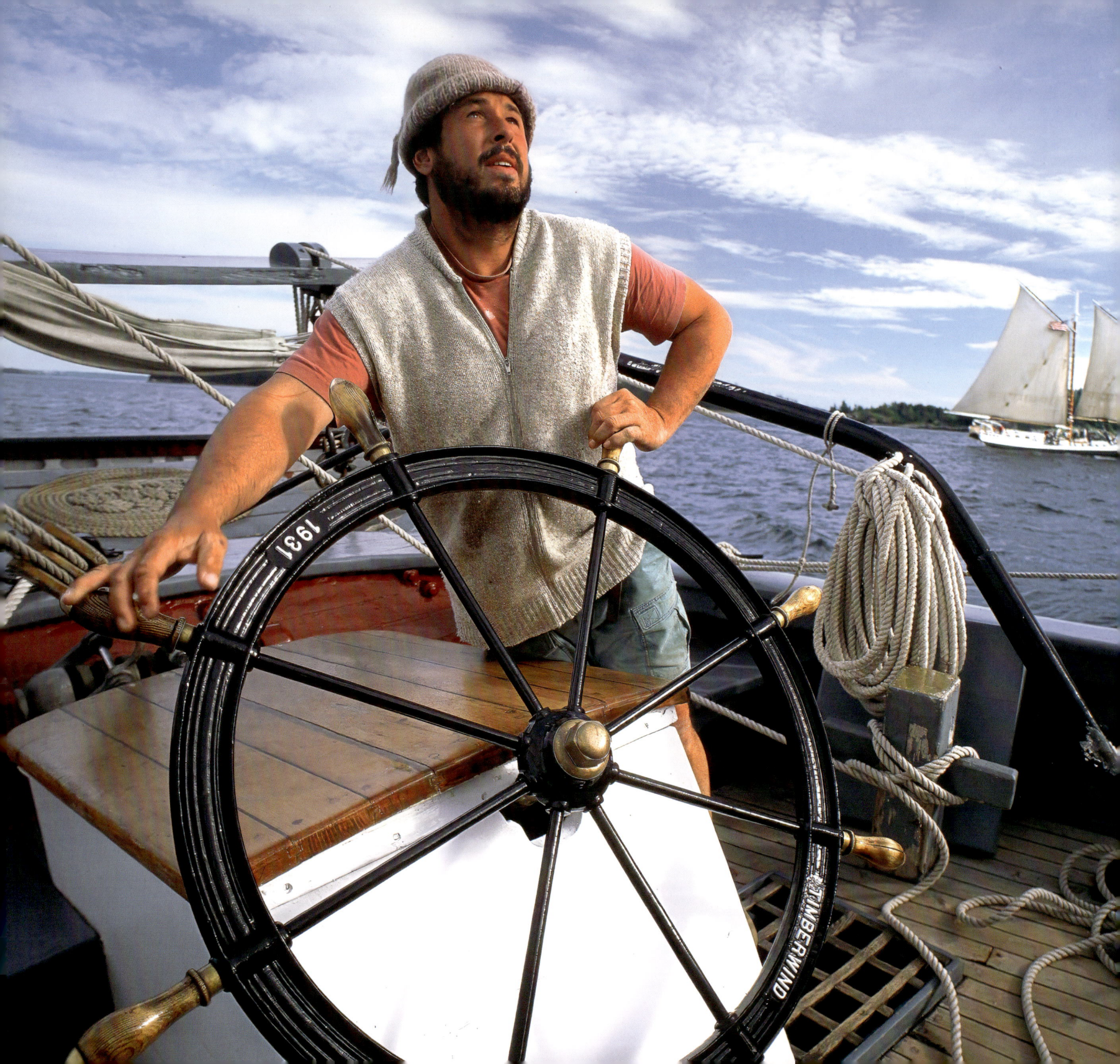

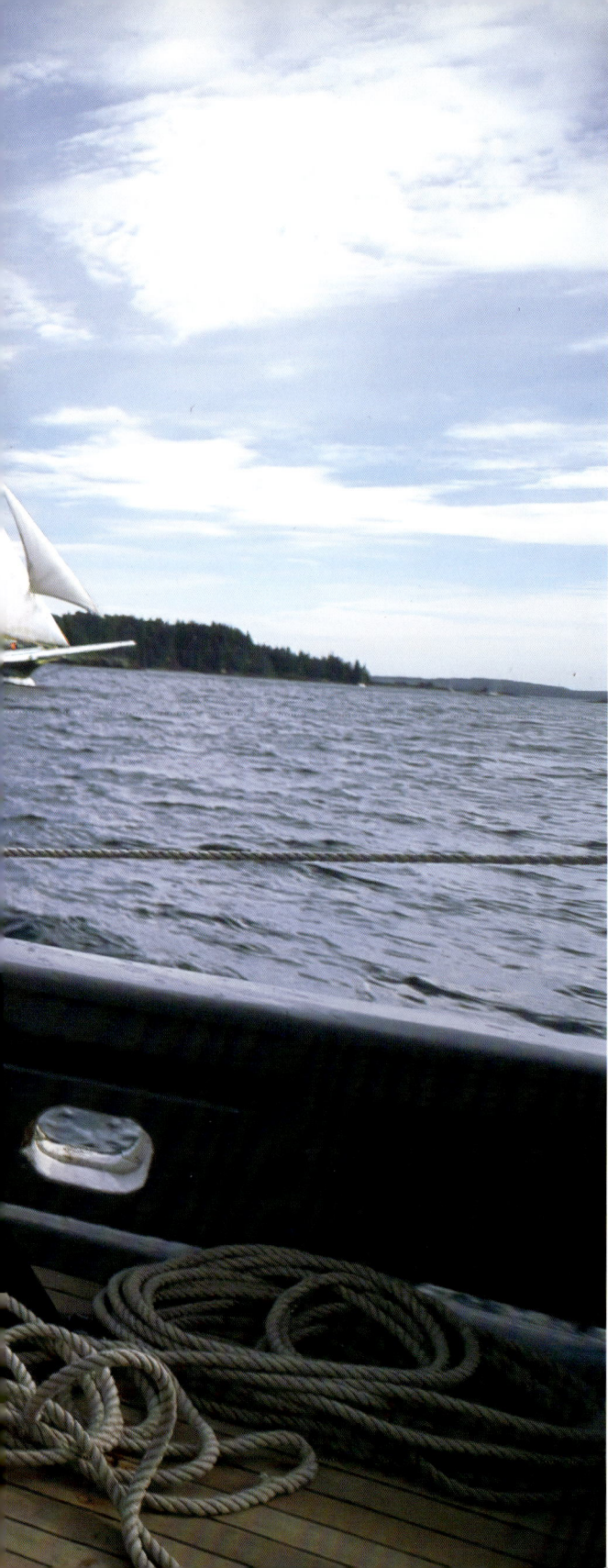

WINDJAMMER CAPTAIN

Penobscot Bay, Maine

Granitic fingers elongating Maine's severely indented shoreline tickles Penobscot Bay and points to one of the world's great sailing grounds. Down East travel gained its nomenclature from prevailing southwest winds which mandated the downwind direction of travel, and for centuries mariners valued that predictable wind-powered current which afforded transport of timber or stone. During the nineteenth century, rich supplies of coastal white pine helped Maine become the number one shipbuilding state in this nation. Meanwhile, so many banks, monuments, and bridges were created by granite, first cut from over a dozen seaside quarries and stowed in the holds of stone sloops or steamers, that modern streetscape filling major eastern cities from Boston to Washington was primarily forged by this valuable cargo shipped on these graceful vessels. Recreational sailors on schooners and classic yachts delight in the bay's diversity of sheltered harbors or secluded coves. These sparkling waters are filled with 200 spruce-clad islands, some decorated by rich colonies of flitting puffins and barking harbor seals.

Beneath cirrus-brushed skies, determined Captain Rick Miles orders an untying of halyards and hoisting all that canvas, as the almost century-old creaking masts on his windjammer *Timberwind* surrender to salty breezes. Steering his course astride another racing historic vessel under full sail adds some maritime pressure, as muscles strain on the heaving crew, their lines rhythmically tugged in syncopation with a catchy sea chanty chorus.

LAND YACHTER

Lancaster, California

Out on vast playas formed in the rain shadow of Sierra Nevada's cracked expanses is El Mirage Dry Lake, which seems to form an endless desert speedway. Tightly interlocking hexagonal polygons of dried mud are ironed smooth by scorching breezes that toss errant tumbleweed dashing toward the distant Shadow Mountains. Drawn by these parched landscapes, an intrepid breed of sailors gathers with their multi-colored land yachts. These sailing vehicles are updated versions of early nineteenth-century wind wagons, which transported workers and their equipment to remote desert gold mines. As blowing currents fill their mainsail, cement-hard ground slides beneath them at speeds of up to sixty miles an hour. They'll skitter across uninterrupted barrens, chasing the horizon's mirage and wafting across this moonscape like errant dandelion spores.

Seeking the holy gale, a courageous terrestrial yachtsman reflects unblinking desert sun which helps to power those intensifying winds. Gloved and fastened into his aluminum craft's bucket seat, he prepares to hitch a daredevil ride on runaway gusts. When captured with adept sailing agility, he might manage to propel his craft at triple the wind's velocity, or perhaps when changing directions teeter that three-wheeled contraption at precarious angles. He'll bravely cavort in casual competitions till sundown when the nighttime racing venue is monopolized by scores of kangaroo rats chased by hungry predators.

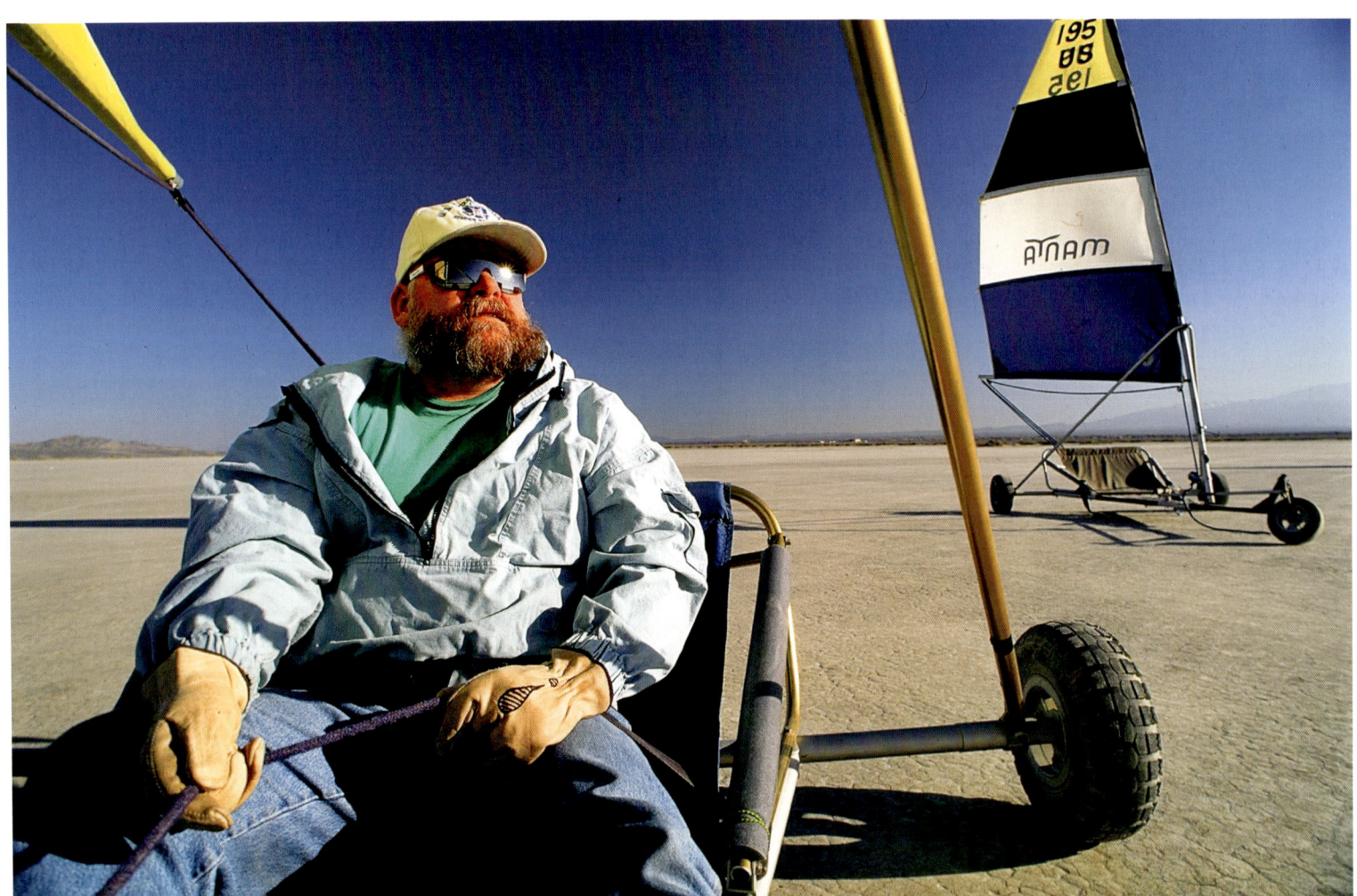

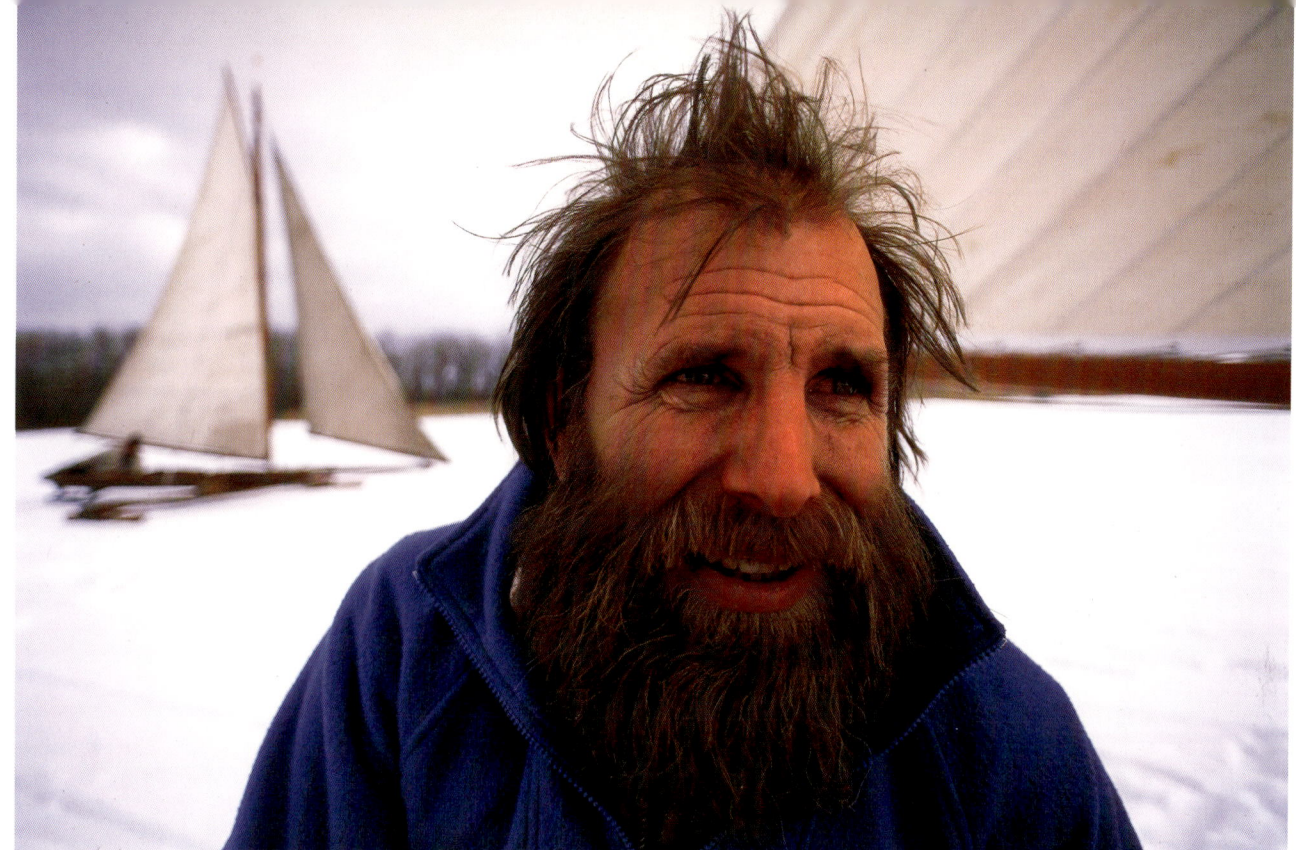

ICE SAILOR

Barrytown, New York

Flying along on blades across icy Dutch canals, iceboaters appear as visions sprouted from both fairy tales and the 1865 classic named *Hans Brinker, or the Silver Skates*. They inspired nineteenth-century Hudson Valley aristocrats who erected conspicuous mansions along the river's edge to suddenly pursue an obsession for iceboats. With a bowsprit and gaff-headed mainsail, these handsome mahogany yachts saluted the graceful lines of their seagoing cousins. Franklin Delano Roosevelt famously helmed his estate's ice yacht *Hawk* across the mansion's frozen riverine backyard in 1905, more than a decade before contracting polio. These days, meticulously restored handcrafted wooden vessels whiz across a solid river during the year's most bitter weeks. Beneath bear-skin throws, a skipper sails at right angles to prevailing winds, sliding over crusty, tide-warped glaze faster than air currents clawing ferociously at the sail. In fact for a brief time before modern aircraft development, these vessels were this planet's fastest transportation, attaining three times the speed of air currents. Out on an immensity of frozen riverfront, kinetic action heats up as wind-chill temperatures plummet and adrenaline-fueled adventurers engage in the world's coldest sport. At full tilt, which sometimes hits almost 100 miles per hour, ice shaved from knife-edged cast iron runners can prick cheeks as vicious gusts snatch tears off eyelashes.

Tousled hair and headwind-blasted complexions accompany iceboat captain John Sperr's insulating beard as he takes a brief warming break from giving free rides to willing throngs while enjoying some Chardonnay by his outdoor stove. Sperr has overseen the Hudson River Ice Yacht Club for forty years, restoring craft, coordinating activities, testing ice conditions, or monitoring weather forecasts, an increasingly fraught challenge as earth continues to warm and threaten this Victorian-era pursuit. When springtime melts yield to nourishing rains, nearby vineyards provide a different valley pastime and an opportunity for advancement of his time-honored viticultural skills.

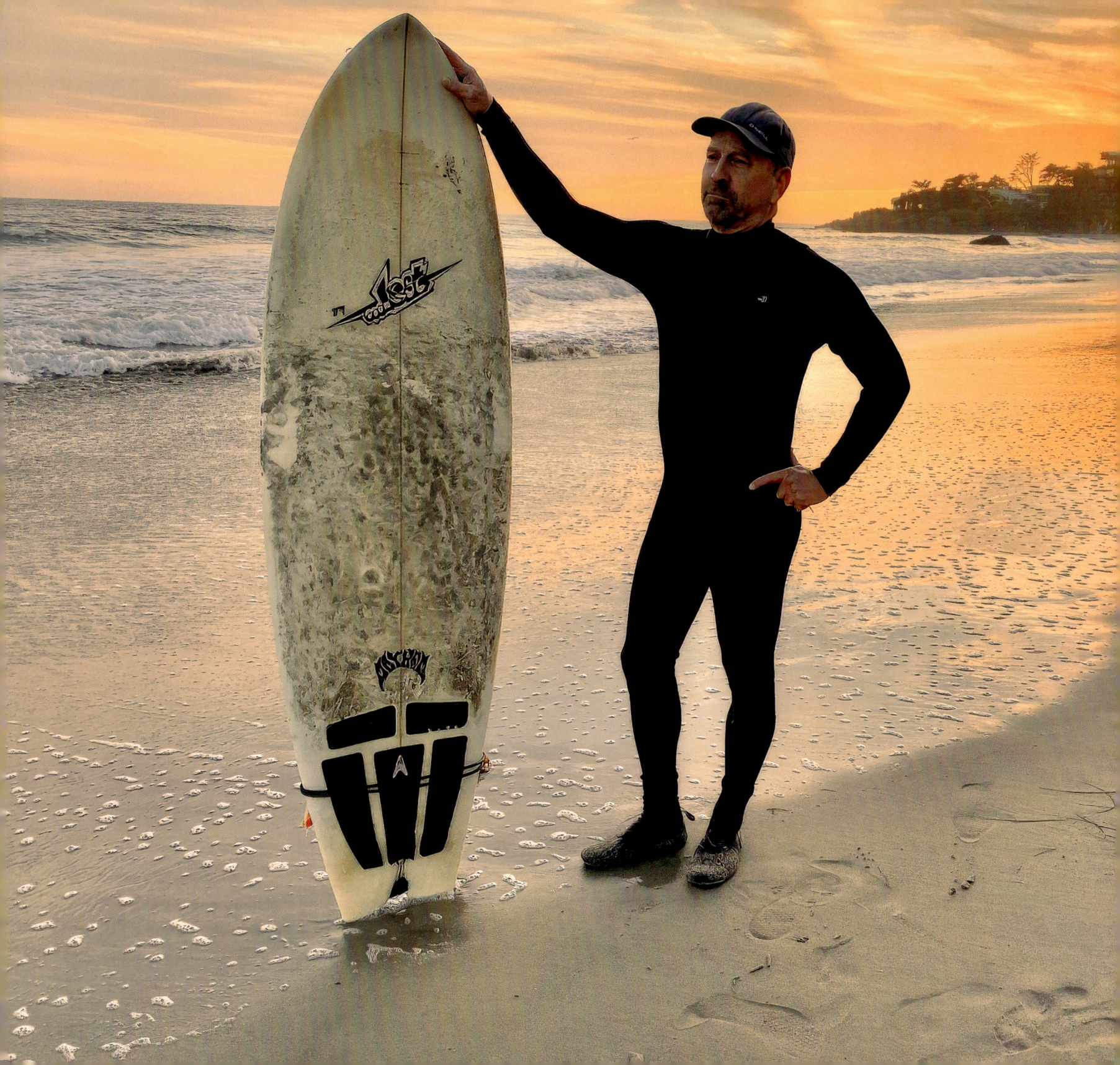

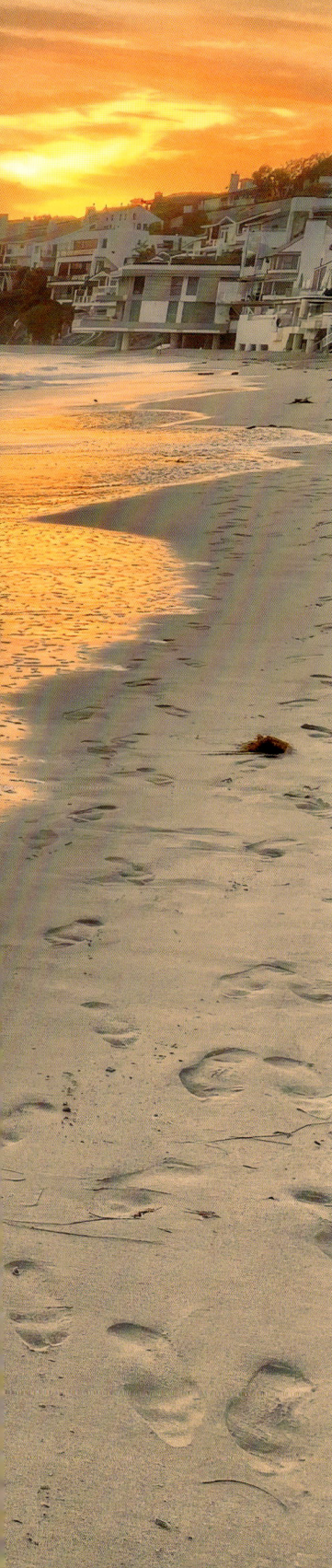

SURFER

Malibu, California

If we listen carefully there's a story of our planet being told by roaring ocean waves that keep licking the shores along Southern California. Water levels are rising as currents shift route directions resulting in changing weather patterns. A quarter million miles away, our moon yanks at the sea with its gravitational tug responsible for tides that rhythmically pulse along their edge. The adrenal glands of surfing aficionados are activated by a syncopated dance with those tides. While ancient sailors learned to exploit wave energy with their boats, that modern art of standing atop surfboards emanates from one apex cornering the Polynesian triangle. Born into a prominent ohana family during the precolonial Kingdom of Hawaii, Duke Kahanamoku trained in Waikiki on traditional olo boards that were fashioned from koa trees and primarily meant for chieftains or kings. Without a fin-like skeg providing directional stability, they were meant to surf huge waves and even tsunamis. Swimming and surfing talents earned him his first gold medal at the 1912 Olympics while heroic rescues of capsized victims completely transformed models for lifeguard recoveries by surfboard. Around that time, California railroad magnate Henry Huntington arranged a publicity stunt demonstrating surfing skills at Huntington Beach, effectively introducing this sport to the mainland. Its notoriety exploded after Hollywood flicks like *Gidget* and were further popularized by infectious surf anthems by the Beach Boys.

The swells in surfer Randy Olson's life journey are fairly circular, like curls of a breaking wave. A marine biologist and scientist who hooked an enviable tenured professorship, he nevertheless drenched himself in a brand-new passion when deciding to relocate across the country, lured by Hollywood's filmmaking possibilities. After graduating from film school there, Olson directed motion pictures that appeared at New York's Tribeca Film Festival including *Sizzle*, the first comedy about global warming . In attempting to bolster a legacy in compelling storytelling, Olson's numerous published books explained his distinctive system for enhancing the effectiveness of narratives. Near the shoreline where *Gidget* was filmed and beneath an O'Neill cap honoring a man who created surf shops and invented neoprene body suits, Olson's driving passions seem most at home on the beach, getting tubed while honing stories of our planet.

BODYBUILDERS

Venice, California

During the Great Depression as unemployment soared, Franklin Roosevelt's New Deal established a Works Progress Administration to create jobs that included construction of exercise and aerobic equipment just south of Santa Monica Pier. The facilities began to attract athletic equilibrists and stunt performers practicing for their scenes in nearby film productions. An earthquake in 1935 created conditions that lured people outdoors, where this site continued growing with regular gymnastic performances, as gawping crowds gathered for the flexing of pecs, glutes, and abs. What eventually became known as Muscle Beach developed into the birthplace of America's physical fitness movement. Startling aerial acrobats and human pyramids displayed their skills as preening show women ripped fat telephone books in half. After attracting mobs of spectators that included television personality "Godfather of Fitness" Jack LaLanne, health club pioneer Vic Tanny, and future gymnasium impresario Joe Gold, this conservative city of Santa Monica purged the increasingly rowdy venue, soon benefiting nearby Venice Beach, almost four miles south. Picking up the mantle, weight pens in this new location retained that notoriety of its earlier incarnation with regular workout visits by Arnold Schwarzenegger, pumping iron and glistening in posing oil during competitions.

Buffed and bronzed in California's late afternoon sunshine, two bodybuilders take a break from their clanking barbells to display eye-popping biceps or bulging pectorals, aspiring for definition along with abdominal striation. Their almost religious devotion to attaining more shredded appearances provides a compelling peek at the narcissistic pop culture of Southern California.

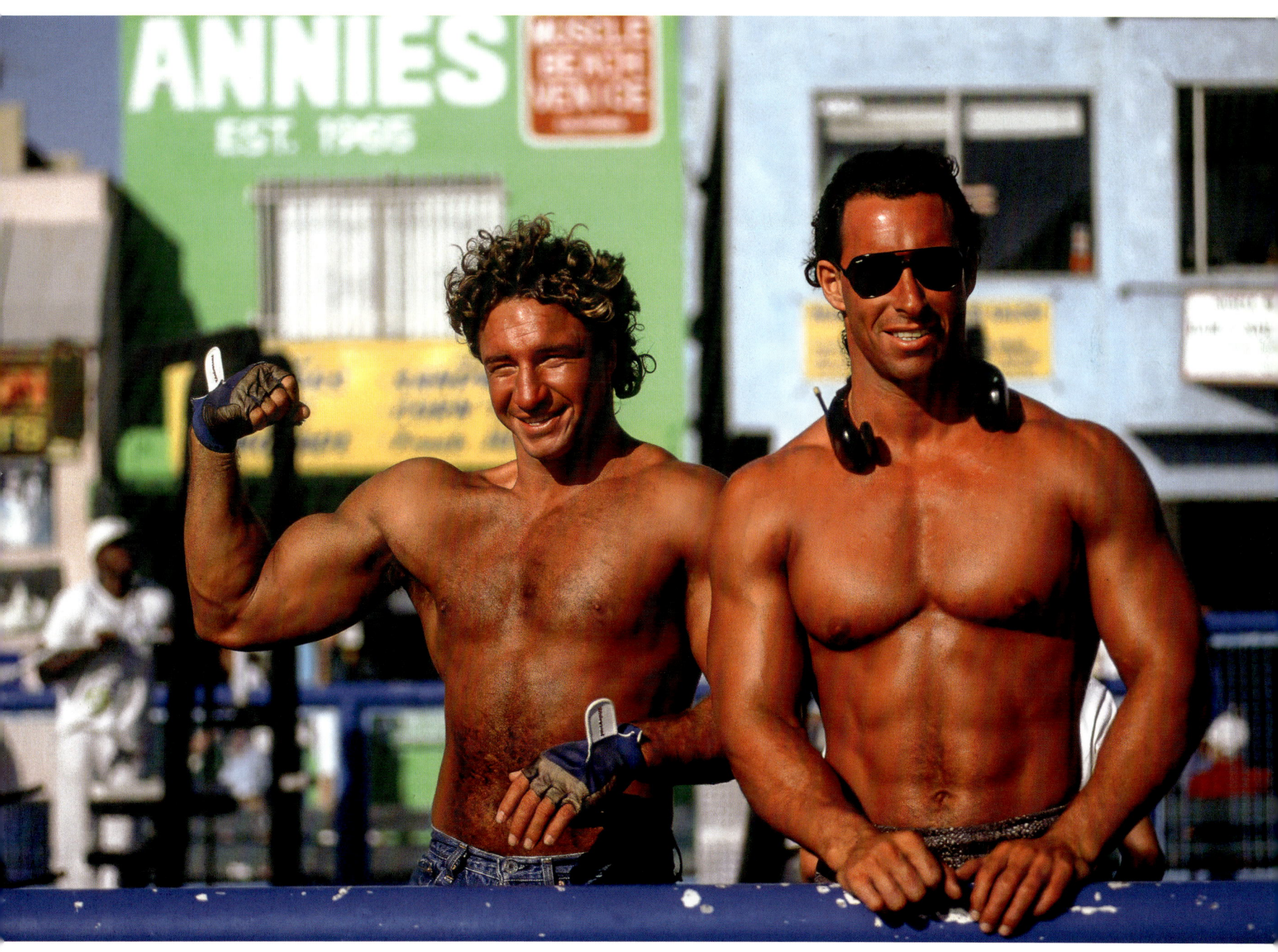

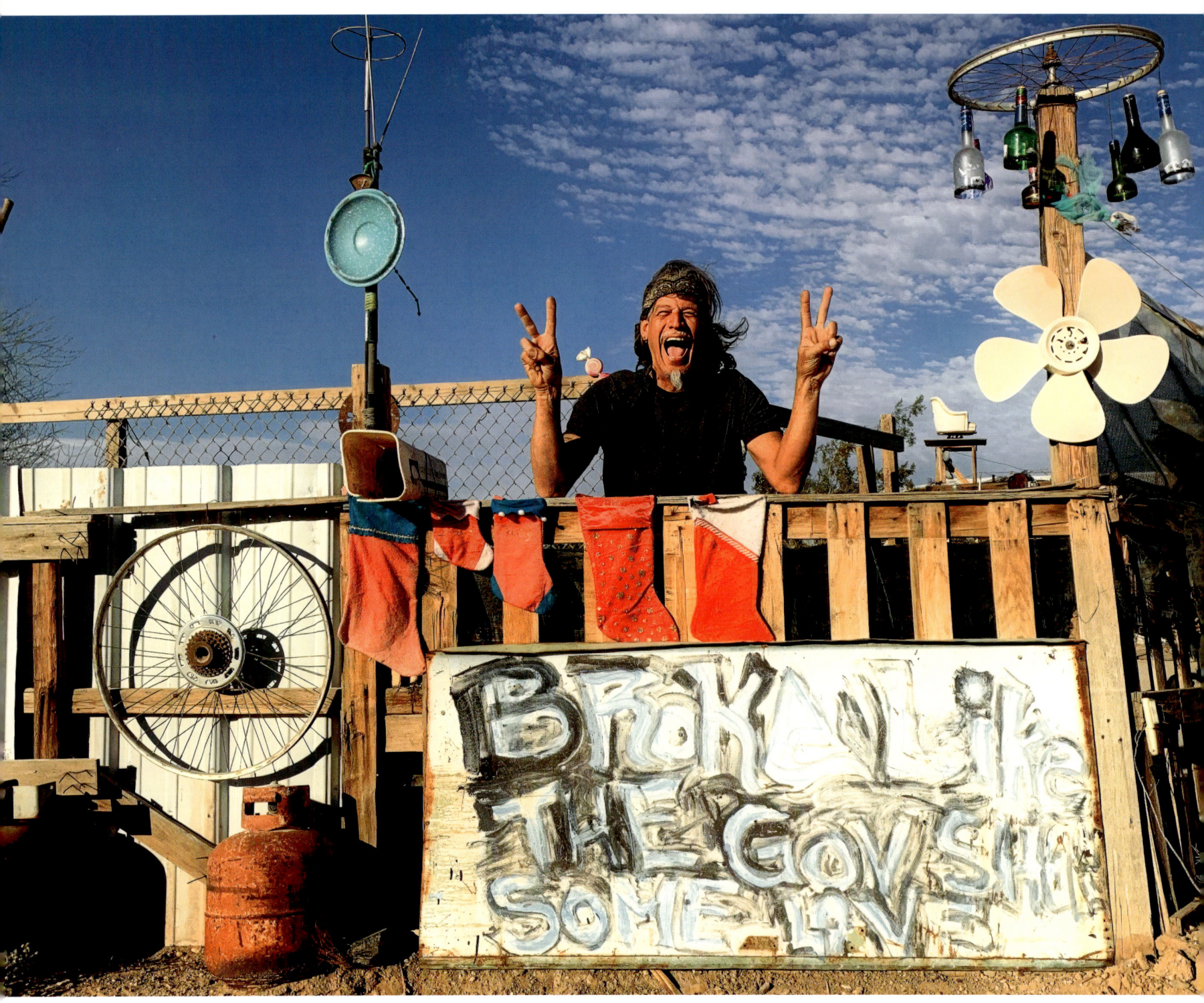

SQUATTER

Slab City, California

As late nineteenth-century frontiers shrank away, an overlay of increasingly modernized and regulation-obsessed civilization expanded to virtually every nook and corner in this country. Visionary loners, disconnected outcasts, and self-segregating pariahs found it increasingly difficult to locate restrictions-free outposts for their own comfortable residential existence. It turned out that many of these misfits of society managed to secrete themselves in a remote corner of the Sonoran Desert in Southern California. When a defunct World War II marine training base, Camp Dunlap, was being torn down, the only traces that remained were old concrete slabs that served as those buildings' footprints. Somehow that locale seemed inviting, even though temperatures might soar to 130 degrees in summer, with no water, plumbing, gas lines, or electricity for support, as squatters, anarchists, drifters, addicts, and outlaws apparently made themselves at home in their beloved 640-acre, heat-scorched wasteland. The allure of an unregulated life, hardships notwithstanding, proved great enough that they were soon joined by retirees, snowbirds, and campers. Their unpoliced utopia nurtured self-styled artists who transformed sandy streets into impromptu outdoor art installations that sometimes doubled as living shelter depending on the configuration of detritus and discarded objects. In this post-apocalyptic haven, tilted telephone poles loom over wooden palettes that are adorned by discarded dolls, old bicycle parts, and broken furniture to create compelling spectacles of desert folk art. An apotheosis of Slab City's artistic development rose on the western edge of town as Salvation Mountain took form with its dazzling polychromed facade, a spiritual fantasyland created over decades by its religious desert rat visionary. Across town, the anarchic suburb East Jesus offers a dizzying jumble of pop art puzzlements awaiting an appreciative audience. As dusk softly approaches and unmerciful daytime heat releases its alarming grip on the 150 or so residents of this community, small coffee shops lure residents out from the shade where an open-air theater space welcomes villagers awaiting evening's musical jam session performances.

Apparently delighted to greet the occasional visitor, this local fixture commands a rickety front deck amidst the trappings of his existence. A hubcap serves as wannabe satellite dish, while his comfy easy chair looks unoccupied atop its aerial podium. Empty stockings seem to await a contribution as his hand-painted sign indicates some reference to impoverishment. A military veteran originally from Puerto Rico who christened himself Caribe, he seems to have adapted into his perspiration-inducing environment, equipped with sweat-mopping bandana and fan blades that perhaps one day could become operational.

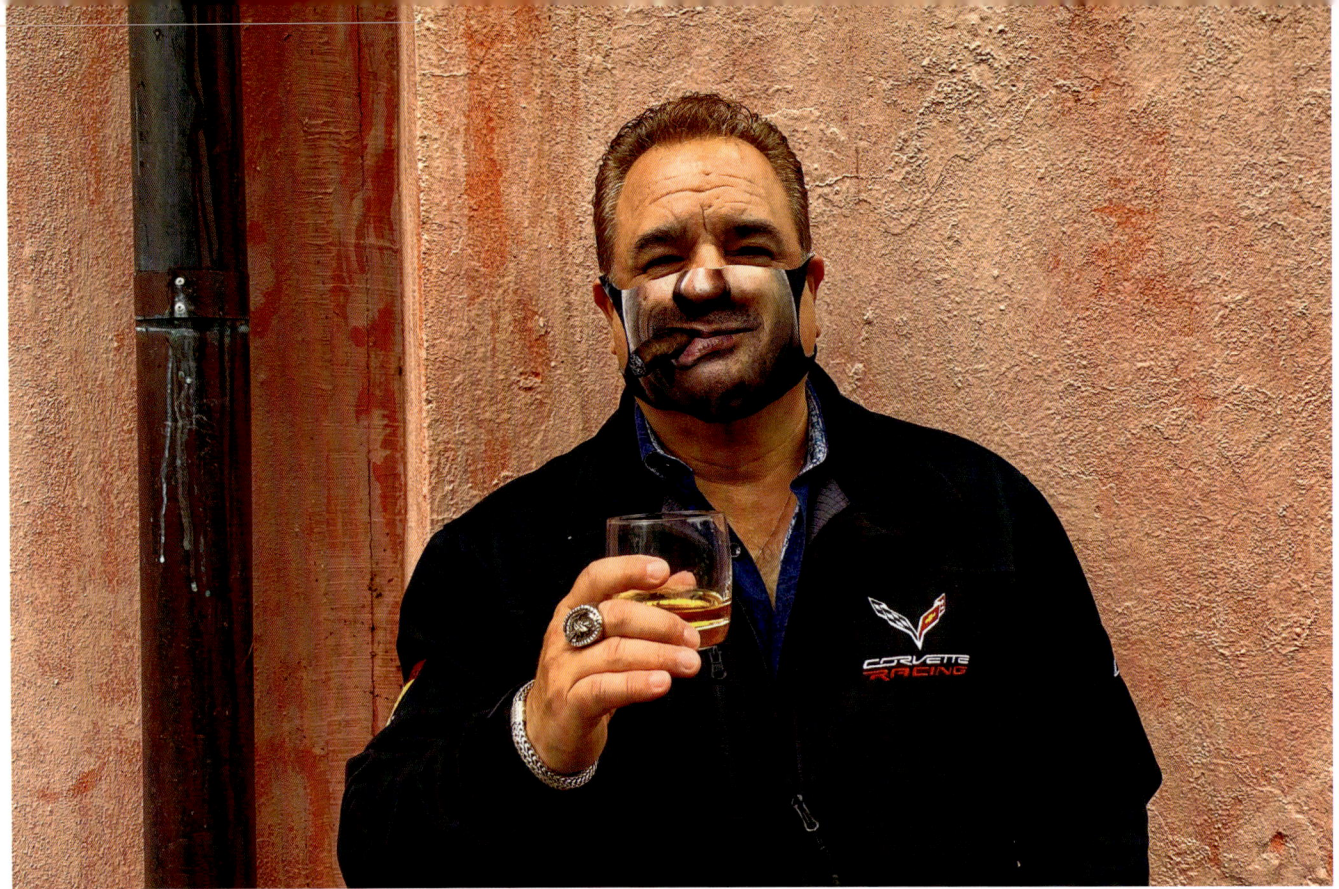

COVID-MASKED RESTAURANT PATRON

Savannah, Georgia

The brilliance of James Oglethorpe's unprecedented design mapping Savannah's park-checkered urban grid has been lauded for promoting both social equity and cooling evapotranspiration effects from vegetation gracing this hot, muggy city. Honoring the inspired genesis of Methodism that was sparked here, a statue honoring John Wesley centers Reynolds Square, one such plot amongst Savannah's twenty-two downtown green spaces. Guarding that square is the 1789 Olde Pink House, one of Georgia's oldest buildings. Its name is derived from red bricks that were long covered in white paint but kept getting stripped by the locality's high humidity, revealing a pinkish hue. Interior challenges were far more concerning. Purportedly, haunted innards housed at least one dozen unleashed ghosts of slaves or servants who labored here atop creaky pine floors spanning some twenty rooms now converted to a famed restaurant. Known for its cornbread fried oysters along with grilled pork tenderloin beneath bourbon molasses, the establishment has survived earthquakes, floods, hurricanes, fires, and Civil War occupations, but recently had to contend with perhaps its greatest challenge yet, an international pandemic of COVID-19. As the nation's 2020 lockdowns, regulations, death tolls and social tensions grew, many dining establishments closed or adapted to outdoor dining.

Beneath pastel exteriors, one masked diner seems to enjoy this restaurant's patio with signature bourbon delivered by a bar manager who has witnessed bottles flying out of their cubbies in the haunted cellar. A racing enthusiast portrays the visual oxymoron that presents itself whenever public protection and personal ingestion meet. Society's daunting years-long monotony plastered behind white facial coverings were occasionally relieved by innovative adaptations like the one here, springing from an idea about nurses comforting bedridden patients with facsimiles of their face printed on masks, surely a bit more nurturing than this cigar-puffing facade.

ROLLER SKATING CARHOPS

West Hollywood, California

Though long promoting contested claims to have invented an onion ring when one of its chefs accidentally dropped a sliver into his bowl of batter, the Pig Stand in Dallas, Texas, certainly made gastronomic history by their earliest known food deliveries to automobiles in 1919 when bow-tied, white-capped curb boys rushed barbecue toward hungry motorists. Car culture's epicurean landmarks quickly shifted to California, the state with America's largest automobile ownership, when Roy Allen created a creamy root beer. With his partner Frank Wright, they opened a Lodi stand in 1923 where tray girls would dash out with frosty mugs to serve thirsty customers waiting inside their vehicles. A&W Root Beer became the nation's first restaurant chain when it started franchising two years later. An explosive growth in highways and their accompanying vehicular patronage ignited demands for drive-ins where intrepid carhops would leap up onto the auto's running board to get a head start on their orders. Mel's Drive-in became a legendary presence on the Californian scene and equipped their busy carhops with roller skates to quicken delivery of their paper-wrapped delicacies jammed onto window-clinging trays. Though fast-food chains began hollowing out drive-in profits, there was a nostalgic revival for these classic eateries when *American Graffiti* appeared in 1973, premiering the first major motion picture directed by George Lucas. This blockbuster was followed that next year by *Happy Days*, the television comedy which first introduced The Fonz. Both featured Mel's Drive-in during numerous scenes and helped cement its reputation as a fiercely romantic 1950s evocation.

Beneath palm trees and the poster blue skies of always sunny Southern California, sunglasses shield two knee-high sock-wearing carhops hoisting miniature 1957 Ford Fairlane Skyliners while enjoying a Sunset Strip moment with their tightly clad friend. The 1962 Googie architecture announcing Mel's 24-hour operations is a much noted mid-century building style featuring upswept rooflines, swooping parabolas, and space age signage. It was named after an eponymous coffee shop less than a mile away on the very same Sunset Boulevard where some Buick Roadmaster or Chevy Aerosedan is cruising for another meal.

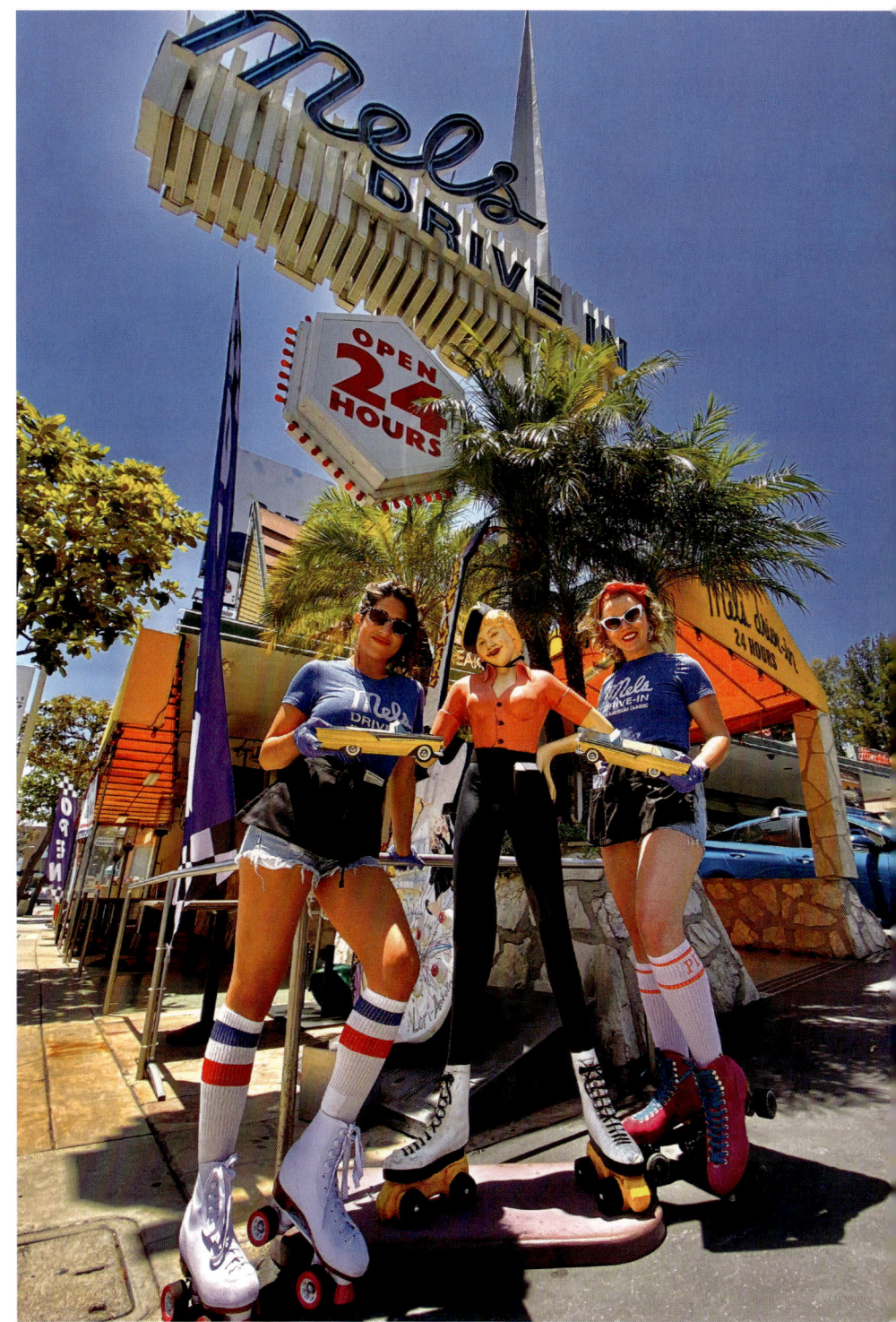

SWEDISH WAITSTAFF

Sister Bay, Wisconsin

Halfway between our North Pole and earth's equator while crowning Wisconsin's northeastern-most tip, the largest Icelandic settlement in this nation is on tiny Washington Island. A Danish dance hall operator here kept his business thriving during Prohibition by purveying his Angostura bitters as a stomach tonic, and Nelsen's Hall to this day has been the world's largest dispenser of that spirit. The isle is a mere dot topping an upside down-shaped exclamation point of land that comprises Door County. It received its name when Native Potawatomi casualties convinced residents that perilous straits separating this island from the mainland should be considered Death's Door. The passage claimed 275 shipwrecks from rocky shores battered with the kind of changing winds and swirling currents which would have found a medicinal drink mighty handy. Maritime disasters here have reputedly promulgated more lighthouses per mile than anywhere else in the contiguous states. This skinny Scandinavian-infused peninsula separates aptly named Green Bay, earth's largest freshwater estuary, from the rest of Lake Michigan. Dotted by Norwegian stave churches and farm stands offering lingonberry or cherry jams, this place is a bucolic evocation of the Nordic world. A leisurely motor journey across the county reveals deeply ancestral ties like Danish gnomes and Norwegian trolls that speckle this landscape. Winding country roads pass traditionally carved Dala horses before converging on Baileys Harbor where the White Gull Inn has regularly performed Scandinavian fish boils for over a century. During this theatrical outdoor dining ritual, bubbling cauldrons host chunks of red potatoes and fresh whitefish that are brought to a kerosene-sparked fiery explosion, spilling the fish oils and creating perfect mouthwatering morsels. Rustic cabins at nearby Little Sweden Resort in Fish Creek precede the decidedly storybook village of Ephraim known for their Norwegian Fyr Bal festival. It celebrates a midsummer solstice where flower-bedecked hair swirls atop Nordic dancers before an immense effigy-burning bonfire, lit by their Viking chieftain and roaring away along its shoreline. Just up the road is Sister Bay, anchored by one renowned livestock-capped eatery that presents a delectable roster of Sweden's gastronomic favorites.

Over at Al Johnson's Swedish Restaurant, decorative rosemaling designs embellish dining rooms where hungry customers consume Swedish meatballs and pancakes or tuck into heaping platters of pyttipanna. Pickled herring and Lake Michigan walleye at this hygge outpost might be followed with sweet notes of molasses-made limpa bread with lingonberry, a native ruby fruit that flavors milkshakes, lemonade, schaum tortes, or their famed flapjacks. What truly distinguishes this gustatory landmark, however, is not the masticating activities beneath its ceiling, but rather eager munching taking place along its rooftop. Up there, a small herd of goats dine on their all-vegetarian menu, trimming errant grass thriving atop the traditional sod roofing. By its ground level entrance, three blonde-haired, dirndl-clad waitstaff beam with joyful amusement from working just underneath the enthusiastic grazing of bleating kids, billy, and nanny goats. After a peaceful overnight at one nearby 40-acre farm, the ungulates return to ascend ramps daily so their performance of caprine activities can play starring roles during eagerly watched webcam viewings.

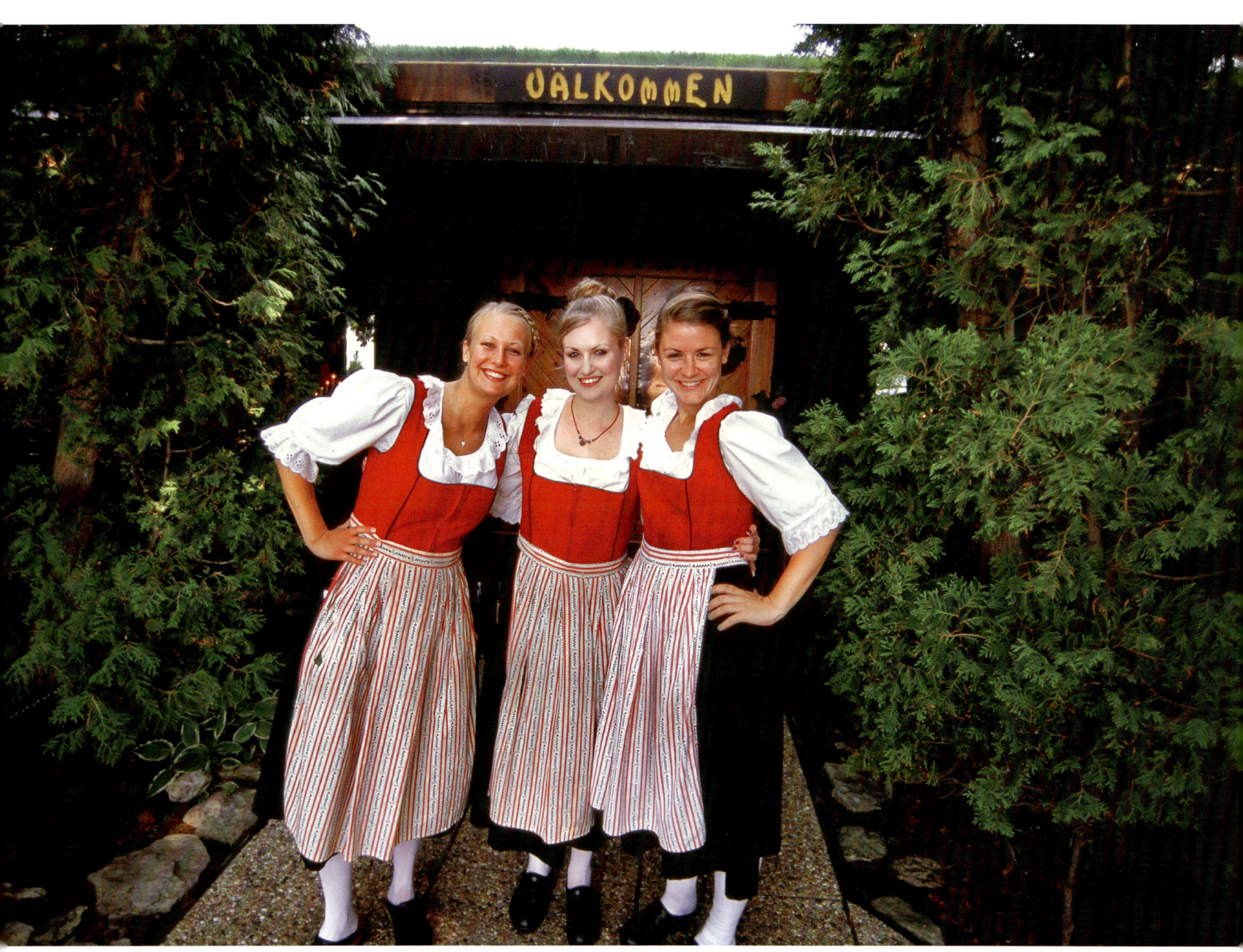

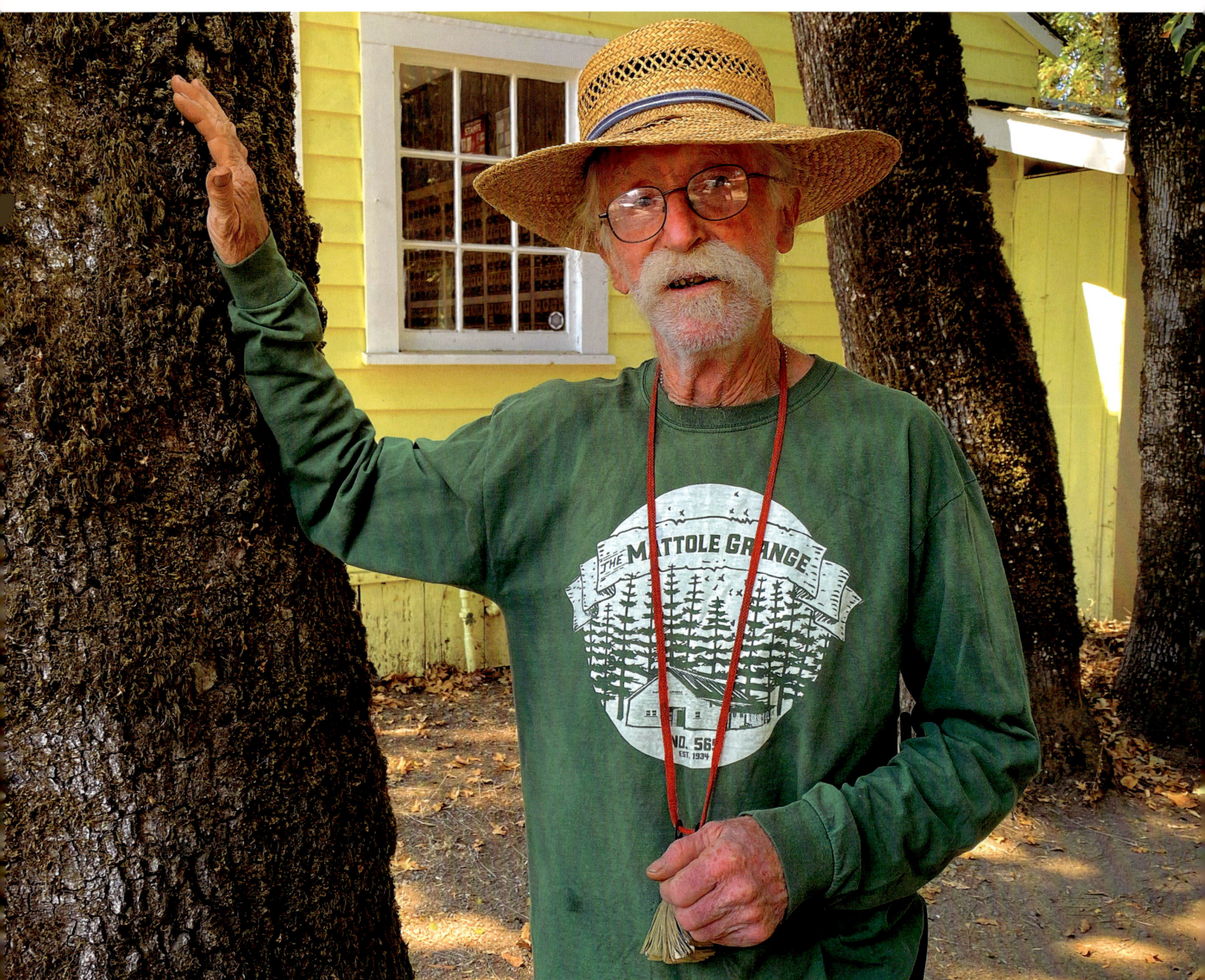

RETIRED POT PRODUCER

Honeydew, California

That most storied, yet third longest coast in this country, California's stunning 840 miles of shoreline is traced by the Pacific Coast Highway providing motorists sweeping views of towering cliffs, craggy sea stacks, dramatic spandrel-arched bridges, and endless golden beaches jammed with surfers or growling elephant seals. Stumping even the most imaginative civil engineers, this shoreline's one interruption of accompanying roadway is along its Lost Coast, an impossibly corrugated stretch known for rugged fog-caressed topography. The primordial Siskiyou wilderness in this region is scratched by waterfalls, dense stands of redwood trees and wandering gangs of majestic Roosevelt Elk. Its relative inaccessibility and few paved roads beckoned a pharmaceutically induced generation populated by self-exiled hippies who fled the squalor inundating San Francisco's psychedelic Haight-Ashbury neighborhood. Here they shoveled their urban culture into a growing Back to the Earth movement. This new rural lifestyle embraced the region's fertility, where cannabis plants thrived amidst a terroir of cool coastal climate and rich, nutrient-dense volcanic soil. Proximity to the ocean's salty air only enhanced terpene flavor profiles of this crop. Hidden, off-the-grid homesteads along dirt roads twisting through Humboldt County hosted vegetable and herbal gardens, many cultivating marijuana as part of a thriving covert industry supplying reliable income for their residents. That dizzying horticultural success within this Emerald Triangle created the most flourishing cannabis-growing region in these United States. Subsequently, the Reagan administration's strict crackdown on pot usage in the 1980s drove an active hide-and-seek game with swooping helicopters and stalking federal agents determined to eliminate these clandestine farms amidst perceptions of menacing threats against domestic tranquility. Ironically, this state's 2016 ballot initiative legalizing marijuana usage initially devastated the area's economic engine as black-market prices plummeted, bankrupting cultivators and bud-trimmers, while new legalized operations faced a torrent of suffocating fees and regulations. These days, weed tours usher cannasseurs and tourists alike to explore the high tech agronomic world of pot cultivation.

Just aside a one-lane planked bridge spanning the Mattole River, this self-described retired pot farmer relaxes by an historic wooden-floored general store and post office in Honeydew, one of very few teeny hamlets sprinkled throughout Siskiyou's wilderness. Oddly, wads of cash seem to dangle from the lanyard over his sweatshirt announcing a nearby grange. It catered to growers in this region whose economy once hinged upon tanning bark harvests before being overshadowed by more lucrative enterprises.

PRAIRIE LEK GUARDIAN

Wray, Colorado

Indigenous peoples across the heartland of America once thrived amongst immense tallgrass prairie where 60 million bison freely grazed and cultivated their land. Discoveries of gold out west lured white frontiersmen who flooded the plains in quantities outnumbering native tribes by three to one. Soon work on the first transcontinental railroad was completed, allowing large quantities in both equipment and soldiers to be moved by US Cavalry, who plotted to exterminate buffalo, separating Native people from their source of food or shelter. Homesteading and agricultural development by pioneering settlers further eradicated native tallgrass ecosystems, where other less conspicuous species also shrank in numbers that dramatically endangered their existence. Never migrating, territorial prairie chickens filled fascinating colonies with one of the animal kingdom's strangest mating rituals but are now challenged by increasingly shrinking ancestral leks. These coveted, slightly hilly rises allowed for observation of approaching predators while providing an arena to view their romantic early morning escapades. At dawn's arrival, their haunting murmur of cooing sounds gradually increases in volume, as the greater prairie chicken begins engaging in a dramatic dance competition. When skies start pinkening, males erect hornlike pinnae feathers atop their relatively small heads, as neck plumage seems to swell up with bright orange air sacs resembling an inflated balloon. While producing whooping and cackling calls, they'll pop tail feathers as their feet start furiously stomping the ground at twenty times per second, dancing like their love life depends on it. Then comical, stylized moves display urgent spins halfway in one direction before twirling back to the opposite side. Rapidly strutting quicksteps precede their cackling leaps into the air, confronting other nearby males. Meanwhile, seemingly unimpressed female spectators observe this ruckus from afar while planning out their eventual rendezvous with the most impressive dancer. As an early spring sun continues to rise, those participants slowly wander away from their booming grounds that will remain eerily quiet until the following dawn. Usually located on private ranchlands, these secret patches of virgin prairie are zealously protected and remain unannounced to the general public.

A concerned rancher about to escort some guests for inspection of the nearby ancestral lek, Russ Seward observes his livestock before climbing into an old pickup truck, then enduring some bouncing drives along rut-strewn dirt roads. Beneath towering sky-scratching trees still bare in late March, his ranch house looks out on a spinning Aermotor windmill changing directions as sweeping cirrus clouds hint at gusty winds brushing the Great Plains.

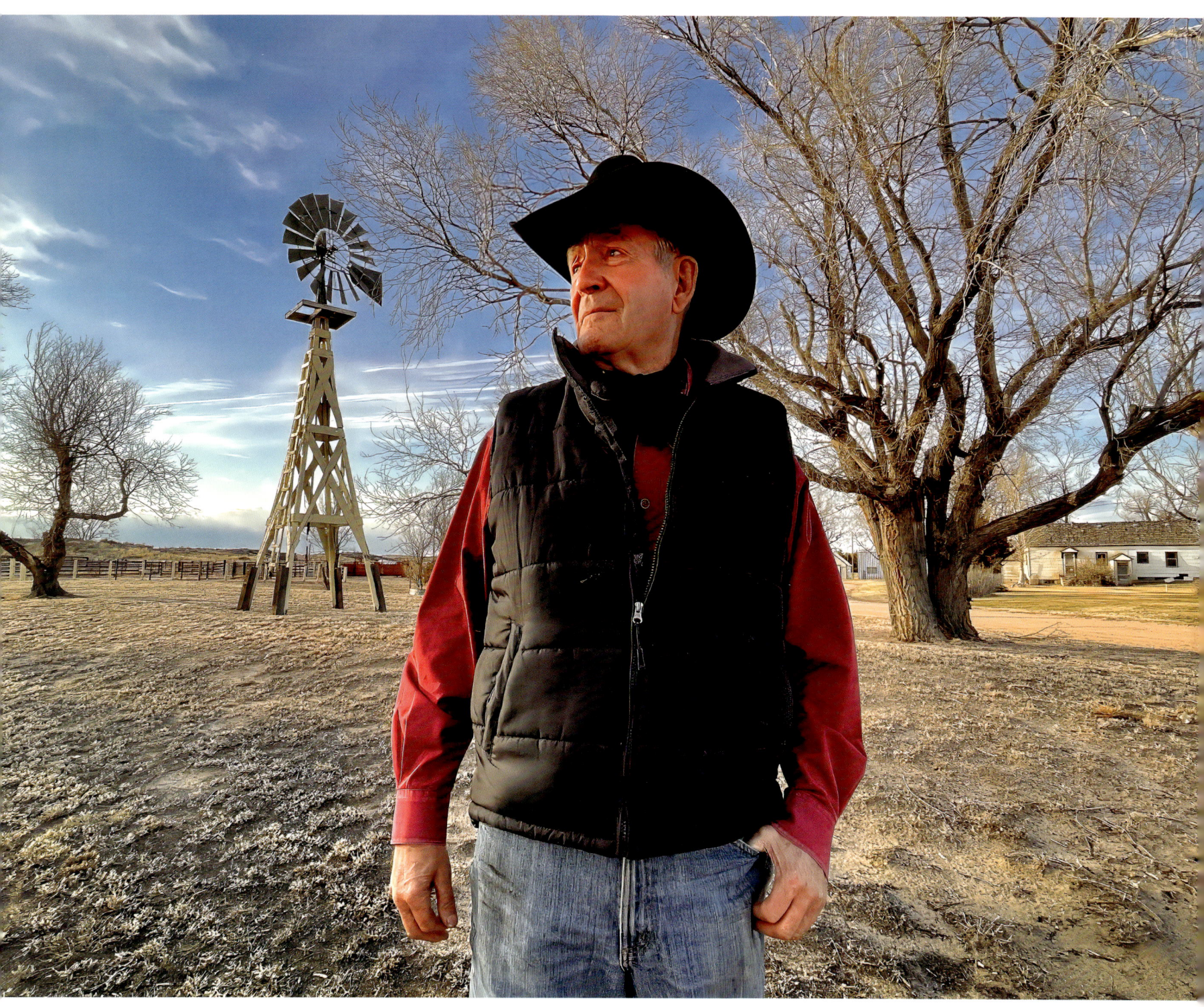

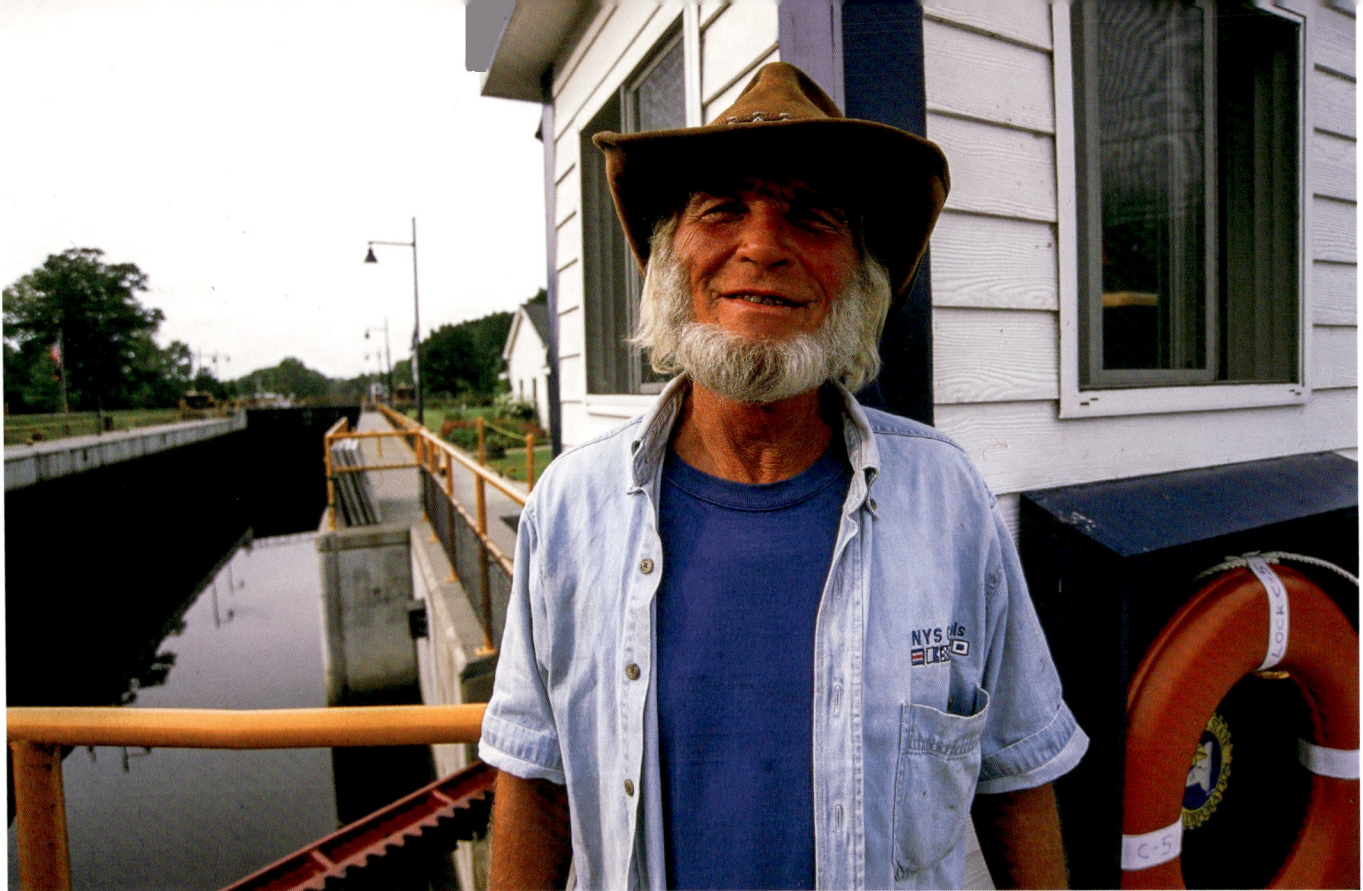

LOCK TENDER

Montezuma, New York

The country's very earliest superhighway connected its Great Lakes to Atlantic waters and helped put on steroids westward expansion across this country. Forging a national identity, the continent's longest artificial waterway provided America's first major triumph of civil engineering. Originally envisioned by an imprisoned, debt-ridden flour merchant, the Erie Canal was seen as a way to rush products to market. Slicing through rocky cliffs, forests, and swamps, the water channels crossed above rivers on aqueducts and lifted boats over hills through a sprawling network connecting eighty-three elevator-like lift locks. This 363-mile liquid passage was at first denigrated as a folly by opponents of then Governor De Witt Clinton, who lent his political muscle to the project. While horses were first employed to pull passenger packets, eventually it was realized that mules led by its crew's children required less grain. Harnessed to their tow rope, the beasts of burden would plod their way alongside a 40-feet-wide ditch filled with water that was often only shoulder height in depth. Though a bit slower, they were capable of hauling freight weighing 30 tons and eventually became the engine of choice. Numerous low bridges crossing the canal inspired a popular 1912 anthem about canal life, imploring travelers enjoying their rooftop perch to avoid decapitation from those structures with only 15-foot-high clearances. An explosion of trade and proliferation of boom towns soon sparked economies across the Empire State, where even today virtually all its major cities naturally lie near paths traced by these original waterways.

Projecting delight behind his chin curtain beard, a canal lock tender awaits the next vessel to enter through miter locks, swinging canal doors first invented by Leonardo da Vinci. Upon the boat's arrival, gates enclosing this maritime chamber will yawn open along ratcheting gears. When the vessel is entirely enclosed inside its watertight container, sluices are opened as water floods in, raising all contents of this rectilinear tub until the craft finally gets disgorged at a higher level. In the meantime, pauses in activity allow some enjoyably quiet moments before that certain arrival of gongoozlers, a delightfully fanciful term describing those who are obsessed with observing details of canal activities.

STATIONMASTER

North Creek, New York

Railroads were once vital lifelines for trade and shipping in the United States, spreading like a cobweb across this country and endowing most towns with at least one train station. In rail's heyday, at least 80,000 depots were actively in use, providing localities with their only connection to the outside world. The stations themselves became mini cathedrals of commerce, social hubs for neighborly interaction and welcoming terminals for visitors and gossip distribution. As avatars for their communities, architects attempted to design train stations as aesthetic works of lovingly crafted art. Regionally distinctive facades would characterize these structures, as architects might employ adobe-coated Spanish Revival styles to sprinkle across southwestern regions or Victorian Gothic's steep rooflines for northeastern areas. In upstate New York an 1872 train depot built in the Stick-Eastlake style capped rural North Creek, filling its need for transporting recently discovered garnet as well as moving hides for a flourishing tannery industry amongst vast, remote stretches of Adirondack wilderness. It was very different cargo, however, that put this tiny station on the map of history. When President William McKinley was shot in 1901 at Buffalo's World's Fair, his Vice President Theodore Roosevelt was alerted while deep in the wilds after summiting Mount Marcy, New York's highest mountain. During a valiant overnight endeavor, he made a 40-mile midnight ride atop an old creaking buckboard wagon on dark, rutted dirt roads through black bear–studded backcountry. Roosevelt arrived just before dawn at North Creek's toylike train station where the monocled leader first learned of McKinley succumbing to his wounds and posthumously handing him the presidency. He then boarded the next train, reaching that site of McKinley's demise and on to a rushed, never photographed inauguration.

These days North Creek's contented stationmaster unwinds with a pipe following an active afternoon of monitoring schedules and maintaining his bejeweled depot. It now cradles historic exhibits about Theodore Roosevelt and the role this station played in seeing him off for the last time as Vice President. This gable-roofed railway depot is one of only 1,000 remaining in the country and continues to stage vintage train journeys or occasional rail bike excursions, a newly hatched adventure where pedal-powered carts spin down forested railway tracks to its trestle bridge crossing over an emergent Hudson River hosting excited whitewater rafters below.

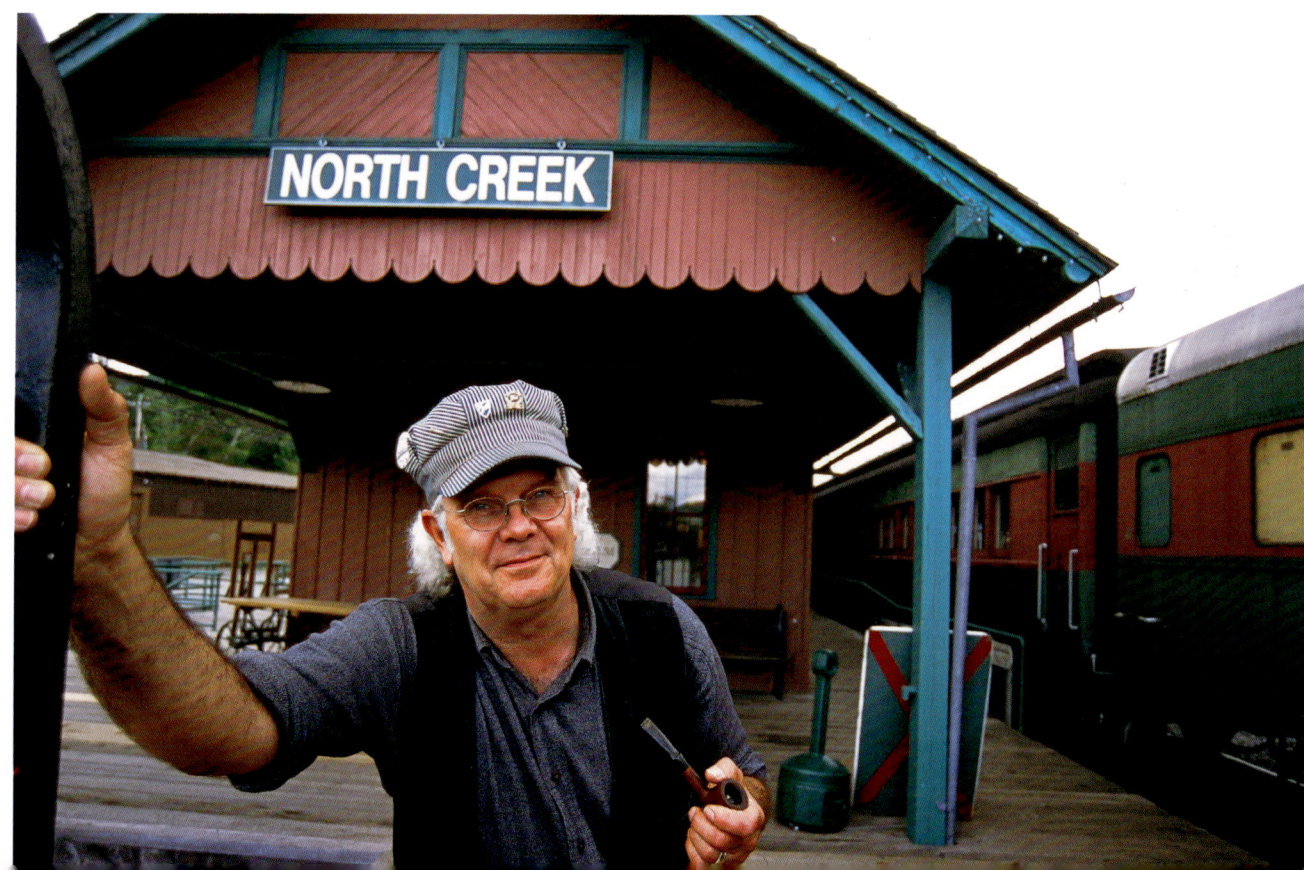

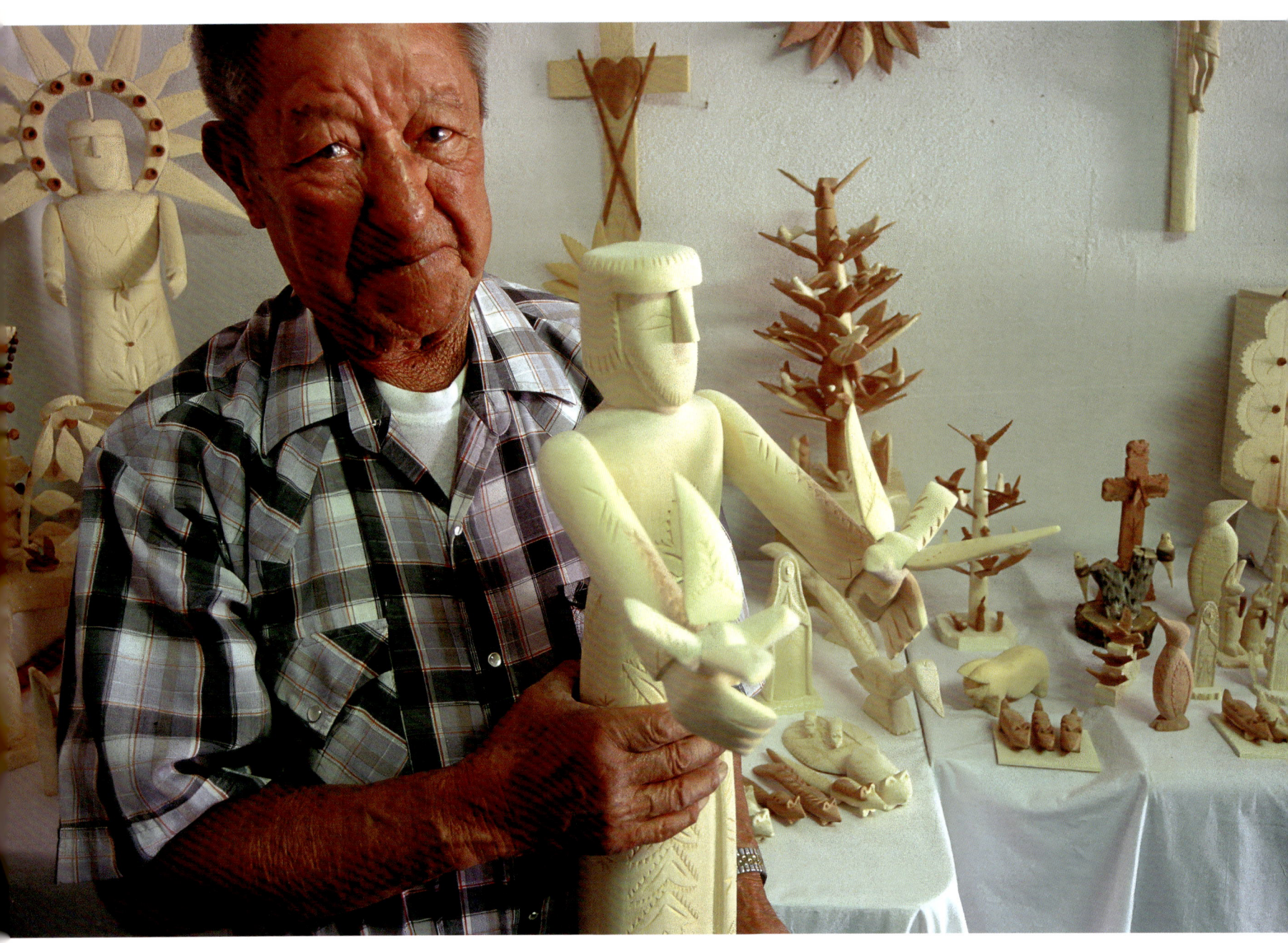

SANTOS CARVER

Cordova, New Mexico

Beneath New Mexico's cerulean, cirrus-brushed skies, a mystically redolent high road to Taos snakes its way along 8,600-foot-high ridges rising toward the snowcapped Sangre de Cristo Mountains. It plunges through fragrant stands of piñon or juniper past remote Spanish colonial villages and Indigenous pueblos. Along its way, mud-baked, centuries-old churches pepper the landscape, most notably two particularly significant spiritual destinations. During Eastertime, Rancho de Chimayó lures this country's largest ritual procession to its sanctuary where devout miracle-hungry pilgrims flock into a dim inner chamber for healing clay soil scooped from El Pozito's floor and meant to be ingested or rubbed on afflicted body parts. At Rancho de Taos, 45 miles north, unadorned, sculpturally striking lines trace St. Francis of Assisi Mission Church as it organically flows from the earth while massive adobe buttresses appear to gesture their support, a vision inspiring both Georgia O'Keeffe's paintings and Ansel Adams's photography. Just off this roadway somewhere between these two palaces of piety, a narrow street's small workshop in Cordova's pocket-sized Hispanic village seems to provide the holy glue connecting hallowed spaces within all these saint-filled edifices. Made there, and reflecting devout Spanish heritage, lovingly carved santos are simple wooden representations of St. Francis grabbing fish or Peter holding keys to heaven. They are made by descendants of celebrated George Lopez, the late patriarch amongst an ever-growing seventh generation that carves santeros. Though his hewn totems are coveted by international museums, many of the whole family's bultos figures are prominently displayed as altar pieces in numerous tiny Catholic chapels all throughout this area. Settled to offer a remote buffer zone protecting northern Mexico's silver-rich treasure from incursions, this mountainous region was among the farthest reaches of Spain's kingdom.

In a small showroom at George Lopez's former home, one family member who picked up the tradition proudly displays an artistry that captures within wood's grain many centuries worth of devotion to Spanish Catholicism. Santeros have religion in their fingertips and are expected to lead an existence of holiness. That weathered hand reveals a lifetime of concerted effort chiseling aspen while breathing an emerging life into his folk-art figures. In artistic styles unknown outside of the Land of Enchantment, santos were originally created to educate prayerful congregations inside their sacred havens about beloved saintly figures and help imbue worshippers with a religious backbone.

TAXIDERMIST

Greenpoint, New York City, New York

Although earliest forms of animal preservation harken back to ancient Egyptians and their expertise with embalming and mummification, they never actually removed skins during the process. Taxidermy literally means movement and rearrangement of skin, often utilizing carved clay or foam molds to replace the innards. Achieving a convincing mimesis of specimens usually requires fleshing tools, scalpels, tweezers, and needles to be employed with surgical precision, while bravely turning the animals inside out. Carefully scooping out brains, excising organs and soft tissue, the repositioned exterior of these creatures seems to offer a second existence with an unrequested chance for immortality. After initial appearances in medieval apothecaries, stuffed animals truly gained currency during the Victorian era which saw private museums and collections featuring an unsettling menagerie of beasts or birds. That may have lured famed naturalist John James Audubon to take up a stint as taxidermist, while explorer Henry Augustus Ward achieved renown preserving bison upon request by Buffalo Bill and elephants for P. T. Barnum.

In her whimsically cramped Greenpoint workshop, Amber Maykut proudly displays impressive ornithological creativity with a playground-strutting species that even unaccomplished birdwatchers should recognize. Behind her an anthropomorphic scurry of poker-playing squirrels, top-hatted mice, or Ouija board-attentive frogs oversee a tableau containing zoological reincarnations featuring Dall sheep, white-tailed deer, and wary raccoons striking their final pose. Often teaching at the Morbid Anatomy Museum, she has lectured at the birthplace of Theodore Roosevelt, who was himself active in taxidermy from the early age of twelve. She proudly utilizes only ethically sourced animals that might arrive from zoos, wildlife refuges, roadkill or even from grieving owners wishing for an alternative to the pet cemetery.

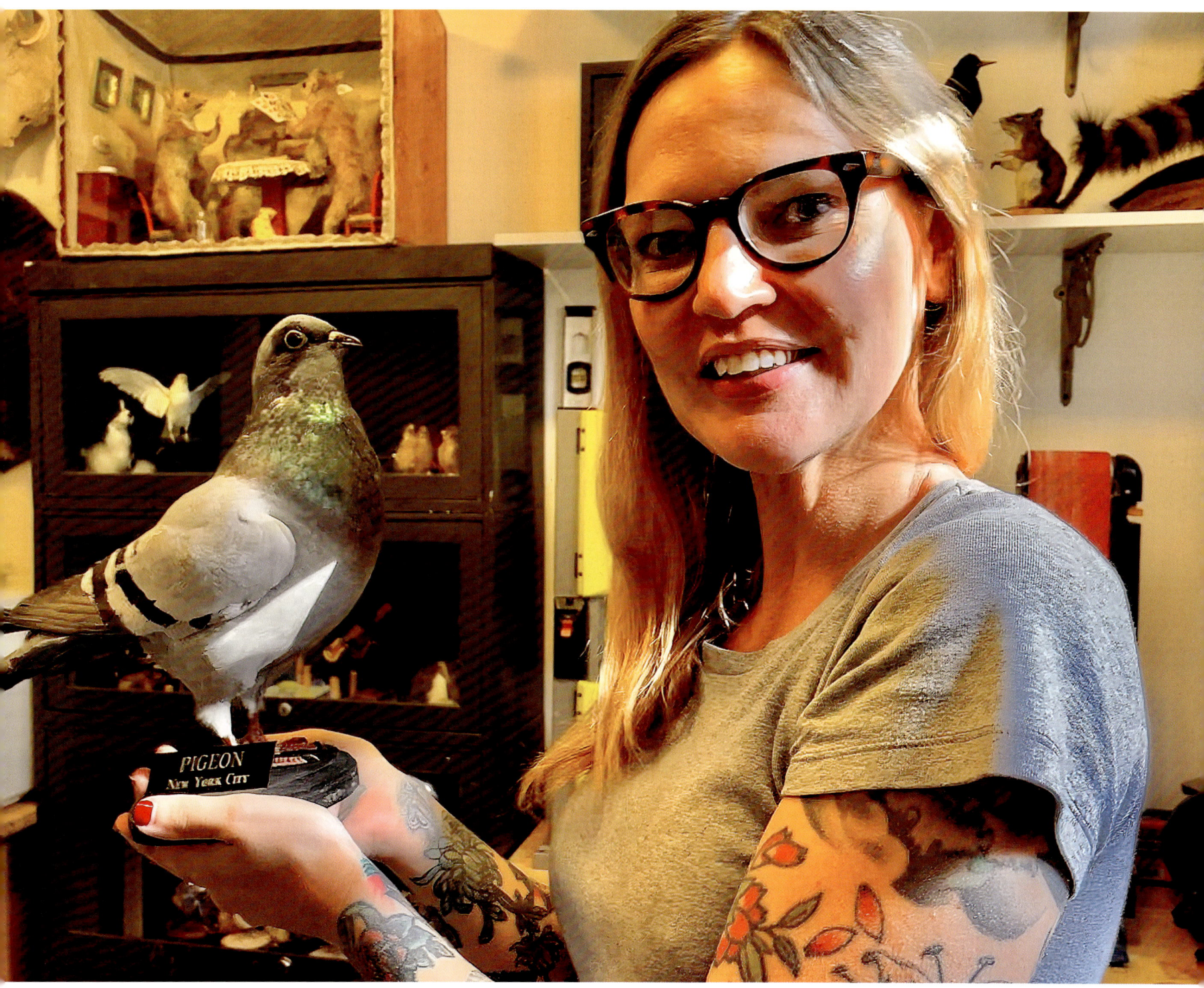

BARBECUE JOINT OWNER

Willow City, Texas

When in 1965 an unusually involved First Lady actively pushed for legislation to create a Highway Beautification Act, it was in part to soothe her ailing nation, then anguished by the ugliness of its Vietnam War. Lady Bird Johnson's projects were sometimes promoted by her husband in State of the Union addresses. Their native Texas had long named the Lupinus texensis as state flower, though added seeding of those bluebonnets along with widespread billboard removal now bring numerous additional springtime visitors down Hill Country roads to enjoy its exuberant floral spectacle. The vibrant sapphire petals of those flowers were said to resemble sun-shielding bonnets worn at that time by Texan pioneer women. Perhaps the most celebrated drive in America for viewing wildflowers is Willow City Loop, a fragrant odyssey dipping into meandering creeks splashed with blooming colors that interrupt sprawling ranchlands. Their fenced domains are dotted by craggy granitic boulders whose rain-moistened soil instigated prolific blooms of bluebonnets, Indian paintbrush, wild poppies, and firewheels. At the start of the route, an 1896 weathervane-capped roadhouse called Harry's on the Loop welcome visitors famished for a hog's ass sandwich with award-winning sauce. Beef or pork normally spend the day cooking for at least eight hours in the smoker. Crackling footsteps traverse a bottle cap-studded parking lot, alerting staff to another arriving customer. Though sometimes warmed by his old iron stove, current, sharp-eyed visitors might be left cold when spotting some of the Old South's unappealingly racist accouterments—one Confederate flag blankets a distant wall while an apparently unused noose dangles next to wine racks.

As his jukebox spits out tunes, highly spirited owner Harry Hickman seems to be enjoying some quality time with his stuffed nine-banded armadillo, the state's official mammal. There are more armadillos in Texas than any other state, but sadly visitors wishing to spot that animal usually only succeed in finding the legs up variety by the side of busy highways. Nonetheless, it appears that this particular mammal's very final incarnation is markedly more distinguished than that of those smothered in barbecue sauce and ingested between bun slices.

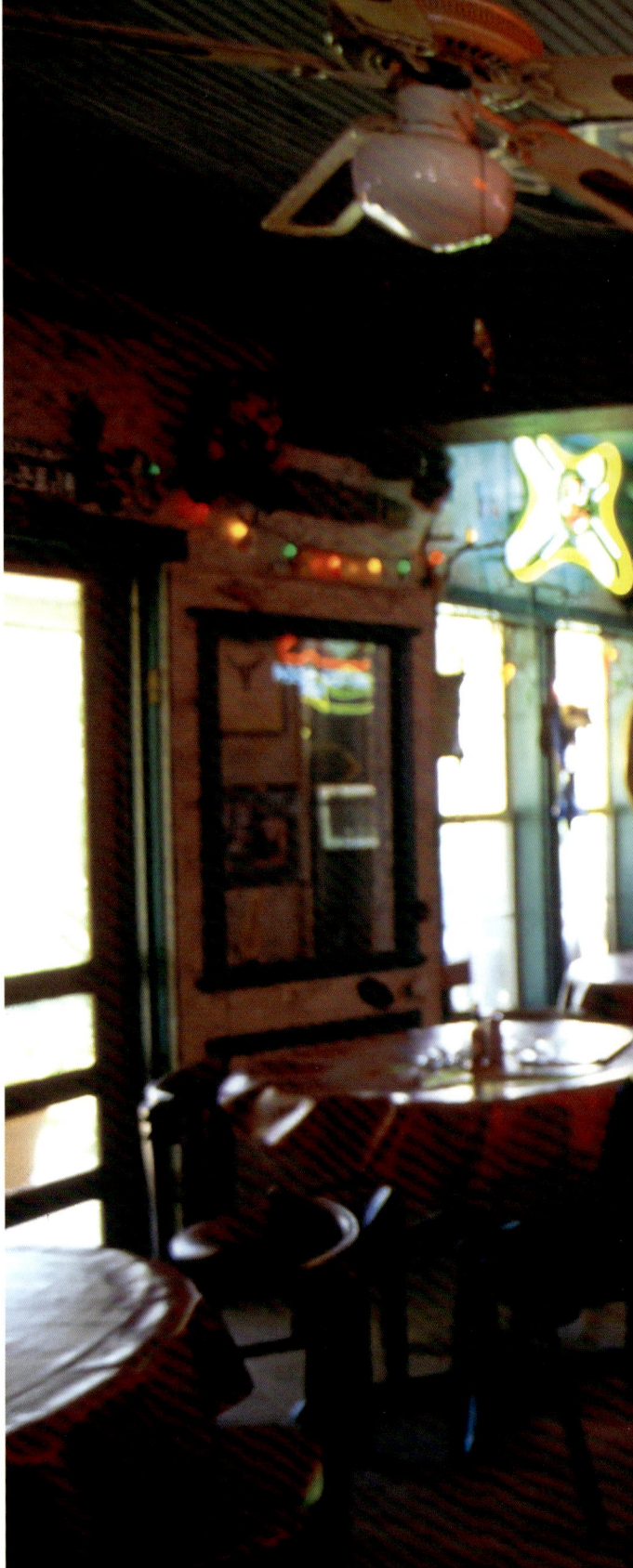

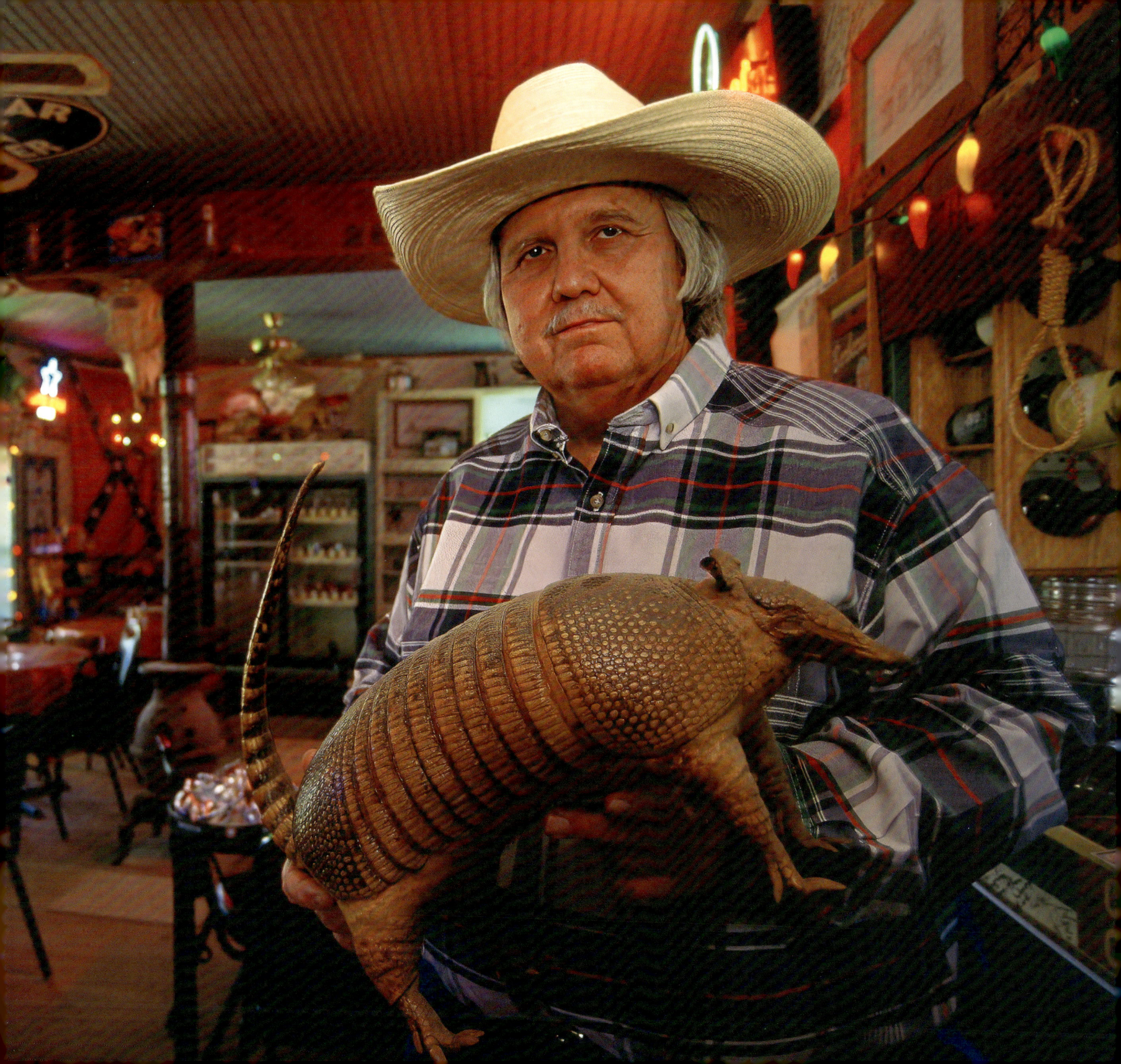

WRANGLER

Marion, Montana

Shortly after the Civil War, Armour and Company's meatpacking plant opened in Chicago. That triggered an exploding demand for beef, which previously was not a major part of American diets. Prices for meat skyrocketed, spurring proliferations of profitable, long-distance cattle drives headed toward the nearest railhead for eastbound shipment to awaiting abattoirs. Prior to barbed wire sewing up remaining corridors of the Western frontier, these Great Plains served as wide boulevards for seasonal movements of bovine traffic. With huge herds, vast territory was usually necessary to fulfill competing appetites and nutritional requirements. The drives became a balancing act between maintaining efficient speed for heads of beef to reach markets and conserving valuable weight on cattle that would otherwise be shed with their quicker workout. As cowboys sought greener pastures, bellowing herds would evoke Remington paintings as they kicked up golden trails of swirling dust heading toward the evening's encampment.

These days, after cattle have feasted on the last remains of summer's grassy vegetation, they will overwinter at ranches once they've been funneled inside their corrals and shuffled into pens. When whoops or whistles attempt to dislodge bulls from their insistent comfort zones, punching, roping, branding, and six-shooter vaccine guns will come with the territory. Here in this lush Thompson River valley, hemmed by ponderosa-dotted sierra and verdant meadows, the 86,000 acres of the Hargrave Cattle and Guest Ranch raised large-framed Charolais. The one-ton, cream-colored cows were bred for their efficient feedlot growth, heavily muscled haunches, and well-marbled beef. When dinner bells rang, that would surely be atop the servery's limited menu, which awaited this steely but exhausted wrangler, finally having shuttered his wooden stock gates at trail's end.

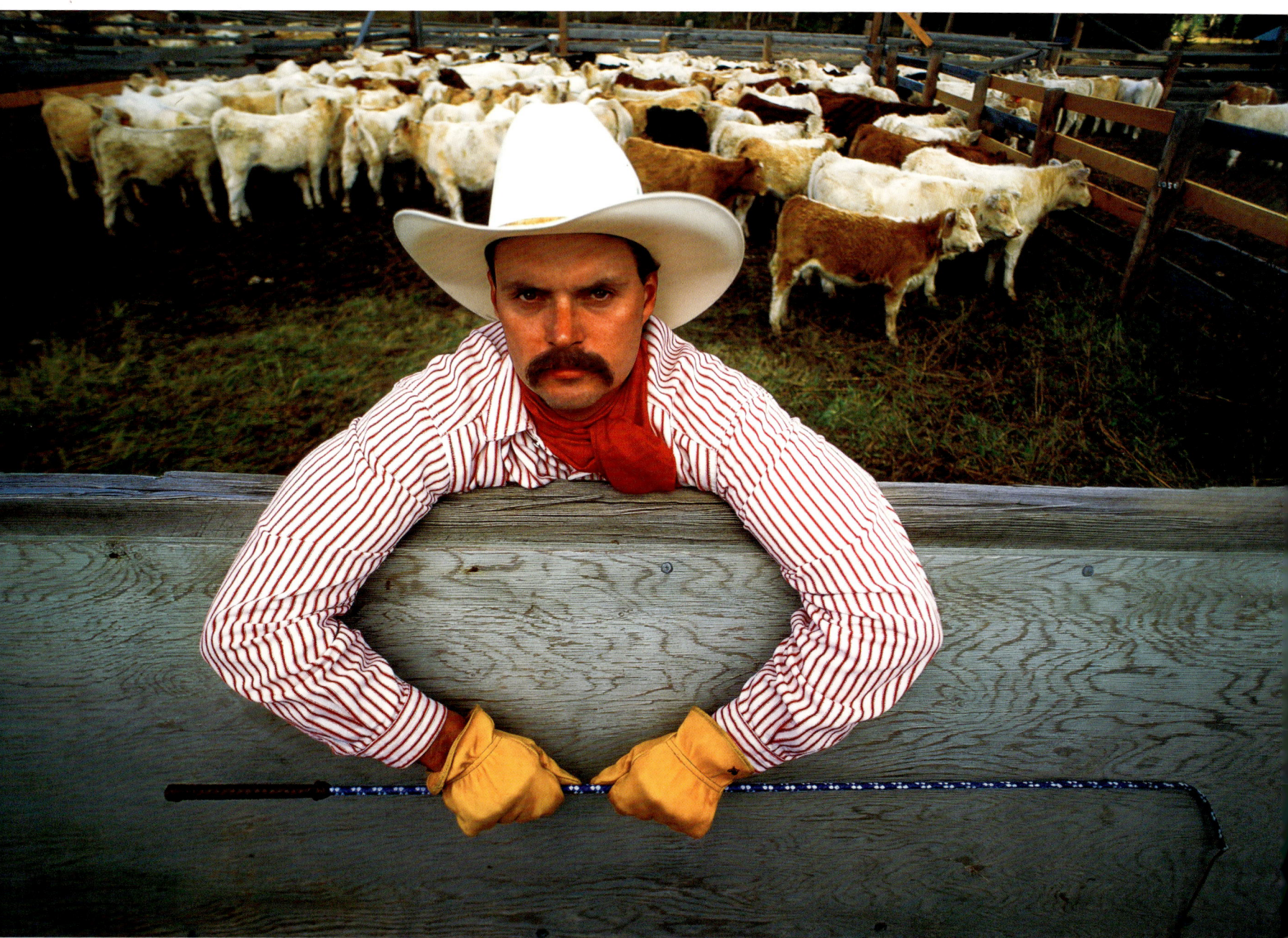

HOLLYWOOD SCREENWRITER

Hollywood, California

Perhaps projecting the world's greatest impact on popular culture, motion pictures have only been around for a century and some change. Though Thomas Edison in America or brothers Auguste and Louis Lumière from France are most often credited with its invention, that cast of characters edits out the first actual originator of this art form. A name few recognize, Louis Le Prince on October 14, 1888, using a hand-cranked single lens camera created the first motion picture ever filmed in human history. He shot a promenading scene at 12 frames per second outside Roundhay Cottage in Leeds, England, starring himself, his in-laws, and son Adolphe. Its running time was less than two seconds. Barely two years later, he waved goodbye to his brother in France at the Dijon station, got aboard the chugging train, and was never seen again. He would have shortly departed for America and an exhibition touting his invention while perhaps cementing a legacy. Many have suspected Edison's involvement in his disappearance, as the two were involved in bitter litigations to attain legal and financial credit for this brand-new technology. Le Prince's son Adolphe then resolved to promote his late dad's achievement, but he was soon found dead of an unsolved gunshot wound in Fire Island, New York. It's a plot juicy enough to grab the attention of some screenwriter, who might often be a launching pad for major Hollywood motion pictures. Much like symphonic orchestras, this cinematic art form is a collaborative enterprise. Usually when creating films, it's actually the fevered, overlooked imagination of screenwriters who orchestrate creative direction or emotional impact within compelling stories that will eventually fill both silver screen and its theater's reclining seats.

Enjoying his backyard's steamy hot tub while accompanied by percolating ideas and improvisational creativity, screenwriter Mitch Klebanoff generated uproarious laughter during a number of his madcap action or slapstick comedy films. In Klebanoff's number one box office hit, the absurd *Beverly Hills Ninja*, a laughingly awestruck bellman played by Chris Rock encounters Christopher Farley, who stars in that bumbling role during his last non-posthumous movie before an early demise. *Disorderlies* features the three Fat Boys, a rap group who tally up more than one thousand pounds. They manage to spill an octogenarian Ralph Bellamy into a swimming pool for the initial delight of soap opera heartthrob Anthony Geary. In a town where art imitates life and vice versa, perhaps scenes like these first inspired Klebanoff while he was relaxing inside his own bubbling perch overlooking this garden's outdoor natatorium in the storied Hollywood Hills.

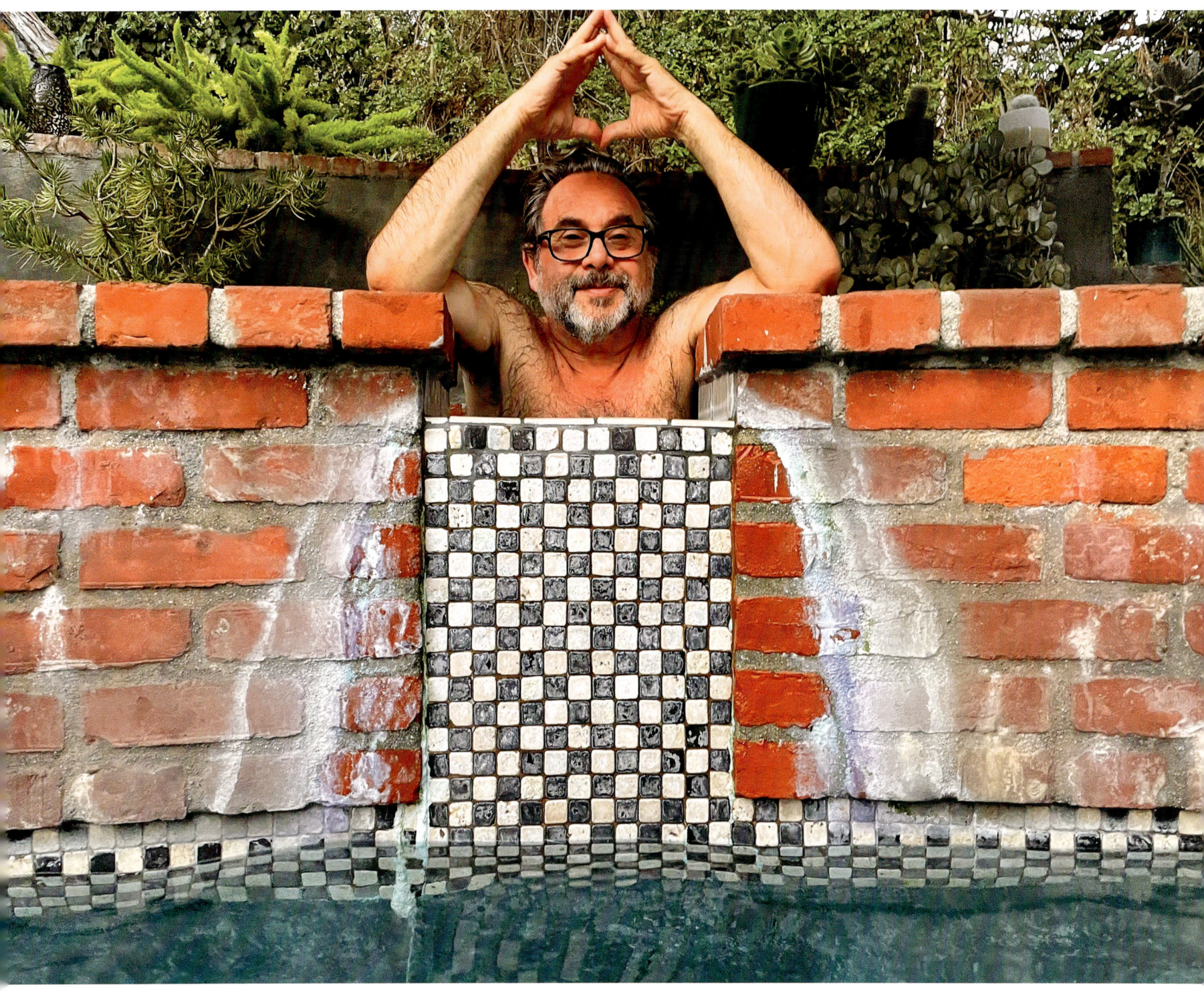

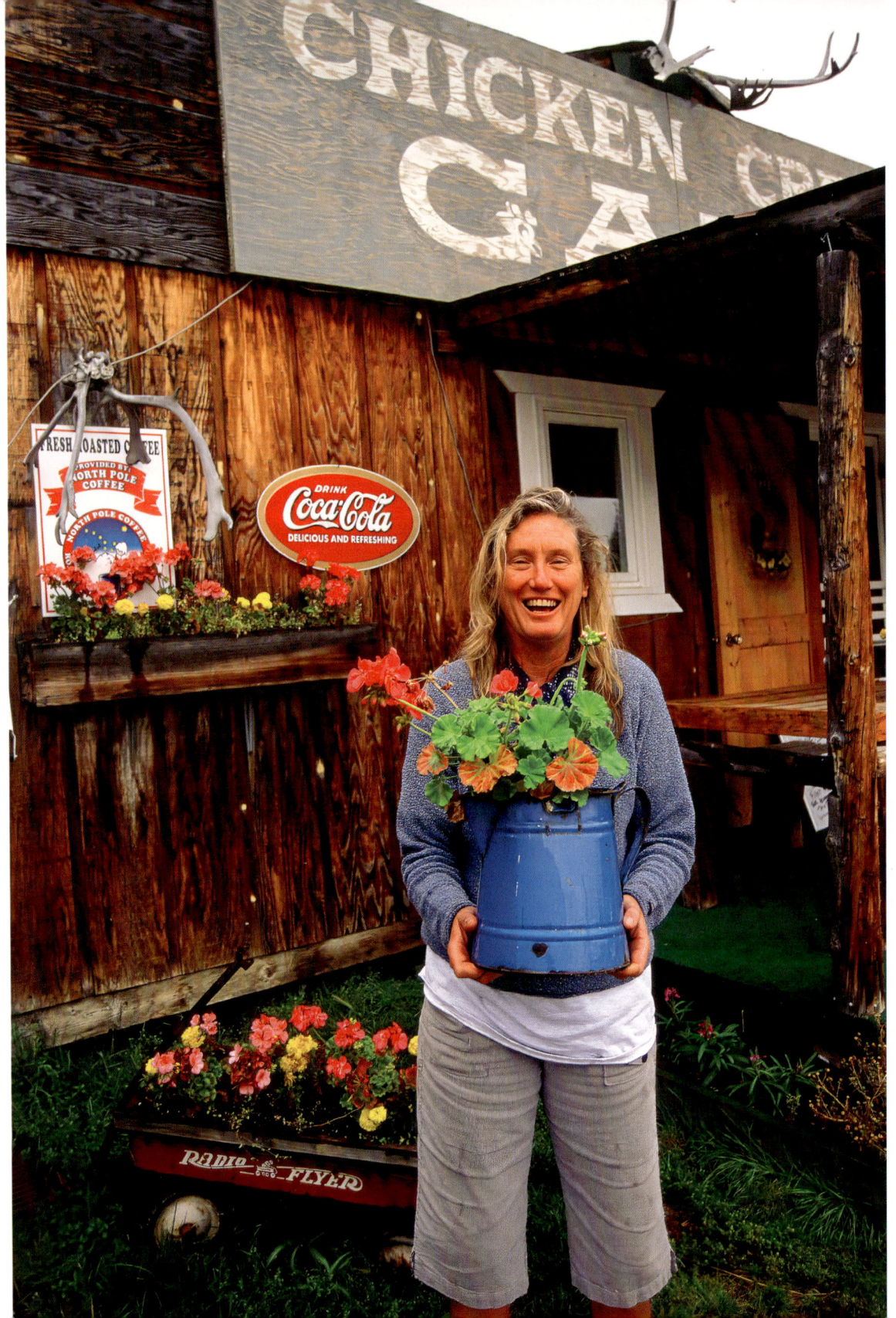

MAYOR

Chicken, Alaska

Among those northernmost roads on this planet, an aptly named gravel-paved Top of the World Highway flirts with the Arctic Circle as it squiggles along dramatic ridges that brush across a Yukon-Alaska frontier. Poker Creek station is the continent's highest latitude border crossing, where a moose-engraved passport stamp might prove consolation for its unpredictable hours of operation. Along with a total absence of guardrails or shoulders, tight turns, frost heaves, potholes, and washboard corrugation are prominent landmarks along this exhilarating, crest-hugging thoroughfare which peers across the treeless infinity of scarlet bearberry tundra, occasionally stomped by migrating caribou. The mesmerizing emptiness of this remote wilderness slowly dissipates as occasional dredges and historic gold mining equipment suddenly disrupt endless horizons, evoking Franklin Creek's nearby 1886 gold discovery. Predating by ten years this mad rush into Klondike territory, it nonetheless was responsible for the creation of Chicken, a rough and ready settlement whose name served as concession to unschooled prospectors who just couldn't spell ptarmigan, that similar looking fowl destined to be named Alaska's state bird.

Upon puttering into Chicken, hours driving through unrelenting wilderness suddenly seem worthwhile as a mirage-like megalopolis consisting of gas station, saloon, cafe, liquor store, and mercantile emporium beckons exploration while seeming to support the year-round population which usually fluctuates somewhere around 12. A three-door outhouse known as the Chicken Poop serves as lone public restroom, a necessity after quality time spent at that saloon, where women's underwear are employed for cannon shooting out back. The restaurant utilizes its pulled rubber chicken to signal a meal's readiness. When a rare warm day rolls around the self-appointed mayor appears in her shorts to water geraniums. For over three decades, Susan Wiren has run this downtown district with the help of her son, greeting intrepid travelers who seek out the only road that crosses a Chicken.

PROMINENT SWAMP RACONTEUR

Palmdale, Florida

This nation's largest subtropical wilderness area and one of its last unpopulated frontiers, the Everglades sits amidst jerry-rigged landscapes sliced and diced with canals or dykes. Its spongy scars were forged by greedy developers and misplaced understandings about this unique waterlogged geography spanning America's largest peninsula. During Florida's rainy season, waters from Lake Okeechobee spill into slowly flowing rivers of grass moving at half a mile per day down the gently sloping limestone peninsula towards Florida Bay. Prolonged nineteenth-century warfare with Seminoles in this humid swampland resulted in the nation's longest and most costly conflict with Native people. As white settlers began to infiltrate these inhospitable wetlands, lands were cleared to permit sugar cane cultivation or making charcoal from buttonwood and draining swamps for housing. These supposedly civilizing actions were superimposed upon the world's only true everglades ecosystem, often besieged by catastrophic flooding and hurricanes. A new environmental awareness about fertilizer and chemical corruptions in this delicate habitat was first set about by Rachel Carson's 1962 landmark book *Silent Spring*, which helped narrow huge perceptual imbalances between the lodging needs of human beings and those required by alligators. In fact, this Everglades wilderness remains the world's only place that hosts both alligators and crocodiles, in addition to 23 species of snakes, rare orchids, roseate spoonbills, manatees, plus the highly endangered Florida panther. Yet perhaps the most uncommon of all creatures here is an original Florida cracker, a term that's not actually an unwelcome racist slur, but a self-embraced description for those original European settlers along with their descendants who have thrived their whole life here in these swamps prior to air conditioning, mosquito repellant, and screen doors.

Celebrating the essence of his snake-littered, insect-studded backyard, swamp entrepreneur and barefoot raconteur Tom Gaskins epitomized an essence of that meme Florida Man decades before its introduction into America's lexicon. Living on the edge of endless cypress wilderness, a life's passion for swamp living blossomed upon recognizing creative and economic opportunities that lay in his vast cypress knees collection. Perhaps to inhale oxygen, these deformed otherworldly protuberances seem to wiggle up from beneath the drowned roots of cypress trees, and when removed, spoke loudly to knee-hatted Gaskins. They'd spark that fertile imagination and earn both a zany moniker and coveted position in his eccentric rural museum. His knees were first exhibited at New York's 1939 World's Fair and leased to Robert Ripley's Odditorium. Later his own hand-built Cypress Knee Museum attracted curious motorists through a series of tree-carved highway signs, then forking over one dollar admission fees, a rate which remained unchanged through decades of inflation. At Fisheating Creek, frighteningly skinny, planked catwalks led visitors eight feet above rarely viewed oak and cabbage hammocks, through a cypress swamp and bay head. He dined exclusively on swamp cabbage and passionately licked wood cell fibers on freshly peeled cypress knees while extracting its carcinogenic creosote. Gaskins wore shoes only going to funerals or patent lawyers certifying his invented versions of grass cutters and tire pressure gauges. His unique manufacturing process involved him cutting, boiling, peeling, and licking knees before gouging out a dry hole cavity. Writing three books on wild turkey hunting, he was apparently the nation's foremost expert. His turkey caller was apparently quite effective as its strange gobbling noise resulted in six of its users being shot. Gaskins's exploits were profiled in *Field & Stream* and entertained Johnny Carson twice on the *Tonight Show*.

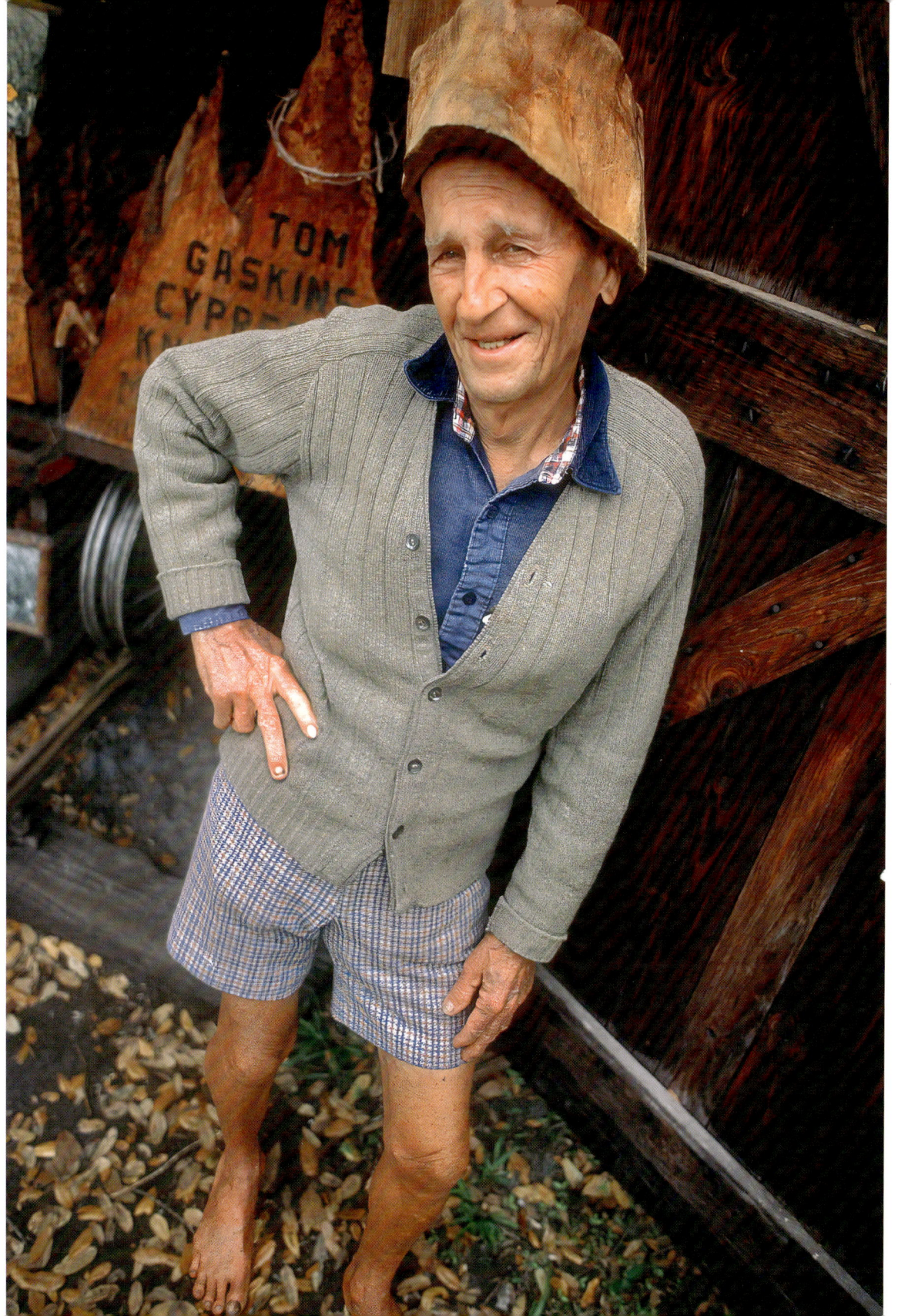

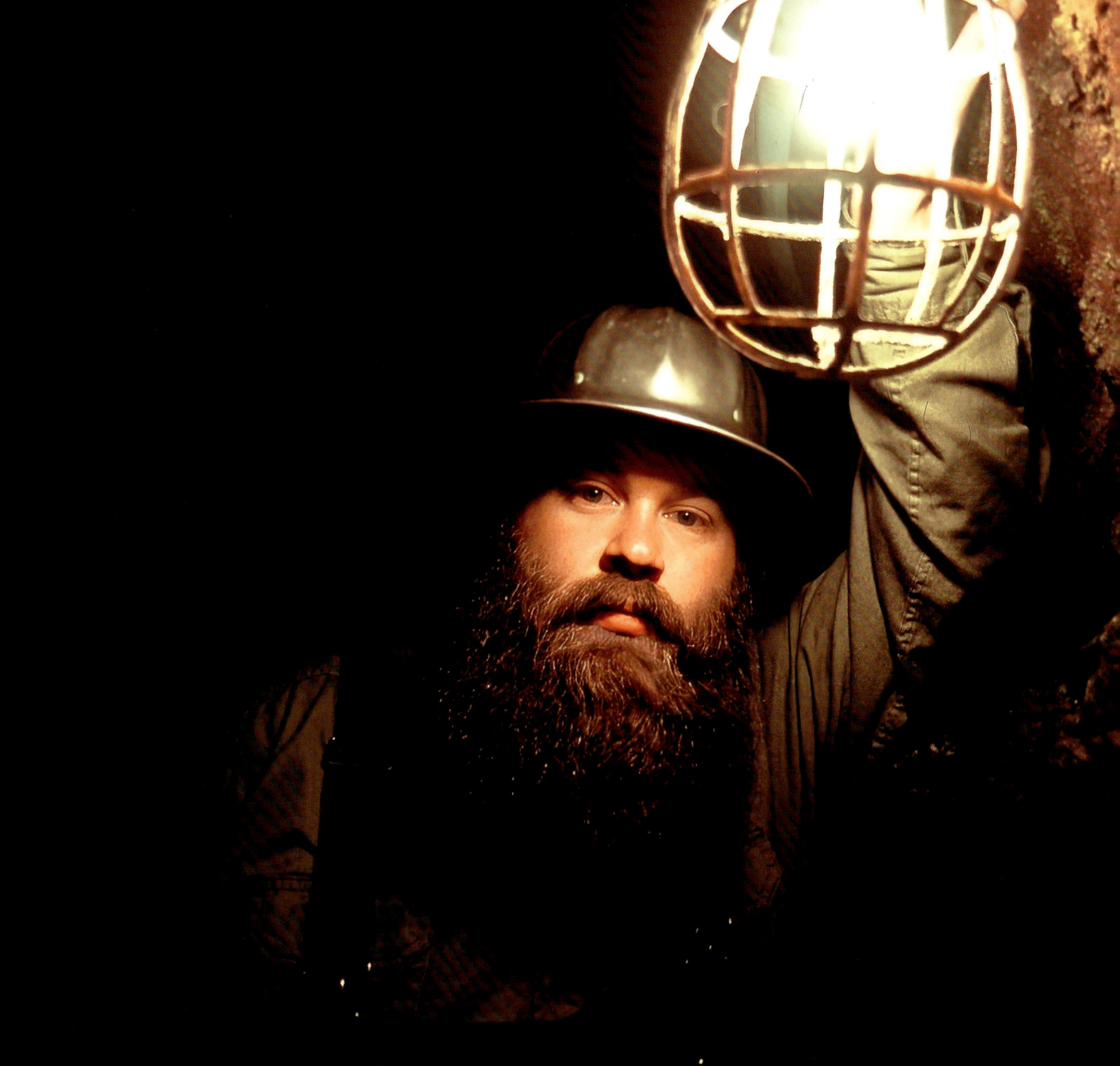

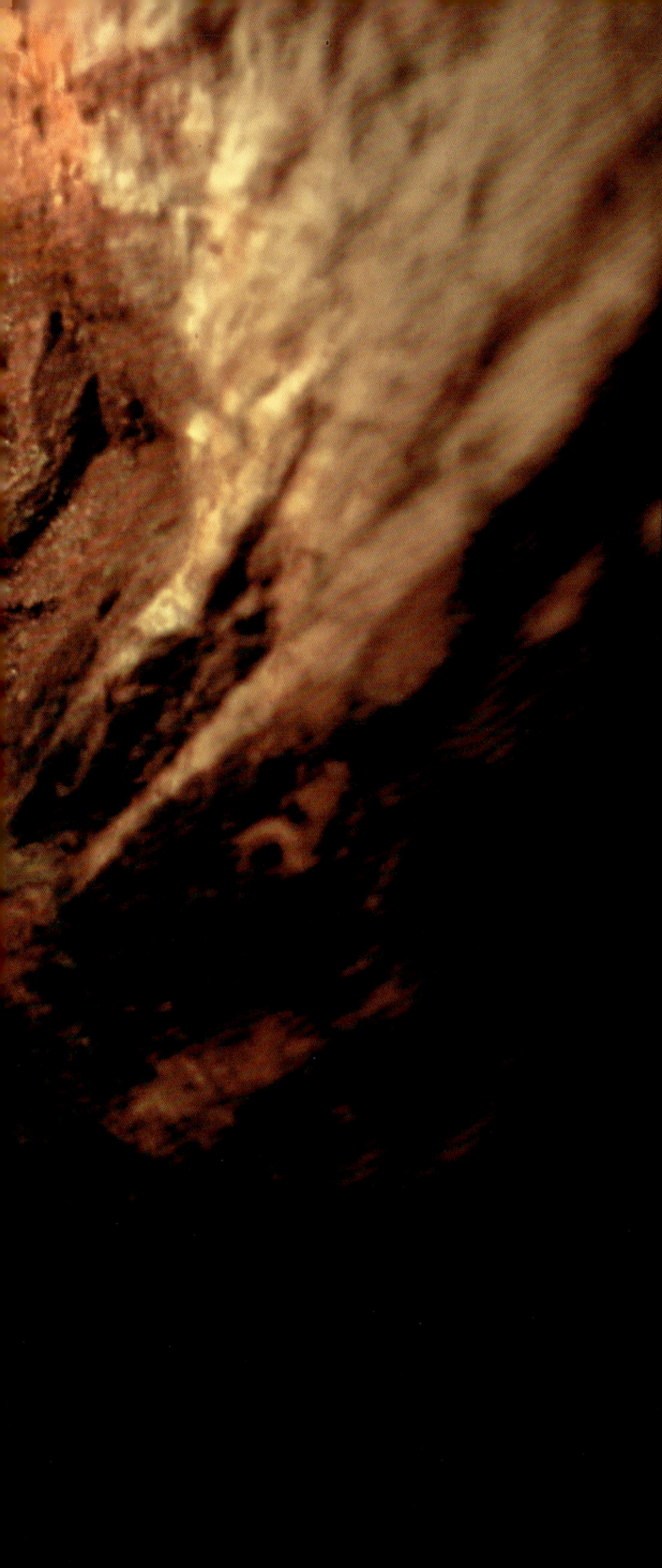

GOLD MINER

Dahlonega, Georgia

In the forested Blue Ridge mountains, a deer hunter in 1828 stumbled across an odd rock, which upon closer inspection was blotched with yellowish metal hues. Thus began the first ever gold rush in this country. Nearly two decades later an additional stampeding exodus by profit-hungry prospectors to California's newfound lode of gilded minerals was dissuaded by local Georgian officials with the famed catchphrase that just nearby "there's gold in them thar hills." That copious gold, initially just scraped off surface rock, had spurred an eager United States government to establish a branch mint in Dahlonega, producing from bullion the bulk of America's shining currencies. During this time precious metals were sifted through trickling water channels within gravity powered sluice boxes, coaxed by the sweating toil of 15,000 dirt-covered gold miners. Many were eventually employed by the newly formed Dahlonega Consolidated Gold Mining Company, seeking their now subterranean geologic quarry, deeply embedded into rich veins of quartz. This outfit overseeing their grueling extractions became the east's first-ever systematic deep underground mining operation. Stamp mills in the region are still employed to crush quartz rock into ore.

Today retired gold miners and expert panners lead visitors 200 feet beneath earth's surface and through claustrophobic warrens of hand dug tunnels, where dangers from this hellishly excruciating work are reflected in the hard-hatted, lamp lit expression of this bearded worker.

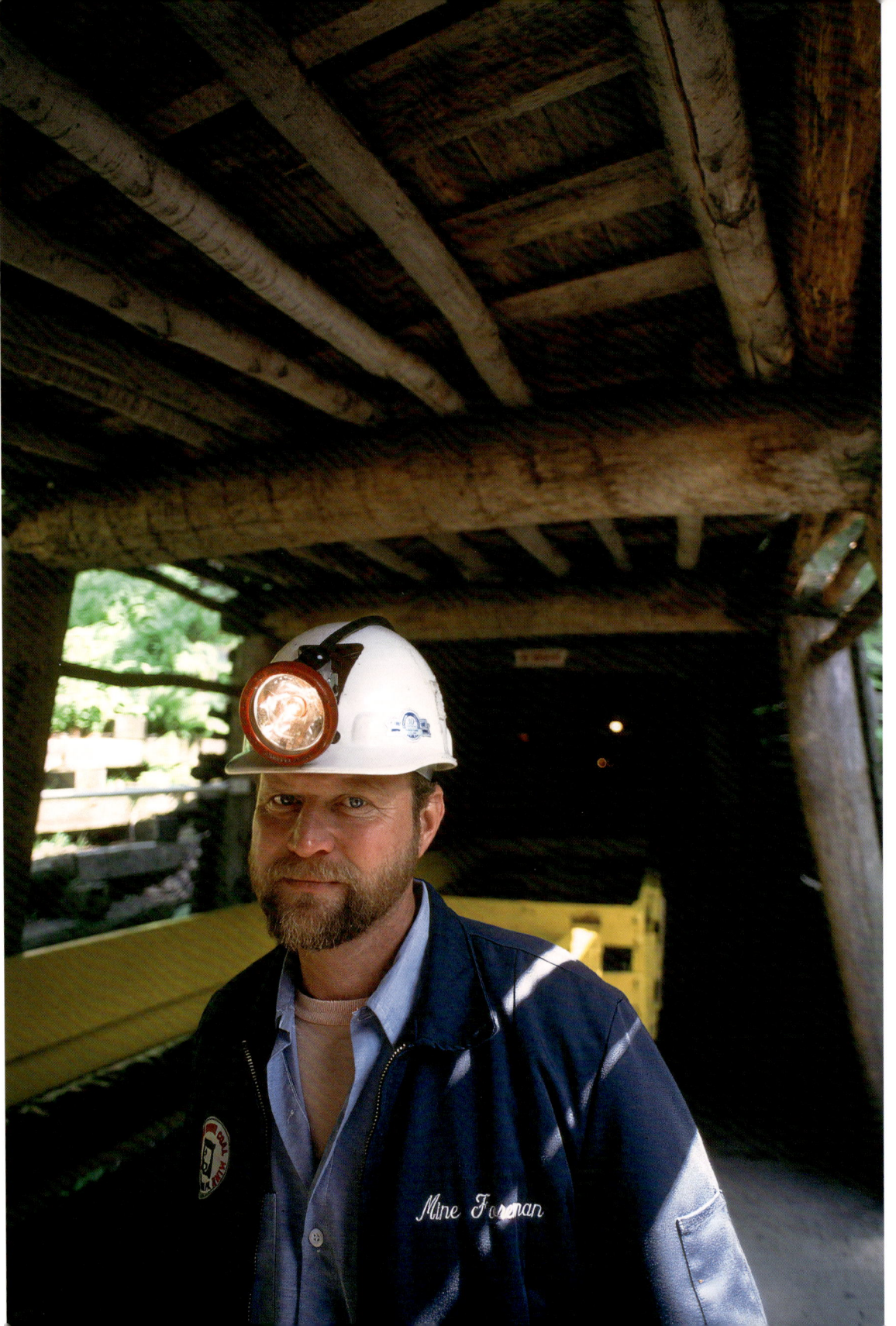

COAL MINE FOREMAN

Scranton, Pennsylvania

With an estimated reserve representing more than seven billion tons, earth's largest deposits of anthracite coal lie deep beneath the ground within seams that stretch across eastern Pennsylvania's Poconos. Sedimentary layers along flanks of imposing mountain ranges produce coalification from the thick forest vegetation once buried within and stressed under severe pressure. The flammable carbon-rich fuel was discovered here in 1790 when a sleeping hunter awoke nearly immolated after his campfire accidentally ignited an outcropping of anthracite. On the outskirts of Ashland, the Pioneer Colliery began operating in the late nineteenth century. After laying rails and opening chutes, the Philadelphia and Reading Coal and Iron Company started overseeing operations in 1911. Rickety railcars rolled beneath timber-braced ceilings into a year-round 52-degree void of darkened recesses. As coal was laboriously removed from its mine, an above-ground anthracite-fueled steam locomotive transported this sooty cargo past bootleg mines enroute to a colliery while aboard the 1920 Henry Clay, named after that Victorian-era politician who did much to promote coal's subterranean industry. When Delaware, Lackawanna and Western Railroad began using cleaner, more expensive anthracite, this line began advertising using one of the world's first model-based fictional characters. Named Phoebe Snow, she wore a white dress and would emerge from her rail travels unblemished by soot as was common during earlier bituminous coal-driven journeys. Her character's name was famously pilfered and adopted by the Grammy Award-winning musician, known for performing "Poetry Man" in 1973.

Preparing to penetrate 1,800 chilly feet into Mahanoy Mountain's core, a hardened mine foreman fires up his headlamp and the open battery-powered mining railcars at Pioneer Tunnel. An eerie wood-framed warren of passageways darkened by coal seams exposes its rocky anthracite bounty, which is harvested with pickaxe, blackened hands, and backbreaking labor. Still being mined today, anthracite coal is the hardest, cleanest, and most metamorphosed type of coal. Until the 1950s it was a chief source of heating homes in this country before oil- and gas-burning systems were introduced, presumably to someday be supplanted by solar collection, its source deep in outer space rather than inner mountains.

TRANSGENDER ACTOR

Hollywood, California

Though untutored common wisdom erroneously suspects that notions of both gay behavior and transgender roles are an emerging, brand-new phenomenon created from societal permissiveness emanating from American culture wars, the actual truth is significantly different. The first recorded same-sex couple in history was displayed with full-color prominence, unashamedly touching noses and embracing on inscribed walls that graced a Saqqara temple from ancient Egypt. Khnumhotep and Niankhkhnum were royal manicurists for King Niuserre and are buried together in the same tomb. Over 2600 years ago in Lesbos, Greece, one of the great lyric poets Sappho wrote much admired elegiac poetry exploring mutual longing between women and was subsequently honored on coins. She and her island home helped supplement our modern vocabulary that gave rise to descriptive notions of sapphic attraction and lesbian behavior. Even the premier mythological god Zeus is portrayed as having abducted that young Trojan man Ganymede for romantic trysts atop Mount Olympus. In fact, all around this planet, from gender-bending fa'afafine drawn from matriarchal Samoan society or effeminate third gender nádleehi in Navajo cultures, a wide, non-conforming spectrum of sexual and gender roles were embraced with tender feelings about their culturally accepted behavior. In the 1920s, German clinics performed those first gender reassignment surgeries until the Third Reich took power and stopped these procedures. Many non-binary people, at cross purposes to inner, biologically instinctive impulses and reluctantly heeding legal barriers along with restrictive religious teachings that had taken firm root in modern societies, lived out their shadowy secret while suffering the stressful toll of gender dysphoria. After seemingly endless delays, there was suddenly a surprisingly rapid evolution of moral and political thought, as the Supreme Court in 2015 finally caught up with popular culture and legalized gay marriage, prompting President Obama's White House to be lit up with rainbow colors that same evening. Almost two decades earlier, comedienne Ellen DeGeneres on her eponymous show came out publicly as the first gay lead character on American network television.

Seen in a dramatically lit kitchen on a Hollywood set at Universal Studios, gifted young actor Isaiah Stannard similarly struck an early triumphant chord for trans representation as he came out acknowledging his gender on the well-reviewed network show *Good Girls*. This character's mom was pregnant with an upcoming sibling, sparking sensitively acted bedside conversations that actually mirrored personal experiences with a real-life supportive mother who lovingly embraced his newly evolved identity. Stannard was originally cast for the show when he told producers about his just-adopted gender, inspiring writers on this daring drama to incorporate that plot twist and raise awareness about an unfairly ostracized segment of society.

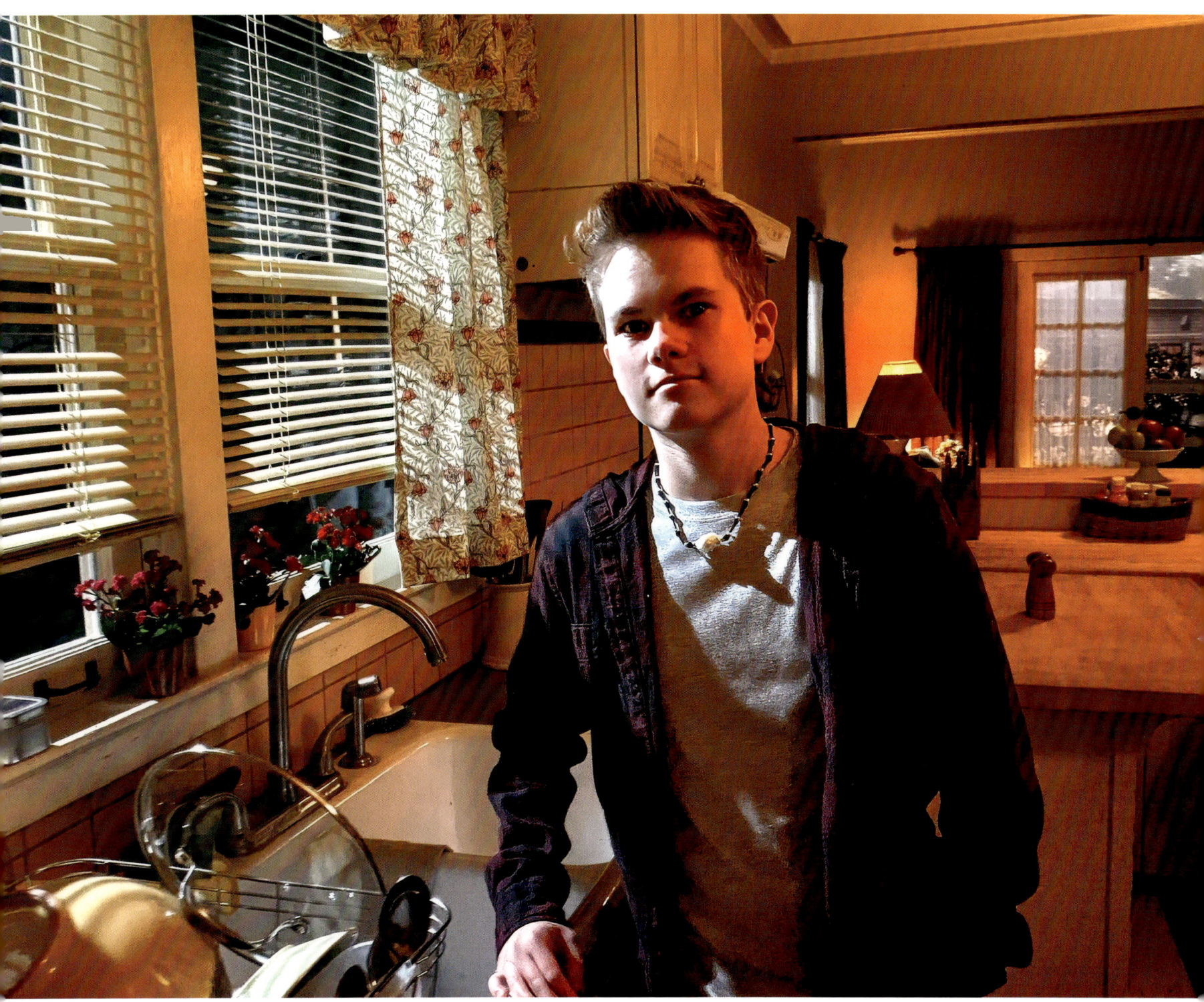

CHURCH PASTOR

Hi Vista, California

Driving past the outskirts edging Lancaster, California, an unsettling sense of civilization's abandonment envelops a newly visiting motorist. Homes and businesses seem to disappear along paved streets, which are lovingly named after letters in the alphabet and become narrower before deteriorating into sandy lanes. Luxuriant displays of towering palms are soon replaced with Joshua trees, actually a yucca-like plant, whose uplifted spiky arms inspired Mormon settlers to name the enormous growth after that Canaan-conquering biblical figure. After passing a few relics of mid-century gas stations and bars, it becomes apparent that these rented, self-styled movie ranches are located in photogenic settings whose vast landscapes are quickly dissolving into the Mojave Desert. Just before the journey seems to require four-wheel driving, an empty, distant horizon reveals haunting profiles of a Spanish Mission–style chapel, first constructed in 1934 as Hi Vista's community hall. This structure was later transformed into an eerie tabernacle for a number of Hollywood movies, most notably as that setting for one of the most notable scenes in film history. The site, now indicated on official maps as the *Kill Bill* Church, was used by Quentin Tarantino in his 2003 film to stage an upsetting, Golden Globe–nominated vision of a wedding ceremony's bloody massacre.

Pastor Oscar Castañeda purchased a peeling building, completely unknowledgeable about its earlier history, and established the Sanctuary Adventist Church whose congregation would meet on Saturdays for their traditional Sabbath day of worship. After realizing that his swollen, well-attended congregations contained many foreign visitors, he learned that many were lured by the site's cinematic pedigree. He eventually embraced the new situation, reluctantly appearing as a religious figure in "Be Careful," Cardi B's crucifix-obsessed, vulgarity-laced music video, now said to be his biggest regret.

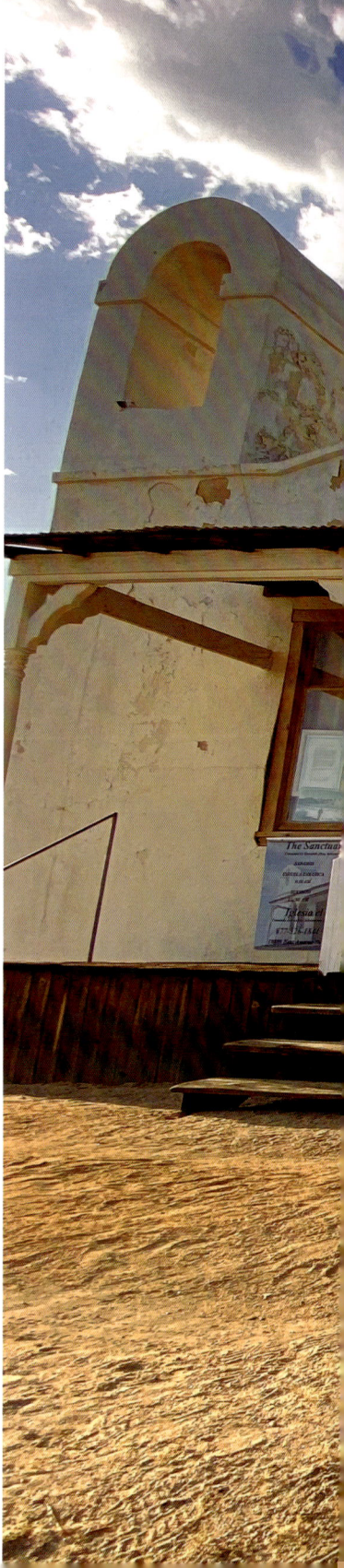

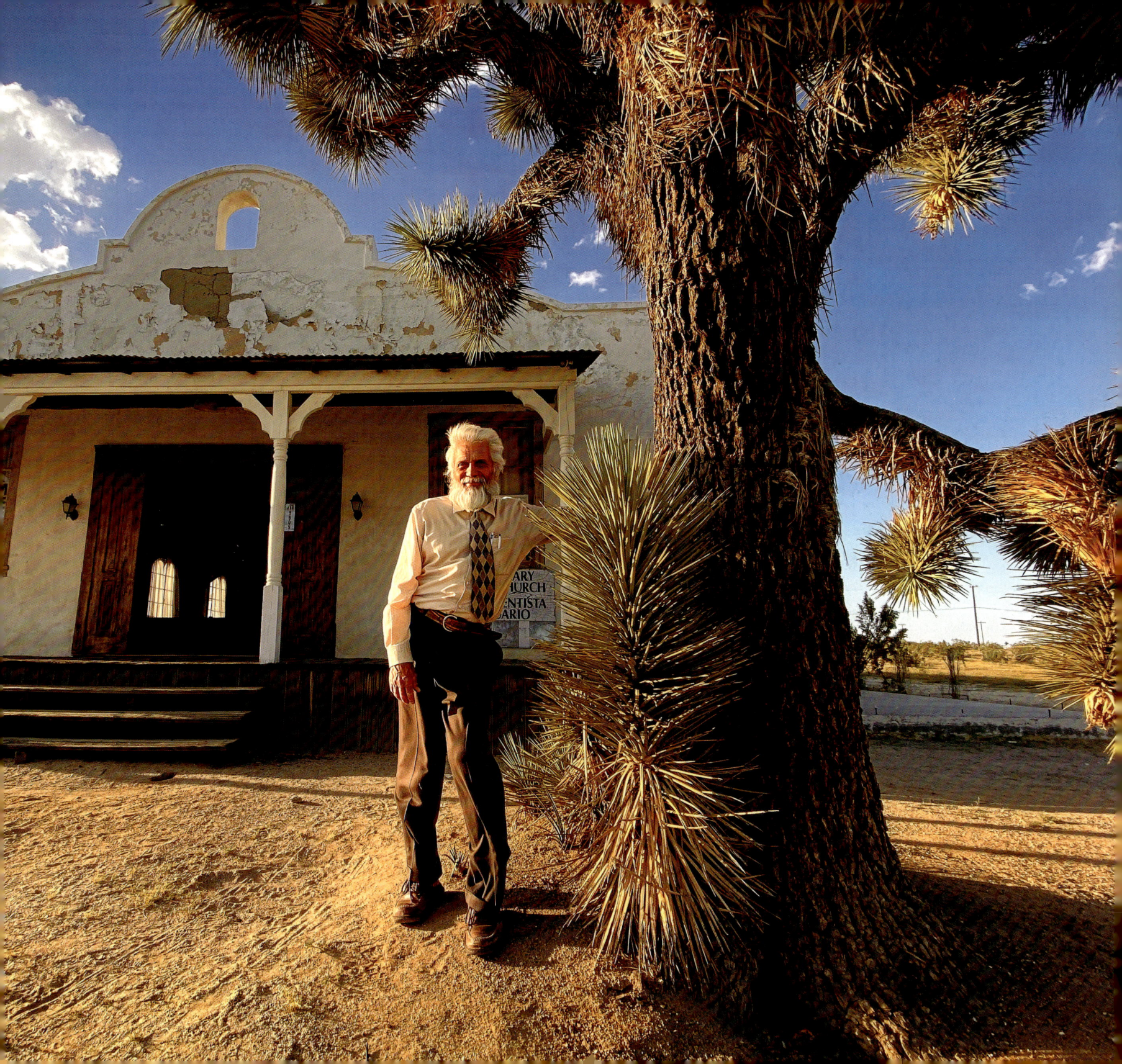

SHOE COBBLER

Bakersfield, California

San Joaquin Valley's fertile southern end cloisters California's vast agricultural fields and its laboring farm workers near the fifth-largest Hispanic majority population of any big city in this country. Bakersfield, also known for its Basque restaurants and sheep raising heritage, nevertheless benefitted from the region's newfangled mid-century craze promoting a wacky building style known as programmatic architecture. During the last century's first several decades, theatrical amalgams of Hollywood imagination, Southern California eccentricity and West Coast optimism sparked a movement to create giant, eye-popping roadside symbols, an expressly American take on European trade signs hung outside shops lining narrow lanes. Across a sprawling grid traced with ever-growing freeways and an exponential explosion of automobile usage, these Brobdingnagian structures were meant to grab drive-by attention that would activate car brake lights. Pullovers offered through-the-looking-glass experiences where caffeinated drinks were served within giant coffee pots, frankfurters got dispensed from 18-foot-long, bun-encased hot dogs, and a behemoth drive-thru donut cloistered its own bake shop.

Two hours north of Los Angeles along Bakersfield's shop-lined drag, a 25-foot-tall Big Shoe Repair shop stepped onto the scene in 1947. A white low top with thick orthopedic insoles, its 32-foot length would make this black-soled footwear roughly size 768. Popping out of the toes to proudly display a newly mended boot, lifelong cobbler Felipe Torres has been repairing shoes since his father taught him as an eager child in León, Mexico, this continent's footwear capital. The genial shoe repairman toils away in a cramped, 380-square-foot workshop on antique equipment inside this imposing stucco footwear, 50 feet long with 3-inch-thick shoelaces. Torres says it's all he knows, but with expertise in stitching purses, jackets, suitcases, and even dog collars from customers that hail from Oregon to Texas, one gets the feeling that eventually he might become pretty well heeled.

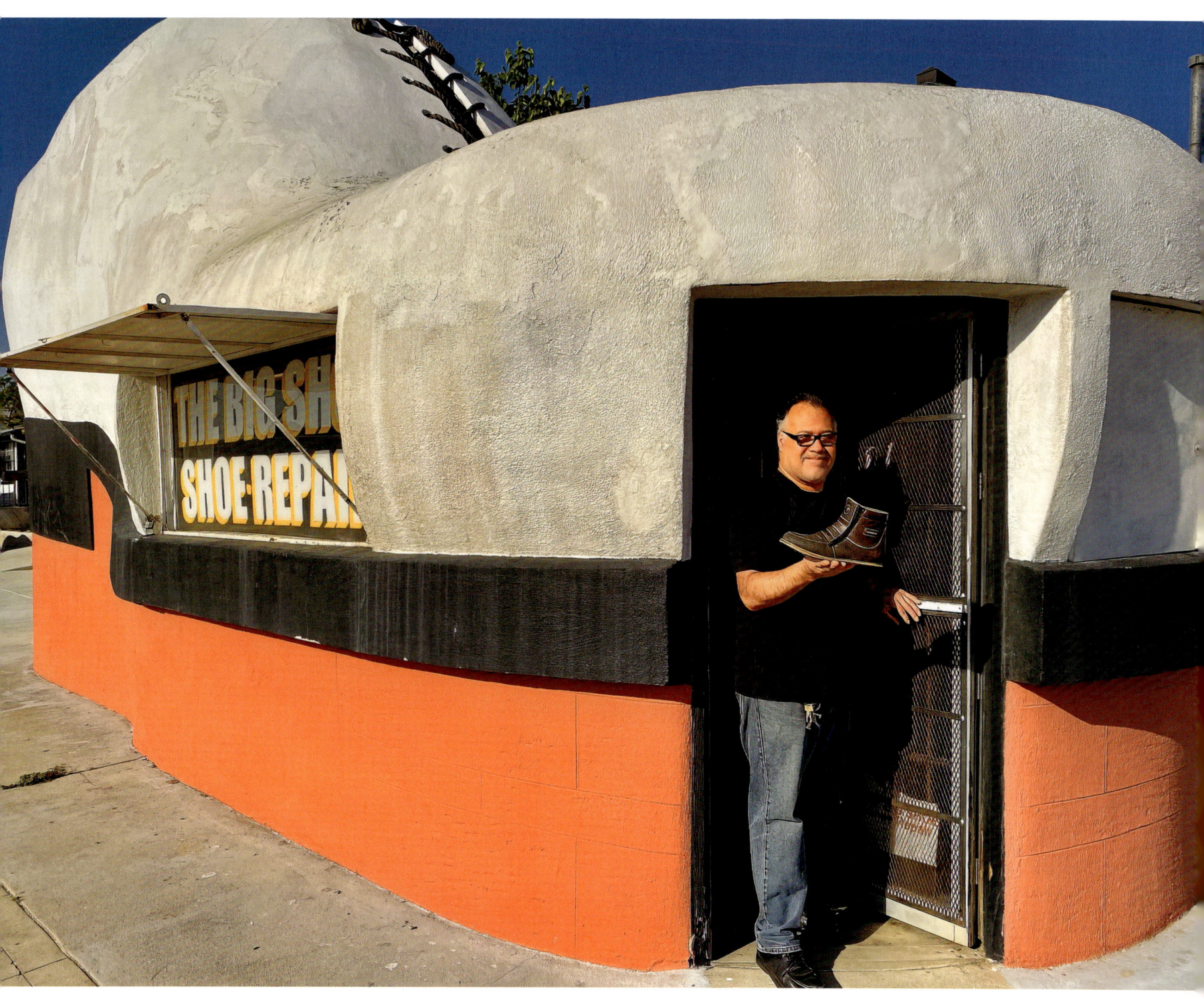

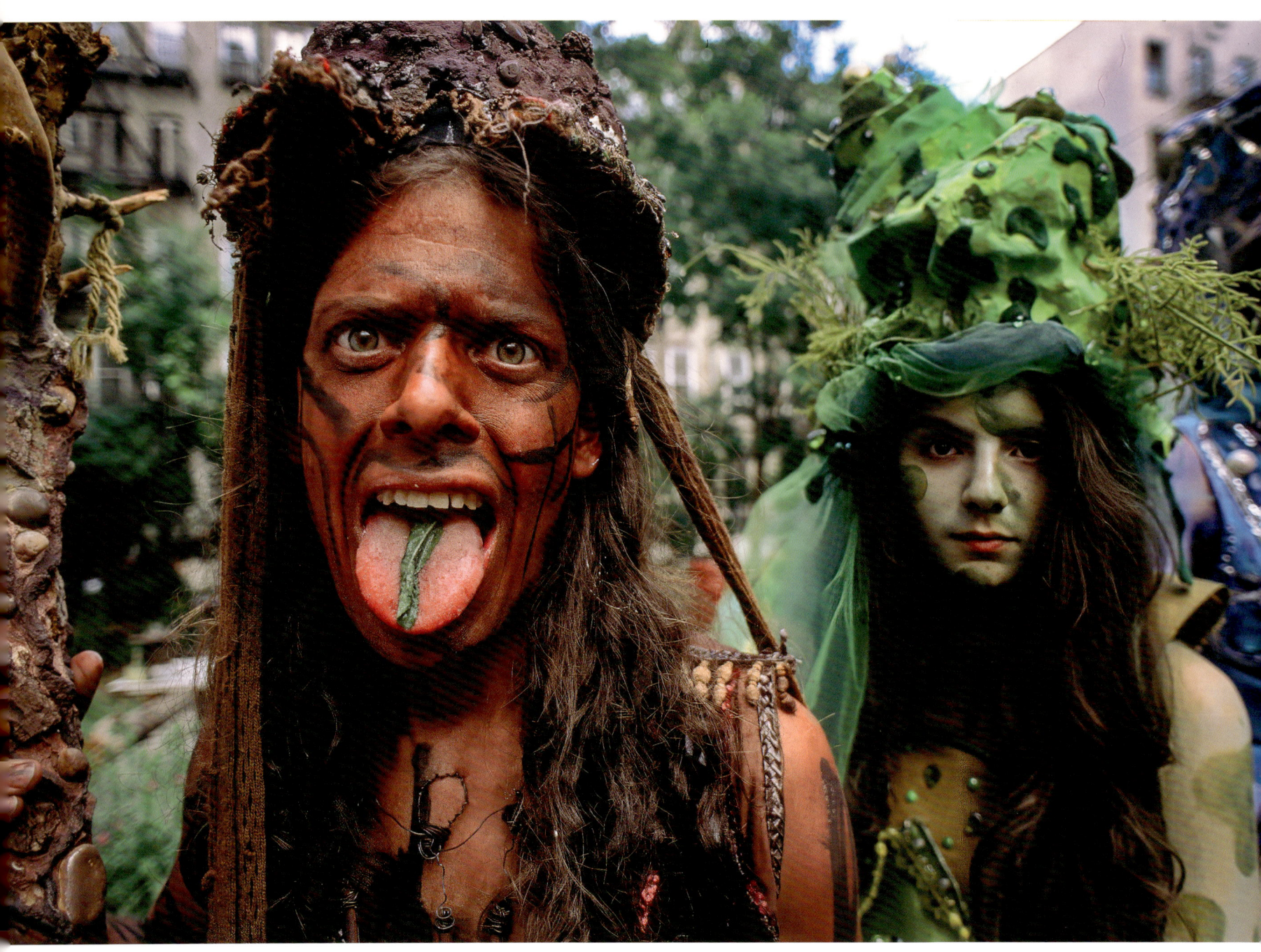

URBAN GARDEN ACTIVISTS

Lower East Side, New York City, New York

Some dozen millennia ago, glaciers retreated as estuaries with inviting harbors formed around a newly emerged island of Manhattan, first settled by Lenape people living in bark-covered homes and surviving off plentiful shellfish supplies or small game hunting. Current-day Times Square was then a lush green forest with an active beaver pond. As time marched on, there's been a breathtaking metamorphosis of changes on this island, but few neighborhoods have changed more dramatically than the Lower East Side. After established Dutch plantations briefly lost their ownership to British occupants, settlements thickened and those very first tenements in this city popped up during early nineteenth-century development along the East River at Corlears Hook. Its crowded, disreputable streets were clogged with thieves and prostitutes, first giving rise to the term "hooker." The high density housing here was soon flooded with a progression of Germans, Italians, and Eastern European Jews. That ushered in chaotic scenes of Yiddish theaters, pickle stands, jammed pushcarts, and multilingual storefronts. When this frenzied social structure began to unravel in the mid-twentieth century, crime plus vandalism took its toll on residents and their properties. Arson destroyed buildings, leaving vacant lots in its wake. Strewn with rubble, rusting vehicles, and sometimes even dead bodies, these numerous plots were eyed jealously by land developers as a favorable economy finally arrived. In the meantime, concerned residents had started cleaning up these empty lots while creating small urban oases of vegetable gardens and sculpture parks. A determined coalition joining artists and political activists organized together, drawing attention to the perceived greed of real estate developers along with this neighborhood's urgent need for humanizing park space. To dramatize their demands, Earth Celebrations' annual procession starring giant puppets and costumed participants wove their way around the city blocks, performing imaginative rituals at each vest pocket park while drawing upon traditions or mythologies of the neighborhood's ethnic populations.

Beneath hulking apartment building facades, garden gnomes, forest spirits, and a particularly fearsome rainforest shaman gather together during their sacred pageant ceremonies. Clutching his gnarled, mystical cane, an intense facial expression appears to project a mouthwatering appetite for greenery. These vernal ceremonies eventually made their mark since a new mayoral administration transferred 200 lots to the Parks Department and saved them from an awaiting real estate auction block. The Lower East Side now has arguably more gardens per square foot than any urban neighborhood in this country. As the superimposition of community transitions roll on, this newly revitalized community has now become a trendy hub for hipsters, entrepreneurs, and an ostentatious bevy of boutique latte emporiums.

DRAG QUEEN BINGO EMCEES

West Hollywood, California

Celebrity sightings along Santa Monica Boulevard are commonplace as rainbow-hued pride flags that flutter atop trendy LGBTQ+ dance clubs populating the colorful thoroughfare. Even before neon-lit clubbing crowds arrive, eye-squinting sunset conditions are endured by westbound traffic heading past this neighborhood toward the Pacific Ocean and its colorful pier where Route 66 officially ends. Along the way, Hamburger Mary's is one nightly venue evoking that mischievous essence of West Hollywood. The name Mary is a slang descriptor used to describe gay men dating back to the early 1900s. The self-described open bar and grill filled with open-minded people often attracts a drag-theme clientele. Though female impersonation actually dates to ancient Greek theater, drag is a theatrical exaggeration of gender, challenging what we think and assume about the sexes. This art form explores fluidity of gender roles, seeking to redefine what it means to live authentically. An initial drag queen bingo event during the early 1990s made its splash in Seattle to help fundraise for gay victims of a rapidly growing AIDS epidemic.

Beneath vibrantly chromatic coiffures, a gurning visage and tumescent lips adorn the naughty hosts of Drag Queen Bingo, who with rambunctious aplomb pull balls from atop their spotlit throne, entertaining boisterous crowds through campy vulgarity served up alongside its famed juicy hamburgers. Red-dressed Ingenue was featured in a 2022 comedy *God Save the Queens* and was inducted into The Hollywood Museum as one of its "Legends of Drag." Copper-wigged Roxy Wood was catapulted into a new career during participation alongside *The Rocky Horror Picture Show*, appeared on the screen in *Supergirl* and *The Rookie*, and now hosts her own online bingo tournament, *Roxy's Got Balls*.

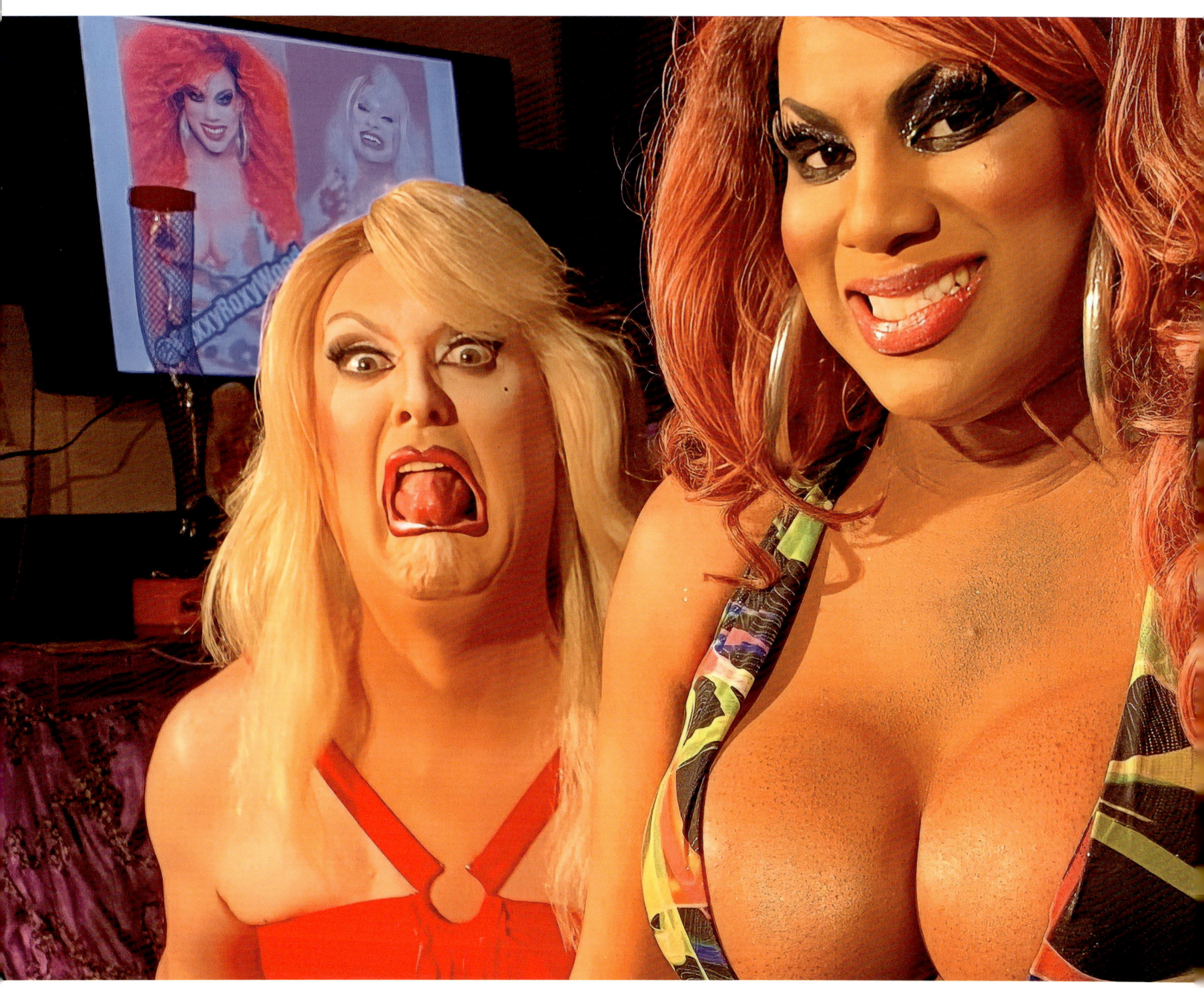

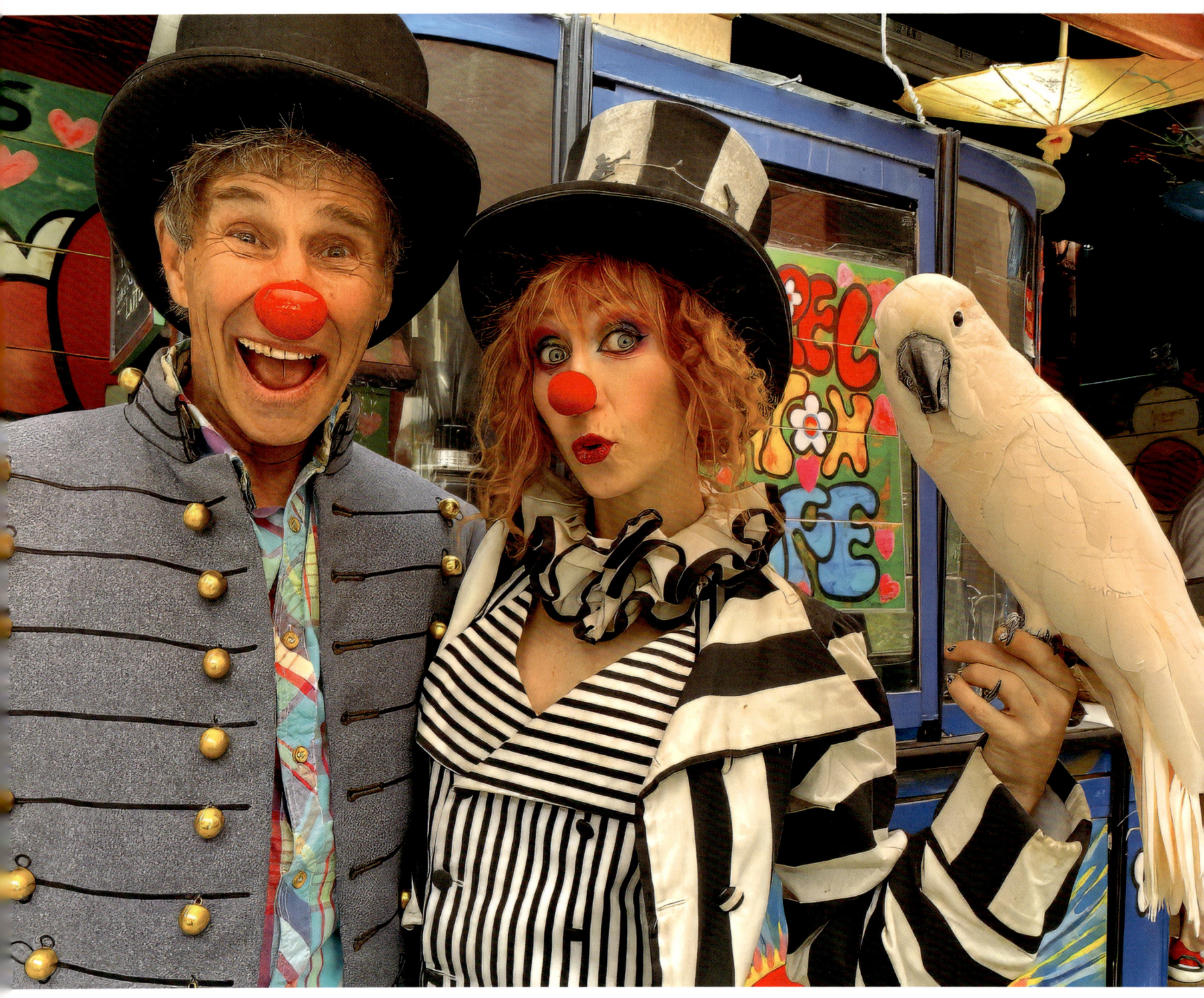

CONTORTIONISTS

Laurel Canyon, Los Angeles, California

Though originally famous for sporting this nation's first rubber-wheeled trolley buses at the beginning of our last century, Laurel Canyon became destined for a much different form of notoriety six decades later. Hosting perhaps America's greatest concentration of musical luminaries and creative sorts, this magical canyon's winding, dead-end lanes cloak many intriguing bungalows. Front porch guitar jams echoed forth along steep eucalyptus-scented ravines where backyard pools became venues for the making of cultural history. David Crosby brought Joni Mitchell to Laurel Canyon for the first time and produced her debut album. Crosby, Stills, Nash, and Young initially met each other at Mitchell's house. She soon became romantically involved with Graham Nash who, as a countercultural homage to domestic tranquility, wrote "Our House," which was then recorded by the entire group. Mitchell remembers looking out her window below to spot three naked women floating on rafts in Frank Zappa's duck pond, perhaps before his nocturnal basement gigging with neighborhood resident Jimi Hendrix. Just down the road, Laurel Canyon Country Store was this neighborhood's psychedelic vortex and sole commercial venue. There, members of The Byrds first learned about nearby housing options, while Carole King, The Eagles, or those harmonizing Mamas and the Papas might shop for sundries along with tuna salad sandwiches before making sleepover arrangements, often involving all-night drug sessions. Just behind that store Jim Morrison sat on his balcony composing "Love Street" for The Doors. Not far from the spot Jackson Browne lived, in a laundry room of an ambitious Columbia Records talent scout, is the house where Linda Ronstadt courted then-Governor Jerry Brown. With famed escape artist Harry Houdini inhabiting one mysterious hilltop estate, it's little wonder that a circus family of contortionists and stunt doubles would claim a castle-like idyll atop an adjacent summit.

Down at the flower-power-themed Laurel Canyon Country Store, its annual neighborhood get together finds Gary Morgan and his agile, red-headed daughter Bonnie enjoying an outing with Picasso, their pet cockatoo. The Flying Morgans are a multigenerational family of entertainers. Gary's parents performed with the USO, and his mother opened for Frank Sinatra in 1942. He and his wife practically raised their children at the Renaissance Faire where they honed their own theatrical performance skills. Atop their carnivalesque abode filled by circus memorabilia and outfitted with a trapeze for Bonnie's aerial workouts, they might babysit kangaroos or practice juggling routines. Gary's television appearances include *Naked City* and *The Partridge Family* while his stunt work has been seen in films like *Batman Forever, Logan's Run*, and *Cujo*. Among many movies, Bonnie's contortions are seen in films such as *Minority Report* or *Fright Night* and she holds the Guinness World Record for her three-minute stuffing into an incredibly tiny, two-foot-square box alongside a couple of other flexible humans.

IDIOTAROD MIMES

Bushwick, New York City, New York

One of history's greatest rescue adventures occurred during the fierce grip of winter in 1925, when northern Alaska's largest city was suddenly hit by an explosive diphtheria epidemic. A vital serum was desperately needed while ice-locked harbors in Nome and the inability of planes with water-cooled engines to fly at that time created a grueling dilemma for saving this city's population from widespread death. A daring plan was hatched to deploy twenty mushers and 150 Siberian huskies hauling lifesaving ampules of antitoxin serum along the legendary, Athabaskan-blazed Iditarod trail. Through numbing ice fog and fierce blizzards, these dogsled teams braved –40-degree temperatures, then after only slightly more than five days that included 674 grueling miles, the heroic relief triumphantly arrived at Nome, led by a failed gold prospector and his lead dog Balto. Overlooking other dogs, Balto immediately became this nation's most admired canine celebrity and a bronze statue celebrating the husky stands proudly on rocky outcrops in New York City's famed Central Park. A little over three miles away from this statue, in Brooklyn's McCarren Park, a modern-day comedic homage to the original Iditarod gathers annually during winter's coldest weeks for their own urban version of that Alaskan relay race. The irreverently named Idiotarod features zany, wildly modified shopping carts as contemporary stand-ins for dogsleds that careen down Bushwick's avenues drawing bemused stares from unsuspecting spectators watching their neighborhoods invaded by costumed racers piloting rolling phone booths and soaring pirate ships. In tribute to those log cabins that offered sheltering warmth to Alaskan mushers between legs of their wilderness race, tap rooms and dive bars serve as race checkpoints providing libations and spirits before the return onto windy Brooklyn streets.

At the ironically named Bushwick Country Club, two silent pranksters seem to enjoy a mime's respite from that Idiotarod's intense competitions after indulging in their pickleback, reputedly first invented at this not-so-exclusive establishment. This beverage now known worldwide, most often involves a shot of Jameson Whiskey chased by another with only pickle brine, helping to neutralize alcohol's burn. Its fame spread through local bartenders and into finer dining venues. Fortunately, it seems to pair perfectly with the wagyu burgers cooked up by racing competitors on a shopping cart's built-in stove. Suspender-clad Charles Harvey Knisely and green-capped Scott McBride epitomize the silly gravitas decorating an Idiotarod checkpoint. McBride proudly claims a diploma from the Ringling Brothers Clown College. For two years he traveled on rails across this country in a literal clown car, backflipping on trampolines, circling around Ringling's hippodrome while walking backwards atop an enormous ball, and performing for the Reagans on their White House lawn during its annual Easter Egg Roll.

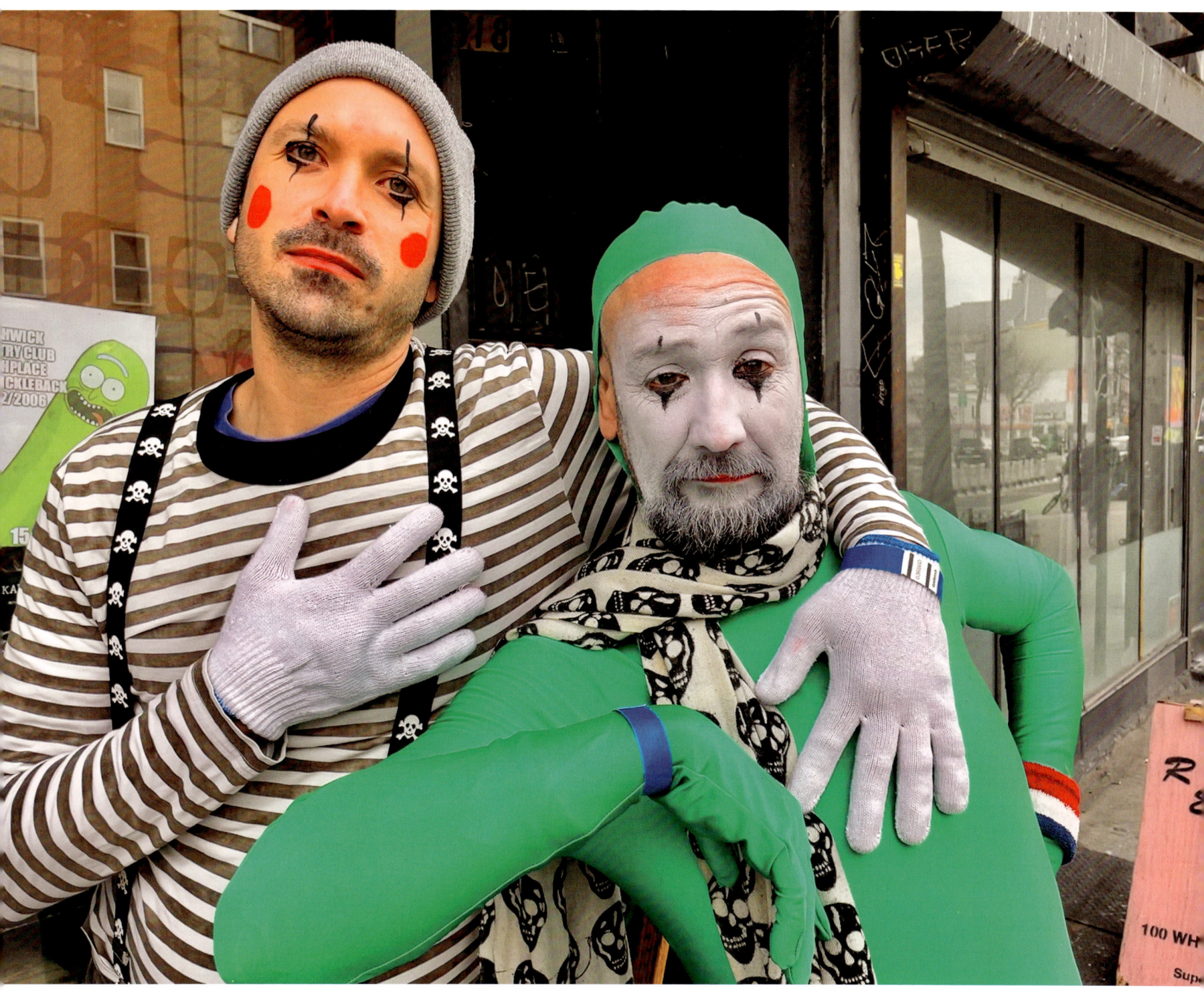

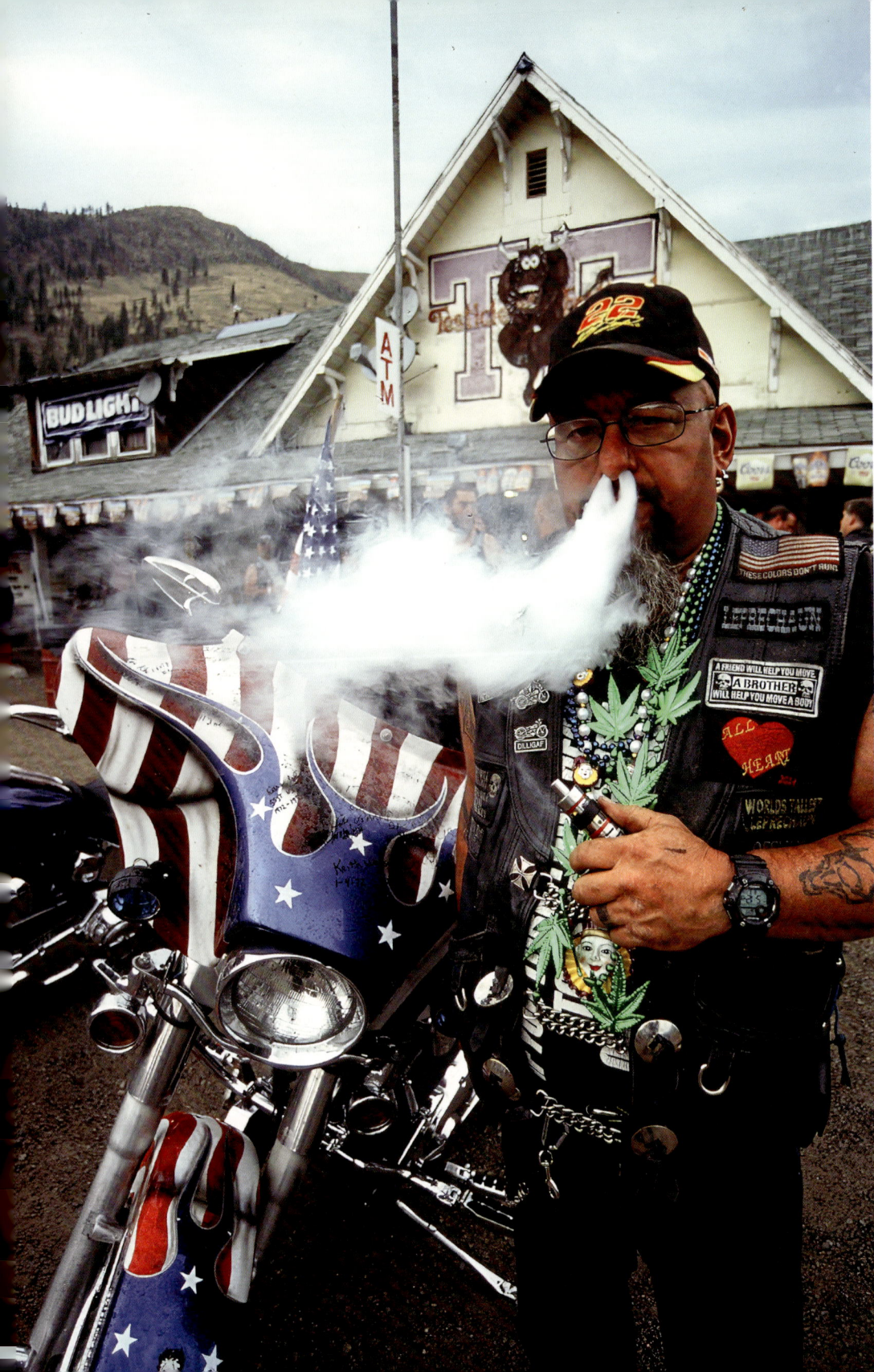

TESTICLE
FESTIVAL
ATTENDEE

Clinton, Montana

Near a convergence of five mountain ranges, the rugged landscape beyond Missoula contains white-tailed deer, grizzlies, black bear, and moose. They provide mere hints of an unusually wild environment that reflects the no-holds-barred speed limit on the nearby interstate, this nation's longest. Just barely off a rural exit ramp from Interstate 90, the annual five-day Testicle Festival is a notoriously raucous celebration. It offers deep-fried bull testicles that attract the gastronomically fearless, who no doubt were heeding highway billboard insinuations that visitors would have a ball. That offal truth can be found at Rock Creek Lodge, whose steamy kitchen is busy cooking up two tons of beer-marinated, well-breaded Rocky Mountain oysters, a cowboy delicacy salvaged from branding and castration practices carried out on neighboring ranches. Amidst pig wrestling and bull-chip throwing contests, an actual beauty competition for this festival's namesake is staged for its human contestants while being judged by females of the species.

Arriving en masse atop roaring choppers just in time for all this debauchery, a goateed biker astride his patriotic machine emits a fierce, dual tailpipe worth of vaping smoke from his nostrils. Replete with a shiny necklace of metallic marijuana, he proudly wears rebelliousness on his sleeves, where the biking culture's obscenity-capped acronym DILLIGAF decorates that leather vest's end, while one rectangular patch on another side helpfully explains those subtle differences between friends and brothers.

MOTORCYCLIST

Sturgis, South Dakota

Mankind's very first motorcycle was a steam-powered velocipede, demonstrated at fairs and circuses in the 1860s. These early vehicles, known as bone-shakers, had wheels of unequal size with a retrofitted coal-fired steam engine wedged between them. Its inventor died from an apparent heart attack while riding atop his creation. Within several years, four-stroke internal combustion engines were developed, encouraging William Harley, along with his friends Arthur and Walter Davidson, to devote the rest of their lives to perfecting motorbikes during its continued evolution, with each new generation of chop-pers proving themselves through the growing popularity embracing this racing sport. Competitive clubs soon developed and in 1938 one such entity, the Jackpine Gypsies Motorcycle Club of Sturgis, staged a Black Hills Motor Classic beneath those granitic spires of South Dakota's dramatic, tunnel-punc-tured Needles Highway. That first rally, viewed by a humble crowd numbering only about 175 people, featured nine riders performing stunts, including one daredevil cyclist crashing through walls of burning pine boards. In the near century since, that simple event exploded into an annual ten-day celebra-tion that has attracted over half a million visitors. They'll flood lodgings in this area and spill over into its local Buffalo Chip Campground, patronizing the biker-thronged Full Throttle Saloon and a host of other cycle-themed establishments. The world's largest motorcycle rally usually provides an apparent neutral zone, as rival biker clubs and gangs seem to rub shoulders with minimal friction, notwithstanding their loyalty oaths or hard-earned patches.

Amidst the metallic forest of Harley pipes and ape hangers that clog congested streets throughout Sturgis, this taciturn, leather-vested motorcyclist basks amongst his fellow rally bikers' roaring din. After returning from exhilarating ventures spent canyon carving across nearby Black Hills terrain, it's no easy riding trying to gingerly navigate bike-choked avenues that spread like spokes in every direction from the center of downtown. His do-rag appears to indicate club involvement with Empire of Defiance, a brotherhood of men that share their love for motorcycles and who were evidently born to be wild.

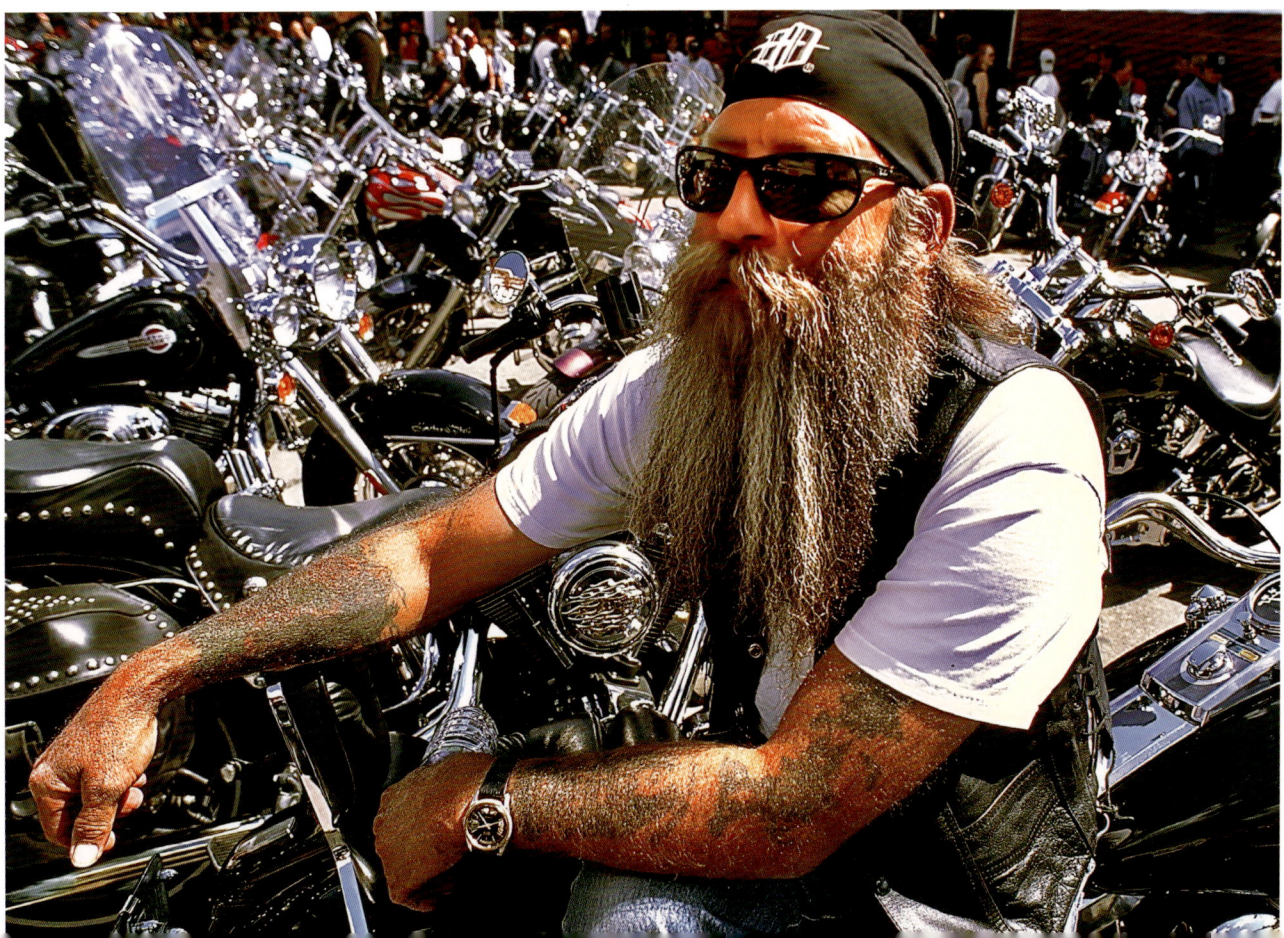

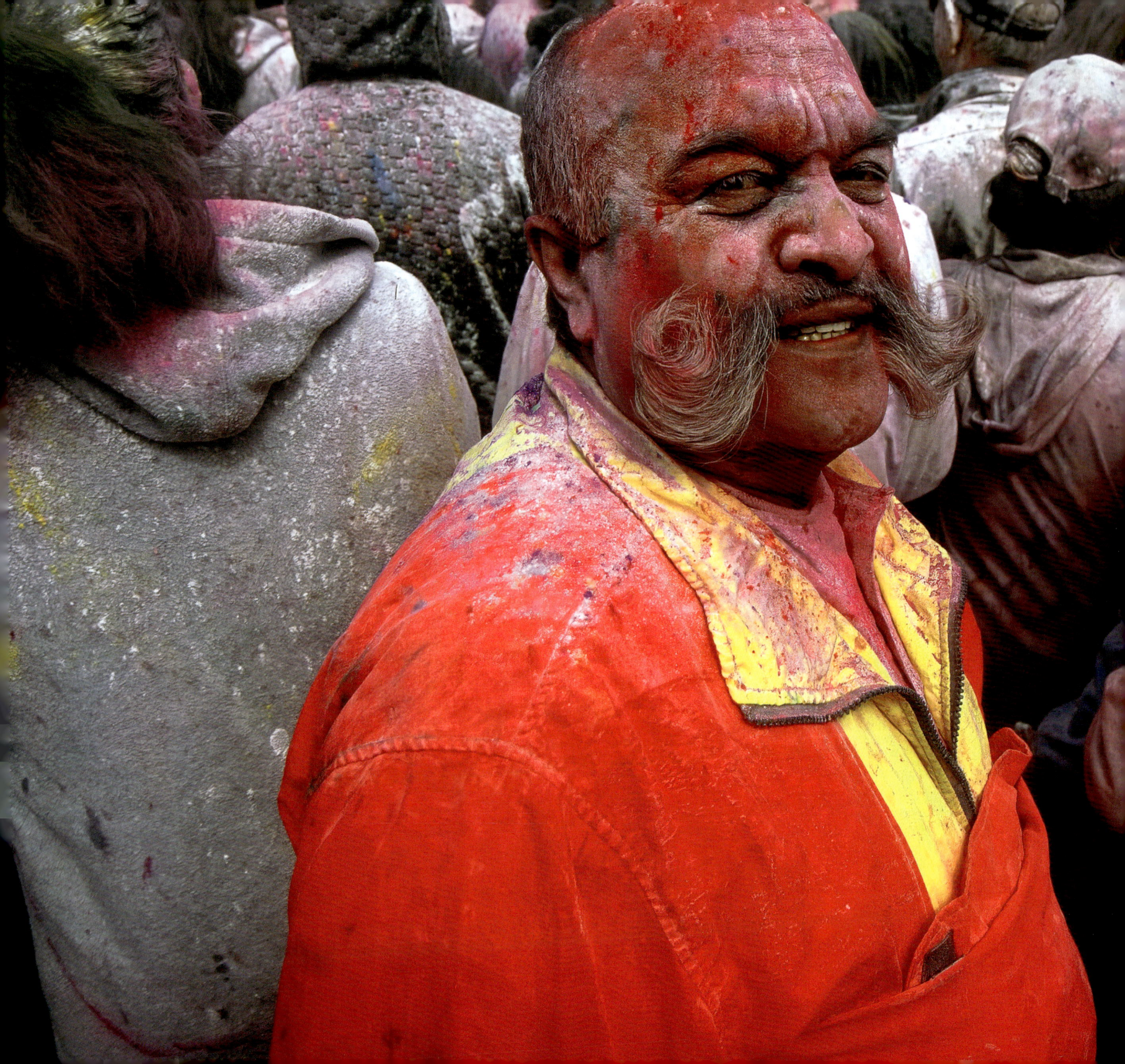

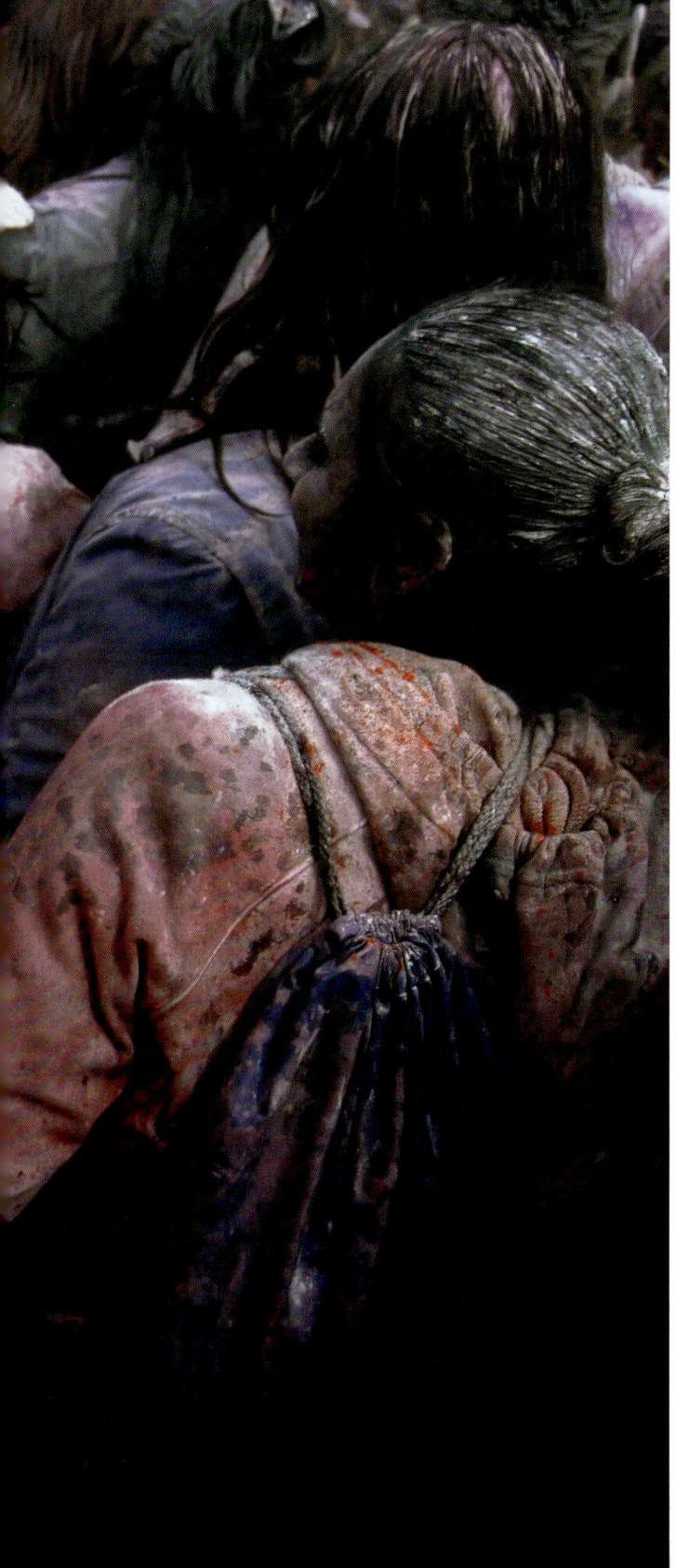

PHAGWAH PARTICIPANT

Richmond Hill, New York City, New York

Among the least understood South American nations is Guyana, spreading outward as this world's largest diaspora in relation to its share of native-born population. Its complex demographics are largely a stew of African slave descendants and the Indians later brought over as indentured servants to replace them in their thankless labors. Over 360 languages and dialects are spoken in the immigrant-friendly New York City borough of Queens, so it's not surprising that a very large Guyanese population has settled there, many within its sedate Richmond Hill neighborhood. As springtime approaches and only a mere inkling of budding begins to tip tree branches in Smokey Oval Park, an explosive riot punctuated by vivid pigments will shortly fill the air. Those honoring their Indian heritage will gather on a full or new moon to celebrate Phagwah, named after its originating month of Phagoon in the Hindu calendar. This joyous festivity is rooted in agriculture, meant to spur regrowth and fertility, yet commemorates ancient Hindu mythology when evil princess Holika's ashes are now gleefully thrown in the form of perfumed abir, along with sprays of Ayurvedic herb-based colored dyes that mix with thick clouds tinted by pastel powder. These vivid coatings harken Holi's ancient stories regarding Lord Krishna's attempts to transform the facial complexion of Radha, his Shakti consort. After devotional songs fill flower-decked neighborhood mandirs, decorated floats and blue-faced deities lead paraders to the raucous festivities several blocks away, where dizzying rhythms of goat-skinned tassa drums lure arriving throngs.

Amongst a speckled painting filled by crowded attendees, this celebrant's facial canvas sports his rakishly swirling handlebar mustache, an enduring Indian symbol of maleness dictating caste equations and social standing. His vibrant vermillion jacket, echoing hues from the Guyanese flag, is splotched with granules of blooming palash and turmeric at this annual pharmacological color war.

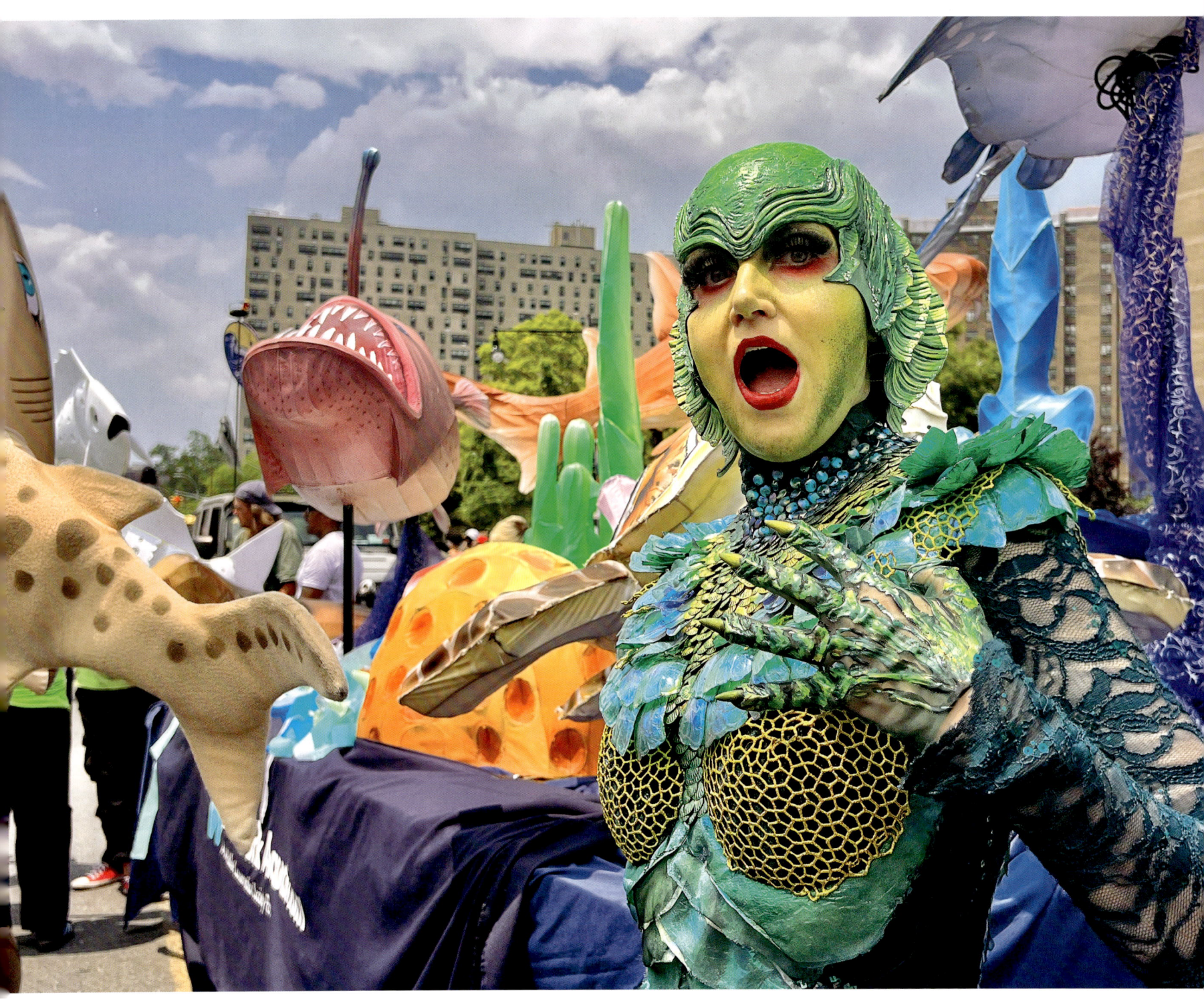

MERMAID PARADE SEA CREATURE

Coney Island, New York City, New York

Ever since our Neolithic era, the year's longest day has been recognized through glorifying celebration and symbolic pageantry. The summer solstice occurs just when our sun is at its farthest point from earth's equator, helping determine seasonal rhythms for growing crops and signaling a new planting cycle. Across ancient Egypt, their sun deity Ra helped predict the Nile's annual flooding and was worshipped in soaring, colonnaded temples, while an axis of carefully positioned stone circles in Celtic culture precisely marked solar passages during solstice days. As midsummer approached, pre-Christian pagan rituals prescribed bonfires to ward off evil spirits and welcome fertility. In the United States' largest city, the solstice-triggered Mermaid Parade has for over four decades drawn a hallucinatory ensemble of several thousand participants toward its boardwalk and streets tracing Coney Island's amusement park neighborhood. Gliding those iconic ipe-planked boardwalks, antique wicker rolling chairs dating back to 1923 host King Neptune and Queen Mermaid, their last names borrowed from titles of nearby avenues. These oceanside luminaries lead a surrealistic honky-tonk procession of tattooed sailors flirting with nearly topless mermaids, while Poseidon and Triton wannabes pull up the rear. Handcrafted mythological creatures emerge from each direction as fantastical representations of maritime and seashore life. Their vivid procession led by brass bands, antique automobiles, and crowded floats entertains throngs of spectators who'll witness concluding ceremonies at the ocean's edge, inaugurating another lifeguard-protected swimming season.

On Surf Avenue, menacing sharks and floating stingrays appear alongside surrealistic menageries of marine biology wading through spectators, as a fishnet-sleeved, amphibian-fingered mermaid seems to gasp for oxygen through gills encrusted with barnacles. Her horseshoe crab bra appears smothered by kelp, providing little real-life assistance in staying cool when ocean breezes subside during the solstice's sizzling summer heat.

UFO FESTIVAL ALIENS

Roswell, New Mexico

As America's Cold War began to dawn, a sudden spate of unusual reported sightings claimed mysterious atmospheric phenomena and filled breathless newspaper headlines across this country. In late June, 1947, a level-headed pilot flying near Mount Rainier reported spotting a chain of flat, brightly flashing pie-pan objects threading their way along the Cascades range. It was the resulting press which first coined that term "flying saucer," and an ensuing national uproar sparked a wide array of copycat claims and hoaxes. Into this charged atmosphere, an official Roswell Army Air Field press release was issued on July 8 of that year announcing a mysterious craft had recently crashed at the remote Foster Ranch north of town. The announcement was quickly retracted, falsely attributing the objects recovered as fragments of a weather balloon. For three decades that incident lay dormant in public imaginations until 1978 when retired lieutenant colonel Jesse Marcel was interviewed by a prominent ufologist and admitted that the original story was an attention-diverting coverup. Marcel speculated about the extraterrestrial origin of the recovered debris, igniting a mythic cultural phenomenon centering around Roswell. That only intensified over the next couple of decades as the city embraced its notoriety and a cluster of eyewitness accounts emerged, including one mortician's claim to witnessing alien autopsies. Documentaries followed, along with a number of eponymously named movies and TV programs. In addition, Emmy Award-winning *The X-Files*, at that time television's longest-running science fiction series, featured a sprawling mythology that drew heavily from the Roswell incident.

At Roswell's UFO Festival, empty stares on alien-headed lamp posts illuminate the way to coffee shops dispensing ET-themed lattes or the flying saucer-shaped McDonald's. Silvery creatures with tinfoil hats stroll down the block toward spaceship simulators at the International UFO Museum, which hosts realistic dioramas spotlighting dissections of space beings alongside heated symposiums that feature paranormal aficionados, conspiracy theorists, space nerds, and survivors from extraterrestrial abduction. Amidst the outdoor costume contest, feline pupils and metallic eyebrows blink at an otherworldly mélange of eerie, unearthly species reuniting during their annual invasion of this once-quiet western ranching community.

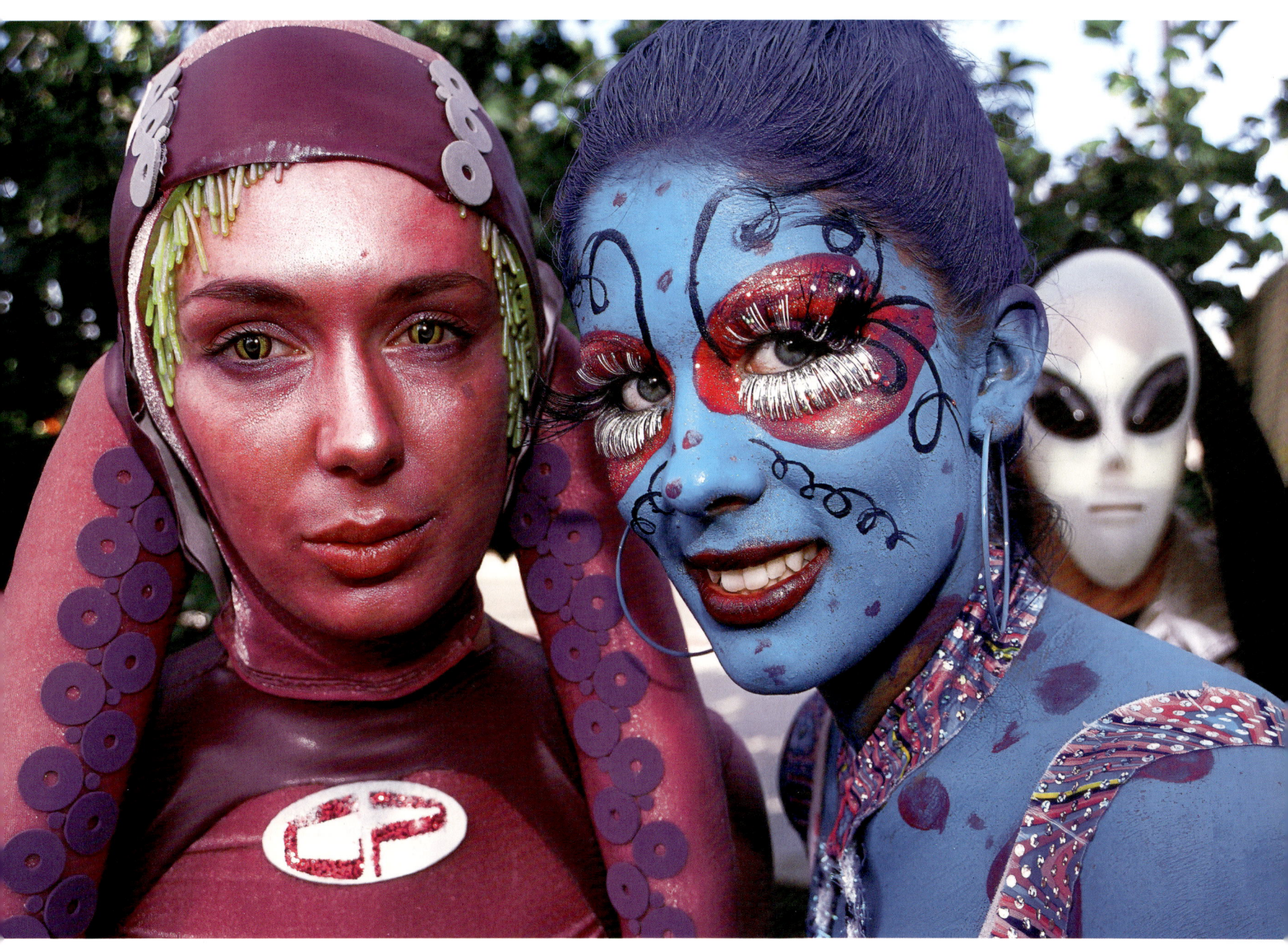

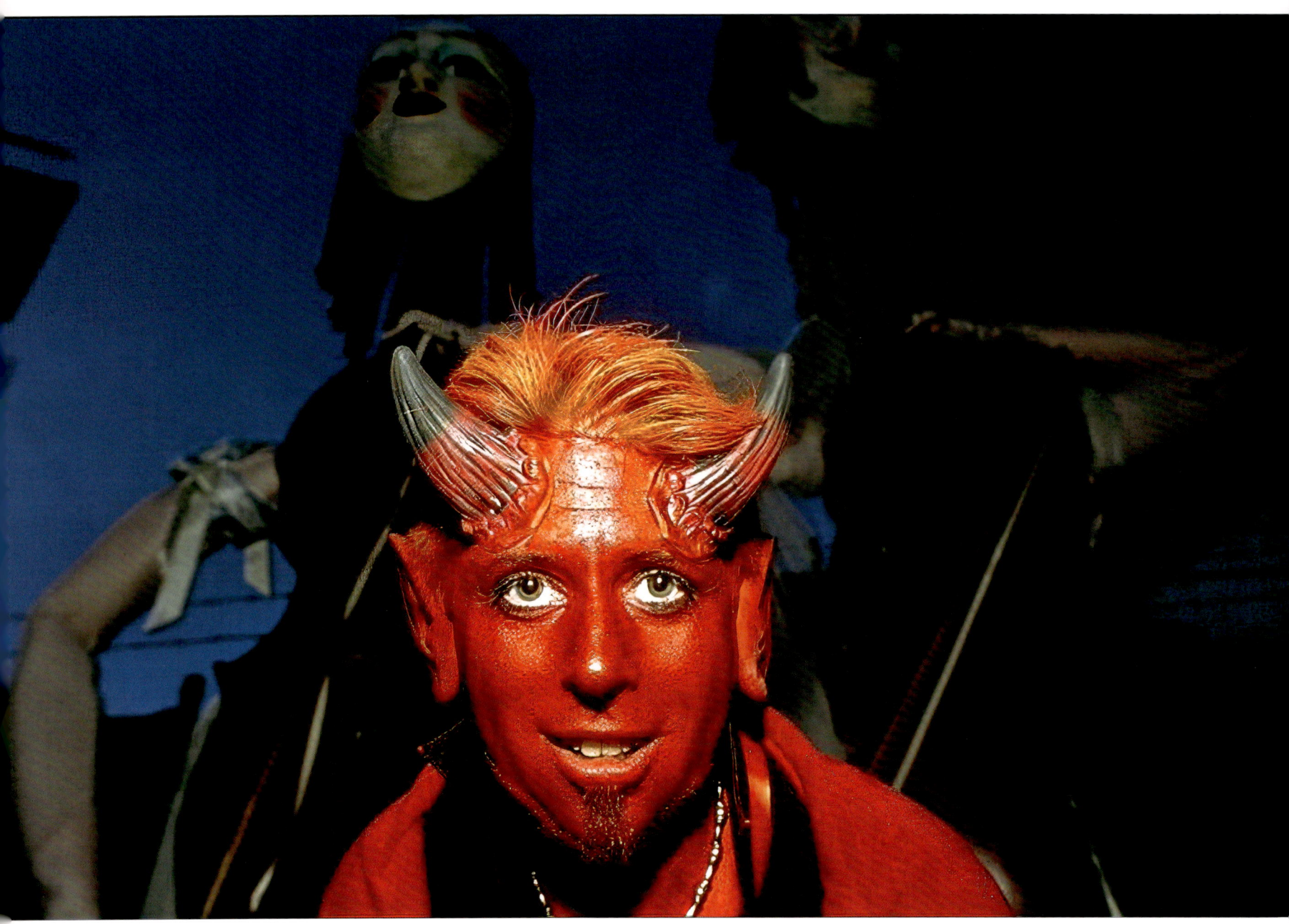

HALLOWEEN DEVIL

Greenwich Village, New York City, New York

Two millennia ago, northern Britain's high latitude Celtic culture celebrated the extremes of seasonal light. Summers there would see the sun setting well after bedtime, while winters only experienced some short glimpses of daylight. Pagan superstitions marked the midpoint between autumnal equinox and winter solstice, so Samhain celebrated an end to summer's harvests, and beginnings of a cold, dark winter, often morbidly associated with death. The first of November was a time fraught with danger and absorbed by fear. They believed that veils between life and death were thinnest then, allowing demons to freely inhabit the earth. Masks would be worn by guisers to impersonate ancestors and confuse malevolent spirits. Bonfires were set to ward off evil, guide souls seeking the afterlife, and illuminate darkness, in turn attracting insects that lured hungry bats for dinnertime. Medieval folklore envisioned these winged mammals as frightening harbingers of doom. In the eighth century, Pope Gregory III attempted to transform these pagan rituals into holy celebrations of heavenly saints for converting Christians. All Saints' Day still grasped onto some of Samhain's traditions and was preceded on October 31 by All Hallows' Eve. Known also as Hallowmas, this holiday was referenced by William Shakespeare, and in 1785 Scotland's national poet Robert Burns described witches, devils, and mischief-making within his saga-length, 28-stanza work entitled Halloween, first introducing that portmanteau into today's lexicon. Ghostly legends were seriously believed, like that of Stingy Jack whose soul was prohibited from heaven before outsmarting the devil to avoid hell, and so became destined to wander the land along with a troubled spirit. To avoid frightening encounters, Irish villagers lined streets with scary faces carved into turnips or potatoes, innards stuffed with burning coal. When Ireland's 1845 potato famine sent populations fleeing to America they brought their holiday customs along, adapting distinctly American pumpkins for their carvings and creating jack o' lanterns. The country's first Halloween parade in 1920 took place in Anoka, Minnesota, where townsfolk hoped to dissuade mischievous holiday pranksters who upended outhouses and let cows loose on their main street. Last century in the United States, when Halloween treats helped quell vandalism's tricks, this mostly agrarian society moved on from nuts, coins, or toys and quickly latched onto sweet traditions of tricolored candy corn, a confection evoking seasonal harvests and first known as chicken feed. In the 1970s, parents concerned about the safety of unwrapped pastilles created a boom for candy bar makers, who churned out this eagerly sought currency for masked neighborhood trick-or-treaters.

Originally a small community stroll through Greenwich Village led by puppeteer and mask maker Ralph Lee, the world's largest Halloween celebration now attracts 50,000 costumed participants which for over five decades has featured scary processions of werewolves, vampires, and zombies snaking their way past sinister hobgoblins, rattling skeletons, or ghoulish poltergeists. Ghostly phantoms serenade vengeful witches and meander through wonder-struck crowds now numbering almost two million spectators. The mad impresario orchestrating all this nocturnal grotesquery is celebration artist Jeanne Fleming, tirelessly creating a dizzying urban hallucinogen of eerie mayhem. Beneath two-story rouge-cheeked dancing apparitions, a crimson-horned, hazel-eyed demon bedevils onlookers as dusk reluctantly surrenders to an eccentric night of fright.

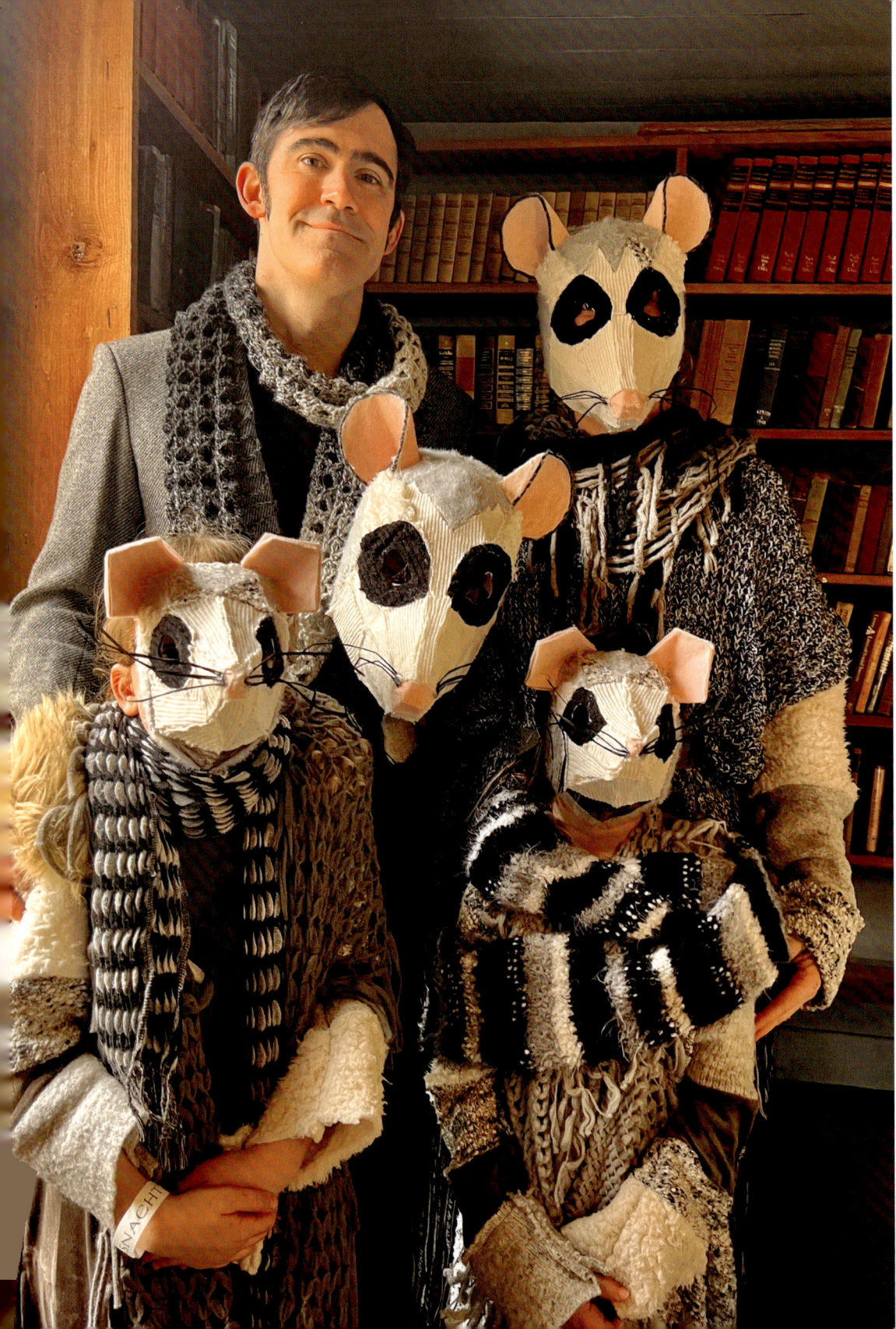

FASNACHT MASQUERADERS

Helvetia, West Virginia

Deep within bulging folds of forested alps, chimneys on ramshackle cabins belch smoke, slowly rising to mingle with wintry clouds that stubbornly grasp onto rugged ridge lines. In hollers below, coal and lumber trucks navigate treacherous serpentine curves twisting endlessly across the sprawling Mountain State. At least an hour in all directions from any traffic light is one tiny settlement of just a few dozen people named Helvetia, the Latin name for Switzerland that's engraved on its golden coins along with her edelweiss-garlanded personification. Joyously clinging to its Swiss ancestry, this usually flower-bedecked village sits by Buckhannon River's Left Fork Right Fork whose nascent flows will eventually end up deposited into the Gulf of Mexico. The riverbanks are anchored by The Hütte, a heartwarmingly humble gastronomic palace of heritage foodways where female servers scurry past potbellied stoves, timeless cuckoo clocks, mounted deer heads, and family heirlooms to deliver tasty plates of sauerbraten, hot apple sauce, or peach cobbler. While visitors come from afar to indulge in steaming platters of Swiss cuisine, a true draw to this fairytale outpost is this nation's sole Fasnacht carnival celebration. With deeply embedded roots tracing back to medieval German-speaking pre-Lenten festivities, startling costume-studded revelry infiltrates this shutters-decorated rural pocket of Appalachia one day a year. Fiddle-filled bluegrass melodies spill from the pocket-sized Helvetia Star Band Hall and signal revelers who gather across rustic wooden bridges, beneath its melody-chiming church spire and in front of a general store-*cum*-post office that triples its functions as an oddball mask museum. When dusk approaches, fantastical figures of handmade mythical varmints and cryptid beasts begin their exuberant promenade across the meadow as a burgeoning lampion parade congeals into candlelit formations. An effigy of Old Man Winter is then released from imprisonment within a village gazebo to lead illuminated processions down the road toward their crowd-rimmed roaring bonfire where this ghostly specter will soon meet his fiery demise. Along the route, chanting spectators make known their eagerness to symbolically dismiss bleak wintertime weather and welcome in a rapid coming of spring. After the immolation, throngs will retreat into an adjacent Community Hall, where a rousing square dance and polka hoedown entertain novice goblin-masked hoofers. Just outside, the bonfire's dwindling embers send sparks soaring skyward to compete with this hamlet's curling chimney smoke.

Atop creaky rafters in the Helvetia Star Band Hall, a nest of mice congregate by aging bookshelves before scurrying off to join gathering menageries in this village's historic square. The momentarily unveiled patriarch of this enigmatic, wool-crocheted family, Daniel Schumacher is an editorial director at *Taste of the South* magazine in addition to being a small batch roaster for his Wired Possum Coffee business. Later on, as candlelit townsfolk gather by that general store for an annual lampion parade, a surrealistic googly-eyed creature prepares for the procession. His hand-held glowing illumination reveals that of the 84 staring eyeballs, at least two include actual retinas.

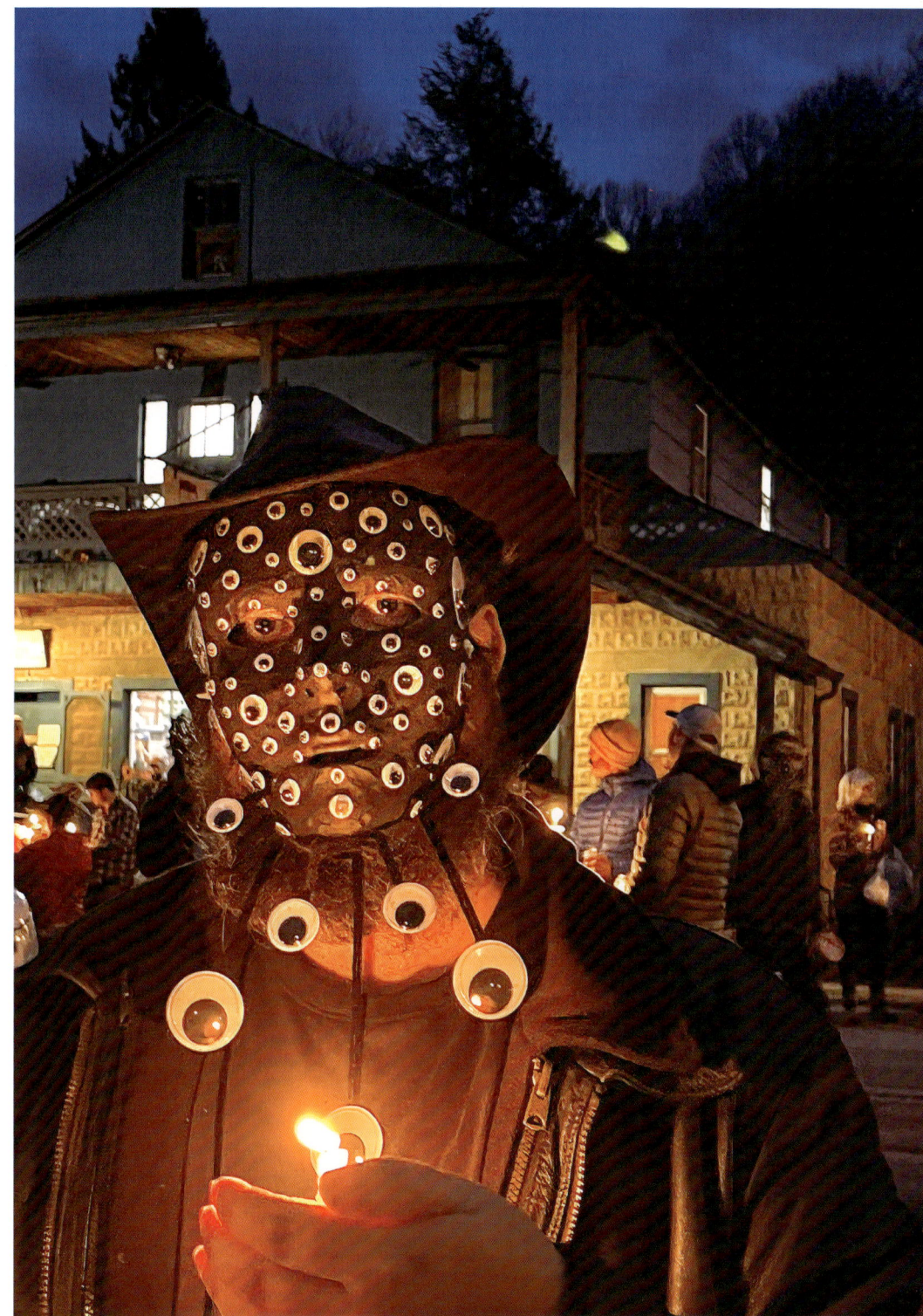

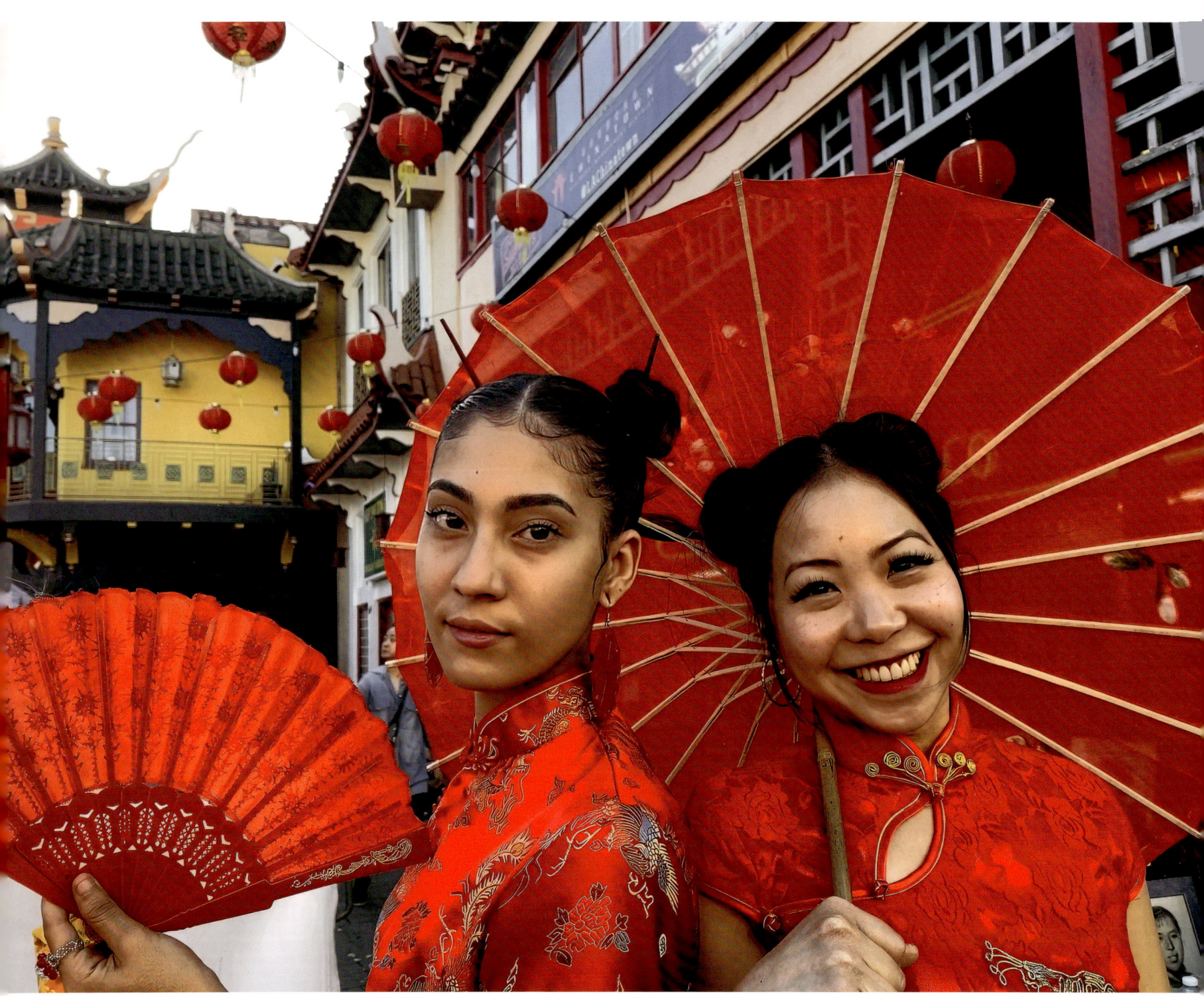

CHINESE NEW YEAR CELEBRANTS

Los Angeles, California

In the nation's first Chinese-owned neighborhood, a warren of lantern-strung alleyways are lined with herbal shops, fragrant bakeries, and incense-filled temples. This reincarnation of Los Angeles's original Asian settlement, demolished to make way for the downtown Union Station, was actually developed in 1938 by Hollywood set designers creating its Central Plaza as a visual homage echoing old Shanghai. The entertainment industry further stamped its character here exactly at an intersection where Sun Mun Way meets Jung Jing Road, anchoring a fairly imposing, 1,600-pound bronze statue of iconic martial artist and film star Bruce Lee, who ran his Jeet Kune Do fight school here. His alert, nunchuck-wielding stance draws waves of admirers and amused visitors aping for their cameras.

During the confetti and fireworks-sprayed Chinese New Year, money-stuffed hongbao envelopes are exchanged as fiercely scowling dragons twist past animated, tandem-staffed lions whirling beneath towering pagodas. Their syncopated dance accompanies a clangorous cacophony of crash cymbals and shigu drums which aspire to defeat evil spirits and usher in auspicious fortune for the eager revelers. Such desires for prosperity are evidenced in these two hopeful celebrants, their jackets brocaded with peacocks, a Ming Dynasty symbol of luck and nobility. The brilliant reds of their garb, umbrella, and fan signify a culture's millennia-old beliefs about that color's power to boost prosperity for an upcoming year.

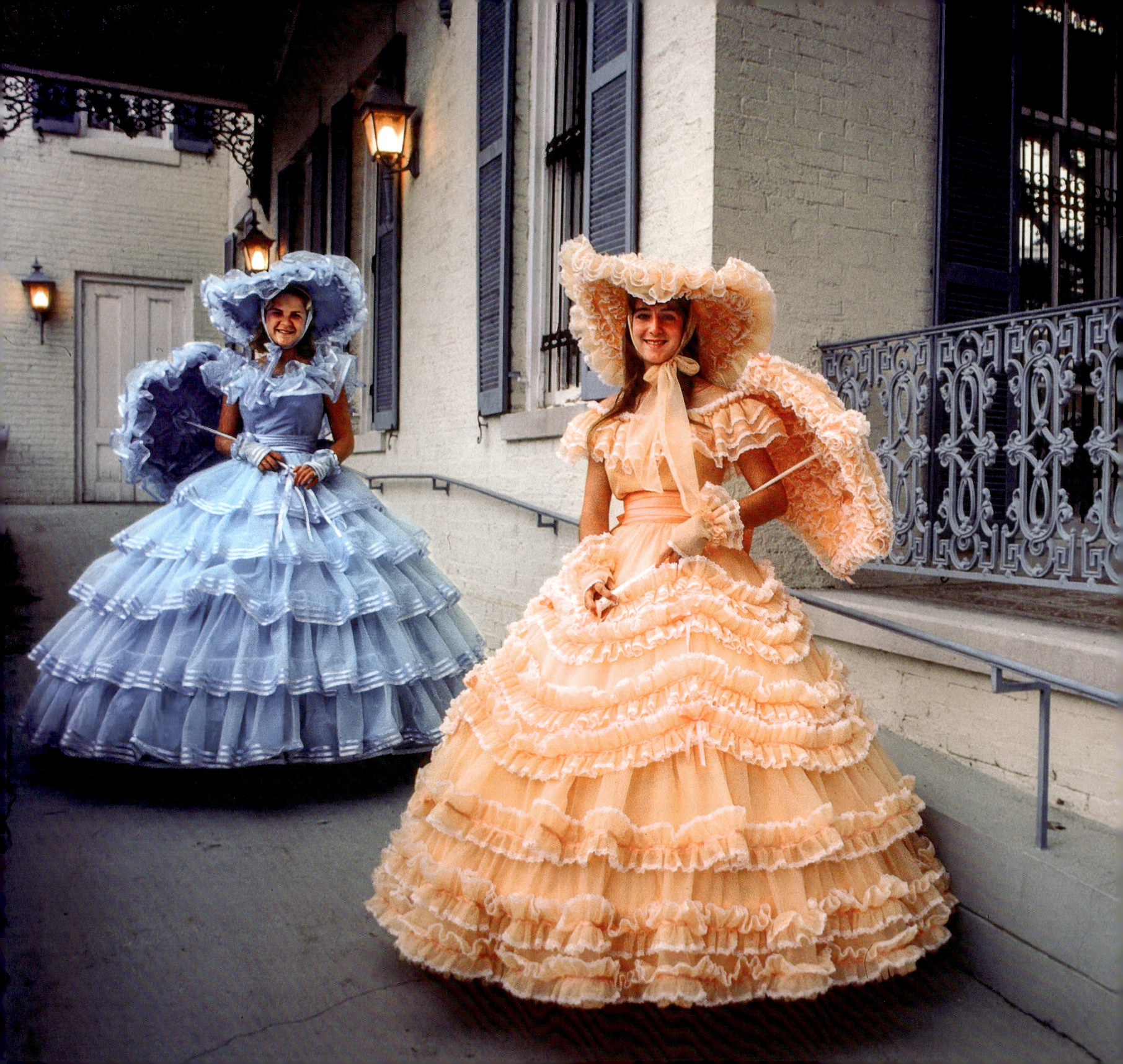

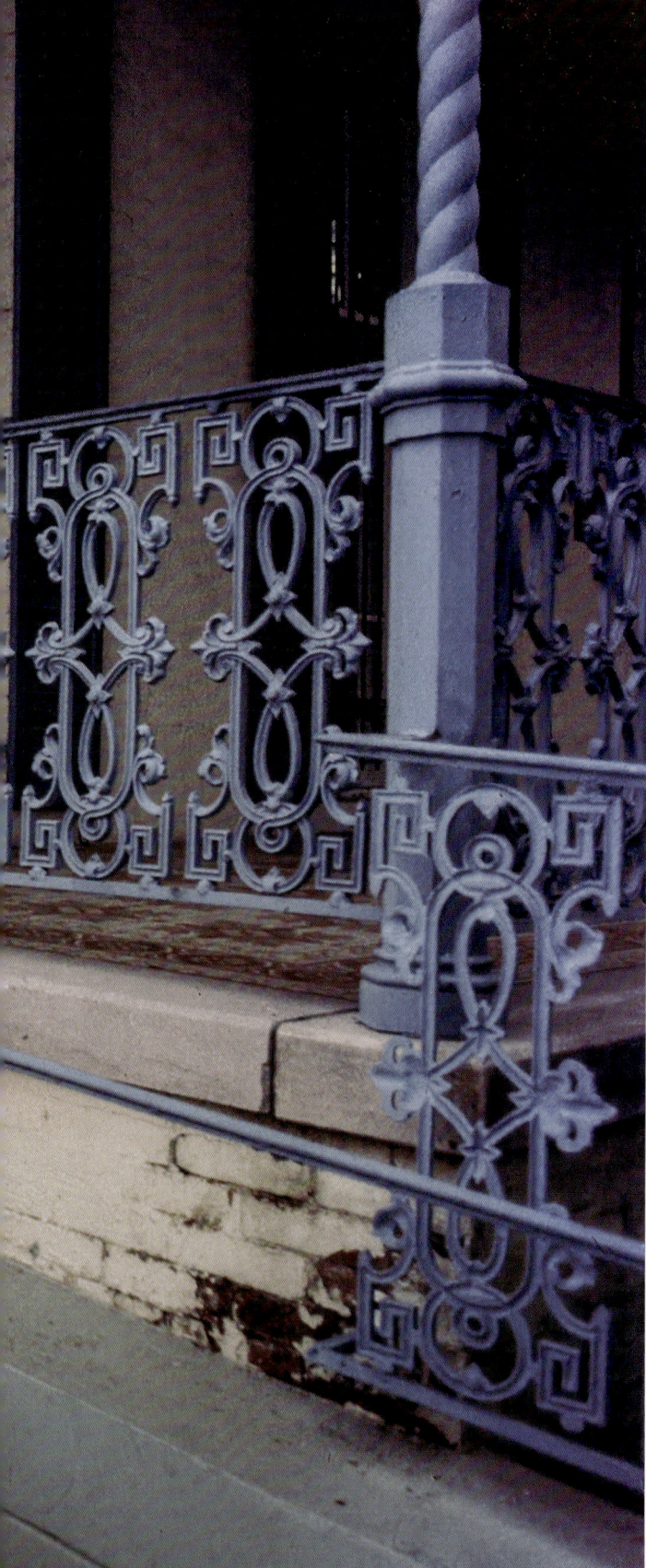

AZALEA TRAIL MAIDS

Mobile, Alabama

Defying an entrenched belief about Mardi Gras' origination in New Orleans, it was actually first hosted in Mobile, Alabama, this celebration's earliest known home in the New World. French Catholic settlers commemorated the Boeuf Gras (fatted ox), brought in 1703 to this city, where its first parade featured a cart pushed by sixteen men and carrying one rather large papier-mâché cow's head. Exactly three centuries of mystic societies and thrown beads later, Mobile finally showcases in all its jester and doubloon glory, a museum created from the wrought-iron clad Bernstein-Bush House, an historic 1872 Creole cottage.

Decorating a side along the gas lamp-lit facade are two pastel-cloaked Azalea Trail Maids, enthusiastic ambassadors to this fragrant city, and emblematic of those flowers that brought Mobile its botanical renown. Their iconic, floral-themed dresses are designed to be emblematic of that graceful charm and hospitality often envisioned about the South. Following lifelong dreams for many who endured their rigorous interviewing process, one select group characterized by valedictorians and honor students are eventually recruited to form a fifty-member, garden-inspired troupe of modern-day Southern belles. Their garments may cost up to $5,000, as an eager army constituted by eighteen seamstresses is employed for individual custom creations of ten-part ensembles that include a three-steel ring hoop skirt, pantaloons, gauntlets, cummerbund, parasol, hat, bow, and sash. Decked out within an astonishing fifty-pound garment, they seem to defy gravity, floating across antebellum porches and softly rebutting uneducated, controversial notions that this country's universal dress style of the early nineteenth century is in any way indicative of slavery-era plantation culture, promulgated by myth-pursuing films like *Gone with the Wind*.

SHOWGIRLS

Las Vegas, Nevada

Deemed by NASA to be earth's brightest spot, the Las Vegas Strip stabs a nighttime desert skyline with shimmering neon cavalcades of winking cowboys, glowing comets, and thirst-quenching martinis. Much earlier, in one of the continent's most parched regions, federal agencies envisioned its largest civil engineering feat when construction of Hoover Dam was initiated in 1930 to provide drinking water, irrigation, and hydroelectric power for this Mojave Desert region. Erecting earth's tallest dam required an enormous infusion of laborers as 25,000 single male workers flocked here to escape the Great Depression, taking residency in newly created Boulder City. While jackhammer-wielding human pendulums swung from canyon cliffs, a massive sixty-story-high concrete wall arose and impounded this nation's largest reservoir, drowning the Mormon town of St. Thomas whose last holdout finally departed his home by rowboat atop Lake Mead's rising waters. Meanwhile, dam workers snuck away on weekends from their highly restrictive settlement to nearby Las Vegas, where they eagerly spent their paychecks at newly legalized casinos, showgirl theaters, and bordellos. Once only a piddling, dusty railway stop, the city's thriving activities soon attracted Mafia operations to this criminally wide-open town. Not surprisingly the dam's very first electrical recipient was downtown Las Vegas along Fremont Street, which became known as "glitter gulch" when establishments bathed themselves in jolting, customer-luring neon lights, a relatively new technology. Downtown's energy spilled onto the strip as fledgling lodges were replaced with a mob-fueled game of one-upmanship. Larger entertainment emporiums boasted air-conditioned rooms with their own television sets that adjoined windowless casinos, devoid of clocks or any hints of daylight, thrumming away with bell-ringing slot machines and dealer-shuffling blackjack tables. Notorious mobster Bugsy Siegel became a founder and beating heart of swanky Flamingo Hotel, the

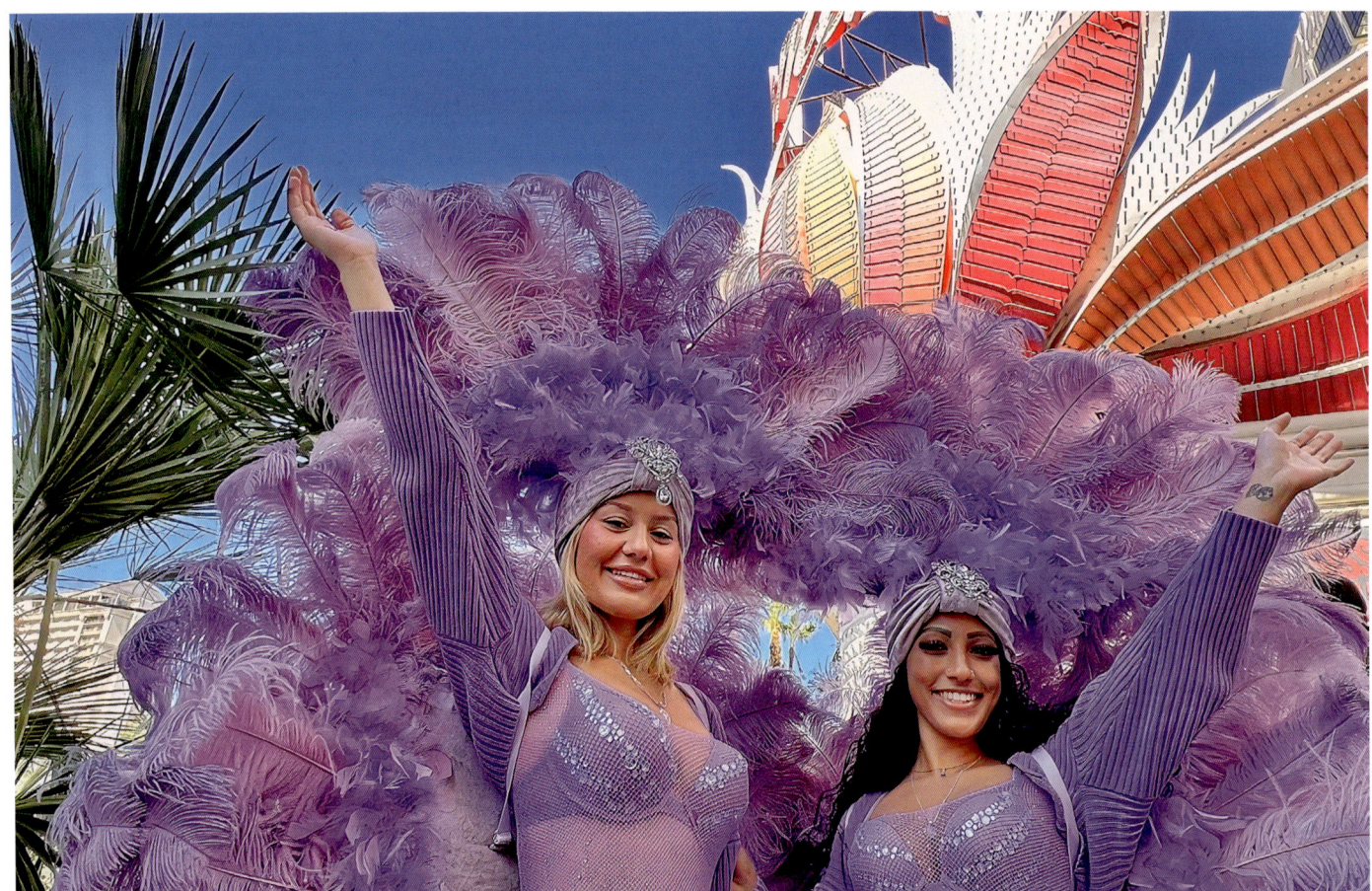

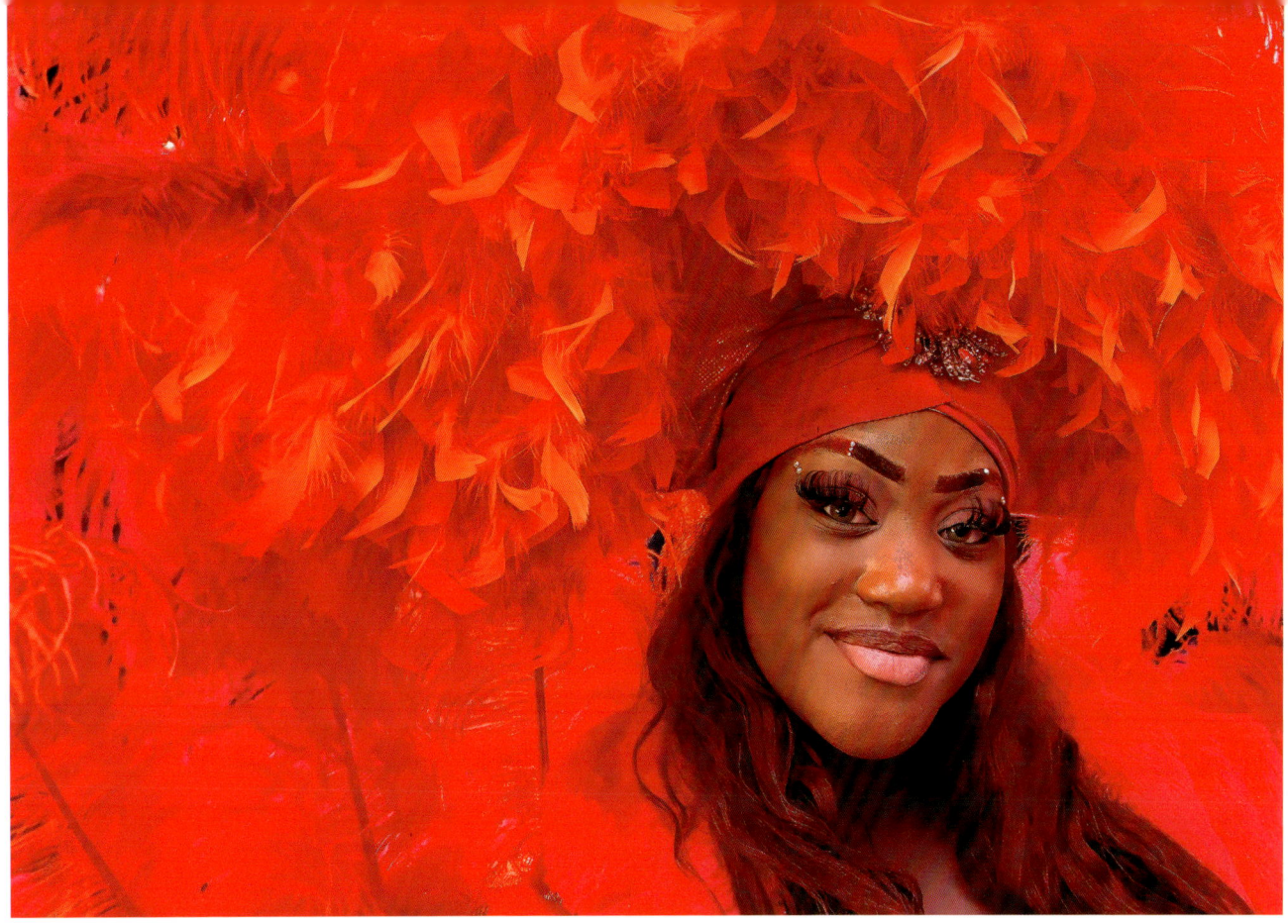

strip's longest operating casino, where tuxedo-clad servers doted on an exciting constellation of celebrities who threw dice while attending its 1946 gala opening, hosted by legendary star Jimmy Durante. Bedazzled showgirls adjusted flamboyant ostrich-adorned headdresses before preening for elaborate onstage performances. Today nonchalant flamingos wander the grounds, apparently unaware that this property's name was actually first inspired by Siegel's red-headed and long-legged girlfriend. An iconic fixture of Vegas pop culture, the ritzy establishment made constant cameos in Hollywood's motion pictures, from Elvis Presley's *Viva Las Vegas* to depictions as a prime heist target in *Ocean's Eleven* with Frank Sinatra and Sammy Davis. As for that mobster founder of this fabled playground for wealthy high rollers, he quickly checked out when shot in the head by probably disgruntled repayment-deprived gangsters, propelling one eyeball fifteen feet onto a tiled dining room floor. Perhaps more troubling still were nearby nuclear blasts that prompted hotels to stage rooftop viewing parties in the early 1950s, when explosive testings helped promote cancer-taunting tourism with atomic-themed cocktails and beauty pageants.

Awash in plumage and boas, two beaming showgirls strike a classic pose and seem to be fitting adornments to the 70-foot-high bouquet of fuchsia and tangerine neon-veined feathers that crown an entrance into this historic Las Vegas Strip landmark. One upraised wrist seems to suggest her affinity to local gambling culture with an inked tattoo of rolling dice. Beneath a scarlet fountain of quivering feathers, luxuriant eyelashes and dramatic etchings of mascara fail to distract from one showgirl's searing gaze along Fremont Street. She echoes a showgirl tradition stretching back to high-kicking late nineteenth-century Parisian cabarets of froufrou-swaying joie de vivres at Moulin Rouge and Folies Bergère. Its Roaring Twenties Americanization infiltrated stage revues during Broadway's Ziegfeld Follies, subsequently followed by highly choreographed dancing kaleidoscopes swirling away in Busby Berkeley's filmed musicals the following decade.

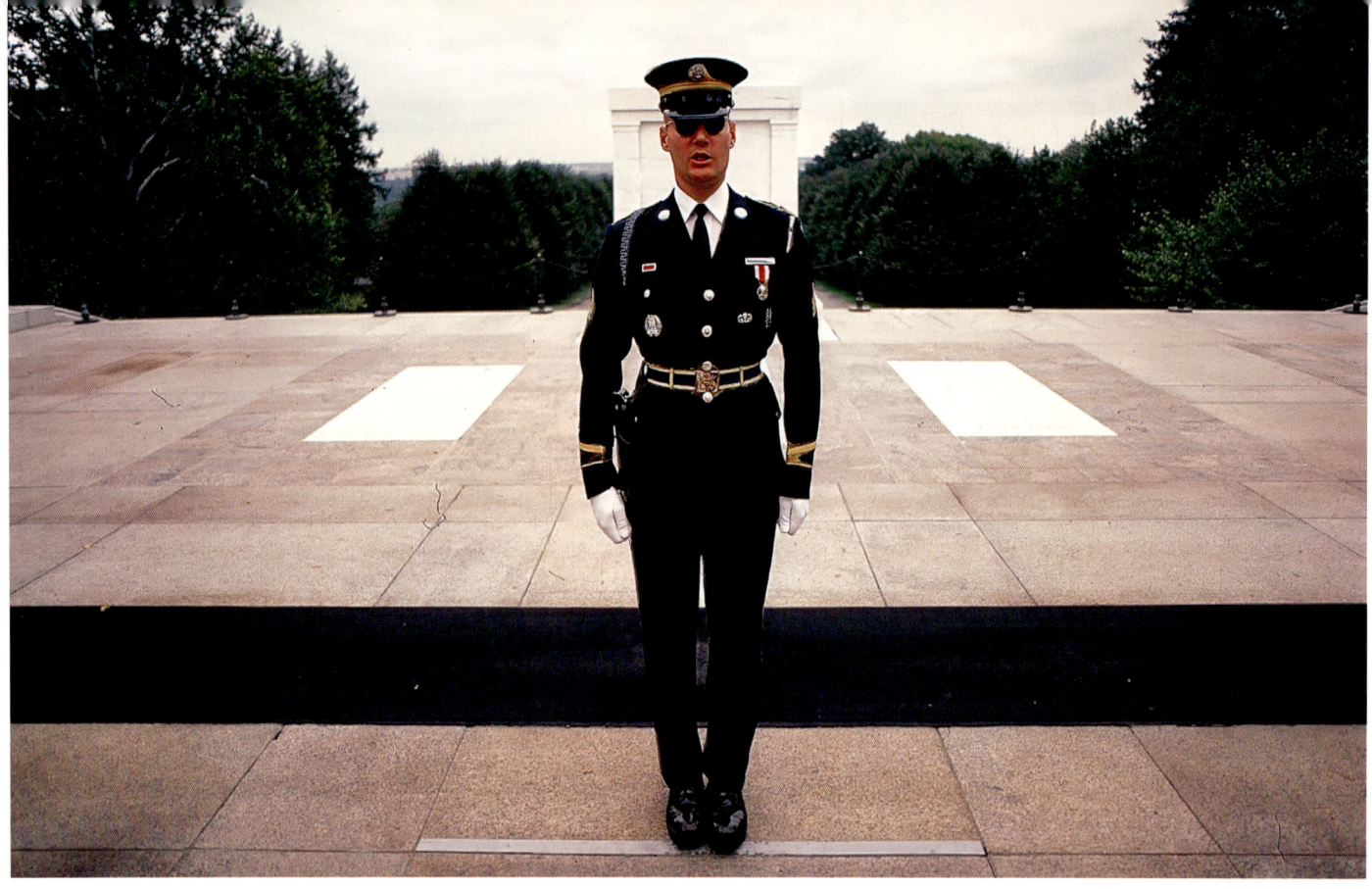

TOMB SENTINEL

Arlington, Virginia

During America's Civil War, the 1864 Battle of the Wilderness resulted in massive death tolls for Union troops. Need for an additional cemetery near Washington, D.C., soon focused on confiscating a hilltop Arlington Estate, privately owned by family members of Confederate general Robert E. Lee. Arlington National Cemetery became a final resting ground for many highly notable Americans, including astronauts, Supreme Court justices, and presidents of the United States. There is no celebrity name, however, at that precise landmark drawing the largest visitation to this national memorial ground. Geographically located precisely in the middle of a cemetery spanning almost 500 football fields, The Tomb of the Unknown Soldier honors those brave and selfless acts of wartime soldiers who left this world with nobody bearing witness to their departure. Beneath a 79-ton marble neoclassical sarcophagus lie the intended remains of unidentified soldiers from both world war conflicts, plus the Korean and Vietnam Wars. As one result of modern DNA testing, a heroic body from Vietnam, the only anonymous one ever recovered, was identified and removed by family wishes to their closer military cemetery. Those remaining three soldiers are dutifully looked after by an extremely elite corps of Tomb Guards. These sentinels must commit to at least two years, while living beneath that tomb in barracks and forswearing cursing or drinking alcohol for an entire lifetime at the risk of losing a sacred wreath pin. Since 1937, the tomb has been guarded continuously in half-hour shifts, 24 hours per day, 365 days a year with absolutely no exception, blizzards and hurricanes notwithstanding.

Rigid and immaculately groomed, a sunglass-guarded tomb sentinel prepares for his Changing of the Guard ceremony. With exacting tribute to the sacred 21-gun salute, he will march precisely those many steps, then halt for that same duration of seconds before repeating this process in reverse. Subjected to excruciating inspection for wrinkles, folds, and lint, this medal-honored uniform supplements polished, heavily insulated shoes with metal heel plates that provide a satisfying click during their halts. Though his gloves are deliberately moistened to prevent slippage while handling his firearm, it's virtually guaranteed he won't lose a grip on his demeanor.

GUNNERS MATE

New York City, New York

In all American history it was only George Dewey that was ever named Admiral of the United States Navy. Under his command American warships delivered a decisive victory in the Philippines at Manila Bay. Returning a year later in 1899 from one of the most significant maritime battles in history, American warships sailed triumphantly into New York's harbor. There a weeklong commemoration of their success during the Spanish-American War included parades and hobnobbing with city residents. That celebratory lineup of nautical might eventually kicked off an annual tradition known as Fleet Week. A cultural exchange of sorts between military and civilians, this event welcomes visitors to watch onboard martial demonstrations while eager sailors await nightfall when they might view their ship's outside for the first time in months. Armed with a bucket list for shore leave, some will head downtown toward tattoo shops for a dermal register of recent high seas emotions. Others might seek out less documented outlets with ladies of the night or pursue more saintly objectives, taking in cultural sights and museums for which Manhattan is justly famous.

Recently deployed overseas, pennant-waving battleships converge along the Hudson River during their port side rendezvous. After a ceremonial wreath-laying, this gunners mate third class, aside his vessel's rear gun mount, proudly hoists an oversized cartridge case for medium range, large caliber artillery shells. His plans for the evening appear largely unresolved.

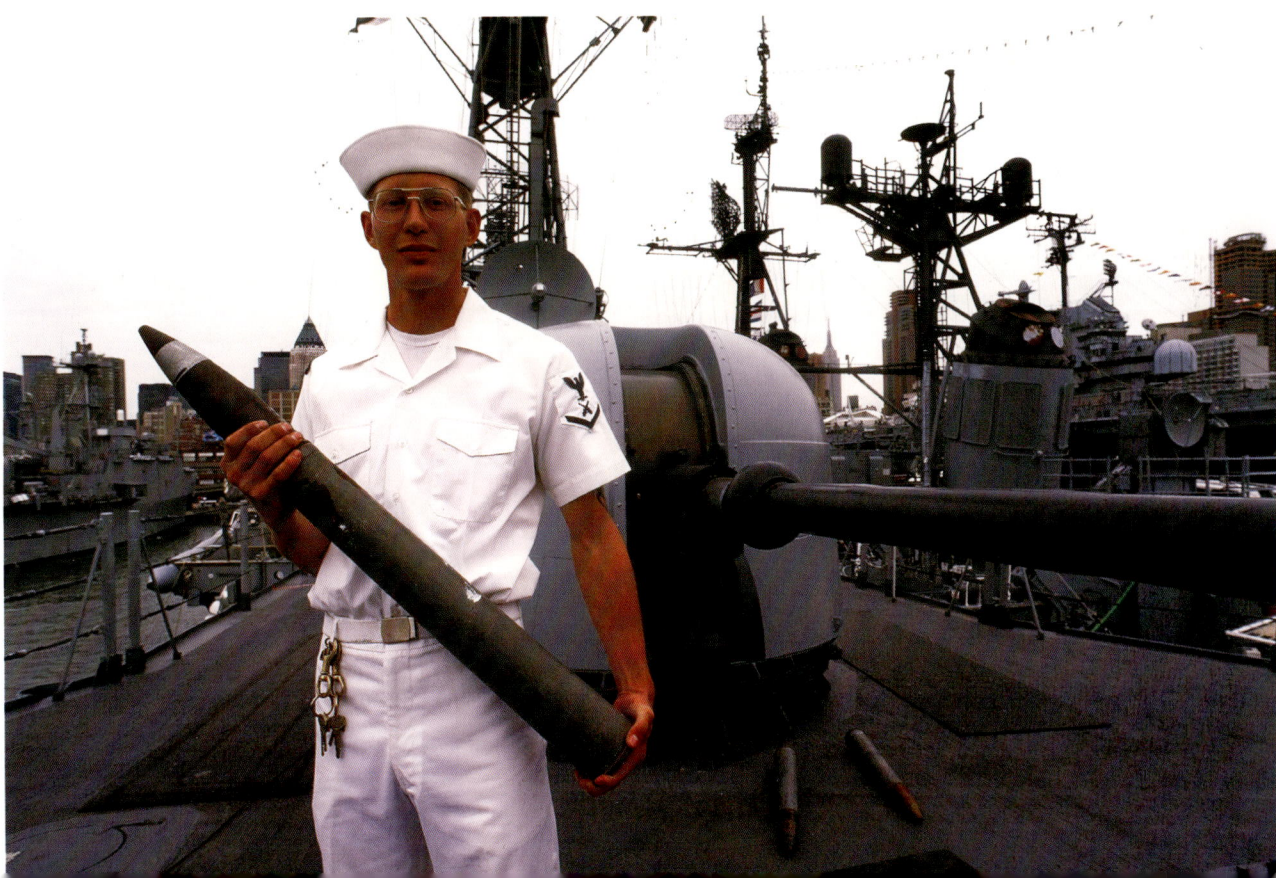

PUMPKIN CHUNKER

Bridgeville, Delaware

Out amongst Delaware's bedsheet-flat fields of soybean and alfalfa, the 600-acre Wheatley Farm diverts its attention from produce recently harvested just beneath their soils to that bright orange crop sailing high above it. As October's page is ripped from the calendar, and with Halloween in the rear-view mirror, all eyes in rural Sussex County turn to the skies for a zany manifestation of American ingenuity. Advantaged by a national obsession with weaponry, pumpkin chunkin is the annual sport of hurling gourds by employing an army of homemade slingshots, catapults, trebuchets, centrifugals, and soaring air cannons. Resembling front lines for a medieval battlefield, gargantuan assemblages of armament wait in turn to display their fierce power while ejaculating pumpkins the distance of approximately eleven football fields. Under the steady observation of obsessive backyard technicians, mass, yield limits, pitch, and wind are calculated as it appears that this science obsessed with flinging squash combines in equal parts da Vinci inventiveness with Gallagher recklessness. Careful selection of the thick-rimmed La Estrella, a smooth-skinned, super-dense, aerodynamic hybrid is instrumental in achieving an optimum launch without any inadvertent pie-shattering mishaps. A blacksmith shop's conversation spurring one-upmanship between four men around 1986 resulted in the first-ever pumpkin-tossing contests, and ultimately evolving into an event meriting one Science Channel special and capable of luring 80,000 spectators. Stocky all-terrain vehicles stand at the ready for a dash across fields and an identification of each splattered orb, beaming lasers back to document distances flown while validating anxiously awaiting contestants. Five-ton torsion catapults with fifteen-foot throwing arms powered by a high tension, twisted-rope bundle generating 180,000 foot-pounds of torque will compete against 60-foot-long aluminum barrels jammed with explosive pent-up compressed air for aerodynamic supremacy and the kind of acclaimed glory that can only be attained at an event with such importance.

With tinted safety glasses firmly in place, a looney rocket launch engineer monitors crosswinds, gauge pressure and pumpkin dimensions during the annual World Championship Punkin Chunkin competition while readying his immense pneumatic air cannon. The Great Emancipator will soon be loaded and aimed to explosively blast an autumnal gourd at almost sound barrier velocities aiming for well over 4,000-foot distances.

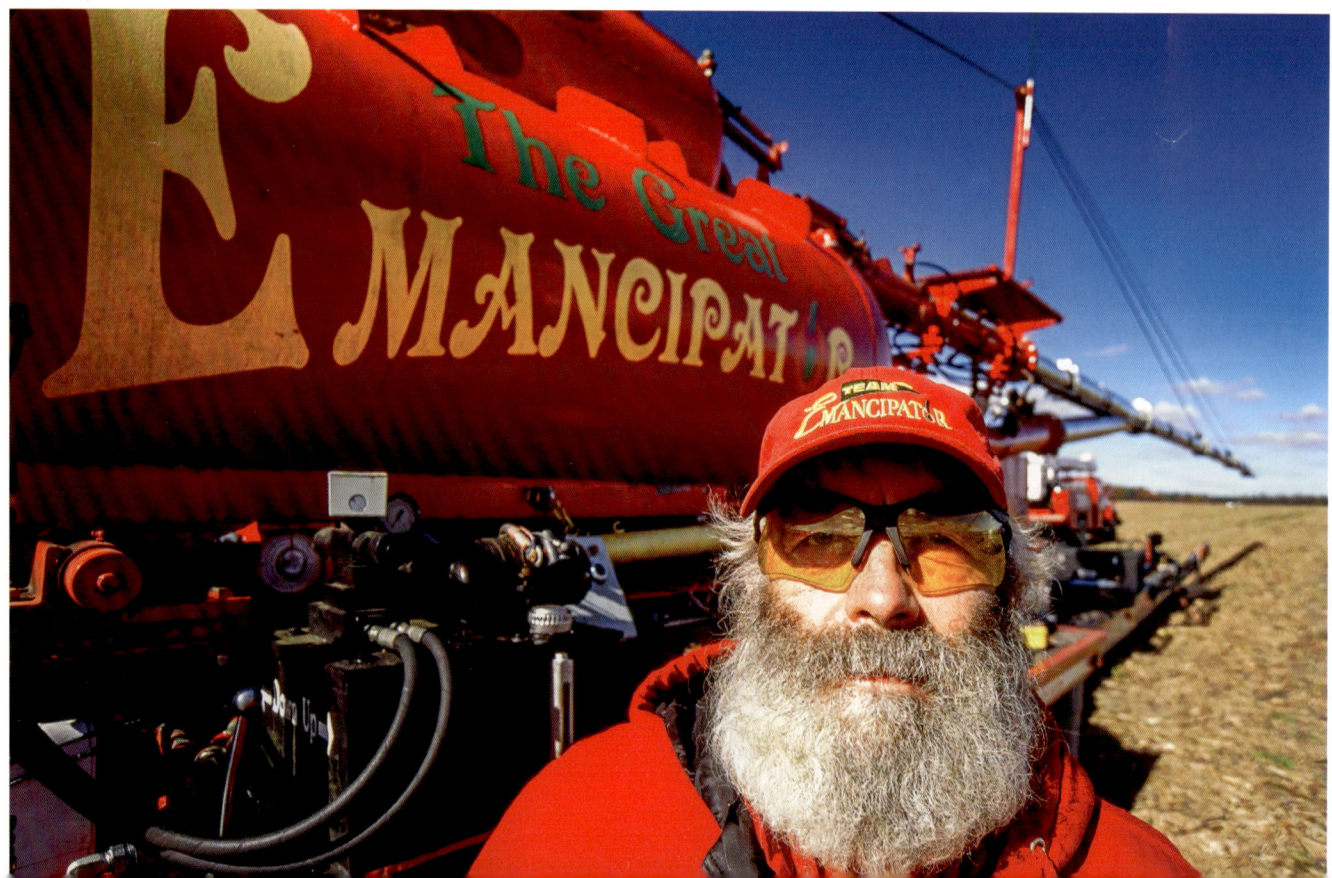

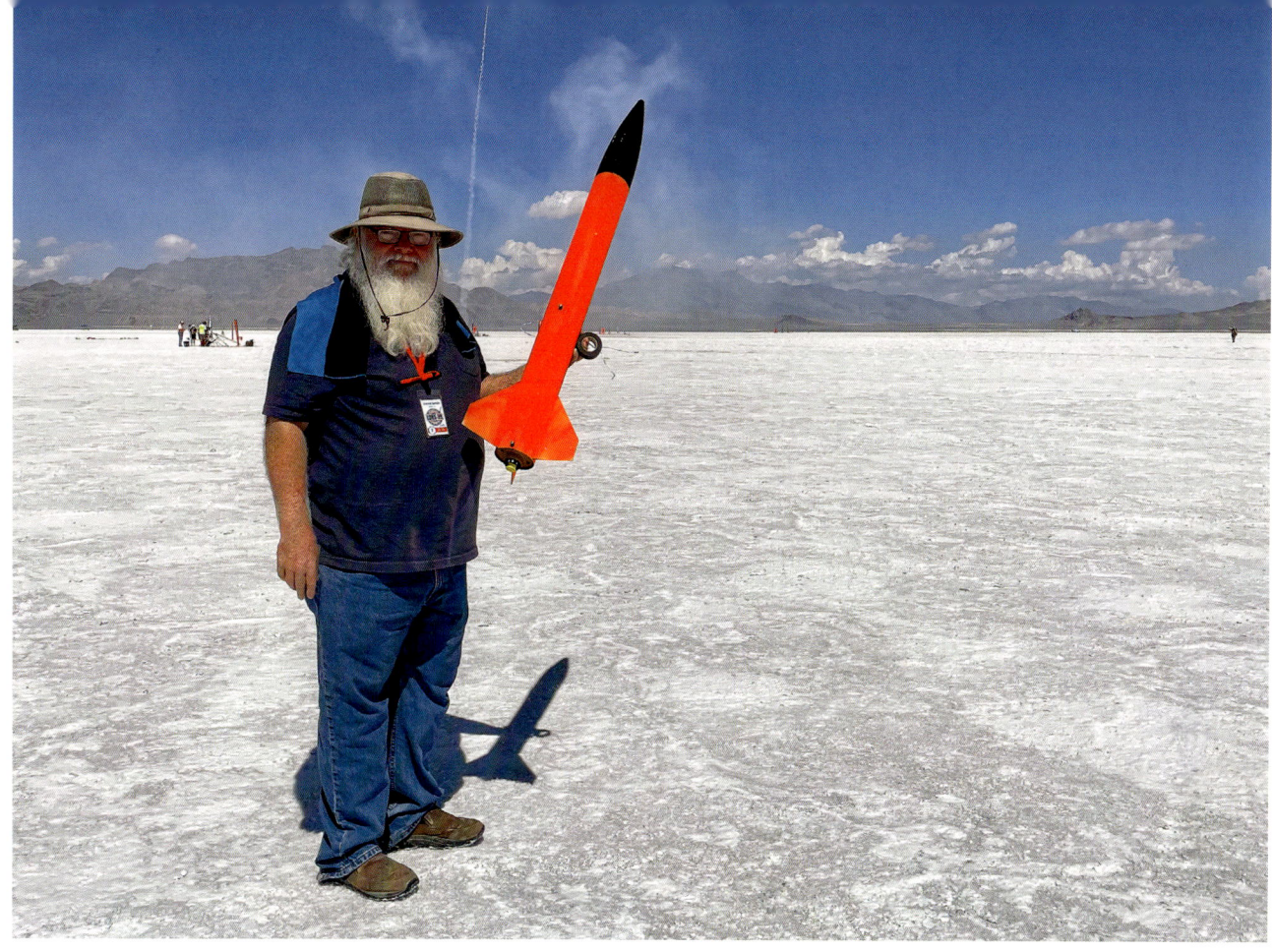

ROCKETRY ENTRANT

Bonneville Salt Flats, Utah

The blindingly white Bonneville Salt Flats are remnants of a Pleistocene-era paleolake. Its ancient lakebed is now a five-foot-thick saline crust, as 90 percent of its almost 150 million tons is basically common table salt. Though known for hosting that fastest motor speedway on earth, where horizontal velocities of over 500 mph have been clocked, it is actually the speeding vertical movements at an annual rocket festival here that draw enthusiasts from all around this planet. This event climaxes deep fascination with astronomical propulsion first kicked off in 1957 with that launch of *Sputnik* and a Cold War–era race to the moon. At this 12-mile-long salt pan, unimpeded geography and limitless sightlines set the table for up to 750 pounds of pure thrust shaking the ground with rocket launchings, some reaching 25,000 feet altitudes in less than one minute. These largest rockets may weigh up to 100 pounds and include complex clustered or staged motors, multiple parachutes, and propellant similar to that used on the space shuttle. Accessing this site requires a dry lakebed, so the aptly named HellFire event takes place in August when temperatures may soar into triple digits.

Sunblock, a sweat-mopping towel, and wide-brimmed hat are de rigueur here for helpfully name-tagged entrant David Smith, who seems to enjoy additional protection from his huge beard, blocking intense sun bouncing off the prismatically reflective crust. Amongst a humbling vastness that encircles these scorching flats, morning skies are scratched with soaring launch plumes, which may tally in the hundreds after just one day of aeronautical exhilaration.

TORNADO CHASER

Harper, Kansas

Hosting a meteorological rarity on this planet, Tornado Alley is the flattened immensity of plains, annually visited in late spring by enemy weather fronts poised for violent conflict. Storm chasers armed with GPS, tattered road maps, laptop weather radar, and an exquisite instinct in reading severe skies will jockey for close-up seats to one of nature's most striking spectacles. After a hell-bent race across an agricultural checkerboard of blowing wheat and alfalfa fields, they'll arrive at their targeted area and initiate the hunt searching for an evident dry line boundary. This marks that spot where warm, sultry air from the Gulf of Mexico confronts moisture-drained forces surging from an Arctic system blowing frigid air. Distant, floating mountains of boiling cumulonimbus angrily bloom to twice the height of Everest. Windshield-protecting hail guards are deployed before a scowling wall cloud begins its menacing pirouette. If conditions persist, unleashed lightning bolts and screaming winds announce a tightly whirling spindle of deadly energy whose finger descends to scrape the earth.

After studying meteorology at Texas A&M and Oklahoma University, avid storm chaser Charles Edwards assisted the Federal Emergency Management Agency with community relations. He was also a stringer for an Oklahoma City news station and his footage has been seen on many television networks including CNN. Yet he most certainly made his most lasting mark after creating the very first commercial storm chasing company in 1996. Cloud 9 Tours took off just as a Hollywood blockbuster disaster movie *Twister* thrilled theater audiences, becoming at that time the highest-grossing Warner Brothers movie in its annals. The film, co-written by Michael Crichton, centered its climax around a seemingly insane quest to deploy equipment into the direct path of an oncoming tornado. Creating his own non-scripted milestone in meteorological history, Edwards hand-forged an 80-pound, lead Dillocam, and at 8:35 p.m. on May 25, 1997, near Harper, Kansas, he became the first ever nonfictional person to actually accomplish that motion picture's bullseye recording of a tornado. With rapidly darkening skies, aside muddy shoulders tracing a rural dirt road, an F2 wedge funnel loudly roared directly over his deployed device, spurring legions of chasers to look beyond the silver screen's staged horizons and reimagine their own close encounters.

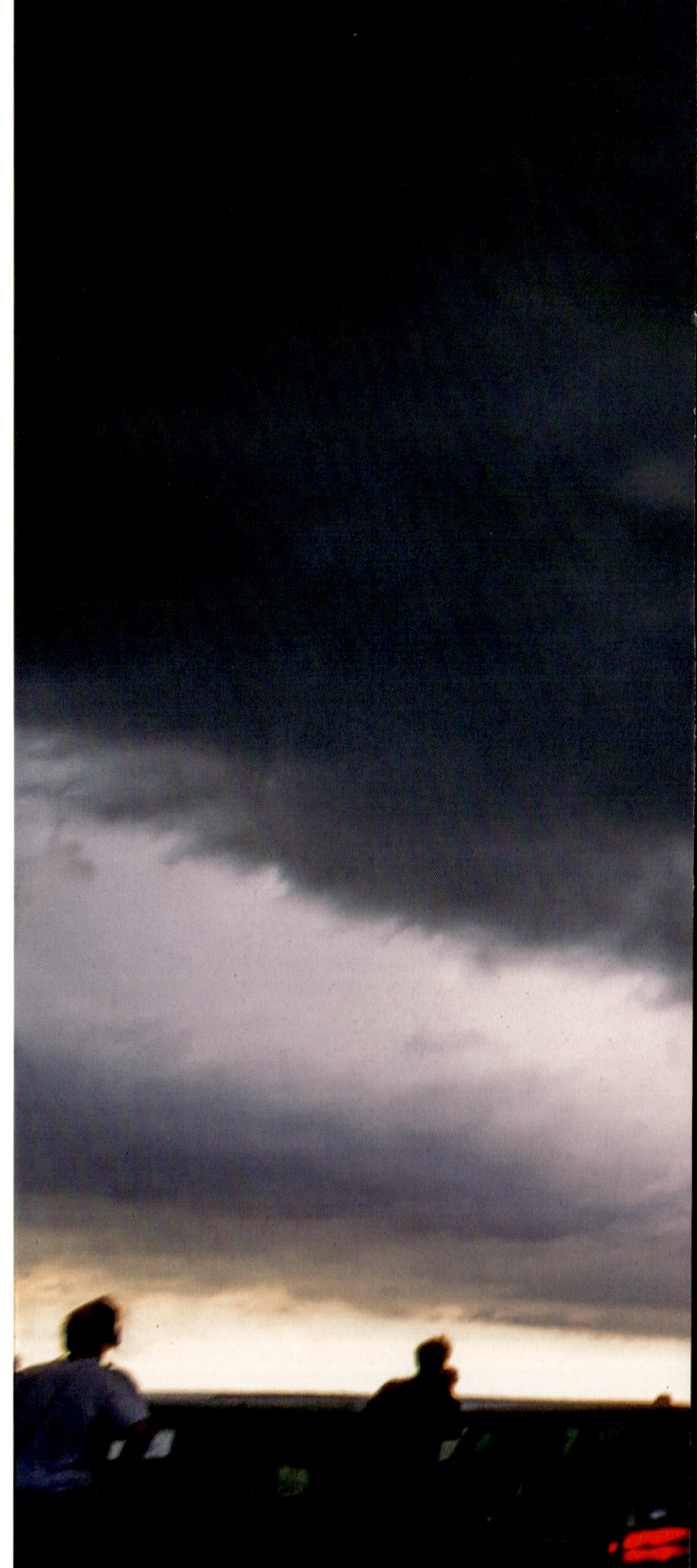

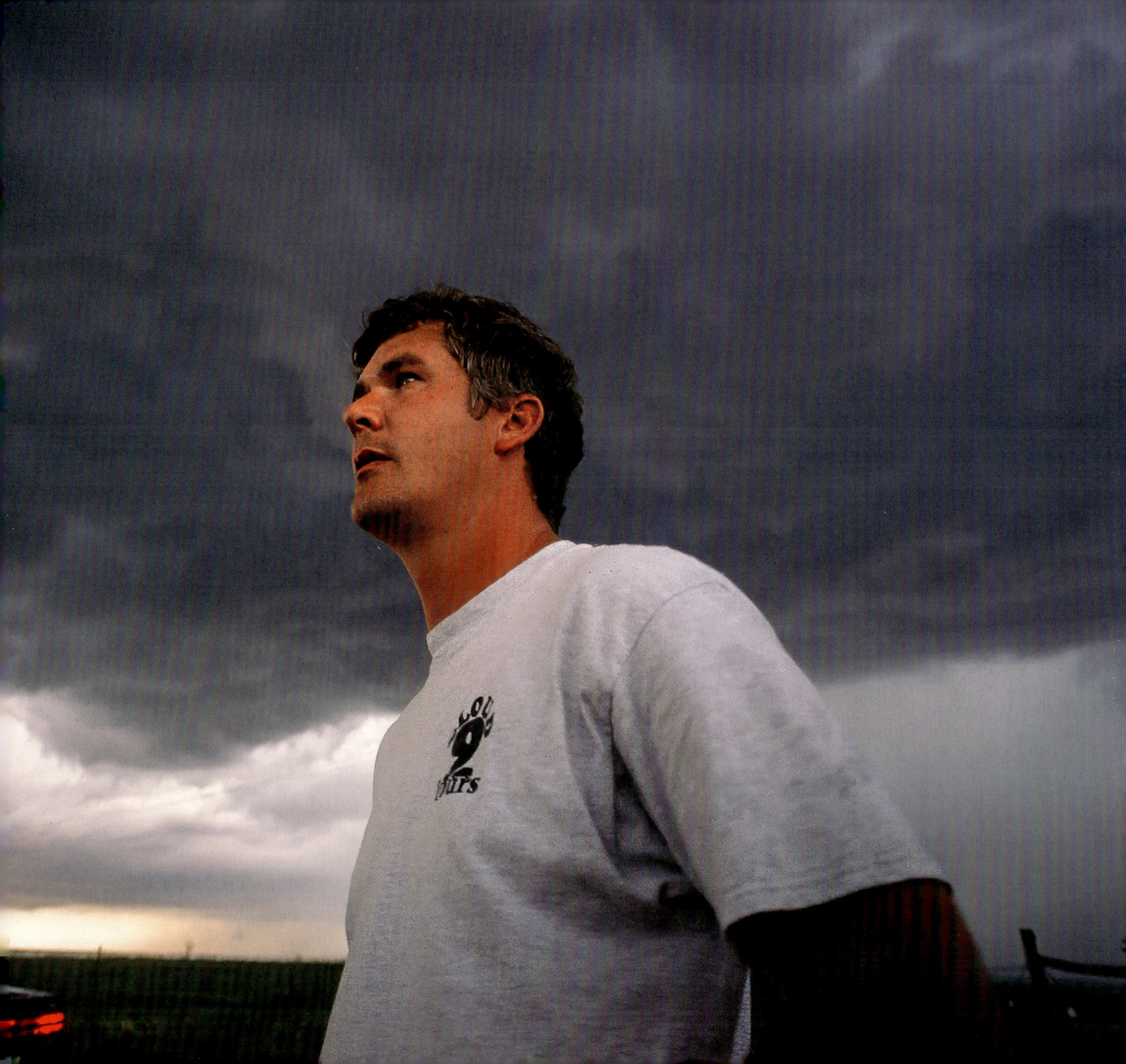

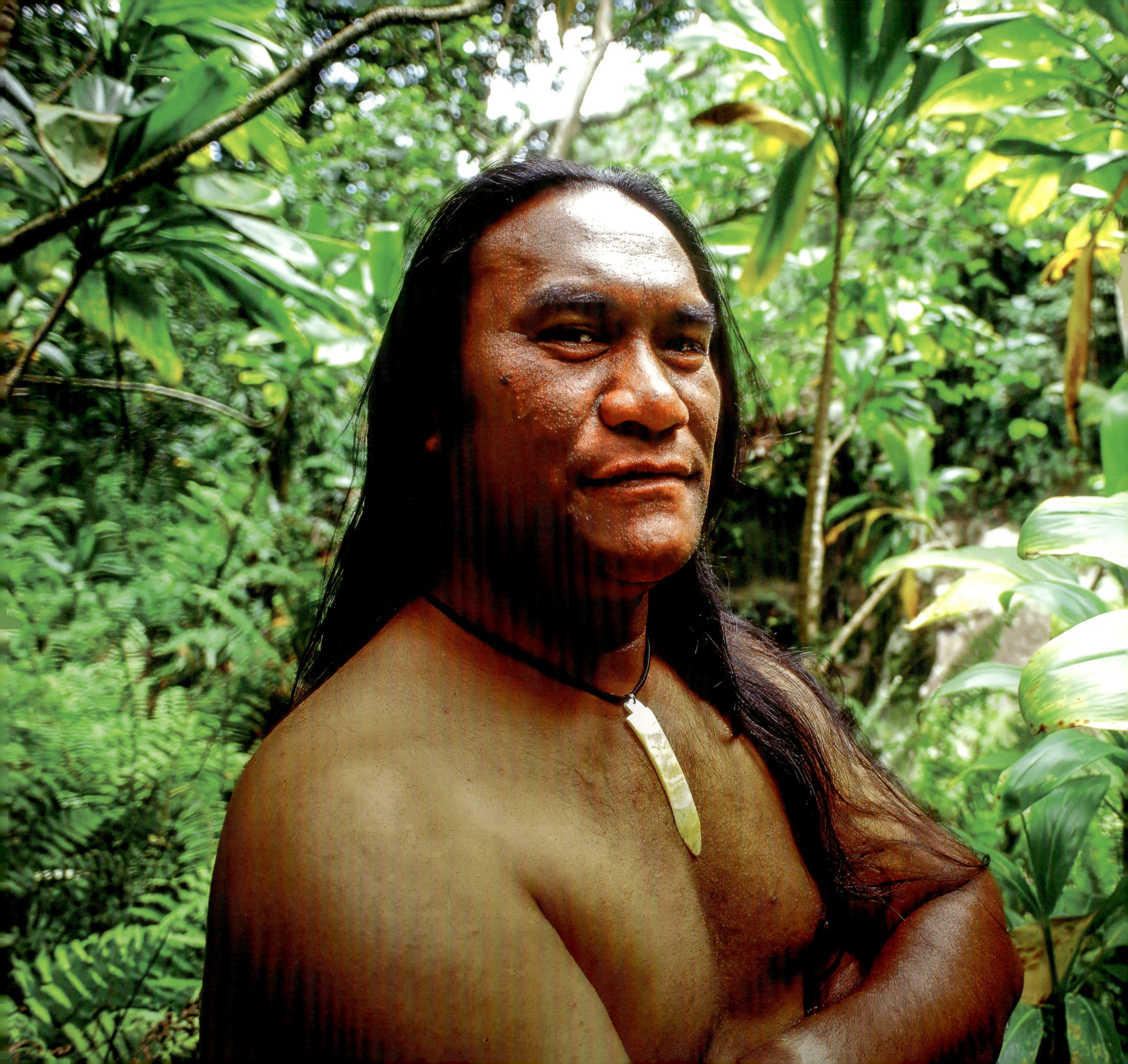

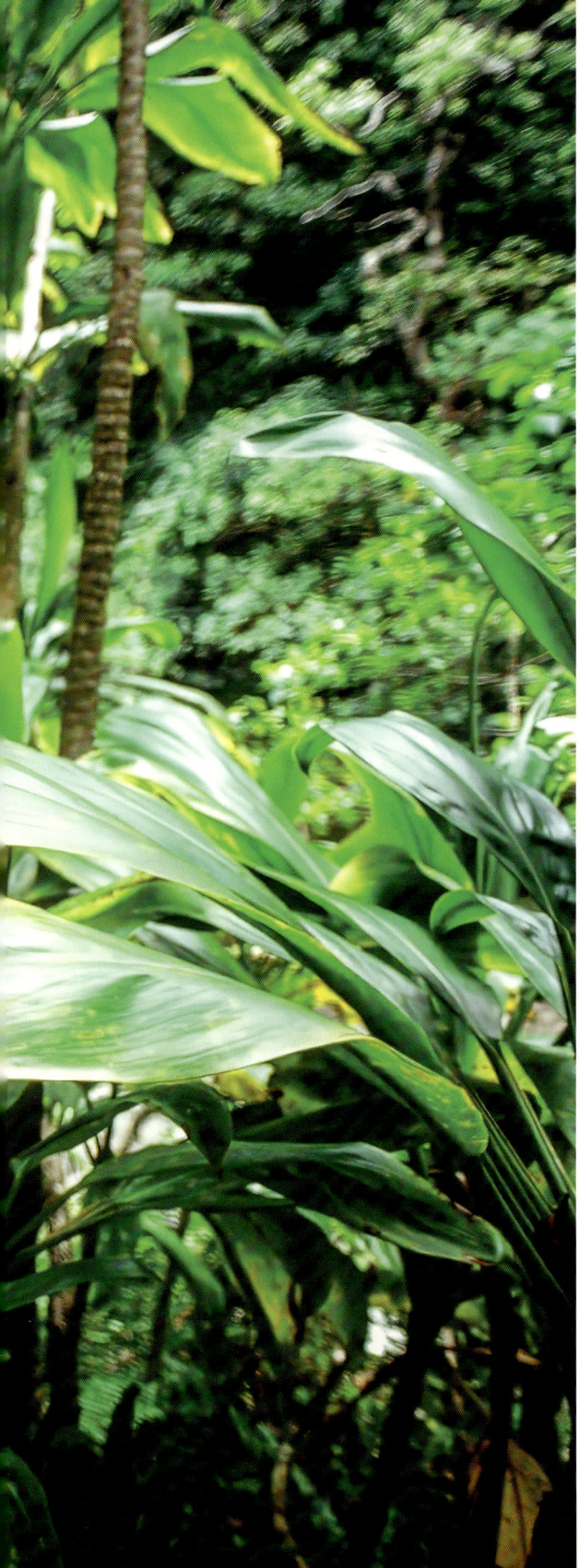

POLYNESIAN TARO CULTIVATOR

Halawa Valley, Molokai, Hawaii

Anchoring a keystone position in earth's most remote island chain, rugged terrain crowning Molokai boasts one hallowed knoll that reputedly spawned the birthplace of hula. Their sacred dance is an unspoken Hawaiian language filled with graceful hand gestures swaying toward a coastline girdled by both this nation's longest fringing reefs and the planet's highest sea cliffs. To penetrate its rarely visited rainforest interior, a stream-fording odyssey is required through jungly endemic vegetation into the Halawa Valley, scratched by waterfalls and alive with ancestral spirit. The island's one ragged thoroughfare meanders past fifteenth-century heiau temples, while nearby cleverly designed basalt and coral fishponds once trapped ocean fish for its Polynesian inhabitants, now numbering only about a dozen year-round residents.

There, revered elder Lawrence Aki, a fiftieth generation storyteller, has resurrected his grandparents' practice tending to the cultivation of traditional taro fields, while wading into muddy paddies whose starchy crop is mashed into worn, wooden bowls creating paste-like poi, an ancestral sweet staple that's ready to eat or be cooked further in earthen imu ovens.

TWINS

Twinsburg, Ohio

Not so coincidentally, Twinsburg, Ohio was founded by identical twins Moses and Aaron Wilcox, believers in their own mental telepathy, secretly swapping during dates, each marrying twins, dying on precisely the same day from alike diseases, then buried together in a grave. The only city on earth named after its twin founders, it decided almost a half-century ago to stage an eye-popping summer event that unprepared visitors might wander through in a surrealistic daze of double vision. Diplopia only intensifies as the Double Take Parade heads off down Ravenna Road accompanied by bubbly calliope music. During the Twins Festival's sure highlight, marching twosomes who have flocked here from all around the world are cheered on by gobsmacked spectators. Their tandem strolls eventually reach the food booth–filled fairgrounds where talent competitions along with lookalike contests seem to overshadow tented medical studies where biometric researchers recruit subjects or conduct DNA and trait analysis. Over these past four decades, advancements for fertility treatments and in vitro procedures have increased a likelihood of twins by over 70 percent. Identical or monozygotic twins are created when a single egg is fertilized before splitting in two, each ovoid harboring the very same genetic material. The world's largest gathering of twins occurs annually in a Cleveland suburb where it finds its usually modest population made pregnant with swelling crowds delighting to this Midwestern frat party during August's first weekend.

Cigar-chomping Spencer and Skyler Nick borrow personas from Babe Ruth's Big Bambino as they grab bats to take the plate in front of Twinsburg's First Congregational Church. Whether participating on *Twinning*, a VH1 reality show, or cooking with Tyler Florence and Anne Burrell during their Food Network program *Worst Cooks in America*, they appear to pull their weight in celebrity-driven, high-visibility venues. By Twinsburg Township Square, where a Noah's ark worth of twins muster by the thousands, Allan and Anthony, looking much like smock-clad butcher shop owners from the 1920s, break away from milling assemblages clustered with like-minded siblings to proudly display their handlebar mustaches.

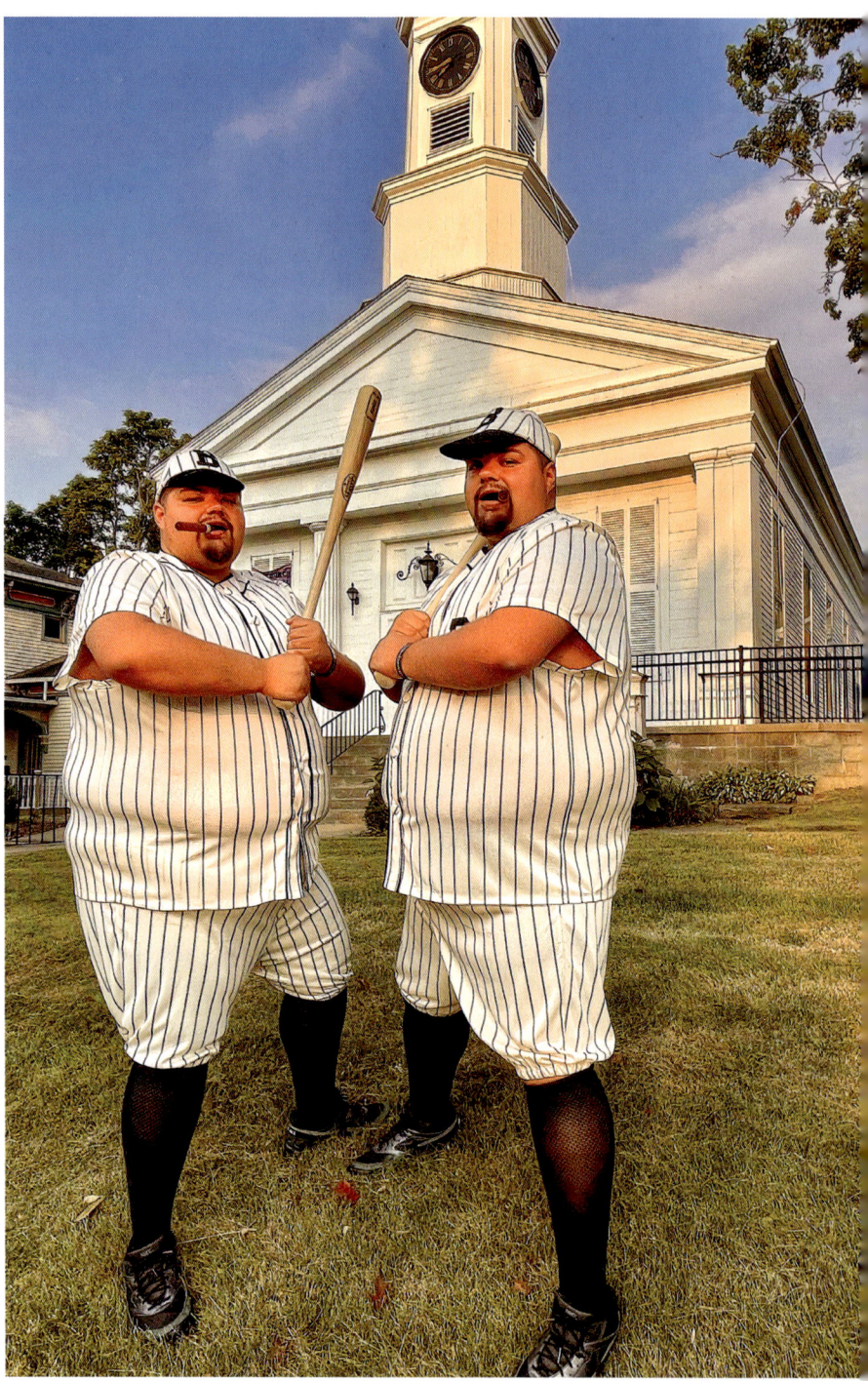

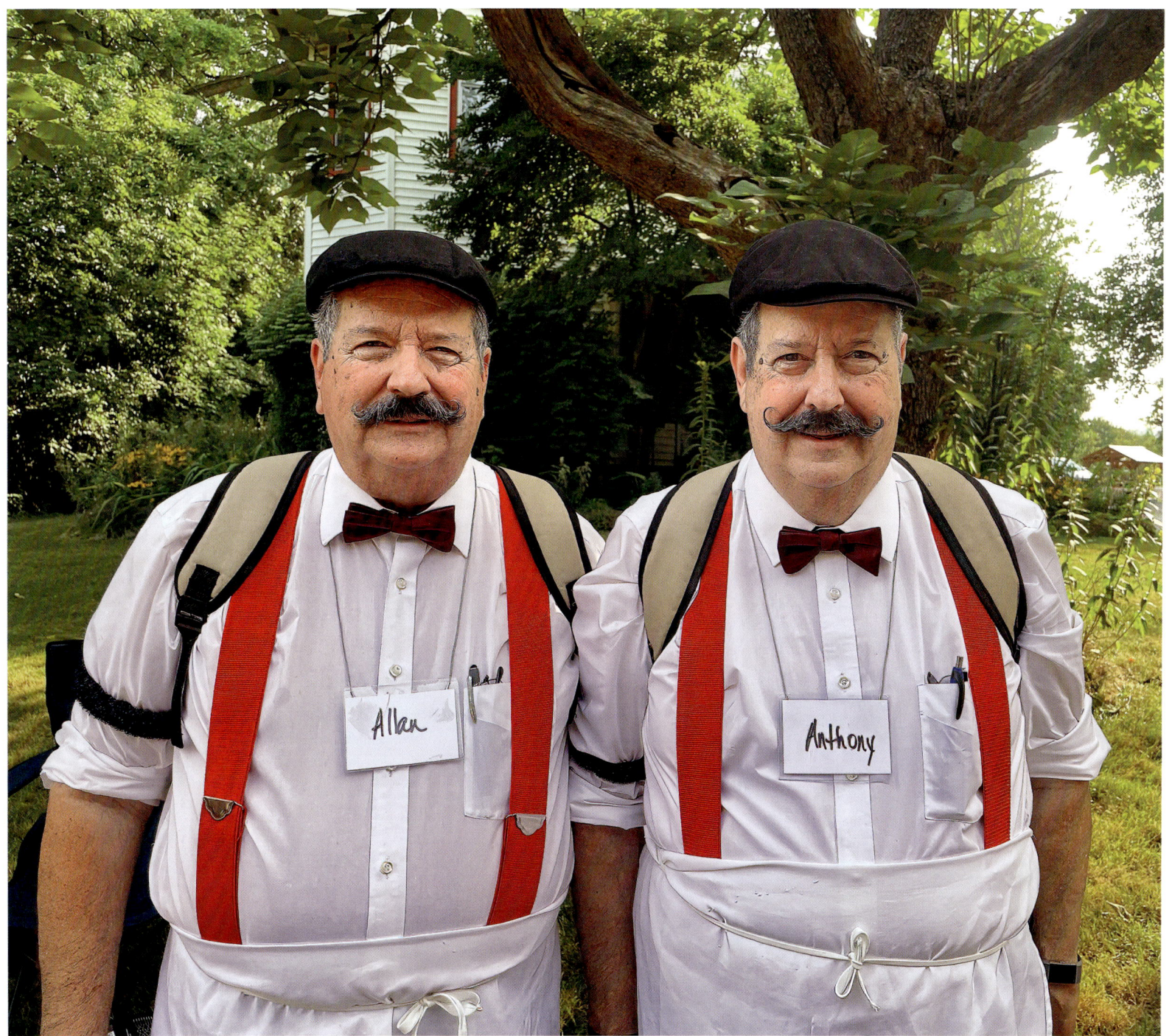

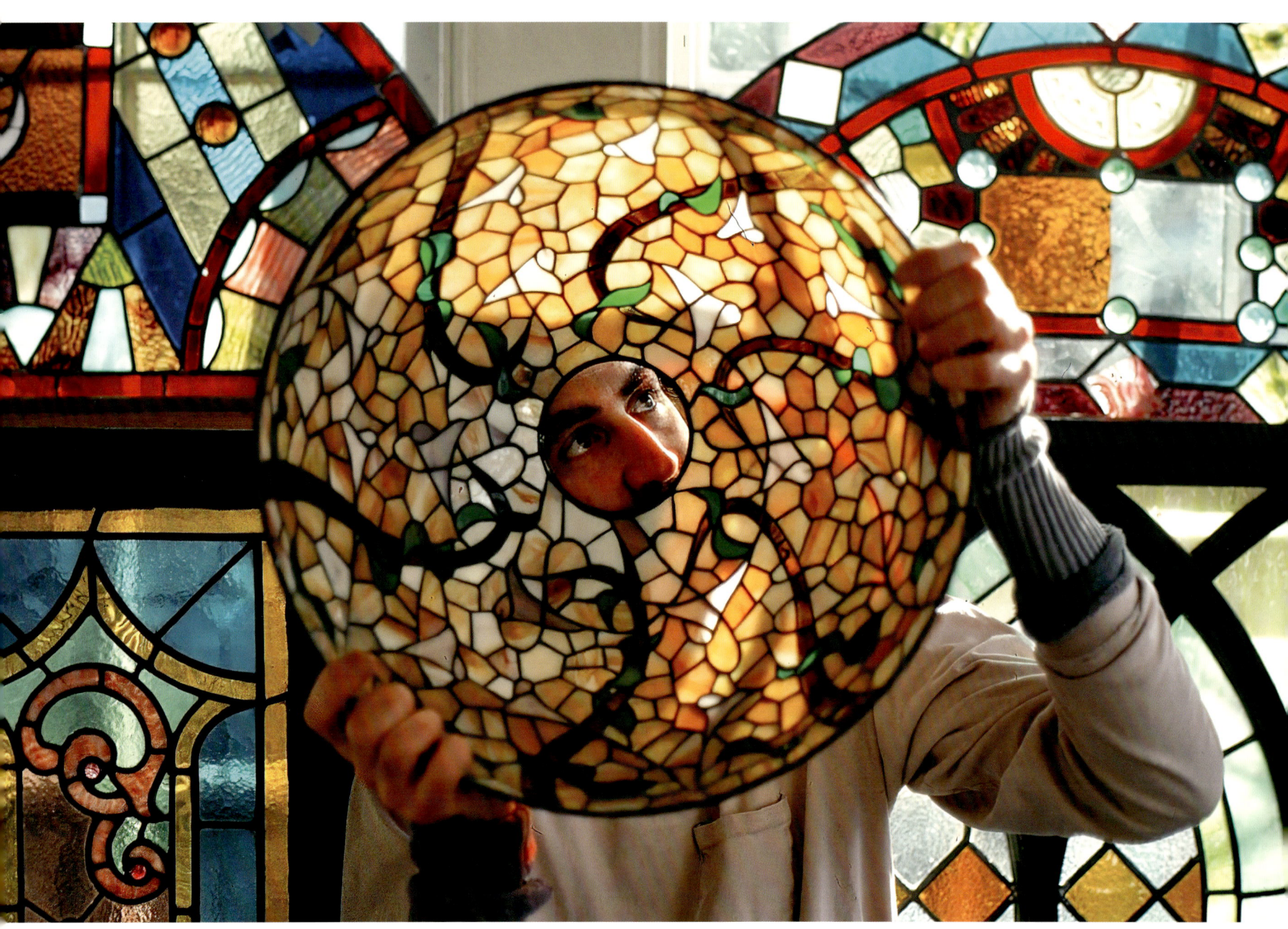

STAINED GLASS RESTORER

Washington, District of Columbia

The depths of our planet belch volcanic lava flows, which when rapidly cooled form obsidian, that igneous rock which provided Paleolithic humankind its very first interaction with glass. This sharp substance helped knap and flake the very first tools into existence and allowed for weapon sharpening. Amulets and crude beads were fabricated in Mesopotamia around 2500 BCE, while during the first century BCE glassblowing was advanced by ancient glaziers in Syria. Forged through fiery creativity, glass creations are fusions combining earth's geology as sand, soda, and lime are melted together. Its atomic structure creates brief moments when the liquid state fuses into clear, non-crystalline incarnations of transparency. Glass has allowed scientists to peer far off into distant galaxies or to look inward while examining biological cells. By the time of eleventh-century Crusades, Roman Empire influences spread glassmaking skills to Murano in the Venetian lagoon, and with cessations of global hostilities impressive Gothic churches in England began installing breathtaking stained-glass windows. Pointed arch and flying buttress architecture allowed their hallowed spaces to support huge walls of light featuring colored panes while producing a stunning medieval jewel box. Within a calming forest spiked with soaring stone pillars, dazzling panels present liturgical lessons illuminating both pew-filled spaces and the minds of often illiterate worshippers seated there, infusing reverence and imagination into their ritual prayers. Above them, sunlight streams through critically timed melting of wavelength-absorbing cobalt which might result in brilliant blues, while iron manifests various shades of green, manganese offers a pinkish purple hue, or costly gold produces red colorations. Most significantly, that stain referenced in the window material's name is derived from an oxide of silver applied to outward facing glass, triggering a chemical reaction coaxing ions to migrate into the panes and creating a golden yellow shade to suggest halos and gates to heaven. Learned through grueling trial and error, these coloring processes were carefully guarded secrets that were handed down through generations. Glass-joining lead came developed during the Middle Ages, are groove-sided strips flexible enough for fittings, yet contain enough strength to hold most of that assembled weight, its joints tin-soldered and then finished off with waterproofing calcium carbonate mixed with linseed putty. In relatively recent times, painter Marc Chagall and architect Frank Lloyd Wright both wove their artistry into stained glass designs. Louis Comfort Tiffany, son of the famed jewelry store founder, along with often uncredited assistants, utilized stained glass techniques for his trademark milky opalescent glass in Art Nouveau windows and lamps, creating enameled, swirling remains from chemical impurities. These textured surfaces brought three dimensionality, which helped suggest folded draperies or angel wings. Perhaps surprisingly, Tiffany also designed the interlocking NY symbol that the New York Yankees have sported on their uniform for nearly a century.

Laboring in his stained glass workshop, diligent master artisan Daniel Goldon Wolkoff trains a discerning eye on the domed Art Nouveau lampshade he meticulously crafted with over 550 tightly fitted pieces expertly cut, foiled, and soldered together, creating a striking motif of blooming calla lily vines. In the style of Renaissance-era practices, Wolkoff is assisted by apprentices toiling away at his Adams Morgan Stained Glass studio. Utilizing historic techniques learned through a half-century of experience, he has lovingly restored major pieces for Smithsonian Castle, Mayer of Munich windows in Catholic University's chapel apse found inside its original 1889 Caldwell Hall, and an 1868 Victorian ensemble within the Calvert Vaux–designed President's Residence at Gallaudet University, originally chartered by Abraham Lincoln. Wolkoff's distinguished work has been featured in *Restore America* on HGTV and within the pages of *Architectural Digest*.

QUILT SQUARE MAKER

Green Bank, West Virginia

Geography is most often destiny. During five years of the nation's Civil War, as most states had firmly chosen sides, this country experienced only one additional admission into its statehood. Corrugated mountainsides and unfarmable landscapes in the Mountain State employed much less slavery-fueled field labor than in regions where plantations sat amongst fertile valleys of arable land. In present day West Virginia, where three states converge at a confluence of both Shenandoah and Potomac Rivers, perhaps the most contentious spark to America's civil war was John Brown's ill-fated insurrection in Harpers Ferry, meant to arm slave revolts by unloading its armory's ammunition arsenal. Resenting political power exhibited by eastern slave holders, Virginia's western region split this state in two by leaving the Confederacy in 1863 to rejoin the Union. With West Virginia no longer part of the South's slavery culture, escapees increasingly utilized an Underground Railroad, relying on their wits, word-of-mouth meeting points, and covert assistance from sympathetic locals. These residents clandestinely maintained safe house stations and helped thwart determined slave catchers enticed by well-advertised rewards. An escaped slave herself, brave conductor Harriet Tubman from nearby Maryland guided scores of fleeing refugees navigating by the North Star to eventually reach their freedom. At the beginning of this millennium, a published book collaboration between an historian and partnering scholar, *Hidden in Plain View*, reveals one quilter's oral narrative from her grandma about quilts containing hidden messages for runaway slaves. Supposedly, their patterned quilt blocks contained secret clues that enabled freedom seekers to navigate the Underground Railroad and were strategically displayed on clotheslines, fence posts, or porch railings. Predetermined symbols, cryptic messages, and suggested directions were embedded within rhythmic shapes and motifs. Though that recent revelation was analyzed during *The Oprah Winfrey Show*, discussed on National Public Radio and featured in numerous museum exhibitions, many skeptical historians cast doubt upon this theory. They insisted on written documentation while perhaps discounting the notion that unwritten stories often telegraph meaningful history amongst societies that were forcefully transported from another continent while not being taught any written languages. Nevertheless, quilting has indeed played a major role in the culture and folk art of rural mountain living for centuries. Even today, quilting guilds, bees, and raffles are found throughout West Virginia as painters often enlarge these geometrically inviting patterns to display them along the sides of barns and farmhouses.

In agrarian Pocahontas County, the Green Bank Art Center nurtures folk art traditions and skills of its rural artisans. Clad in a smock still smeared with drying clay, versatile potter and painter Kathryn Gillispie joyfully exhibits her dazzling eight-pointed star quilt square, painted using water-based enamel on canvas panel boards primed by latex. Traditional designs that she employs are carefully selected from an 80-year-old catalog displaying patterns created before 1902. The prolific artist has received numerous juried awards at Mountain State Forest Festival and her work is included in West Virginia's State Museum art collection. The arts cooperative founded by Gillispie lies just outside Green Bank Observatory, where one of earth's largest radio telescopes tirelessly searches our heavens for intelligent life, just as desperately determined freedom seekers once sought that North Star.

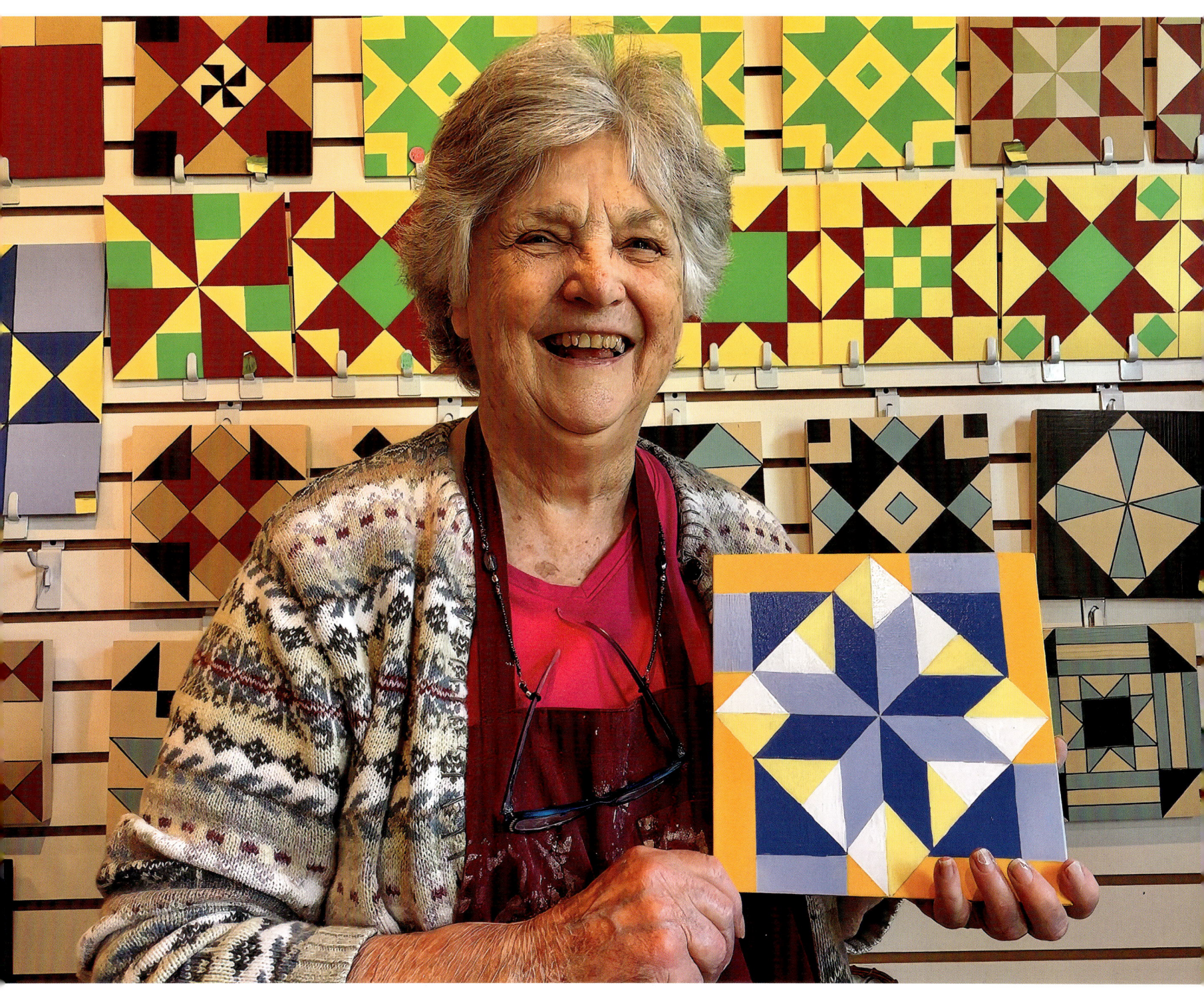

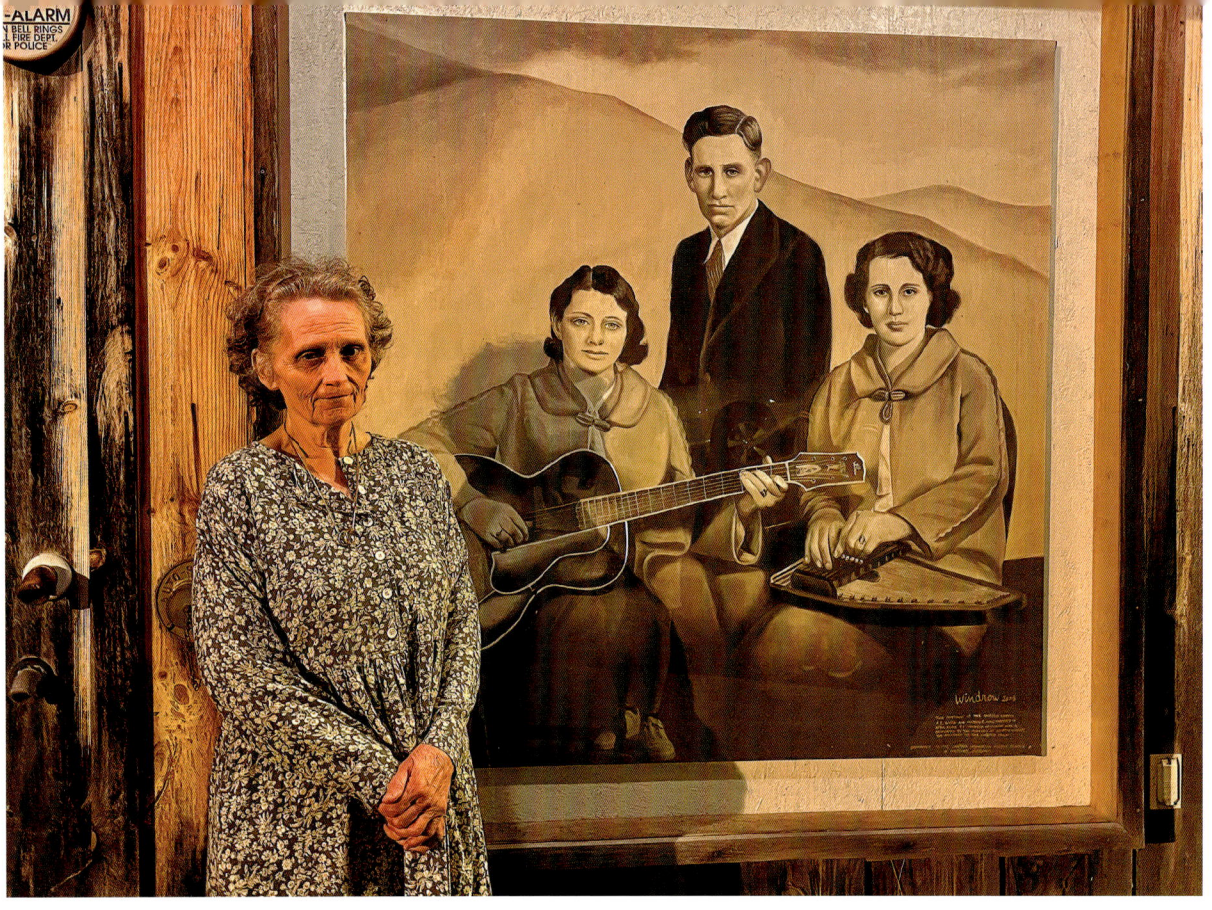

COUNTRY MUSIC DOYENNE

Hiltons, Virginia

Tucked within Blue Ridge Mountains' topography, a bright yellow line down the middle of State Street in Bristol is an actual border between Virginia and Tennessee. Both sides claim the proud mantle of country music's birthplace, a title officially stamped by Congress. In 1927 while talent hunting down south, one representative of Victor Talking Machines lured rural musicians from distant hills into town to make a series of recordings for which bands were paid $50 per song. The tunes were performed in a makeshift studio, capturing sounds of what was then called hillbilly music. Now known as the Big Bang of country music, these historic Bristol Sessions were meant to promote fledgling vinyl records as a brand-new concept. Appearing most prominently in these recordings were the Carter Family, who had traveled from their home sometimes across roadless hills, battling a broken vehicle and carrying an eight-month pregnant member over raging streams. A.P. Carter, his wife, Sara, and sister-in law, Maybelle, became lauded pioneers of a new music genre and helped launch the country music industry.

Back at the Carters' home grounds in Hiltons, an appealingly rustic, 800-seat music shed was constructed as a pilgrim-drawing tabernacle to preserve the roots of country music. A Saturday night outbreak of Appalachian buckdancing along with staccato clogging erupts as the banjo-inflected mountain strains of Haint Hollow Hootenany or Hogslop String Band echo through rafters that stretch over a strictly no-smoking-and-drinking crowd. Acoustic music always prevails, save for Johnny Cash, who married Maybelle's daughter June Carter and performed his last-ever concert here. Overseeing the weekly toe-tapping jamboree is Rita Forrester, granddaughter of A.P. and Sara, who strikes a remarkable resemblance to her painted family portrait. After booking talent she'll emcee fiddle-wielding performers and is often up until 3 a.m., when Forrester will still be cooking chili, soup beans, or cornbread for her audience with recipes that were featured by Rachael Ray on Food Network.

BARBER

Mount Airy, North Carolina

Just one month before John Kennedy was elected president, a situation comedy aired on CBS Television and ran for eight seasons. It ended its run as the number-one rated series, a feat only equaled by *I Love Lucy* and *Seinfeld*. *The Andy Griffith Show* depicted vignettes of an ideal rural life in Mayberry, a fictional small town set in the hills of northern North Carolina, and provided welcome respite from this nation's brewing domestic troubles. In this Emmy Award–winning series, the level-headed Griffith, often volleying wisdom with Aunt Bea, played a humble sheriff needlessly assisted by one bumblingly inept deputy Barney Fife. His earnestly curious young son, acted by future Hollywood director Ron Howard, goofy gas station attendants Gomer and Goober Pyle, and the overly talkative Floyd the barber were woven into plots thick with eccentric townspeople. In the show, this unarmed sheriff's problem-solving talents were constantly tested while confronting local drunks and out-of-town ne'er-do-wells. In Mount Airy, the wholesome North Carolina town where Andy Griffith was born and said to be this program's inspiration, vintage police cars patrol its main street from another era, where Snappy Lunch serves up famed pork chop sandwiches and business at the barber shop seems to move at a fairly good clip. During their annual Mayberry Days, jailhouse tours and checker competitions preface the whistling contests paying tribute to this series' catchy opening tune.

At Floyd's City Barber Shop, Russell Hiatt, a skillful, much beloved barber is poised with comb and clippers, lording over his warm, recently occupied chair while he awaits another customer. He remained busy shorning scalps right up to the ripe age of ninety. Snapshots of satisfied patrons or noted visitors fill walls and mirror reflections permeated by the aroma of Barbasol and Mayberry memories.

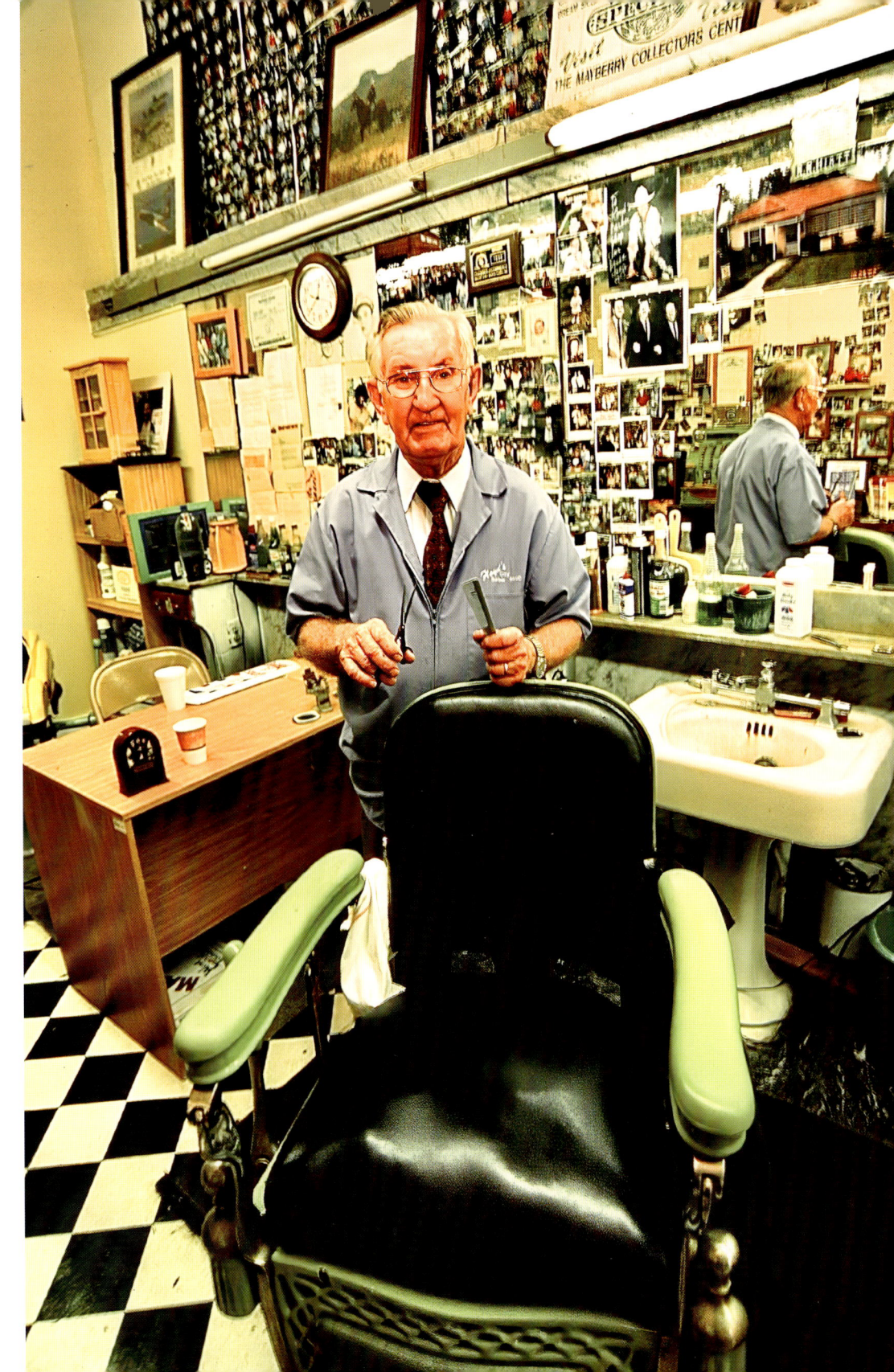

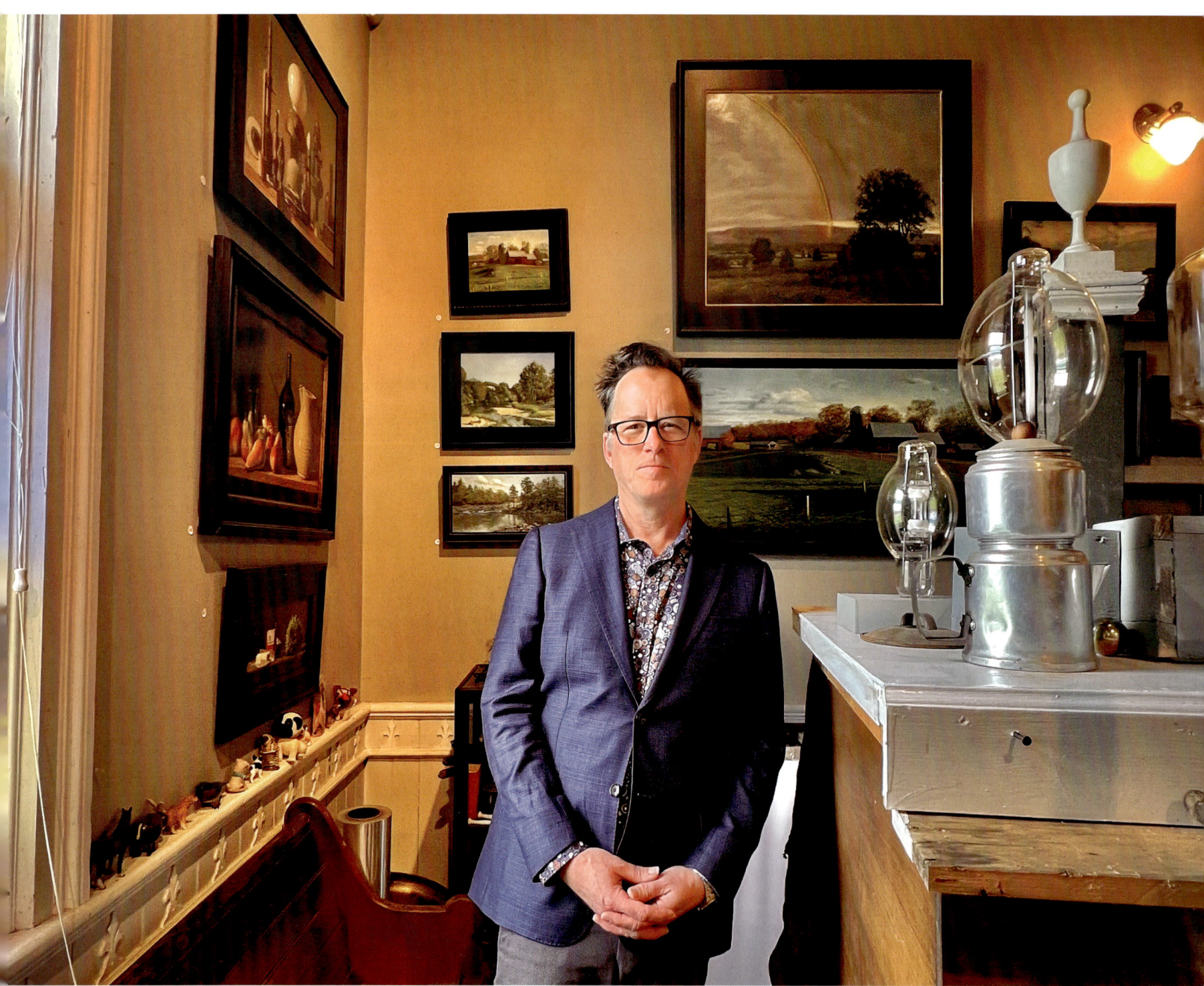

EMINENT FINE ART PAINTER

Stuyvesant, New York

At the beginning of Europe's industrial revolution, coal-choked skies and grimy factory conditions in northern England induced a failed businessman to escape his doomed ventures. Seeking brighter horizons, he relocated his family across the ocean to America's east coast. His teenage son, Thomas Cole, had been a calico factory textile worker, but soon began an itinerant career painting portraits. In 1825 he caught an especially lucky break when a gilding shop on Bleecker Street in Greenwich Village displayed three of his paintings from its window. They grabbed the eye of one wealthy patron who bought a steamship ticket for Cole to widen his visual repertoire. Steaming up the Hudson River, he got his first glimpse of glowing autumnal colors springing from this fabled valley's rolling deciduous forests and craggy mountains. After one stopover in West Point, he continued toward the town of Catskill and transferred onto a coach and then later horseback to penetrate that wild mountainous hinterland. Transfixed by tranquil vistas, dramatic storm clouds, and raging waterfalls, his paintings explored a luminosity that bathed landscapes in golden light, imparting an awed feeling of nature's serenity. As early nineteenth-century urbanization in an increasingly industrial country intensified, city dwellers developed deep nostalgia for unspoiled wilderness during this era of angry divisions brewing across a pre–Civil War nation. Cole gave the country its first signature style and his Hudson River School of Art became America's earliest artistic movement. Along with his prized pupil Frederic Church, artists like Albert Bierstadt, Jasper Cropsey, and Asher Durand, who had been an accomplished engraver slated to become a lifelong friend, all used their paintbrushes to help advance notions that the wilderness was meant to be revered rather than conquered. Their work, imparting moral or sacred values, offered the spiritual power of nature's raw beauty that was meant as a godlike rebuke to urban growth and worship of money.

Today, a mere dozen miles further upstream along the Hudson River from Thomas Cole's disembarkation into art history, the 1884 Methodist Episcopal Church in Stuyvesant cloisters an elegantly repurposed art studio evoking religious overtones. Laboring away inside this towering Carpenter Gothic landmark, spiritually insistent resident John Morra, one of the nation's most accomplished realist oil painters, suffuses divine evocations into his work, manifesting highly polished renderings in both Hudson Valley landscapes and studio arranged compositions. Above Holy Trinity–inspired fleur-de-lis molding, just one small sampling of Morra's work grace walls that include the region's rolling farmland and rainbow-swept Copake meadows, while exquisite Vermeer-level observations imbue lovingly intertwined objects with a sense of reverence. Cathode-ray tubes, opalescent ostrich eggs, lemon juicers, and eggbeaters, all with comical or menacing personalities, create beguiling still-life skylines. With hands clasped in almost prayer-like devotion, Morra reflects on his exacting Cole-like details revealed in both nature and found objects that seem infused with a profound meaning of heavenly revelation. Seeking even deeper immersion into a sacred life, he sings regularly inside yet another church with his wife Isabelle Bosquet-Morra, herself an often noted floral designer.

ACCOMPLISHED POLITICAL CARTOONIST

Upper West Side, New York City, New York

In the eighteenth century, as visual arts became commercialized, engravings began appearing amongst London's taverns and being sold inside print shops. Gifted with keen perceptions of his world, painter William Hogarth began engraving morality-based subjects, injecting humorous dimensions into theatrical portraitures and astute observations of street life. In 1721 he created an image widely considered the first political cartoon. Hogarth depicted richly detailed eviscerations of political characters responsible for an economic bubble's collapse and the disastrous stock market crash that followed. A French Revolution decades later prompted James Gillray's oft-imitated motif portraying Napoleon Bonaparte and Prime Minister William Pitt seated for an enormous meal while fighting to the death for control of the globe, which they were each carving up onto their elegant dinner plates. As newer printing presses helped widely disseminate ideas, the incorrect notion that Napoleon was significantly shorter than average heights during those times was emphatically advanced by Gillray's caricatures. Overseas, Benjamin Franklin's pamphlets debuted one masterpiece of political messaging through his graphic woodcut presenting a chopped-up snake, its eight pieces representing colonies and suggesting that unity was necessary to defeat the French during their Seven Years' War. *Punch* magazine first helped coin the term cartoon in 1843 to describe its many humorous political sketches, then *Harper's Weekly* became noted as home for political cartoonist Thomas Nast, famed for takedowns of corrupt Tammany Hall politicos. He created the initial Republican elephants and Democratic donkeys, not to mention that first depiction of Santa Claus as a bearded roly-poly embodiment of jollity. The founding of *Puck*, an American gazette filled with lively political satire, helped redefine political cartooning. Adorned by giant, pen-wielding golden statues of Shakespeare's mischievous pixie, New York's Puck Building housed the world's largest lithography facilities. Their deft caricatures denied Ulysses Grant a third term in 1880, and by his own admission elected Grover Cleveland four years later. A *Washington Post* newspaper cartoon portraying Theodore Roosevelt's 1902 hunting trip developed the notion of a teddy bear, while Theodor Geisel's newsprint cartoons encouraged American efforts during World War II before he became known as Dr. Seuss.

Maverick thinkers with barbed points and biting sarcasm continue the excoriation of establishment rule for its injustice and hypocrisy, now enlisting computers with digital tools to disseminate visual ideas online. At his studio's drafting table, political cartoonist Steve Brodner finds his comfort zone amongst taped sketches, scrap notations, photo studies, and mounted excerpts of published work, assisted in no short measure by his trusty schnoodle canine Jazz. Brodner was the house artist for *Esquire* magazine, regularly contributing to *The Atlantic*, *The New Yorker*, and *The Nation* among many others. The recipient of numerous awards and solo exhibitions, his masterwork book *Freedom Fries* features his vast career's notable oeuvre.

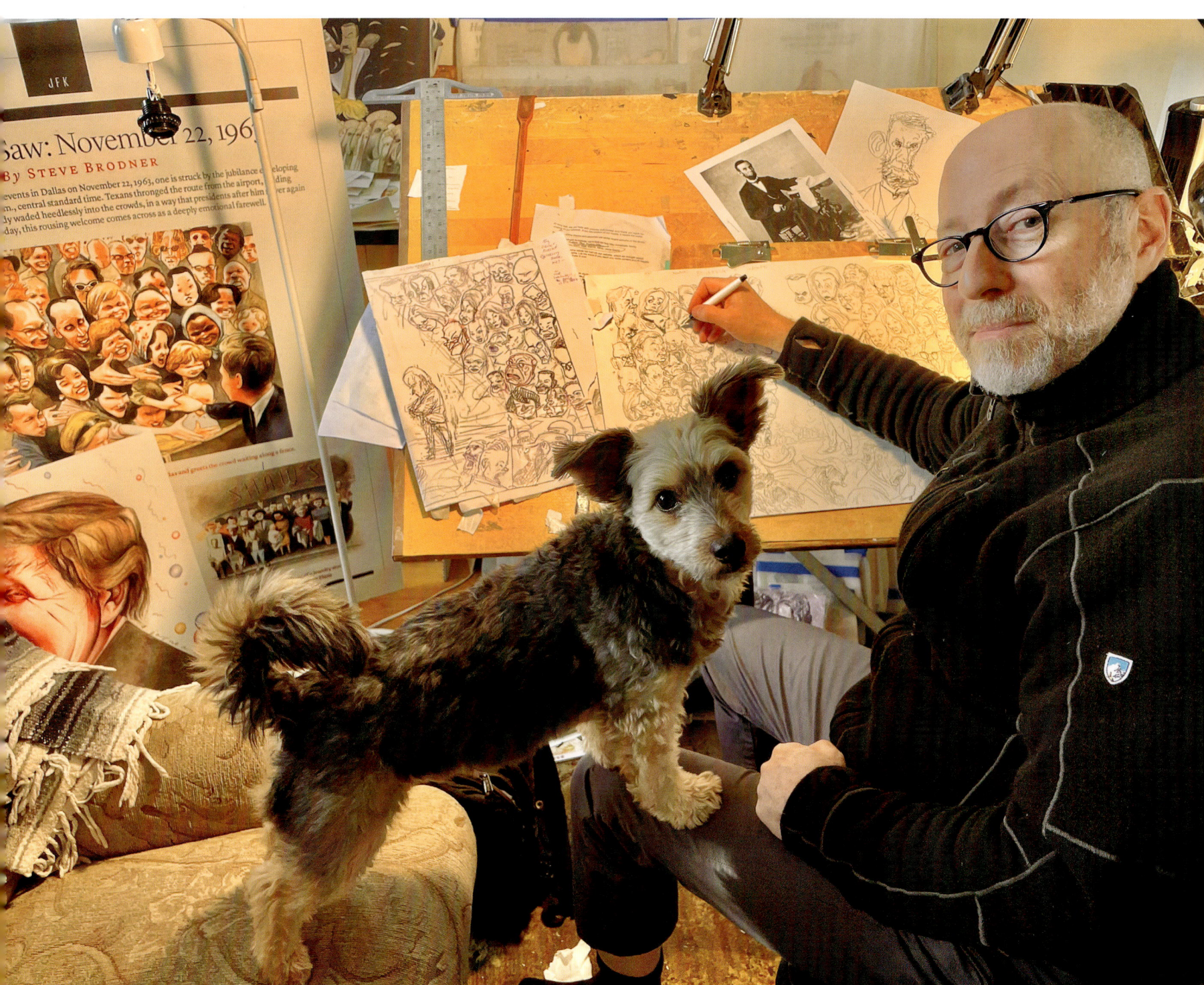

Saw: November 22, 196[?]

By STEVE BRODNER

[?]vents in Dallas on November 22, 1963, one is struck by the jubilance d[?]eloping, [?]m., central standard time. Texans thronged the route from the airport, [?]lding [?]ly waded heedlessly into the crowds, in a way that presidents after him [?]ver again [?]day, this rousing welcome comes across as a deeply emotional farewell.

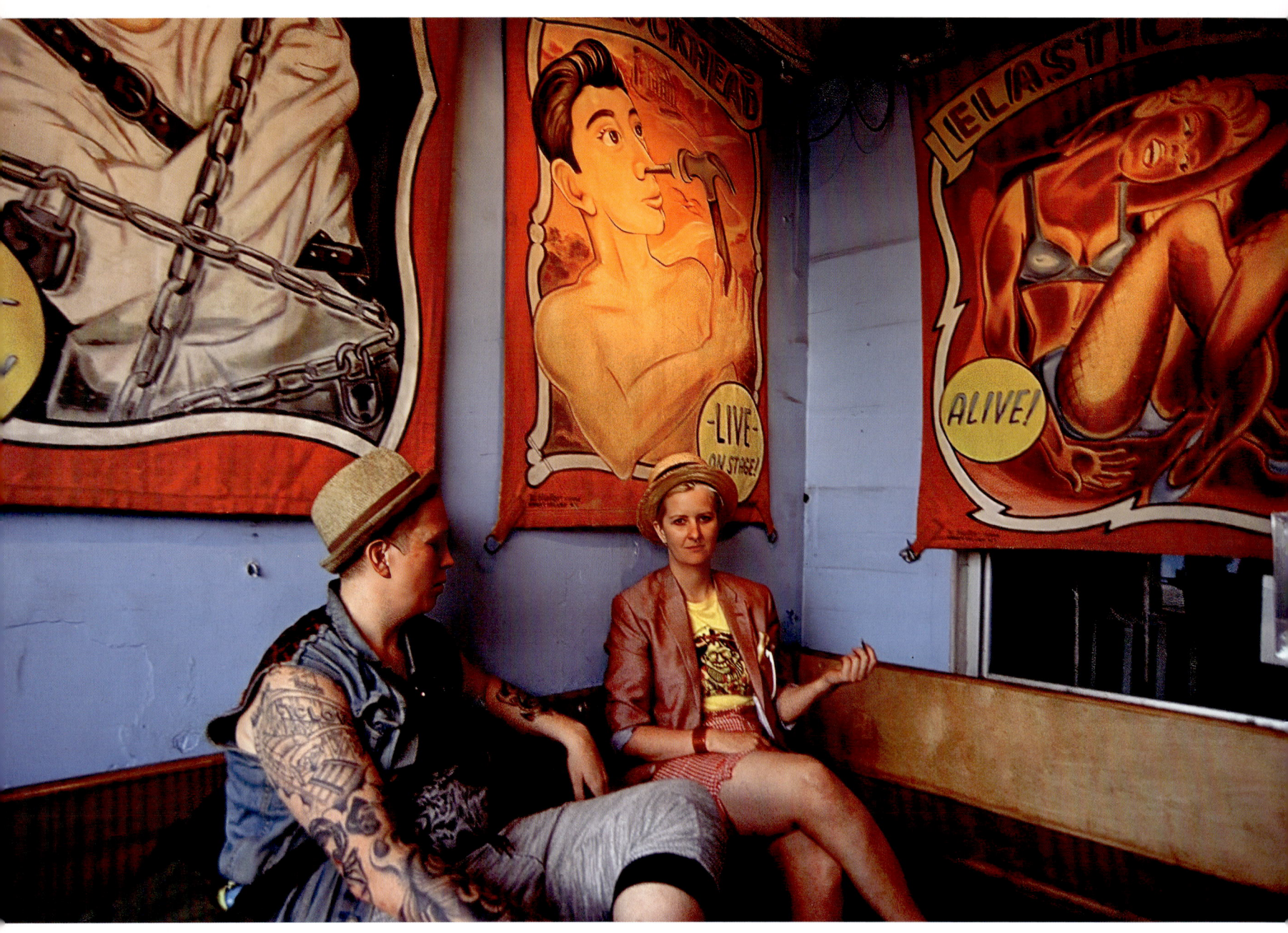

FREAK SHOW PERFORMERS

Coney Island, New York City, New York

The spectacle-hungry Victorian-era society loved viewing magic lantern and stereopticon images exhibiting world oddities along with human freak shows. People with biological anomalies were first featured in medieval courts, kept as entertainment for royalty, and later provided amusement in carnivals or even at British taverns. The craze migrated across the ocean where, mostly due to an acclaimed impresario and promoter, for almost a hundred years freak shows became one of America's most popular entertainment forms. At that time, with this nation quickly expanding from wilderness to townships, marketable human deformities were not yet viewed the way some do today as a pornography of disability. Understanding nineteenth-century American appetites for curiosity, the hyperbolic P. T. Barnum became this nation's most lauded showman and eventually left a widespread legacy. On Broadway within lower Manhattan he established Barnum's American Museum in 1841, which soon became a popular showplace displaying jugglers, fire eaters, exotic women, and stuffed animals while launching hot air balloons from its rooftop. America's greatest showman made global phenomenons of Chang and Eng Bunker, famous original Siamese twins; Prince Randian, better known as a "human torso," who apparently was very skillful at using his only remaining appendage since he married before spawning four children; plus Jo-Jo the Dog-Faced Boy, whose facially hairy hypertrichosis affliction was said to be an inspiration behind *Star Wars*' Chewbacca character. Barnum's newfound friend, fully grown, three-foot-tall Charles Stratton, was denoted General Tom Thumb and for several years the two traveled Europe together, hobnobbing with heads of state and entering Buckingham Palace to entertain Queen Victoria herself. Along with James Bailey, Barnum created The Greatest Show on Earth circus where a given name, that of his immense African elephant Jumbo, entered the national lexicon and ultimately gained international awareness as an adjective to describe large jet airplanes. These days medical advances curing abnormalities and obsessions with television's pop culture ultimately led to the near demise of freak shows, except at Coney Island, once site of this nation's largest amusement park.

By the entrance alcove of an historic 1917 Spanish Colonial Revival building, two relaxed freak show performers take a break on wooden benches during sword swallowing featured inside their Ten-in-One sideshow acts. A passion for carny life is worn with tattoos of Coney Island's Cyclone rollercoaster and Zippy the Pinhead tee shirt. Encircling the walls are circus banners depicting one daring escape artist, an elastic lady, and a truly cringe-inducing human blockhead who happily hammers large nails deeply into his nostrils.

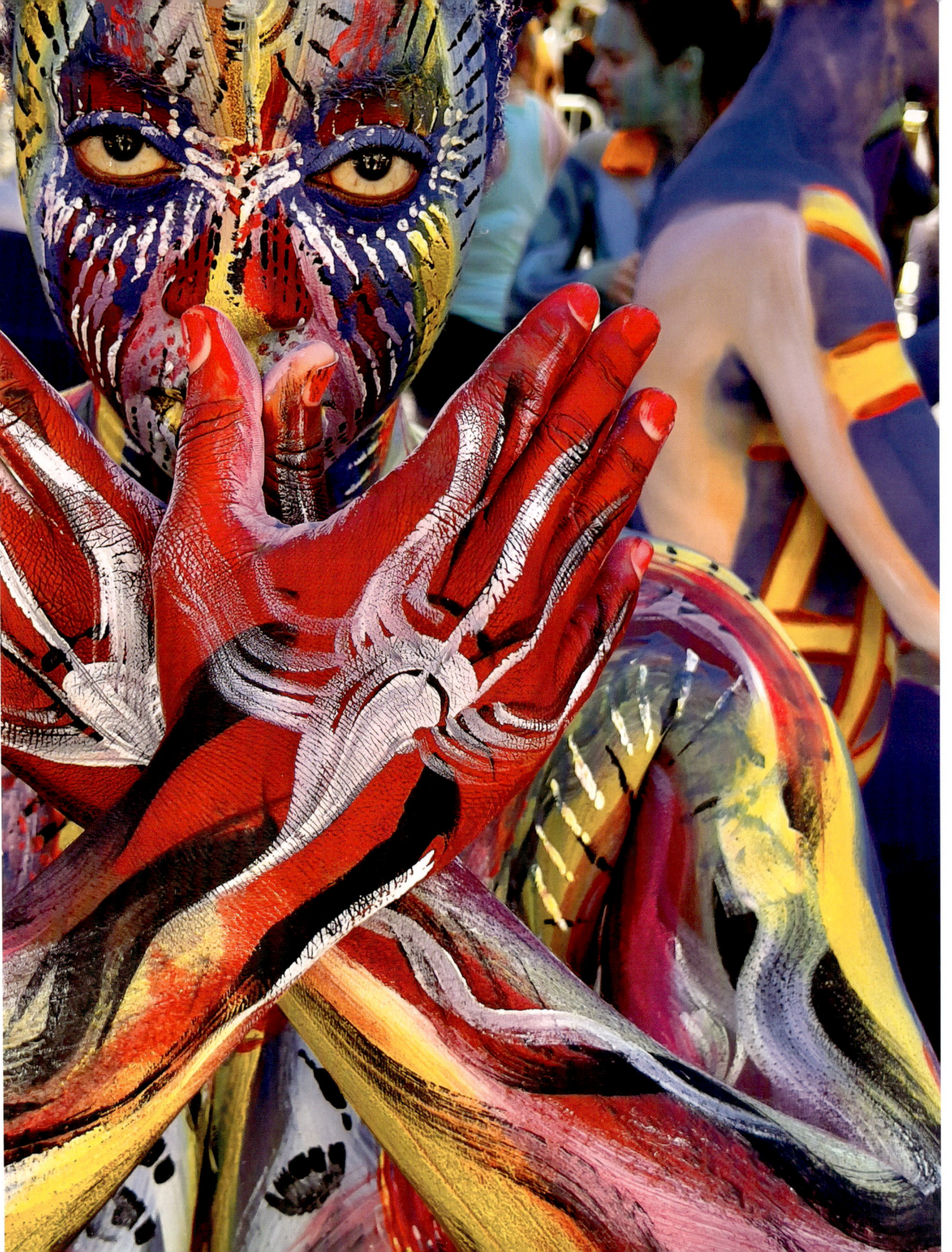

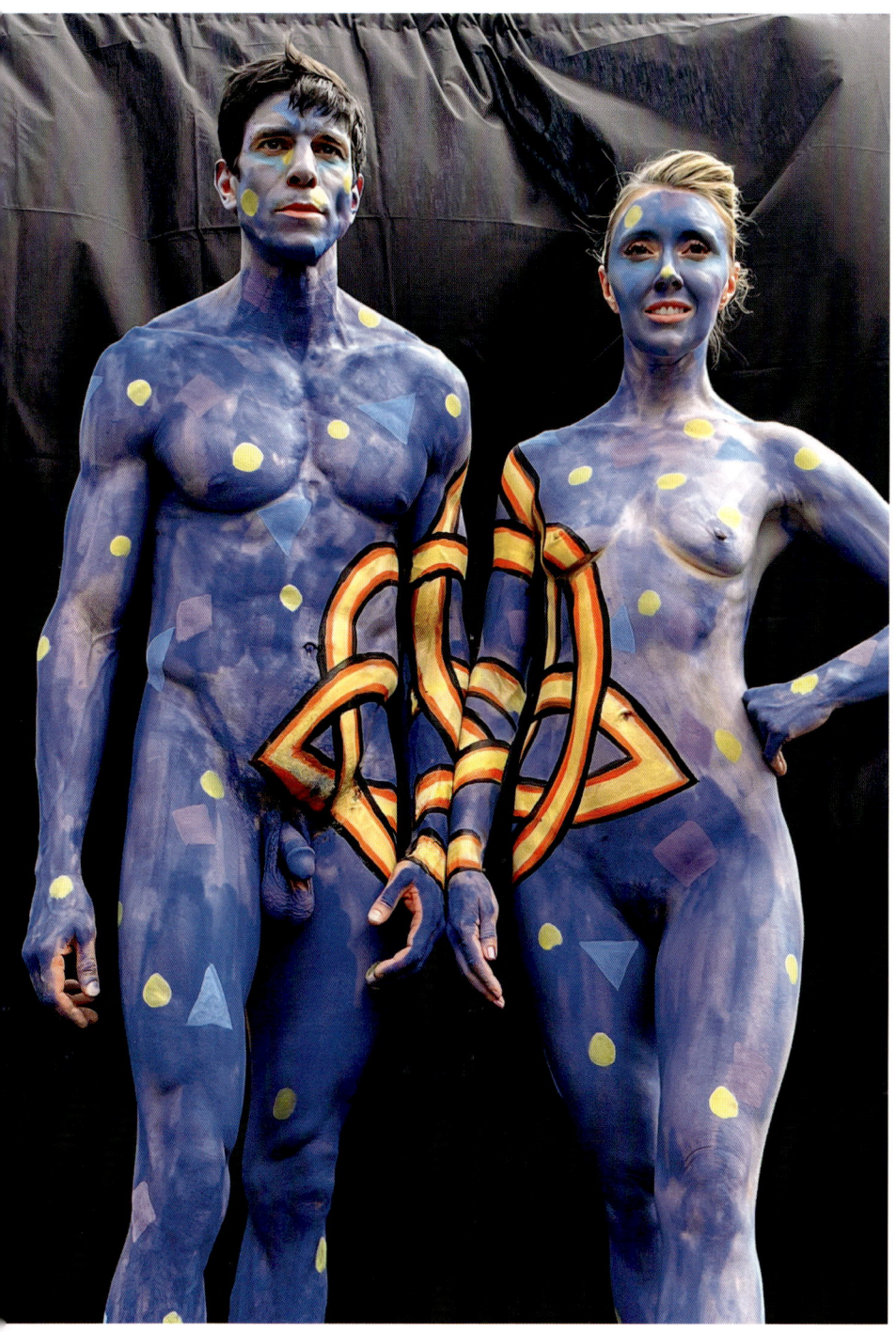

PAINTED HUMAN CANVASES

Union Square, New York City, New York

Amongst 370 million Indigenous people in ninety countries, a rich array of cultural body painting may still be witnessed though their traditions actually stretch back millennia. Tribal applications that coated their skin with colored pigments are thought to uphold power, order, and protection, while being used in warfare, identifying status or initiating rites of passage. In Papua New Guinea, its remote Wahgi valley shielded Kuman-speaking Chimbu people from discovery by outsiders until the mid-twentieth century. Their bodies are completely painted in white clay and ash, intimidating their enemies by the skulls or bones that present tromp l'oeil skeletons. The nomadic, cattle-herding Wodaabe tribe in Niger stage male beauty contests for women to choose preening mates, their vividly painted vermilion faces topped by bulging eyeballs and setting a standard of beauty within this African region. Australian Aborigines paint themselves with animal fat, colored charcoal, ochre, and manganese dioxide to maintain their body temperature while camouflaging their scent during hunting sessions in the bush. In America, polite society seemed shocked at the 1933 World's Fair in Chicago when Maksymilian Faktorowicz, son of a rabbi and later known better as Max Factor, sent burlesque dancer Sally Rand onstage dressed solely with his zigzagging body paint job. In pursuit of cosmetic adornment, he developed flexible greasepaint and popularized the noun "make-up" while creating an industry dedicated to painting film celebrities for their silver screen appearances. Flower power movements during the 1960s spawned a psychedelia that dressed both rock concert attendees and caged go-go dancers in painted regalia.

Within the bustling heart of Manhattan's Union Square, penetrating eyes emerge from inside expressionistic brushstrokes during National Bodypainting Day, an annual decade-long event created by accomplished body painter Andy Golub, bravely confronting authorities and arrest numerous times. Nontoxic hues applied with brush and sponges coat this couple of exhaling canvases wearing nothing but their bravery but mutually brandishing the triquetra, a Celtic trinity knot often viewed as an iconographic symbol of protection.

223

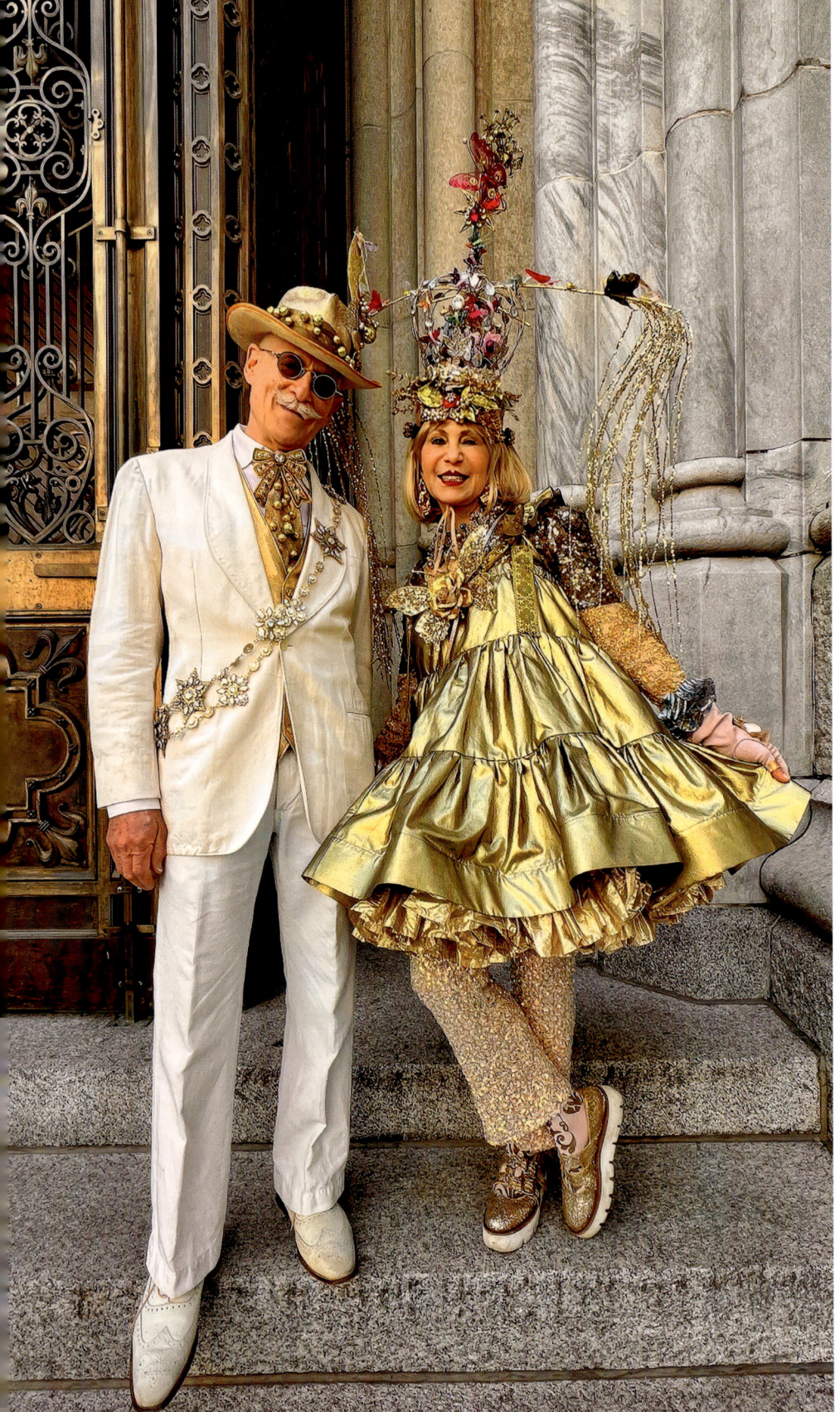

EASTER PARADERS

Midtown, New York City, New York

Directed by a battlefield vision, fourth century's Constantine the Great became the first Roman emperor converting to Christianity and later decreed that his subjects wear their finest clean garbs to parade in celebration of Christ's resurrection. Springtime's natural rhythms of renewal further prompted worshippers into dressing up for Easter during solemn processions toward their church, and in 1597 *Romeo and Juliet*'s ill-fated Mercutio made reference to Eastertime couture. As European immigrants made their way to the New World, they brought their cultural inclinations and customs that were embraced by upper class society who dwelled along Manhattan's Millionaire Row during elegant top-hatted strolls to worship at newly built Gothic churches lining Fifth Avenue. Emulating elegant flower festoons and pyramids of lilies displayed amongst church altars, flaunting ladies in the 1870s garnished their refined wardrobe when promenading to Easter service. Dressmakers and milliners took notice while sketching these outfits, introducing their creations to newly hatched department store windows along Fifth Avenue. That growing spectacle inspired composer Irving Berlin to spend 15 years perfecting his classic tune "Easter Parade," which later spawned the highest-grossing musical of 1948, an eponymous film starring Judy Garland and Fred Astaire. Today's Easter Parade and Bonnet Festival is a creative, jaw-dropping display of ostentatiousness, where over-the-top pastel hats adorned with bunny rabbits, caged taxidermied birds, or precariously stacked painted eggs upstage their models as they valiantly attempt to strut their finery down streets choked by gawking paparazzi.

This bedazzled couple outshines even ornate golden doors that since 1879 have served as a side entrance to religious services at the Neo-Gothic St. Patrick's Cathedral. Taking a brief respite from hordes of angling, bulb-flashing photographers on Fifth Avenue, Howard Chezar and Patricia Fox capture the essence of the Easter Parade after drawing crowds that are rendered agog by their strolling art installation. Atop Fox's phantasmagorical headwear, butterflies hover while a finch appears to alight amongst the bouncing tinseled tentacles. As successful assemblage artist, interior designer, and onetime national training director for Estée Lauder, her fearless fashion sense enhanced by bold sartorial accouterments have been featured in style magazines, while she pairs perfectly with a dashing, mustachioed partner who is also an eagerly collaborative master builder.

SANDCASTLE COMPETITION JUDGE

Rockaway Beach, New York City, New York

Ever since erosive waves have crashed atop rocky shores, the resulting sandy expanses have provided tempting sculpting grounds for visiting beachgoers. The first real documentary evidence of purposeful sand creations dates to medieval Hinduism when fourteenth-century Odia poet Balaram Das forged devotional sculptures in his native India. When a New Jersey railroad conductor first conceived plans in 1870 for an elongated boardwalk along Atlantic City, it was to keep sandy pedestrians from marring railroad cars and hotel lobbies. Strollers promenading the wooden thoroughfares would toss spare coins to artistically bent sunbathers who created fantastical sculptural figures along its edge. Oceanside resorts staged sandcastle competitions to entertain their overnight guests and the beachgoing public. Slowly emerging from sandy seashore floors, mermaids and sea creatures took form while often joined by mammoth castles drawing inspiration from sprawling Victorian structures just across the way. Today shovels and buckets seem to be the critical construction tools of choice, assisted by correct proportional recipes for mixtures with water, as sand grains adhere best with surface tension created from added moisture. Those raw materials for all this beachfront manufacturing would seem to be in greatest abundance aside the longest island in these continental United States. From Suffolk County's Montauk Point to Brooklyn's Verrazzano-Narrows Bridge, the 118 miles across Long Island include dune-carved national seashore and endless uninterrupted shoreline featuring tiny crystals of quartz mineral.

Along that stretch in Rockaway Beach, near the site of amusement park Playland for almost 90 years, a strict two-hour limit of frenzied construction has come to an end as judges begin their final deliberations. They'll evaluate the entrants based on criteria of creativity, composition, and wow factor. That last category if applied toward fashion choices would surely go to Owen Loof, standing at the ready for coronations of prestigious medals onto their worthy recipients. Self-dubbed the "Best Dressed Man in Rockaway," a partial title of his latest book, Loof had been raised just several blocks away, was an Army vet wounded in Vietnam, worked as New York City's subway station agent, and spent twelve years teaching American history in Hawaii. Returning to his birthplace after losing a spouse, he once again reinvented passionate purpose. In partial retirement, when not spotted as background actor on *The Greatest Showman* or *The Marvelous Mrs. Maisel*, show-stopping attire and flamboyant sartorial choices are portable credentials for this man about town who seems to be a dancing partner's hot ticket gracing the floor at his local Knights of Columbus lodge.

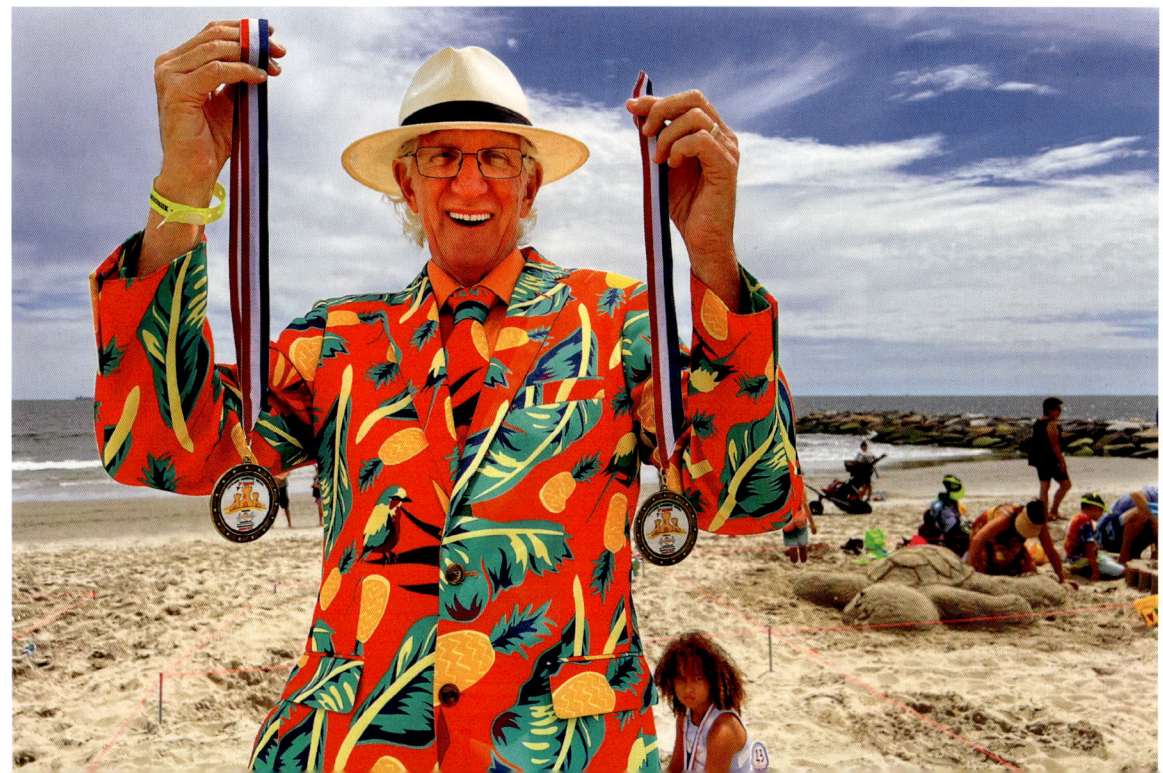

COUNTRY FAIR RIBBON WINNER

Chester, Connecticut

America's earliest country fair was held only about 100 miles from the Nutmeg State's charming town where a newly formed Chester Agricultural and Mechanical Society attempted to showcase this area's hillside farmers and valley factory workers. Since 1877, an annual time-honored tradition held here boosted both town spirits and the region's economy during summertime's sweltering dog days. Early events featured boys' bike races, tug-of-war, plus parade floats sporting Rube Goldberg–style whirligigs, a concoction of gears, flying arms, and swirling balls. These days, cotton candy, cheesesteaks, or fried desserts fill bellies, and dunking booths cool off overheated visitors while blinking Ferris wheels spin above shrieking midways that brim with dizzying amusement rides. After several rounds of frog-jumping competitions, quilting contests pull visitors away from the sun and into tented structures. Outside, yoke-harnessed oxen strain to tug nearly 3,000-pound loads of stone cargo filling sleds in the pull ring, while squealing pigs race around their course fascinating spectators that go hog wild over all the fanfare. Just across the lawn, ushered livestock preen for admiring farm families while heavyweight vegetables inspire growers looking to improve their horticultural know-how.

This young farm girl jubilantly displays her yellow Reserve Junior Champion ribbon after a hectic round of judging Jersey and Holstein dairy breeds. Able to pick their noses or open gates with their muscular tongue, this lip-licking, ear-tagged heifer calf requires being under four months of age for eligibility in these muddy competitions most unlikely to leave mandatory white pants and shirts unblemished.

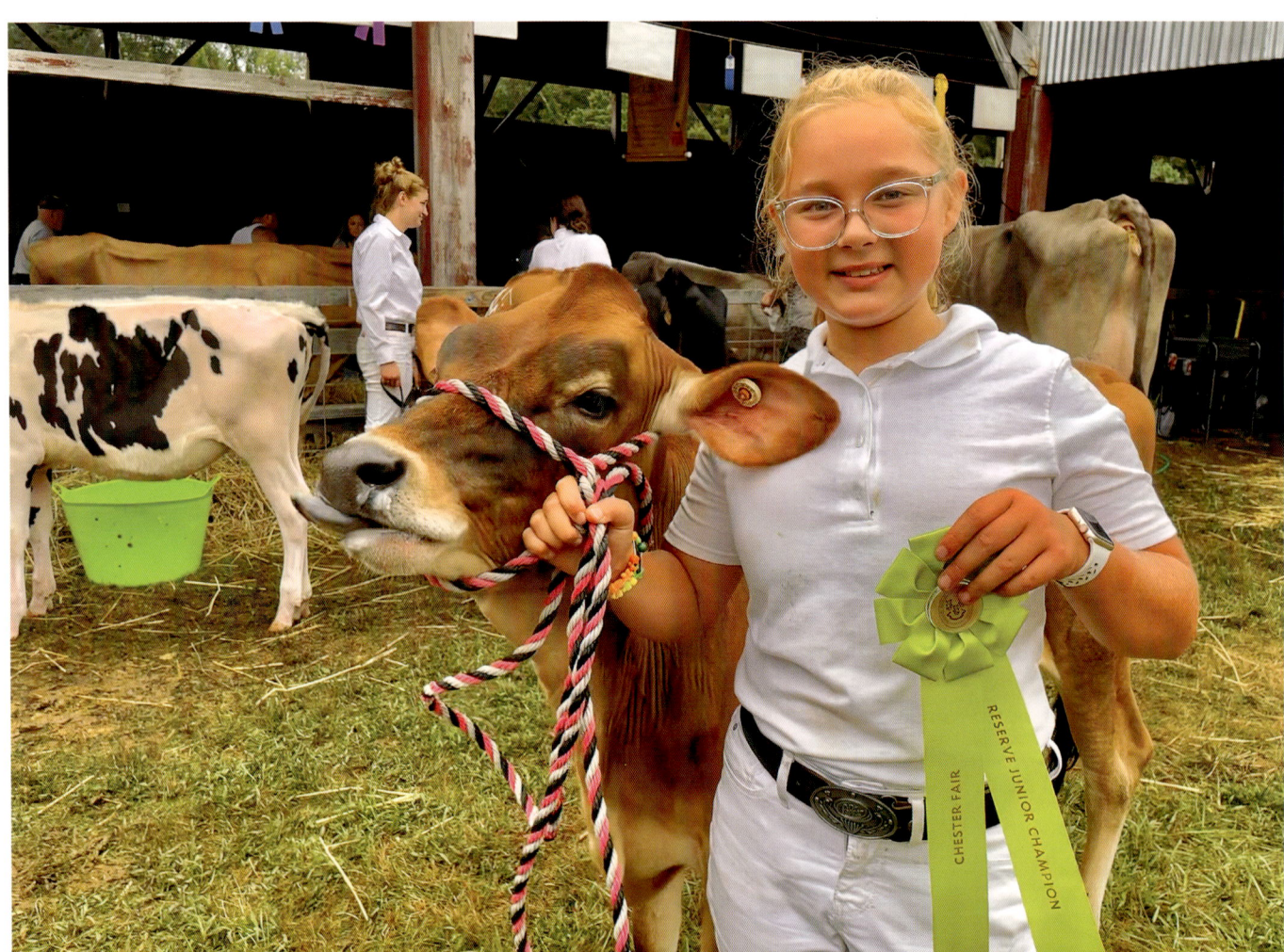

LIGHTHOUSE KEEPER

Saugerties, New York

Trickling out from Lake Tear of the Clouds's glacial tarn, the Hudson River's nascent waters begin a 315-mile, gravity-driven search for an eventual ocean. Uniquely, the river gushes variously along whitewater rapids, dramatic gorges, elongated fjords, sprawling tidal estuaries, and soaring palisades cliffs. Its scenic banks are still dotted by seven lighthouses, each winking differently patterned beams notifying alert mariners as to their precise fogbound locations. Near Saugerties, a formerly thriving paper- and iron-manufacturing village, this red brick lighthouse, originally lit with whale oil lamps, was constructed in 1869 to alert nautical traffic of an upcoming channel-bending peninsular appendage. Its idyllic location is reachable on foot only by sauntering through cattail-filled wetland marsh and loosestrife-lined boardwalk, which can get wetter than an otter's pocket when caught during the wrong moments of a tidal cycle. With its beacons now powered with solar panels, the shoal-alerting lighthouse, presided over by an intrepid keeper, serves double duty as a bed and breakfast. There a brocaded couch greets romantic guests who can play records on an old Victrola, cozy up to an invitingly toasty coal stove, or hop into their clawfoot basin shower.

Ending speculation as to whether owners can wind up resembling their pets, Alexander Wade and his loving pug companion ably steward the successful operation of this landmark beacon. As lighthouse keeper, he resides in the quarters and oversees its museum, parlor, and kitchen activities. Ready to solve any engineering or architectural issues that arose onsite, Wade was an accomplished high school valedictorian, often considered a walking encyclopedia, and was called upon frequently to assist in the renaissance of Saugerties, including bluestone sidewalk restorations, now lined with antique stores that thrive alongside charming vintage shops.

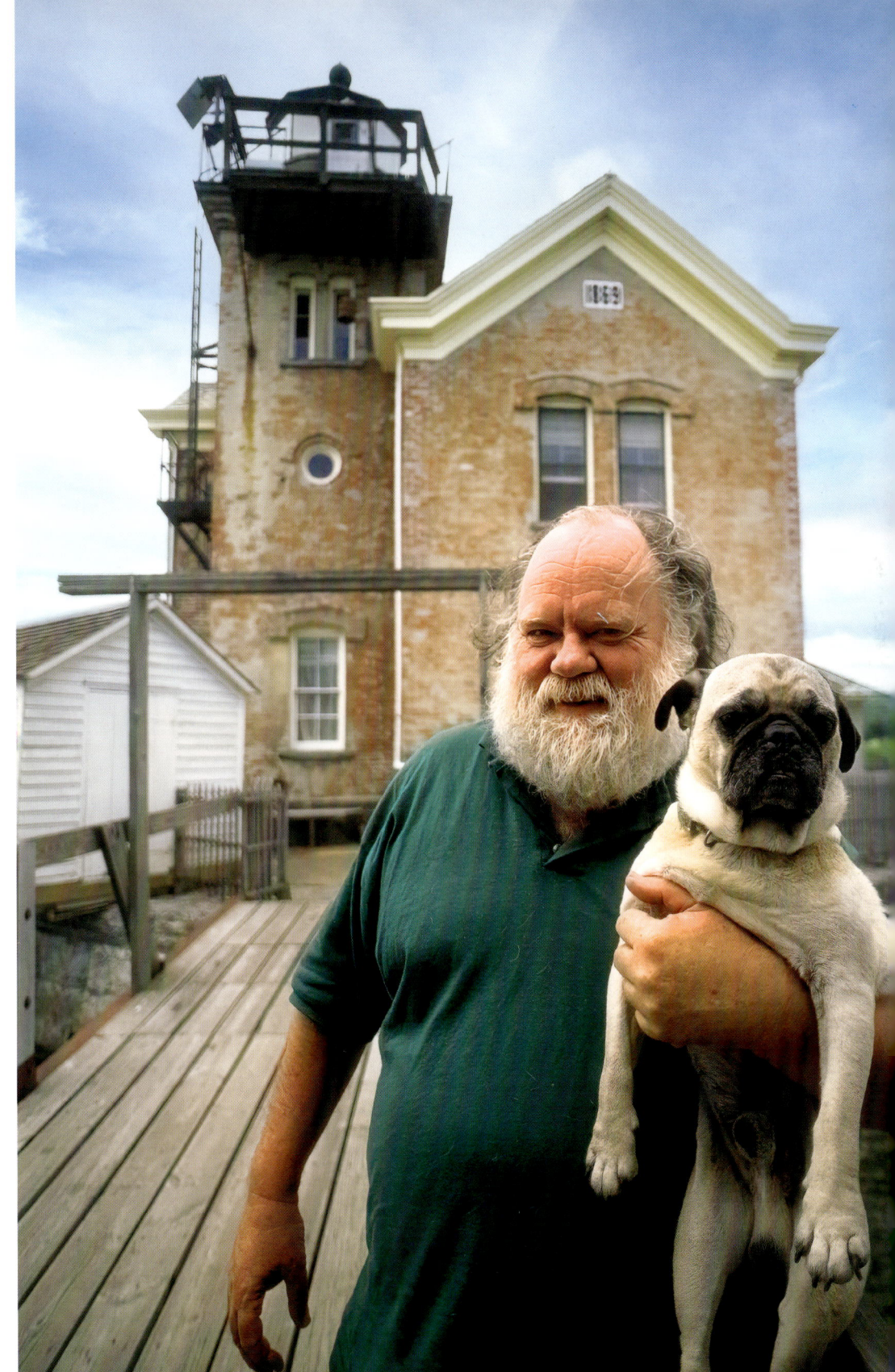

TWINE BALL CUSTODIAN

Cawker City, Kansas

Amongst widely stretched corn and wheat field patchwork, just a handful of miles from the precise geographic center of the United States, a farmer in 1953 fed small hay bales to his cows and began to save loose bale strings made from sisal twine. As a thrifty child of the Great Depression, he decided to consolidate those fibrous strings into one huge ball, which soon grew larger than his barn door. Neighbors began donating extra cordage and the accumulating project soon grew into a local sensation. Regional newspapers picked up this story which then spurred the curious to see it with their own eyes. Cawker City thought it might be a neat idea to create an obvious public display in their downtown right along the well-trafficked path of US Highway 24. After first claiming one Guinness World Records title for the largest ball of sisal twine while attempting to fight off rivals competing for this title, the town began ensuring its record in perpetuity by sponsoring an annual Twine-a-Thon in conjunction with a parade and picnic.

School librarian Linda Clover volunteered to be caretaker and, as belle of the ball, is always ready with extra sisal twine for passing motorists who might eagerly whorl their own efforts at personally contributing to that record. Her kitty-emblazoned tee shirt echoes an enlarged cat on a stick. That treasured gift was apparently a tribute epitomizing the feline's need to chase balls of twine, as their instinctive feral-hunting techniques were spurred pursuing prey with long, stringy tails. Currently, a pavilion in town shelters this colossal sphere, which currently brags about its bulging 9-ton, 40-foot circumference, and has attained status as iconic roadside attraction for inquisitive vacationers from all across the country.

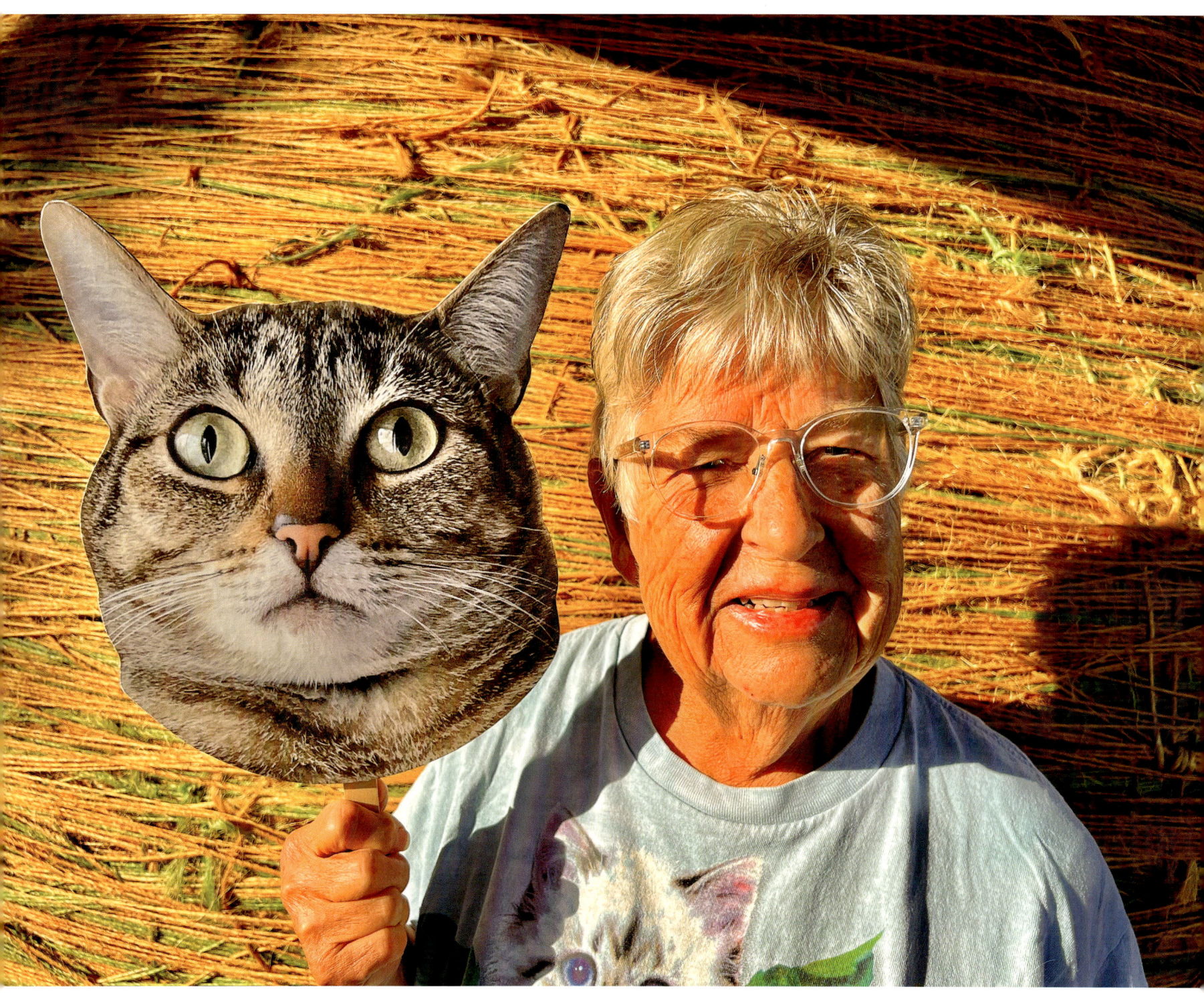

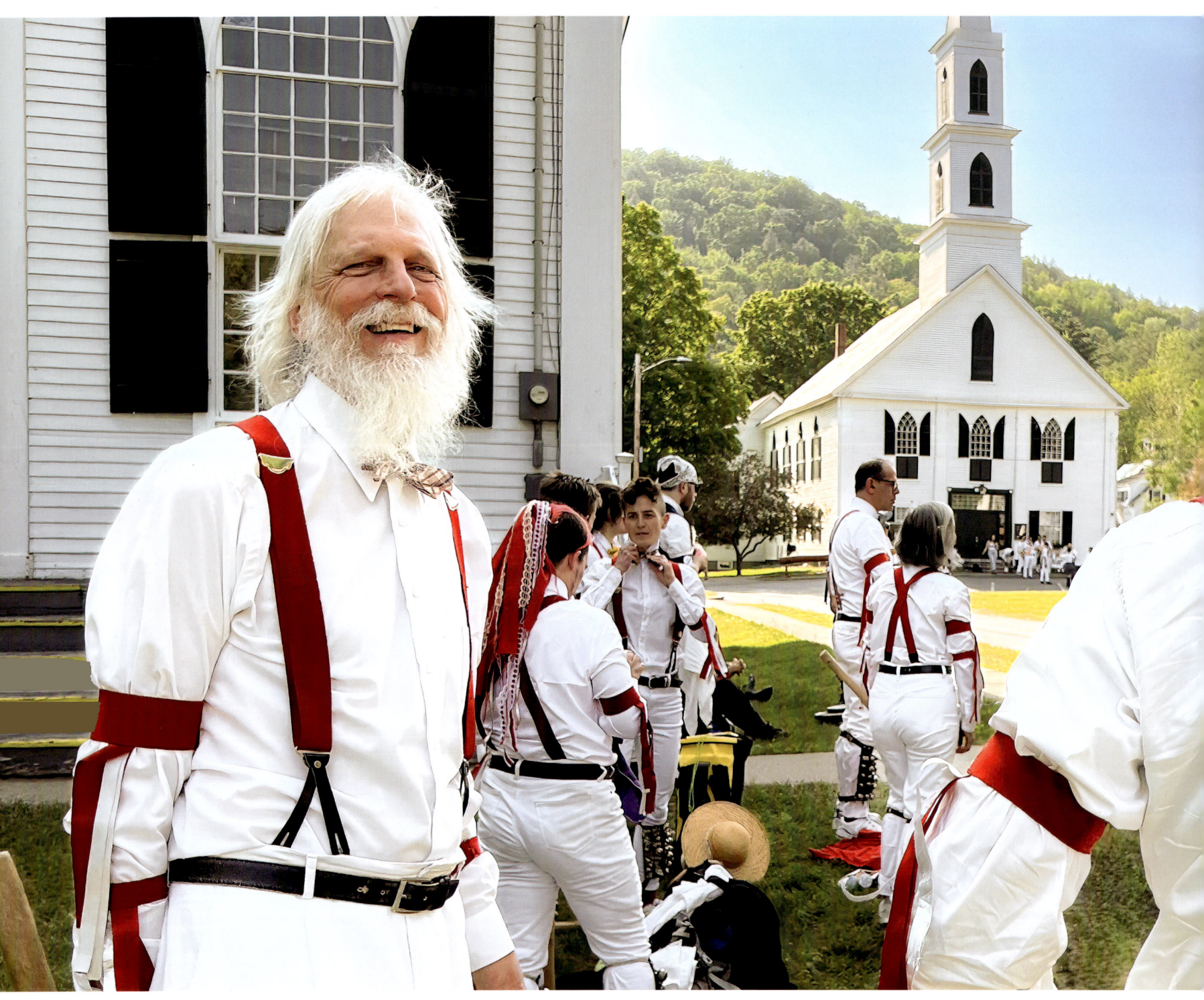

MORRIS DANCER

Newfane, Vermont

Confused notions about the exotic nature of Moorish culture helped christen Morris dancing, a folk tradition first developed in rural England. Accompanied by fiddle and fife tunes, rhythmic stepping, energetic gamboling, along with synchronized stick-battling characterize a vernal tradition whose precise origins remain unclear. An earliest known reference to Morris dancers was from payments made of seven shillings by the Goldsmith Guild for a spring cleaning feast day in 1448. At least in part one remnant of pre-Christian fertility rites, Morris dancing became a fixture at church festivals across medieval and Renaissance England. These fairs, many concentrated amongst the sylvan Cotswold region, would brew and sell ale to raise funds for parish upkeep. In Act 2 of *All's Well That Ends Well*, William Shakespeare celebrated these dancers' fitness, strenuously leaping in choreographed unison during what is perhaps the only athletic pursuit ever centered around handkerchiefs. With jingling bell pads strapped to their shins, these suspenders-clad, hankie-waving troupes exuberantly leap about while rhythmically announcing the demise of winter's dreary gray. Once these frolicsome dances spread and attached themselves to village fetes, Morris dancers became scorned by seventeenth-century Puritans as their flower-bedecked celebrations were considered heathenish or profane. Though the industrial revolution sent young men to factory towns and caused an eventual decline in these springtime frolics, a resurgence during the last century helped spread this tradition abroad and today Morris dancing may often be found in pastoral regions across America.

By the village green in bucolic Newfane, Vermont, a bow-tied, stick-wielding Morris dancer still glows after strenuous displays of airborne calisthenics and his musical procession down spectator-lined side streets. As bonnets, beribboned wands, and accordions are temporarily laid to rest, large congregations of white-clad performers loiter around the village's Congregational Church aside rolling green mountains that are this state's namesake. The Marlboro Morris Ale is an annual rendezvous of dance lines who had spent their entire day cavorting in different villages throughout southern Vermont. After some thoughtful consideration, they'll top off the day quaffing a pint or two of ale in some nearby pub.

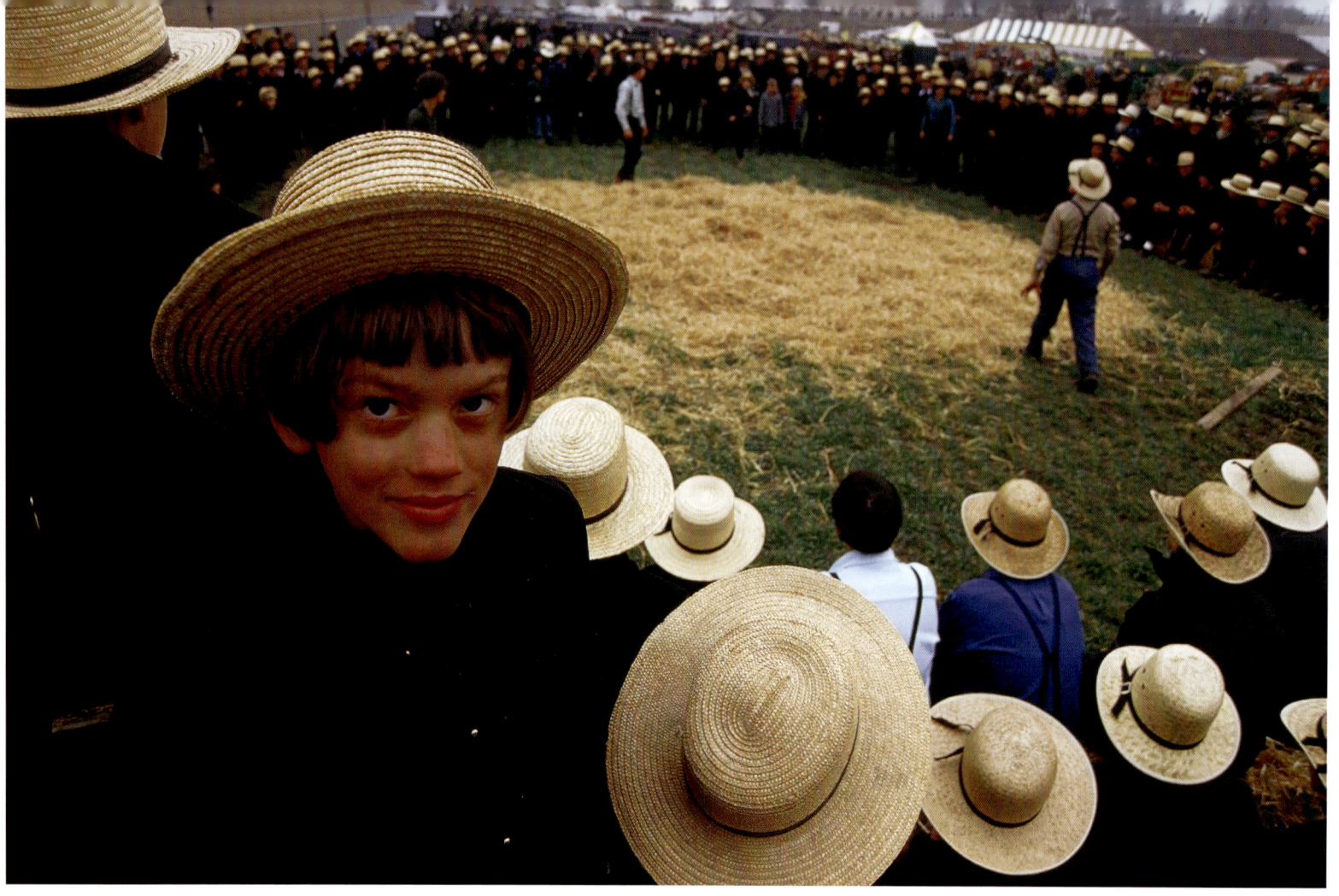

AMISH CORNER BALL SPECTATOR

Peach Bottom, Pennsylvania

In fertile Lancaster County, a fifth season seems added to the complex farming calendar used by Amish people. Just as winter snows are almost melted, yet before springtime's slowly thawing soil gets plowed, striped fairground tents sprout up near small village crossroads celebrating their mud season with a lively gathering of the button-eschewing plain people, busy auctioning off buggies, horses, and hay bales. Amongst rolling fields sprinkled with tagged farm equipment and clapboard sheds offering sticky shoofly pies or warm, freshly baked pretzels, a swarm of young boys tug at their wooden hand wagons, pitching the mud sale's departing shoppers instant valet service for their unwieldy purchases. From all directions, a rapid-fire tidal wave of nearly indistinguishable sounds emanates from the energetic mouths punctuating Old Order Amish auctioneers.

During one brief afternoon lull, youthful crowds picnic or break into spontaneous games of corner ball, a curious athletic concoction that somehow balances those sly evasions seen in dodgeball with the spirited innings-based assertiveness denoting baseball. Gathering around an impact-softening, straw-strewn ballfield, and amongst a bobbing sea of suspender-strapped, straw-hatted spectators, a youthful, crudely shorn sports fan appears to find some competing intrigue beyond the field of play.

MAY BREAKFAST HOSTESS

Cranston, Rhode Island

The country's smallest state punches way above its belt-loosening weight. Only 38 miles wide and conceivably fitting inside Texas 222 times, diminutive Rhode Island serves an inordinately large amount of local cuisine indigenous to the state. Very commonplace on menus there but virtually unavailable outside this state are skillet-cooked johnnycakes made from stoneground cornmeal, clam cakes whipped up using the battered mollusk, chowders packed with that same bivalve, sausage-stuffed quahogs known as stuffies, striplike tomato pie, scungilli snail salad, baked zeppole doughboys, creamy milkshake cabinets, and syrup-sweetened coffee milk which is Rhode Island's official beverage. Even more exclusive to the Ocean State is an entire meal called a May Breakfast. Well known to virtually every Rhode Islander but completely unheard of outside its borders, the meal is a rite of spring when fellow villagers finally mingle after their winter hibernations. Usually offered during just the first week of May, fire stations, community centers, churches, and grange halls follow more than a sesquicentennial tradition which originated at Oaklawn Community Baptist Church in Cranston. At the Old Quaker Meeting House in 1869 an active church elder, inspired by England's traditional May Day festivities, proposed a breakfast fundraiser featuring local staples to build their new house of worship. As sunlight streams through stained glass windows onto begonias gracing long white tables weighted down by fluffy scrambled eggs, hand-sliced honey ham, piping hot clam cakes, freshly baked cornbread along with apple pie, vernal appetites and neighborly conversations flourish during this anxiously awaited annual event.

As at dozens of Rhode Island communities, lines that might reach up to 1,000 guests start forming outside the church by 6 a.m. A freshly scrubbed, porcelain-cheeked face backed by an aproned battalion of church members garbed in Quaker costumes appear ready to serve the meals and perhaps 90 apple pies, all prepared on premises.

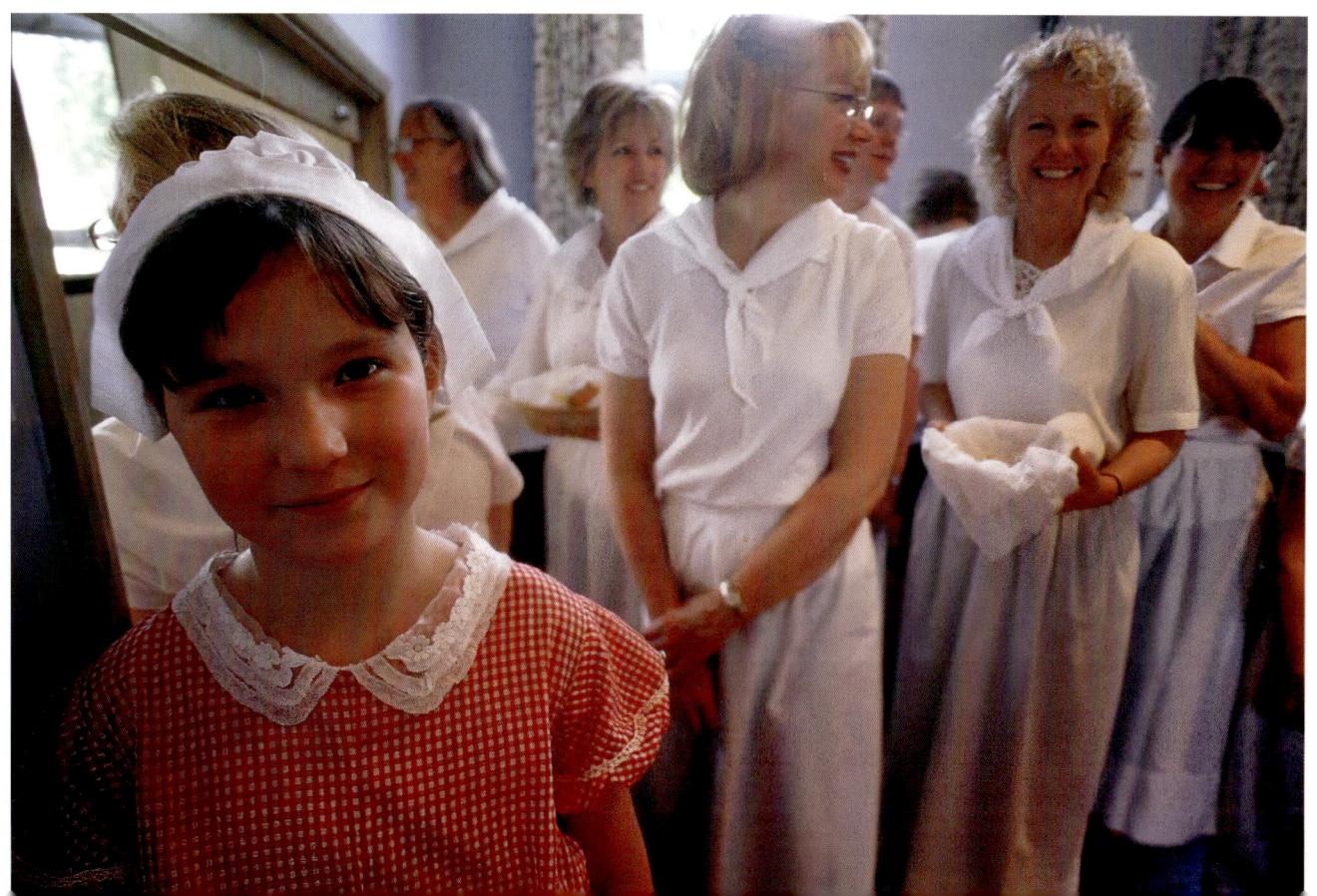

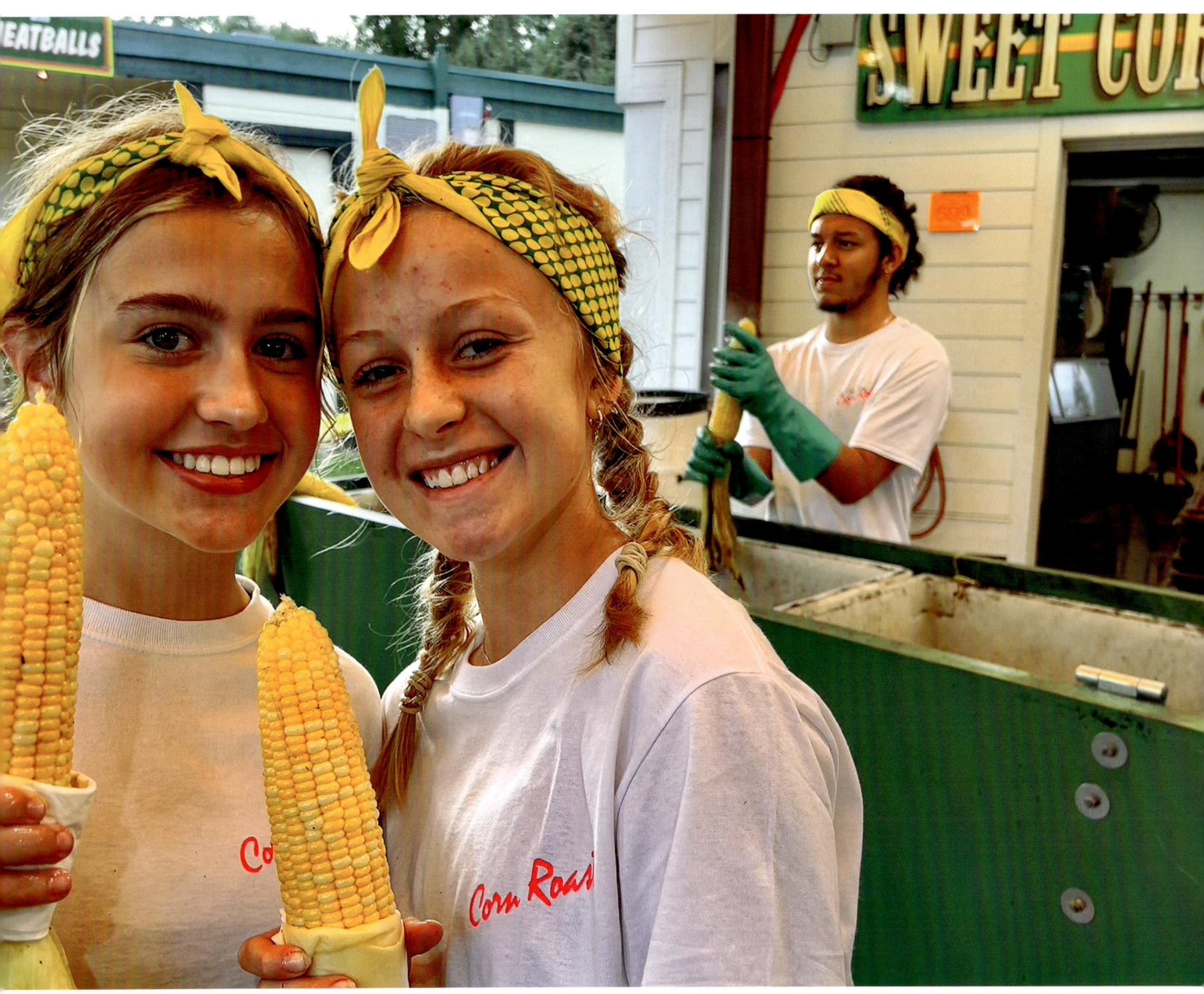

CORN ROASTERS

St. Paul, Minnesota

Over the centuries, fairs have evolved significantly since their earliest incarnations as spiritual events. Its Latin root *feria* meant "holy day," when time was set aside for recreation and religious celebration. The first fairs held across this country were almost entirely agricultural in nature with competitive exhibitions of livestock and displays featuring novel farm products. They afforded rural families some opportunity to break from chores, share family recipes, enter contests with their draft animals, and learn about the newest inventions. As this nation evolved from its agrarian roots toward an industrial society, amusement rides, midways, and food booths added a bit of urban sparkle to the fair's humble pastoral roots. Since 1885, the Minnesota State Fair has provided Midwestern spectacles during a dazzling ten-plus days of events. Boasting the country's largest attendance for any state fair, this 322-acre fairground provided an impressive venue for Theodore Roosevelt in 1901 to first utter that famous phrase "speak softly and carry a big stick." It's a bit unclear whether that stick he was referring to resembled the one that many decades later hoisted deep-fried pork chops or chocolate-dipped bananas for voracious fairgoers. Perhaps one of the healthier food items available at this fair can be found alongside its iconic Corn Roast, held beneath a towering pop art rendering that depicts naked sweetcorn. Because of Mother Nature's volatile thermal temperament, corn is first planted in May at time-staggered intervals to ensure that one of these plantings will perfectly hit this fair's ten-day window over three months later. During its moment of peak perfection, a highly acclaimed Mirai corn variety must be picked by hand only one day before it's eaten at the fair. After being dunked in water, corn is roasted inside its husk at 575 degrees over a bed of hot coals and an open flame, yielding rich flavors as those burnt kernels caramelize the sugars. Brittle husks and charred ochre ears signal the ideal moment for public consumption.

With smiles bright as the sunshine that first nourished their produce, two pleased corn roasters wield post-shucking ears just prior to a dousing in melted butter. Glistening fingers attest to that cob's baptism into just a fraction of the two-ton butter supply used up here during this fair's short run. Racing at 2,400 ears per hour, quick agility is necessary to evade the outdoor kitchen's 130-degree temperatures where roasting human beings can wind up being an occupational hazard.

LITTLE MISS BEAN SOUP

McClure, Pennsylvania

A second-floor reunion in an agrarian Pennsylvanian blacksmith shop brought together Civil War veterans in 1883 where their traditional wartime bean soup was served up with hardtack. Within one decade, the popularity of this savory broth spurred a public invitation to sample the soup during their newly hatched community gathering. Beneath its steam-filled pavilion, a wood-fired battery of furnaces are able to simultaneously boil up sixteen cast iron kettles that simmer away with thirty-five gallons comprising an identical time-honored recipe. Into clear spring water, percolating inside its bubbling pot, twenty pounds of beef are unloaded alongside an equal bucketful crammed with dry navy beans, eight pounds containing suet, and a quick salt sprinkling. Like an oversized human whirligig come to life, a dedicated army of kitchen-hardened villagers toil away in two-hour, twenty-minute shifts, their large ten-pound wooden paddles stirring continuously while brushing beans and creaming the soup.

Across the midway, a spinning Ferris wheel soars above this lively festival of milk-chugging and wheelbarrow-decorating contests. The annual merriment accompanies its signature soup tastings, overseen by a white-sashed Royal Court, including this tiara-crowned Little Miss Bean Soup, proudly standing sentry for thousands of hungry chowder hounds who will arrive over those next four days.

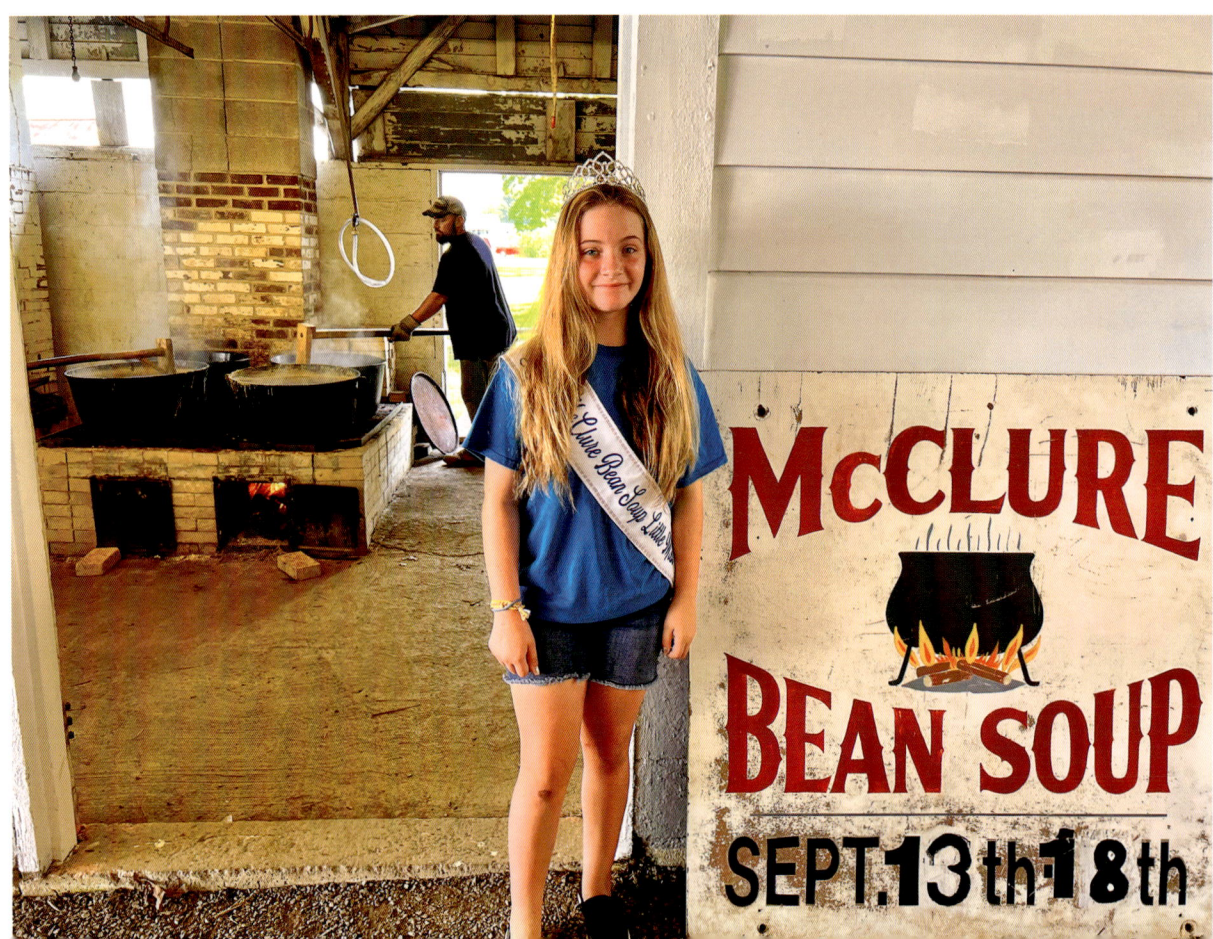

PURIM MERRYMAKER

Williamsburg, New York City, New York

Enfolded within Williamsburg's patchwork of ethnic enclaves, the Satmar know how to throw a god-fearing party. On Purim, very observant Jews convene for celebrations during a Mardi Gras for this Hasidic world where they toss behavioral taboos to the wind and let their payos down. Purim celebrates the defeat of Haman, an evil rapscallion who plotted for elimination of Jews in Babylonia two and a half millennia ago. Queen Esther, niece of Jewish leader Mordecai, was coronated through an ancient version of *The Bachelor*. She schemed with her uncle to defeat Haman through a decree from King Ahasuerus because of Mordecai's earlier heroic efforts spoiling the deadly conspiracy against him. Today, that complicated circular plot is recounted during raucous recitals of the Megillah scriptures, when noise-making graggers and jeering boos drown out his name while echoing throughout synagogue congregations. Out on the streets, wine-splattered revelers join prowling gangs of joyous teenagers who spill from party buses for street dancing to rhythmic Yiddish anthems. Meanwhile, a curiously preposterous junior crowd rivals Halloween trick-or-treaters as they scurry along sidewalks crowded with walking Torah scrolls and double-headed rabbis. Inflated hand-standing clowns, weirdly inappropriate Raggedy Ann dolls, and tin soldiers dodge other street corner children cadging charity-bound paper currency from their elders. Adults rapidly shepherd their numerous costumed children toward brief visits with relatives where they present shrink-wrapped holiday delicacies trimmed by hamantaschen. This triangular pastry is named for one of the villain's two external hearing organs, jammed with a variety of possible fillings, like poppyseed paste (*mohn*), fig, or apricot preserves.

By the doorway of a visiting relative, this rouge-cheeked boy wearing a faux military jacket hugs his diminutive poppet simulacrum, replete with similar outfit, yarmulke, payos, and buckled shoes. Though they bear some striking resemblance to one another, the little wide-eyed mini-me somehow seems a bit more gung-ho about this ancient annual holiday.

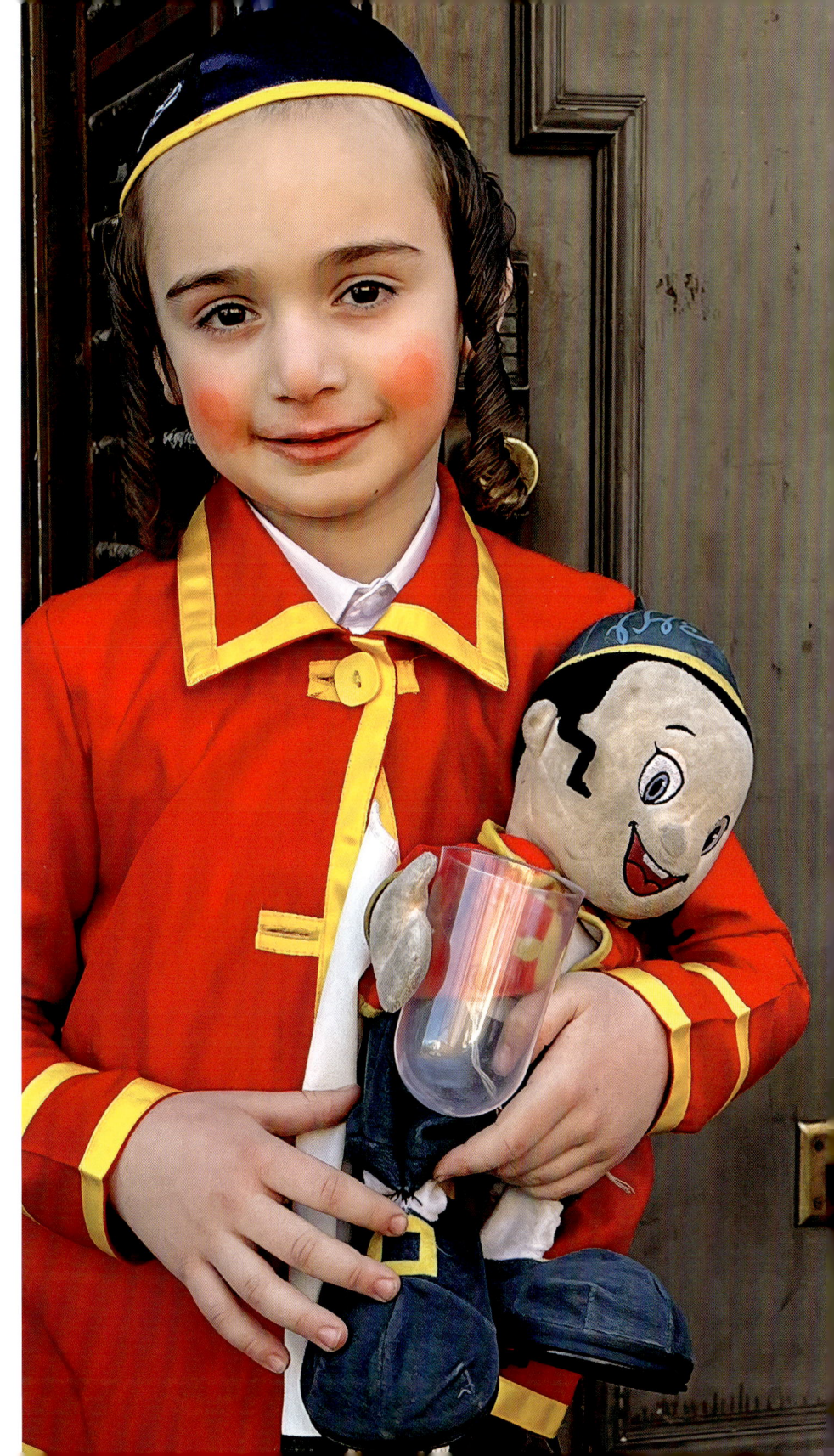

VENTRILOQUISM MUSEUM DIRECTOR

Fort Mitchell, Kentucky

Archaeological evidence from Egypt suggests that far back in 2000 BCE, popular superstitions were exploited by ventriloquizing to suggest familiar spirits, while in ancient Greece priests would emit sounds from their stomachs, using diaphragm muscles for applying pressure onto their vocal cords. The British Isles developed an entertainment industry of thrown voices that arose at traveling carnivals during the late eighteenth century, when performers utilized dolls and puppets as a conduit for their disguised vocalizations. Vaudeville helped popularize the carved dummy during mid-twentieth century decades as wooden sidekicks like Edgar Bergen's Charlie McCarthy or Paul Winchell's Jerry Mahoney became big hits on radio and television. Their rambunctious alter egos would spring to life as expertly employed levers and control sticks activated tilting heads, raised eyebrows, and hinged mouths.

Overseeing this world's largest collection filled with these jokester acolytes, the eye-popping, slack-jawed expressions on exhibition director Lisa Sweasy and her loyal friend sets a good example for an assembled entourage of frighteningly alert dummies. Housed inside earth's only such dedicated museum, a well-behaved congregation is crowded with ligneous characters that appear quite content to be seated in actual chairs rather than on the laps of their manipulative companions.

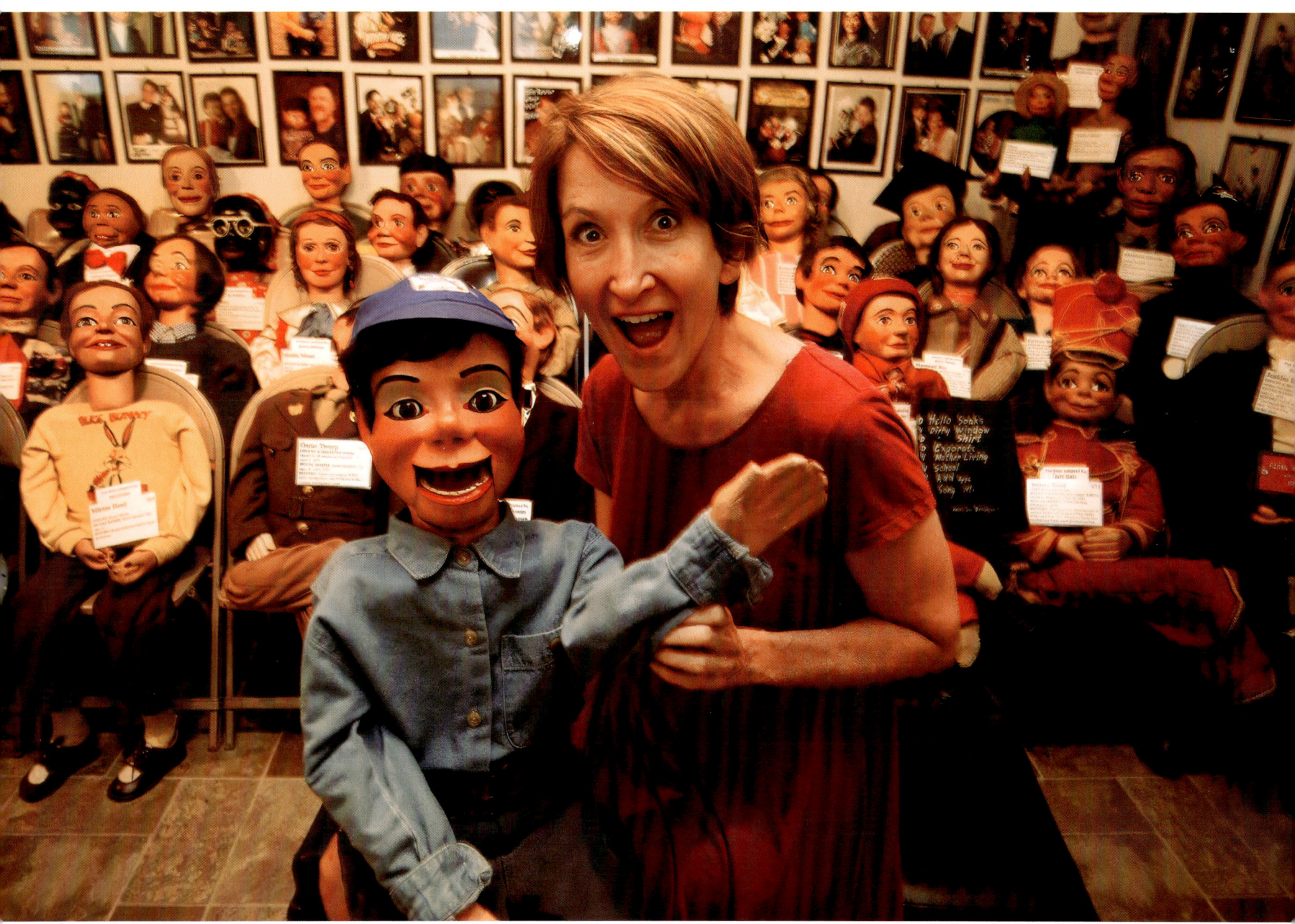

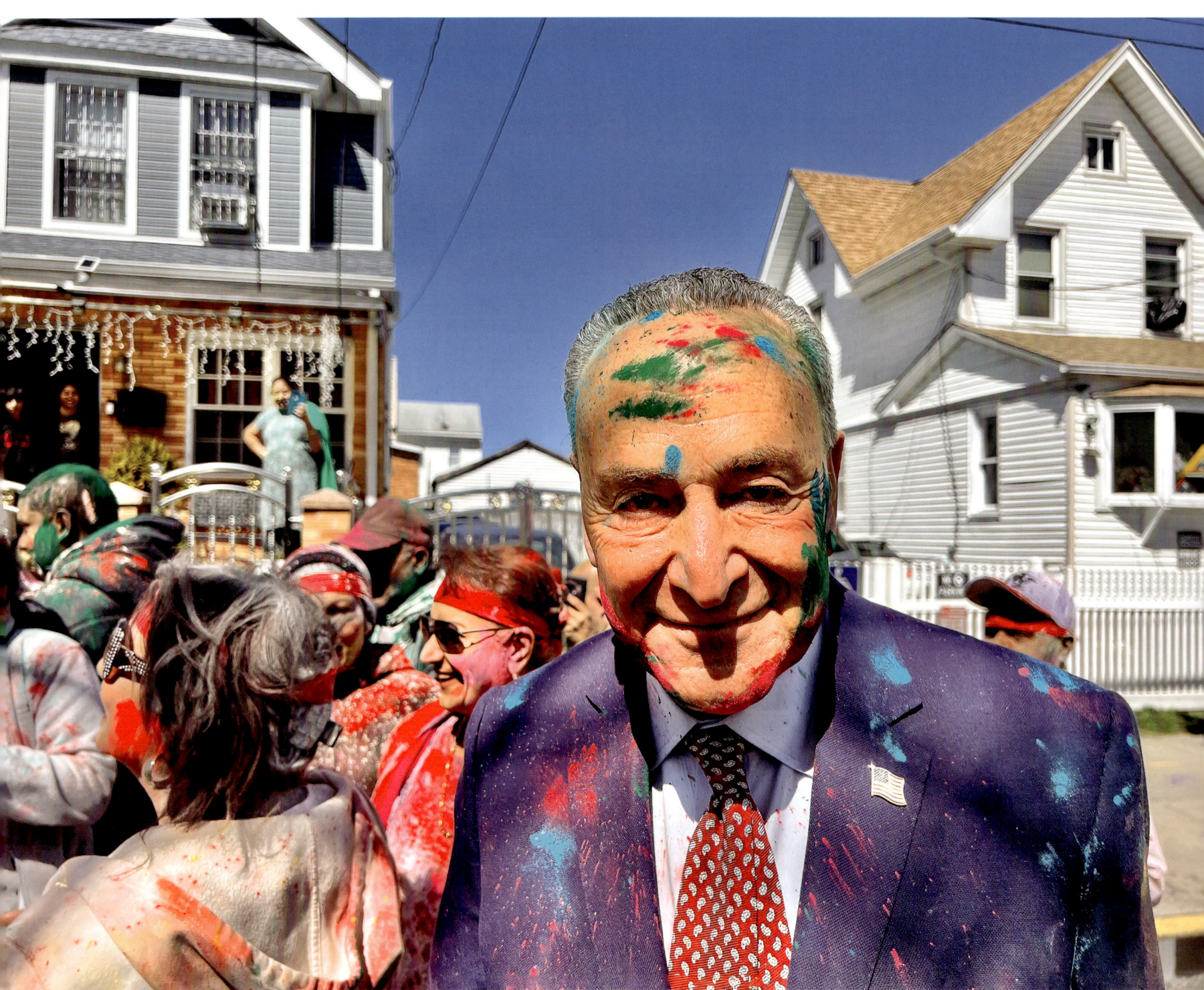

SENATE MAJORITY LEADER

Richmond Hill, New York City, New York

Politics can be a very messy business. Its carnival-like pageantry in the United States of America has usually arisen as a result of passion for this country's Constitution. Though not actually forged until more than a dozen years after the nation's independence, this civic bible will be confronting its semiquincentennial celebration in 2037, somehow still surviving as template for America's political business. Cobbled together in large measure thanks to that brilliance of 37-year-old James Madison, a scrawny, slightly over five-foot-tall, sickly hypochondriac who nonetheless outlived all other Founding Fathers. In 1787 he led a contentious convention of 55 white men meeting in secret proceedings over several months inside the Pennsylvania State House, managing to finally crank out four parchment pages containing 4,500 words blueprinting this country's future governance. These words never included slavery, which through desperately grievous desires for compromise would offer an amoral accounting that each slave be tallied as three-fifths of one human being. One of those momentous discussions held inside this loaned out Assembly Room is immortalized on the back of America's cotton-, linen-, and silk-papered two-dollar bill. Striking a delicate balance between nurturing personal liberty and maintenance of public order, this document was the world's very first constitution. The landmark charter outlined one strong federal government comprised of two very different congressional bodies counterbalanced by a judiciary and an executive. His presidential election would be determined by the not-so-democratic Electoral College, which arose out of concern for ordinary citizens' supposed provincial thinking. Remarkably, only one delegate to this Philadelphia convention, James Wilson, actually proposed direct election of a president by the people. In attempting to weave together dissimilar, yet supposedly united states, the Senate embodies a collective will of each sovereign state, while that population-based House of Representatives represents their individuals. As the result of all this, America is considered an actual republic rather than a pure democracy. Meant to be seriously deliberative bodies, Congress has since seen on its floor a fair share of angry arguments, scandal revelations, censures, impeachments, cane beatings, and even an indecorous 30-member melee that ripped the hairpiece off of an astonished representative during fractious times before America's Civil War. Then came the convulsive nation-shaking violence of January 6, 2021.

While a trip to the dry cleaners is probably within his near future, Senate Majority Leader Chuck Schumer meets celebrating constituents far more concerned with honoring Hindu god Vishnu by flinging colored dye than glad-handing politicians at this neighborhood Phagwah celebration in Queens. Proudly claiming annual visits into each of New York's 62 counties, he, like all American politicians, is almost constantly engaged with the indignities required for fundraising to help finance upcoming campaigns. The nation's highest elected Jewish official wore that same laundered jacket less than a year later when he led his congressional delegation to Ukraine for on the ground assessments of its war needs. An exterminator's son, he now attempts to eliminate political opposition inside halls of Congress, as he's busy shepherding important legislation onto the presidential desk for signing. Schumer served nine terms in the House of Representatives before his election as Senator in 1999 plus was a major sponsor to a Violence Against Women Act and co-author for an Assault Weapons Ban.

DISGRACED CONGRESSMAN

Lower Manhattan, New York City, New York

Sunglasses do little to distract attention from these almost thirty other lenses trained on then-congressman George Santos. He managed to get elected after a ceaseless blizzard of fabricated biographical claims that when uncovered enraged his voters and attracted intense media obsession. Constantly seeking the televised limelight, he pointlessly attended history's first-ever arraignment of an American president at a camera-thirsty downtown courthouse. Santos effortlessly wove twisted webs of absurd lies or unnecessarily cockamamie stories that only partially included shamefully exaggerated circumstances involving his mother's death, degrees from universities that weren't even attended, misfortunes while serving as landlord though not ever owning any property, producing Broadway shows despite remaining unknown to their real producers, scamming a disabled veteran's GoFundMe campaign, and boastings over collegiate volleyball player stardom although never having played. After a scathing House Ethics Committee report, he was indicted on multiple federal charges and expelled from Congress, the sixth such expulsion in the annals of this nation.

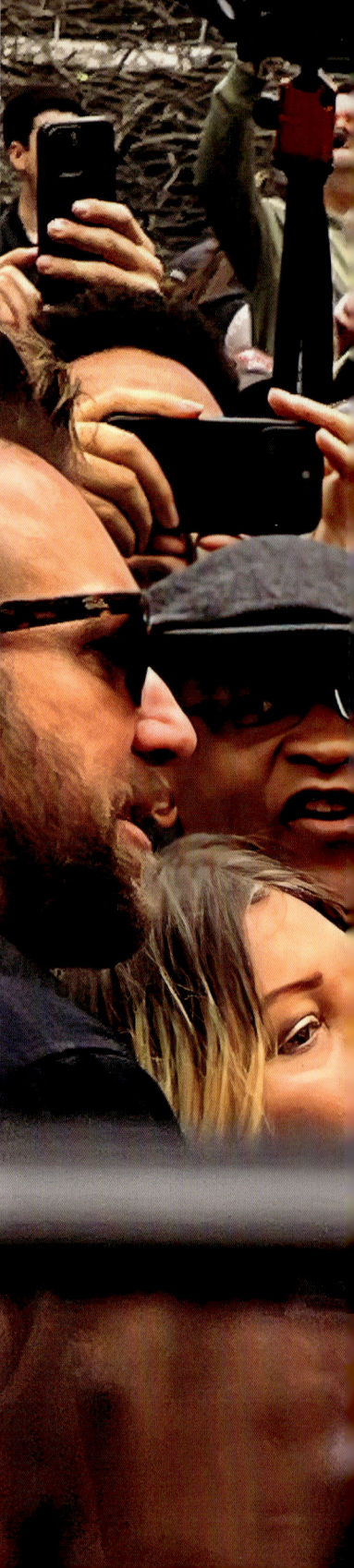

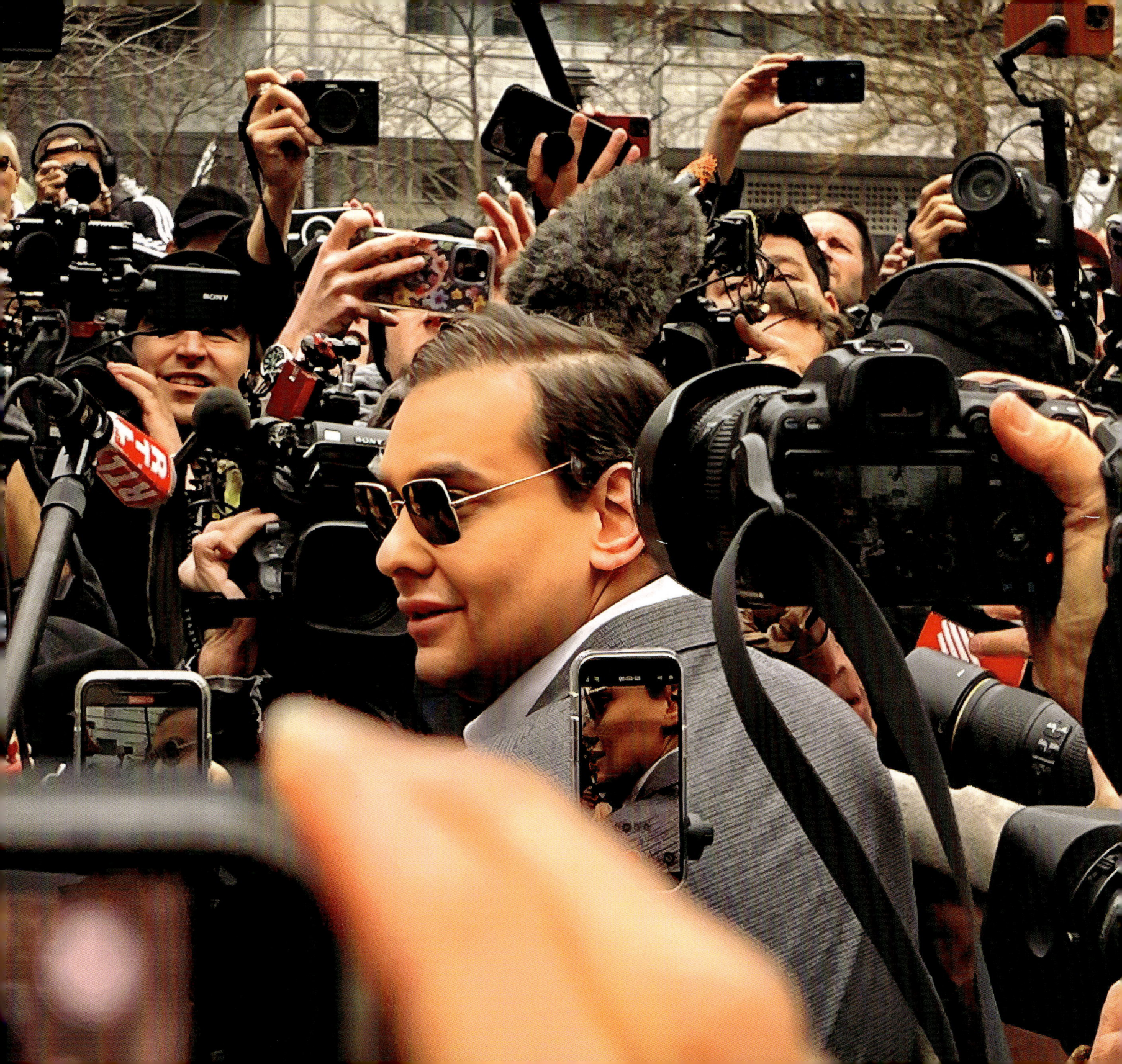

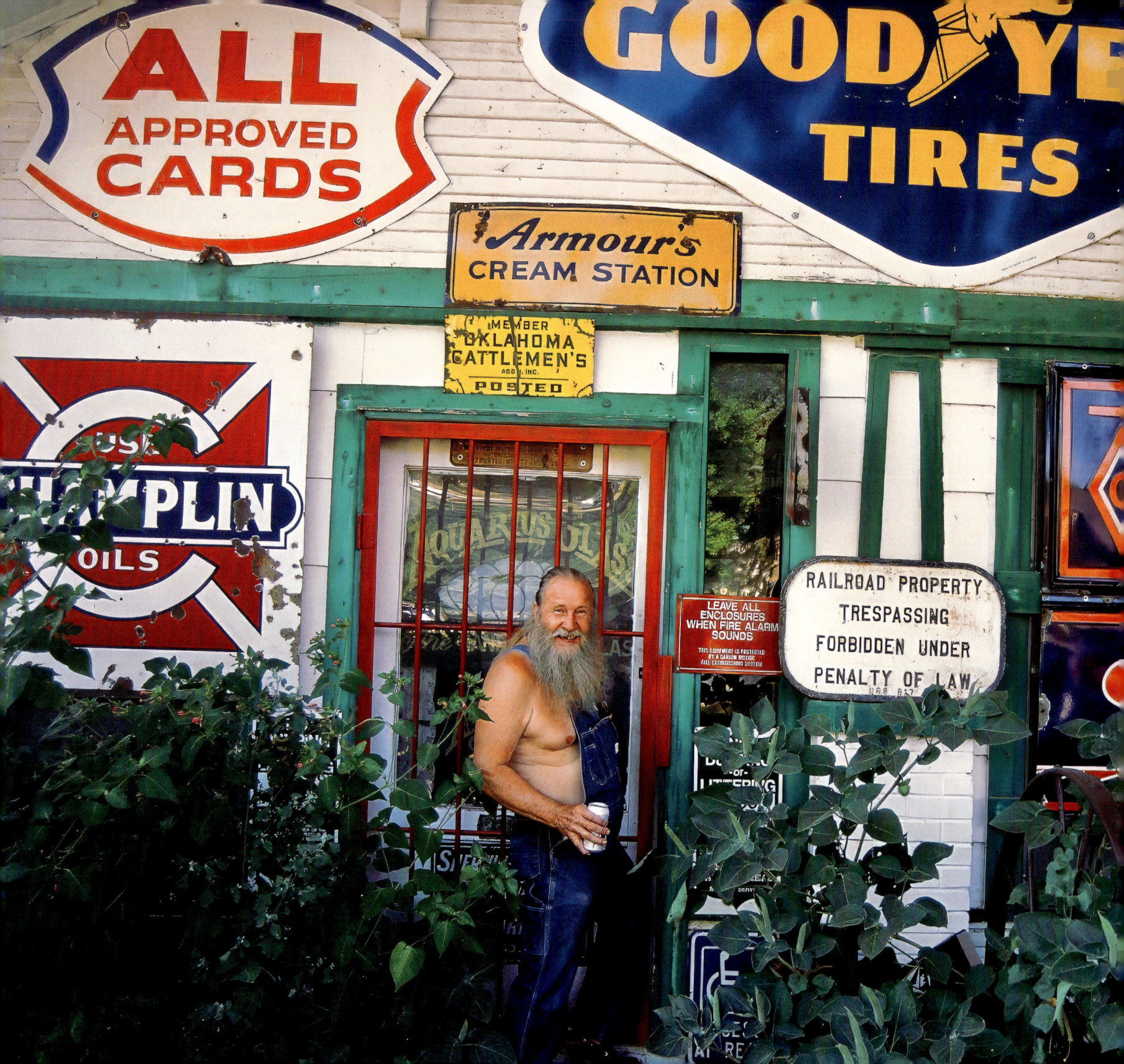

SELF-DESCRIBED REDNECK

Erick, Oklahoma

Six miles from its Texas border, Erick, a small Oklahoma settlement was said to be that first town encountered by westbound motorists moving along the National Old Trails Road to project some western feel, as its wide, sunbaked main street filled up with horsemen going about daily business. In the early thirties, notorious gangsters Bonnie Parker and Clyde Barrow kidnapped law enforcement officers, then left them tied up to a tree here with barbed wire. Later that decade not far away, black blizzards of the Dust Bowl left this region impoverished, its atmosphere obscured by dislodged topsoil. Upon clearing, growing traffic along the newly designated Route 66 brought with it needs for cafes, shops, filling stations, hardware stores, and even meat markets. When Route 66 was eventually bypassed by modern four-lane Interstate 40, this town began to dry up as it lost its businesses, a common story all along the Mother Road. So, Erick created a corner museum dedicated to Roger Miller, that acclaimed honky-tonk singer known for his Grammy-winning song "King of the Road," about an ambling hobo of no means. Just barely down the street from the museum stands one remaining remnant of an old meat market where a hobo-like figure holds court. For many travelers exploring those faded riches on Route 66, he is indeed a king of the road. This bearded man whose smile reveals some missing teeth transformed that aging meat market into the Sandhills Curiosity Shop where absolutely nothing inside is for sale and curious visitors are startled when its proprietor suddenly locks the door behind them. Whipping out an electric guitar and his string of profanity-laced proclamations, he'll launch into a shockingly vibrant rendition of "(Get Your Kicks on) Route 66." This emporium's self-proclaimed "redneck capital of the world" touts insanity at its finest atop a swinging sign above the porch at this still-operating Greyhound bus stop now chockablock with vintage gasoline or soda pop signs,

When Disney created animated motion picture *Cars*, all about the sad collapse of towns bypassed by interstates, they sent research scouts scouring that historic 2,400-mile highway. Encountering Harley Russell, an inspired crew realized they had discovered the real deal around which to focus their plot. Avoiding spoiler alerts, Tow Mater is the gap-toothed anthropomorphic embodiment of a joyfully optimistic, rusting tow truck, whose voice is performed by Larry the Cable Guy. In readying for his role, he was asked to spend time with Russell, observantly acquiring his colorful hillbilly expressions and intonations. Wearing overalls and little else, he hoists a beer while opening his "redneck castle" residence tucked away behind the shop. Bedecked in service station ads, he'll soon warn invited guests about his bathroom's nicknamed sewage lagoon and roach infestations in the kitchen, decidedly not referring to any insects.

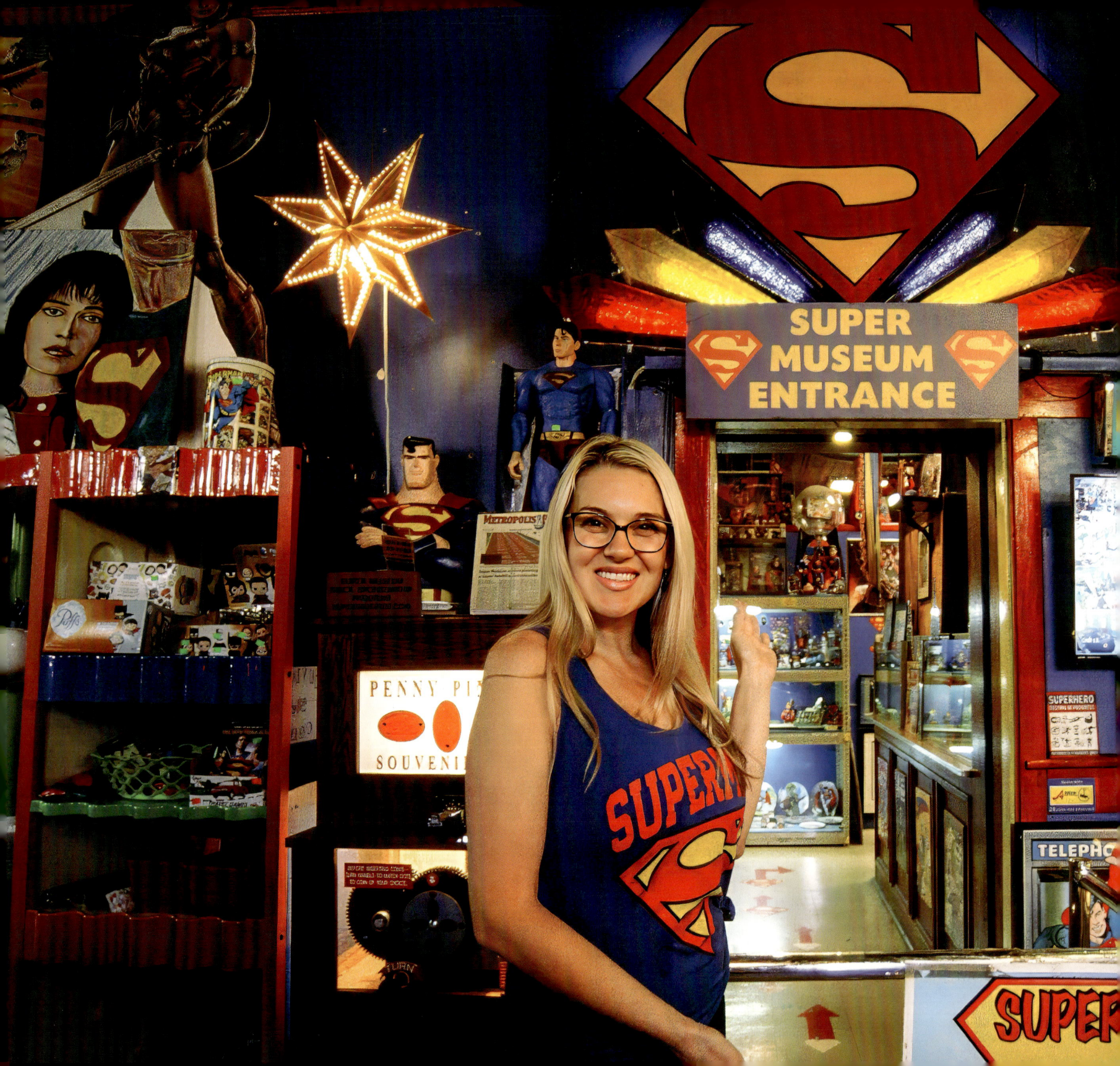

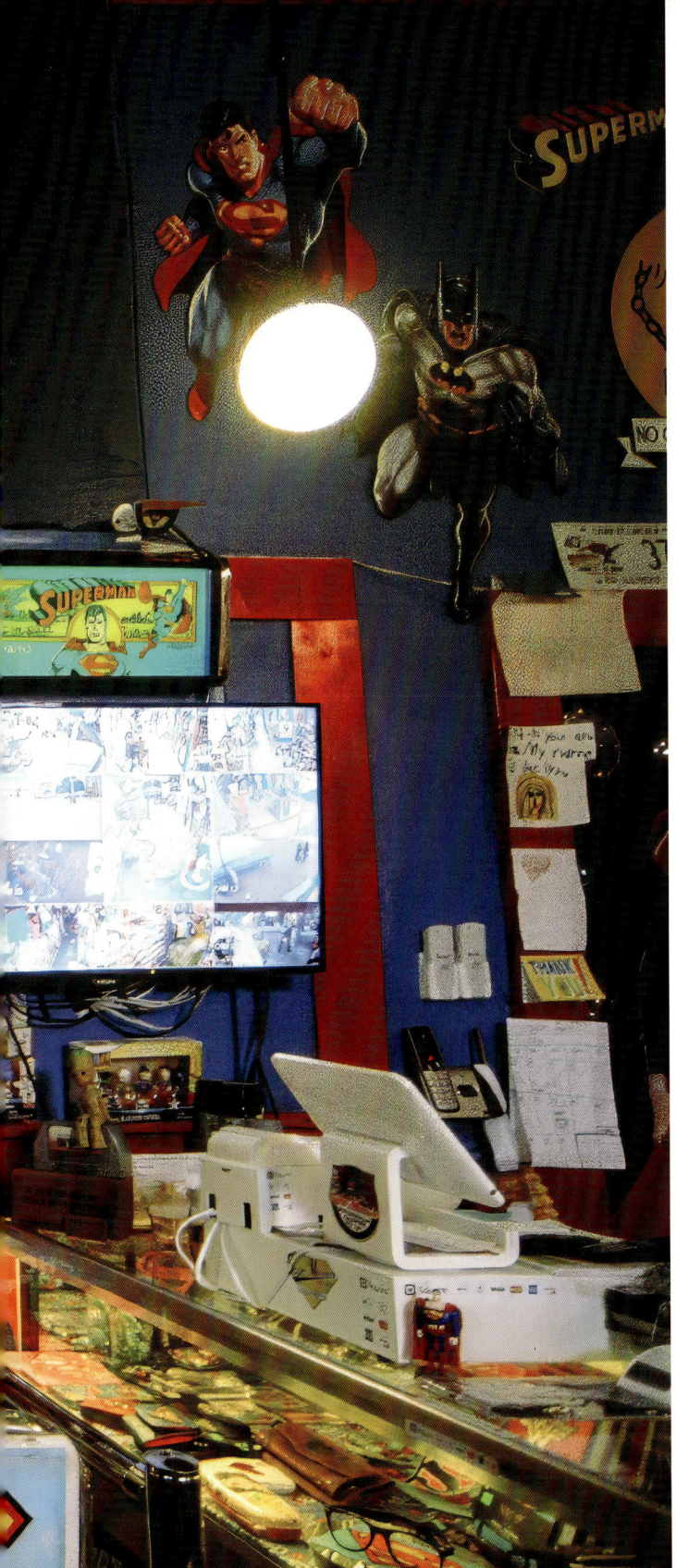

SUPERMAN MUSEUM TOUR GUIDE

Metropolis, Illinois

While myths appear throughout every ancient culture, in the United States robust American expansion and its sense of manifest destiny for a newly forged nation helped assemble an astonishing roster featuring greater than life-size heroes, both hewn from whole cloth or sculpted around actual historical figures. Frontiersman Davy Crockett actually perished at the Alamo, horticulturist Johnny Appleseed gardened feverishly throughout Midwestern precincts, and John Henry, that fabled Black steel-driving man, may have met his actual demise in West Virginia's North Bend Tunnel. Conversely, both Paul Bunyan and the Lone Ranger were completely fabricated to reflect valiant lumberjack or marshal traditions of their respective regions. Just prior to World War II, as popular culture accompanied mass consumption and began leaking into American consciousness, comic book writer Jerry Siegel teamed with Joe Shuster and was inspired by the Torah during Hebrew school lessons about infant Moses being launched adrift in his mother's basket, a buoyant vessel of concealed identity. Drawing parallels to a Superman from another world, they crafted history's very first flying superhero, notwithstanding an unfortunate decision that ultimately sold the publisher their rights for only $130.

Subsequent fame of this cape-clad, soaring champion offering truth and justice eventually motivated Illinois's State Legislature to declare Metropolis, founded on the Ohio River with that hopeful name in 1839, to be Superman's official hometown. It so happened that the comic book's flying superhero resided within an identically named fictional city on his newly adopted planet Earth. America's largest collection of Superman memorabilia may be viewed even without any X-ray vision inside The Super Museum. By its entrance, an enthusiastic staff member ushers in visitors to explore colorful, meandering aisles at this otherworldly, kryptonite-resistant exhibition, featuring in one corner the television actor's eventual suicide. After museum hours, as that sun slowly sets outside by the courthouse square, an imposing three-ton, fifteen-foot-high painted bronze statue of Superman seems poised to ensure evening's tranquility amongst any wannabe villains.

NUCLEAR PHYSICIST

Brookhaven, New York

In the beginning there was that Big Bang. Eons later, out on this contiguous nation's longest island, Brookhaven National Laboratory was established in 1947 for peacetime nuclear research. It was deliberately sited within a proximity to the greatest number of Ivy League researchers studying nearby. Magnetic levitation, mRNA vaccines for COVID-19, and video game technology were all first developed on the 5,300-acre campus, where comprehensive research eventually was rewarded with seven Nobel Prizes. With scientists seriously determined to better understand those very origins of existence, a Relativistic Heavy Ion Collector (RHIC) was constructed after two decades in the making. An outline revealing its submerged circular 2.4-mile-circumference tunnel may actually be seen from outer space. The RHIC is the world's only machine with an ability to collide beams of polarized protons and investigate its missing spin. Crisscrossing these beams containing superconducting magnets will accelerate nuclei of heavy gold atoms to nearly light's speed, smashing together deliberately engineered opposing traffic in this tunnel, while yielding vivid imagery that display quarks and gluons. These experiments help recreate that birth of nuclear matter thought to have existed only 13.8 billion years ago at the time of our universe's initial explosion.

If comprehension of those life-defining concepts seems a bit daunting, that might help explain the serious facial expression on this determined nuclear physicist, flashlight in hand, exploring and maintaining complex circuitry within an exceedingly gargantuan supercollider. Closed to outsiders for much of the year, occasional short, highly regulated visits are permitted only in unrestricted areas, usually on Sundays during July.

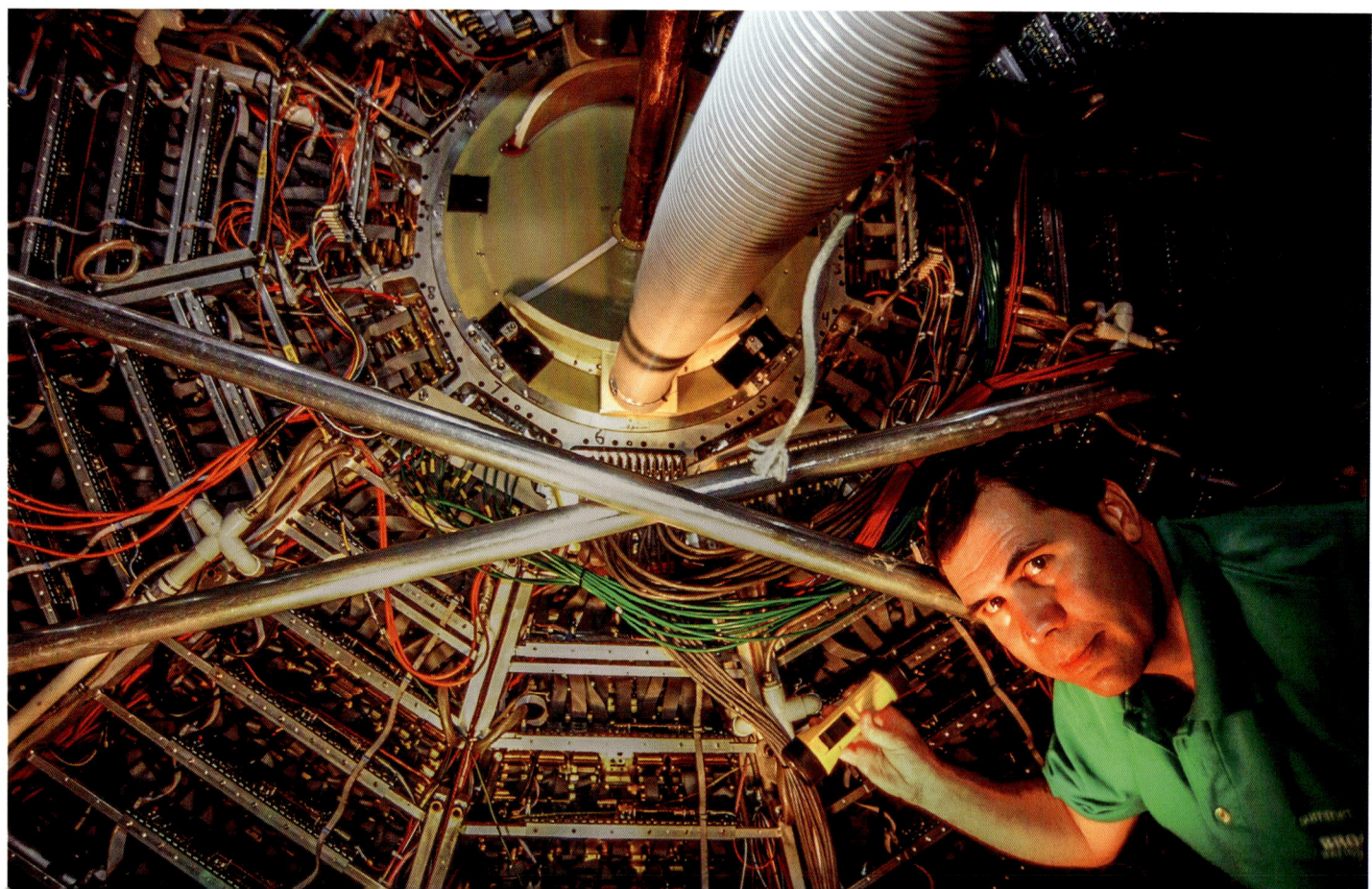

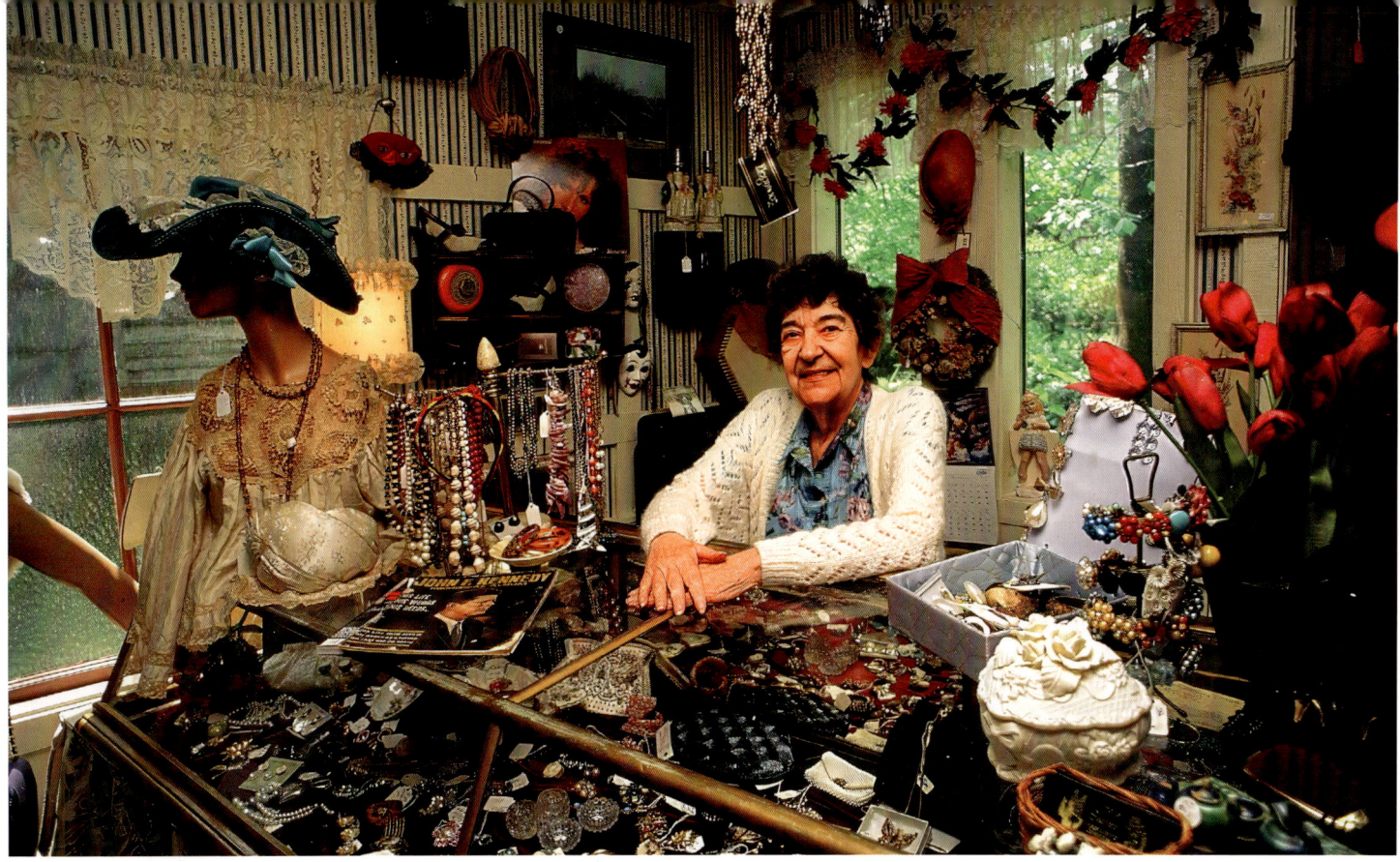

SHOPKEEPER

Nashville, Indiana

Straddling two time zones, the Hoosier State is wedged between three of its fellow Great Lakes states. Indiana has one of the oldest state nicknames, its oddball portmanteau derived from an often garbled response to a door knock. Imagined stereotypes about this Midwestern region's tabletop-flat farmlands are turned upside down in Brown County, by far the most forested of all Indiana's 92 counties. Sheltered within steeply rolling hills, charming spots cluster near one another, like the quaint 1880 Bean Blossom Covered Bridge, crossing its babbling eponymous creek within one of this nation's very few Howe Truss spans. Deep in woods that are barely reachable down a long and winding road, the entirety of Story, Indiana, is its namesake inn, an 1851 former grocery store with rusting gas pumps that once helmed this now deserted lumbering community. The inn is only slightly less renowned for its tasty food than ghostly apparitions vividly described in overnight guest books. During peripatetic wanderings across this area, legendary horticulturalist Johnny Appleseed would bury his fruit tree seeds and help further spread nurseries throughout the state, where he himself was buried in 1845. Spreading images instead of trees, acclaimed photographer Frank Hohenberger was attracted to the region after glimpsing scenes bursting with rustic village life. He was perhaps inspired to settle here after visits to Bear Wallow or Gnaw Bone, a disappearing remnant of Americana where now only one bakery remains within an old sorghum mill. Publication of his images created an enticing tourist draw for this region, where he took up residence within The Olde Bartley House in nearby Nashville, its three traffic lights the only ones to be found anywhere across Brown County.

At one cramped corner inside The Olde Bartley House, built in 1886, memories of a bygone era are for sale amid this bijou showcase chock-filled with vintage baubles, fandangles, and gewgaws. A contented shopkeeper's floral blouse echoes the patterned couture cladding an antique mannequin. Adorned by nostalgic millinery that also ornaments the wallpapered environs, creative sensibilities here no doubt indicate Nashville's nineteenth-century heritage as one of America's original art colonies.

TIRELESS COLLECTOR

Bloomsburg, Pennsylvania

Across their empires, ancient civilizations of Egypt, Babylon, China, and India erected temples and tombs that gathered within dimly lit inner sanctums an extensive collection containing objects meant to glorify a ruler, culture, or religion. During the Roman Empire, especially through those reigns of Emperors Augustus and Hadrian, collections featuring statues or sculptures grew in importance as art markets were first developed. Then industries of restoration and reproduction flourished during the Renaissance era in artistic centers throughout Italy, where keen observations by Leonardo da Vinci promoted a greater thirst for discovery. Deeper knowledge of the world was soon advanced during global expeditions led by land-conquering explorers as their collected natural oddities and plundered objects were delivered to European institutions. They established *wunderkammers*, or cabinets of curiosity, which emphasized the classification and arrangements displaying exotic items. Donations by private collectors helped spark numerous openings of grand museums in Europe, like the Louvre in Paris or London's National Gallery. In the United States, financiers or great titans of industry like Andrew Carnegie, William Vanderbilt, along with J. P. Morgan amassed impressive fortunes bolstered by extensive art collections which made their way into institutions like New York's Metropolitan Museum of Art and Washington D.C.'s Smithsonian Institution, considered this nation's attic. Smaller museums and local, family-owned collections mushroomed across the country, spurred by capitalism's driving forces of acquisition, creativity, and curiosity. In a definite league by itself, but somehow well beneath the radar is Bill's Old Bike Barn, an astounding find just off one of Pennsylvania's major interstate highways, yet somehow hiding in plain sight. Beneath the disguise of an industrial looking metal storage shed, a pains-takingly reassembled 220-year-old barn cloisters beneath its rafters unending collections featuring America's industrial heritage. Amongst two-stories of bus-long wooden beams, 55,000 square feet contain the East Coast's largest collection featuring vintage bicycles, motorcycles, tanks, and air-plane displays only interrupted by a carousel serving as metaphorical symbol for those dizzying exhibits that envelop it. Head-scratching layers of collections and acquisitions ramble endlessly through the complex. Extended along an indoor brick-lined street jammed with vintage vehicles, a firehouse, barber shop, tool shed, gas station, and toy store dominate this pretend town filled by dozens of similar antique emporiums. All are completely stuffed to the rafters with mind-boggling displays related to their business.

Like peeling the layers within an onion or disassembling Russian nesting dolls, a seemingly inex-haustible compilation of objects pays extravagant tribute to one compulsive man's tireless pursuit. The crazed genius behind all this noble stockpiling is Bill Morris, who has amassed the world's largest collection of Harley-Davidson parts and seems to be equal parts biker, builder, mechanic, museum curator, collector, and dreamer.

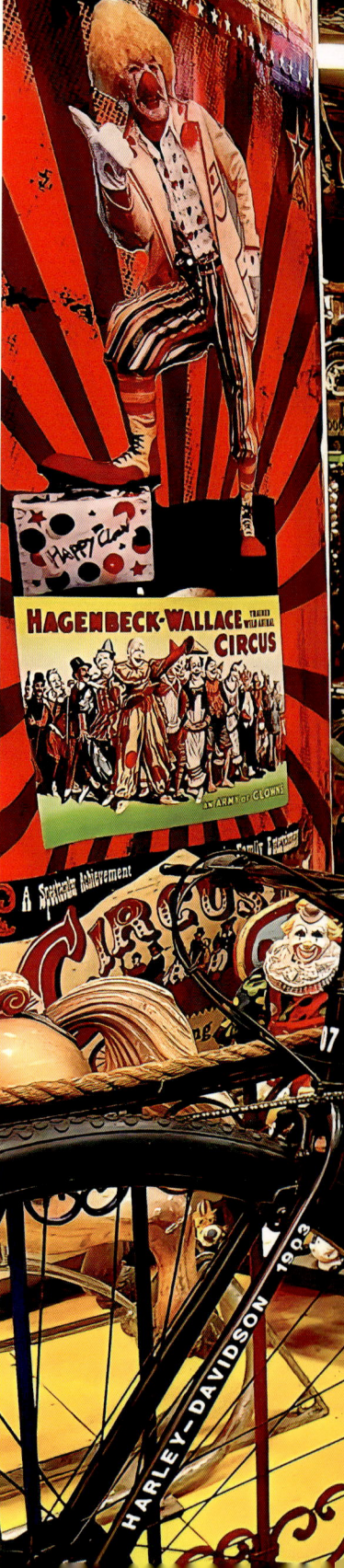

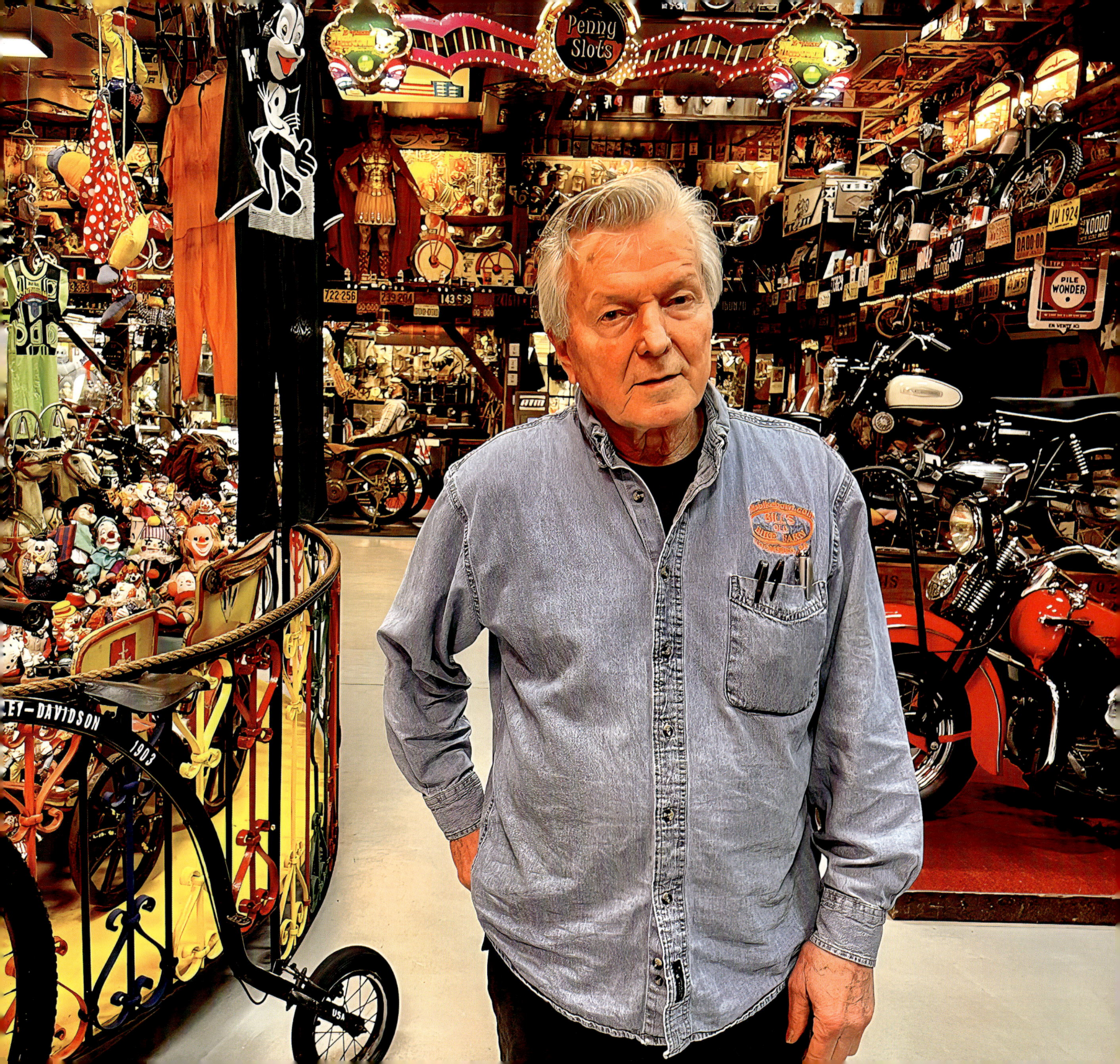

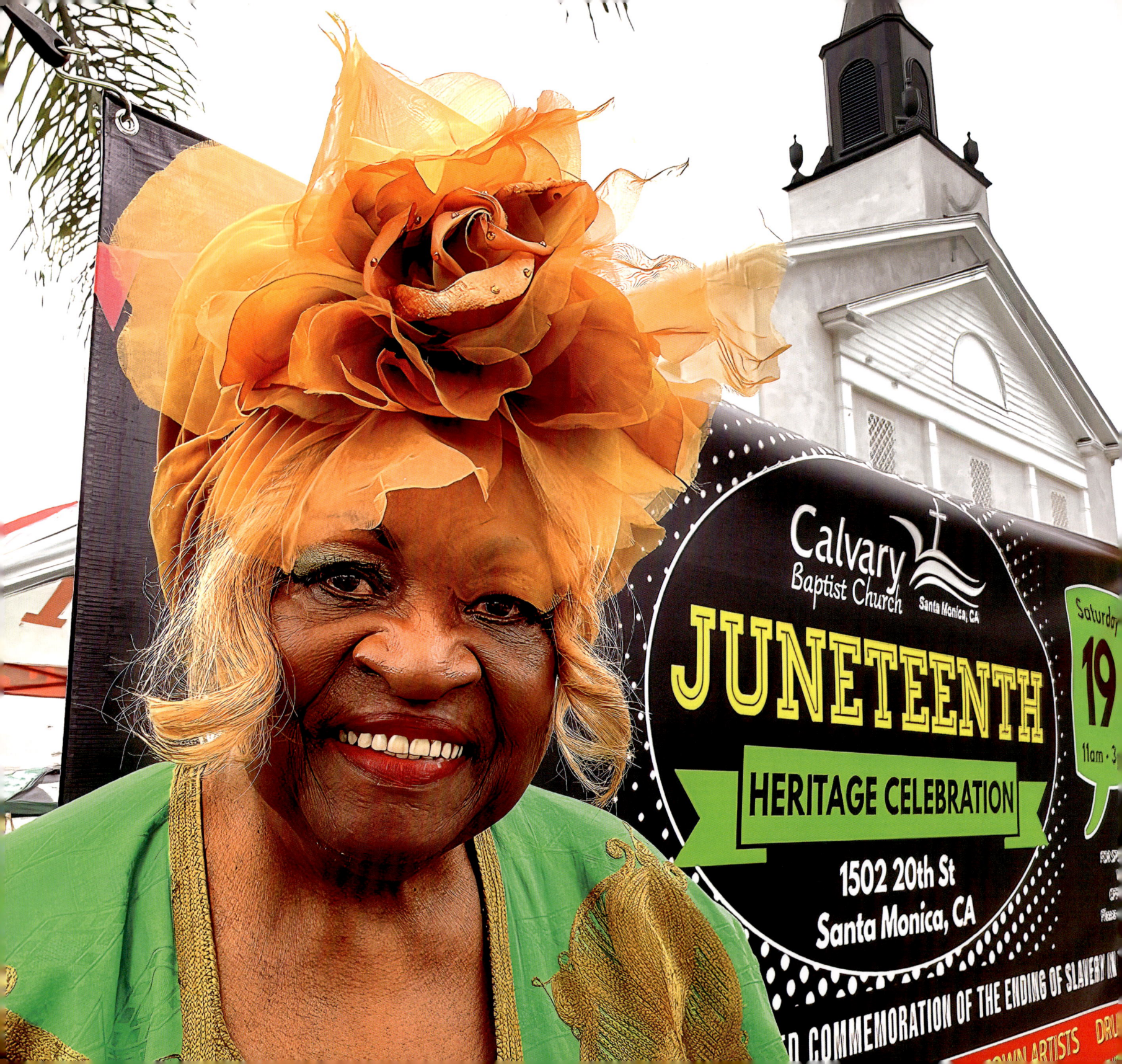

JUNETEENTH ORGANIZER

Santa Monica, California

The most revered phrase in the Declaration of Independence stated that "all men are created equal" despite the fact that a majority of signers to this document were slaveholders, and its author Thomas Jefferson owned over 600 people during his lifetime. Four of the first five presidents were slaveholders. Apparently, those unalienable rights of liberty were not self-evident truths as described in that founding document and once were far from the reach of Black people who had been captured, tortured, and shipped in cramped vessels from western Africa. This abhorrent enterprise was part of a sad, trade wind-powered triangular conveyor belt between continents to ensure profits for cotton, tobacco, and sugar. The stubborn blight of human enslavement in America precipitated a civil war, sparked by a clash between economic and moral imperatives. Even that mid-conflict Emancipation Proclamation issued by Abraham Lincoln was motivated less by altruistic notions of humanity than as a war strategy to deprive the Confederacy of their financial engine. Although officially eradicated throughout Confederate states, many enslaved workers in Texas, the distant westernmost reaches of the Confederacy, remained unaware of their emancipation until June 19, 1865, when 2,000 Union troops under Major General Gordon Granger finally arrived at Galveston to announce their freedom more than two months after General Lee's surrender inside Appomattox Court House. Euphoric jubilation broke out as Juneteenth, a portmanteau of that momentous month and date henceforth marked this significant church-centered celebration whose spirituality was soon bolstered by culinary or cultural revelries. Aside from hypnotic rhythms of djembe drum circles, red velvet cake along with strawberry soda, fruit punch, or kola nut tea is often served. That became a gustatory mainstay at these events as those vivid hues represented the transformational embodiment of spiritual power embraced by enslaved Yoruba and Kongo tribes, first dragged to Texas generations earlier. Though enslaved labor in Southern states ended that Juneteenth, slavery farther north continued until a ratification of the Constitution's Thirteenth Amendment many months later.

A beloved fixture at the gospel-infused Calvary Baptist Church, LaVerne Ross, community activist and organizer, approached the city of Santa Monica three decades ago to commemorate this holiday that her family had first celebrated in Texas. After 64 years as a master cosmetologist, Ross helped revive fading strands of history when she founded a committee that swept the holiday's prominence over to the West Coast. Her efforts contributed to forging the country's eleventh national holiday, which was signed into law by President Joseph Biden in 2021.

LEPIDOPTERIST

East Meredith, New York

Alive on earth for more than a thousand times longer than man, the 1.5 million species of insects collectively weigh over one billion tons. Although a quarter of the earth's human population living mostly in its tropical zone now eat protein-rich insects within their regular diet, that nightmarish fear involving these diminutive creatures seems widespread among first-world countries. While just the thought of wasps, cockroaches, or scorpions might make their skins crawl, entomophobic people still find butterflies their most beloved insect. Evoking breathless wonder, these arthropods with wings transport a dazzling color catalog of ravishing designs and patterns. With taste bud sensors on their feet, they'll determine exactly where to lay eggs, measuring the perch's scrumptiousness for feeding newly hatched caterpillars. Their clever antennae tell them the time each day, enable midair courtships and help maintain balance while flying at a top speed of 12 miles an hour. The mysterious 3,000-mile multi-generational migration of monarch butterflies is among the world's longest, utilizing their time-compensated compass which also perceives polarized light to orient themselves on even cloudy days. Over 20,000 species of these gossamer-winged miracles flutter worldwide and set alight a deep fervor for gathering the colorful specimens. Butterfly collecting had been a passion first sparked by cabinets of curiosity established in Edwardian conservatories. Those exhibits were established during the golden era of exploration when returning ships unloaded a hefty inventory filled with curious plant and animal specimens. Imaginative Victorian children, inspired by the ineffable magic of their natural universe, would head off with muslin, kite-shaped butterfly nets to ramble through nearby meadows. Winston Churchill as a youth chased butterflies at his prep school and later stocked his estate gardens with the fluttering insects. Butterfly hunting became an activity requiring the wrist action-bolstered agility demonstrated by nimble tennis players, and was considered a sport akin to fly fishing, catching darting swallowtails instead of plunging salmon. Across the pond, an unlikely Butterfly Farm and Museum was established in 1953 by Max Richter who imported his German childhood obsession with insects to upstate New York. Breeding and selling butterflies, he nurtured thousands of their eggs through metamorphosis into chrysalises, stored in protective sheds. Butterfly collections like his have offered priceless genetic data while swallowtail coloration studies led to development of more efficient light-emitting diodes. Richter passed away five months after reaching 100 years of age and his own final metamorphosis.

Inside an 1830 boarding house transformed into a chrysalis and pupae-fueled butterfly exhibition, lepidopterist Helen Richter Kruppenbacher, daughter of the museum founder, guides her visitors through many rooms boasting kaleidoscopic assemblages filled with diaphanous-winged insects. Those include its impressive collection containing immense Attacus atlas moths with the world's largest Lepidoptera wingspan of up to ten inches. The museum sits amongst flower-dappled Catskills meadows where live versions of these mounted specimens are now busy fertilizing mountain wildflowers.

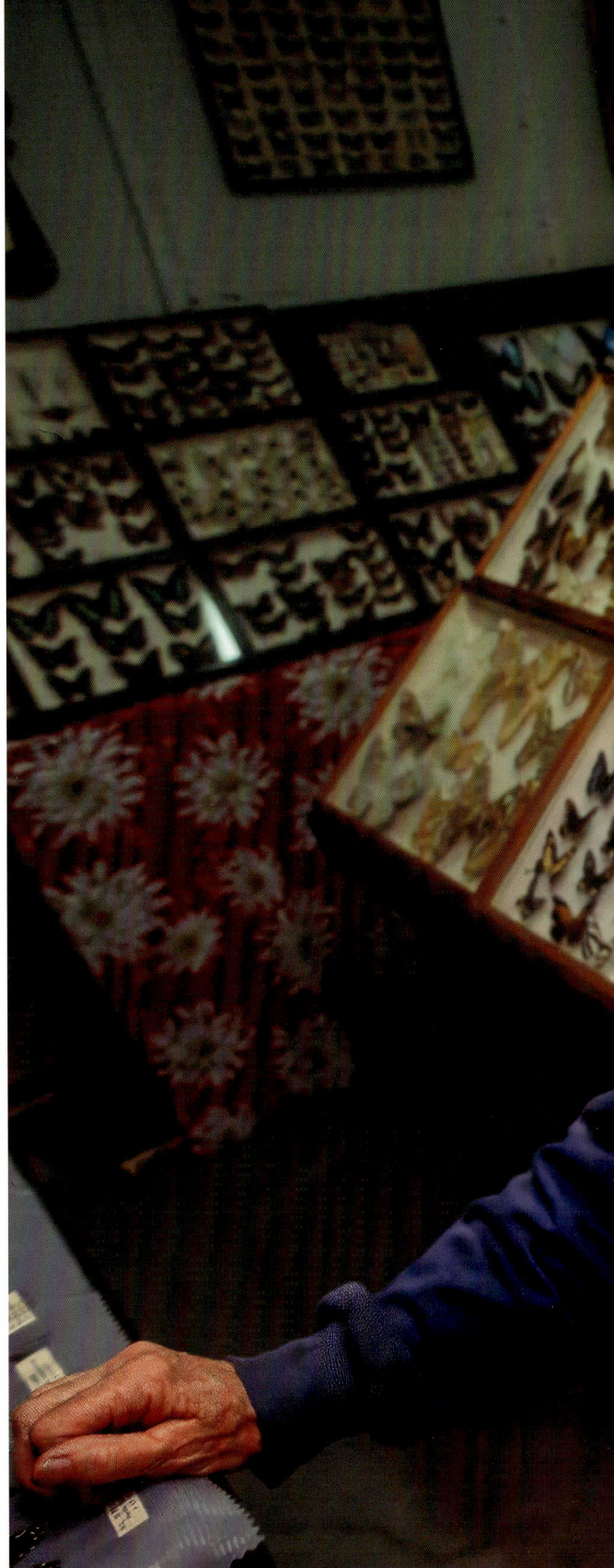

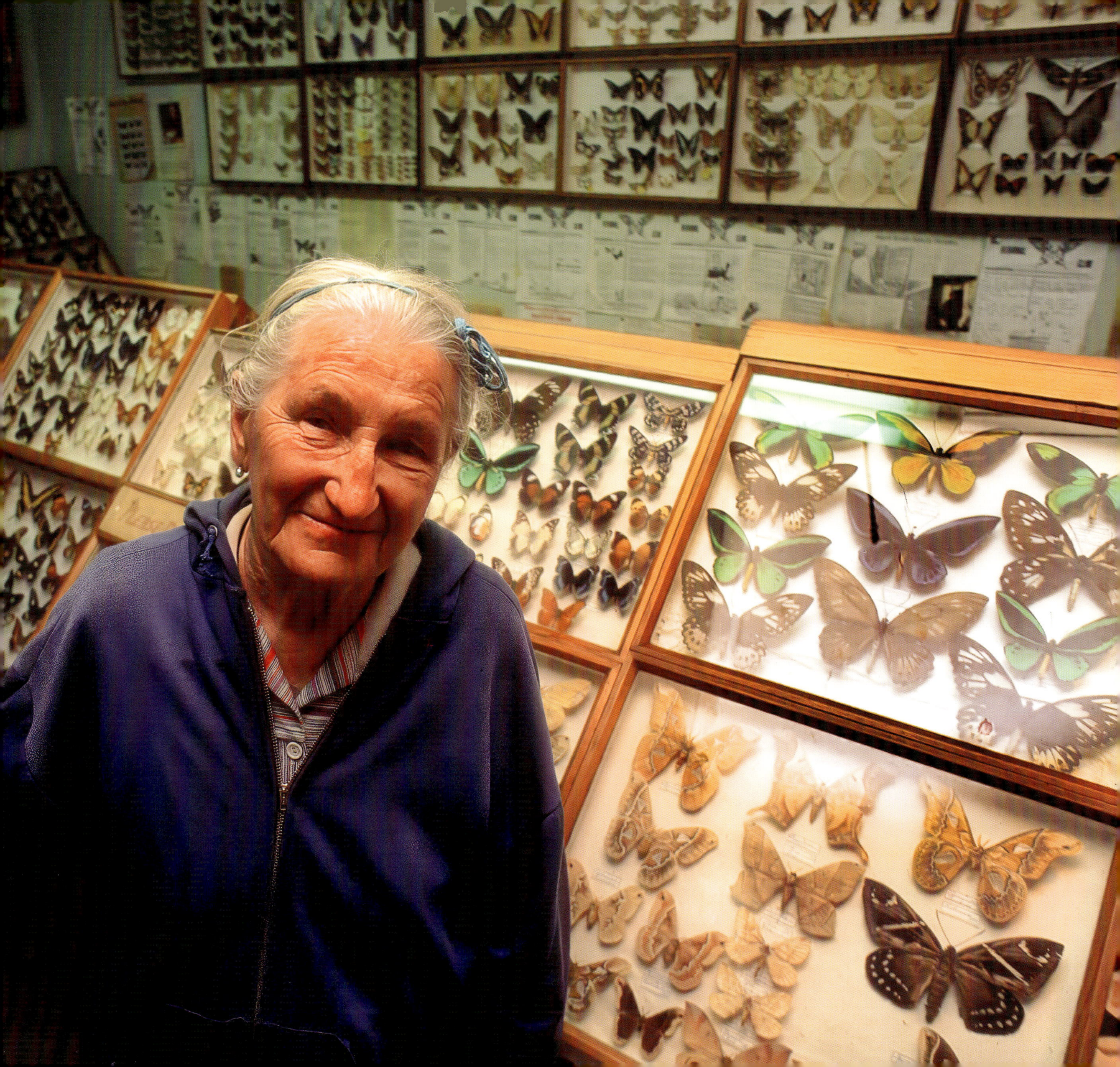

ACKNOWLEDGMENTS

With deepest gratitude to my amazing friend Clifford Pickett's remarkably selfless efforts and indefatigable dedication toward enhancing the beauty of this book's photographic imagery. My incredible wife Lori Greene's reliably skillful editing insights and clever suggestions proved absolutely invaluable. I'm very grateful to friends Curt Middleton's brilliant design guidance and Guido Caroti's discerningly perceptive counseling whose talents both proved instrumental. At Skyhorse Publishing, I'm so humbled and extremely grateful for insightful publisher Tony Lyons's steadfast belief in my creative visions and feel deeply fortunate to work with gifted editor Sarah Janssen, who has generously shared her adroit guidance, providing critical keys to this book's complex evolution. I'm particularly struck by her unflappable reactions to my admittedly outlandish, possibly creative, and likely futile, determined quest that this text should never repeat any single word within its individual sentences. It seems perhaps for better or worse that I myself might be quite a character. Lastly, and probably most importantly, I am truly thankful to the enormous cast filled by remarkably captivating characters profiled here who so generously gave either seconds, minutes, hours, or days of their time. It's been such a soul-enriching blessing and privilege to have shared at least one brief moment of their very distinctive lives.